# Capt. Thiago Brenner

# Aircraft Performance

# Weight and Balance

**4th Edition – English Version**

2024

Book title: **AIRCRAFT PERFORMANCE WEIGHT AND BALANCE**
Edition: 4th (Hard Cover - English Version) – Original
Author: Thiago Lopes Brenner
Copy Editor: Luiz Armando Silveiro Susin
Cover and chapter intro illustration: Marketing Aeronáutico
Originally published on Nov 30th, 2024
Printed by Amazon
Number of pages: 374
ISBN: 9798345111147

# Acknowledgments

A pilot's life is challenging. Some airlines around the world offer the opportunity to sleep at home every day without layovers! Unfortunately, that is an impossible dream for me. Airlines in Brazil have always published rosters with long days away from home. Layover after layover, that's what I hate most about my job. It wasn't always like this. There was a time I really enjoyed being paid to visit other places, but after getting married, and especially after the birth of my kids, I started to struggle with this difficult part of the job. Still, I love flying and teaching.

When I decided to rewrite the book for the third time (second revision in English), I inevitably ended up using time I could have spent with my family working on this project. Once more, I owe the success of this endeavor to the enormous sacrifices made by them. I must thank them very much for giving me all the support I needed to complete this difficult task. My beloved wife, **Eliza Brenner**, and my wonderful children, **Gustavo Brenner** and **Rafael Brenner**, played a key role in the process. They understood right from the start how difficult such a task was and were always supportive. Many thanks also to my parents, **João Batista Brenner** and **Maria Cristina Brenner**, and my sister, **Ana Carolina Brenner**, for all their support and motivation since I was a child, in pursuing my dream of becoming an aviator. My mother and my wife, by the way, were the ones responsible for pushing me towards the idea of writing the English version of this book. I am also grateful to my mother-in-law, **Ilza Castanho**, and my sister-in-law, **Paula Castanho**, who have been very helpful in taking care of my young children. With their help, I could devote the time I needed to write this book.

I am deeply indebted to my dear university professors, who have helped me acquire expert knowledge over the years, some of whom I have developed a beautiful friendship with: Rodrigo Coelho, Éder Henriqson, Cláudio Scherer, Elones Ribeiro, Hildebrando Hoffmann, Lucas Fogaça, and Guido Carim. I would like to thank two new friends as well: Doctor David Esser, a professor at Embry-Riddle Aeronautical University who has helped promote the book within the University, and the Boeing 737 guru, Captain Chris Brady, from whom I learned so much about this airplane. They are both great supporters of the English version of this book!

Many thanks to Luis Filipe Santos, a course partner at Boeing and also a good friend. I would also like to extend my gratitude to friends who have shared the flight deck with me at various times: Gustavo Libardi, Rafael Brandelli, Felipe Abreu, Leonardo Munhos, João Centeno, Arthur Pettersen, Everaldo Telles Jr, Filipe Kisiolar, Thiago Forti, Rodrigo Castanheira, and many others.

Many thanks also to Luiz Armando Susin, my copy editor, who took on the task of revising this edition once again and helped me improve its readability and clarity. Being a layman, he asked me questions about extremely technical concepts, and we discussed points that needed further clarification – which was definitely a good test to ensure this book serves its purpose.

Without the support and teachings from all of you, I could not have possibly written this book. With all my heart, thank you very much.

# Table of Contents

# Foreword

Let us be honest, a book about Aircraft Performance Weight and Balance could be a very dry read, but let me assure you that this is not; it is actually a page-turner. This is very well written and engaging book, written by a highly respected Boeing 737 Captain. Furthermore, it is also very well illustrated containing hundreds of explanatory diagrams, graphs, tables and photographs, all of which help the reader to grasp the concept being conveyed in the text.

Some 30 years ago I used to teach performance to both new and current 737 pilots, I wish this book had been available then to offer to the pilots as background material rather than my own course notes. I cannot recommend this book highly enough.

Captain Chris Brady

Author of The Boeing 737 Technical Guide
www.b737.org.uk
https://www.youtube.com/c/ChrisBrady737

# Briefing

After intensive work, I released the first version of this book in March 2018. It has several illustrations and a great deal of details, and I had excellent feedback from those who had purchased the material. However, I also received many questions from my readers and I realized that I needed to expand the content. A second edition was published in early 2019, after a thorough revision, which attempted to respond to all the points previously made by my readers. After all, their feedback is greatly appreciated.

In the second edition, the book had many more details, and its content had matured, but it was published only in Portuguese. In late 2019, I finally felt confident enough to go ahead with the development of the English version of the book and spent a bit over one year working on it. It had over 100 more figures than the previous edition, and a lot of extra content. Initially, the book would be released just on paper, as with the previous two, but I decided to go digital with this one as well! So, it became a reality in May 2021. Two years later, and after a big success (at least comparing to my original expectations), I decided it was time for a new edition. And in early 2024, I started to develop this new and once again expanded version of the book. Now I am very proud to present the fourth edition of "Aircraft Performance Weight and Balance"! I hope you enjoy it!

The first edition of this book offered readers nearly 30 pages with exercises, but the second, the third, and the current (fourth) edition provide a wider context. In comparison, the first edition had 260 pages while this edition has more than 360! Having said that, keeping the exercises would make this book even longer and more expensive (at least for the paper version)! As I did not wish to raise the price of the book too much, I decided to remove most of the exercises (but I still left some examples). However, not to disappoint those willing to put into practice what they have learned here, a list of free questions and answers is available in digital format.

Although this is a fourth edition, I made a complete revision of the content, updating information that has changed, editing or adding illustrations, and, of course, creating new topics that readers of the previous editions had asked for. Once again, I did my best to make a complex subject clearer in a foreign language.

This book was originally created to be used as the textbook of the "Aircraft Performance Weight and Balance" course, which I taught in the Aeronautical Sciences Degree Program at Pontifícia Universidade Católica do Rio Grande do Sul, PUCRS, in Brazil. It has all the theoretical content that students need to complete the above-mentioned degree, but it takes a step further. To reach a larger audience, the book also includes an opening chapter that deals with aerodynamics at a more basic level, just to provide readers with a foundation on the topic.

As with the course, the book is also based on performance class A aircraft – the class with the most demanding requirements – built under Federal Aviation Regulation (FAR) Part 25 regulations for Transport Category Airplanes. Even though I have mostly focused on the rules of operation under FAR Part 121 (regular passenger transport), I occasionally mentioned some details of other regulations to demonstrate the basic differences between them.

**FAR Part 25**

Transport Category Airplanes

Operating according to

**FAR Part 121**

*Figure 1: The main focus of this book.*

To make the content easier to understand, I have given several examples of real aircraft, with the vast majority referring to Boeing 737-800. Although this aircraft is used as a model, the data presented here are for illustrative purposes only and should not be used for actual flights.

Class A aircraft, the target of our book, are all jet engine aircraft, as well as all turbo-propeller multi-engine aircraft with seating capacity of more than 10 passengers or maximum takeoff weight over 5,700kg. One major difference between Class A and Class B aircraft is that the former must be able to handle engine failure at any point between takeoff and landing without requirement for a forced landing. They must also be able to operate on contaminated runways without jeopardizing safety.

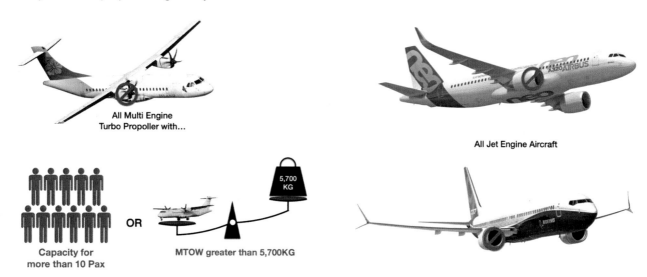

*Figure 2: Class A aircraft.*

My main goal in creating this material is to make a traditionally complex and tiring theme (like aircraft performance) somewhat enjoyable and objective, from the practical perspective of an airline pilot, while stressing the importance of studying this subject matter. Pilots must understand the requirements behind each part of their flight and what can be expected from the airplane at every moment. Then, flying accordingly is the only way to ensure operational safety and efficiency. Pilots, engineers, and flight dispatchers need to reach common ground. In other words, they need to learn about each other's work to avoid unintentional deviations in flight conduct that could downgrade safety of the aircraft and its occupants.

The material is very detailed and rich in illustrations, and it is intended for any reader interested in aviation, but especially for pilots (professional, recreational, or student pilots), flight dispatchers, and engineers working in the operations engineering office of any airline.

Although the book is written in English, the reader should be aware that the author is not a native speaker of that language. Therefore, if you are in doubt about any part of the book, please let me know so that I can improve the quality of this material in further editions. If you have any questions, criticism, compliments, or suggestions regarding this book,  please email me at performance.brenner@gmail.com.

Happy reading!

Intentionally left blank.

**Aircraft Performance Weight and Balance** – 4th Edition (English Version)

# Physics of Flight

As I mentioned in the Briefing, this book is not designed exclusively for pilots, but for anyone interested in studying Aircraft Performance, including engineers, flight dispatchers, and aviation enthusiasts. However, some knowledge of basic aerodynamics, flight controls, and onboard equipment is required for readers to keep up with the subject matter.

I would like to stress that the primary goal of this book is to study the performance of class A aircraft, not to serve as a comprehensive guide on physics or aerodynamics. I will approach these subjects superficially, with the sole intent of making lay readers more familiar with the topics that will be addressed throughout the chapters. So, let's move on and take a look at some concepts of physics that will be important for the study of aircraft performance.

### 1.1.1 Temperature

As far as temperature is concerned, the most important item that I would like to highlight is the difference between absolute temperature and relative temperature, as these concepts will be useful for developing our calculations.

In physics, temperature is slightly different from how it is perceived by people at large. If you ask a child what their understanding of temperature is, their answer is likely to be related to the amount of heat in an object. For physics, however, temperature and heat are distinct concepts. Heat is a measurement of energy. Temperature, on the other hand, is a measure of the level of molecular agitation in a body. When these molecules are at rest, the temperature is 0. We call this point "absolute zero," and there are two scales that measure temperature from zero: Rankine (R), an

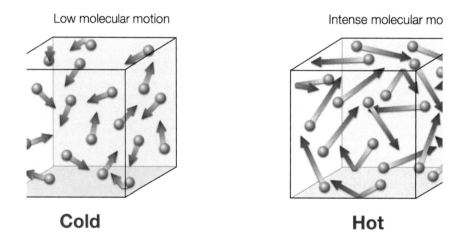

Figure 3: What is temperature?

Temperature, as we know it when measuring ordinary things in our daily lives, is a relative scale within an absolute one. When we measure something in degrees Celsius (°C), we are using a relative scale based on the absolute Kelvin scale. The difference between the freezing and boiling points of water is divided into 100 units, with the freezing point set at 0°C. It has not always been like that, but this is not a history book anyway.

When measuring temperature in degrees Fahrenheit (°F), the relative scale is based on the absolute Rankine scale. In this case, the difference between the freezing and boiling points of water is divided into 180 units, with the freezing point set at 32°F. The Fahrenheit scale was also not originally created using water as a reference, but rather winter and human body temperatures.

Both are great stories that I highly recommend you explore further.

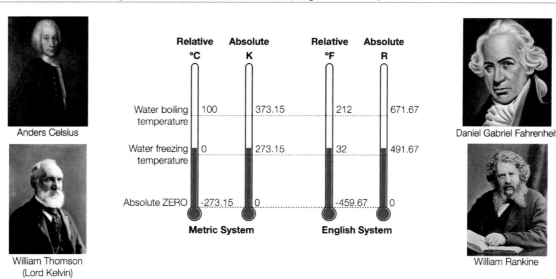

Anders Celsius

William Thomson
(Lord Kelvin)

Daniel Gabriel Fahrenheit

William Rankine

*Figure 4: Relative and Absolute Temperature scales.*

To make performance calculations, the temperature used in equations should always be set to an absolute scale — never a relative value. In our studies, we will use the metric unit (Kelvin). To convert degrees Celsius to Kelvin, simply add 273.15 to the value indicated in °C. For example, 22°C is equivalent to 295.15K.

To illustrate the importance of working with absolute temperatures, consider a simple example: Is 40°C twice as hot as 20°C? The answer is no. It is hotter, no doubt, but it is far from being twice as hot. Figure 5 shows the reason: 20°C on the absolute scale is equivalent to 293.15K. Doubling that temperature gives you 586.3K or 313°C, which is much more than merely 40°C.

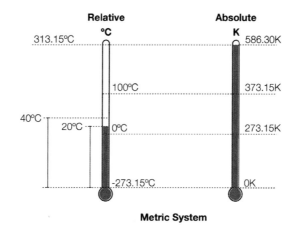

*Figure 5: Twice as hot as 20°C is definitely not 40°C.*

## 1.1.2 Weight versus Mass

There is a great deal of confusion over the terms weight and mass. Weight is a force that depends on both mass and the acceleration of gravity. Mass is a slightly more difficult concept, but we can say that it is the amount of matter in a body. However, what really matters at this point is to explain how the terms will be used throughout the chapters.

The metric unit of weight is Newton (N), but in this book, we will use the concept of kilogram-force (kgf) to define the weight of objects. The book will purposely consider the "kg" unit to define weights and refer to weight as what should technically be called mass. For example, the term Takeoff Weight will be used instead of Takeoff Mass, and Landing Weight instead of Landing Mass, Zero Fuel Weight instead of Zero Fuel Mass, and so on. It was a difficult decision to maintain this "physically colloquial" language, but I think it is important to keep the terms that are used in everyday life rather than being physically correct and potentially creating confusion with the practical application of what we will learn.

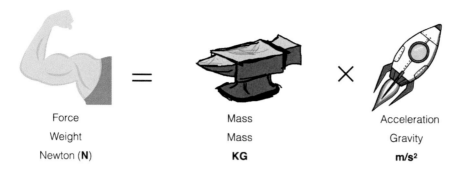

| Force | Mass | Acceleration |
| Weight | Mass | Gravity |
| Newton (**N**) | **KG** | **m/s²** |

*Figure 6: Weight versus Mass.*

Still, there are equations that we will learn that require the weight variable (W). In these equations, we need to remember the actual definition of weight and that the value of acceleration of gravity must be multiplied by mass to find the correct result.

The value of gravity acceleration at sea-level at a latitude of 45° is 9.80665m/s².

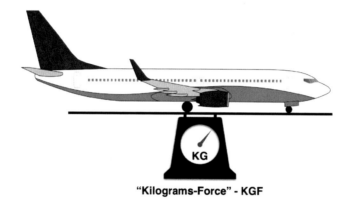

**"Kilograms-Force" - KGF**

*Figure 7: Weight is KG, KGF or N?*

## 1.1.3 Pressure

In the following sections of this chapter, we will be working extensively with air pressure, and you should know at least two things about this physical property: what it depends on and how it can be measured.

Pressure is the amount of force exerted in a given area. The international system unit for measuring pressure is Pascal (Pa). One Pascal is equivalent to one Newton of force exerted over an area of one square meter. We can increase pressure on a particular body in two different ways: either by increasing the force on it or by decreasing the contact area. In either case, pressure will increase.

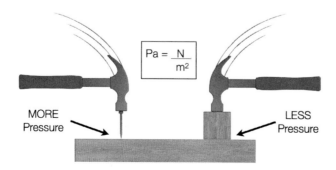

$$Pa = \frac{N}{m^2}$$

MORE Pressure

LESS Pressure

*Figure 8: How to increase pressure.*

The pressure we are now interested in measuring is the one over our heads. Although we cannot feel it, mostly because we are adapted to it, we are under some air pressure all the time. When determining how to measure the value of such pressure, the issue was resolved by using an element called mercury. After a long test tube was filled with this material and then inverted into an open container, it was found that not all of the content spilled out. The conclusion was that the amount of mercury that remained inside the test tube exerted the same downward pressure as all the air above us.

The sea-level atmosphere exerts pressure that is equivalent to that of a test tube with mercury in it up to a height of 760mm or 29.92in. This value is also called "One Atmosphere" and is equivalent to 101,325Pa or 1,013.25hPa, as it is most commonly used in aviation.

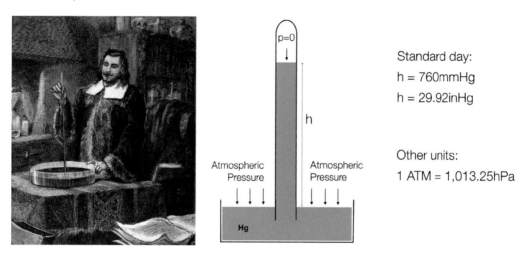

Standard day:

h = 760mmHg

h = 29.92inHg

Other units:

1 ATM = 1,013.25hPa

*Figure 9: Evangelista Torricelli measuring atmospheric pressure.*

## 1.1.4   Trigonometry

Finally, let's look back at some basic trigonometry: sine, cosine, and tangent. There are numerous applications for these functions, and I will explain some of them throughout the book. But what exactly is this so-called "sine"?

Sine, cosine, and tangent are mathematical properties of the angle ø shown in Figure 10, established by the relationship between the hypotenuse and the sides of a right-angle triangle. In the illustration, "x" is the adjacent side, "y" is the opposite side, and "z" is the hypotenuse. Sine is the relationship between the opposite side and the hypotenuse of the right-angled triangle. Cosine is the relationship between the adjacent side and the hypotenuse, and finally, tangent establishes the relationship between the opposite and adjacent sides of this triangle.

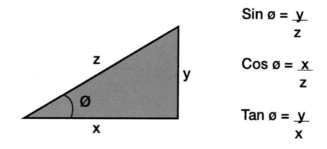

$$\text{Sin } \o = \frac{y}{z}$$

$$\text{Cos } \o = \frac{x}{z}$$

$$\text{Tan } \o = \frac{y}{x}$$

*Figure 10: Relationship between sides and angles of a right triangle.*

A curious fact that is worth noting is how these concepts were framed. Although, in practice, they represent relationships between the sides of a right triangle, the initial study was performed within a circle with a radius of one unit, as shown in Figure 11. The vertical axis was called sine, the cosine is the horizontal axis, and a vertical tangent line was drawn to the right side of this circumference.

The sine, cosine, and tangent values are the projections that a radius drawn at any given angle measured from the horizontal axis (measuring the angle counterclockwise) makes on the axes and the tangent. See the following example for an angle of 60°. The sine and cosine range from -1 to 1, and the tangent can be any positive or negative number (from minus to plus infinity).

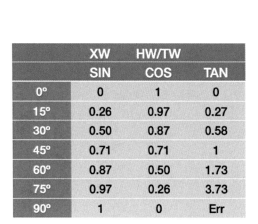
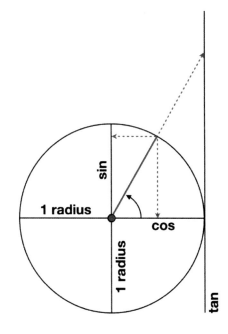

| | XW | HW/TW | |
|---|---|---|---|
| | SIN | COS | TAN |
| 0° | 0 | 1 | 0 |
| 15° | 0.26 | 0.97 | 0.27 |
| 30° | 0.50 | 0.87 | 0.58 |
| 45° | 0.71 | 0.71 | 1 |
| 60° | 0.87 | 0.50 | 1.73 |
| 75° | 0.97 | 0.26 | 3.73 |
| 90° | 1 | 0 | Err |

*Figure 11: Origin of sine, cosine, and tangent.*

Let me show you a practical application. Consider an airplane lined up for takeoff on runway 20R (runway course is 200°). The tower reports that the wind is blowing from 140° at 16 knots. What is the value of the headwind component (HWC) and the crosswind component (XWC) of this wind? As you can see in Figure 12, the sine of the angle between the runway track and the wind direction will represent the percentage of crosswind, and the cosine establishes how much headwind or tailwind there is. This is also shown in Figure 11, where we can see "XW" on top of Sine and "HW/TW" on top of Cosine in the table that contains the values for these mathematical properties.

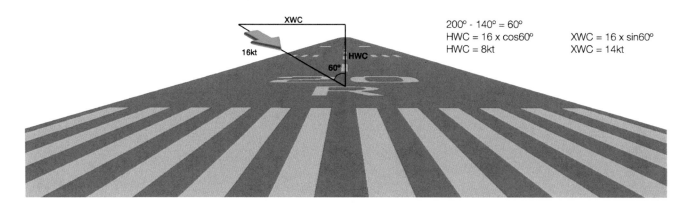

*Figure 12: Decomposing wind into head/tailwind and crosswind.*

In studying gas behavior, the behavior of air in the atmosphere is what matters most for performance. To this end, we need to make some assumptions, such as understanding the fact that the atmosphere is dynamic and constantly changing. For this reason, there is a need to define a standard atmosphere model to allow us to compare and estimate results for aircraft and engine performance, as well as to compare data obtained from "test flights" in wind tunnels, for example.

Several standard atmosphere models have been created over time, but it was not until the 1960s that the International Civil Aviation Organization (ICAO) defined a model of its own, which was eventually adopted by all aircraft and engine manufacturers around the globe. This model of the atmosphere was called the International Standard Atmosphere (ISA) and corresponds to an average of data collected over a long period of time, mostly in the mid-latitudes of the northern hemisphere. While there are expected to be large variations from this model, especially in polar and equatorial regions, the ISA has been used as a reference ever since.

Our next step is to discuss altitude settings. Importantly, some terms have different meanings when comparing technical literature on aircraft performance with meteorological literature for pilots, for example. Don't worry about these differences! The important thing is to make it clear how those terms will be used in this book.

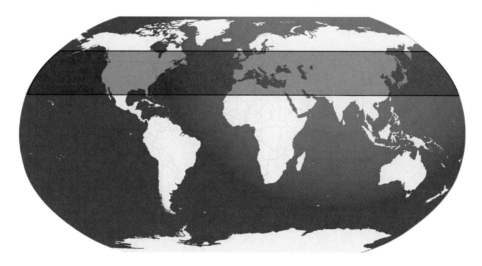

Figure 13: Area where data was collected to establish the International Standard Atmosphere - ISA

## 1.2.1 Absolute Altitude

The first altitude we will focus on is what we will call Absolute Altitude (AA). In this context, AA is the distance measured between the point where the aircraft is and the center of the Earth. You will see another definition using the same name when we talk about how high an airplane can fly. If the Earth were a perfect sphere, considering any two aircraft flying at the same altitude relative to sea level, their absolute altitudes would also be equal. However, the Earth is not a perfect globe. In fact, the radius from the center of the Earth to the Equator is approximately 21.5km greater than the radius from its center to the poles.

This considerable difference in the Earth's radius makes the acceleration of gravity also considerably different at these two points on the globe (Equator and poles). However, since we are not studying spaceflight and rocket launching, absolute altitude is more of a "nice to know" concept for our study than knowledge with a relevant practical effect.

By the way, considering Absolute Altitude, Mount Everest is not the highest point on Earth. In fact, it is almost 2,400 meters lower! The highest point in the world is located in Ecuador, in the middle of the Andes, and it is called Mount Chimborazo. Off topic, but an interesting point to note!

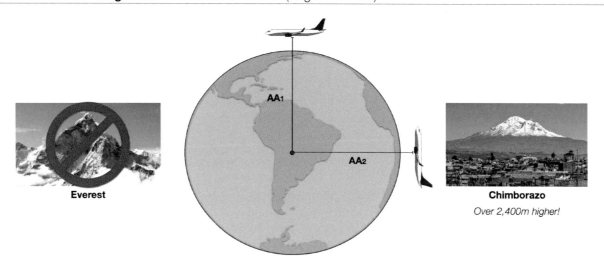

Figure 14: Absolute Altitude (AA).

## 1.2.2    Tapeline Altitude

Tapeline Altitude (TA) – also known as geometric altitude or true altitude – is the distance between the aircraft and sea level at any point on Earth. Two equal TAs at different latitudes will result in different AAs due to the Earth's flattening near the poles. It is called Tapeline Altitude because one can imagine measuring the altitude using a tape measure between the plane and sea level, which is, of course, impossible to do. To measure altitude, another solution needs to be proposed, as this is only a theoretical concept. A radio altimeter would work in some parts of the globe, but it would be subject to indication errors owing to variations in the terrain below the airplane.

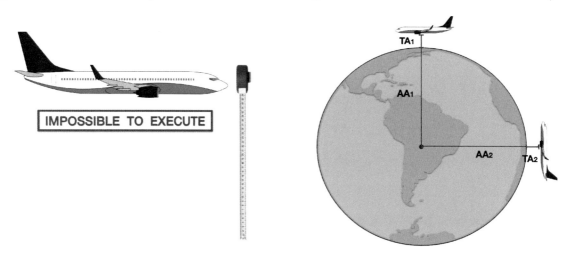

Figure 15: Tapeline Altitude (TA).

One possible solution to establish altitude would be to measure air pressure. However, as we saw earlier, the atmosphere is extremely dynamic, which complicates such measurement. And this is not the only problem. Let's take a look at the next item.

## 1.2.3    Geopotential Altitude

When trying to establish a pressure variation model to correlate it with altitude, one of the challenges was that the acceleration of gravity is not constant as altitude increases, nor is it the same at the same altitude (TA) at different latitudes.

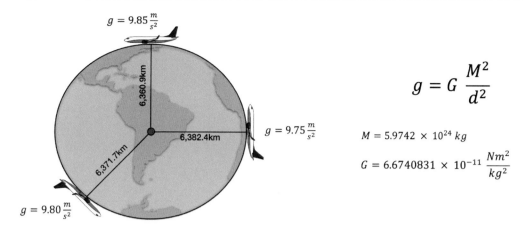

$$g = G \frac{M^2}{d^2}$$

$$M = 5.9742 \times 10^{24}\ kg$$

$$G = 6.6740831 \times 10^{-11}\ \frac{Nm^2}{kg^2}$$

*Figure 16: Acceleration of gravity at sea level at different latitudes.*

With this in mind, the solution was to create a model that considers the acceleration of gravity, "g", as constant at 9.80m/s². It was concluded that the error generated by this model was acceptable for aviation studies, as it was very small when compared to the theoretical Tapeline Altitude, reaching only 1% at 65,000 meters in height. The altitude based on this constant "g" model is called Geopotential Altitude (GA). It was named "geopotential" after the potential energy of air molecules, as this type of energy is directly linked to the acceleration of gravity, which was considered constant for the purpose of measurement.

### 1.2.3.1 Temperature Variation on the Geopotential Altitude Model

The geopotential altitude model used by manufacturers to set engine and aircraft performance parameters is ISA. Within this model, the part of the atmosphere that is relevant for our study is the troposphere and a portion of the tropopause, which begins at 36,089ft in this standard model. ISA also established a standard temperature behavior as a function of altitude, starting at 15°C at sea level and dropping 1.9812°C for every 1,000ft climbed until reaching the tropopause, where the temperature becomes constant.

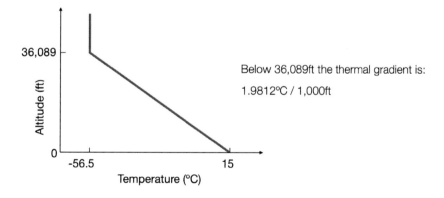

Below 36,089ft the thermal gradient is:

1.9812°C / 1,000ft

*Figure 17: Temperature variation within the Troposphere and the Tropopause in the ISA model.*

### 1.2.4 ISA Deviation – Temperature

One technical term we need to become acquainted with is the reference of current temperatures to ISA deviation; we call this value ΔISA. In the standard atmosphere model, sea level temperature is expected to be 15°C. If, at any location with 0ft elevation, the temperature is 25°C, we refer to this condition as ISA+10, with "+10" being the ISA variation measured in degrees Celsius. The same is true for other altitudes. In the standard atmosphere, the temperature at 35,000ft is expected to be -55°C. If the temperature at this altitude is -58°C, we say that it is ISA-3. Once again, the index next to the acronym ISA represents the variation from what was expected, which in this last example is 3°C colder.

## 1.2.5    Pressure Altitude

Using the geopotential altitude model to correlate pressure and altitude, we encounter a new problem: pressure variation. We have already seen that the atmosphere is in constant motion and atmospheric pressure at the same point can vary greatly between days and even within the same day. Thus, the altimeter was built and calibrated to represent the ISA atmosphere, considering sea level pressure equal to 1,013.25hPa (29.92inHg).

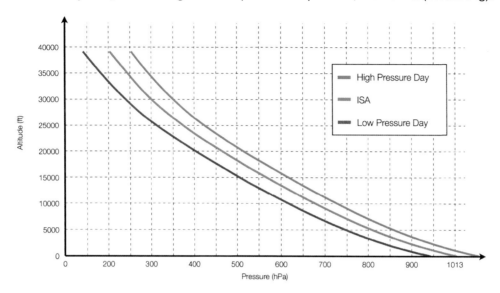

*Figure 18: Pressure variation in the atmosphere.*

Of course, the fact that the altimeter is calibrated to identify sea level as a 1,013.25hPa pressure location will cause reading errors every time sea level pressure differs from this value. This error can be up or down depending on the actual sea level pressure. On low-pressure days, the altitude read on the instrument will be higher than the actual one, and on high-pressure days, the altitude read on the instrument will be lower than the actual one.

This error may or may not be dangerous depending on the purpose. If the intention is to keep airplanes separated from each other by a minimum height so that they do not collide when crossing the same point at the same time, it is not a problem to fly with incorrect altitude information as long as they all fly with the same error, i.e., the separation between them must be maintained at all times. In aviation, when we are in this situation, where all that matters is the vertical separation between airplanes, we say that we are flying at a Flight Level (FL) and the altitude values are expressed in hundreds of feet. For example, FL120 means 12,000ft, FL310 means 31,000ft, and so on.

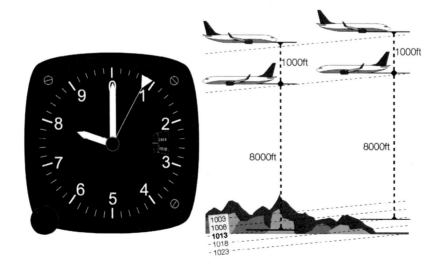

*Figure 19: Flying at different flight levels using pressure altitude.*

## 1.2.6 Indicated Altitude

But what are we supposed to do when we are approaching an airport to land? We need to ensure that the airplane's separation from the ground is as accurate as possible. For this purpose, a device has been installed in the altimeters that allows pilots to change the reference sea level pressure, giving them a much more accurate indication of the actual altitude. All we need is someone to tell pilots what the sea level pressure is at the location they are approaching to land. This is one of the roles of the control tower. The adjustment we make to this altimeter device (known in analog altimeters as "Kollsman's window") is named using the "Q" language, originating from Morse code. When the setting represents the standard atmosphere (1,013.25hPa), we say that the altimeter is set to QNE and, as I said previously, we will refer to altitudes as flight levels.

By changing the value in Kollsman's window on the altimeter to reflect the actual sea level pressure, we say that the altimeter is now set to QNH. With this altimeter setting, we no longer refer to flight levels, but to flight altitudes. It is a relatively accurate way to measure altitude, and by knowing the elevations around us, we can maintain a safe separation from the terrain. I used the expression "relatively accurate" because there are still important errors that we need to account for.

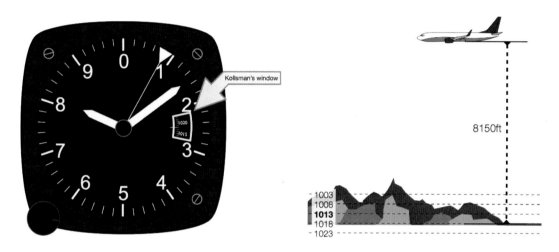

*Figure 20: Flying with QNH setting to maintain terrain clearance.*

Let's look back at some important concepts about gas behavior. By increasing the temperature of a given gas while keeping a constant pressure on it, the volume of this gas expands. Owing to this gas behavior, looking at a vertical path, isobaric lines will be closer together when the air is cold and farther apart when the air is hot. Since the pressure altimeter is calibrated with a fixed altitude scale between each isobaric line, an indication error will occur. For example, the altimeter calibration is adjusted to indicate that, near sea level, every 1hPa of pressure variation is equivalent to about 28ft of altitude variation. If the day is warmer than ISA, this ratio changes, and 1hPa may be worth 30ft, while it may change to 26ft on a cold day.

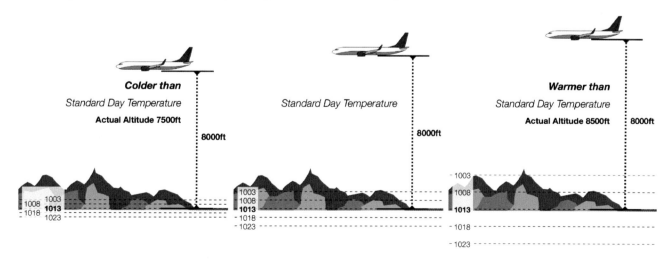

*Figure 21: Indicated Altitude errors owing to temperature variation.*

These errors can be either safe or unsafe. A safe error occurs on days with temperatures higher than the International Standard Atmosphere (ISA), i.e., on hot days. In this case, the altimeter will show a lower altitude than the actual one. Since the plane will be higher than indicated, there is no risk of impact with the ground. On the other hand, when the day is colder than ISA, the indicated altitude is higher than the actual one. This means the pilot's separation from terrain elevations decreases, posing a major safety hazard. To address this danger, there are tables that correct altitude values when temperatures fall below a certain threshold.

Let's look at an example of how to correct the temperature error in a landing procedure. Suppose the procedure specifies that the minimum altitude over a given waypoint is 4,400ft, the aerodrome has a temperature of negative 20°C, and an elevation of 1,000ft.

**Altitude Correction Table (Heights and Altitudes in Feet)**

| Airport Temp °C | Height Above Altimeter Reference Source | | | | | | | | | | | |
|---|---|---|---|---|---|---|---|---|---|---|---|---|
| | 200 feet | 300 feet | 400 feet | 500 feet | 600 feet | 700 feet | 800 feet | 900 feet | 1000 feet | 1500 feet | 2000 feet | 3000 feet |
| 0° | 20 | 20 | 30 | 30 | 40 | 40 | 50 | 50 | 60 | 90 | 120 | 170 |
| -10° | 20 | 30 | 40 | 50 | 60 | 70 | 80 | 90 | 100 | 150 | 200 | 290 |
| -20° | 30 | 50 | 60 | 70 | 90 | 100 | 120 | 130 | 140 | 210 | 280 | 420 |
| -30° | 40 | 60 | 80 | 100 | 120 | 140 | 150 | 170 | 190 | 280 | 380 | 570 |
| -40° | 50 | 80 | 100 | 120 | 150 | 170 | 190 | 220 | 240 | 360 | 480 | 720 |
| -50° | 60 | 90 | 120 | 150 | 180 | 210 | 240 | 270 | 300 | 450 | 590 | 890 |

*Figure 22: Altitude Correction Table.*

Solution:
4,400ft (Waypoint) – 1,000ft (Aerodrome) = 3,400ft (height) => Search for this value in the table above.
420 + 60 = 480ft is the correction value to apply to the Waypoint.
4,400ft + 480ft = 4,880ft.

## 1.2.7   Density Altitude

Density altitude addresses the issue of temperature in altitude readings. It determines the equivalent altitude we would have if the air temperature and pressure matched ISA conditions. I often say that when calculating density altitude, we are determining the altitude that the airplane 'feels' it is flying at in order to assess its performance.

Air density varies as a function of temperature and pressure. While keeping one of these values constant, density drops as pressure decreases, and it rises as pressure increases. Density is lower when the temperature rises and higher as the temperature drops. The equation below is valid when assuming the air is dry. "P" stands for the air pressure at the current elevation in hPa, and "T" stands for the air temperature in Kelvin.

In the following example, we will compare two different airports: one at 5,000ft with a QNH of 1028hPa and a temperature of -5°C, and another at sea level with a QNH of 1002hPa and a temperature of 42°C. The figure illustrates that the plane 'feels' as though it is at a higher altitude when at the airport at sea level compared to the one at 5,000ft elevation. This is a result of adjusting for QNH and temperature.

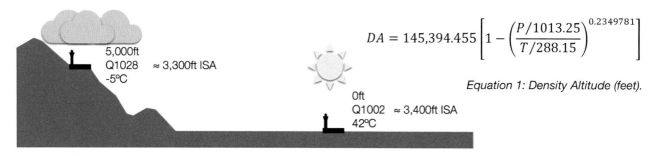

$$DA = 145{,}394.455\left[1 - \left(\frac{P/1013.25}{T/288.15}\right)^{0.2349781}\right]$$

*Equation 1: Density Altitude (feet).*

*Figure 23: Density Altitude example.*

## 1.2.8    Differences between OAT, SAT, and TAT

We have already discussed altitude; now, let's talk about temperature. In the previous section, we saw that temperature in performance equations must always be an absolute temperature, i.e., never relative. Here, however, we will discuss something slightly different: how to obtain the outside air temperature value when we are in flight.

*Figure 24: Different temperature probes. TAT probe on the right.*

Installing a thermometer (like the one shown on the left side of Figure 24) on the airplane might seem like a good idea, but it is not, at least not for the airplanes that we are studying. When the aircraft is stationary, this thermometer can accurately read what we call Outside Air Temperature (OAT), which is the static air temperature outside the aircraft. However, at higher speeds, when air can no longer be considered an incompressible fluid (around 190 knots or 30% of the speed of sound), increasing air pressure raises air temperature. Additionally, the friction of the air "scraping" the thermometer will further increase the temperature, resulting in a reading that is completely different from the actual static air temperature outside.

Fortunately, there is an equation that shows how much the temperature will increase as a function of our speed. However, the thermometer that we must use is a TAT probe, a type of sensor that measures what we call Total Air Temperature (TAT).

This sensor has a hole that allows air to enter at an extremely low velocity (almost stagnation), causing air pressure and temperature to rise as predicted by the equation. The efficiency of the thermometer is known as the Recovery Factor (RF). In most modern sensors (like the one on the right side of the previous illustration), the RF is 1 and can be eliminated from the equation. The equation then depends on the airplane's speed relative to the speed of sound (Mach number, which will be studied in more detail later) and the static air temperature to determine the total air temperature. Since the thermometer measures the TAT and we wish to find out the static air temperature, we simply invert the equation and isolate the desired variable.

It is important to note the difference between the terms OAT (Outside Air Temperature) and SAT (Static Air Temperature). The numerical values of the two temperatures are always the same when the aircraft is stationary, but OAT is obtained from a direct reading on a thermometer when the air is actually still, while SAT is calculated for air moving through the second type of thermometer (TAT probe). The difference between SAT and TAT is known as Ram Rise, which indicates how much the air temperature increased owing to compressibility.

To understand the magnitude of Ram Rise, consider a Concorde flying at twice the speed of sound (Mach 2) in a location where SAT is -59°C. The pilots would see an indication of 113°C in the cabin, measured by the TAT sensor. Yes, that is a positive number: 113°C, representing a difference (or Ram Rise) of 172°C.

$$TAT = SAT \times (1 + 0.2 \times C_T \times M^2)$$

└──→ *Recovery Factor*

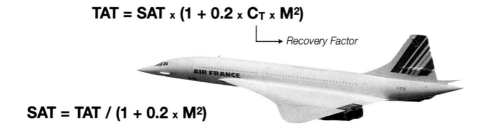

$$SAT = TAT / (1 + 0.2 \times M^2)$$

*Equation 2: Determining TAT on the basis of SAT and vice versa. Temperatures are always in Kelvin!*

On the next page of this book, you will see what is known as the Standard Atmosphere Table. This table contains reference values that are used in various calculations of aircraft performance. Below, I explain what the values in the Table represent.

$$\delta = \frac{p}{p_0}$$

**Delta**: Pressure at present altitude divided by pressure at sea level on a standard day (**1,013.25 hPa**).

$$\theta = \frac{T}{T_0}$$

**Theta**: Absolute temperature at present altitude divided by temperature at sea level on a standard day (**288.15 K**).

$$\sigma = \frac{\rho}{\rho_0}$$

**Sigma**: Air density at present altitude divided by air density at sea level on standard day (**1.2250 kg/m³**).

$$\sigma = \frac{\delta}{\theta}$$

$$\frac{a}{a_0}$$

Represents the speed of sound at present altitude divided by the speed of sound at sea level on a standard day (**661.4786 kt**).

*Figure 25: Meaning of Delta, Theta, and Sigma.*

## 1.2.9    Standard Atmosphere Table

| $h_p$ | OAT | $\theta$ | | Atm Pressure | | $\delta$ | $\sigma$ |
|---|---|---|---|---|---|---|---|
| feet | °C | $T/T_0$ | $a/a_0$ | inHg | hPa | $p/p_0$ | $\rho/\rho_0$ |
| 0 | 15.0 | 1.0000 | 1.0000 | 29.921 | 1013.2 | 1.0000 | 1.0000 |
| 1000 | 13.0 | 0.9931 | 0.9966 | 28.855 | 977.1 | 0.9644 | 0.9711 |
| 2000 | 11.0 | 0.9862 | 0.9931 | 27.821 | 942.1 | 0.9298 | 0.9428 |
| 3000 | 9.1 | 0.9794 | 0.9896 | 26.816 | 908.1 | 0.8962 | 0.9151 |
| 4000 | 7.1 | 0.9725 | 0.9862 | 25.842 | 875.1 | 0.8637 | 0.8881 |
| 5000 | 5.1 | 0.9656 | 0.9827 | 24.896 | 843.0 | 0.8320 | 0.8617 |
| 6000 | 3.1 | 0.9587 | 0.9792 | 23.978 | 812.0 | 0.8014 | 0.8359 |
| 7000 | 1.1 | 0.9519 | 0.9756 | 23.088 | 781.8 | 0.7716 | 0.8106 |
| 8000 | -0.8 | 0.9450 | 0.9721 | 22.225 | 752.6 | 0.7428 | 0.7860 |
| 9000 | -2.8 | 0.9381 | 0.9686 | 21.388 | 724.2 | 0.7148 | 0.7620 |
| 10000 | -4.8 | 0.9312 | 0.9650 | 20.577 | 696.8 | 0.6877 | 0.7385 |
| 11000 | -6.8 | 0.9244 | 0.9614 | 19.791 | 670.2 | 0.6614 | 0.7156 |
| 12000 | -8.8 | 0.9175 | 0.9579 | 19.029 | 644.4 | 0.6360 | 0.6932 |
| 13000 | -10.8 | 0.9106 | 0.9543 | 18.292 | 619.4 | 0.6113 | 0.6713 |
| 14000 | -12.7 | 0.9037 | 0.9507 | 17.577 | 595.2 | 0.5875 | 0.6500 |
| 15000 | -14.7 | 0.8969 | 0.9470 | 16.886 | 571.8 | 0.5643 | 0.6292 |
| 16000 | -16.7 | 0.8900 | 0.9434 | 16.216 | 549.1 | 0.5420 | 0.6090 |
| 17000 | -18.7 | 0.8831 | 0.9397 | 15.569 | 527.2 | 0.5203 | 0.5892 |
| 18000 | -20.7 | 0.8762 | 0.9361 | 14.942 | 506.0 | 0.4994 | 0.5699 |
| 19000 | -22.6 | 0.8694 | 0.9324 | 14.336 | 485.5 | 0.4791 | 0.5511 |
| 20000 | -24.6 | 0.8625 | 0.9287 | 13.750 | 465.6 | 0.4595 | 0.5328 |
| 21000 | -26.6 | 0.8556 | 0.9250 | 13.184 | 446.4 | 0.4406 | 0.5150 |
| 22000 | -28.6 | 0.8487 | 0.9213 | 12.636 | 427.9 | 0.4223 | 0.4976 |
| 23000 | -30.6 | 0.8419 | 0.9175 | 12.107 | 410.0 | 0.4046 | 0.4807 |
| 24000 | -32.5 | 0.8350 | 0.9138 | 11.597 | 392.7 | 0.3876 | 0.4642 |
| 25000 | -34.5 | 0.8281 | 0.9100 | 11.103 | 376.0 | 0.3711 | 0.4481 |
| 26000 | -36.5 | 0.8212 | 0.9062 | 10.627 | 359.9 | 0.3552 | 0.4325 |
| 27000 | -38.5 | 0.8144 | 0.9024 | 10.168 | 344.3 | 0.3398 | 0.4173 |
| 28000 | -40.5 | 0.8075 | 0.8986 | 9.725 | 329.3 | 0.3250 | 0.4025 |
| 29000 | -42.5 | 0.8006 | 0.8948 | 9.297 | 314.8 | 0.3107 | 0.3881 |
| 30000 | -44.4 | 0.7937 | 0.8909 | 8.885 | 300.9 | 0.2970 | 0.3741 |
| 31000 | -46.4 | 0.7869 | 0.8870 | 8.488 | 287.4 | 0.2837 | 0.3605 |
| 32000 | -48.4 | 0.7800 | 0.8832 | 8.106 | 274.5 | 0.2709 | 0.3473 |
| 33000 | -50.4 | 0.7731 | 0.8793 | 7.737 | 262.0 | 0.2586 | 0.3345 |
| 34000 | -52.4 | 0.7662 | 0.8753 | 7.382 | 250.0 | 0.2467 | 0.3220 |
| 35000 | -54.3 | 0.7594 | 0.8714 | 7.041 | 238.4 | 0.2353 | 0.3099 |
| 36000 | -56.3 | 0.7525 | 0.8675 | 6.712 | 227.3 | 0.2243 | 0.2981 |
| 37000 | -56.5 | 0.7519 | 0.8671 | 6.397 | 216.6 | 0.2138 | 0.2844 |
| 38000 | -56.5 | 0.7519 | 0.8671 | 6.097 | 206.5 | 0.2038 | 0.2710 |
| 39000 | -56.5 | 0.7519 | 0.8671 | 5.811 | 196.8 | 0.1942 | 0.2583 |
| 40000 | -56.5 | 0.7519 | 0.8671 | 5.538 | 187.5 | 0.1851 | 0.2462 |

*Figure 26: Standard Atmosphere Table.*

## 1.3.1   Airspeed Unit - Knot (kt)

In the past, during the era of great navigations, naval explorers faced many challenges. Ingenious solutions were developed to address these problems! For instance, a unit of measurement for distances had to be established (there was no metric system at the time, and even today, it is not used in air or marine navigation, except in China and Russia). The solution was brilliant. The globe, like any circumference, has 360 degrees. Each degree can be divided into 60 equal parts called minutes, and each minute is divided into 60 equal parts called seconds (just like we measure time on a clock).

To determine positions on the globe, a geographic coordinate system known as latitude and longitude was created. Latitudes indicate how far north or south we are from the Equator (0° being the Equator and 90° being the poles, either North or South). Longitude tells you how far east or west of a reference point we are (180° to each side, East and West). This reference became known as the Greenwich Meridian, named after the English town that this imaginary line passes through.

If we imagine cutting the Earth horizontally as if it were a lemon, a cut right through the middle would result in two equal halves, and a certain circumference would be visible from the top. With a higher or lower cut, the parts would be different, and the circumference would always be smaller than the one measured with the cut in the middle. We say that this middle cut results in a great circle.

On the other hand, making vertical cuts in the lemon, which can occur in any direction when viewed from above but always passing through the "poles" of the lemon, will always result in two equal halves with a great circle. On Earth, the same principle applies. Among the parallels (latitudes), only one is a great circle: the Equator, but all the meridians pass through the poles and all of them are great circles.

Thus, it was established that every minute of a great circle on the globe would represent a unit of measure for distance. This unit was named a "mile", but since the name was already in use and the measurements were different, we call this mile the "nautical mile" (nm). Therefore, we can deduce that each degree is worth 60nm, meaning that the Earth's maximum circle (the Equator or any meridian) measures 21,600nm in circumference (360 times 60). This is not 100% accurate since the meridians are slightly shorter than the Equator owing to the flattening of the Earth at the poles, but it is sufficient for our purposes here.

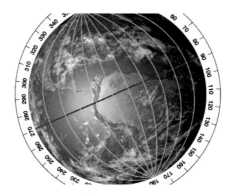

*Figure 27: Maximum Circles.*

Now that a unit of measure  had been established for distances, a unit had to be determined for speed. What could be more practical than knowing how many nautical miles were traveled in an hour? Thus, the nautical mile per hour quickly became the unit used to define speed at sea. But how could this be measured without GPS or other modern systems? Mathematicians developed a very ingenious method for measuring speed on the high seas. They would tie knots in a long rope at regular intervals (approximately 14 meters in today's metric system), and this rope was thrown overboard with a triangular-shaped wooden plank, called "log", attached to the end.

As the boat sailed away, the log remained relatively still in the water, pulling the rope (known as log line) from inside the ship into the sea while a sailor counted the number of knots that passed through his hand. When the hourglass ran out (about 28 seconds), the person responsible shouted out the result: "seven knots". That meant the speed was seven nautical miles per hour. Of course, this did not take into account sea currents and only measured the vessel's speed relative to the water, but we must acknowledge the ingenuity and simplicity of the process.

The term "knot" to define speeds has been inherited from sea navigation and is still commonly used in aviation today. In short, 1kt means the same as 1nm/h.

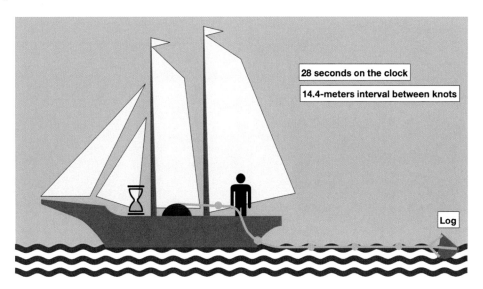

*Figure 28: Measuring speed in knots.*

## 1.3.2 Indicated Airspeed - IAS

As soon as humans began to fly, two things became clear. First, there was a need to develop a method to measure airplane speed, which would be quite different from the one used on 15th-century boats. Second, since an airplane flies because its wings interact with the air passing through them, the crucial velocity to measure is the one relative to the air moving through the aircraft, regardless of the aircraft's speed relative to the ground. This was just like the primitive vessels mentioned earlier, which measured their velocity relative to the water, disregarding any currents.

Various methods of measurement were attempted, for example, fitting a speed scale next to a metal bar on the wing, which would bend with the relative wind and indicate the speed to the pilot. After some time, it was realized that total air pressure, which increases because of the impact of the air caused by the aircraft's movement, could be compared to static air pressure. The key was determining how to make these two measurements, and most small aircraft use a single sensor for this purpose, known as the pitot-static system.

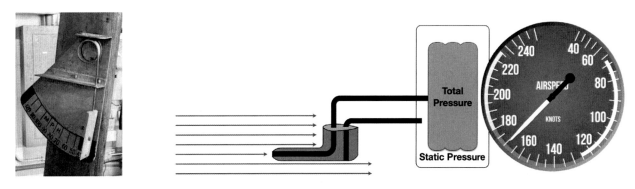

*Figure 29: Metal bar speed indicator on the left and the Pitot-Static System on the right.*

In Figure 29 (on the right side), you can see how this system operates. Moving air impacts the hole in front of the sensor, which registers the total air pressure, while a side or bottom hole that does not receive the air impact measures the static pressure, as if the air were stationary around the sensor. The capsule shown inside the instrument is a diaphragm that expands with higher velocity and contracts when the aircraft decelerates. By assigning a scale to the pressure difference that causes the diaphragm to expand and contract, a basic airspeed indicator was developed. While primitive, it remains highly reliable and is still widely used in many small aircraft. In more complex aircraft, the indicated airspeed is determined not by the expansion of a capsule but by a mathematical equation based on total and static pressure readings — a slightly different approach achieving the same goal through the same method.

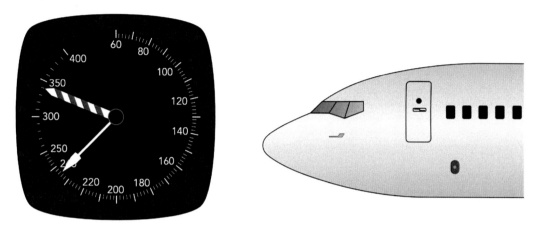

*Figure 30: Airspeed Indicator (ASI) and the pitot tube (green) and static port (red) sensors.*

As we have seen in our study of altitude measurements, nothing is that simple. This Indicated Airspeed (IAS) is used by pilots in flight, but they know that there are certain errors inherent in the measurement process. Therefore, IAS is just the speed read directly from the instrument. Let's see others.

## 1.3.3   Calibrated Airspeed - CAS

The first deficiency we can identify in the accuracy of speed measurement by the airspeed indicator is the fact that the pitot-static system is fixed to the aircraft. Its position is established when the equipment is installed and cannot be changed; thus, some errors caused by this position are expected to occur owing to the incidence of air in the total pressure of the sensor (pitot tube).

In Figure 31, the blue lines represent the air passing through the airplane. The incidence of air in the pitot tube mounted on the underside of the wing is different in both aircraft. This is one of the factors that can lead to errors. Another possible error is associated with the static pressure sensor, especially when it is in the fuselage, separate from the pitot tube, like the one in Figure 30. In this case, the aerodynamic shape of the fuselage changes the air pressure near this point and another reading error occurs. Finally, we can cite errors related to imperfections in the mechanisms, such as friction between gears or other similar things. When we can correct all these errors, we say that we now have the Calibrated Airspeed – CAS.

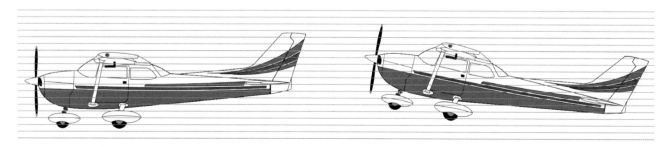

*Figure 31: Pitot tube position causes reading errors by the airspeed indicator.*

The only way to measure such errors is through test flights with a sensor that is not affected by these aerodynamic disturbances. A device called "trailing cone" is normally used. It is located at the tail of the plane at a certain distance from it to collect the data needed for measurement. We can usually see this device very close to the tail of test aircraft during takeoff and landing situations when the cable is retracted.

*Figure 32: Trailing Cone.*

With data collected by the trailing cone in hands, the manufacturer can build a chart to be able to show pilots the calibrated airspeed instead of the indicated airspeed. Have a look at the example below. The main airspeed indicator on the primary flight display shows CAS data from an Air Data Computer (ADC) that generates speed information based on pieces of information other than pressure, such as angle of attack and temperature. On the other hand, the standby instruments work the simplest way possible, collecting data only from total pressure and static pressure sources to display the indicated airspeed.

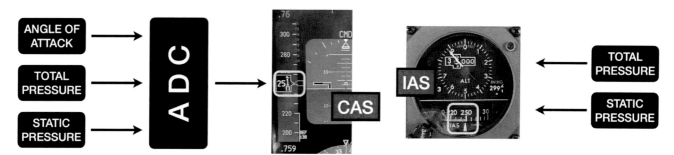

*Figure 33: Airspeed displayed by primary (CAS) and standby (IAS) instruments on a modern jetliner.*

The data used by the manufacturer to transform IAS into CAS is published on graphics or tables in the Airplane Flight Manual (AFM), stating how much error was identified in several situations (altitudes, weights, and speeds) during test flights. The errors are relatively small, as shown in the following chart. In the example, IAS is 290kt and altitude is 15,000ft. The error identified here is only 2kt, so CAS is 292kt.

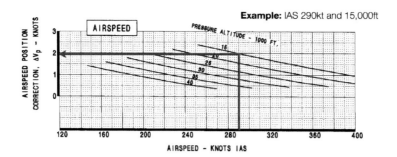

*Figure 34: In the example, CAS is 2kt greater than IAS.*

## 1.3.4 Equivalent Airspeed - EAS

This is one of the least understood speeds when it comes to ASI errors. It turns out that as speed increases, the pressure waves traveling in front of the airplane begin to get more and more compressed. This compression raises the air pressure at that point (pitot tube inlet).

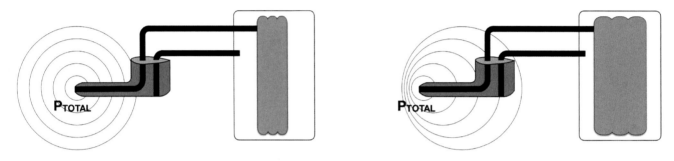

$$P_{Total} = (P_{Impact} + P_{Compressibility}) + P_{Static}$$

*Figure 35: Compressibility Error (Equivalent Airspeed - EAS).*

This phenomenon is well-known and taken into consideration when calibrating the airspeed indicator to show the airplane speed. Dynamic pressure, used to define velocity, is the result of total pressure minus static pressure. This dynamic pressure, however, is made of two parts: pressure resulting from air impact and compressibility pressure, which we have just mentioned.

When calibrating the ASI, the manufacturer considers the phenomenon at sea level. The problem is that compressibility intensity is different at altitude because of the Mach number (the speed of sound, which we will see soon).

When we refer to equivalent speed (EAS), what we are doing is to make a correction to eliminate this reading error caused by a different level of compressibility from the one the airspeed indicator was designed for, leaving the compressibility pressure equivalent to the one measured under ISA condition at sea level.

The equivalent speed will always be lower than CAS when at altitude and equal when flying in standard conditions at sea level. EAS = CAS - ΔVc. Equation 3, below, shows that we can measure the equivalent airspeed using two different variables: the calibrated airspeed and "delta" (local pressure divided by standard sea level pressure). Correction factors were applied in this equation so that speed values can be expressed in "knots".

$$EAS = 1479.1 \sqrt{\delta\left[\left(\frac{1}{\delta}\left\{\left[1 + 0.2\left(\frac{CAS}{661.4786}\right)^2\right]^{3.5} - 1\right\} + 1\right)^{\frac{1}{3.5}} - 1\right]}$$

*Equation 3: Determining EAS using CAS and Delta.*

Next, there is a graph that can be used in place of the equation to define ΔVc and correct CAS as a function of Mach number and altitude.

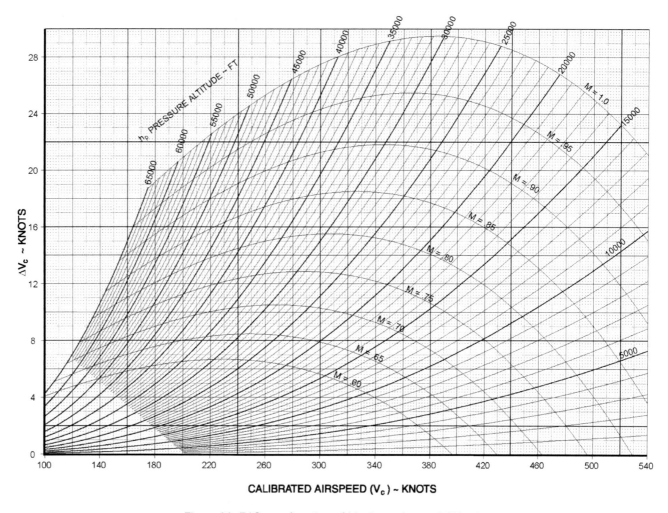

*Figure 36: EAS as a function of Mach number and Altitude.*

## 1.3.5   True Airspeed - TAS

True Airspeed (TAS) can be physically explained by using calculations or diagrams that I would prefer not to reproduce here. Forgive me if you enjoy extremely technical explanations, but my intention is to explain the meaning of TAS in simpler terms, as I promised to do in this book.

First of all, let me point out that this explanation is not technically correct; it is an analogy about the speed measurement process. Therefore, we must first understand how air particles are spread apart at sea level compared to at altitude. As pressure decreases with altitude, so does air density. With fewer air molecules per unit volume, we can say that they are more separated from each other.

Based on this premise, let's imagine that the airspeed indicator works as follows: there is a sensor inside it that records the arrival of each air particle. Suppose it has been calibrated with the premise that the particles are 1 cm apart. If the time interval between two particles hitting our imaginary sensor is one second, I can conclude that the plane travels at a speed of 1cm/s with respect to the air. This information is displayed on my Airspeed Indicator (ASI).

As we climb, the particles become further separated. Imagine a certain altitude where the particles are 2cm apart. If two particles hit the hypothetical sensor at a 1-second interval, my actual speed will now be 2cm/s. However, the airspeed indicator does not account for the new distance between the air molecules. For the ASI, the distance between those molecules is still 1cm, as previously calibrated. Therefore, even if my real airspeed is 2cm/s, the indicated airspeed will be 1cm/s.

And there you have it! TAS aims to correct our Calibrated Airspeed (CAS) based on factors that change the space between particles, i.e., altitude and temperature. The final result is the true airspeed of the airplane. The equation for calculating TAS (in knots) is shown below the illustration. Note that the equation requires Theta and Delta values, meaning it takes into account temperature and pressure variations, just as we had deduced.

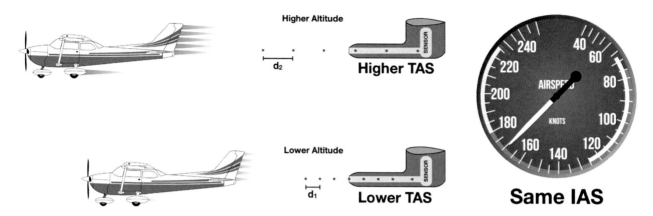

Figure 37: True Airspeed (TAS).

$$TAS = 1479.1 \sqrt{\theta \left[ \left( \frac{1}{\delta} \left\{ \left[ 1 + 0.2 \left( \frac{CAS}{661.4786} \right)^2 \right]^{3.5} - 1 \right\} + 1 \right)^{\frac{1}{3.5}} - 1 \right]}$$

Equation 4: TAS calculated on the basis of CAS, Theta and Delta.

## 1.3.6   Mach Number

Perhaps the simplest of speeds, Mach number is just a ratio of actual true airspeed (TAS) to the speed of sound. What is complicated is to determine the speed of sound itself as it depends on air temperature. In the ISA atmosphere and at sea level (15°C), the speed of sound is 340m/s or 661.4786kt. To find out the speed of sound (in knots) at any other temperature, use the equation below:

$$a = 661.4786 \ \sqrt{\theta}$$

Equation 5: The speed of sound in knots. Temperature must be in Kelvin!

"Theta" is the ratio of current flight level temperature to ISA sea level temperature. Remember that temperature values must be in Kelvin, not in degrees Celsius nor in Fahrenheit. With the speed of sound established and knowing your TAS, Mach number is the ratio of the latter to the former.

$$MACH = \frac{TAS}{a}$$

Equation 6: Mach number.

## 1.3.7   Ground Speed - GS

Finally, ground speed. The plane travels within a mass of air. In terms of aerodynamics, lift, drag, etc., this is all that matters. But if this air mass moves relative to the ground, this will change, for example, the flight time between two points. Ground speed (GS) is equal to true airspeed (TAS) plus the influence of the wind on it. If the wind is against its displacement (headwind), GS will be TAS minus the opposite component of the wind. If the wind blows in favor of the displacement (tailwind), GS will be equal to TAS plus the favorable wind component.

The speed indicated on the airspeed indicator does not change with the wind. It remains the same and all that makes the pilot realize that the wind holds or pushes the airplane is the ground passing below the airplane more slowly or rapidly. Of course, in addition to this rudimentary perception, we currently also have inertial reference system instruments, GPS, among others.

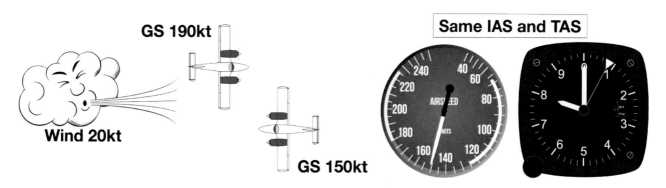

*Figure 38: Different Ground Speeds, but same TAS and IAS.*

## 1.3.8   Air Miles versus Ground Miles

To calculate the flight time between two points, we need to know the distance to be traveled and the speed at which this distance will be covered. There are two options here. When planning your flight, the predicted wind along your route can be used to adjust the True Airspeed (TAS) to obtain Ground Speed (GS) or to correct the distance to be flown.

Imagine a hot air balloon taking off on a day with no wind at all. The balloon would climb but not move in any direction other than up and down. It has no engine to propel it from point A to point B. It goes wherever the air mass goes, and in this case, nowhere. Now, if the wind is blowing from A to B, in a given amount of time, it will cover the distance, but once again, the balloon will have done no work at all! The air mass did the job for it.

Now let's look at what happens to an airplane. Although the ground distance remains unchanged, a headwind will effectively increase the air distance. The airplane moves forward while the air mass moves backward, much like swimming against a current. Conversely, a tailwind will effectively reduce the air distance. At some point in this book, readers will encounter the term "NAM", which stands for "Nautical Air Miles". This term refers to a distance that has already been corrected for wind conditions along the route.

In the end, flight time is equal to Ground Distance divided by Ground Speed, or Air Distance divided by True Airspeed.

$$\text{Flight Time} = \frac{\textbf{GND} \text{ Distance (NM)}}{\textbf{GND} \text{ Speed (kt)}} \qquad \text{Flight Time} = \frac{\textbf{AIR} \text{ Distance (NAM)}}{\textbf{AIR} \text{ Speed (kt)}}$$

*Equation 7: Calculating flight time.*

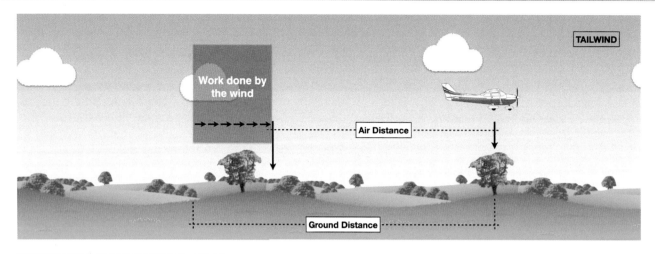

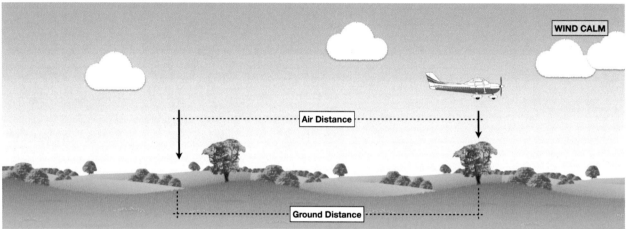

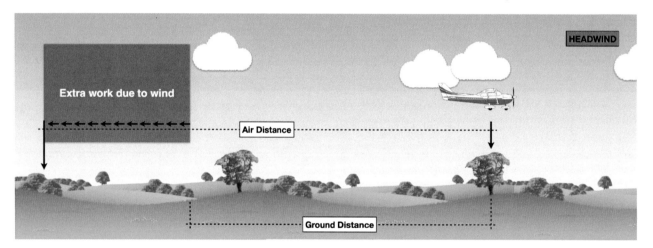

*Figure 39: Effect of wind on air distance.*

I would like to remind you that this book is not about aerodynamics, but we do need to understand a few things about it to conduct our study of performance. Therefore, I will cover some topics that I think are fundamental for developing the main content later.

## 1.4.1   Viscosity

Viscosity can be explained as the property of a fluid that causes it to adhere to and flow around an object when passing by it. By the way, this effect is known as the Coanda effect. To visualize this, place a cylindrical glass bottle under a stream of water, for example, from a kitchen faucet, and observe how the water "sticks" to the glass and follows the curvature of the bottle for some distance before detaching and falling away. Higher viscosity indicates that a fluid can adhere to the surface of an object more easily and bend around it, but it also means that the object will encounter greater resistance when moving through the fluid.

Figure 40: Example of viscosity of water.

### Influence of Temperature

All fluids are viscous, and viscosity varies with temperature. This variation differs between gaseous and liquid fluids. For gases, such as air, higher temperatures increase viscosity, while lower temperatures decrease it; thus, air temperature and viscosity are directly proportional. This occurs because viscosity depends on the ability of gas molecules to transfer momentum. When it is hot, these molecules are more agitated and collide more frequently, making energy transfer easier.

Liquids, however, have an opposite behavior. Lower temperatures increase their viscosity. This is because viscosity in liquids is much more dependent on intermolecular bonds, which become stronger at lower temperatures.

### Boundary Layer

If there were no viscosity when a fluid passes over an object, there would be no deformation or resistance, and the fluid would maintain a uniform path regardless of how far the molecules were from the surface of the object. However, this is not what happens. Molecules that come into contact with the surface tend to reduce their velocity to nearly zero and adhere to the object. Adjacent molecules also experience a reduction in flow rate as they try to adhere. However, the further away a molecule is from the surface, the smaller the effect of speed reduction on it, until the flow becomes free and uniform again.

The fluid layer whose speed is reduced by this effect is called the "boundary layer". The size of this layer depends on three main factors: fluid viscosity, distance along the surface, and the nature of the flow.

The nature of the flow can be either laminar or turbulent. For simplicity, let's use an analogy with a wave at sea approaching the shore. Initially, the wave exhibits laminar behavior, maintaining a smooth shape. However, soon the water molecules that are farther from the seabed, moving at higher speeds than those in contact with the bottom, "roll over in front of the wave" and cause the water flow to become turbulent as they continue moving.

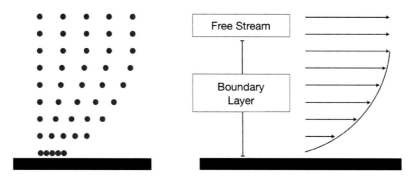

*Figure 41: Boundary Layer.*

Speaking of air, when it flows over any surface, such as an airplane wing, the airflow is initially laminar but soon becomes turbulent. The farther away the air flow travels from the leading edge of the wing, the larger the boundary layer becomes, and it tends to increase more rapidly after the transition zone where the flow changes from laminar to turbulent.

### 1.4.1.3 Reynolds Number

There is a parameter that relates the inertial and viscous properties of a fluid (density, boundary layer thickness, transition point between laminar and turbulent flow, and viscosity), and it is called the Reynolds Number. Through this number, we can determine the nature of the fluid at any given point on the surface, as well as the transition point, the thickness of the boundary layer, and something we call frictional drag, which is simply the friction of the flow against the surface, making it difficult for the object to move forward.

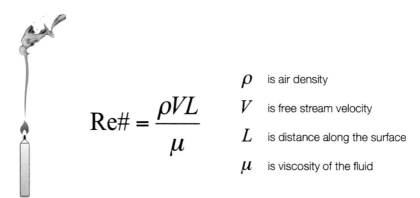

$$\text{Re\#} = \frac{\rho V L}{\mu}$$

$\rho$   is air density

$V$   is free stream velocity

$L$   is distance along the surface

$\mu$   is viscosity of the fluid

*Equation 8: Reynolds Number.*

The Reynolds number is a dimensionless value. By using this number to calculate the transition zone of the airflow on a wing, we can identify that the transformation from laminar to turbulent flow occurs very early on the wing. For this reason, the wing is generally considered to have turbulent flow throughout.

When comparing a laminar flow with a turbulent flow, we see that while the laminar flow has low thickness, low friction, and a low velocity gradient, the turbulent flow is the exact opposite: high thickness, high friction, and a high velocity gradient.

The so-called "velocity gradient" is the ratio between the speeds measured on each streamline of the airflow from the point it contacts the surface and the end of the boundary layer. In laminar flow, there is a gradual increase in velocity, whereas in turbulent flow, this increase happens rapidly.

I would also like to point out that the ability of fluid molecules to exchange energy is very high in turbulent flow owing to the constant collisions between them, whereas it is almost zero in laminar flow. The following illustrations summarize the major differences between laminar and turbulent flows.

| *Laminar Flow* | *Turbulent Flow* |
|---|---|
| Low thickness<br>Low friction<br>Low speed gradient<br>**NO** energy exchange between streamlines | High thickness<br>High friction<br>High speed gradient<br>There **IS** energy exchange between streamlines |

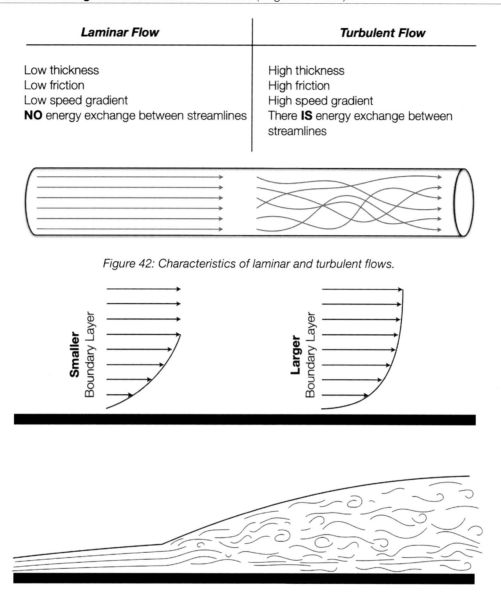

*Figure 42: Characteristics of laminar and turbulent flows.*

*Figure 43: Difference in boundary layer between laminar and turbulent flows.*

### 1.4.1.4   Relation between Speed and Static Pressure

Before we move on to the study of lift and drag, we must first understand the relationship between two properties of a fluid. Whenever flow velocity increases, this necessarily implies a reduction in the static pressure of the fluid. Conversely, when speed decreases, there is an increase in static pressure. Consider, for example, an air mass flowing around a cylinder.

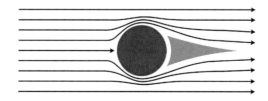

*Figure 44: Streamlines around a cylinder.*

Immediately in front of the cylinder, the airstream speed is zero. At the top and bottom, the curved surface forces an increase in flow velocity (according to Bernoulli's law) and pressure drops. In areas of still air, pressure is high, whereas where the air is moving, static air pressure is lower. Pressure distribution occurs as shown in the following illustration. Note that the vectors are drawn showing the direction from low to high pressure, relating the static pressure at each point to the one measured in free stream.

*Figure 45: Force distribution around the same cylinder.*

The sum of all these vectors can be represented by a single vector which, in this case, will be directed to the right, against the intended motion of the object and in favor of the airflow movement. This single vector that represents the sum of all others is the resultant aerodynamic force.

*Figure 46: Resultant force vector after the sum of all forces.*

By changing the shape of this cylinder into a droplet-like form, the stretching at the back allows the airflow to avoid abrupt disturbances because the viscosity of the gas enables it to circumvent the profile. The boundary layer detaches from the surface almost at the end of the object, and the aerodynamic resultant is substantially reduced.

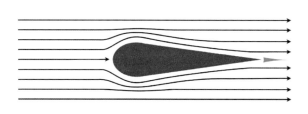

*Figure 47: Shape similar to an airfoil (A).*

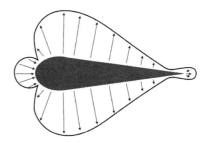

*Figure 48: Shape similar to an airfoil (B).*

*Figure 49: Shape similar to an airfoil (C).*

If we now change the position of this object, as seen in Figure 50, it distorts the flow around it in such a way as to produce some interesting results. The new force distribution will have more vectors pointing upwards than downwards, as shown in Figure 51. What do you think will happen to the aerodynamic resultant? More on that in just a moment.

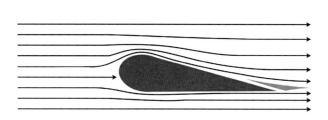

*Figure 50: Airfoil producing lift (A).*

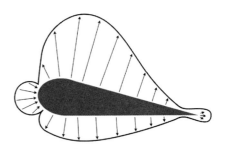

*Figure 51: Airfoil producing lift (B).*

## 1.4.2    Airfoils

The object seen in Figures 50 and 51 is what we might call a symmetrical airfoil. An airfoil is essentially a cross-section of a wing viewed from the side. The following illustration (Figure 52) shows a shape resembling most airfoils used in non-acrobatic aircraft. Note the asymmetry between the upper and lower surfaces. While this model is most commonly used, the symmetrical airfoil is widely used in aerobatic aircraft to facilitate inverted flights (flying upside down) – but let's not deviate from the focus of our study. Here are some properties of the airfoil:

*Figure 52: Parts of an airfoil.*

1. Chord: This is an imaginary line connecting the leading edge to the trailing edge.
2. Thickness: The greatest distance measured between the top and bottom of the airfoil or wing.

### 1.4.2.1    Angle of Attack

To understand the angle of attack, another concept must be very clear: relative wind. If we imagine a stationary plane and change our perspective to think of the air passing by the aircraft rather than the plane moving through the air, the angle of attack will be the angle formed between the relative wind and the airfoil chord. For instance, if a plane is positioned horizontally but falling vertically towards the ground, the angle of attack will be 90°, as the air will pass by the wing from bottom to top. Another way to think about the angle of attack is to measure the angle formed between the aircraft's trajectory and the airfoil chord. In the following illustration, you can see that the angle of attack can be the same on different trajectories such as climbing, level flight, and descending.

*Figure 53: Different trajectories, but same angle of attack.*

### 1.4.2.2    Lift

Lift and drag are concepts created by human imagination! They do not really exist! Please calm down, I will explain what I mean by this statement. Around an airfoil, the air is forced to change its trajectory, and when it changes speed and direction, a force is created. As we have seen, these forces around the airfoil point in every direction, but once we group them all together to be represented by a single vector, we get the resultant aerodynamic force. On the airfoil, this force is averaged at a point called the center of pressure (CP), and, as we are Cartesian thinkers, it will be decomposed into the vertical and horizontal axes. The vertical upward-pointing vector resulting from this decomposition of the aerodynamic resultant is named LIFT, and the horizontal backward-pointing one is named DRAG. Observe the following figure.

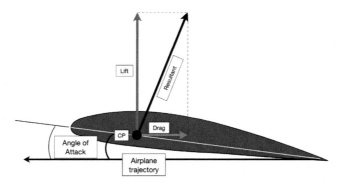

*Figure 54: Creating Lift and Drag!*

In a two-dimensional airfoil, we can focus our study solely on the airflow and the streamlines around it, without concern for interference from other surfaces in the airflow. In Figure 55, you can see images of an airfoil and streamlines around it. Note the lift and drag values for all six different angles of attack.

In the images, we can see that the streamlines above the airfoil are much more deflected than those below it. If we measured flow velocity, we would find a much higher velocity above the airfoil, even though, in both cases (top and bottom), the velocity of the boundary layer flow is greater than that of the free stream (such as in front of the airfoil or beyond the boundary layer). Naturally, we would also observe a higher static pressure below the wing than above it.

We can also note that at the rear of the airfoil, the airflow curvature is much smaller than near the leading edge. This strong curvature of the airstream in front of the airfoil occurs because the airflow approaching the leading edge "senses the obstruction" in its path and anticipates its route, either above or below the airfoil. This advanced perception occurs at the speed of sound, and as the airplane approaches this speed, it becomes increasingly difficult for the airflow to anticipate this movement.

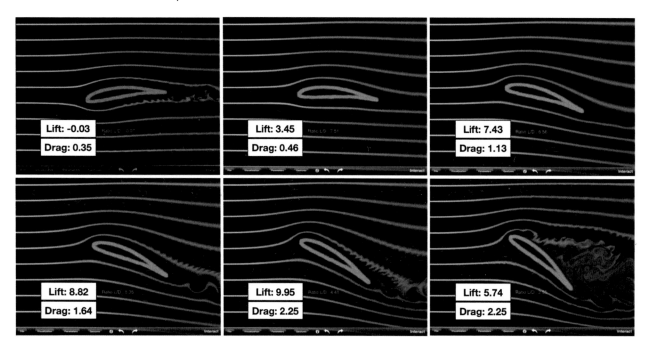

*Figure 55: Streamlines around an airfoil at different angles of attack.*

Still in this sequence of images, we can already see a detachment of the boundary layer in scene number 4, and yet, the lift continues to increase. This detachment occurs in the final half of the airfoil, and as we increase the angle of attack in scene 5, the point at which the layer loses contact with the upper part of the wing shifts forward. This separation of the airflow occurs earlier and earlier to the point where it is almost complete, and the wing is no longer able to produce the necessary lift to maintain flight. We call this scenario a "stall".

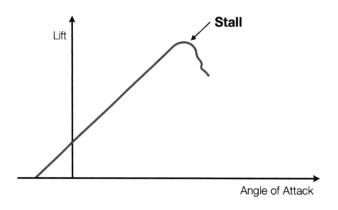

*Figure 56: Lift as a function of angle of attack and stall.*

## 1.4.3 *Three-Dimensional Wing*

There are countless subjects to discuss in the physics of flight regarding the wing of an aircraft: how to measure wingspan, airflow behavior near the fuselage and wingtips, sweepback angle, aspect ratio, among many others. However, I point out again that this is not a book about aerodynamics; the sole purpose is to create a knowledge base for non-pilot readers so that they can understand the main content of this book: performance.

When we abandon the idea of observing a simple airfoil and move on to a real wing, we first need to exercise our imagination and think about an infinite wing. The goal behind this is to be able to ignore all the complications created by the junction of the wing with the fuselage and the wingtip. Later, we will study the wingtip a bit, but we will set aside problems concerning the junction of the wings to the fuselage of the airplane (the so-called area problem). Let's leave that to a book focused on aerodynamics.

Looking at the distribution of lift along a supposedly infinite wing, we see that this force is exactly the same across all sections of the wing. However, in a real and therefore finite wing, lift near the end of the wing is disturbed.

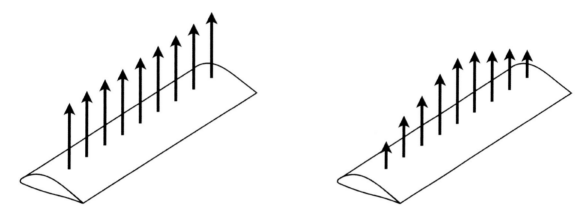

*Figure 57: Lift distribution on infinite and finite wings.*

This disorder that causes a significant drop in lift has a name. Popularly known as 'wingtip drag' and technically called 'induced drag', this phenomenon occurs for a very simple reason. There is a large pressure difference between the underside of the wing (higher pressure) and the topside of the wing (lower pressure). The air 'wants' to flow from high to low pressure and encounters an obstacle in the way: the wing. This pressure difference is one of the factors that generates lift. However, when the air reaches the wingtips, it finds a clear path to move towards the top of the wing, creating a significant disturbance in the airflow.

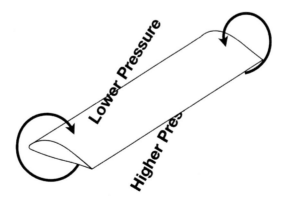

*Figure 58: Airflow scaping from the lower to the upper part of the wing.*

The explanation for the name "induced drag" comes from the reason for its existence. Induced drag occurs because it is caused by lift itself. The drag generated by the wingtip is not the only form of induced drag; it is possibly the most pronounced, but not the only one. In fact, all drag generated as a result of lift is called induced drag, regardless of where it appears.

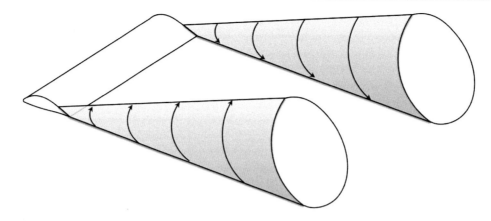

*Figure 59: Wingtip vortex (A).*

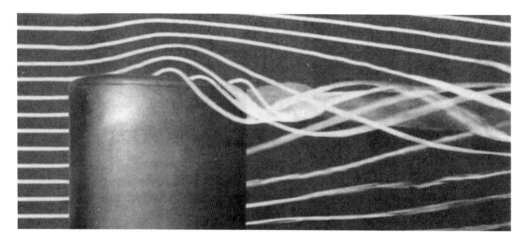

*Figure 60: Wingtip vortex (B).*

To try to reduce the size of this wingtip drag, engineers have developed several interesting solutions. I do not venture to say which one is the best, but I believe there is always one best suited for each project. Winglets, the upward-folded wingtips, are the most famous of all solutions employed, but there are also other possibilities, such as raked wingtips, for example.

Let's now look at the equation that helps us measure the amount of lift on an aircraft.

$$L = C_L \ S \ \frac{\rho}{2} \ V^2$$

*Equation 9: Lift (A).*

In the equation above, L is lift, S is "wing area", V is flow velocity, $\rho$ is air density, and $C_L$ is the lift coefficient. Let's explore some factors in more detail.

You may have noticed that I cited S as "wing area," using quotation marks. I will explain why. However, before my explanation, try to answer the following question: which part or parts of the airplane produce lift?

Although by convention we usually say that lift comes only from the wings, that is not entirely correct. Every part of the plane causes some kind of disturbance in the airstream, and somehow, they all end up generating some degree of lift, whether positive (up) or negative (down).

For this reason, it is not of fundamental importance to make an accurate measurement of the wing area of the airplane. In fact, manufacturers usually set this value in a somewhat imprecise manner, drawing a straight line at about the leading edge and another at about the trailing edge, disregarding any small changes in the actual wing profile. These lines start at the wingtip and go all the way to the axis of the aircraft, ignoring the existence of the fuselage.

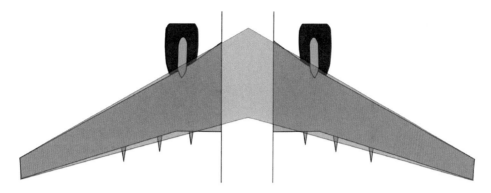

*Figure 61: Wing area.*

The area obtained with this rough "wing design" does not need to be perfect but must be consistent in all other calculations. I promise to explain the reason for this, but please be patient for now. Instead, let's talk about the lift coefficient ($C_L$) that I mentioned earlier.

The lift coefficient ($C_L$) is a parameter in the equation that encapsulates several factors that, individually, would affect the calculation of lift (such as free flow velocity, object shape, fluid viscosity and compressibility, and angle of attack). Since these factors cannot be analyzed individually, we combine them into one parameter called the lift coefficient. But how can we determine the value of this coefficient?

In a wind tunnel test, a dynamometer is placed under the model of the airplane to measure the lift produced at various speeds and angles of attack. Referring back to the lift equation, we isolate all known values from the wind tunnel test (freestream velocity, air density, and lift):

$$\frac{2\ L}{V^2\ \rho} = S\ C_L$$

*Equation 10: Lift (B).*

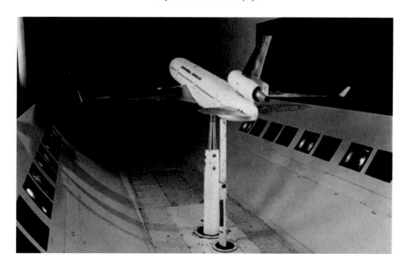

*Figure 62: Aircraft model on a wind tunnel.*

I left "wing area" and $C_L$ as unknown on purpose. By establishing the wing area, the lift coefficient of the aircraft is determined. Remember, I mentioned that the measurement of the area does not have to be exact, and here is the reason why: it only serves as a reference within the equation to establish $C_L$. Larger areas will result in lower coefficients and vice versa. Once the wing area is defined, it must be consistently used for both $C_L$ and $C_D$ (drag coefficient) values. You cannot use one wing area for studying $C_L$ and another for $C_D$. Furthermore, if you set the wing area to 1, you won't need this variable in the equation at all, though the coefficients would be very large numbers and the wing area will be necessary for other calculations later. The equation for measuring drag is the same as the one used for measuring lift, except for the substitution of $C_L$ with $C_D$.

$$D = C_D \; S \; \frac{\rho}{2} \; V^2$$

*Equation 11: Drag.*

We will continue the "study of aerodynamics" shortly; however, let's first cover some concepts related to the wing. We have already discussed wing area (and how its measurement is not precise), and that it is conventionally defined by ignoring the fuselage. Now, other concepts you must be familiar with are:

**Quarter Chord:** This is an imaginary line that connects the points identifying the quarter-length measurement of the chord from the axis of the airplane to the wingtip.

**Sweepback Angle:** This angle is measured between the transverse axis of the airplane and the imaginary quarter chord line. It is sometimes referred to as the "inflection" of the wing. It is considered positive when the wings are swept back and negative when they are swept forward.

**Wingspan:** The wingspan is the straight-line distance between the wingtips, including the winglets if installed.

**Mean Aerodynamic Chord (MAC):** You will see this concept in more detail later in the book. The mean aerodynamic chord is defined using a relatively simple process of imagination. Think of the wing of the airplane as having a rectangular shape with the same area and wingspan as the "real" wing. If the base of the rectangle is the wingspan, its height will be the value of the mean aerodynamic chord.

**Aspect Ratio:** The aspect ratio will also be discussed shortly. It is measured by dividing the square of the wingspan by the wing area.

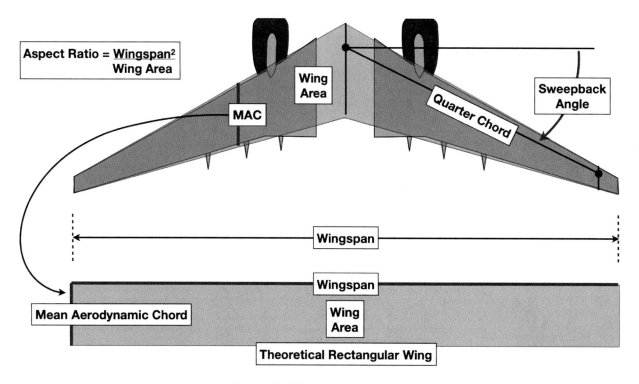

*Figure 63: Different wing aspects.*

### *1.4.4    Wing Stall at High Altitude*

One phenomenon that has caught many pilots off guard is that stall speed at high altitudes is significantly higher than at lower altitudes. Although stall is often related to speed, remember that wing stall is primarily linked to the angle of attack of the wing. Stall occurs when this angle becomes so high that the air cannot flow smoothly over the top of the wing, causing the airflow to disrupt.

In the four images of Figure 64, I will illustrate why stalls occur at higher speeds when flying at high altitude. First, consider that all images show the same calibrated airspeed (CAS). As we studied earlier, the same CAS represents a higher Mach number at higher altitudes because the temperature is lower (ISA conditions in the troposphere).

In the first scene, we see that the detachment of the boundary layer on the top of the wing occurs at about three-quarters of its length. In the following scene (same CAS at higher altitude), two factors are noticeable: at the leading edge of the wing, the streamline deflection is slightly more pronounced, and on the top of the wing, the boundary layer detachment occurs earlier. This pattern is repeated in scenes three and four, resulting in a stalled wing at high altitude for the same CAS, while the wing is not stalled at lower altitudes. But why do these two things happen?

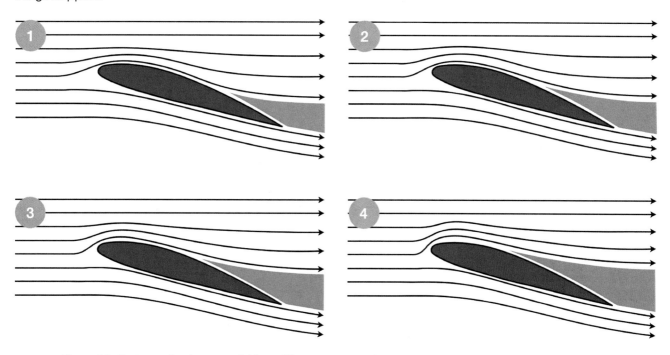

*Figure 64: Airstream for the same CAS at different altitudes, from a lower altitude (1) to a higher altitude (4).*

Regarding the increasingly sharp curvature of the streamlines at the leading edge, this is happening owning to the Mach number. As we mentioned earlier, the air does not simply reach the wing and then bend over. It anticipates the deflection by choosing its path before encountering the object. This anticipation occurs at the speed of sound, so when flying at Mach 1 (exactly the speed of sound), there would be no anticipation at all. This is what we call the sound barrier: compressing air in front of an object without giving it time to decide whether to go over or under it.

Since the same CAS represents a higher Mach number at higher altitudes, this delays the "decision-making" of the airflow, causing the choice to go above or below the wing to be made closer to the wing itself. With this late decision, the air is forced to make a more aggressive turn and loses a significant amount of energy.

The second aspect visible in the illustrations is the increasingly early detachment of the boundary layer. This phenomenon is linked to another factor that we have previously addressed: the Reynolds number and the viscosity of the fluid. We have seen that air viscosity decreases at lower temperatures (exactly what happens at altitude). With lower viscosity, the ability of the airflow to stay attached to the wing also decreases. Considering that the airflow also has less energy, the detachment will certainly occur earlier.

## 1.4.5   Sweepback Wing Stall Characteristics

Every aerodynamic feature has both advantages and disadvantages. Within each project, we need to balance the benefits and drawbacks to determine whether such a feature is worthwhile. In the case of sweepback wings, one of the major disadvantages is stall. Airplanes with this wing design tend to have high stall speeds, and the flow detachment characteristics of the wing are also challenging.

A stall does not occur simultaneously across the entire wing. The detachment of the boundary layer happens partially, and in positive sweepback wings, it occurs first at the wingtips and then spreads towards the root. The problem with this characteristic is that the first part of the wing to stall is the one that contains the flight controls known as ailerons (more details about flight controls are coming soon). To ensure the pilot maintains control of the plane until a complete stall occurs, one solution found by engineers was to install a device that forces the boundary layer to detach first at the root of the wing. However, this significantly anticipates the occurrence of the phenomenon, allowing it to happen at even higher speeds. In the case of the Boeing 737NG, a small device called a Stall Strip was installed on the leading edge of the wing, between the fuselage and the engine, as shown below.

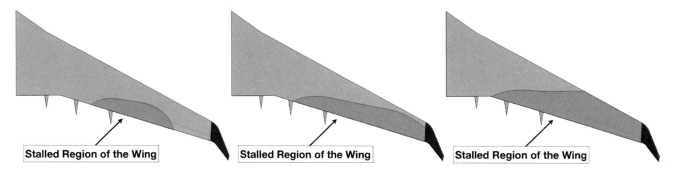

*Figure 65: Stall happening on a wing without stall strip installed.*

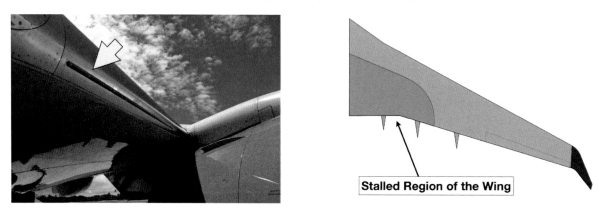

*Figure 66: "Stall strip" shown on the left picture and how stall occurs on wings with this device on the drawing.*

## 1.4.6   Drag Polar

Previously, we examined the behavior of the airflow passing over the airfoil as we increase the angle of attack. The change in lift force with this upward movement of the angle of attack is virtually linear until stall occurs, whereas the increase in drag generated by increasing the angle of attack is exponential. Initially, drag decreases (due to the asymmetrical profile of the wing, with lift measured from a negative angle of attack where $C_L$ is zero) and then grows rapidly. Figure 67 shows a graph of lift and drag coefficients as a function of the angle of attack.

Now, if we combine the two coefficients in a graph and set aside the angle of attack, we can identify the best ratio between lift and drag by simply plotting a tangent to the graph from the origin of the system. Identifying this point will be important for future performance calculations, such as determining the lowest angle of descent speed. This new chart is known as a drag polar (Figure 68).

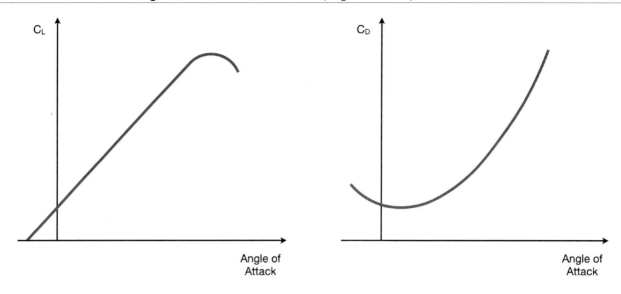

*Figure 67: Lift coefficient versus angle of attack (left) and drag coefficient versus angle of attack (right).*

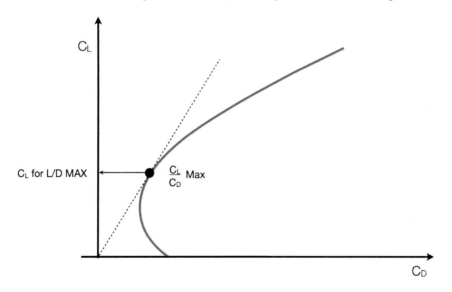

*Figure 68: Drag polar and $C_L$ for best L/D.*

## 1.4.7   Drag

Induced drag, as previously discussed, is all drag generated as a result of lift, but it is definitely not the only kind of drag on an airplane. Let's explore some others.

### 1.4.7.1   Drag-Divergence Mach Number and Critical Mach Number

Another type of drag is produced as a result of airflow behavior when it reaches the speed of sound. As a matter of fact, the airflow reaching the speed of sound is not a problem, when it returns to subsonic speed. However, it creates what we know as a shockwave. The shockwave causes the boundary layer to detach and significantly increases the overall drag of the airplane. Note that I mentioned the airflow exceeding the speed of sound, not the airplane itself. Air accelerates as it passes over the wing owing to wing curvature; thus, the airflow may become supersonic at some point on the aircraft even if the airplane is traveling at subsonic speed (which is very likely at higher Mach numbers).

The speed of the airplane when the airflow first becomes supersonic somewhere around it is called the Critical Mach Number. In the following example (Figure 69), the Critical Mach Number of the aircraft is M0.79.

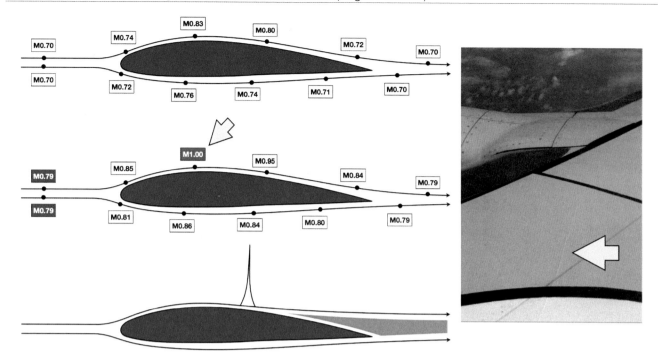

*Figure 69: Critical Mach Number.*

For the same $C_L$, $C_D$ remains relatively constant at any Mach number below the point where the shockwave forms. Beyond this speed, CD increases rapidly as the Mach number rises. Arbitrarily, it was established that the speed at which $C_D$ increases by 0.002 units would be called the Drag-Divergence Mach ($M_{DD}$).

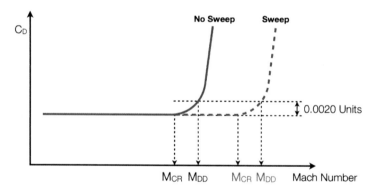

*Figure 70: Drag Divergence Mach.*

The graph in Figure 70 illustrates another objective behind sweepback wings. This aerodynamic feature delays the occurrence of the Critical Mach Number ($M_{CR}$) and, therefore, the Drag-Divergence Mach ($M_{DD}$) occurs at a higher speed. This delay allows for relatively economical flight at high speeds.

**Interesting discussion:** Let's consider two aircraft from the same manufacturer and generation, such as the Boeing 737 and 747. The first is designed for short-haul flights, while the second is intended for very long flights. From the manufacturer's perspective, the 737 should be able to operate on short routes where cruising speed does not significantly affect travel time between origin and destination owing to the short distances involved. As such, this aircraft was developed with a relatively small wing sweepback angle, allowing it to have low stall speeds and to take off from and land on short runways. On the other hand, its larger counterpart, the 747, has the greatest sweepback angle on a wing among subsonic commercial airplanes. This design choice was intentional. To cover long distances, the ability to fly fast is a significant advantage. However, the 747 is not capable of flying at low speeds like the 737, but this was not considered a serious problem, as it is designed to fly between major airports that serve as hubs for airlines to distribute their passengers. Generally, these airports have long runways and do not limit the operation of jumbo jets. Note that each wing design was focused on the primary mission the plane was intended to accomplish, which reinforces what I mentioned earlier: there is no perfect aircraft, only one that best suits the intended type of operation.

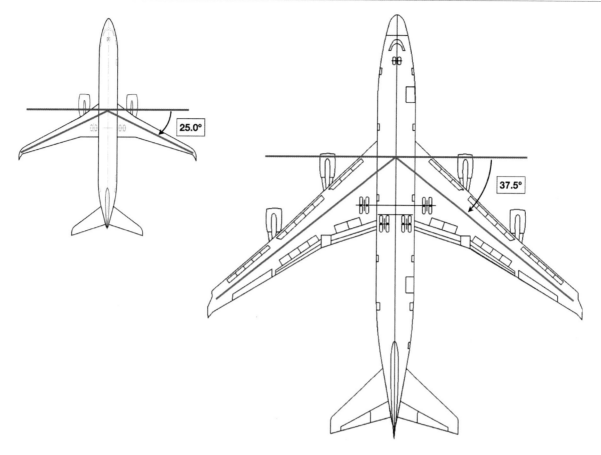

*Figure 71: Sweepback angle comparison between Boeing 737 and 747.*

### 1.4.7.2 Parasite Drag

All other factors that influence the overall drag of an aircraft and are not related to lift are called parasitic drag. Some types include: skin friction drag (caused by the viscosity of the air in friction with the surface of the airplane), excrescence drag (produced by parts of the airplane that are not intended to produce lift, such as an engine, an antenna, or the fuselage), and interference drag (generated by the connection of structures such as wing and fuselage), among other things like misaligned control surfaces.

The sum of parasite drag and induced drag results in the total drag of the aircraft, and the proportion of each type of drag (in the total amount produced) varies as a function of speed, as shown below. Note that parasite drag is directly proportional to speed and induced drag works the opposite way, that is, it is reduced as speed increases.

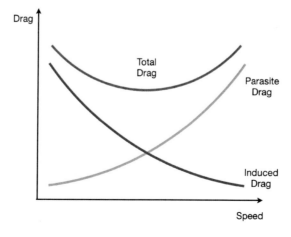

*Figure 72: Total drag as a function of airspeed.*

## 1.4.8 Wing Aspect Ratio

I promised to talk more about the wing aspect ratio, and I will do that now by proposing a problem-solving task: imagine a tow plane and a glider that will make a ferry flight between two cities. Each aircraft carries up to two occupants, meaning that there are four seats available. There are three pilots weighing 90 kg each on this mission. The question is: which aircraft would you seat two pilots in, and which would go with just one? The goal is to make your flight as fuel-efficient as possible.

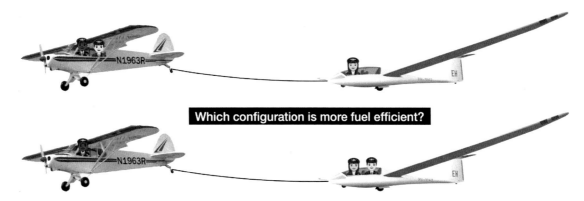

*Figure 73: The glider ferry flight issue.*

To make the problem more interesting, let's consider that both the tow aircraft and the glider have the same wing area. However, the first has a 10-meter wingspan, while the second has a distance of 20 meters between wingtips.

Aspect ratio is the key to solving this problem. The glider has a very high aspect ratio, while the tow plane has a very low one. Practically, this means that to produce the same lift, the glider generates much less drag than the airplane. To further illustrate the concept, let's start with two simple sheets of paper of the same size.

Fold the two sheets in half so that they retain identical areas. However, fold them in different directions, as shown below.

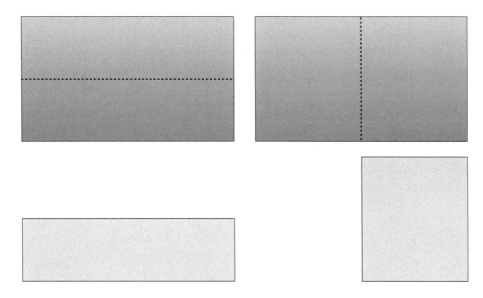

*Figure 74: Folded sheets. Same area, different aspect ratio!*

Assuming that those sheets represent two wings, let's compare their efficiency. Take a closer look at the wingtips. The wing chord on the left wing of the figure is much smaller than on the right wing. If you remember the beginning of our study of three-dimensional wings, you know that lift decreases near the tips because of the air that passes from the bottom to the top of the wing, generating the traditional vortex.

The thinner wing has a larger aspect ratio, and it will put in "much less effort" to produce the lift needed to carry the extra weight of the aircraft. This is because it has smaller wingtips, so its "aerodynamic loss" is also small. This is the solution to our problem: put two pilots in the glider and leave the solo pilot in the tow plane! The tow-glider system will be much more efficient this way.

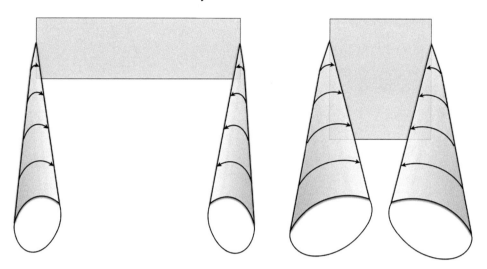

*Figure 75: Folded sheets. Less drag on the one with higher aspect ratio.*

## 1.4.9   Flight Controls

### 1.4.9.1   Flaps and Slats

The wing of a high-performance aircraft, like the ones we are going to study, has to be efficient at both high and low speeds and altitudes. This requires such aircraft to undergo significant transformation to adapt to each new situation. Flaps and slats are two of the devices responsible for this aerodynamic metamorphosis, making a wing designed for high-speed and high-altitude flights also capable of flying at low speed and altitude, as in takeoff and landing situations.

Flaps are devices located at the trailing edge of the wings that can move backward and downward (in less complex aircraft, they typically only move downward, not backward), increasing wing area and curvature. With this transformation, the same amount of lift can be generated at much slower speeds.

There are different types of flaps that can be used in aircraft designs, each known by a different name. I cannot say that one is better than another. The flap chosen by the manufacturer will largely depend on the objectives behind each airplane design. Cost, structure, maintenance complexity, type of aircraft operation, among other factors, need to be evaluated for flap selection and design.

Slats have the same goal of increasing lift, but unlike flaps, they are situated at the leading edge of the wings and, when activated, move forward and downward. These two structures are called high-lift devices. Curious note: there are also leading-edge flaps known as Kruger flaps. These flaps are fitted on aircraft such as the Boeing 727, 737 (on this one, just in a small part of the wing between the engine and fuselage junction), and 747.

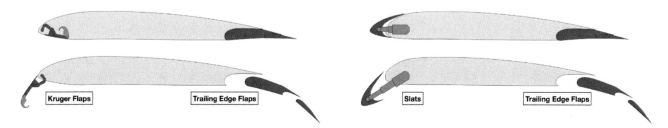

*Figure 76: Flaps, slats, and Kruger flaps retracted on the top and extended on the bottom.*

### 1.4.9.2 Ailerons, Rudder, and Elevator

So, we already know how the wing produces lift in such different situations, but we have not yet seen how pilots are able to control the airplane.

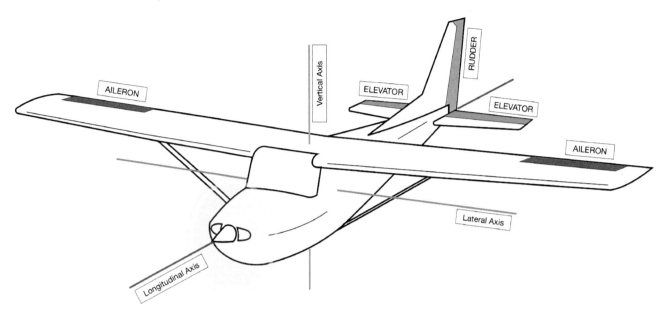

*Figure 77: Three axes and controls.*

The airplane is controlled along three axes: vertical, lateral (or transverse), and longitudinal. Changing the attitude of the plane along these axes requires that wings, horizontal stabilizers, and vertical stabilizers be capable of the same metamorphosis mentioned when we talked about flaps and slats.

The aerodynamic surfaces that allow control of the airplane are always at the trailing edge of the airfoils and are capable of moving both ways: up or down for those installed on the wings and horizontal stabilizer, and right or left when installed on the vertical stabilizer.

Every time this portion of the trailing edge of the airfoil moves, its curvature changes and the force it produces also changes. This force will increase in the opposite direction of the deflection of the surface. Such a surface is given different names depending on where it is mounted: an aileron (if it is mounted on the wings), an elevator (if it is mounted on the horizontal stabilizer), or a rudder (if it is mounted on the vertical stabilizer).

Consider a wing as an example. If the aileron descends, the upward lift increases and the wing rises. If the aileron rises, the upward lift decreases and the wing descends. This explanation alone supports the notion that ailerons will always work in opposite ways to control the aircraft along its longitudinal axis, making the aircraft roll left or right.

*Figure 78: Aileron on different positions: up, neutral, and down.*

As far as the elevator is concerned, when the pilot pulls the stick, this surface is deflected upward, and the airplane rotates around its transverse axis, lifting the nose. The reverse command is made to lower the nose. Although we are talking about the movement of the airplane using the nose as a reference, attention should be drawn to a detail here. The upward movement of the nose of the plane is a consequence of an action made on its tail. As mentioned before, pulling the stick causes the elevator to rise, which causes a downward lift (opposite direction of surface movement). This downward lift will bring the tail down and the nose will pitch up as a result.

The same goes for commands applied around the vertical axis. They are made with the rudder and resemble the way a ship is steered in water. The rudder deflects right or left and yaws the plane to one side or the other along its vertical axis. The control is applied at the surface through pedals in the flight deck. Pressing the pedal causes the rudder and nose of the plane to move the same way. Of course, what happens to the nose is again a consequence. The real act occurs in the tail, where the vertical stabilizer is. Pushing the right rudder pedal makes the rudder surface go right. A left-pointing lift will be generated on the stabilizer, and if the tail goes left, it is obvious that the nose goes right.

When the nose of the airplane moves sideways, we say that there is a YAW movement. When it moves up and down, we say there is a PITCH movement. Finally, when it banks to a side, we say that this is a ROLL movement of the aircraft.

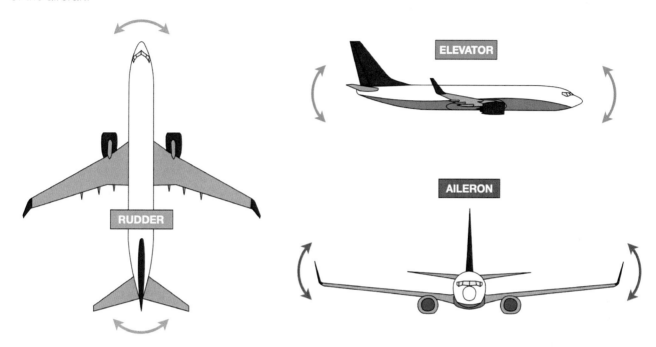

*Figure 79: Movement caused by all of the control surfaces.*

Dutch roll happens when lateral stability and directional stability are basically out of sync, meaning that the airplane has more lateral stability than directional stability. Explaining this with a video would be way easier than putting it into words, but I will do my best here. Picture this: a plane cruising along at a steady altitude and speed, with a pretty wing with a steep sweepback angle of 35 degrees.

Now, let's follow a train of thought where we link each action to its consequences. Let's kick things off with simple turbul...

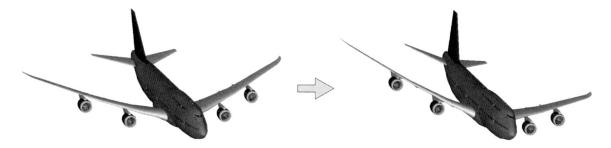

*Figure 80: Right hand wing moving up due to an upward wind gust.*

So, when that roll happens, the right wing goes up and the left wing goes down. The right wing goes up because it catches a gust of wind that gives it extra lift during the turbulence. And since lift and drag go hand in hand, that wing also ends up creating more drag. This excess drag on the right wing makes the plane yaw slightly to the right.

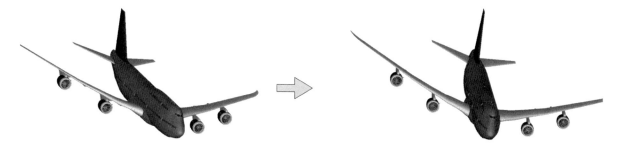

*Figure 81: Yaw to the right owing to excess drag on the right-hand wing.*

As the plane yaws to the right, the left wing moves forward, picking up speed and lift. And thanks to the sweepback angle, the left wing is hit harder by the relative wind compared to the right wing during this yaw. With the extra lift, the left wing that was down now moves up, and the right wing moves down as a result.

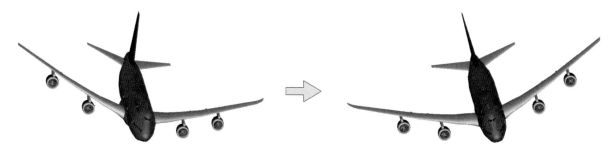

*Figure 82: Now the left wing has more lift and that is the one moving upwards.*

And so, the cycle continues. The wing that moves up (the left one) generates more lift and drag. This drag pushes the left upper wing back and the lower right wing forward.

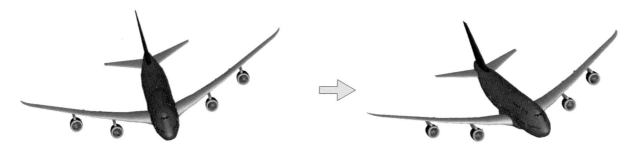

*Figure 83: More lift equals more drag, so a yaw to the left is created.*

Next, the right lower wing gets more lift, moves up, creates more drag, and leads us back to the original problem of the plane rolling to the left (right wing up). This back-and-forth dance in the air is what we call the Dutch Roll.

*Figure 84: Yawing to the left will force the right-hand wing back up and things will start over.*

If an airplane has an unstable behavior, this Dutch Roll can be a serious safety concern. However, the tail fin of the plane is the aerodynamic hero that helps stabilize the aircraft by damping out some of that Dutch Roll in each cycle, bringing the plane back to steady flight.

Most commercial airliners are stable when it comes to Dutch Roll, but just stability is not enough for passenger comfort. Even if the plane could suppress that movement in just three cycles each time, I bet 90% of passengers would feel queasy. That is why manufacturers developed the Yaw Damper system, among other things, to prevent Dutch Roll entirely.

The Yaw Damper quietly does its job behind the scenes, nudging the rudder (without the pilot even moving the pedals) to squash any Dutch Roll before anyone even notices. I won't dive into the nitty-gritty details here since each airplane model may have its own system specifics, but in all cases, the Yaw Damper is the system responsible for preventing Dutch Roll from happening.

To explain what Mach Tuck (also known as Tuck Under) is, we first need to take a few steps back and talk about airplane stability. Imagine you are a pilot flying your Cessna 172 at a constant speed and altitude. The aircraft is properly trimmed, and even though there is no autopilot, you do not need to touch the controls.

Now, when I say that the aircraft is trimmed, can you tell me what it is trimmed for? Some pilots might say they have trimmed the attitude of the airplane, but that is not true! The airplane is always trimmed for its speed, regardless of its attitude. Let's prove it!

I said you were flying at a constant altitude and speed with no need to touch the flight controls. Now, let's throttle down to idle. If the airplane were trimmed for attitude, it would lose a lot of speed. If it were trimmed for altitude, it would stall. But as I mentioned, it is actually trimmed for speed. So, it will lose just a bit of speed and then lower its attitude to recover that lost speed. Maybe it will gain more speed than intended and pitch up to dissipate this excess velocity. Maybe it will lose too much in this process and pitch down again to accelerate. This up-and-down movement will eventually disappear and the airplane will be back to its original speed at a different attitude, and this time on a descent path. That is the longitudinal stability of the airplane!

Let me back off for one second. The airplane is not trimmed for speed, per say. It is trimmed for angle of attack, but as we have seen on the lift equation that those things are connected. To produce a given amount of lift you have a given angle of attack and speed. Should you change one, you would have to change the other to keep lift constant. Then yes, although I said trimmed for speed instead of angle of attack, the final result is the same. You need to keep speed constant to keep angle of attack and lift also constant.

Back to the subject, all commercial airplanes (as far as I know) have longitudinal stability, which means this up and down movement will dampen a little bit with each cycle, eventually letting the airplane settle at a new stable attitude at the same constant speed it was at before being disturbed by the reduced thrust. The same idea applies to a thrust increase! The airplane will pitch up and look for a new stable attitude, but now climbing at the same speed it was before.

You might now ask where this stability comes from. Well, many things contribute to it, but let's narrow our study to a relationship among three forces: weight, positive wing lift, and negative horizontal stabilizer lift. In the following figure, I took out the engine of the aircraft to ease the view of the vectors, but what is important is that you can see the equilibrium created by equal momentum between weight and wing lift (pitch down momentum), and between horizontal stabilizer lift and wing lift. Both are of equal intensity and opposite rotation, nullifying each other ................................................................................ance, with tł

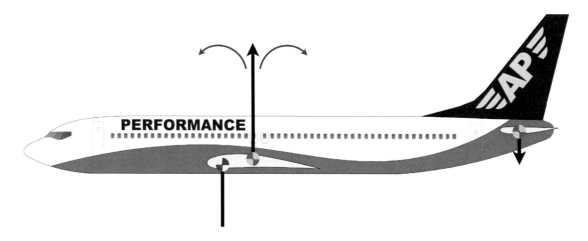

*Figure 85: The airplane is like a see-saw in perfect balance.*

So, here we are in flight school, learning to fly, and that is what we learn and feel: once the airplane is trimmed, if it gains speed, it will pitch up to dissipate this extra energy. If it loses speed, it will pitch down to recover that energy. Ok, lesson learned. How can I accelerate in level flight? Using what we have studied, I can deduce that we will need to add some thrust and use some way to prevent the airplane from climbing, which I can do by pushing the yoke forward. Perfect! I have settled for a new speed and a new angle of attack. And it works similarly the opposite way. To reduce speed in level flight, we reduce thrust and pull back on the stick to avoid losing altitude, changing our angle of attack, and trimming the airplane for this new steady condition.

Now, what about Mach Tuck? Wait for it! We are getting there!

Remember what happens when we start to get close to the speed of sound? At a speed called Critical Mach Number ($M_{CRIT}$), the air reaches Mach 1 for the first time over the airplane, and at speeds over $M_{CRIT}$, we start to see a shockwave forming over the wing. This shockwave first appears where the wing is thickest and starts to move backwards as the airplane accelerates. As the shockwave moves to the rear part of the wing, it also shifts the CP aft, increasing the pitch down momentum, as illustrated in the next figure.

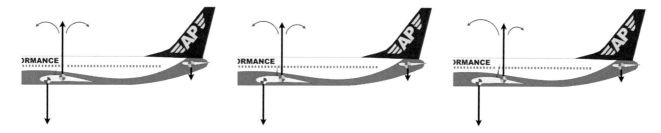

*Figure 86: Form left to right showing the effect of speed increase.*

You might think this shift in the position of the CP is no big deal, but let's take a closer look at the consequences. Say you are perfectly trimmed, flying at a constant altitude and speed. The speed you are currently flying is just above $M_{CRIT}$. Suddenly, a gust of wind makes your speed increase a bit. What will happen now? We have seen that all commercial aircraft have longitudinal stability, so we expect the airplane to pitch up and return to the original speed. However, at this range of speeds, that is not going to happen!

Once you gain a bit of speed because of that wind gust, the center of pressure will move backwards. Moving that way, the CP will create a pitch down momentum, increasing the arm between itself and the center of gravity. With the nose down, the aircraft will accelerate even further, moving the CP to an even more rearward position, and again increasing the pitch down momentum. You have just fallen into a trap! It is a vicious circle that is retro-feeding itself, aggravating the nose down situation as time goes by. More speed equals more pitch down that equals more speed that once again equals more pitch down and so on.

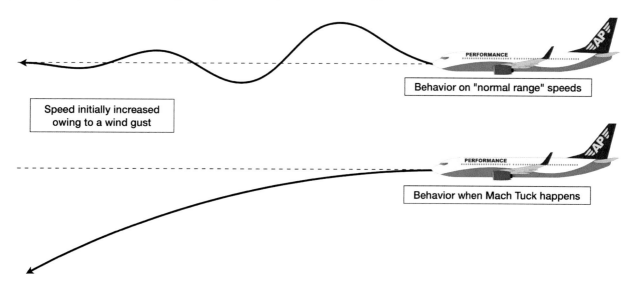

Speed initially increased
owing to a wind gust

Behavior on "normal range" speeds

Behavior when Mach Tuck happens

*Figure 87: Mach Tuck or Tuck Under.*

Wait a minute! I said every commercial airplane has longitudinal stability. How can they be allowed to fly at speeds where they would behave unstably, like in the Mach Tuck speed region? Well, when flying at those speeds, the airplane is artificially stable! All of them must have a system that provides speed stability at higher Mach numbers. This system may have different names on different aircraft models, but it is often called the Mach Trim System.

For example, the Mach Trim System of the Boeing 737NG is completely transparent to the pilot and operates in a way that the pilot would never notice this change in airplane pitch behavior because of Mach Tuck.

Finally, let's put ourselves in the place of an engineer responsible for the design of the aircraft. Our mission: ensure the airplane can continue to fly safely should the Mach Trim System fail in flight. What would you do? How would you design the non-normal checklist for that situation?

Mach Tuck is when the airplane reverses its "natural" behavior of longitudinal stability. Would it be feasible to tell the pilot to "flip a switch in the back of their head" and start flying in the opposite way as any pilot was ever trained? That is, pulling the yoke as you gain speed to maintain altitude instead of pushing it. Well, I do not think this is the safest way to address this problem at all! And I believe you agree with me! In fact, by now, I believe you have come to the same conclusion as the engineer did: limit the airplane speed!

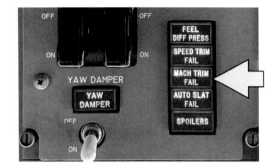 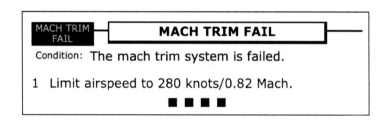

*Figure 88: Checklist for Mach Trim Fail on a Boeing 737NG.*

For the purposes of performance studies of Class A aircraft, we will focus exclusively on issues related to jet aircraft propulsion. Propeller engines will not be covered in this book.

The thrust of a jet engine is produced by applying Newton's famous third law: for every action, there is an equal and opposite reaction. The action force that generates the reaction is produced according to Newton's second law: F = ma (force is equal to mass times acceleration).

In the following illustration, you can see how an engine produces thrust by picking up a mass of air in front of it and accelerating it. The mass that exits the engine is slightly greater than the mass that enters because it has been mixed with fuel.

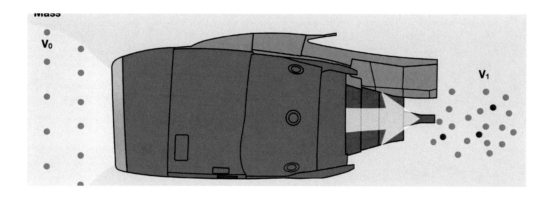

Figure 89: Jet Engine accelerating an air mass and producing forward thrust.

If we divide the speed difference between the incoming and outgoing air by the time it took to gain this speed, we obtain the acceleration of the air mass. Multiplying this value by the mass gives us the force produced by the engine. The complete equation for jet engine thrust measurement can be seen below. "F" is force, "m" is mass (either from the air or the fuel, as indicated), "V" is velocity (either from the jet exhaust or the airplane), and "g" is the acceleration of gravity.

$$ F_{Thrust} = \left( \frac{m_{air} + m_{fuel}}{g} \times V_{jetexhaust} \right) - \left( \frac{m_{air}}{g} \times V_{airplan} \right) $$

Equation 12: Thrust produced by a jet engine.

For now, it is important to understand which factors change engine thrust. Later in the course, we will examine the internal parts of the jet engine and how this thrust variation affects performance. At this point, we can highlight two important factors: speed and air density (which can be influenced by temperature variation, altitude, or a combination of both).

Every time the plane starts to accelerate, the engine becomes capable of receiving more air per unit of time. This is beneficial because increasing the air mass increases the force. However, it becomes increasingly difficult to add speed to the air intake, as this air already has relative velocity. The force comes from the ability of the engine to impart more speed to the air passing through it, and this capability is drastically reduced with speed.

In older jet engines, these two factors virtually canceled each other out, and thrust could be considered constant as a function of speed. Modern engines, however, behave differently. While older engines accelerated a small amount of air at a high speed, modern engines accelerate a large amount of air at a slower speed. This inversion of priorities has resulted in an enormous increase in efficiency, leading to higher thrust and lower fuel consumption. However, the engine behavior regarding speed has changed, and thrust is no longer constant for any airspeed. We will explore this engine efficiency issue in more detail in the Specific Fuel Consumption section of the Enroute Performance chapter.

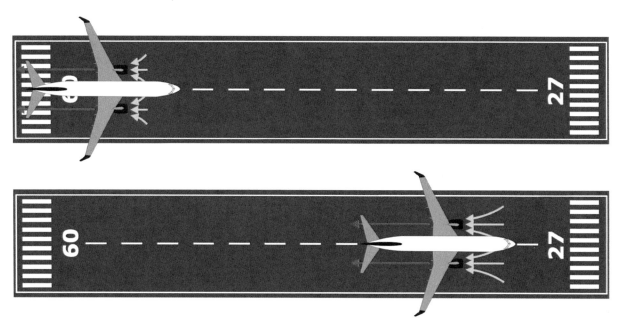

*Figure 90: Airplane static (above) and with speed (below). There is more air intake with speed, but less acceleration of the air mass.*

As we gain speed and approach the speed of sound, a new factor begins to stand out: the Ram Effect in front of the engine (similar to the compressed air effect in front of the pitot tube when we studied EAS). As the previously compressed air enters the engine, it improves the efficiency of the compressors, and thrust increases with increasing speed, reversing the initial behavior. This situation is illustrated in the following figure.

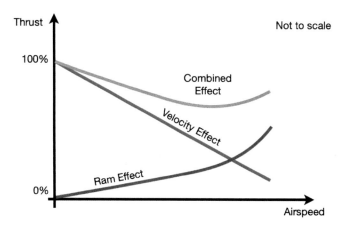

*Figure 91: Engine thrust as a function of speed.*

The other factor that affects thrust, as we mentioned previously, is air density. Here, the effect is simpler to understand. As the plane climbs, there is less air available, and the mass that will be accelerated decreases. If the air mass decreases, the result is that less thrust is produced.

By understanding this logical sequence, we can conclude that temperature also affects thrust because higher temperatures result in lower air density. Lower density means fewer particles per volume, or simply less air. With less air, the engine produces less thrust. There are some exceptions to this statement, which will be addressed at the appropriate time, specifically when we discuss the concept of Engine Rate and Reduced Takeoff Thrust.

To make the topic clearer, let's exemplify it with numbers. In fact, we will do this frequently throughout this book. In Figure 92, observe the maximum thrust developed by a 27,000-pound thrust engine at the start of the takeoff roll, and compare it to the amount of thrust as the airplane leaves the ground at 165 knots. Then, in Figure 93, look at the comparison made between an aircraft with the same engine as in the previous example, but flying with a calibrated airspeed (CAS) of 300 knots at sea level and then flying at Mach 0.78 at 39,000 feet.

Figure 92: Loss of thrust as a result of speed.

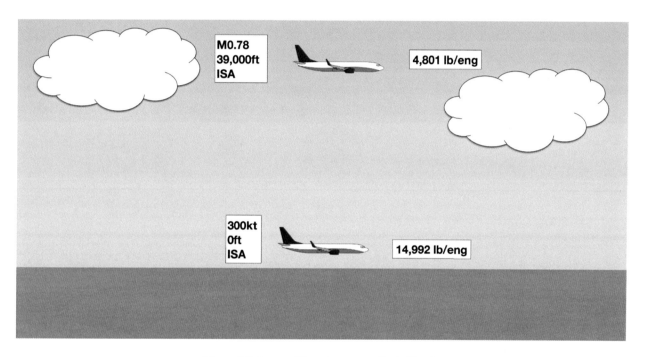

Figure 93: Loss of thrust as a result of altitude.

### 1.8.1    Maneuvering Speed – $V_A$

Transport category and standard category aircraft have very different requirements when it comes to the load factor that they can handle without breaking their wings. While the focus of this book is on the transport category, let's kick things off by delving into the VG diagram and the information you can get from the airspeed indicator of a standard category plane.

First off, let's quickly revisit the concept of a stall. Imagine you are cruising at a steady speed and altitude with a specific weight. At an angle of attack of 2 degrees, you start decreasing your speed while maintaining altitude. As the speed drops, the angle of attack increases to balance lift and weight, thus keeping your altitude constant. This continues until you hit the critical angle of attack, let's say 18 degrees in this example. At that point, the air is no longer capable of following the curvature of the wing, leading to a stall. It is important to note that a stall is not about speed, but it occurs when the critical angle of attack is reached, and it can happen at any speed. In our example, we have demonstrated a stall with a load factor of 1G.

*Figure 94: Demonstration of 1G stall.*

Now, what would happen if instead of keeping constant altitude and gradually reducing speed the pilot simply pulled very hard on the stick? The airplane would change the angle of attack, keeping the airspeed constant (at least initially) and significantly boosting lift. The ratio of lift to weight is called the load factor. For instance, if lift is twice the weight, we have a load factor of 2G. Standard category planes are designed to withstand 3.8G positive and 1.52G negative loads. With this in mind, let's revisit the scenario of pulling hard on the stick and explore its potential consequences.

Say we are back to previous scenario, with the same weight, and we are at constant altitude and speed, but this time speed is slower. And to compensate for the slower speed, our angle of attack is now 6°. Every time we double the angle of attack that was stablished for constant speed and altitude, lift is also doubled (remember that we are now keeping the speed constant and pulling hard on the stick here). So at 12° we have 2G and at 18° angle of attack we have 3G. It is impossible to go any further because 18° is the critical angle of attack and at this point 1

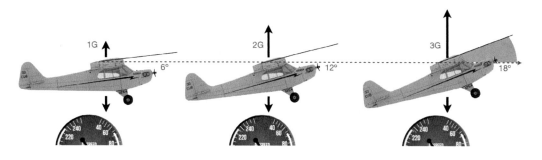

*Figure 95: Pull hard on the yoke at 120kt.*

I believe you may have figured out what I mean by this demonstration. Let's now repeat it, but changing our starting point to a higher speed. Say 140kt. To be able to maintain altitude at a higher speed but with the same weight, we will need a smaller angle of attack. In this case, it will be 4°. Remember that every time this angle doubles it doubles our load factor. Now, after pulling hard on the yoke, let's see what happens. When the angle of attack reaches 8°, we have a load factor of 2G. Coming to 12°, we have 3G. Getting to 16°, we have 4G! Wait a minute! The limit that this aircraft is able to withstand is 3.8G. We are overstressing the structure of the aircraft already and there is still room to do more! In fact, this aircraft will only stall at 18° and that means 4.5G!

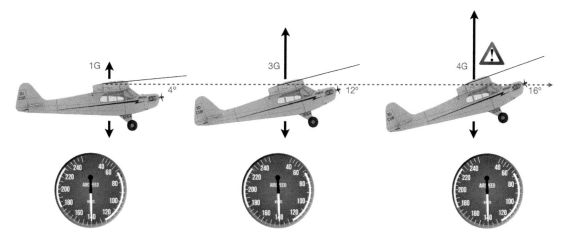

*Figure 96: Pull hard on the yoke at 140kt.*

We have seen two different situations. In the first one, the airplane stalled before reaching its limit load factor. In the second, the airplane was overstressed and likely damaged during the maneuver. What was the fundamental difference between both scenarios? Speed! And the minimum speed in which full application of flight control will result in exceeding the limit load factor is known as Maneuvering Speed ($V_A$). At speeds below $V_A$, the airplane will stall first and therefore not exceed the maximum load.

However, $V_A$ is not a fixed speed! It varies with weight. To understand that, let's go back once again to our demonstration using 120kt, but this time we will do it at a lighter weight. If we are lighter, we need a smaller angle of attack to keep that speed at constant altitude. Say we need only 4° of angle of attack now. If that is true, what is going to happen once we pull hard on the yoke is exactly what we saw in Figure 96, that is, the airplane will overstress, reaching up to 4.5G before stalling!

Sometimes the manufacturer will provide a table with several weights and their corresponding $V_A$; however, if only one $V_A$ is published, keep in mind that it is always presented for maximum takeoff weight and be aware that this speed may be much lower than you think at your current weight. Have a look at the figure below. The part of the diagram that was highlighted in blue is the same presented on your airspeed indicator (ASI) – green band, yellow band, and red line. All information is there considering Maximum Takeoff Weight! For different weights, you will have different diagram, but unfortunately you will not have a different airspeed indicator.

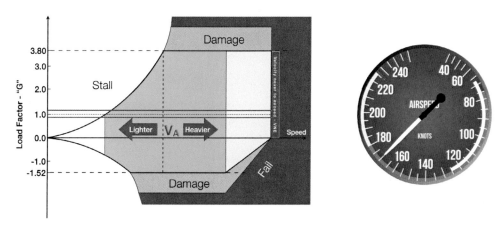

*Figure 97: VG diagram and the airspeed indicator (ASI) – FAR Part 23.*

Some people think that "VG", on the VG diagram stands for "Velocity" and "G load". But G in fact stands for GUST. Every corner of this diagram has a maximum vertical wind gust that the airplane must withstand. For standard category airplanes, the green band ends at the point where a vertical gust of 50ft/s (positive or negative) will make an airplane reach its maximum load factor (+3.8G or -1.52G). We call that seed $V_{NO}$. From that speed onwards, you will find a yellow band indicating you can only fly that fast on smooth air (no turbulence). A red line is drawn at the speed at which the maximum load factor is reached with a vertical gust of 25ft/s. We call this red line the Velocity Never to Exceed, $V_{NE}$.

To clarify the terms "damage" and "fail" on the diagram: "Damage" indicates overstressing the aircraft up to 50% above the load limit, causing the structure to bend beyond its elastic limit. "Fail" means the structure breaks apart, leading to wing separation!

Now back to transport category airplanes! They must be able to withstand a load factor ranging from 2.5g positive to negative 1g when the flaps are retracted. When they are extended, the range changes to 2.0g positive, and no negative g load tests are performed.

Within these legally established margins, a speed envelope is created in which the airplane must be able to fly. Please note: the boundary speeds of this envelope are not intended for normal aircraft operation. They will be used as a reference to prove that the aircraft is capable of meeting regulatory requirements. The minimum speed of this envelope is related to the stall speed that will be discussed in a later section in this book. The other speeds are known as $V_A$ (already discussed but we will make a quick review), $V_B$, $V_C$, and $V_D$. As I said previously, every corner of this diagram has a specific vertical gust speed.

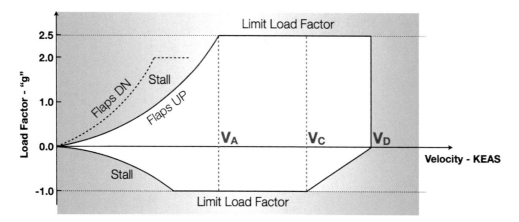

*Figure 98: Load limit envelope.*

An important remark should be made here. Manuals of large commercial aircraft often give pilots a warning:

*Even below $V_A$, do not apply sharp and full deflection of controls. This action may cause the aircraft to run out of control and, if repeated, it will lead to structural failure.*

An accident like this happened to an American Airlines Airbus A300 on November 12th, 2001: after taking off from New York, it faced wake turbulence from another aircraft that took off in front of it. The pilot repeatedly applied full rudder deflection to both sides and the vertical stabilizer eventually separated from the plane, leading to the crash and death of all occupants.

Important note: as we mentioned aircraft manuals, the concept of maneuvering speeds has a different meaning on some flight operations manuals (such as Boeing models) than the one discussed here. Despite the same name, that maneuvering speed and this one are two separate things. By the way, that FCOM (Flight Crew Operations Manual) maneuvering speed represents a speed at which you could bank the airplane up to a minimum of 40° bank before stall warning (stick shaker) is activated.

## 1.8.2    Maximum Gust Speed – $V_B$

$V_B$ is the speed at which the gust value is the highest (66 feet per second). Normally, this speed is set by the manufacturer as $V_{RA}$ (Rough Air Speed or Turbulent Air Penetration Speed).

## 1.8.3    Design Cruising Speed – $V_C$

$V_C$ is a speed equal to or less than 80% of $V_D$ and is usually defined as the $V_{MO}/M_{MO}$ (Maximum Operating Speed or Mach) of the airplane. $V_C$ must be sufficiently higher than $V_B$ to allow the pilot to fly at $V_B$ and face an inadvertent speed increase in severe turbulence without exceeding $V_C$.

## 1.8.4    Design Dive Speed – $V_D$

$V_D$ is the speed achieved in a 20-second dive starting from $V_C$ with 7.5° downward trajectory and engine applied producing 75% of maximum cruise thrust. At this speed, the airplane may not exhibit characteristics of high vibration, flutter, or any other that may jeopardize the integrity of its structure.

In the previous section, we discussed the load limit envelope, which determines the maximum speeds at which a certain load can be supported by the structure. The term "envelope" is used because the chart has an enclosed shape, indicating the allowable flight regime for the aircraft. The aircraft can only operate within the boundaries of this envelope. The speed envelope for normal airplane operation is much narrower but is directly related to the load limit envelope that we discussed previously.

In the operating envelope, represented by the illustration below, we have speed and altitude limits. In Figure 100, we see the environmental envelope that defines the altitude and temperature limits within which the airplane can operate. The example provided is from a Boeing 737NG, but naturally, these limits vary from model to model.

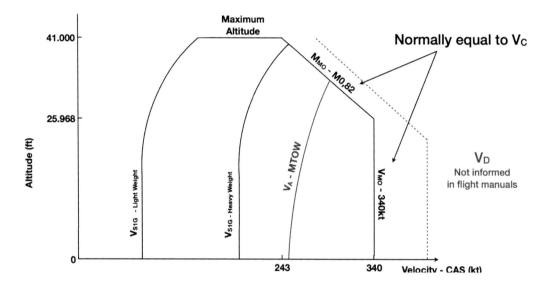

Figure 99: Speed and altitude envelope of normal flight operations.

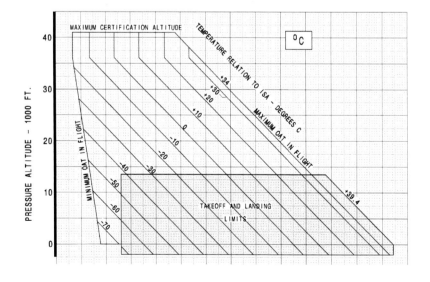

Figure 100: Environmental envelope.

02

# Weight
# and Balance

Any pilot making their first flight in a small single-engine airplane goes over a weight and balance sheet which introduces the Maximum Takeoff Weight (MTOW). "The objective is clear", says the flight instructor: "the actual takeoff weight must be below this limit (MTOW)". However, as airplanes increase in size and complexity, new weight terms and limits emerge: basic operational weight, payload, maximum landing weight, maximum zero fuel weight, and so on. To understand which items are included in each term, as well as the rationale behind all weight limits, let's start from scratch and consider the airplane as it rolls out of the factory hangar for the first time.

When the airplane leaves the assembly line, it is weighed for the first time (this is figurative, as the aircraft does not actually go on a scale at this moment — the weight is assumed to be known by the manufacturer since all airplanes assembled are the same at this point). At this stage, the airplane is still in its raw state, and all we have is:

## 2.1.1   Manufacturer Empty Weight – MEW

This includes the aircraft structure with its fuselage, wings, and engines, as well as enclosed fluids, flight crew seats and seat belts, and minimal emergency equipment, such as fire extinguishers.

From this starting point, we add blocks of items, and each time we insert one of these blocks, we assign a new name to the resulting weight.

## 2.1.2   Basic Empty Weight – BEW
### Standard Items – SI

Standard items include unusable fuel from tanks, oil and other engine fluids, unusable water from washbasins, first aid kits, flashlights, megaphones, portable oxygen bottles, galley frame, and some electronic equipment requested by the aircraft operator.

Adding SI to MEW results in the Basic Empty Weight (BEW), also called Dry Empty Weight (DEW).

## 2.1.3   Basic Operational Weight – BOW
### Operational Items – OI

Operational items include pilots and cabin crew with their luggage, navigational manuals and charts, onboard service materials (food, drink, dinnerware, napkins, onboard magazines), drinking water, life jackets and lifeboats, portable ELT (emergency locator transmitter), containers, and cargo pallets.

Adding OI to BEW results in the Basic Operational Weight (BOW), also called Dry Operational Weight (DOW).

## 2.1.4   Zero Fuel Weight – ZFW
### Payload

Payload includes passengers and cargo (all flight revenue).

Since all that is left for the plane to be able to takeoff is fuel, adding Payload to BOW will result in something that we call Zero Fuel Weight (ZFW).

## 2.1.5   Takeoff Weight and Landing Weight – TOW and LW
### Total Fuel

Total fuel includes all fuel on board the aircraft at the moment of engine start. It can initially be subdivided into 3 parts - Taxi Fuel, Trip Fuel, Fuel Over Destination. This third part involves some portions that will be dealt with in detail later, but as an example, we can mention Contingency Fuel, Alternate Fuel, Hold Over Alternate Fuel, and Extra Fuel.

Total Fuel plus ZFW results in the Taxi Weight or Ramp Weight.

By subtracting the fuel needed for taxi-out (taxi from the tarmac to the runway – taxi fuel), we now have our Takeoff Weight – TOW, also known as Brake Release Weight (BRWT). We can also say that TOW is the sum of ZFW and Takeoff Fuel. Below is a graphical representation of these weights and the name given to each new part created by the sum. Importantly, these are just one of the names by which the sum is known.

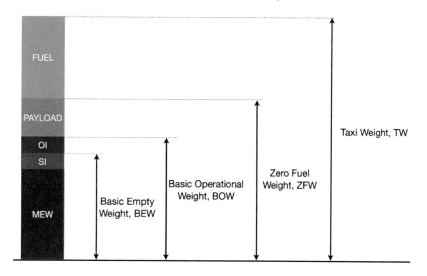

*Figure 101: From BEW to TW.*

### 2.1.5.2    Takeoff Fuel

Fuel on board at the beginning of takeoff roll. This is the total fuel loaded minus taxi fuel.

### 2.1.5.3    Trip Fuel

Fuel required to get from origin to destination considering all phases between takeoff and landing. Subtracting that from Takeoff Weight results in the predicted Landing Weight on the destination airport. Predicted Landing Weight should always include all fuel that has been loaded except the parts just mentioned (taxi fuel and trip fuel).

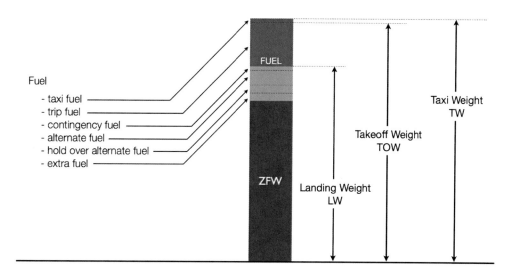

*Figure 102: TW, TOW and LW.*

## 2.1.6 Maximum Takeoff Weight and Maximum Landing Weight – MTOW and MLW

Maximum takeoff and landing weights are set by the manufacturer based on specific aspects of the landing gear structure. To this maximum value, the manufacturer can (and usually does) apply some decrements to sell weight certification as an option.

Let's use the Boeing 737-800 as an example. Boeing sells this model with several maximum certified takeoff weight options: 70,500kg, 72,500kg, 75,000kg, and 79,000kg, for instance. There is absolutely no technical difference among these aircraft. The only thing that changes is the price. The operator will purchase the weight certification that best fits the missions it wishes to accomplish. You will find more details about this in the Takeoff Performance chapter, Maximum Takeoff Weight section.

Let's focus on the highest takeoff weight that will ever be offered (79,000kg). What is it based on? As stated earlier, the landing gear plays a decisive role in this definition. FAR 25.473 states that the aircraft must withstand a landing at its maximum takeoff weight (MTOW) where ground contact occurs at a rate of descent of 6ft/s or 360ft/min. The maximum landing weight is also set as a function of landing, but with an even steeper descent rate. The aircraft must withstand a landing with a vertical velocity at the time of touchdown of 10ft/s or 600ft/min.

To put into perspective how "hard" a landing with this sink rate is, on average landings, touchdown happens at a rate close to 2ft/s (120ft/min). Anything beyond 4ft/s and very bad words would be yelled all over the cabin and flight deck, for sure!!

Avarage pilot touches down at a rate of descent between 120 and 180 ft/min

*Figure 103: Maximum Takeoff Weight and Maximum Landing Weight.*

This discussion makes the manufacturer's objectives clear in establishing a maximum takeoff weight and a maximum landing weight, but it still does not clarify why there is a limit called Maximum Zero Fuel Weight.

## 2.1.7 Objectives behind Maximum Zero Fuel Weight – MZFW

This limitation is related to the wing structure of the airplane, especially near the root, where it attaches to the fuselage. The following graphs show how the effort applied at this point of the aircraft varies with the weight of the cargo loaded and the amount of fuel on board.

For this demonstration, we will assume a large capacity center tank in the aircraft and disregard the effect of engine weight on the calculation. We will also consider that the aircraft is in level flight and is producing lift equal to its current weight.

The required lift will be distributed between both wings, with each wing producing half the amount needed. The weight of the aircraft is a vector located in its longitudinal axis and pointing downwards. The lift is represented by two vectors that point upwards on each wing. As a result, there is a tendency for the wings of the aircraft to bend upwards during flight, causing significant strain on the root of the wing (where it joins the fuselage). Observe the sequence of figures below.

Figure 104 shows the airplane without fuel, in flight as a glider. Although it is not a realistic scenario, let's go on with it. The next step is to load the aircraft to its MZFW. The more weight we add to the plane, the more lift is generated to maintain the airplane flying, and consequently, the greater the stress on the wing-fuselage junction (increasing the moment of force), as shown in Figure 105.

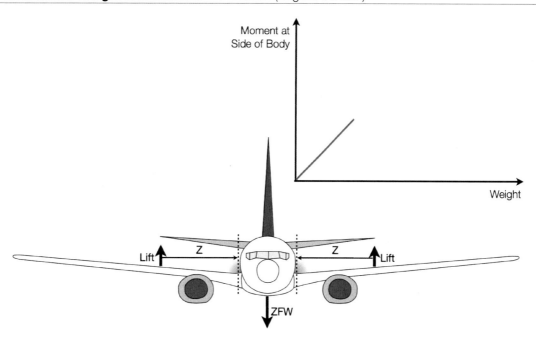

*Figure 104: Airplane in flight with no fuel and ZFW below maximum.*

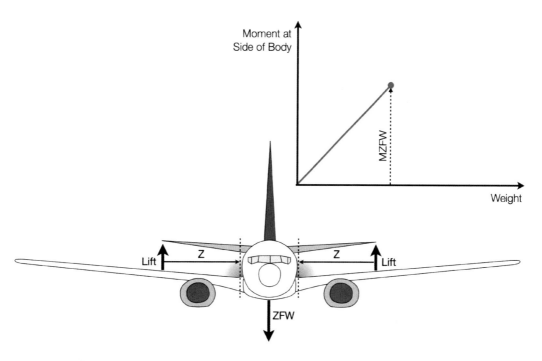

*Figure 105: Airplane inflight with no fuel and at maximum zero fuel weight.*

It is time to start fueling this plane. As we add fuel, initially to the wings, the lift generated by them will increase in the same proportion. However, because the fuel weight is closer to the wing root at this time, it generates a smaller bending moment than that of lift. For this reason, the total bending moment at the wing root increases. In Figure 106, "Y" and "Z" indicate the fuel weight arm and lift lever arm, respectively.

As we continue fueling the wing tanks, the average weight force that represents the fuel moves towards the wing tip. At some point during this process, even before topping off the tanks, the fuel weight force will pass through the exact spot where the center of pressure of the wing is. At this moment, both forces exert the same bending moment on the wing, as can be seen on the stress graph when the blue curve, representing this effort as a function of fuel, stops rising and levels off (Figure 107).

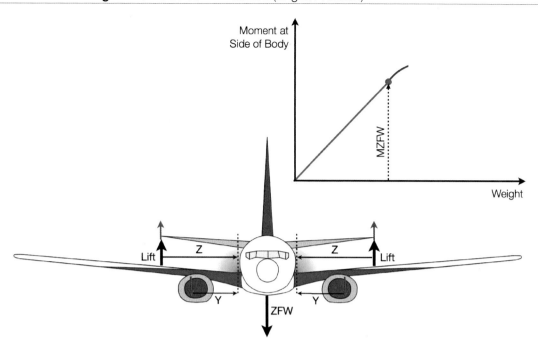

*Figure 106: Airplane at MZFW with wings partially filled with fuel (1).*

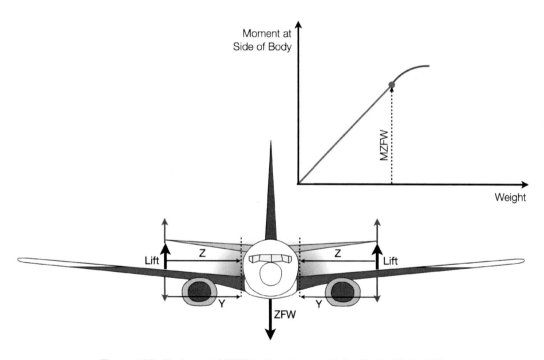

*Figure 107: Airplane at MZFW with wings partially filled with fuel (2).*

Finally, when topping off the main tanks with fuel, the weight force moves even closer to the wingtip, while lift is still applied at the same point as before. This distribution of forces causes the downward moment generated by fuel weight to be greater than the upward moment generated by increasing lift, so stress on the wing root now decreases. Figure 108 shows the aircraft with its main tanks full. Observe the behavior of the graph indicating the bending moment of the wing.

Figure 109 shows that the center tank is now fueled. Because it is located in the fuselage, adding fuel (weight) to this tank generates the same stress behavior that we observed when increasing payload – there is a linear increase in force moment. With all tanks topped off to their full capacity and the aircraft in flight, this results in the greatest bending moment for this type of aircraft.

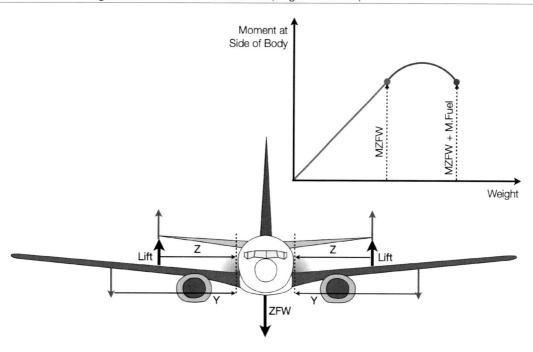

Figure 108: Aircraft at MZFW and main tanks full.

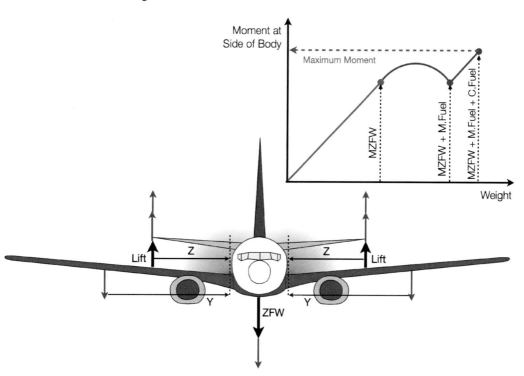

Figure 109: Aircraft at MZFW with main tanks and center tank full.

When engineers design an aircraft, they consider the highest zero fuel weight that they want and scale the wing structure to withstand the stress that will occur at the so-called maximum bending moment. For regulatory reasons (FAR 25.303), the aircraft must be able to withstand this bending stress with a load equivalent to 2.5g (2.5 times the acceleration of gravity), and a safety factor of 1.5 should be added over this maximum. So, the plane is made to withstand 150% of the maximum load it should ever encounter in the worst imaginable turbulence. If you do not remember these concepts, just reread the topic "Design Speeds".

Let's assume the role of these engineers. Figure 110 shows a given aircraft and the bending moment graph that we have just studied.

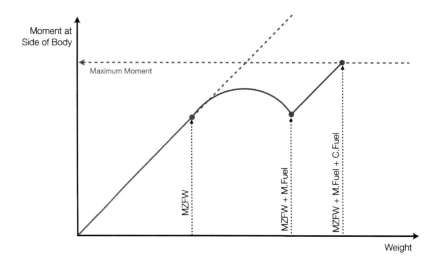

*Figure 110: Starting point. Maximum bending moment.*

In Figure 111, I illustrate what would happen if engineers were to review the wing design and launch a new version of the same airplane with a reinforced structure capable of withstanding a greater bending moment. The MZFW (Maximum Zero Fuel Weight) could be increased. In contrast, Figure 112 shows an aircraft that was reported to have early material fatigue. To ensure that the service life remains sufficiently long, engineers review their calculations and establish a lower maximum bending moment than that of the initial design. The result would be a reduced MZFW.

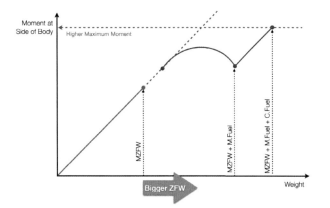

*Figure 111: Greater bending moment.*

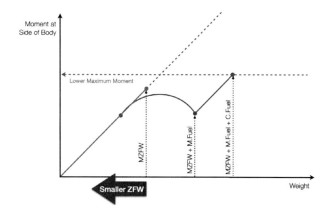

*Figure 112: Smaller bending moment.*

## 2.1.8 Fuel Burn – Why Center Tank First, then Main Tanks

By comparing the two following illustrations (Figures 113 and 114), we can understand why it is essential to burn the center tank fuel before the fuel in the wing tanks. In the first illustration, observe the blue line representing the fuel. If you scroll from right to left, you will see a straight line indicating fuel in the center tank and a curved line representing fuel in the main tanks (wings). You can see the force moment decreasing as the fuel burns until the center tank is empty. Then, the moment increases when the wing tank fuel begins to burn, eventually reversing and decreasing again.

Figure 114 shows what would happen if we chose to burn the wing tanks first and then the center tank: the maximum bending moment would be exceeded, jeopardizing the safety of the aircraft structure if this inverted fuel burn pattern were repeatedly used.

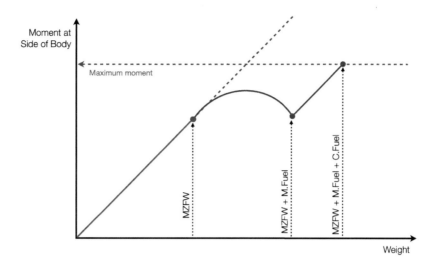

*Figure 113: Normal fuel burn sequence. First center tank, then main tanks.*

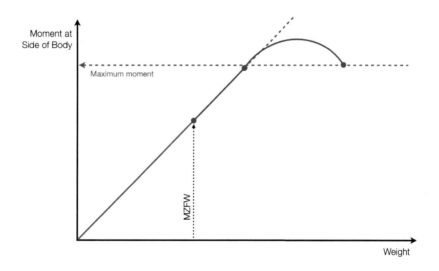

*Figure 114: Inverted fuel burn sequence. First main tanks, then center tank.*

Of course, this inverted fuel burn pattern does not instantly compromise flight safety. Remember that the maximum moment is designed to support a 2.5g load with an additional 50% safety margin. So, rest assured that if, after takeoff, any malfunction of the fuel system occurs and makes it impossible to burn the fuel in the center tanks, you will definitely face issues with the endurance and range capacity of your flight. You will probably not be able to reach your final destination and will most likely require a technical landing. However, there is absolutely no immediate risk of the wings breaking in flight.

## 2.1.9   Keeping an Eye on Weight

Under US regulations (FAA), the plane must be weighed every 3 years. European regulations (EASA) provide for a longer weighing interval: 4 years. In any case, operators must keep a continuous, complete, and always up-to-date record of the empty weight of their aircraft.

This document should always record any change in weight or the position of the center of gravity. This occurs when, for example, we perform maintenance services that alter the weight of the aircraft, change the internal seating configuration, or install new devices on the aircraft.

There is no need to change the original BEW value in the documents of the aircraft every time a change occurs. We must keep records of these changes, but the document only needs to be modified with each new weighing (every 3 or 4 years, depending on the regulator) or whenever the records show a weight variation greater than 0.5% of the maximum landing weight (MLW) of the aircraft. The same applies to CG offset. The documentation will need to be updated whenever records indicate that, by calculation, the CG shifts more than 0.5% of the mean aerodynamic chord (MAC). Later, we will see why we use MAC as a reference to identify the CG position.

Figure 115 shows an example of how small services may change the weight of an airplane and re-establish the basic empty weight through calculations and re-weighing on scales.

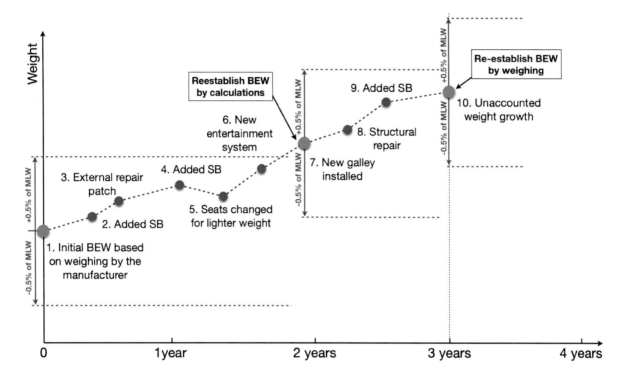

*Figure 115: When do we have to put the aircraft on a scale?*

In this section, we will study the effects of changing the CG position on various aspects of our flight, starting with an intriguing question: two identical airplanes are supplied with the same amount of fuel and cargo, fly the same route, at the same altitude, and under the same weather conditions. At the end of the flight, will they both always have the same amount of fuel remaining?

## 2.2.1 Effects of CG Position on Fuel Consumption

To answer the proposed question, let's take a step back and consider another one first. In the scenario presented above, are both aircraft producing the same lift during cruise flight? Well, not necessarily, and let's explore why.

When pilots attend their first aerodynamics class in private pilot training, they are told that, to maintain level flight, lift must equal weight. While this statement is sufficient for the basic understanding required by a private pilot, it is not entirely accurate. Figure 116 shows an aircraft with lift and weight vectors distributed on it. Lift acts at the center of pressure while weight acts at the center of gravity.

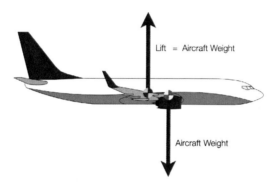

*Figure 116: Like an unbalanced seesaw: weight is on the right, but there is nothing on the left.*

In Figure 116, the plane resembles an unbalanced seesaw. There is a force in the center, like the seesaw pivot (represented by the lift on the wing), and someone sitting on one side (represented by weight at the CG), but no one on the other side. Consequently, this plane would lower its nose.

To remain stable during cruise flight, there must be a force on the opposite side of the weight, generating an equal but opposite moment. To balance the seesaw, engineers installed a second pair of wings on the aircraft called the horizontal stabilizer. This stabilizer acts as a wing positioned upside down on the tail of the aircraft, generating downward lift, which we will refer to as "negative lift" from now on. Note that there are now two vectors pointing downward and only one poin

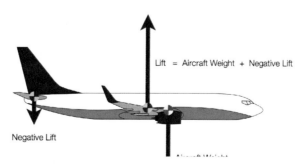

*Figure 117: Balanced seesaw.*

Although we have stabilized our seesaw, the positive lift produced by the wing must now match not only the weight of the aircraft but the sum of that weight and the negative lift produced by the horizontal stabilizer.

Given these considerations, we can address how lift can differ between two identical aircraft. Figure 118 shows two aircraft. The CG (center of gravity) of the aircraft on the left is in a forward position, while the CG of the one on the right is in a more aft location, closer to the center of pressure. For the sake of maintaining equilibrium, a forward CG requires an increase in negative lift and, consequently, an increase in the positive lift generated by the wings. With an aft CG, however, the pitch-down moment decreases, and the negative lift from the horizontal stabilizer can be smaller to balance the aircraft, resulting in smaller positive lift requirements.

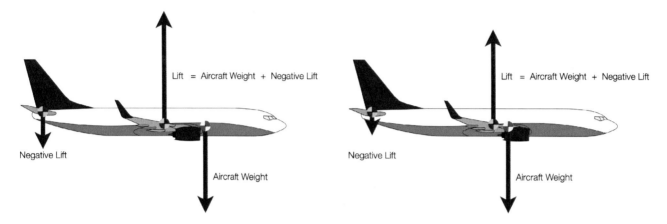

*Figure 118: Positive lift is smaller with aft CG position.*

To reach a conclusion regarding the initial question, let's examine the consequences of each situation presented in Figure 118. Follow this train of thought with me: a forward CG requires more negative lift; more negative lift needs greater positive lift from the wings; greater positive lift generates more drag; more drag requires more thrust; producing more thrust leads to increased fuel consumption. Therefore, identical aircraft with the same weight may have different fuel consumption rates depending on the weight distribution on board. Conclusion: a forward CG leads to higher fuel burn while a rear CG results in lower fuel consumption, provided the CG remains within specific limits (the envelope), which we will discuss later.

## 2.2.2   Effects of CG Position on Lateral Control

Next point to discuss: How does CG affect aircraft lateral control?

In assessing lateral control, we need to make a few assumptions. First, let's consider a twin-engine aircraft and try to control thrust asymmetry by assuming that one engine is inoperative while the other is at maximum thrust. We will use only the rudder to control the airplane. Second, the rudder will be at maximum deflection, and we will change the force generated by the vertical stabilizer by varying the airflow velocity over its surface (which means changing the speed of the airplane).

Based on the proposed scenario in Figure 119, observe the following details: the "F1" force generated by the engine is exactly the same on both airplanes. The CG is in a forward position on the aircraft on the left and in an aft position on the one on the right. The CG position does not change the engine arm (d1), but it significantly alters the value of "d2", which represents the arm of the vertical stabilizer.

The moment produced by the engine is the same on both aircraft (same force and same arm), and to nullify it, we need either a very large force with a small arm or a large arm with a much smaller force. Since force is determined by the airstream velocity passing over the stabilizer, the conclusion is that a forward CG increases the lever arm and allows the required force to be lower (lower speed). With an aft CG, the opposite occurs: we have a small lever arm and thus need more force (higher speed) to achieve the same moment.

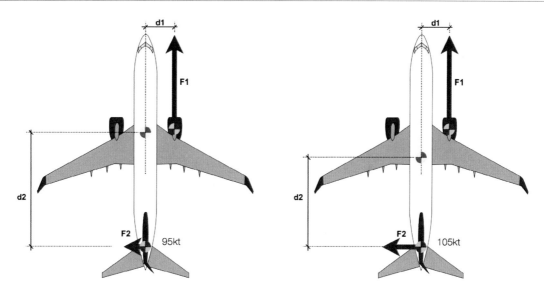

*Figure 119: How CG position changes required speed for directional control.*

Note that directional control of the aircraft becomes easier (we need slower speeds to achieve the desired result) with a forward CG. On several occasions, you will see statements that say: "the CG must be considered in the most unfavorable position". The most unfavorable position depends on what is being evaluated. The most unfavorable CG for directional control is the aft CG, but when discussing fuel consumption, the most forward CG is the least favorable, as discussed in the previous topic.

## 2.2.3  CG informed in % of MAC

Now that we have seen how CG position affects some flight characteristics, let's look at how it is reported on large aircraft.

The first step is to establish a line that will serve as a reference for all arms to be measured from. This reference line is known as the "Datum Line" (Datum is Latin for reference) and is usually located in front of the aircraft. The plane is then divided into stations described as distances from the Datum Line. Every time we place some weight at a station, a moment is generated. The CG is a single point on the airplane where, if lifted with a jack, it would not tip to any side, i.e., it would be in perfect balance. This is obtained by summing all moments and dividing them by the total weight, with the result given as a distance from the Datum Line that we mentioned earlier.

On smaller aircraft, the CG position is often represented as a distance from the Datum Line. However, on the larger aircraft that we are going to study, another measure is usually taken. The CG is normally reported as a percentage of the mean aerodynamic chord (MAC) of the wing of the aircraft. Remember: the chord is an imaginary line that connects the leading edge to the trailing edge of the wing.

To find the mean aerodynamic chord of a wing, the process is quite simple, and we have already covered it in a previous chapter (1.4.3), but let's review it quickly. The manufacturer determines the wing area that will be used as a reference in performance calculations and divides it by the wingspan of the wing. The result is the MAC.

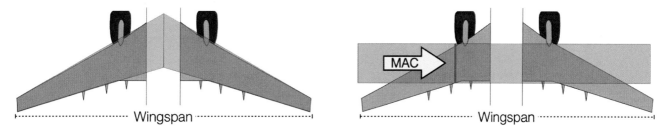

*Figure 120: The blue line is the mean aerodynamic chord (MAC).*

Once the MAC has been established, we arbitrarily define its leading edge as the beginning of the chord (0%) and its trailing edge as the end of the chord (100%). In the following figure, you can see LEMAC (Leading Edge of MAC) and TEMAC (Trailing Edge of MAC), and how the front and rear limits that allow CG movement are indicated as percentages of the total MAC length. The example shows a Boeing 737-800. To scale this up and give the reader a better idea of the measurements, this plane has a MAC of about 4 meters in length and it is allowed to fluctuate over 1.2 meters between the front and rear limits (5% front limit equals 0.20 meters and 36% rear limit equals 1.44 meters). We will cover more details about the CG envelope later in this course.

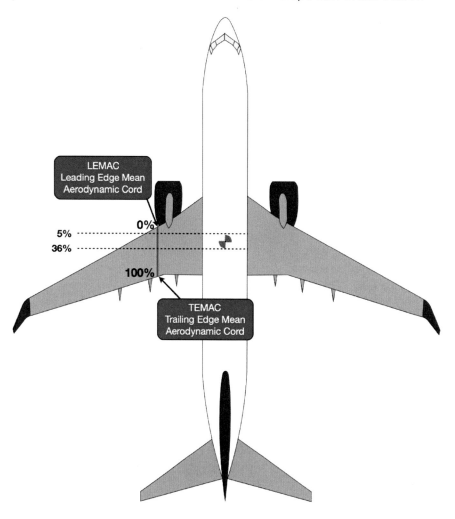

*Figure 121: CG travel on a Boeing 737-800.*

Although it seems obvious, it is important to note that even if the CG is reported as a function of the mean aerodynamic chord (MAC), that is not where it is actually located. The CG must be somewhere near the longitudinal axis of the aircraft and is represented as a MAC projection at this point on the aircraft, as shown in the previous illustration.

### 2.3.1  Cargo Distribution Limitation

Looking at the floor structure of an aircraft, one might easily assume that, despite its capacity to carry a large amount of cargo, the entire load cannot be supported by a single point. This could potentially lead to breakage of the floor or damage to the fuselage walls.

With this in mind, manufacturers publish the Weight and Balance Manual (WBM), which includes two types of load limitations: a maximum load per unit of area and a maximum load per unit of length. Let's explore this concept further with an example in the sequence of images below.

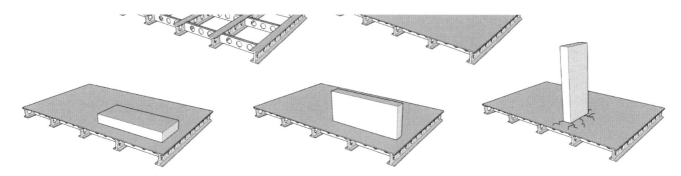

Figure 122: Why is there an area load limit?

You might notice that when placing a load on the floor of the aircraft, the pressure exerted by this load on the floor depends on how it is arranged. In this illustration, the major concern is with load distribution on the floor, and a weight limit per unit of area is imposed by the manual, for example: $300kg/m^2$.

As mentioned earlier, the airplane is similar to a seesaw. In its structure, there is a significant bending effort that represents the sum of two other efforts: tension on the top of the surface and compression on the bottom. When heavy loads are placed farther from the bending point, i.e., the wing, this effort increases. Conversely, as they approach this point, the bending effort decreases.

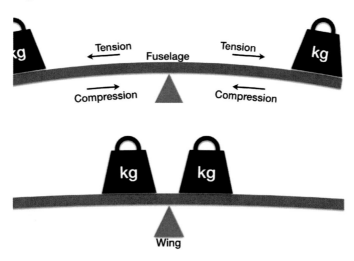

Figure 123: Different bending moments, depending on cargo location.

For this reason, aircraft also have a load constraint per unit length, which represents measurements along their longitudinal axis, for example: 1,250kg/m. The closer you are to the wing, the higher the allowable linear load value may be. Please note that the maximum linear load refers not only to the cargo itself, but to everything that is boarded and placed in the same station. In the fuselage cross-section in the following figure, we need to consider the cargo container, the passengers, the carry-on luggage in the overhead bins, and even the crew using the so-called "sarcophagus" to rest on long flights. In this example, the sum of all these weights in this station could not exceed 1,250kg.

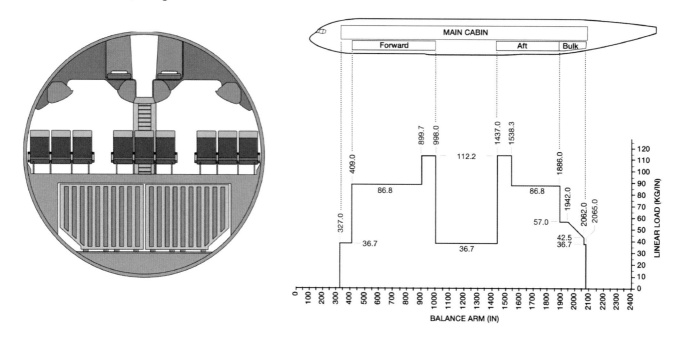

Figure 124: Load limit per length. Example of a Boeing 777.

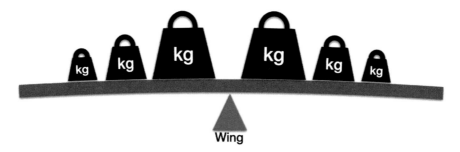

Figure 125: Cargo distribution along the aircraft.

## 2.3.2 Finding CG Position

Before moving on to the next step and learn how to build an operational envelope for the center of gravity, let's do some exercises to calculate CG position using simple momentum equations.

Example 1: Find A and B.

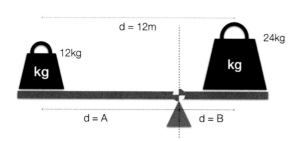

| At rest, | Then |
|---|---|
| A + B = 12 | 2 x B + B = 12 |
| 12kg x A = 24kg x B | 3 x B = 12 |
| | B = 4m |
| Isolating A, we get: | |
| A = 2 x B | A = 12 – B |
| | A = 8m |

Example 2: Find A.

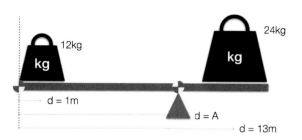

At rest,
$1 \times 12 + 13 \times 24 = (12 + 24) \times A$
$12 + 312 = 36 \times A$
**A = 9m**

Example 3: Find A.

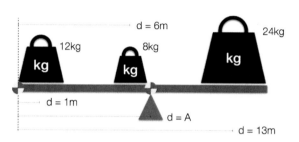

At rest,
$1 \times 12 + 6 \times 8 + 13 \times 24 = (12 + 8 + 24) \times A$
$12 + 48 + 312 = 44 \times A$
**A = 8.45m**

Example 4: Consider an aircraft with a basic empty weight of 700kg and a CG arm of 248cm from the Datum Line. Onboard will be two pilots weighing a total of 180kg (220cm arm), two passengers weighing a total of 170kg (310cm arm), 200 liters of fuel weighing 156kg (270cm arm), and luggage weighing a total of 25kg (430cm arm).

A) What is the CG position on takeoff?
B) If we remove one pilot (90kg), what will be the new takeoff CG?

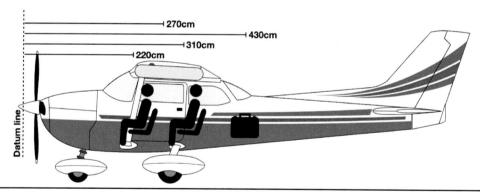

A)
$700 \times 248 + 180 \times 220 + 170 \times 310 + 156 \times 270 + 25 \times 430 = $ Momentum
Momentum = 318,770kg.m
CG = Total Momentum / Total Weight, that is,
CG = 318,770 / (700 + 180 + 170 + 156 + 25)
**CG = 258.95cm from datum line**

B)
$318,770 - 90 \times 220 = $ New Momentum
New Momentum = 298,970kg.m
CG = Momentum / Weight, that is,
CG = 298,970 / (700 + 90 + 170 + 156 + 25)
**CG = 262.02cm from datum line**

Example 5:

Imagine the aircraft below weighs 35,000kg on the main gear and another 7,000kg on the nose gear. LEMAC is 16m from the Datum line and TEMAC is 21m from the same reference. What is the CG position in %MAC?

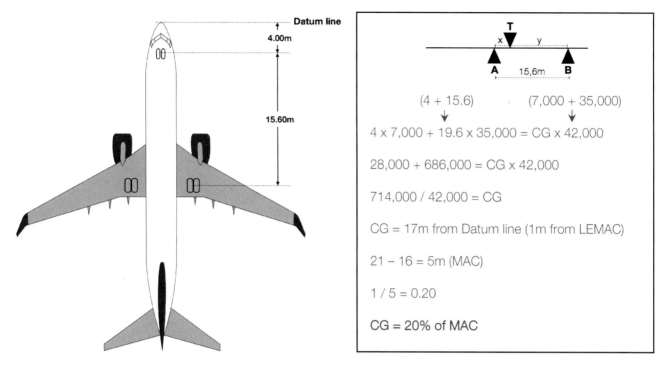

Datum line

4.00m

15.60m

T
x      y
A    15,6m    B

(4 + 15.6)          (7,000 + 35,000)
↓                        ↓
4 x 7,000 + 19.6 x 35,000 = CG x 42,000

28,000 + 686,000 = CG x 42,000

714,000 / 42,000 = CG

CG = 17m from Datum line (1m from LEMAC)

21 – 16 = 5m (MAC)

1 / 5 = 0.20

CG = 20% of MAC

Of course, there are always other ways to do the proposed exercises and achieve the same result. Here, I have demonstrated just one way to solve them.

## 2.3.3 Replacing Momentum by Index

When calculating example number 4, you may have noticed that the biggest problem with working with momentum is how large those numbers can get! As the plane becomes longer, the arm increases significantly, and momentum values increase as well. To make this task easier, someone had the brilliant idea of working with an index. The index is simply the momentum values divided by a constant. However, there are a few more details that I will cover soon.

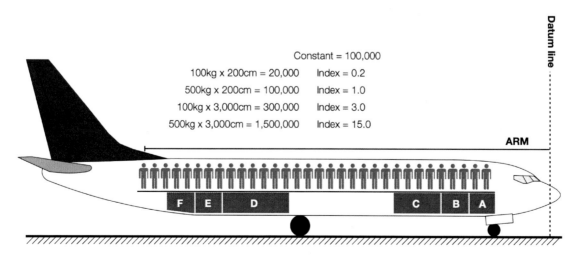

Datum line

Constant = 100,000
100kg x 200cm = 20,000      Index = 0.2
500kg x 200cm = 100,000     Index = 1.0
100kg x 3,000cm = 300,000   Index = 3.0
500kg x 3,000cm = 1,500,000 Index = 15.0

ARM

F  E  D          C  B  A

*Figure 126: Why should we use an index?*

When using the index instead of momentum, manufacturers often make adjustments so that the final values, which we will use to set the takeoff and landing CG, are always positive. One of the strategies to achieve this is to use a sample BOW CG as a reference instead of the Datum Line. Thus, whenever cargo is loaded in a way that shifts the CG forward of this reference, it will result in a negative index, while cargo that shifts the CG backward will have a positive index. Here, "cargo" refers to any weight loaded onto the aircraft, such as luggage, passengers, fuel, etc.

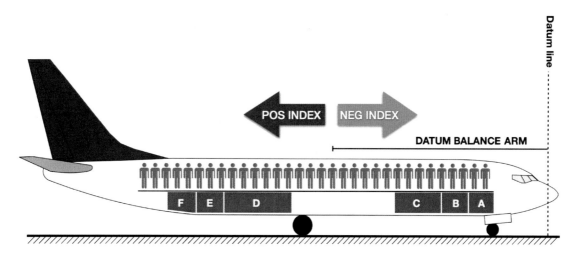

*Figure 127: Meaning of negative and positive index values.*

The "few more details" that I mentioned just now about how to transform momentum into index are two fixed values in addition to that constant by which the momentum will be divided.

$$\text{Index} = \frac{\text{Weight} \times (\text{Balance Arm} - \text{Datum Balance Arm})}{\text{Moment Constant}} + \text{Datum Constant}$$

*Equation 13: Index on weight and balance calculations.*

In this equation, the "Datum Balance Arm" is a constant that helps give the envelope the shape desired by the manufacturer (I promise to show you what this means with an example in a moment), and the "Datum Constant" is a value that ensures all final results will be positive.

These values for any aircraft model can be found in Jeppesen manuals. To illustrate, let's take a look at the values for the Boeing 737-800.

Datum Balance Arm: 658.3in

Datum Constant: 45.0

Moment Constant: 35,000 (considering that weight is in kilograms and arm is in inches)

### 2.3.4 Defining CG Envelope

Now let's look at the CG envelope of our reference plane. Remember that each plane will have specific design specificities, but overall, the assessments made to define the curtailments are the same.

Engineers typically start from a point where the envelope would be a simple rectangle referencing weight and CG (% of MAC). At this point, only two assessments are made. The first concerns the maximum weight at which the aircraft must be able to takeoff, and this is defined on the basis of the type of mission for which the aircraft was designed. The second aspect deals with stability and controllability of the aircraft in flight. As we saw in the previous topic, depending on CG position, the negative lift generated by the horizontal stabilizer will be different to counteract the tendency to lower or raise the nose of the aircraft, and the elevator must be able to allow full controllability whatever the CG position might be (within the flight envelope limits).

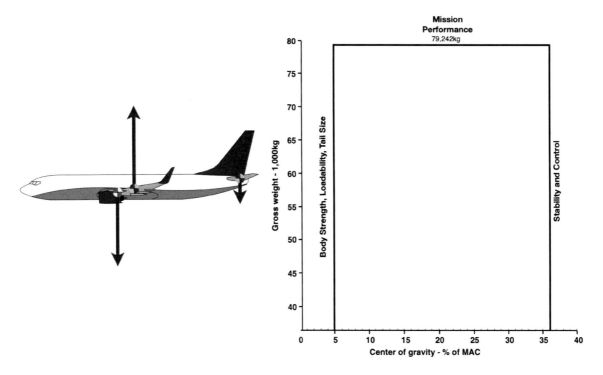

*Figure 128: Starting point to design the CG envelope.*

Now, this initial rectangular CG envelope will undergo several cuts that will shape it quite distinctly at the end. Items that engineers typically evaluate to get to the final envelope format are described next.

### 2.3.4.1  Wing load limit.

Every time CG is moved forward, the airplane must increase negative lift on the horizontal stabilizer. This downward vector makes the plane "heavier" and requires greater positive wing lift. Increased lift yields a greater bending moment, and with a very heavy aircraft, it is common for designers to narrow the front boundary of the envelope further back, thus relieving maximum load on the structure.

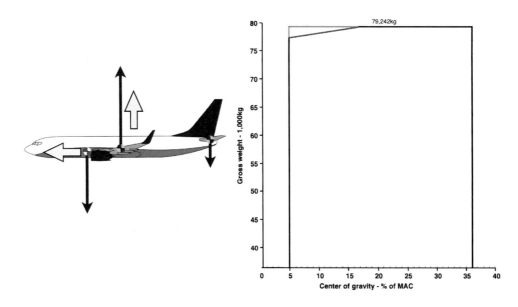

*Figure 129: Wing load limit curtailment.*

### 2.3.4.2    Tail load limit.

Let's follow the same train of thought as before but shift our focus to the tail. From this point of view, the negative lift required from the horizontal stabilizer is greater with a forward CG, so the aim of cutting the envelope now is not to exceed the load limit that must be supported by the tail of the aircraft.

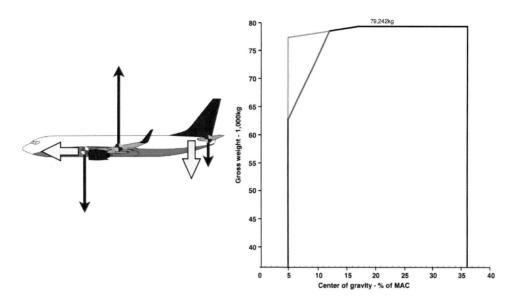

*Figure 130: Tail load limit curtailment.*

### 2.3.4.3    Gear load limit.

CG position changes the load distribution on the landing gear assembly. The more forward the CG is, the greater the weight supported by the nose gear will be, and with an aft CG, there is a greater load on the main gear. This will require a curtailment at the front and at the back of the envelope for heavy weight conditions. The front cut is usually not noticed because it is beyond the cuts made by previous items. The rear cut of the envelope, however, is easily identifiable on most aircraft.

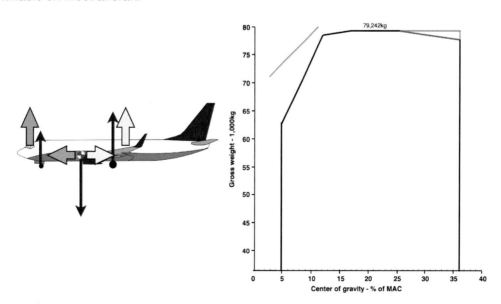

*Figure 131: Load curtailment for nose and main gear.*

### 2.3.4.4    Fuel burn vector.

Most significant travel of the CG in flight is due to fuel burn. Each aircraft has its own characteristic CG behavior while fuel is burned during a flight, but variation in this behavior is small. For most jets, burning fuel from the center tank will force CG to shift backwards, while burning fuel from the wing tanks will shift it forward, mainly owing to the swept-back shape of the wings. Some aircraft that have a tail-mounted fuel tank, are able to keep CG in a relatively constant position for a long time. These aircraft are commonly used on long-haul flights, e.g., the A330, B747 or MD-11, and they do so by automatically transferring fuel from one tank to another.

Since CG will actually move backwards at the beginning of the flight (considering a full tank on takeoff) and it cannot come out of that rectangular envelope that we saw at the beginning of this chapter, a new cut is made in the rear section of the envelope. With this limitation imposed, the manufacturer mitigates its concerns in the area of operation, which needs to be proven safe to operate.

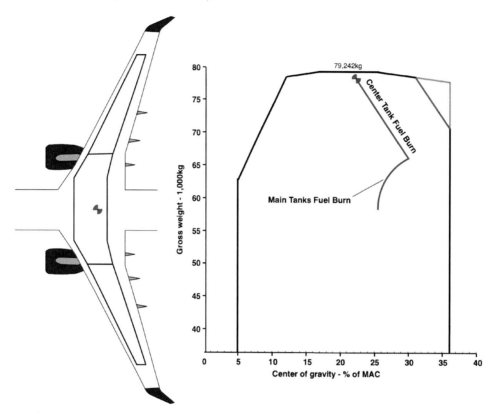

*Figure 132: Fuel vector curtailment.*

Some aircraft that I mentioned, whose fuel tank is located on their tail, might use it to store fuel on takeoff, but, in other cases, the tank exists for the sole purpose of being used in flight and ensuring a more favorable CG position during the cruise phase of the flight.

Remember, with respect to fuel consumption, the best position for the center of gravity to be is as aft as possible within the flight envelope. The system usually works as follows: after the plane takes off and during climb, fuel begins to be transferred from the center tank or from the wing tank to the tail tank. The amount transferred is only the one required to place the CG of the aircraft at a predetermined point in the envelope (at the rear). As the airplane burns fuel, the amount in this tank is always adjusted and CG position is kept in the most favorable location for a good portion of the flight. Such a system guarantees a significant increase in the endurance and range of the aircraft.

### 2.3.4.5   Tail power protection.

When applying thrust, airplanes with engines mounted below their center of gravity have a "nose up" momentum. With CG in front of the center of pressure of the wing, the weight of the aircraft causes a "nose down" momentum. The required force to balance this situation is generated by the horizontal stabilizer. It generates a downward force that is less and less needed as the airplane gets lighter and the CG is in aft position. In extreme situations, with a very rear CG position and a very light aircraft in a high thrust regime (such as a go around, for example), almost zero negative lift would have to be produced at the horizontal stabilizer. For this reason, a further curtailment in the envelope is made to guarantee full controllability in every situation.

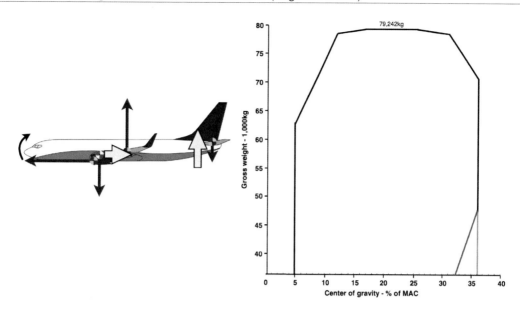

*Figure 133: Tail power protection for low weight and high thrust.*

### 2.3.4.6  Brake release tip up.

For the same reason as described in 2.3.4.5, one more cut is made to prevent the plane from lifting its nose when setting takeoff thrust. This cut is often much more pronounced than the one we have just seen, and for a simple reason: the aircraft is on the ground and standing still. The horizontal stabilizer is unable to produce any lift at this time, whether positive or negative. Therefore, the weight of the aircraft alone must be able to keep the nose gear on the ground when takeoff thrust is applied. In this case, however, momentum is not referenced to CG or CP but to the main landing gear. Depending on the level of engine thrust produced on takeoff (we call it engine rate), the envelope may have a different curtailment. It will be further forward with higher takeoff thrust. We will talk about Takeoff Rates later in this book.

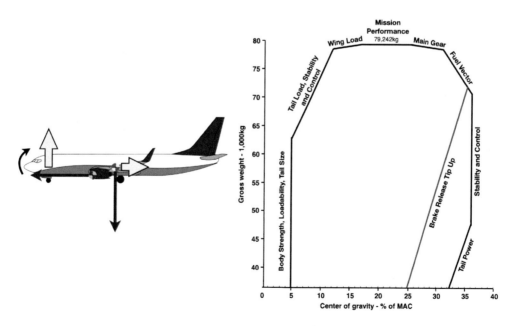

*Figure 134: Brake release tip-up protection curtailment.*

Finally, when writing the weight and balance manual (WBM), the manufacturer must assess two other issues. Remember that the envelope we have drawn so far considers aspects of flight operation (from takeoff to landing); however, when boarding or deplaning passengers, or when loading or unloading cargo, CG will travel far beyond this envelope. The main concern is that the airplane may sit on its tail during this process (we call that a "tip-up" situation). Well, it can happen, although unwanted, and it has happened on several occasions. To avoid this situation, the manufacturer publishes two other limits in the WBM.

The first is the "ground stability limit". With CG, at this point, the aircraft should be able to stay in normal position (no tipping) even while sitting on a 3% pitched tarmac with headwinds blowing near 35kt.

The second is a limit CG to avoid tipping on level ground and with no wind at all. Beyond this point, the aircraft will fatally lift its nose. It is simply called the "tipping limit".

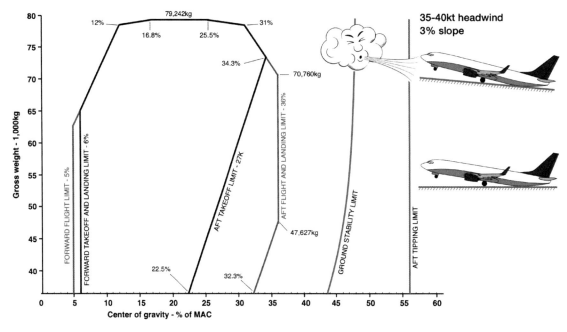

Figure 135: Ground stability and tipping limits.

Figure 136: To tie down the nose landing gear or use the tail stand is a good way to avoid tipping when loading and unloading cargo from the aircraft.

## 2.4.1   General Loading Report

A load sheet (also known as balance sheet, load manifest, or even loading report) contains various information regarding aircraft loading. The point that gathers the most important information is the CG envelope. In addition to loading data, smaller aircraft usually have a field detailing mission fuel and payload. Let's start by looking at this type of manifest.

Although the names of each line indicated in fuel planning may be different depending on the aircraft operator, the important thing is to emphasize that all lines above the first totalizer, named in the example "Minimum Fuel Required (MFR)", have what we call a "priority over payload". This means that this amount of fuel is absolutely necessary to accomplish the mission and that it will be on board even if that means that we need to remove passengers or cargo from the airplane. The lines below MFR and before Takeoff Fuel are an amount of fuel that will be in tanks at the operator's discretion, but only if there is weight available for takeoff. This fuel quantity has no priority over payload and no passengers or cargo will stay on the ground for this portion of fuel to be filled.

| | Endurance (hh:mm) | Fuel Qty (Gal) | |
|---|---|---|---|
| Trip Fuel | | | |
| Alternate Fuel | | | Priority over payload |
| Reserve Fuel | | | |
| Ballast Fuel | | | |
| Technical Fuel | | | |
| Min. Fuel Required | | | |

*Figure 137: Which one has priority? Fuel or payload?*

The regulatory minimum fuel on board before takeoff will be mentioned in the next topic. It varies from regulator to regulator, but for the time being, let's assume that our flight requires the amount of fuel as shown in the table below, with 6 gallons included as technical fuel owing to poor weather forecast on destination.

| Endurance and Fuel Quantity | Endurance (hh:mm) | Fuel Qty (Gal) |
|---|---|---|
| | 01:50 | 44 |
| Fuel | 01:12 | 29 |
| Fuel | 00:45 | 18 |
| uel | 00:00 | 0 |
| Fuel | 00:15 | 6 |
| Required | 04:02 | 97 |
| l | 00:00 | 0 |
| uel | 04:02 | 97 |

Considering this quantity and the fact that our maximum takeoff weight is equal to the maximum structural weight of the aircraft, we can go on to assess available payload.

Our sample mission will have a pilot weighing 100kg and that will occupy the front seat; a passenger weighing 70kg, who will occupy one of the two center seats; two passengers weighing a total of 200kg, who will seat on the rear seats. There are 40kg of cargo going on the rear baggage compartment and 10kg in the smaller forward hold. When filling the next table, we will find out if we are able to perform this mission. The available traffic load (maximum payload in Figure 139) must be 320kg, which is equivalent to the sum of weights of passengers and cargo.

| Maximum Payload | |
|---|---|
| Maximum Certified Takeoff Weight | **2,155 kgf** |
| Basic Empty Weight | - 1,447 |
| **Allowable Traffic Load** = | 708 |
| Min. Fuel Required (MFR) | - 265 |
| Flight Crew Weight | - 100 |
| **Maximum Payload** = | 343 |

*Figure 139: Maximum Payload (fuel density equal to 2.73kgf/Gal).*

In this example, we are left with an underload of 23kg (maximum payload, 343kg, minus actual payload, 320kg). When this value is identified, it can be used for two evaluations. First, I can take 23 extra kilograms of cargo in case there is any last-minute change. Second, I can add 23kg of fuel as long as I deem it necessary to take this additional amount. If our available payload were lower than the one contracted, we would have a situation that we call an "overload". If this happens, we need to rethink our mission strategy. We will have to remove fuel by opting for a closer alternate airport, give up additional fuel (technical fuel) or plan an intermediate landing if previous options are not possible. The last resort is the refusal of cargo or passengers.

Having defined the amount of fuel and cargo that we are able to carry, we now have to think about how to distribute cargo on our airplane. We will initially try to arrange the items as requested by the exercise. Consider the front limit of our CG envelope to be equal to 2.083m and the rear limit to be equal to 2.403m.

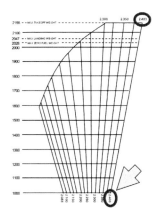

**Weight and Balance**

| Items | Weight (kgf) | Arm (m) | | Moment (kgf x m) |
|---|---|---|---|---|
| Basic Empty Weight | 1,447 | 2.21 | | 3,197.87 |
| Front Seats | 100 | 2.17 | + | 217.00 |
| Center Seats | 70 | 3.00 | | 210.00 |
| Rear Seats | 200 | 4.00 | + | 800.00 |
| Front Baggage Hold (Max 45 kgf) | 10 | 0.57 | + | 5.70 |
| Rear Baggage Hold (Max 45 kgf) | 40 | 4.54 | | 181.60 |
| Zero Fuel Weight | 1,867 | 2.47 | = | 4,612.17 |
| Takeoff Fuel (___ Gal x 2.73 kgf/Gal) | | 2.41 | + | |
| Takeoff Weight (Max. 2,155 kgf) | | (1) | = | |
| Trip Fuel (___ Gal x 2.73 kgf/Gal) | | 2.41 | - | |
| Landing Weight (Max 2,047 kgf) | | (1) | = | |
| | | | | (1) - Moment / Weight |

*Figure 140: Load distribution. First attempt.*

You noticed that ZFW CG (2.47m) was outside the envelope (maximum 2.403m) and we have seen the risks posed by this situation with a possible loss of control being the most serious of them. Let's redo the calculation by swapping passengers in the center and rear seats and observe the effect of this possible solution. Next, you will see the manifest completely filled with this change and you will notice that CG remains within the limits of the envelope the whole time. Takeoff, landing and zero fuel CG were in the same place (2.38m), but this is no rule, it is a mere coincidence showing that the fuel balance arm is roughly at this exact point, therefore not changing the CG position as fuel is burned. The final step for filling in the manifest is plotting the data in the envelope.

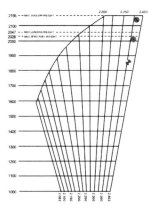

**Weight and Balance**

| Items | Weight (kgf) | Arm (m) | | Moment (kgf x m) |
|---|---|---|---|---|
| Basic Empty Weight | 1,447 | 2.21 | | 3,197.87 |
| Front Seats | 100 | 2.17 | + | 217.00 |
| Center Seats | 200 | 3.00 | | 600.00 |
| Rear Seats | 70 | 4.00 | + | 240.00 |
| Front Baggage Hold (Max 45 kgf) | 10 | 0.57 | + | 5.70 |
| Rear Baggage Hold (Max 45 kgf) | 40 | 4.54 | | 181.60 |
| Zero Fuel Weight | 1,867 | (1) 2.38 | = | 4,442.17 |
| Takeoff Fuel (___ Gal x 2.73 kgf/Gal) | 265 | 2.41 | + | 638.65 |
| Takeoff Weight (Max. 2,155 kgf) | 2,132 | (1) 2.38 | = | 5,080.82 |
| Trip Fuel (___ Gal x 2.73 kgf/Gal) | 120 | 2.41 | - | 289.20 |
| Landing Weight (Max 2,047 kgf) | 2,012 | (1) 2.38 | = | 4,791.62 |
| | | | | (1) - Moment / Weight |

*Figure 141: Load distribution. Second attempt.*

We will now move to the weight and balance manifest of larger aircraft to check for the differences. First thing we will see is the CG envelope, now working with index value instead of large numbers of momentum.

## 2.4.2   *Operator CG Curtailments*

As we have seen previously, in larger aircraft, it is common practice to replace the use of momentum with an index in calculations. However, when we discussed the initial curtailments of the envelope, you could see that they were shown in a graphic that cross-references %MAC (horizontal axis) and weight (vertical axis). The index was not mentioned at all. A redesign is necessary, and the chart will have an additional axis of information.

In this new envelope, the horizontal axis now represents the index, the vertical axis continues to inform weight and an additional piece of information has been created with its own pattern lines (neither vertical nor horizontal) that informs CG position in %MAC. This movement will redesign the shape of the envelope, as shown below.

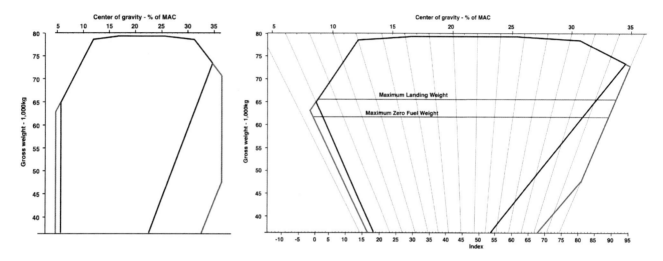

*Figure 142: Weight and %MAC on the left. Weight, %MAC and the index on the right.*

This new graph format shown in Figure 142 has brought us very close to the envelope model that will be used by operators, but an important final step is still missing. Each airline around the world has its own operation characteristics and needs to identify them for the next step that I will discuss. I emphasize that the manufacturer's envelope must never be exceeded, either upwards or sideways.

The operations engineering team of the airlines must determine how to ensure that CG is always kept within limits. Will passengers be weighed individually, or will they have their weight estimated? How will ramp personnel ensure the correct load distribution? When CG is close to a side limit, how does changing the configuration of the airplane (landing gear and flap) affect CG position? Will CG be calculated while considering passenger weight distribution by row, or will the airplane be divided into three, four or five larger sections to ease the process?

Based on the answers to these questions, the operations engineering team will make new curtailments to the manufacturer's envelope to get to the one that will actually be used in flight operations. These new curtailments can occur on the sides (limiting CG travel) and at the top of the envelope (limiting maximum takeoff weight). How "deep" this cut will depend solely on operators and even though manufacturers advise that these cuts should be made, they are not responsible for them. They will even teach operators how to do it, but operators must execute the cuts themselves.

In the following example, our fictitious engineering team has applied new curtailments to the front and rear parts of the envelope – identified by the green line on the envelope. Using known measurement errors of daily operations, these restrictions ensure that CG never extrapolates the limits established by the manufacturer.

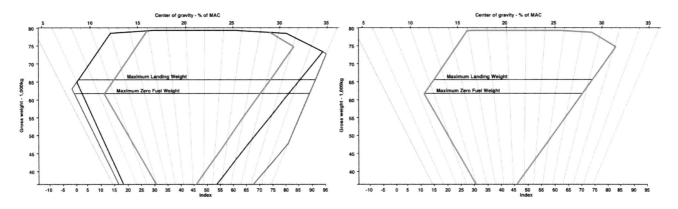

*Figure 143: Manufacturer envelope with operator curtailment on the left. Final envelope on the right.*

Maybe it took a bit too long, but I will finally do what I had promised: explain the Datum Balance Arm of the index equation. Remember, this variable is intended to give a proper "shape" to the envelope.

In the following two illustrations, you will see the final CG envelope shown in Figure 143 with different shapes, produced by a different Datum Balance Arm.

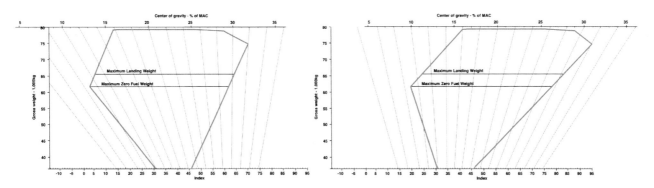

*Figure 144: Different envelope shapes with different Datum Balance Arm values.*

## 2.4.3   Fulfilling a sample Load Sheet

On the next page, there is a weight and balance manifest similar to those used by an airline that operates our model aircraft (737NG). It is filled in accordance with the following data. Note that the passenger cabin is divided into 3 large sections and the index for each section is established according to the number of passengers in it.

Passenger distribution by section (Adult 80kg / Child 40kg / Infant 20kg – Brazilian average weights):
   Cabin A: 42/2/2   Cabin B: 50/4/0   Cabin C: 54/6/0
Forward cargo compartment: 1,000kg     Trip fuel: 6,457kg
Aft cargo compartment: 1,100kg      Dry Operational Weight: 42,957kg
Takeoff fuel: 11,457kg        Dry Operational Index:  49

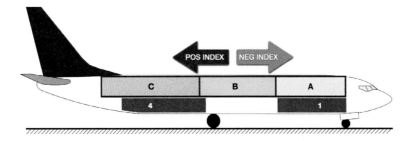

*Figure 145: Index influence on CG movement.*

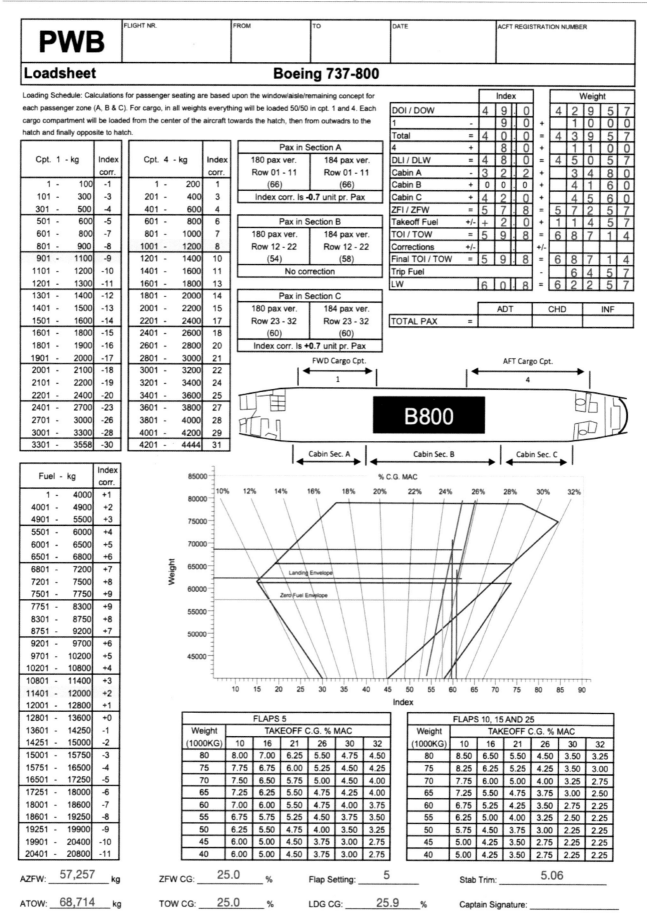

*Figure 146: Load sheet from example exercise.*

## 2.4.4   Trim Sheet

Another way to determine an aircraft's takeoff and landing CG is through a Trim sheet. This is a weight and balance sheet that leads to the final result through a sequence of straight segments to one side or the other, representing CG movement every time a weight is loaded on the airplane. See the example below for a Boeing 777-200 Trim sheet.

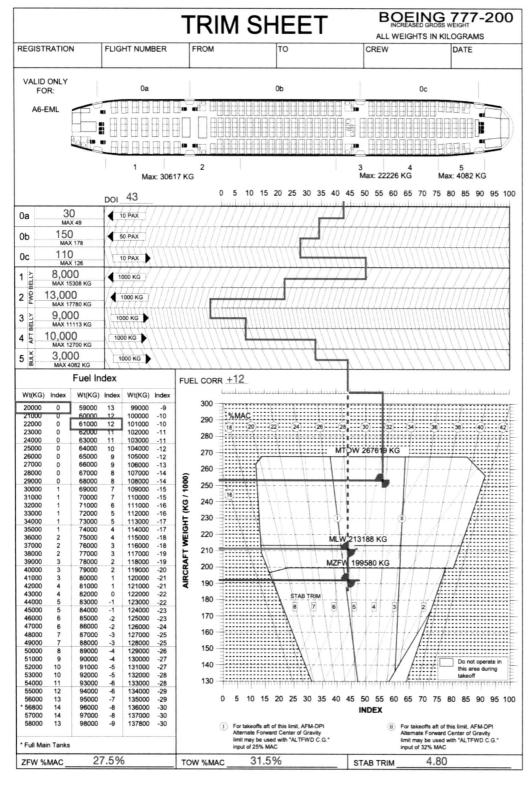

Example:

Cabin A: 30/0/0
Cabin B: 150/0/0
Cabin C: 110/0/0
1 Cargo: 8,000kg
2 Cargo: 13,000kg
3 Cargo: 9,000kg
4 Cargo: 10,000kg
5 Cargo: 3,000kg
Adult: 80kg
Child: 40kg
Infant: 20kg
DOW: 125,800kg
DOI: 43
TO. Fuel: 61,000kg
Trip Fuel: 42,000kg

*Figure 147: Trim Sheet example from a Boeing 777-200.*

# 2.5 Last M

Before departure, the weight and balance documentation must accurately reflect the aircraft's loaded state. However, if you're already in commercial aviation, you've likely encountered passengers who fail to board. They've purchased a ticket, checked in, dispatched their luggage, but didn't show up at the gate. Additionally, when multiple flights are heading to the same destination on the same day, there are often passengers who booked later flights but arrive early and wish to board the earlier flight. Does that sound familiar? To comply with legal requirements, it's often necessary to adjust the loadsheet after completion. These adjustments are called last minute changes (LMC).

The last minute change process allows for late updates to a finalized loadsheet (manual or electronic) without revising the main document or preparing a new one. There's no regulation specifying how to perform an LMC or the acceptable differences between the final documentation and the actual weight and balance at departure. However, regulators require airlines to develop and submit their LMC policies for approval. Once submitted, these policies are enforced by the regulatory agency. It's important to note that each airline's policy can differ, even within the same airline for different aircraft types.

Although airlines are responsible for developing their own policies, they must ensure that after any LMC:

1. The aircraft's takeoff weight is below its maximum allowable takeoff weight (see topic 3.10 for more on maximum allowable takeoff weight).
2. The aircraft's zero fuel weight is below its Maximum Zero Fuel Weight (MZFW).
3. The aircraft's new center of gravity is known and remains within the envelope limits.
4. No compartment limitations are exceeded, in terms of volume or weight.
5. The new takeoff weight does not reduce fuel endurance below the minimum required for the flight.

When changes to fuel quantities or locations are needed, most airlines require a full recalculation of weight and balance, with new documentation due to its significance. However, some operators allow fuel LMCs for smaller quantities. In such cases, fuel weight and index data must be available, and the new center of gravity should be checked.

Remember, margins may be further reduced as many operators request significantly aft trims for better fuel efficiency. Operators might manage the effects of LMCs with stricter flight envelope curtailments. Maximum allowable adjustments for passenger sectors, cargo holds, and compartments can ensure center of gravity limitations are not exceeded.

If unsure about the aircraft's limitations, use the weight and balance system to produce a new loadsheet. For manual loadsheets, use a balance chart to ensure compliance.

Anyone responsible for LMC calculations must be appropriately trained, with weight and index data readily available. They must understand the aircraft's weight and balance condition before and after changes to prevent exceeding limitations due to the LMC.

The LMC should include the following minimum information:

1. The load to be changed (bags, passengers, cargo, etc.)
2. The weight of the load to be changed
3. The location of the load to be changed (cabin/bay area, hold, compartment, etc.)
4. The nature of the change (+ or - as appropriate)
5. The intended location of the load (if remaining onboard)
6. The total weight and index change of the LMC

Ensure any change in the loading position of dangerous goods complies with the operator's instructions for segregating incompatible goods. Amend the notification to captain (NOTOC) accordingly and provide it to the captain before departure, who must confirm receipt. A copy must be kept accessible to the flight operations officer, flight dispatcher, or ground personnel until the flight arrives. Many aircraft have more restrictive flight envelopes at lower weights. Thus, while a lighter aircraft might seem to accommodate larger load changes, it affects the center of gravity more significantly, so LMCs must be carefully checked.

Additionally, with passengers carrying more hand luggage, items may need relocating to a cargo hold. If this occurs, complete the necessary calculations as part of the LMC.

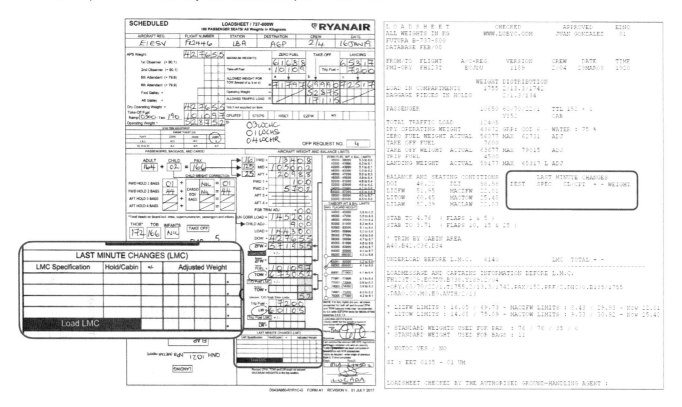

*Figure 148: Example of LMC fields on a manual and electronic loadsheet.*

When student pilots are having their first flying lessons, the flight instructor might tell them that for every local flight (takeoff, training a few maneuvers, and coming back for landing at the same airdrome), a fix amount of fuel is required for takeoff. If a pilot is taking off for a cross-country flight, regardless of destination, most flight schools (in Brazil, at least), may try to play on the safe side by asking their students to take off on full tanks. Well, this is not the way we do it on commercial flights. We now need to make a precise plan for how much fuel we should have on board the aircraft at brake release to accomplish our mission and, to do so, we need to evaluate the mission itself.

The rule changes according to the type of flight that will be performed. This rule also varies considerably from regulator to regulator, and we will see here a complete set of Brazilian regulations, as well as FAA and EASA rules for jets operating commercial flights, only.

To facilitate the description, we will consider the airport of origin as being airport "A", the destination airport as "B", and the alternative airport as "C".

In any of the cases listed in this topic:

- the pilot must add enough fuel for engine start, taxi from tarmac to the active runway, and an eventual APU (auxiliary power unit) fuel burn as well as any additional fuel required by MEL/CDL (see chapter 6.4) dispatch;
- actual takeoff weight must be used for fuel planning;
- fuel must be added considering air traffic control procedures and any predicted delays;
- the best available weather data (turbulence, wind, and temperature) must be used when computing fuel requirements;
- fuel must be calculated considering the predicted flightpath either from A to B and from B to C – SID (Standard Instrument Departure), airways to be flown, STAR (Standard Terminal Arrival) and IAP (Instrument Approach Procedure), whenever applicable;

That being said, let's have a look on the specifics of every regulation.

## 2.6.1   Brazilian Regulation
### Visual Flight Rules – VFR (RBAC 91.151, General Aviation)

At brake release point, the aircraft must have enough fuel to go from A to B plus 30min of fuel endurance computed with a thrust setting for normal cruise flight. This is valid only if every single portion of the flight is carried between sunrise and sunset (during daylight).

If any portion of the flight happens after sunset or before sunrise, the additional fuel must be equivalent to 45min instead of 30min.

### Instrument Flight Rules - IFR (RBAC 91.167, General Aviation)

At brake release point, the aircraft must have enough fuel to go from A to B, go around at B, and divert to C, plus 45min of fuel endurance computed with a thrust setting for normal cruise flight.

### Jet and Turbo Prop Airplanes (RBAC 121.645, Domestic and Flag Air Carriers)

At brake release point, the aircraft must have enough fuel to go from A to B, go around at B, and divert to C, plus a contingency fuel equivalent to 10% of the fuel amount (mass) required to fly between A and B, plus 30min of fuel endurance computed on holding speed, 1,500ft above the alternative airport (C).

The operator might be eligible for 5% contingency fuel instead of 10% if it has a fuel data monitoring system. In any case, contingency fuel should be equivalent to at least 5min of fuel endurance flying on a holding pattern 1,500ft above the destination airport in standard weather conditions.

**Note:** before 2020, this regulation was a bit different, more in line with others around the globe. Fuel reserve was equivalent to <u>a period of 10% of the time required to fly between A and B</u> computed on the basis of fuel flow that is observed just before top of descent is reached. I am honestly not sure if this change in understanding from "10% flight time" to "10% fuel mass" was on purpose or occurred by a kind of typo on the document when adding the rule that allowed some operators to be eligible for using 5% instead of 10%. Anyway, that is what is in effect today (November, 2024).

The flight may be dispatched without an alternate airport. In this case, at brake release point, the aircraft must have enough fuel to go from A to B plus 2 hours of fuel endurance computed with a thrust setting for normal cruise flight. However, some criteria must be met to allow that rule to be followed:

- it must be an international flight;
- flight time between A and B must be less than 6 hours;
- weather data must indicate that between 1 hour before and 1 hour after ETA (estimated time of arrival):
  - predicted celling is at least 1,500ft above the lowest MDA (minimum decent altitude) or 2,000 above field elevation, whichever is higher;
  - predicted visibility is 3km above the one required by the IFR procedure or 5km, whichever is higher.

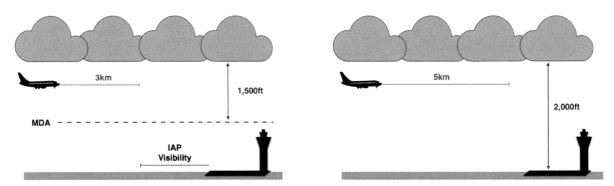

*Figure 149: Weather requirements for dismissing an alternative aerodrome (ANAC).*

## 2.6.2 FAA US Regulation

### 2.6.2.1 Domestic Operations within the 48 contiguous states and DC

At brake release point, the aircraft must have enough fuel to go from A to B, go around at B, and divert to C (if an alternative aerodrome is required), plus 45min of fuel endurance computed on the basis of fuel flow that is observed just before top of descent is reached (FAR Part 121.639).

### 2.6.2.2 International Operations (or domestic operations outside the 48 contiguous states)

At brake release point, the aircraft must have enough fuel to go from A to B, go around at B, and divert to C (if an alternative aerodrome is required), plus a contingency fuel equivalent to a period of 10% of the flight time between A and B computed on the basis of fuel flow that is observed just before top of descent is reached, plus 30min of fuel endurance computed on holding speed, 1,500ft above the alternative airport (FAR Part 121.645).

### 2.6.2.3 Supplemental Operations

Similar to flag operations, but the specific requirements can vary based on the type of operation and the regulations. Those specifics will not be covered in this book.

### 2.6.2.4   When the Alternative Aerodrome is not Required

Similarly to Brazilian regulations, an alternate aerodrome may not be needed. If so, minimum fuel is the amount required to go from A to B plus 2 hours of fuel endurance considering normal cruise flight.

The requirements are almost the same as the Brazilian ones; however, the flight does not need to be international, and the unit used for visibility is the statute mile instead of the kilometer:

- flight time between A and B must be less than 6 hours;
- weather data must indicate that between 1 hour before and 1 hour after ETA (estimated time of arrival):
    o predicted celling is at least 1,500ft above the lowest MDA (minimum decent altitude) or 2,000 above field elevation, whichever is higher;
    o predicted visibility is 2 miles above the one required by the IFR procedure or 3 miles, whichever is higher.

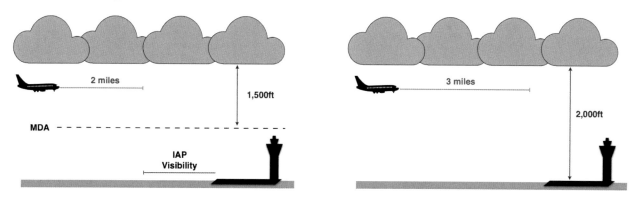

*Figure 150: Weather requirements for dismissing an alternative aerodrome (FAA).*

## 2.6.3   EASA Regulation

### 2.6.3.1   Jet Airplanes (Domestic or International Operations)

At brake release point, the aircraft must have enough fuel to go from A to B, go around at B, and divert to C, plus a contingency fuel equivalent to a period of 5% of the flight time between A and B computed on the basis of fuel flow that is observed just before top of descent is reached, plus 30min of fuel endurance computed on holding speed, 1,500ft above the alternative airport. Those 5% should not be less than 5min of fuel endurance flying on a holding pattern 1,500ft above the destination airport in standard weather conditions (basic rule, only – there are some "ifs" that you can look for in the following document: AMC1 CAT.OP.MPA.191).

The same aspects of the Brazilian rule apply for flights for which an alternate aerodrome is not feasible, such as flying to remote islands.

## 2.6.4   Fuel Considerations for Every Regulator

### 2.6.4.1   Minimum Fuel Over Destination (MFOD)

When the pilot has enough fuel on board to go from B to C, plus 30min of fuel endurance at holding speed, 1,500ft above C, we say that the airplane is on its Minimum Fuel Over Destination (MFOD). That does not necessary imply that an airport diversion must be performed, but, by this time, the pilot must have committed landing somewhere.

Either at the destination airport (B) or at an alternative one (C), in which case he/she must be already heading to this airport.

When you start burning fuel from this amount (MFOD), that means you have run out of options, and that is why you need to make this commitment to land in the airport you had chosen.

### 2.6.4.2    Final Reserve Fuel

The final reserve fuel is the amount equivalent to 30min of fuel endurance at holding speed 1,500ft over the alternative airport. Here, we have two different scenarios to consider.

In the first scenario, the pilot, on his/her best judgement, figures that current ATC clearance is enough to land at the intended airport (regardless of whether it is the original destination or an alternative) with a fuel endurance just over the bare minimum of 30 minutes. All planned landing-site options have been reduced to that specific aerodrome and no other operating site is available. In this case, a MINIMUM FUEL message must be sent to ATC to make them aware that current clearance is OK, but any further delays will certainly force the pilot to declare a fuel emergency.

Now, whenever the pilot realizes that landing will be made with 30min or less of fuel, an emergency must be declared! Attention: do not wait for having 30min of fuel on board! It does not matter how much fuel you have got now, either 60min or 100min. If on your best judgement you can predict that the remaining fuel upon landing will be 30min or less, declare a MAYDAY!

Important note: in both cases I mentioned "on the pilot's best judgement". That is not an exact science. No one will blame you for declaring an emergency because you thought you would land with 30 minutes of fuel remaining and then it happens that you have landed with 45 minutes of fuel still left in your tanks. That is all right! However, should the opposite happen, and you land with 25 minutes of fuel on board without having declared an emergency, well, the authorities will certainly not like that.

To sum up: when you have run out of options, but on your best judgement you are still going to make it to the airport safely above the minimum fuel reserve, declare MINIMUM FUEL to air traffic control. When you are at risk of getting to the airport with 30 minutes of fuel or less declare a MAYDAY.

# 30min

## FINAL RESERVE FUEL

The moment the pilot figures landing will happen with
30min or less of fuel endurance…

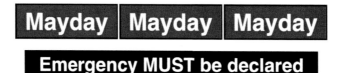

### Emergency MUST be declared

*Figure 151: Mayday Fuel Status.*

To study takeoff performance in more detail, we need to know the different speeds that are involved in the process, how they are determined and what they are used for. For this study, we can divide the speeds that we will examine into two categories: demonstrated speeds and operational speeds. Within the operational ones, there are also two types: the operational speeds themselves and those that are related to them.

### 3.1.1 Demonstrated Airspeeds

#### $V_S$ – Stall Speed

By definition, an aircraft stall speed ($V_S$) is the one recorded when the aircraft is no longer capable of maintaining flight. The problem is, to define this speed on test flights, we depend on the pilot's skill and perception to identify the moment when they consider the plane to be stalled. Elementary instruction aircraft have a well-defined stall characteristic, and aircraft stability causes the nose to fall at the time it stalls, even if the stick is fully pulled. On the other hand, on big commercial aircraft, stall is much more difficult to be perceived by the pilot. When the wing stalls, the plane starts to sink without changing much of its attitude. In this way, different pilots flying the same aircraft, under the same conditions, will perceive different stall speeds.

#### $V_{S1G}$ – Stall Speed at 1G

To resolve the impasse created by $V_S$, the term $V_{S1G}$ has been coined. $V_{S1G}$ is obtained through an accelerometer installed on the plane under the pilot's seat. The plane loses speed to the point where the sensor registers a drop on G-force, which becomes less than 1G the exact moment the airplane starts to descend. The speed recorded at this very moment is that airplane's $V_{S1G}$ for that particular weight. In fact, a fine adjustment is made to the measurement system during test flights that identifies $V_{S1G}$ only when the accelerometer registers a drop of 0.05G. This tolerance is only intended to avoid an inadequate record caused by some small turbulence, but by definition, $V_{S1G}$ stands as the speed recorded when load factor is still equal to 1G.

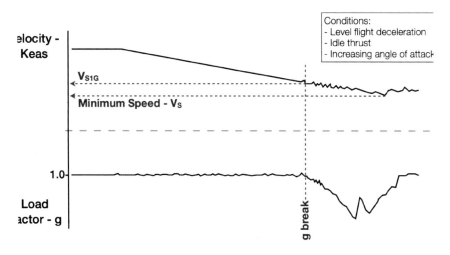

*Figure 152: VS1G definition.*

#### $V_{SR}$ – Reference Stall Speed

FAR Part 25 allows the manufacturer, on discretion, to use any reference stall speed for performance calculations, provided it is greater than or equal to $V_{S1G}$. The one that will be used will be called $V_{SR}$. But honestly, I do not know of any aircraft maker using any value higher than $V_{S1G}$.

$$V_S < V_{S1G} \leq V_{SR}$$

### 3.1.1.4 Stall Warning

Stall warning with sufficient margin to prevent inadvertent stalling with the flaps and landing gear in any normal position must be clear and distinctive to the pilot in straight and turning flight. The warning may be furnished either through the inherent aerodynamic qualities of the airplane or by a device that will give clearly distinguishable indications under expected conditions of flight.

If a warning device is used, it must provide a warning exceeding the speed at which the stall is identified by not less than 5kt (five knots) or 5% (five percent) CAS, whichever is greater. Once initiated, stall warning must continue until the angle of attack is reduced to approximately that at which stall warning began.

*Figure 153: Types of stall warning - aural and stick shaker.*

### 3.1.1.5 V_MU – Minimum Unstick Speed

In the early 1950s, commercial aviation entered the jet era with the introduction of the DeHavilland Comet. This British airplane was a milestone in the world of aviation for several reasons, including some accidents. One occurred when the pilot rotated the airplane too early during takeoff, reaching an attitude in which the plane touched the ground with its tail. This is the highest angle of attack physically possible to be reached with the plane still on the ground. But with this angle of attack, the plane generated so much drag and had so little thrust that it was not able to accelerate, and even if it were, this attitude was beyond this airplane's stall angle of attack. Of course, it could not takeoff before the end of the runway and crashed. Luckily there were no fatalities.

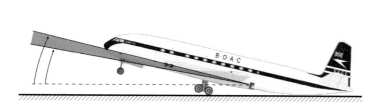

*Figure 154: Comet 1, tail number G-ALYZ crashed at Ciampino Airport, Rome.*

After the accident, it was demanded that airplane designers should foresee such a situation, and that the aircraft should be able to continue accelerating and taking off in this attitude safely. Minimum unstick speed ($V_{MU}$) emerged. The term unstick refers to the act of "taking off". The aircraft is stuck to the ground up until this moment and it unsticks at that speed. So, this is the lowest possible speed for an aircraft to get off the ground.

$V_{MU}$ must be established when the CG is in the most unfavorable position (in this case, forward) and for all flap configurations that are intended to be certified for takeoff. Engine thrust must have the least possible influence when determining this speed, and that is why test flights are performed with considerably low thrust setting. This is due to the fact that, with a high pitch attitude, the engine thrust component pointing upwards would help to make the plane airborne.

*Figure 155: Greatest angle of attack possible to be achieved on the ground.*

### 3.1.1.6    V<sub>MCG</sub> – Minimum Control Speed on the Ground

Check the next figure. It is from a small piston-prop twin airplane built according to FAR part 23 regulations. Every airplane from this category has to publish and show a speed known as the minimum control speed (VMC) on the airspeed indicator. But, did you notice there is no A (air) or G (ground) next to the acronym? And if there is no such information, which VMC is this one?

*Figure 156: Is light twin prop VMC equal to VMCA or VMCG?*

To answer that, let me ask another question: what should the pilot do if one engine fails during takeoff on these light twins? This is a very important question with only one answer: STOP the takeoff. Even if you are airborne, but the landing gear is still down, reduce power and land straight ahead! These airplanes are not meant to fly single engine with the gear down and the failed engine's propeller not feathered, and nor they are requested to fly that way by the regulator.

So, in this type of airplane, if the pilot always aborts the takeoff when an engine fails on the ground, there is no use for a minimum control speed on the ground. Such a speed parameter is pointless. Thus, the red line on the airspeed indicator shows the speed of minimum control in the air!

You certainly understand that there is no point in having V<sub>MCG</sub> on a light piston-prop twin, but you might be wondering why I am bringing that up. Well, do you remember what class A aircraft must be able to comply with? They must be able to handle an engine failure at any point between takeoff and landing without any requirement for a forced landing. But when, during takeoff, must we commit to takeoff? The idea of V1 was coined for pilots to comply with that regulation. Before V1 we can stop, after V1 we must fly – not exactly that, but V1 will be explained later. Anyway, V1 must be a speed that allows pilots to continue takeoff should an engine fail at that speed. And to be able to do that, the pilot must be able to have control over the airplane while still on the ground, hence the need to stablish a new speed called velocity of minimum control on the ground, V<sub>MCG</sub>.

So, V<sub>MCG</sub> is the lowest speed at which the pilot is able to control the aircraft on the ground, using only aerodynamic control surfaces, in the event of a sudden failure of the aircraft's critical engine (a term explained in Section 3.1.1.8). To establish this minimum speed, several criteria must be met. Some of them are mentioned below:

1.   The CG must be in the most unfavorable position – in this case, aft.
2.   Operating engine(s) must be at maximum takeoff thrust.
3.   The airplane must be at the maximum takeoff weight.
4.   Wind effects are not considered.
5.   During the aircraft control process, a maximum deviation of 30ft from the runway centerline is allowed.

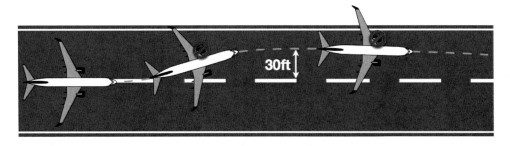

*Figure 157: Maximum allowable deviation from the runway centerline.*

The $V_{MCG}$ published on performance manuals is a speed that will basically vary depending on the thrust produced by the engine. Considering that CG is always in the most rear position and the application of the directional rudder is always at maximum, whenever thrust is reduced, the momentum will also decrease, and a lower speed will be necessary for the pilot to be able to control the aircraft. Remember the topic 2.2.2, when we discussed Effects of CG Position on Lateral Control? You can revisit that if you feel you need to.

Anyway, now we can assess what causes the engine to vary its thrust. Here are two examples:

Altitude – as altitude increases, air density decreases. This reduces engine thrust and thrust asymmetry. So, higher altitude means lower $V_{MCG}$.

Temperature – when temperature is higher, air density is lower. This reduces engine thrust and thrust asymmetry. So, higher temperature means lower $V_{MCG}$.

### 3.1.1.7  $V_{MCA}$ – Minimum Control Speed in the Air

$V_{MCA}$ has almost the same definition as $V_{MCG}$, but it happens in the air instead of on the ground and with slightly different parameters. The pilot now can bank wings up to 5° away from the inoperative engine to maintain control of the aircraft. In addition:

1. The CG must be in the most unfavorable position – also aft.
2. Critical engine inoperative and operating engine(s) must be at maximum takeoff thrust.
3. The airplane must be at maximum takeoff weight or at a weight that allows it to demonstrate this speed.
4. Ground effect cannot be considered.
5. During the aircraft control process, a maximum deviation of 20° from the initial heading is allowed.

$V_{MCA}$ must also be equal to or less than $1.13 V_{SR}$.

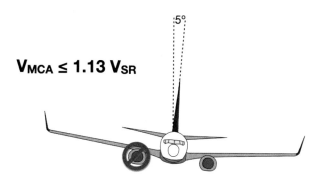

*Figure 158: Speed of minimum control in the air.*

Although it is a demonstrated speed, $V_{MCA}$ cannot be checked in many airplanes . This is because in these aircraft, $V_{MCA}$ is a lower speed than stall speed. The test pilot starts reducing the airplane's speed according to the characteristics above and he or she is able to maintain control until the aircraft stalls. There is no way to fly below this speed and $V_{MCA}$ demonstration fails. For Boeing aircraft, for example, in all models between the 727 and the 787, $V_{MCA}$ is lower than $V_S$ even though they use extremely low weights trying to demonstrate it. In these cases, $V_{MCA}$ is established through calculations.

Please pay attention to a detail about $V_{MCG}$ and $V_{MCA}$: when we talk about control speeds, regulation requires manufacturers to show that the pilot does not need any exceptional skills to achieve control of the airplane.

### 3.1.1.8  Critical Engine

Critical Engine is basically the engine that, if failed (suddenly inoperative), would leave the airplane with the most unfavorable performance. The engine might be different depending on what is being evaluated. If a twin-engine jet has two engines producing different amount of thrust (yes, that can happen), when defining $V_{MCG}$, the critical engine is the one producing less thrust, because the one with more thrust will require a higher control speed (which is bad). On the other hand, if evaluating climb capability of the same aircraft, the critical engine is the one with higher thrust, because the one with lower thrust will lead the airplane to climb with a smaller rate of climb (also a bad situation). For a quad-engine airplane, such as the Boeing 747 or the Airbus A380, any outboard engine is the critical engine (engine 1 or 4). If it fails, the situation will require more deflection on the rudder and, therefore, generate more drag. Assuming all four engines are producing the same amount of thrust, this statement is correct for both: $V_{MCG}$ and climb capability analysis.

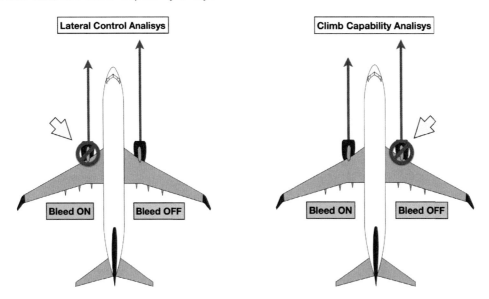

Figure 159: The critical engine might be a different one depending on what is being studied.

Aircraft with propeller engines have an extra issue to be addressed so that we can establish which engine is the critical engine. Consider a twin-engine propeller aircraft. Propeller blades can be counter-rotating (each engine rotates in one direction – one clockwise and the other counterclockwise) or they can both rotate to the same side. You might wonder: why is this important? Well, first, take a look at the following figure. As you can see, the engine is seated on the wing tilting a little bit upward. That has a huge effect on the amount of thrust produced by the propeller blade of the engine, depending on the position of this blade during rotation. The blade moving down has a greater angle of attack than the one moving up, therefore producing more thrust.

Figure 160: Engine position on a propeller engine aircraft.

If the engine were positioned exactly 90° to the displacement of the airplane, the angle of attack of the upcoming and down-going blade would be the same, but as this is not always true, especially during climb, the result is an asymmetric thrust on the blades, as shown in the next figure.

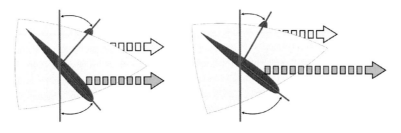

Figure 161: Asymmetric thrust produced by the blades of a propeller engine.

Now, let's take a back and top view of this airplane (Figure 162). On the left there is a twin prop-airplane with both engines rotating clockwise. On the right you can see an airplane with counter rotating propellers. On this latter one, no matter which engine fails, the yaw moment produced by this failure is the same. On the airplane on the left of the picture, however, the yaw moment is much more intense if the left engine fails than if the right engine fails. As critical engine is the one that will let the airplane at the worst possible condition when failed, we can say that the airplane on the right has no critical engine (the situation is the same if either engine fails) and on the airplane on the left, the left engine is the critical engine.

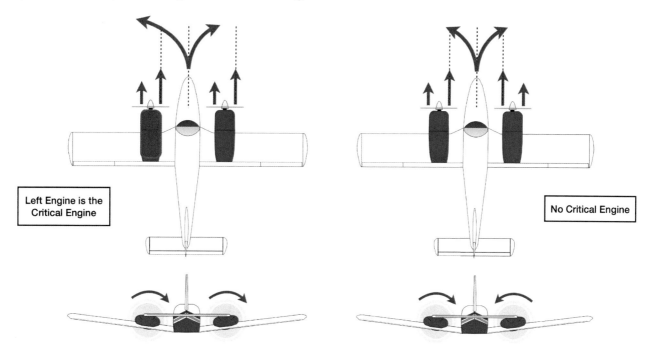

*Figure 162: Critical engine defined by asymmetric load on the blades.*

## 3.1.2 Operational and Related Operational Airspeeds

### 3.1.2.1 V1 – Takeoff Decision Speed

First of all, calling V1 a takeoff "decision" speed is a kind of misnomer, since it is in fact an "action" speed. You will see the reason why in a little while, but let's not hurry. For many aviation enthusiasts or even pilots beginning their career, V1 is probably the best-known speed. "It is the highest speed to abort a takeoff", they say simply. This definition is not wrong, but it is certainly very incomplete.

On the one hand, V1 is a maximum speed. V1 is the highest speed at which the pilot must have already taken the first **ACTION** to stop the aircraft so that it can be stopped within the available runway length (ASDA).

On the other hand, V1 is also a minimum speed. V1 is the lowest speed at which, in the event of a critical engine failure at $V_{EF}$, the aircraft is able to safely continue takeoff and reach the minimum height required at the end of the available runway (TODA). In order not to make anyone anxious about this $V_{EF}$, let's explain it before moving on with the discussion about V1.

$V_{EF}$ or Velocity of Engine Failure is a speed that occurs 1 second before V1. And why 1 second before? Remember that V1, unlike what some may think, is not the maximum speed at which engine failure may occur, but it is the highest speed at which the pilot must have already taken ACTION to stop the aircraft. This action can be: pulling the thrust levers back, applying brakes, lifting the speedbrakes, or any other action as described in the aircraft's Flight Crew Training Manual (FCTM).

When writing the definition of V1 in this way, someone may have wondered: but when something goes wrong, how long does the pilot take to realize the failure, think about what to do and react to the event? Some tests show that this period is 1 second. For this reason, $V_{EF}$ was defined at this moment of takeoff. From this instant on, even if an engine failure happens before V1, the pilot no longer has enough time to reject takeoff and must be able to proceed.

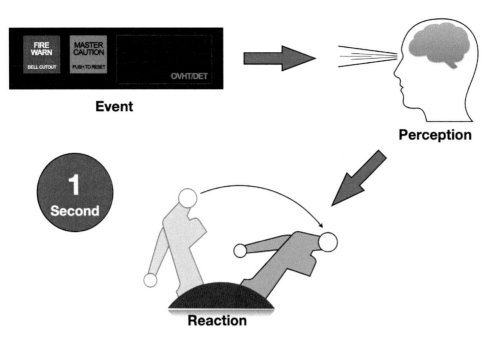

*Figure 163: Why is VEF 1 second before V1?*

Resuming the discussion about V1, even though this speed represents a maximum and a minimum, regulation requires that there should be a single V1 for each takeoff. Establishing which V1 to use for takeoff is a process with so many options and that generates so many different types of impact on operation that I created a separate topic called "V1 Considerations" to promote an extensive discussion on this subject. For now, we will limit ourselves to answering only one question: what are the limits of V1?

## The lowest V1 possible

The lowest V1 possible will be defined on the basis of its maximum concept. After passing V1, the pilot is obliged to continue taking off no matter what happens. It is logical to assume that he/she must be able to maintain directional control of the aircraft in order to proceed. So, the lowest possible V1 is $V_{MCG}$! Well, not quite. Let's analyze the scenario in the next figure.

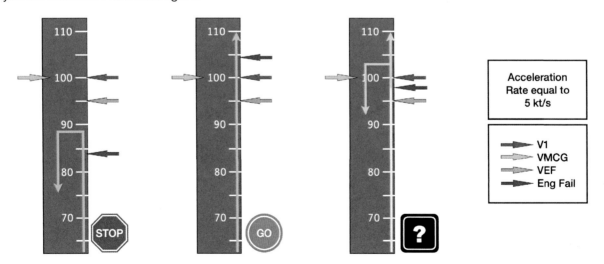

*Figure 164: Engine failure on limbo! No correct answer is possible.*

Figure 164 shows an airspeed indicator and some colored arrows indicating V1 (100kt), $V_{MCG}$ (100kt), and $V_{EF}$ (95kt). $V_{EF}$ is set to 95kt because we have assumed an acceleration rate of 5kt/s. As $V_{EF}$ is the speed that happens

1 second prior to V1, 95kt is our number! Please pay close attention here! $V_{EF}$ is not the speed in which your engine has failed when you tell me a story about an event that has happened to you. $V_{EF}$ is the MAXIMUM speed an engine CAN fail and you will still be able to reject takeoff.

Back to the figure, I proposed 3 speeds for an engine failure. On the left, the engine failed at 84kt. Should you take 1 second to react you would reject takeoff by 89kt. As you would be below V1, all is fine! In the center, I assumed an engine failure at 105kt. Your response to that event above V1 was to continue takeoff, which is also correct! But on the right, there is a challenge. What would you do if the engine failure happened at 97kt?

Some would say GO! You are above $V_{EF}$, so that must be the correct answer, right? Well, no! You are below $V_{MCG}$, therefore you could never be allowed to continue takeoff without directional control of the airplane!

Some would say STOP! You are below V1, so that must be the correct answer, right? Well, still no! You are below V1, but should you take 1 second to react, and by the time you reject the takeoff you would do the first action to commence that process above V1!

I refer to that situation as a LIMBO. There is no possible answer! At least not a correct one. But don't worry. Regulators also thought about this scenario and they have proposed a solution that suits our problem. What if $V_{MCG}$ was not the minimum V1, but the minimum $V_{EF}$? By looking at the next scenario, you will see that this indeed solved our problems and there is no limbo anymore. Now, regulators only need to give a name to minimum V1. They decided to call it $V_{1(MCG)}$! And if $V_{EF}$ is the speed that happens 1 second before V1, this so-called $V_{1(MCG)}$ is simply the speed that happens 1 second after $V_{MCG}$!

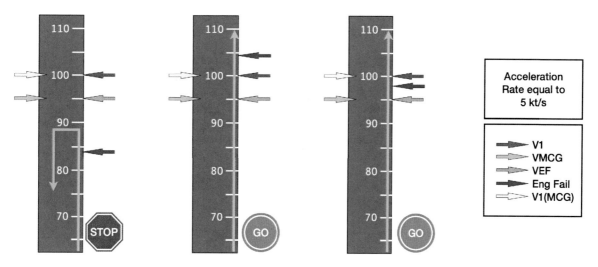

*Figure 165: All problems solved with this new concept - the V1(MCG).*

### The highest V1 possible

The highest V1 possible will be defined according to two parameters. The first is VR (which will be seen in detail next). Once the pilot starts the rotation to make the aircraft airborne, he/she can no longer give up this process, and the plane must fly. The other limit is a speed called $V_{MBE}$, or Maximum Brake Energy Speed.

When a pilot decides to abort a takeoff attempt, the aircraft must be able to stop within the runway limits. All the airplane's kinetic energy is dissipated during the stop maneuver in two different ways: aerodynamic brakes (such as speedbrakes) and wheel brakes. The latter generates a gigantic amount of heat while absorbing the airplane's kinetic energy. $V_{MBE}$ guarantees that the set of brakes will be able to absorb all this energy without jeopardizing the airframe structure safety for at least 5 minutes (time estimated for firefighters to arrive at the scene), in situations like an uncontained fire, a failure in the brake system that prevents the plane from stopping, etc. Small flames on the brakes are expected. Now, to sum up:

$$V_{1(MCG)} \leq V1 \leq VR \text{ and } V_{MBE}$$

### 3.1.2.2 VR – Rotation Speed

Speed at which the pilot starts the rotation of the aircraft (lifting its nose from the ground) while still accelerating to V2 (we will see more details of this speed in a moment).

Assuming that an engine failure has occurred at $V_{EF}$, VR is a speed selected considering that a rotation rate between 2 and 3° per second will be used to reach V2 at 35ft above the runway. VR must be equal to or greater than 105% of $V_{MCA}$ (1.05$V_{MCA}$).

If no engine failure has occurred, the pilot will start the rotation in the same VR; however, when reaching the flight attitude at about 35ft, the speed will be higher than V2 in some knots. In fact, the plane will be flying between 10 and 25kt faster than V2 at this point. This will depend on the aircraft model, and I will explain the difference in the "Stabilizer Trim Setting" section.

### 3.1.2.3 $V_{LOF}$ – Liftoff Speed

This speed results from VR and is the speed at which the airplane ceases to have contact with the ground. It has to be known because aircraft tires have a speed limit that they can withstand before they fail. This limit, established by tire manufacturers (Bridgestone, Goodyear, Michelin, etc.), is known simply as Tire Speed, $V_{TIRE}$. As an example, tires fitted to 737NG have a speed limit of 225mph or 235mph, depending on the model.

$V_{LOF}$ must always be less than or equal to $V_{TIRE}$ and greater than or equal to 1.10$V_{MU(n)}$ or 1.05$_{VMU(n-1)}$ (where "n" is the number of engines on the airplane). Why is that, one might ask. Well, with all engines, your acceleration rate is high and you must be at least 10% above $V_{MU}$ at lift off. However, should an engine fail at $V_{EF}$ your acceleration rate will fall, so that requirement also falls to 5% greater than $V_{MU}$. In any case, being above $V_{MU}$ assures the airplane will be airborne at an attitude less than tail strike attitude.

### 3.1.2.4 V2 – Takeoff Safety Speed

It is the speed that is reached at 35ft above the runway considering that a failure of the critical engine has occurred at $V_{EF}$. This speed will allow the airplane to achieve the minimum climb gradients that were established in takeoff calculations. These minimum gradients will be seen later in this book.

V2 must always be greater than or equal to 1.13$V_{SR}$ and 1.10$V_{MCA}$. It must also be able to allow the aircraft to have a minimum maneuver capability equal to the one defined by FAR 25.143, which, in the case of the aircraft pertinent to our study, is equivalent to 30° bank (wing inclination) before activating the stall warning (this alarm is known as stick shaker on Boeing airplanes – it has this name because there is a small electric motor attached to the control column that makes it vibrate when activated).

Here is an important note! Every time a rule mentions bank angle before stall, it splits this information into two pieces: regular bank plus a safety margin. In this case, 30° is the total amount. The actual rule is 15° plus 15°, so the pilot should always plan to use 15° bank or less while flying at V2. The other 15° is a safety margin in case of turbulence, for example.

**V2 ≥ 1.13 $V_{SR}$ and ≥ 1.10 $V_{MCA}$**

**Allow 30° bank angle**

*(Equivalent to 1.075 $V_{SR}$)*

*Figure 166: Takeoff Safety Speed.*

The summary table for takeoff speeds (Figure 167) shows an example of the possible sequence of events, but it is not written in stone. Some speeds may be reversed depending on the aircraft's model. $V_{MCA}$, for example, comes after $V_S$, but as mentioned earlier, on Boeing aircraft, $V_{MCA}$ is a speed that usually occurs before $V_S$.

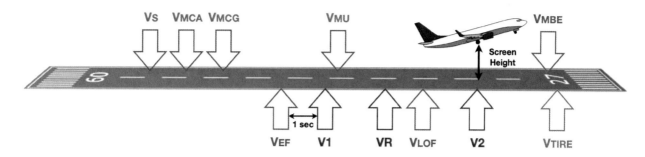

*Figure 167: Takeoff Speeds summary.*

Figure 167 shows Demonstrated Airspeeds in red, Operational Airspeeds in brown, Related Operational Airspeeds in blue and $V_{TIRE}$, which does not fit into any of these subdivisions, in magenta.

### 3.1.3   *Important Historical Note*

Many of the speeds seen so far and others to come are somehow related to stall speed. Before the creation of the term $V_{S1G}$, those relations were different. V2, for instance, was 1.20 times higher than $V_S$, not 1.13, as it is today. The reason for this difference is that $V_{S1G}$ (and $V_{SR}$) is always a higher speed than $V_S$, and the regulator immediately realized that this change in stall definition would have an enormous impact on all others. So, every single speed that has any reference to stall speed was reviewed and those relations changed by 7% for most of them.

V2 was 1.20$V_S$ and is 1.13$V_{SR}$ now. $V_{REF}$ was 1.30$V_S$ and is now 1.23$V_{SR}$. $V_{FTO}$ was 1.25$V_S$ and is 1.18$V_{SR}$ now. And don't worry about these speeds that have not been discussed yet; they will be timely addressed. My intention is just to clarify that if you have read different values somewhere else, those are not "wrong" and many airplanes were built with adherence to those rules, but those books are simply not updated. The reference values in this book are. At least, until December 2024!

## 3.2.1   Declared Field Length Distances

All right, here is a big challenge! I simply hate it when people memorize things without really understanding the subject, and unfortunately, that is what often happens when we talk about declared field length distances. ASDA equals TORA plus STOPWAY, TODA equals TORA plus CLEARWAY, and so on. So, give me a chance to explain that to you in a different way. Let's first discuss the airplane, and then we will move on to talk about the runway.

Takeoff Run (TOR), Takeoff Distance (TOD), Accelerate and Stop Distance (ASD), and Landing Distance (LD). Did you realize that I basically wrote TORA, TODA, ASDA, and LDA but without the final "A"? That "A" stands for Available, hence the runway! Take the "A" off and now we are talking about the airplane, I mean, the runway length the airplane will actually use to complete a given task.

### Takeoff Distance – no clearway

First, let's split this topic into two parts. There is the One-Engine-Inoperative Takeoff distance (also referred to as Engine Out Go, or EO-GO), where the airplane accelerates with all engines until $V_{EF}$, loses its critical engine at this point, and continues takeoff with that engine inoperative. And there is the All Engine Takeoff Distance (also referred to as All Engines Go, or AE-GO), where there is no problem during takeoff.

The EO-GO is the distance measured from brake release until a point where the airplane reaches a screenheight of 35ft if the runway is dry or 15ft if the runway is in any other condition (wet, slippery, or contaminated). The AE-GO is the distance measured from brake release until a point where the airplane reaches 35ft, regardless of runway condition, plus 15% of that reference distance.

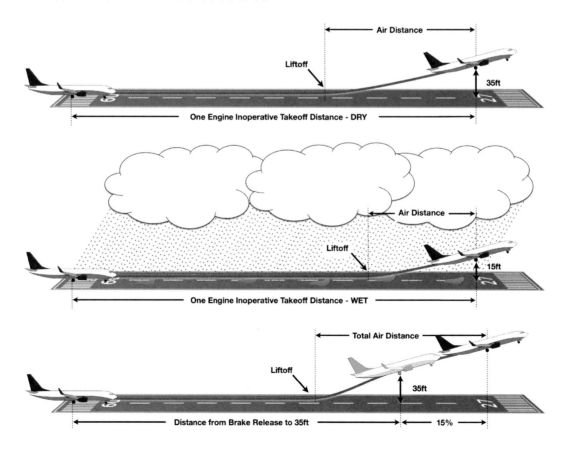

*Figure 168: How to measure the airplane's takeoff distance when there is no clearway.*

### 3.2.1.2   Takeoff Distance – using a clearway

The use of a clearway is allowed for takeoff performance computation following certain criteria. For a DRY runway, there are no restrictions, and it can be used whenever available. For any other runway condition (wet, slippery, or contaminated), a clearway may be used for AE-GO, but using it for EO-GO computation is prohibited.

The next question to be answered is: how much can a clearway be used? FAR part 25.113 states that up to one half (50%) of the air distance computed on EO-GO can be flown over the clearway (if a clearway is available on that runway, of course). Remember that this is only allowed for a dry runway. A clearway must be completely disregarded from EO-GO performance calculations on any runway condition other than dry.

For AE-GO, you can also use a clearway, but this time you can use it for either a dry or a wet runway takeoff. However, it is a bit trickier to understand how much of it you can use. First, we need to measure the distance from brake release to halfway between liftoff and the 35ft point. Then we need to multiply that reference number by 1.15 (that is, 115% of the distance we have just measured). Okay, now look at the length between liftoff and the end of this 115% distance. That is the total air distance in our measurement. Up to 50% of that amount can be flown over a clearway. Looks complicated? I bet it does! But I will provide an example with numbers, and perhaps the next figure will make it easier to understand as well. Please note that the figure is not to scale, and keep in mind that it is perfectly okay to use less than 50% of the total air distance over a clearway (normally that is the case for AE-GO); after all, that is just the maximum allowable distance, not a mandatory amount.

Imagine that an All Engine Takeoff Distance between brake release and the point where the aircraft reaches 35ft is 1,500m. From liftoff to 35ft, we have 200m. Should a clearway exists, what is the maximum length of it we are allowed to use?

Answer:   Liftoff point is 1,500m – 200m = 1,300m
Half way between liftoff and 35ft is 1,500m – 100m = 1,400m
115% of distance from brake release to midpoint between liftoff and 35ft is 1,400m + 15% = 1,610m
1,610m – 1,300m = 310m (Total Air Distance)
310m / 2 = 155m (One Half of the Total Air Distance)

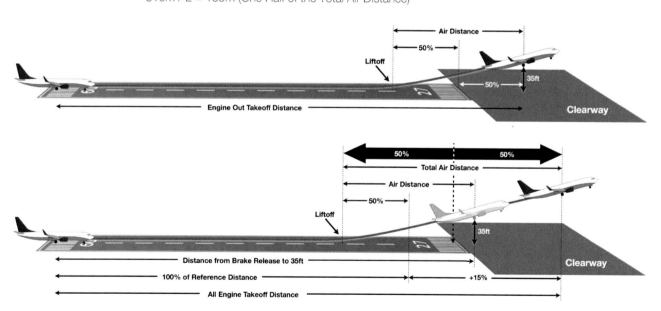

*Figure 169: Use of clearway for takeoff distance.*

### 3.2.1.3   Takeoff Run

The expression "takeoff run" strongly suggests that this would be the distance measured between brake release and liftoff, but unfortunately that is wrong! In fact, takeoff run measurement will depend on the use or not of a clearway in our computation. Should a clearway NOT be used, either because the runway is not dry or because it does not have a clearway available, takeoff run is the same as takeoff distance: distance from brake release to screenheight for EO-GO (either 35ft or 15ft depending on the situation) and distance from brake release to 35ft plus 15% in case of AE-GO.

When there is a clearway available for performance computation and the runway is dry, the one engine inoperative takeoff run measurement needs to be changed. Takeoff run, in this case, is the distance between brake release and a point half way between liftoff and where the airplane reaches 35ft, as indicated by the following figure.

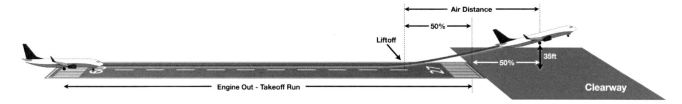

*Figure 170: One engine inoperative takeoff run when a clearway is available and the runway is dry.*

The all engine takeoff run using a clearway is still the same as the all engine takeoff distance with a clearway available. I will write the definition again here just in case: first, we need to measure the distance from brake release to halfway between liftoff and the 35ft point. Then we need to multiply that reference number by 1.15 (115% of the distance we have just measured). Okay, now look at the length between liftoff and the end of this 115% distance. That is the total air distance in our measurement. Up to 50% of that amount can be flown over a clearway. An example of this complex calculation is on the previous page.

There you go! TOR must fit within TORA! And TORA is represented by the whole paved surface of the runway except for any stopway (if available). Certainly, TOR could be smaller, but never larger than TORA. Likewise, TOD must fit within TODA! And as we have seen, TOD might use a clearway, so, it is easy to infer that TODA includes the clearway (if available).

### 3.2.1.4  Accelerate and Stop Distance

This is the distance measured between brake release and a point where the airplane comes to a complete stop after having accelerated until $V_{EF}$, losing its critical engine at this moment, and rejecting takeoff at V1. Just out of curiosity, when observing how much runway is required to execute this maneuver, about two thirds of that distance is used accelerating and one third stopping the airplane. That is no rule, only statistics for an average airplane on a dry runway.

If there is a stopway on a given runway, here is the only moment when it is allowed to be used: during stopping maneuver after aborting a takeoff attempt. Despite the name STOPway, this area is not intended for use during landing when the pilot is also stopping the airplane. I just needed to point that out to avoid any confusion. And, of course, you could never use a stopway to commence takeoff roll.

By the way, a stopway is represented by that yellow chevron painted on the pavement, and below you will find a figure where the airplane has used all accelerate stop distance available to accelerate to V1 and stop.

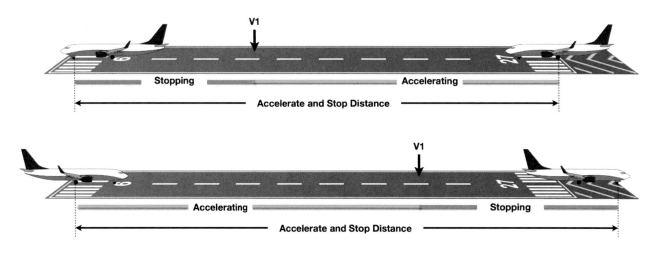

*Figure 171: Accelerate and stop distance.*

### 3.2.1.5   Landing Distance

That is the distance measured from a point 50ft above the runway until a point where the airplane has come to a complete stop. As you can see, as with takeoff distance, there is also an air distance and a ground distance within the landing distance.

A displaced threshold does not affect any of the takeoff distances at all, regardless of the runway in use. However, it does reduce the landing distance available, but only when landing is being performed in the direction that the displaced threshold is. Landing the opposite way, that area painted with white arrows can be used. In the following figure, the airplane has not used all landing distances available to actually land.

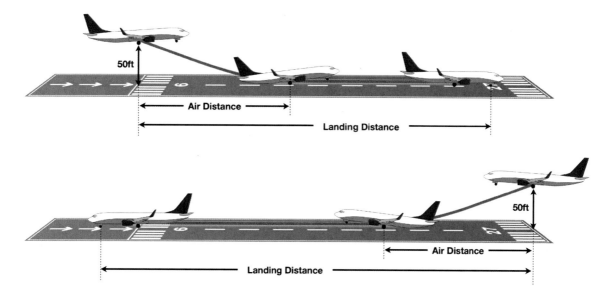

*Figure 172: Landing distance.*

### 3.2.1.6   TORA, TODA, ASDA, and LDA

In the next image, I will show all of the runway assets together: stopway, clearway, and displaced threshold. However, do not think that these assets are related to each other just because they are usually drawn like this in books. They are completely separate and one can exist without the other, or have a different size. For instance, the stopway could be bigger than the clearway.

I created a runway that is 2,000m long and has different assets (stopway, clearway, displaced threshold) to illustrate how they affect the different distance values (TORA, TODA, ASDA, LDA). If the declared length is black, it means it does not change for runway 09 or 27. If it is blue, it applies to runway 09 and if it is red, it applies to the opposite direction, runway 27.

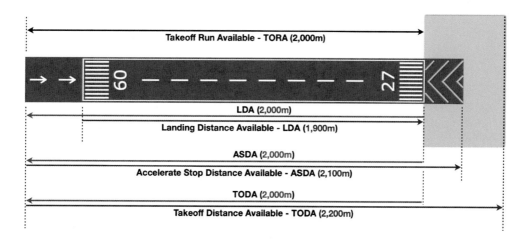

*Figure 173: TORA, TODA, ASDA and LDA.*

### 3.2.1.7 Clearway

It is often said that it is "an obstacle-free area after the runway", but this is not exact. It is an area with minimum and maximum sizes, controlled by the airport authority. Ideally, it would have no obstacles, but they can exist if they stay below an imaginary 1.25% slope up from the end of the runway (TORA). The only exception to this 1.25% slope is the runway's threshold light system, which can be there if it is less than 0.66m (26in) tall and on the sides of the runway.

A clearway has a minimum dimension to the sides, namely 75m for each side of the runway axis (150m total) and a maximum length equivalent to 50% of TORA.

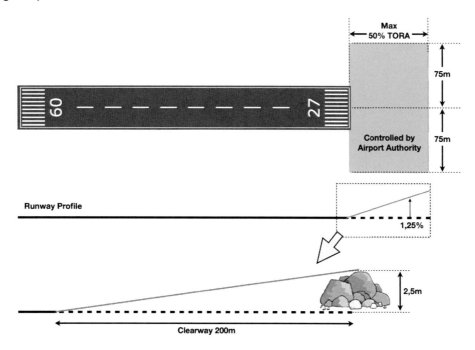

Figure 174: Clearway dimensions and obstacles allowed inside a clearway.

### 3.2.1.8 Stopway

As the name suggests, it is an area designated for stopping the aircraft. However, I must emphasize that it is intended for use only during a rejected takeoff (RTO). It cannot be used for calculating stopping distance during landing, for example. A stopway must be at least as wide as the runway and capable of supporting the aircraft without causing damage. If there are red lights positioned at the end of the TORA (Takeoff Run Available) and at the beginning of the stopway, these lights should be either flush with the ground or designed to break easily upon impact.

Figure 175: Lights to be installed at the end of the runway.

### 3.2.1.9 Runway End Safety Area – RESA

Regarding declared distances, the last item we have to study is called Runway End Safety Area, or simply RESA. This area is currently an ICAO standard for every runway and represents a recommended space located at the end of the runway and should not be computed when defining lengths of TORA, ASDA or LDA. It can be a clearway as long as it meets some requirements (we will talk about them in a moment). Minimum RESA width is twice the width of the runway and has a clear objective: to allow the aircraft, in the event of an overrun (runway excursion), to have an exhaust area that can guarantee the safety of its occupants.

Note that, as opposed to the stopway, the RESA is not required to withstand the aircraft's weight or to avoid damaging the aircraft if it stops over this area. The RESA does not even have to be a paved area. It can be grassed, covered with gravel, or even that kind of soft concrete that crumbles when the plane passes over it, dissipating the kinetic energy and stopping the aircraft – it is called EMAS (Engineered Material Arresting System).

*Figure 176: RESA with EMAS (Engineered Material Arresting System) installed.*

ICAO states that a RESA's minimum length should be 150m, but recommends a length of 240m. In fact, that is not what the text on Annex 14 says, but that is what it means. Every aerodrome has a minimum distance between the end of the runway and the physical limit of that aerodrome, hence, the fence of the aerodrome. That distance is 60m and is called the runway strip. So, if you look at Annex 14, it will say that the minimum length of the RESA is 90m beyond the runway strip, and that means 150m in practical terms. The same applies when the text recommends a RESA with a length of 180m beyond the runway strip, that is, 240m in total.

But what can we do to airports that have existed way before RESA was even mentioned in that document and really have a fence or wall at the end of the runway strip? There is nowhere to grow and implement a RESA. What should we do? Let's put our minds to work on this problem and try to implement a RESA on a fictitious aerodrome that was built long before RESA existed. By the way, this situation has been very common in Brazil since 2016.

Say the runway shown below has 2,000m on all declared distances. The runway has the minimum runway strip of 60m on each threshold. However, let's imagine that this area next to threshold 27 is leveled, but the one next to threshold 09 has a steep downward slope. With that being said, we will now try a strategy to implement RESA on both sides.

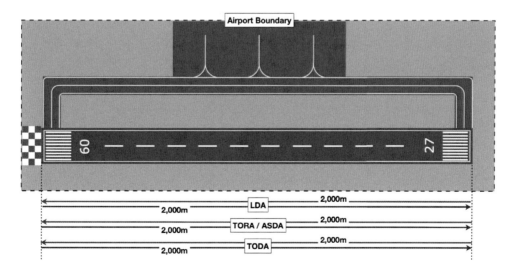

*Figure 177: Original runway.*

First, let's look at the situation for departure and arrival using runway 09. As I said, RESA minimum width is twice the runway width. So, we have to guarantee that in the area defined by the last 150m by 90m, the surface is leveled and free of any obstacles that might cause severe damage to the aircraft structure. By the way, such length includes the runway strip of 60m plus 90m (150m in total) and consider a runway width on 45m, hence the 90m width of RESA.

Okay, we did just that in the next figure, but what should we do with that piece of pavement that is still there? I understand I cannot use it for performance calculations when operating on runway 09, but the E on RESA stands for END. Not beginning! Why should I exclude that length from calculations if departing from runway 27? There is no reason for that. Even the taxiway still connects to the runway at the point.

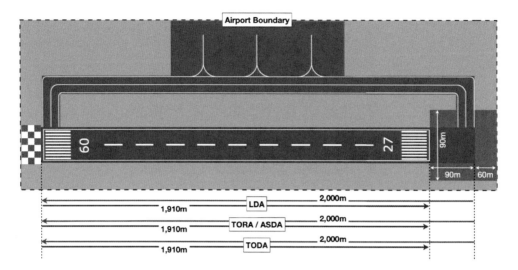

Figure 178: Implementation of a RESA at the end of runway 09.

If we start looking for a kind of paint job that we could do over that pavement to indicate that it cannot be used operating one way, but can be used on the opposite way we will not find anything specific. But we could do something that is the next best thing: displaced threshold! The problem is a displace threshold sign will affect the landing distance for runway 27, but as I said, this is no perfect solution, it is just the best one that we were able to find.

Now, wait a second. Can you remember clearway minimum width? That is 75m to each side of the runway axes. And say we have just that. Can you think of any reason for those 90m lost with a RESA not to be considered a new clearway? The area complies with minimum width, is within maximum length, has no obstacles above 1.25% slope and is within the airport boundaries. At least one piece of good news here! We now have a clearway at the end of runway 09! As I mentioned earlier, a RESA is not a clearway, but it might just happen that both coexist, and that is exactly what happened here.

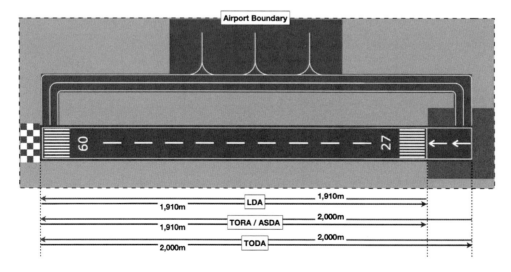

Figure 179: RESA at the end of runway 09 implemented.

Job well done so far. But we still have to implement a RESA at the end of runway 27. And we have an extra challenge here. Remember that steep slope at the end of the runway? Because of that we cannot count the 60m of the runway strip as a RESA, so we will need to get rid of 150m of available runway in this case. The final solution will be the same: create a displaced threshold, but a bigger one.

As it happens, we have TODA unchanged for both runways because we have created a clearway for both. TORA and ASDA were reduced by the amount of pavement we had to give up at the end of each runway. And LDA was the distance most affected after being reduced both at the beginning and the end of the runway.

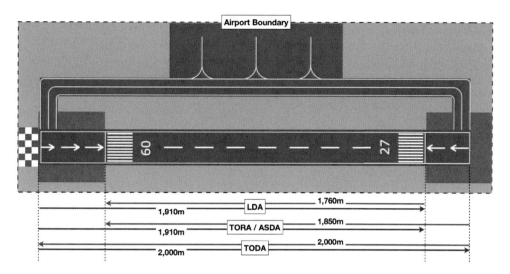

*Figure 180: RESA implemented on both runways (09 and 27).*

I believe you are all wondering now why that displaced threshold at the end of the departing runway could not be used for performance calculations. Well, a displaced threshold is usually on the runway because there was one or more obstacles interfering with the approach path (we will discuss that in detail when talking about landing performance) and could be used as part of TORA and LDA. However, this displaced threshold presented in the example has a totally different reason to be there! It is not a displaced threshold per say, but a runway end safety area, and that is why it cannot be part of TORA or LDA in this example.

Still, some might ask: how would I know the difference? Well, the thing is, you won't! Just by looking at any given runway, you are unable to say if that displaced threshold can or cannot be used. Is it there because of obstacles or is it a RESA? The only way of knowing is looking at the official numbers of that airport. Analyze published values of TORA, TODA, ASDA and LDA and then you can figure out the actual reason behind that displaced threshold. Some will be allowed to be used on takeoff, others you will not, and the RESA is the reason behind it.

With all being said, take a look at Porto Seguro airport in Brazil, where authorities did exactly what we did. They used a part of the runway to implement RESA, painted that part as a displaced threshold, and were able to create a clearway.

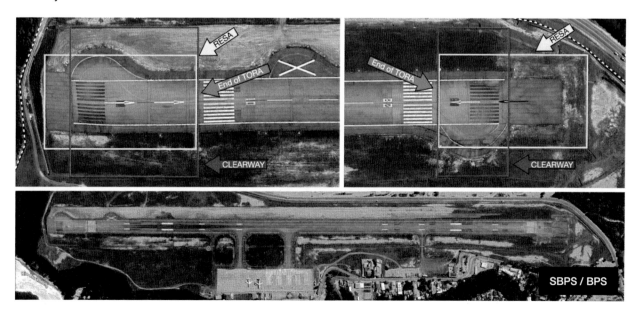

*Figure 181: Implementing a RESA at Porto Seguro airport - SBPS / BPS.*

## 3.2.2   Accelerate and Stop Distance Requirement

Now that we have seen which runway length is available for calculating takeoff performance, we will analyze what aspects should be observed to determine the runway length required for takeoff. We have talked about that briefly but let's dig a little deeper into that subject now.

When we talked about V1, we argued that the aircraft must be able to accelerate to this speed and then stop within the available runway length (ASDA). Well, this is the first calculation that must be done. With our intended takeoff weight as our starting point, we will now study how much runway distance is required for the aircraft to be able to accelerate, have a sudden failure in its critical engine at $V_{EF}$, have the first action to stop at V1, and come to a complete stop.

Legislation requires that we must account for a transition period that occurs owing to the airplane's inertia. The airplane is accelerating and thrust levers are retracted exactly at V1, but the aircraft does not start to decelerate instantly. The speed is expected to increase a little bit more before it actually starts falling. The time interval to be credited to the calculation is 2 seconds between the moment that the aircraft passes through V1, initially still in acceleration and later in deceleration. Depending on the model of the airplane (and how old its design is), the rule changes slightly, considering the transition period as a constant speed (current rule) or still accelerating (previous rule).

An aircraft manufacturer is required to prove that its aircraft is capable of making this transition in less time than required by law. If the transition time is longer than 2 seconds, this longer interval is the one that must be used in calculations. Boeing, at its discretion, uses a time gap of almost 4 seconds between $V_{EF}$ and "V1 decelerating" to compute performance, even though it has proven, for example, that the process only takes about 1.4 seconds on the Boeing 737NG.

To stop the aircraft on a dry runway, we are not allowed to consider the use of reverse thrust. On a wet or contaminated runway, however, it is optional for the operator to consider the use of thrust reversers (all but 1 on a wet runway or even all on a contaminated runway).

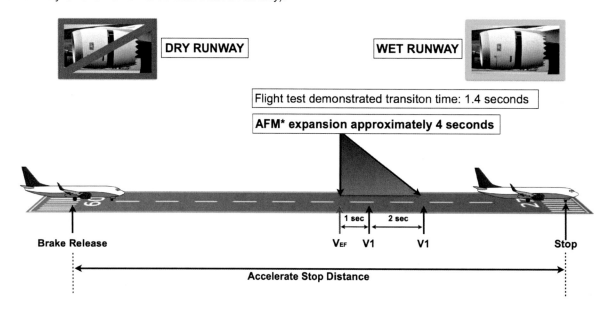

*Figure 182: Establishing the accelerate and stop distance.*

As you can see, there is a certain margin that manufacturers ultimately offer when calculating the accelerate and stop distance. In addition to this margin, legislation requires CG to be considered in its most unfavorable position, that is, the CG will be as forward as possible to put less pressure on the main landing gear and brakes. Considering it all, the chance that the computed distance will be greater than the actual distance is quite strong, as long as the pilot acts correctly when rejecting takeoff. Remember, for example, that the use of the reverser cannot be considered when calculating dry runway takeoff performance, but that does not mean that the pilot will not effectively use it in a real reject takeoff (RTO).

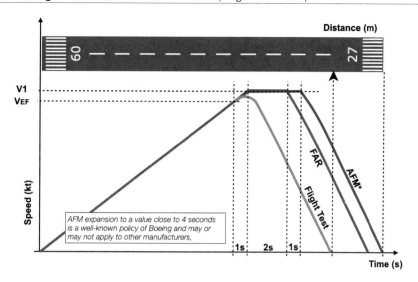

*Figure 183: Calculating acceleration and stop distance. Difference between AFM and Flight Test.*

### 3.2.3    One Engine Inoperative Takeoff Distance Requirements

In addition to the accelerate and stop distance, we must also calculate the field length needed to accelerate, have a sudden failure on the critical engine at $V_{EF}$, and continue takeoff. The plane must be able to reach the screenheight within the limits of TODA.

Screenheight is another factor that deserves attention. As we have seen, legislation offers the possibility of changing its value depending on runway condition. It should be 35ft when the runway is dry, and when the runway is wet, although legislation does not allow to consider any clearway for EO-GO performance calculations, the screenheight drops to just 15ft. The million-dollar question: why?

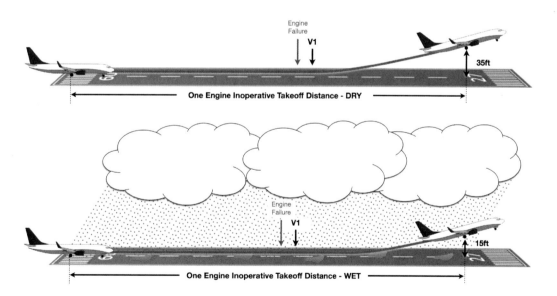

*Figure 184: One engine inoperative takeoff distance on a wet runway (also called Engine Out Go, EO-GO).*

To clarify the reason for the difference in screenheight, we must think about the aircraft's accelerate and stop distance. Although some Hollywood movies and Walt Disney cartoons try to show the opposite, an airplane accelerates because the engines throw air backwards and propel them forward. The airplane's wheels have nothing to do with it. So, whether on a wet or dry runway, an aircraft's acceleration is exactly the same. Stopping the aircraft is a whole different story; it depends heavily on brake efficiency and the friction between tire rubber and the ground surface. The latter is greatly reduced owing to the presence of water over the runway.

This lower braking action makes V1 on a wet runway decrease to allow stop to begin with less speed and with more runway length available. VR and V2, however, do not depend on the runway condition, but on the aircraft's weight, air density and other factors; therefore, they do not change. When comparing two aircraft of the same weight that are taking off from identical runways, but with different conditions (one wet and one dry), we will see that the VR and V2 speeds are identical and V1 is the only different V Speed.

With a wet runway and a lower V1, the "distance" between V1 and VR becomes very large. Assuming the engine failed at $V_{EF}$, acceleration after this point occurs at a very low rate, as it is being performed with one less engine. In a twin-engine aircraft like the 737, acceleration drops from about 4kt/s with both engines operating to approximately 1kt/s after one has failed.

As a result of this much lower acceleration, VR will be reached at a point further down the runway, much closer to the end of it, when comparing wet to dry runways. This is because VR is closer to V1 when the runway is dry. With VR taking place at an advanced point on the track, 35ft cannot be reached before the end of it. Aware of this problem, regulators allowed the screenheight to be smaller, but prohibited the use of the clearway. Note that the speed at the end of the runway will be less than V2, since V2 is the speed that we reach at 35ft, not 15ft.

In the example below, we see a takeoff in two different scenarios: dry and wet runways. The airplane is departing with the same weight and V Speeds are: V1 139kt, VR 141kt, and V2 151kt for the dry runway and V1 130kt, VR 141kt, and V2 151kt for the wet runway. Note that V1 is the only difference between both.

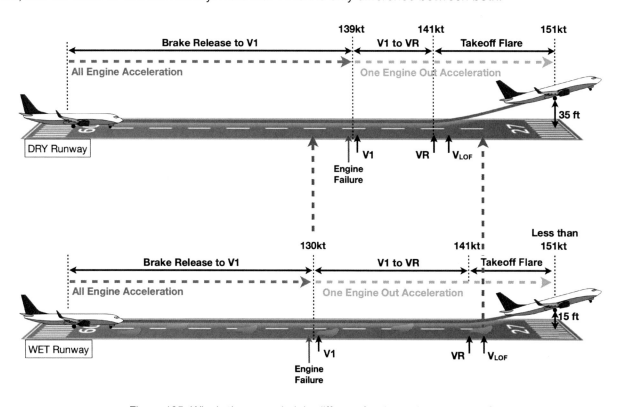

*Figure 185: Why is the screenheight different for dry and wet runways?*

When calculating the accelerate/stop distance and one engine inoperative takeoff distance, we have to think about how "engine failure" will be considered. At the beginning, the event always happened at $V_{EF}$ and takeoff rejection was always due to an engine failure. However, over time, it was perceived that other factors could lead pilots to abort takeoff at that point. If the event that forced rejection left residual thrust on the engine (at idle thrust, for example), the stopping distance ended up being longer than the one calculated for an actual engine failure. As no reverse thrust is used, an all engine RTO takes a longer distance than an engine out RTO.

With that in mind, today there are different ways to study accelerate/stop and takeoff distances with an inoperative engine. As calculations must be made within the worst-case scenario in mind, this is how it is done now: zero thrust is considered for EO-GO, and that means a fuel cutoff on the critical engine. Residual thrust available is considered for ACCEL-STOP, and that means only to throttling back the engines to idle.

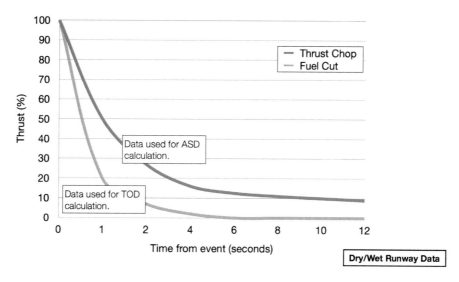

*Figure 186: Engine status to calculate ASD and EOTD.*

## 3.2.4   All Engine Takeoff Distance Requirements

The last aspect that needs to be evaluated to establish the required runway length for takeoff is when the airplane takes off with all engines running. It is surprising that such a topic needs to be evaluated, since it seems logical to infer that this distance will always be less than takeoff distance with an inoperative engine.

The assumption is correct, indeed, but remember that 115% of AE-GO? That is the distance that matters! Again, there is that weird way of computing all engine takeoff distance when a clearway is involved, but anyway, this is the required length that will be used and compared to the others to stablish minimum field length required for takeoff.

## 3.2.5   Field Limited Takeoff Weight

We have analyzed three different aspects regarding the runway length required for takeoff at any given weight. Now, all that needs to be done is to compare the three resulting values. The required runway length will always be the longest among the three.

In the figure below, after defining the Accelerate Stop Distance, the One Engine Inoperative Takeoff Distance (in the current runway condition) and 115% of the All Engine Takeoff Distance, we can see that the highest value among them is the ASD. This value will be called FAR Field Length Required (FAR - Federal Aviation Regulation).

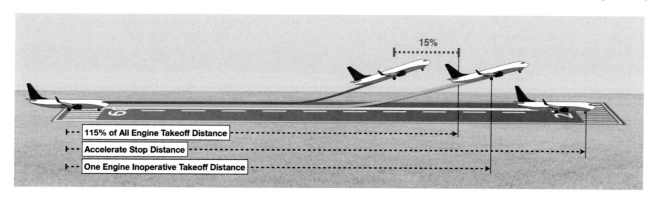

*Figure 187: FAR Field Length Required is the longest among these three.*

Most of the time, medium range twin-engine aircraft (such as B737 and A320) have the longest of three distances as the Accelerate and Stop Distance or One Engine Inoperative Takeoff Distance (considering an average takeoff weight at maximum thrust). So, when is the All Engine Takeoff Distance considered to be a frequent limit?

Well, this happens more often with three- and four-engine aircraft. In the sequence of illustrations below, you can see the reason why. A twin-engine that loses one of its engines ends up with 50% of the takeoff thrust available. This makes the takeoff distance measured with all engines running very different (shorter) from the one measured with one inoperative engine since $V_{EF}$.

A four-engine airplane loses just 25% of its available thrust when one engine fails, so takeoff distance with one engine inoperative is not much greater than the takeoff distance with all engines running. The latter distance is often very long because the airplane is heavy and takes a lot of runway length to gain speed. If we add the regulatory 15% to that distance, the final result (115% of the All Engine Takeoff Distance) will normally be greater than the One Engine Inoperative Takeoff Distance.

I wish to emphasize that this is not a rule! Just statistics. A four-engine airplane may also have EO-GO or ACCEL-STOP distance as the main factor, and a twin-engine airplane may have AE-GO as the longest of the three. But that is not usually the case.

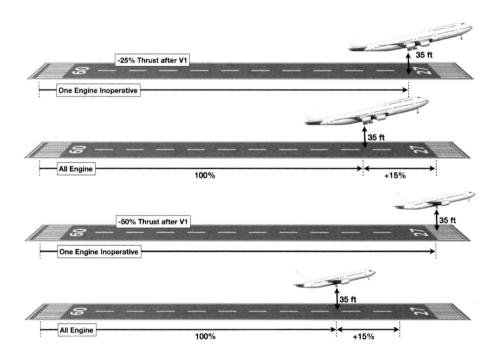

*Figure 188: When is the All Engine Takeoff Distance more often found as a limit for takeoff?*

An evaluation can always be made from two different perspectives. What we have done so far was to find the minimum runway length needed for takeoff with a given weight. The second option is a reverse point of view. What is the maximum weight for takeoff from a given runway? The answer for this question is known as the "**Field Limited Takeoff Weight**".

## 3.2.6   Dry Check

Talking about Field Limited Takeoff Weight, I have to make a very important remark. In very specific cases, when calculating this weight limit for a given runway, the result found with a wet condition may be a greater weight than the one obtained with a dry runway. Even if the calculation is correct, regulations forbid us to takeoff from a wet runway with a greater weight than the one allowed for takeoff on a dry runway. To prevent this situation, we need to do what we call the Dry Check.

This unusual situation can occur, for example, on short and grooved runways (groove is applied to the asphalt to facilitate water drainage) that are certified as Skid Resistant Runways (SK-R). A runway with this certification usually has a similar braking capacity for both conditions, dry and wet. However, thrust reversers cannot be used in calculations while on a dry runway. On a wet one, this credit is allowed when determining the accelerate and stop distance. Because of this small detail, the result of the wet runway analysis is a higher weight than that of the dry runway.

Attention: your calculations would be correct, but you are legally prohibited from using this higher weight for takeoff. If that happens, you must use the dry runway limited Takeoff Weight as the maximum weight for takeoff on the wet runway on this airport.

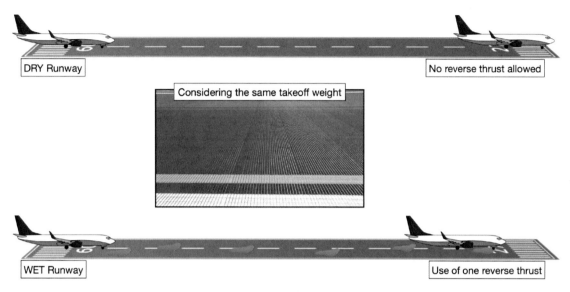

*Figure 189: Why do we need to do a dry check?*

## 3.2.7 Line up Corrections

If you are a kind of meticulous person, by now you have probably noticed that in almost all the illustrations so far, the brake release point is never at the beginning of the runway, but a little bit further on. This is not done out of nowhere. When an aircraft takes position for takeoff, either entering the runway from a 90° taxiway or having to make a backtrack (as shown in Figure 190), a given amount of runway always ends up being left behind when lining up. Shouldn't this missing piece of track be taken into account?

Well, the legislation of most countries does not require this correction to be made (but EASA does). However, a good number of operators around the world voluntarily apply runway length corrections and the table used to perform such adjustments is provided by manufacturers.

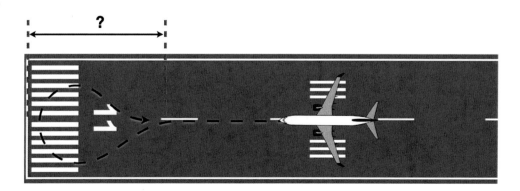

*Figure 190: Line up corrections (1).*

This Line Up Corrections table shows different penalties for TORA/TODA and ASDA. The reason for this difference is explained in the next illustration (Figure 191).

While the aircraft's stopping distance must consider the airplane stopped with its nose gear still on the runway, the takeoff distance is measured with respect to the aircraft's lowest point at 35ft (usually the main gear). So, the difference between the two penalty values is equivalent to the distance between the nose gear and the main gear of the evaluated model.

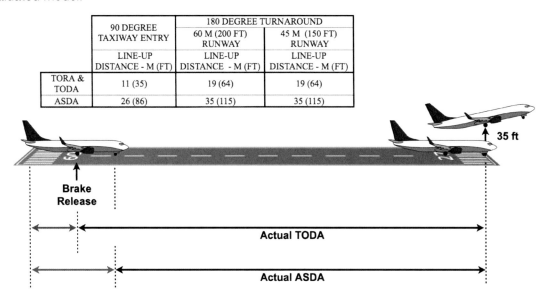

|  | 90 DEGREE TAXIWAY ENTRY | 180 DEGREE TURNAROUND | |
|---|---|---|---|
|  |  | 60 M (200 FT) RUNWAY | 45 M (150 FT) RUNWAY |
|  | LINE-UP DISTANCE - M (FT) | LINE-UP DISTANCE - M (FT) | LINE-UP DISTANCE - M (FT) |
| TORA & TODA | 11 (35) | 19 (64) | 19 (64) |
| ASDA | 26 (86) | 35 (115) | 35 (115) |

*Figure 191: Line up corrections (2).*

Even though the actual length of the runway needs to be corrected (by reducing the penalty distance from TORA/TODA and ASDA), manufacturers agree that pilots should use the rolling takeoff technique on every departure whenever they can. This technique means that pilots do not stop on the runway before applying takeoff thrust and starting to roll. Instead, during the line-up maneuver on the runway, pilots begin to increase thrust and, as soon as they align with the runway, they apply takeoff thrust.

During this process, even though takeoff thrust is finally set with a little bit of runway left behind, the airplane already has some speed when this occurs. For this reason, the difference in the runway length that will be used for takeoff becomes absolutely negligible. With this in mind, there are two major advantages regarding the rolling takeoff technique: it significantly reduces the possibility that the airplane could ingest objects that can cause damage to the engine (FOD – Foreign Object Damage), as well as decreases the chances of engine compressor stall during strong cross-wind takeoffs.

I kindly ask you to pay special attention to the act of lining up on the runway for takeoff. A common mistake among pilots is to follow the yellow line that is in the center of the taxiway into the runway, figuring that this line will take you to the point where you should start your takeoff roll.

No! The yellow line was not meant to lead pilots into the runway, but rather, away from the runway and onto the taxiway. This line has the exact opposite role of what some people have thought.

Following the yellow line can be a serious problem, especially when takeoff occurs from a taxiway intersection that is a high-speed exit. Look at the following two illustrations. In the first, the pilot follows the yellow line. In the second, he/she enters the runway as stated in the aircraft's FCTM (Flight Crew Training Manual). In both situations, there is a loss in runway length, but in the second illustration, the loss is the one we saw in the lineup corrections tables, while the loss in the first illustration is noticeably greater.

The red dashed line in the figure indicates the right main landing gear path during alignment. The blue line is the point from which measurements are taken to indicate how much runway is available for a takeoff.

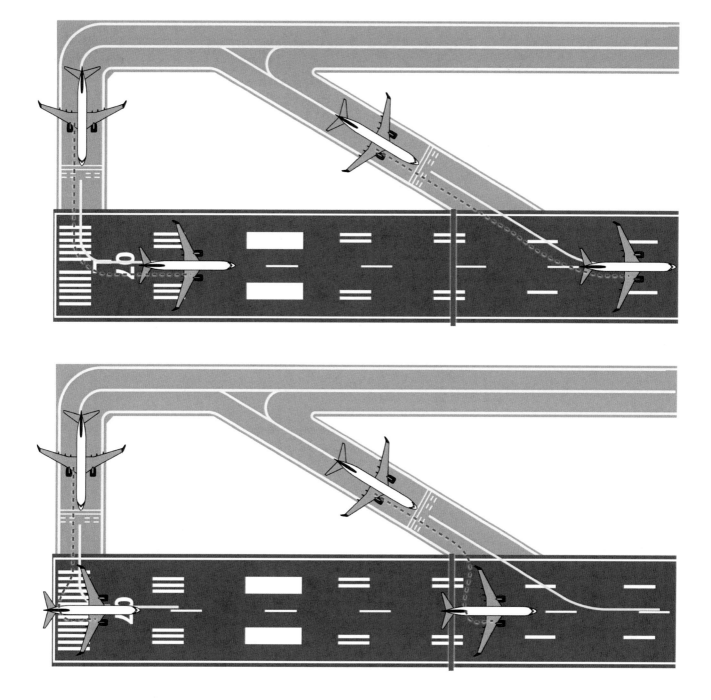

*Figure 192: Entering the runway and lining up. The wrong way on top and the correct way to do it on the bottom.*

### 3.2.8 V1 Considerations

This topic of our discussion is, perhaps, the most important so far. As I said before, although V1 is one of the most famous performance-related speeds, it is also one of the least understood.

Let's start by talking about how much the chosen V1 affects our one engine inoperative takeoff distance.

I will give numbers to the example to make it easier to understand. A given aircraft has a VR of 140kt and V2 of 145kt. We have already talked about how V1 affects runway length when we discussed the issue of lowering the screenheight on a wet runway, but let's get back to this topic anyway. To demonstrate in more detail what happens with the one engine inoperative takeoff distance as a function of V1, I will show you a runway and two rulers. The ruler does not show distance, but speed. By looking at the bottom ruler in Figure 193, you can identify the speed at which the airplane will be at each point along the runway (all engine acceleration). This ruler is linear and a real one would not be, I know, but that does not invalidate the example. We will list 3 different V1s for our analysis. VR and V2 will remain unchanged:

A) V1 130kt      VR 140kt      V2 145kt      (standard V1 – 10kt to VR and 15kt to V2)
B) V1 125kt      VR 140kt      V2 145kt      (lower V1 – 15kt to VR and 20kt to V2)
C) V1 135kt      VR 140kt      V2 145kt      (higher V1 – 5kt to VR and 10kt to V2)

In the illustration, the bottom ruler on the runway shows the exact point at which the plane reached V1. From this moment on, we will consider that an engine has failed, and acceleration has decreased. To see where the airplane reached VR and V2, we should look at the top ruler and check how many knots we need to accelerate until reaching those speeds. Once again, I know the real ruler would not be linear, but it is still ok. It works for the purpose of our mental exercise just as presented.

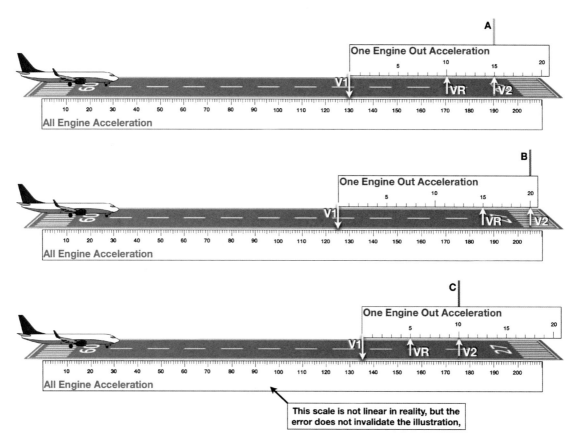

*Figure 193: Effect of V1 on one engine inoperative takeoff distance.*

In situation A, we have the following scenario: the airplane accelerated with all engines until V1 (130kt) and from this point onwards, it continued with one engine inoperative. It needs to accelerate 10kt to get to VR and another 5kt to get to V2 (15kt in total). The green line "A" indicates the point where it reached V2.

In situation B, we have the following scenario: the airplane accelerated with all engines until V1 (125kt) and from this point onwards, it will proceed with one engine inoperative. It needs to accelerate 15kt to get to VR and another 5kt to get to V2 (20kt in total). The red line "B" indicates the point where it reached V2.

In situation C, we have the following scenario: the plane accelerated with all engines until V1 (135kt) and from this point onwards, it will proceed with one engine inoperative. It needs to accelerate 5kt to get to VR and another 5kt to get to V2 (10kt in total). The blue line "C" indicates the point where it reached V2.

Note that the highest V1 caused our plane to shorten the "engine out go" takeoff distance, while the lowest V1 increased that distance.

If we change the focus and study the effect of V1 on the accelerate and stop distance, we will see the opposite. By using a higher V1, the airplane will take more time (and distance) accelerating, and it will take longer to stop as well, so the required runway length will be very long. With a lower V1, the aircraft will reach this speed quickly and stop in a very short distance.

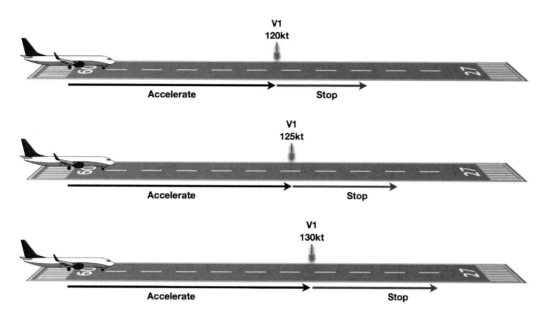

*Figure 194: A higher V1 results in a higher accelerate and stop distance.*

V1 has no effect on the all engine takeoff distance because acceleration is not abruptly reduced in any moment. Choosing a higher or lower V1 leaves that distance unchanged.

Next, I drew a graph containing takeoff distances (ACCEL-STOP, EO-GO and AE-GO) according to the selection of V1. In this graph, take any V1 as an example and you will be able to see the runway length needed to accelerate and stop (red line), to accelerate and go with one inoperative engine (green line), and 115% of the distance required to accelerate and go with all engines running (blue line). As we discussed before, the FAR Field Length Required will always be the largest among them. Check the sequence of illustrations below.

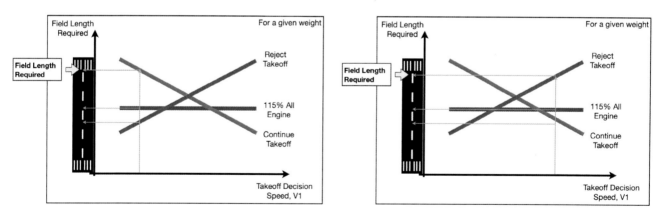

*Figure 195: Effect of V1 on the FAR Field Length Required.*

After a quick analysis of the graph, we can see that, ***in this example***, the All Engine Takeoff Distance will not be our field length required, regardless of the chosen V1. Also, observe that a lower V1 causes the required runway length to be established according to the One Engine Inoperative Takeoff Distance and a higher V1 makes our minimum length required to be the Accelerate and Stop Distance.

Note that the two lines that matter ***in this example*** (red and green) form an "X" and what defines the runway length required for takeoff is only the top of this "X", shaped as a "V".

Finally, choosing the V1 that occurs when the two lines meet gives us the shortest possible runway length for takeoff with this given weight. It is a point at which an interesting fact occurs: the accelerate and stop distance is exactly the same as the one engine inoperative takeoff distance. We call this situation a "**Balanced Field**" and the V1 that enabled this to happen is called "**Balanced V1**".

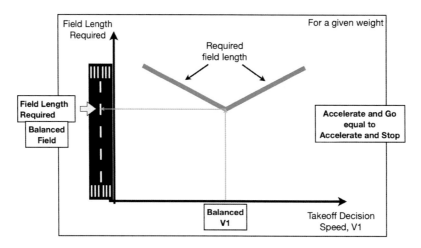

*Figure 196: Balanced Field and Balanced V1.*

And why is it called the Balanced V1? Well, you can think of the ACCEL-STOP and EO-GO distances behaving like an old weighing balance. Every time one rises, the other shrinks. And V1 is the factor responsible for establishing this behavior. I would say that V1 is the element that "can bring balance to the equation"! Star Wars fans, please forgive me for that! I know it was a terrible joke, but if it helps you forever remembering what a balanced V1 is, I believe it was worth it! Look at the following sequence of illustrations.

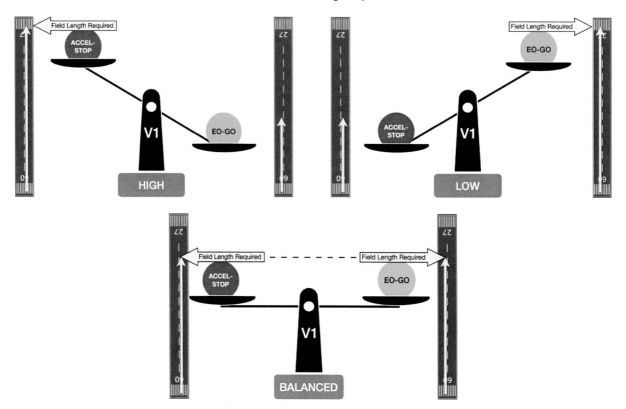

*Figure 197: Balanced V1 and balanced field length.*

Allow me to clarify some common mistakes people make regarding the balanced field length.

First: despite the name "balanced field length", this term has no relation to the runway itself! Some pilots believe that having TORA, TODA, and ASDA with the same values means the runway is balanced. No! Not true! Balanced field length is a condition that refers to the airplane and how much runway it will use in two different scenarios: either for ACCEL-STOP or for EO-GO.

Second: many pilots believe that when you have a balanced field length, it means that you will use all the runway available for a given task. Mostly, they think that you will use all the runway available to accelerate, and stop if a takeoff attempt is aborted at V1. That is also not true! You can have a balanced field length while using much less runway than the length available to you.

Third: there is some confusion when people use the term "balanced field length" when talking about landing distance. This is a big mistake. Balanced field length is an expression solely related to takeoff. There is no such thing as a balanced field for landing.

To make these explanations absolutely clear, the next figure shows a given runway with all declared distances exactly the same and three situations showing ACCEL-STOP and EO-GO distances for an airplane. Only in scenario C we find a balanced field length.

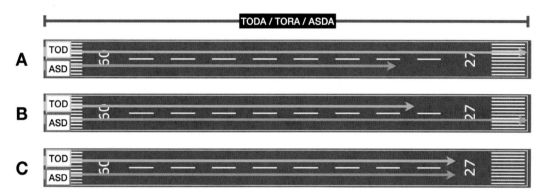

*Figure 198: Balanced field length has no relation to the available field length.*

Now back to the same graph we saw in Figure 196, we can do a reverse analysis. Let's see which V1s are available to be chosen with a given runway length. The figure below shows exactly this inversion and we can identify the minimum and maximum values that can be used. Of course, this is complementary to what we have seen previously (takeoff speed section). Minimum V1 must also be greater than or equal to V$_{1(MCG)}$ and maximum V1 must also be less than or equal to VR and V$_{MBE}$.

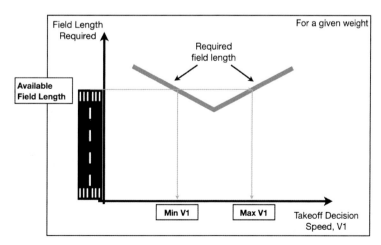

*Figure 199: Minimum and maximum V1 from the point of view of the runway.*

Well, you may be wondering: why would anyone want to use a V1 other than the balanced one if it uses the shortest runway length? To discuss how changing V1 can be beneficial, we will analyze it from a different perspective than we used in the graphs above. So far, we have been looking for a V1 that provides the required runway length for a given weight. Now, we will seek a V1 that, for a given runway, will determine our maximum takeoff weight.

With that in mind, we will conduct an initial study to identify which V1 can be chosen if we intend to continue takeoff after an engine failure at any given weight – we will call this $V_{GO}$. A light aircraft gains speed easily, whereas a heavier one has much more difficulty accelerating. Therefore, we can conclude that for a lightly loaded airplane, $V_{GO}$ can be a low speed, because if an engine failure occurs at this V1, the aircraft will still be able to continue accelerating and reach VR and V2 within runway limits. With higher weights, however, $V_{GO}$ has to be higher, closer to VR, so that the aircraft can take off within the runway limits; after all, the acceleration rate will be much lower after an engine failure.

If we analyze it considering a possible RTO (rejected takeoff) at V1 – let's call it $V_{STOP}$ – we will notice that what occurs is the opposite of what we just discussed. A heavier plane will have more difficulty in accelerating and then stopping. A lighter plane will find it much easier to decelerate to zero. Thus, we conclude that for a lightly loaded aircraft, $V_{STOP}$ can be high, and it would still be possible to stop within ASDA (Accelerate-Stop Distance Available). As the plane gets heavier, we must reduce $V_{STOP}$ to ensure that it can actually stop within the available runway length if the pilot decides to abort the takeoff.

The graphic below summarizes what we have discussed in the last three paragraphs. On the left, you can see that $V_{GO}$ can be almost any speed when the airplane is light and must be increased as it becomes heavier. On the right, you can see the behavior of $V_{STOP}$. The airplane can stop at very high speeds as long as it is lightly loaded. Heavier weights require the use of a lower V1 to stop within runway limits.

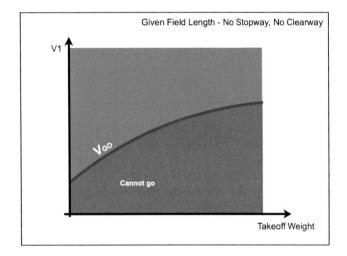

*Figure 200: TOD - Weight as a function of V1.*

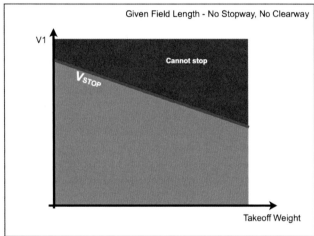

*Figure 201: ASD - Weight as a function of V1.*

Next, we will combine both analyses into a single chart. The green area of this new graph is the result of merging the previous ones, indicating that we can find a V1 that meets both conditions: being able to accelerate and stop, as well as accelerate and continue with an inoperative engine.

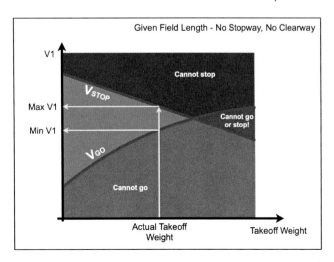

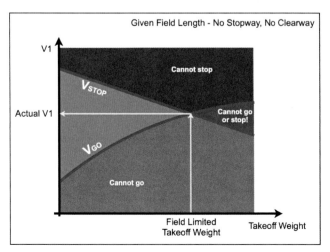

*Figure 202: A single V1 option on field limited maximum takeoff weight (on the right).*

Take the graph's horizontal axis (Takeoff Weight) and select any weight. If you draw a vertical line upwards from this weight and do not intersect the green area, it means you are above the maximum takeoff weight for this runway. If you find the point where the $V_{GO}$ and $V_{STOP}$ lines meet, you will be exactly at the maximum takeoff weight, with only one possible V1 and no options to choose from. In summary, a light aircraft can choose any V1 within several possibilities defined by the green area, but as it gets heavier, these possibilities will narrow down until there is only one possible V1 at the maximum takeoff weight.

By changing a detail in the characteristics of our runway, we can identify why unbalancing V1 may be advantageous. In the next illustration (Figure 203), we see almost the same graphic as before, but with a single difference: a stopway was added to the left graphic and a clearway to the right graphic.

With a stopway, we gain extra runway length to stop, so the $V_{STOP}$ line rises. Observe what happens to the meeting point of the $V_{STOP}$ and $V_{GO}$ lines: it shifts to the right, meaning that a runway with a stopway allows for a higher takeoff weight. To take advantage of the stopway and carry this extra weight, V1 must be increased (compared to the one in Figure 202 – the respective line is shaded in Figure 203 as well).

With a clearway, there is extra space to continue the takeoff and reach 35ft in the event of an engine failure, allowing us to reduce $V_{GO}$ (remember that reducing V1 increases the one-engine inoperative takeoff distance). Note again the vertex of the $V_{STOP}$ and $V_{GO}$ lines: it has shifted to the right, indicating that a runway with a clearway also allows for a higher takeoff weight than one without this feature. To take advantage of the clearway and carry this extra weight, V1 must be decreased (compared to the one in Figure 202 – shadow line in Figure 203). Of course, the runway must be dry as well.

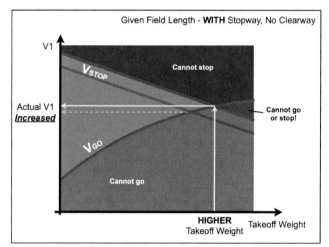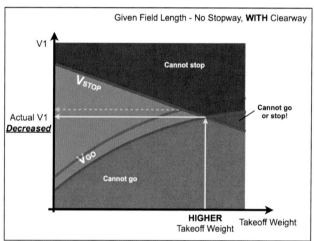

*Figure 203: Change in V1 to take advantage of the clearway and the stopway, thus increasing maximum takeoff weight.*

The next illustration (Figure 204) shows, in a different way, what happens to ASD (Accelerate-Stop Distance) and TOD (Takeoff Distance) when changing V1. This can help readers understand what happened in the previous illustrations, especially if they are not very familiar with interpreting graphics.

However, nothing illustrates this better than an example with actual numbers, as shown in Figure 205. This example demonstrates how changing V1 can result in a weight increase.

Consider a runway that allows a Boeing 737-800 to take off with a maximum weight of 70,200 kg when the air temperature is 30°C and the wind is calm. Keeping V1 balanced prevents the runways in the middle column (which has a clearway) and the right column (which has a stopway) from achieving a higher takeoff weight. This is because the concept behind the balanced field is to keep the "accelerate GO" and "accelerate STOP" distances equal. However, if you allow an imbalance to take advantage of these areas at the end of the runway, the gains are very significant!

The V1 chosen to generate the greatest available weight for takeoff is called the "Optimum V1," and it can be balanced or not.

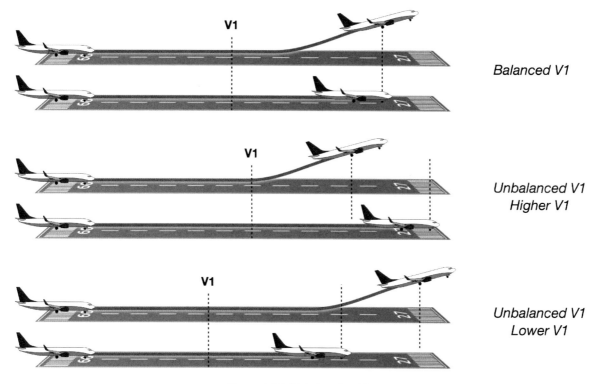

Figure 204: Unbalancing V1.

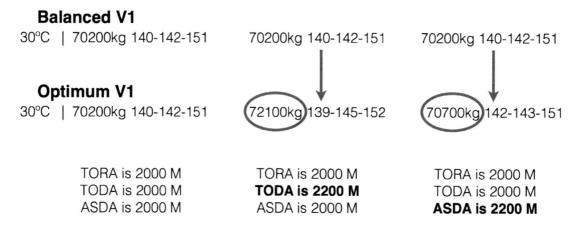

Figure 205: Optimum V1 versus Balanced V1.

On the next page, there is another illustration showing this variation in V1. The first three images indicate a runway with a stopway and the other three, a runway with a clearway. In both cases, there is a red line indicating the Accelerate-Stop Distance and a blue line showing the One Engine Inoperative Takeoff Distance. Each sequence of the three images indicates the following situations:

1st: Maximum takeoff weight for a balanced runway with no advantage taken of the feature presented (stopway or clearway).

2nd: The runway is unbalanced, but it maintains the same takeoff weight as in the first image.

3rd: The runway is unbalanced and its weight was adjusted to take advantage of the available feature (stopway or clearway).

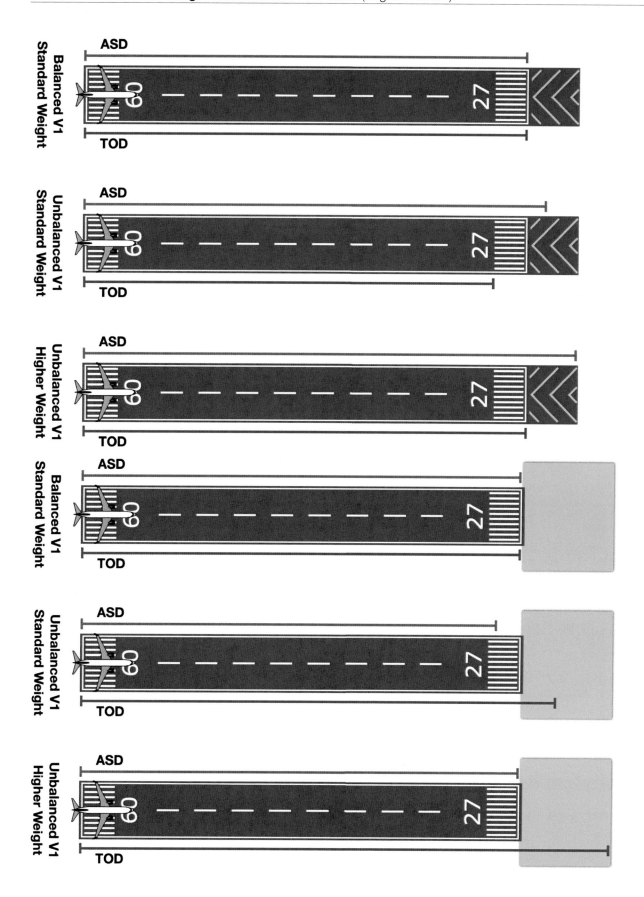

*Figure 206: Effects of changing V1 on TOD and ASD.*

So far, we have seen situations where unbalancing V1 was an operator's choice. However, there are scenarios where an unbalanced V1 is mandatory. I can cite three cases: whenever the balanced V1 is below V1$_{(MCG)}$, above VR, or above V$_{MBE}$.

Explanation: if the V1 value calculated to establish a balanced V1 is below V1$_{(MCG)}$, this result should be discarded, and takeoff is prohibited unless V1 is adjusted to be equal to V1$_{(MCG)}$. Remember, you cannot commit to continuing takeoff without reaching a speed that allows you to control the aircraft in the event of a critical engine failure.

If the calculated V1 is greater than VR, it implies that it would be acceptable to reject the takeoff even after lifting the nose to make the plane airborne. This is absurd! Thus, whenever this result occurs, V1 must be adjusted to be equal to VR, and this is done by reducing the initially calculated V1 value.

Finally, what is the problem when the calculated V1 is above V$_{MBE}$? A huge problem! Accepting this result means allowing a rejected takeoff above the maximum speed supported by the brakes. In this case, stopping within ASDA is not guaranteed, and even if it happens, it is very likely that the brakes will fail. Thus, as was done when V1 was greater than VR, V1 should be reduced to match V$_{MBE}$. In the first and last situations, there may be a penalty for the maximum takeoff weight owing to the V1 adjustment. Whether or not this penalty exists will depend on the length of the runway intended for takeoff.

A question that I am often asked is, what if I miscalculate V1?

This question can be clearly answered with the graphics below, which are valid for a twin-engine aircraft only, as the "GO" graphic is different for three- or four-engine aircraft. Of course, these are only valid if you are performing a field-limited takeoff (where your takeoff weight is limited by runway length). Calculating a V1 as 4kt higher than the correct speed can cause the airplane to reach the end of the runway at about 40kt instead of zero. Missing the correct V1 by 4kt less means passing the opposite threshold at about 20ft instead of 35ft, or even less if the calculation was done for a wet runway. These graphs assume that the engine has failed at V$_{EF}$.

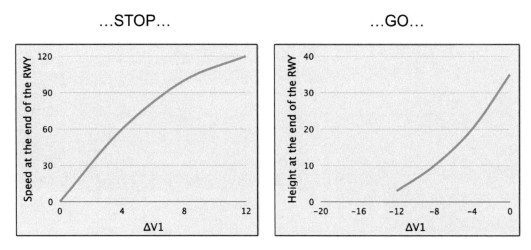

*Figure 207: What happens if V1 is miscalculated?*

### 3.2.9  RTO Statistics and Go No-Go Decision Making

A study on RTO events showed that, between 1960 and 2003, there were about 143,000 aborted takeoffs out of over 430 million flights. Of these, 76% occurred at low speeds, below 80kt, and only 2% occurred in the "dangerous region" of speeds above 120kt.

To put into perspective how uncommon an RTO is, a pilot flying short and medium-range flights, with 50 takeoffs every month (which is a lot), would experience one RTO event approximately every six years. This statistic is believed to be underreported, with several low-speed RTOs below 40kt not being recorded. Nevertheless, over the 40 years covered by the study, 97 runway excursions were registered, all during RTOs initiated above 120kt. Let's delve into those events.

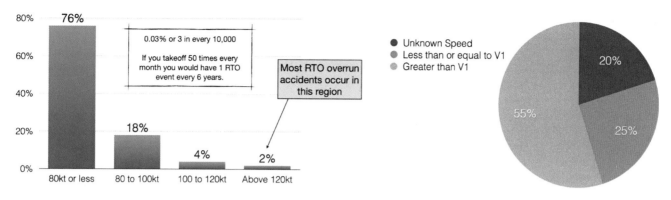

*Figure 208: RTO statistics.*

Above (Figure 208), one fact calls our immediate attention: 55% of the 97 runway overrun events were caused by maneuvers commenced after V1! You have not read anything wrong! More than half of the accidents were caused by pilots rejecting takeoff at a speed higher than the one at which they should have already committed to go. And the following graphic causes as much concern as the previous one.

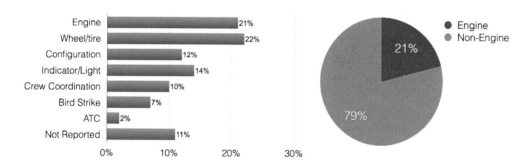

*Figure 209: Reasons for all high energy RTOs from the study.*

See, pilots are trained to split takeoff roll into two different parts. The first one is the low energy region, defined by Boeing as speeds at or below 80kt and by Airbus as speeds at or below 100kt. Above this speed, there is what we call a high-energy region. This division exists to help pilots in a go/no-go decision-making process. In the low energy region, it is agreed that RTO is a very safe maneuver, and any discrepancy should be a reason for aborting the takeoff attempt.

In a high-energy region, however, the risks involved in an RTO maneuver are far higher than to continue takeoff. For that reason, it is stipulated that only safety-critical issues are to be considered when deciding to reject. Those issues are: fire of any kind (engine, APU, cargo, etc.), engine failure (by failure I mean any kind of thrust deterioration) and windshear. Of course, there may be other factors that pilots may judge necessary when they consider interrupting takeoff, and the captain always has the final authority to make this decision, but those three situations are the most studied, and having this in mind is very helpful.

I would like to share a personal note here. A kind of tip for my pilot colleagues. When taking off, I always think of high energy RTO as follows: **I will only abort takeoff if the aircraft <u>YAW</u> or <u>YELL</u>**! Yaw represents engine failure or any kind of thrust deterioration, and yell is used because every fire warning comes with a bell ring, and a windshear alert will also be announced by the airplane – there is an exception for windshear, but I will not talk about aircraft systems. Send me an email with your thoughts on that if you like!

Back to the subject. After presenting the main reasons for RTOs in high-energy regions, go back to Figure 209 and see the reasons that actually led pilots to stop a takeoff attempt. Only 21% are engine-related issues. Although 11% of the cases are unknown, 68% of RTOs were possibly executed for no reason. And let me draw your attention to tire-related incidents. This is one big concern of the industry! Remember that when close to V1, pilots have only 1 second to react to any event.

And I know my tip has a flaw. If you react quickly to any yaw without giving a second glance at engine instruments, you might be cheated by a tire failure situation. When a tire explodes during takeoff roll at high speed, a loud bang is likely to be heard and a yaw will probably be felt (depending on the aircraft's model). So, please, be careful about that! RTOs motivated by tire failure at a high speed are NOT RECOMMENDED!

There are good odds that the runway will be overrun if the pilot executes a high energy RTO owing to tire failure. Aircraft have been designed to stop within ASDA considering that all brakes are working properly, and that is definitely not the case in this scenario. The safest course of action would be to continue takeoff, burn some fuel and land. If the tires are the only problem, maybe the flight can even proceed, and landing will occur at the original destination with significantly less weight. That assures that the stopping distance will be shorter and, therefore, safer!

### 3.2.10 Factors that will affect Takeoff Speeds

See how the factors below affect takeoff speeds (V1, VR and V2):

**Weight:** higher weight requires higher VR and V2. Owing to difficulty in accelerating after an engine failure, V1 will also increase with weight, even if this increases aircraft stopping distance.

**Density:** lower air density decreases engine thrust and, for this reason, takeoff speeds must be closer to each other (it is difficult to accelerate). To compromise, V1 and VR will increase and V2 will decrease.

**Flap:** a larger takeoff flap setting increases lift at the same speed. This, in turn, reduces VR and V2. Since V1 cannot be greater than VR, it also ends up decreasing.

**Wind:** with headwind, it will be easier to stop the aircraft in case of RTO, and tailwind will make this process more difficult. Thus, headwind increases V1 while tailwind decreases it. VR and V2 are not affected by wind.

**Runway slope:** an uphill runway makes it easier to stop the aircraft in the event of an RTO, while a downhill runway makes this process difficult. Therefore, a positive slope (uphill) increases V1, while a negative slope (downhill) decreases V1. However, VR and V2 are not affected by slope.

### 3.2.11 Establishing Runway Slope

Establishing the runway slope to use in our performance calculations is much more complicated than it may seem. One way to determine the average runway slope is to calculate the difference in elevation between the two thresholds and divide this amount by the runway length. The first problem is that at most airports, the only information about elevation comes from the airport chart, and that is not exactly the threshold elevation, but the touchdown zone elevation (TDZE), a point about 300 meters from the threshold.

Take Congonhas Airport as an example. In the airport chart reproduced on the right side, we can see that runway 17R has a TDZE of 2,615ft, while runway 35L is 2,633ft above sea level. This elevation difference of 18ft, when converted to meters, is approximately 5.49m. Given that the runway is 1,940m long, we can calculate the average slope as plus 0.28% (uphill) for those using runway 17R and minus 0.28% (downhill) for those using runway 35L.

I used Congonhas as an example because this is one of the airports that also have a different chart published

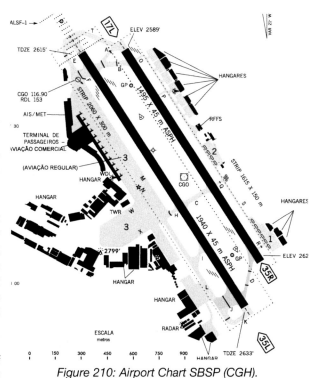

Figure 210: Airport Chart SBSP (CGH).

called AOC (Airport Obstacle Chart). Not all airports have this one, but look at the difference in our result! In addition to obstacles, AOC shows the runway profile with its elevations. In this chart, also reproduced below, the elevations are published in meters, but I edited to feet in order to compare it with the airport's chart.

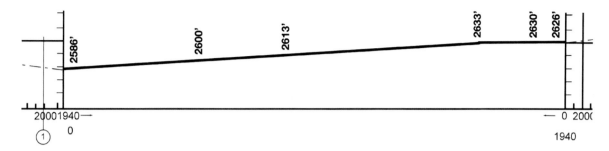

*Figure 211: AOC from the same airport (SBSP/CGH)*

On threshold 17R, the elevation is 788.7m (2,586ft), while on threshold 35L, the elevation is 801m (2,626ft). Using these data instead of the previous ones results in a difference of 12.3m between the thresholds. Dividing this by the same 1,940m of runway length, the calculated slope will be 0.63%, positive or negative, depending on the direction of takeoff. And when departing from a runway intersection a new slope should be calculated too! The problem has been identified, but do not expect a solution from the author. If I were the owner of an airline, I might hire an engineering team to conduct a planialtimetric survey of airports without a published AOC.

The second difficulty is perhaps even more concerning: how to work with runway with slope variations?

There is no definitive solution to this, and all the companies that I know of ignore the problem, that is, they measure the runway slope the way we have just discussed. Allow me to demonstrate the problem we can encounter when calculating the slope in this manner and ignoring its variation along the runway.

First, consider a truly flat (0% slope) and dry runway. We are on a field length limited runway and departing at maximum takeoff weight. The airplane will use its full length for both Accelerate-Stop Distance (ASD) and Takeoff Distance (TOD). This means that during acceleration to V1, the plane will use approximately two-thirds of the runway. Suppose V1 is 135kt and it is reached at this point (two-thirds of the runway) where the RTO maneuver is initiated. In this case, the remaining third of the runway will be used to stop the aircraft, bringing its speed to zero at the exact end of the runway.

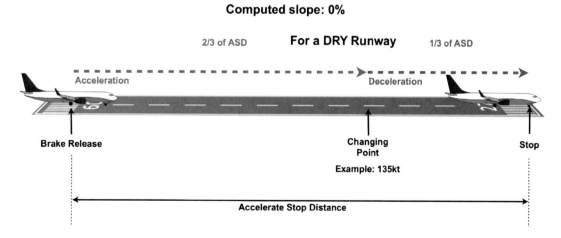

*Figure 212: First part of the study. Slope 0% on a flat runway.*

In a second scenario, imagine a runway in the same condition as the first (dry), except that this time it is not flat. There is an uphill slope in first two thirds and a downhill slope in the last third, but the thresholds are at the same elevation. As there is no difference between them, the calculated slope will be zero as well.

When the computer was informed that the runway slope was zero, it projected the calculations the same way as in the previous example, which resulted in the same takeoff weight and the same V1 of 135kt. However, actual acceleration of this aircraft will be made against gravity, meaning more slowly, and this will cause the speed of 135kt to be reached at a point farther from the brake release point and closer to the end of the runway, compared to the first study.

Since we have reached V1 closer to the end of the runway, it can be obviously concluded that there is less runway left to stop from now on. This, alone, is a big problem, but there is another one ahead. The computer 'believed' that the aircraft would be stopped on flat ground; however, we are on a steep descend and stopping is even more difficult. We will need a longer runway length than the one that was originally calculated. This is the possible result of this study: a runway excursion, even though the pilot had initiated RTO at the right speed.

**Computed slope: 0%**

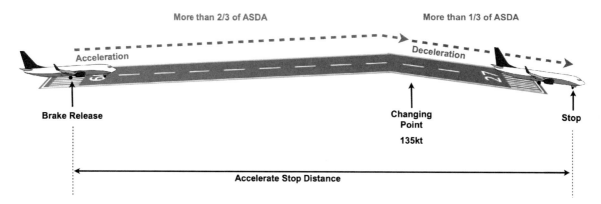

*Figure 213: Second part of the study. Slope 0% on a double sloped (up then down) runway.*

### 3.3.1  Obstacle Accountability Area - OAA

We are finally airborne! It is a big step. But what lies beyond the runway? We need to ensure that all obstacles are overcome by a certain safety margin. Herein lies a significant challenge. ICAO and EASA (CAT.POL.A.210) clearly define an area on the departure path where any obstacle must be cleared by 35ft in height plus a safety margin that we will discuss in detail later. On the other hand, FAA and ANAC (Brazil) regulations state that any obstacle must be cleared by 35ft plus a given safety margin in height (just as ICAO), OR 200ft horizontally whenever inside the airport boundary and 300ft horizontally when flying outside that limit.

Let's be honest, the FAA's instruction is quite clear on vertical clearance, but I believe we have too little information on how to accomplish the horizontal clearance. Clearing obstacles horizontally would strongly depend on altitude and the reason is illustrated in the figure below. Terrain does not rise vertically like buildings; it rises in slopes that can be more or less steep. The point is, you would have to know your exact path and altitude to comply with this rule, and even if you do, can you really keep a precise track like this with thrust asymmetry?

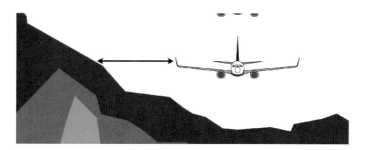

*Figure 214: Kee̦                                                            ɔn it seems.*

For that reason, an advisory circular was published to provide an operationally realistic horizontal clearance plane (AC 120-91A). ACs are neither mandatory nor the only acceptable methods for ensuring compliance with the regulatory sections. Operators may use other methods if those methods are shown to provide the necessary level of safety and are acceptable to the FAA. Anyway, an AC basically makes us focus on vertically overcoming (by 35ft plus the safety margin) any obstacle within a certain area, just as ICAO and EASA do! And for this purpose, there is the Obstacle Accountability Area (OAA).

The FAA's obstacle accountability area starts at the end of the runway with a 200ft half-width until the end of the airport boundary. At this point, it jumps to a 300ft half-width until 4,800ft from the end of the runway. Why 4,800ft, one might ask? Because starting the tip of a cone at the end of the runway and widening up at a rate of 6.25%
will reach a 300ft half-width at exactly 4,800ft. Beyond this point, the area is no longer a corridor but follows this

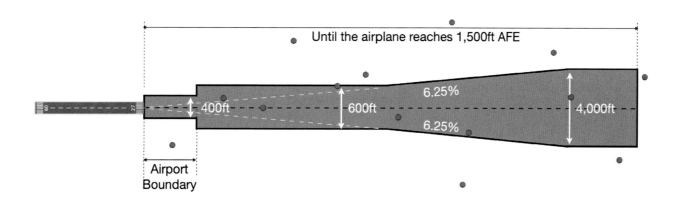

The ICAO/EASA obstacle accountability area is also cone-shaped and becomes wider as you get farther from the runway; however, the splay is significantly different from the FAA's. In fact, it is twice as much and the area is widening 12.5% to each side. That starting point is also different. It begins at the end of the runway with a half-width of 60m plus one half of the aircraft's wingspan or 90m, whichever is smaller. After 60m beyond the end of the runway (the end of the runway strip), it starts to expand in width at the mentioned ratio (12.5%). The maximum width values for ICAO and FAA are essentially the same despite the difference in units — 4,000ft for FAA and 1,200m for ICAO.

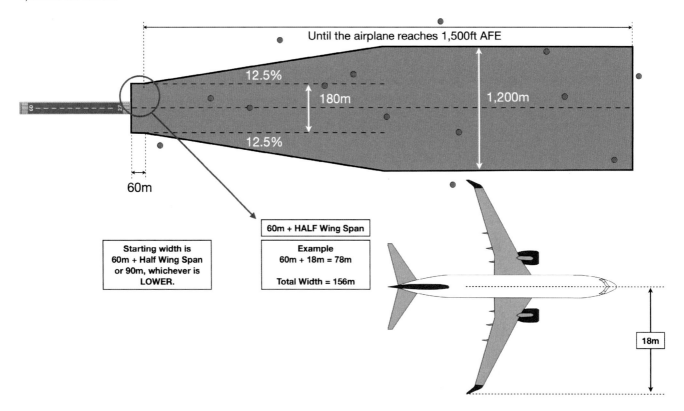

*Figure 216: ICAO's OAA. If the airplane were a B737NG, it could start on 78m half width instead of 90m.*

The width will remain constant at its maximum value up to the point where the aircraft reaches 1,500 feet above the field elevation (AFE) or clears any relevant obstacles and can resume navigation towards its intended destination, whichever altitude is higher. To clarify, obstacles are no longer relevant once you reach certain altitudes such as Minimum Vector Altitude (MVA), Minimum Safe Altitude (MSA), or Minimum Enroute Altitude (MEA).

Attention! The maximum width previously mentioned is only applicable for straight-out departures (no deviations greater than 15 degrees from the runway track). If a turn is necessary, the maximum width will be slightly larger: 6,000 feet for FAA standards and 1,800 meters for ICAO standards (again, essentially the same value, but in different units).

In the case of departures involving turns, obstacle heights must be adjusted. Current software is unable to calculate the reduction in climb performance during turns, mainly because the software does not account for the airplane turning; after all, the engine-out procedure is not part of the software's calculations. Therefore, engineers are expected to artificially increase the height of obstacles to compensate for this limitation. The extent to which obstacle height is increased depends on the takeoff flap setting and the bank angle used during the turn, and that information can be found in the airplane's performance manuals.

In Figure 218, you can see an example of the penalty in climb capability. For a flap 5 configuration and a 15-degree bank, this Boeing 737-800 loses 0.66% of its climb gradient compared to a wings-level climb. What the engineer needs to do in such cases is to increase the height of each obstacle that exists during and after the turn by a specific amount, as illustrated in Figure 219.

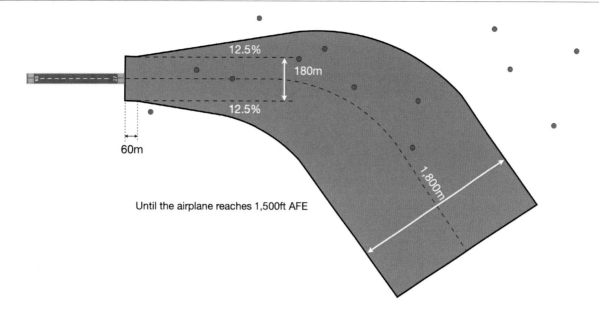

*Figure 217: EASA's OAA when changing heading by more than 15°.*

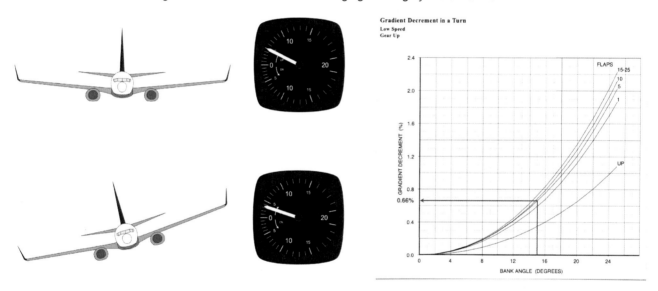

*Figure 218: Climb decrement in a turn - Boeing 737-800 example.*

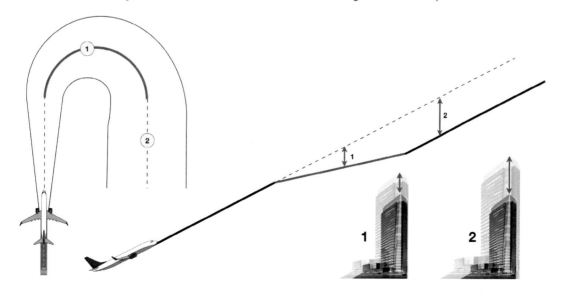

*Figure 219: Adjusting obstacle heights along a path during and after a turn.*

Of course, not every single tree or building within OAA must be plotted on the chart. Only obstacles that remained within this area and surpass an imaginary upward plane of 1.2% from the end of the runway must show. Such obstacles will be plotted on a chart called AOC (*Airport Obstacle Chart*). We talked briefly about it when discussing how to calculate runway slope. This chart has information about location of the obstacles on a kind of blueprint including a top and side view, showing each significant obstacle.

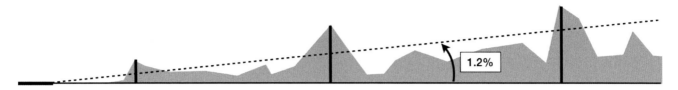

*Figure 220: Obstacles on AOC are those that surpass the imaginary plane with 1.2% upward gradient.*

In the next figure, note obstacle number 35, the highest of all obstacles listed. It is 6,448m far from the end of the runway and it is 210m tall. Remember those numbers as we will use them in a future example for calculating minimum net and gross flight paths.

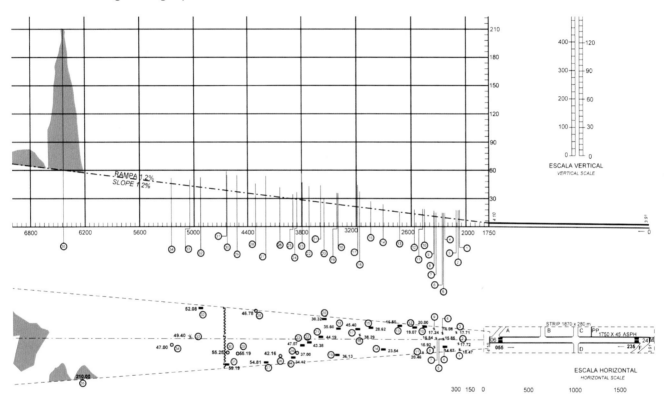

*Figure 221: AOC sample for the departure end of runway 24 in SBVT.*

Now, some things in Brazil are quite weird! I am not sure if this kind of thing happens in other parts of the world, but I will tell you anyway. Aeronautical publications are the responsibility of an agency called DECEA, which is under the jurisdiction of the Ministry of Defense, while legislations, including the analog of FAR Part 121, are established by ANAC (National Civil Aviation Agency), this one, a civilian agency. DECEA publishes AOC charts following ICAO's standard, with that funnel starting at a width of 180m and widening by 12.5%. ANAC, on the other hand, publishes in RBAC 121.189 (Brazilian Civil Aviation Regulation) an exact copy of the text found in the FAA's regulations, that is, the obstacles must be cleared vertically by 35ft plus a given margin (that we are still going to discuss), OR horizontally by 200ft within the limits of the airport and 300ft beyond this limit. However, there is no advisory circular (that I am aware of) to "provide an operationally realistic horizontal clearance plane" as FAA does.

What to do now? As far as I know, most airlines choose to follow ICAO's standards and use the chart provided by DECEA (the AOC) as is, considering every obstacle on it, but that is common sense, not a rule. And forgive me for saying that, but I believe we cannot trust in common sense on that regard.

Anyway, in the following illustration, observe how the OAA proposed by the FAA is less restrictive. In a generic map of obstacles, ICAO's model might require more obstacles to be taken into account for takeoff calculations than the FAA's model. All previous illustrations were not to scale, but the following is, so we have a better idea of the difference between them. OAAs in the figure represent a straight-out departure up to 10km away from the airport.

*Figure 222: FAA's and EASA's OAAs shown independently and overlaying.*

Back to performance calculations. Each obstacle can be considered in its real position or aligned with the intended flight path. There is a great advantage in considering the obstacles in their actual positions when these obstacles are very close to the runway. In case of more distant obstacles, there is no significant difference in doing this. Here is an example:

Suppose a given obstacle is listed as follows: 12/240/-100. The first number represents the obstacle's height, the second indicates its distance from the runway (imagining its position is on the aircraft's trajectory), and the third shows the lateral displacement of this obstacle (positive numbers to the right and negative numbers to the left of the flight path). All numbers may be presented in feet or meters, depending on the operator's choice. Sometimes a combination of both is used, such as height in feet and distance in meters, which is the case in our example.

If we consider that the obstacle is on the aircraft's flight path, a calculation is made to overcome an obstacle 12 feet high and 240 meters away. Placing the obstacle in its actual position, Pythagoras tells us that it is, in fact, 260 meters away from the runway. Considering the same height, the farther the obstacle, the lower the gradient required to overcome it. However, it was worth placing this obstacle in its actual position because it was close. If it were far from the runway, even when measuring the diagonal distance, we would see that there is no significant difference in that distance that justifies the complexity of this process.

In the example, the net gradient required to overcome the obstacle, assuming it is aligned with the runway, will be 5.97%. This gradient drops to 5.51% when the obstacle is placed in its real position. We will explain what "net gradient" means in a moment, so don't worry.

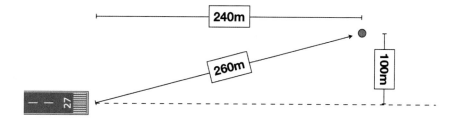

*Figure 223: Close-in obstacle.*

To conclude this topic, I believe that nowadays it is feasible to position every single obstacle in its real location because calculations are no longer done manually but by computers. As engineers' only job is to input the correct data into the software, and I recommend that everyone should do it, regardless of its perceived worthiness.

One more problem – as if those presented so far were not enough: obstacle database! Where to find it? And no, I did not forget the AOC, but if you look at any sample of this chart you will see that most of them will end 10km far from the departure end of the runway. Is that enough? Short answer: no! Take a look at the next figure:

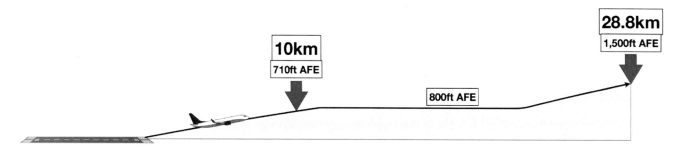

*Figure 224: How far to reach 1,500ft?*

The example above is a real one! That is a Boeing 737-800, thrust rating 24K, departing from SBKP, runway 15. Actual takeoff gross weight is 73,000kg, using flaps 5, wind calm, QNH 1013hPa and OAT 30°C. At the time this airplane flies by the 10km mark, it is still climbing through the second segment. Considering acceleration altitude at 800ft above field elevation (AFE), at the moment that the final segment ends (we will talk about this segment soon), the airplane is already 28.8km far from the runway! What obstacles are there between 10 and 28.8km? That is a big uncertainty area, and FAA recommends a few different sources that might help pilots find them out:

- FAA Form 5010
- Topographical Quadrangle Charts
- Jeppesen/Lido Departure & Approach Charts
- National Flight Data Digest
- Low Altitude Instrument Approach Charts (DoD)
- Aeronautical Information Publication (AIP)
- ICAO Type A/B/C Charts (TPC)
- USGS 3 Arc Second Terrain Data
- USGS 1 Arc Second Terrain Data
- Digital Vertical Obstacle File (DVOF)
- Digital Terrain Elevation Data (DTED)
- National Geodetic Survey (NGS)
- Area Navigation Approach Survey (ANA)
- NOTAMs

I have no idea how to access most of this data and it would be awesome to always have accurate official data to make the analysis, but we all know that such data is not available in some places. So, my final recommendation is: use your best judgment to find out the most reliable source of obstacle data! Sometimes your only option will be Google Earth! Believe me! There is a saying: "no data is better than bad data", but I risk to say that, in this case, "some data is better than no data". Would you agree?

## 3.3.2   Net and Gross Takeoff Flight Path

Now that we know which obstacles need to be considered, let's move on to the second part of our problem: by what margin do they need to be overcome? We have seen that regulations state every obstacle within the OAA must be cleared by at least 35 feet. What else?

If the aircraft is in a turning pattern and this turn is performed with a bank (wing inclination) greater than 15 degrees, the rule changes slightly. The FAA's regulations maintain the 35-foot rule but emphasize that it must refer to the lowest point on the aircraft (usually the wing tip). EASA's regulations, however, state that in a turn of more than 15 degrees bank, the obstacles must be cleared by 50 feet. To simplify our examples, we will work with the 35-foot requirement and assume a straight-out departure that maintains the runway track.

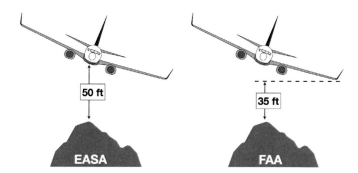

*Figure 225: Margin to overcome obstacles during turns.*

The path that allows the obstacle to be cleared by this minimum margin of 35 feet is known as the **Net Flight Path (NFP)** – this is the net path I mentioned earlier. Net flight path is the same for every airplane. However, regulators (thankfully) decided to add an extra margin to this minimum height in case the pilot makes a handling error or weather conditions differ from the computed ones.

So, although the NFP is the same for every aircraft, the extra margin depends on the number of engines on the airplane. For a twin-engine aircraft, it is 0.8% above the previously measured path. It is 0.9% for a three-engine and 1.0% for a four-engine airplane. NFP plus the extra gradient results in the Gross Flight Path (GFP), and it is this trajectory that the airplane must demonstrate that it can fly after takeoff, considering a sudden failure of its critical engine at $V_{EF}$. Note that, owing to this extra gradient, more distant obstacles are overflown by a greater height margin.

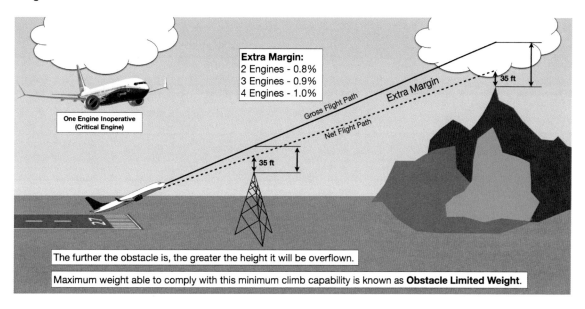

*Figure 226: Minimum obstacle clearance requirements.*

The maximum weight at which the airplane can overcome the obstacle with minimum height defined by gross flight path and with its critical engine inoperative since $V_{EF}$ is called **Obstacle Limited Takeoff Weight**.

### 3.3.2.1 GFP is an Impossible Task to Accomplish!

Every time you calculate the gradient required to overcome a particular obstacle, two things must be noted. First, the starting point for establishing the net and gross flight path is the departure end of the runway, hence, the end of TORA. Second, the aircraft's trajectory is not a straight upward line. As we saw earlier, the engine loses thrust with altitude, and therefore the airplane's climb path resembles a parabola. So, it is automatically impossible to follow a straight path like the GFP. What do we do, then?

The plane defined by the GFP (measured from the end of the runway) should not be invaded by the aircraft's trajectory at any time – an exception is granted when there is a clearway available, and the airplane will end its takeoff distance within this area. In practice, the performance software will look for a target altitude over the obstacle and will work from there, establishing a weight, thrust setting, and speeds to meet that target altitude even with a parabolic climb path. The practical result is shown in the following figure.

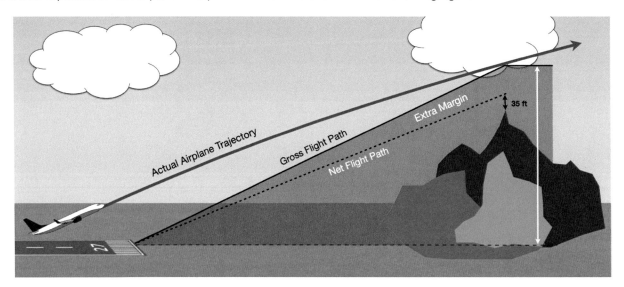

*Figure 227: Difference between computed GFP and the airplane's actual trajectory.*

Having clarified this fact, let's do an exercise: what is the minimum height for a two-engine aircraft to overcome the following obstacle: 210/6448/0? Also indicate what the NET and GROSS flight paths are. Obstacle information is in meters (height / distance / offset) and consider 1ft equal to 0.305m.

| | |
|---|---|
| 35ft x 0.305ft/m = 10,675m | 4.22% x 6448m = 272.11m |
| 210 + 10.675 = 220.675m | 272.11m / 0.305ft/m = 892.2ft |
| 220.675 / 6448 x 100 = **3.42% NFP** | The aircraft must fly over the obstacle at 892.2ft and never invade |
| 3.42 + 0.8 = **4.22% GFP** | the imaginary plane of 4.22% gradient from the end of the RWY. |

### 3.3.3   Effect of V1 on Obstacle Clearance

When we talked about V1 in the topic "V1 Considerations," one of the things we saw was how the chosen V1 affects takeoff distance. Back then, we concluded that V1 has no effect on the All Engine Takeoff Distance, but it greatly changes the takeoff distance with an inoperative engine. The higher the V1, the less runway the airplane needs to use for takeoff in this situation.

When we discussed the optimum V1, we considered the possibility of changing the value of balanced V1 to gain weight, and we saw this being applied on a runway with a stopway or a clearway. Now let's think about how unbalancing V1 can change the maximum takeoff weight when we are obstacle-limited.

Important note: Every obstacle is always considered to be fixed in its position. Ships or cars passing close to the runway are not taken into account. That being said, let's imagine a fixed obstacle that is 129 feet tall and is located 1,110 meters from the departure end of a runway.

After some calculations, we find a net flight path of 4.5%, and for a twin jet, we have a gross flight path (GFP) of 5.3%. This means that this obstacle must be flown over at 193 feet above field elevation (AFE), considering that the jet's critical engine has failed at $V_{EF}$. As noted, the airplane will not fly in a straight line but in a parabolic trajectory. The following figure attempts to illustrate that the airplane's trajectory must be very steep if it becomes airborne near the end of the runway (close to the obstacle itself) and could be much shallower if it becomes airborne sooner.

Increasing V1 will decrease the engine-out go distance (EO-GO), allowing the airplane to become airborne using less runway and increasing its distance from the obstacle. This means it will be able to fly a less aggressive climb path and potentially carry more weight on takeoff compared to lifting off closer to the end of the runway. There you have it! This presents a great opportunity to unbalance V1, seeking a higher value to increase the maximum takeoff weight when that weight is obstacle-limited.

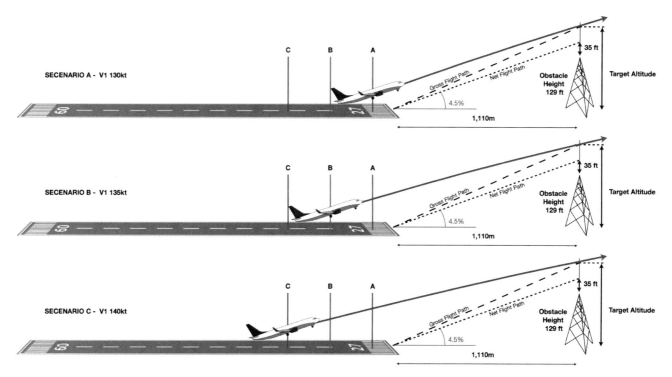

*Figure 228: Influence of V1 on obstacle limited takeoff weights.*

### 3.3.4    *Standard Instrument Departure – Unable to Comply with Climb Gradient*

Another aspect that we must pay attention to concerns the minimum climb gradient published on Standard Instrument Departure charts (SIDs). These instrument departure charts are created under the guidelines of DOC 8168 – PANS OPS, which clearly states that whoever designs the procedures must keep in mind that they will be executed by an airplane with all its engines operating. Airplanes are not required to comply with published gradients in emergency conditions.

The same document states that the responsibility for developing a contingency procedure in the event of an engine failure falls on the aircraft operator, that is, the airline. This contingency procedure must be developed for each runway at each airport the airline wishes to operate from. Therefore, if air traffic control clears you to follow an SID with a minimum climb gradient of 8% and you identify that your airplane, with one engine inoperative, is capable of climbing "only" 6%, it is not necessary to request a different SID from ATC. You just need to ensure that you are able to achieve the published gradient while all engines are running. If this is not possible, then another SID must be requested.

DOC 8168 regulates the design of an SID according to the following rules regarding obstacle clearance: first, an imaginary plane is measured, starting at the departure end of the runway (DER) and reaching the top of the obstacle. This plane is called the Obstacle Clearance Surface (OCS). To this gradient (found in the OCS), a fixed safety margin of 0.8% is added. This margin is called the Required Obstacle Clearance (ROC). The result obtained from the sum of OCS and ROC is called the Procedure Design Gradient (PDG), and this is the gradient that will be published on SID charts.

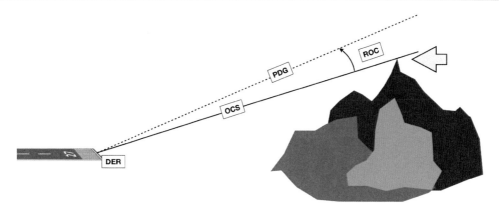

*Figure 229: DOC 8168 - development of SID (1).*

If the obstacle is in a region of the SID that will be flown with the aircraft turning (a curved trajectory), the process I described above undergoes a single change. The initial imaginary plane, the Obstacle Clearance Surface (OCS), will be drawn between the end of the runway and a point 246ft (75 m) above the obstacle rather than right on the top of it.

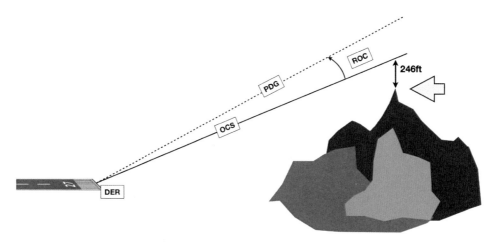

*Figure 230: DOC 8168 - development of SID (2).*

If there are no obstacles on the SID's path, the minimum OCS value will be 2.5%. Adding to this the safety gradient of 0.8%, any SID will always have a minimum published gradient of 3.3%, or 200ft per nautical mile. When a higher gradient is specified, the altitude/height to which it extends is published. Minimum lateral clearance with terrain depends directly on the resources used to fly the departure (NDB, VOR, GPS). Whichever feature gives you the greatest degree of certainty of your position, the SID will require less lateral separation. Details on this will not be covered in this book.

Pilots must be aware that not all elevated climb gradients refer to obstacles on the flight path. Many SIDs are published with significantly high procedure design gradients due to air traffic control-related issues.

Pilots must also know that in the USA, the FAA uses a different rule to create their procedures, and some countries around the globe adopt this American way of designing procedures. This rule is called TERPS (Terminal Procedures). TERPS uses the same terminology as DOC 8168 and has the same minimum OCS (2.5%); however, the Required Obstacle Clearance (ROC) is not a fixed value. The PDG is calculated by dividing the OCS by 0.76. As a result, the ROC is always 24% of the published SID climb gradient. If the minimum gradient is used (3.3%), then the ROC from TERPS matches the one from DOC 8168: 3.3% x 24% = 0.8%. Thinking the opposite way: the minimum OCS is 2.5%, so 2.5% divided by 0.76 equals 3.3% (Published Design Gradient).

### 3.3.4.1 Developing an Engine Out Standard Instrument Departure – EO-SID

As I mentioned, DOC 8168 clearly states that the operator is responsible for developing a contingency procedure for every runway at every airport that they intend to fly from. The question is: how do they do this?

There is no single correct answer. They might do it themselves or hire someone to do it. But one thing is for sure: the FAA, EASA, and any other regulator have no responsibility for that design, and neither do they need to approve it. They just need to know that the operator has one! When there are no relevant obstacles in the departure sector, that procedure could be as simple as a message saying, "if an engine fails, follow the published SID". However, if there are obstacles around, the operator must devise a different solution!

Creating an EO-SID (Engine Out SID) is certainly very challenging, especially when the airport is located in valleys surrounded by mountains. Let's discuss some problems that may arise when developing one.

We have already talked about the obstacle accountability area (OAA) and the fact that elevations must be adjusted if they exist during or after a turn. But depending on how you establish this path to be flown, the OAA can become much, much wider! You see, using a fixed bank angle, when turning toward the operating engine, the turning radius is greater than in normal flight with all engines operating. On the other hand, turning away from the operating engine makes the turning radius smaller.

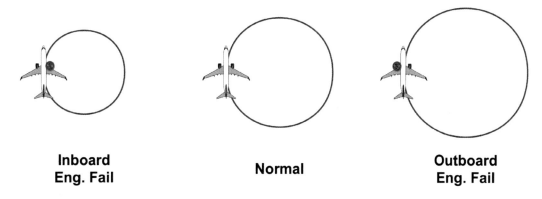

*Figure 231: Turning radius with a failed engine – same bank angle for all scenarios.*

If the instructions on an EO-SID simply say, "after crossing waypoint XYZ, turn right with a 15-degree bank to heading 180," this will create two different track possibilities, one for each engine failure scenario. The area splay of 12.5% (or 6.25% for the FAA) will have to be calculated for both scenarios.

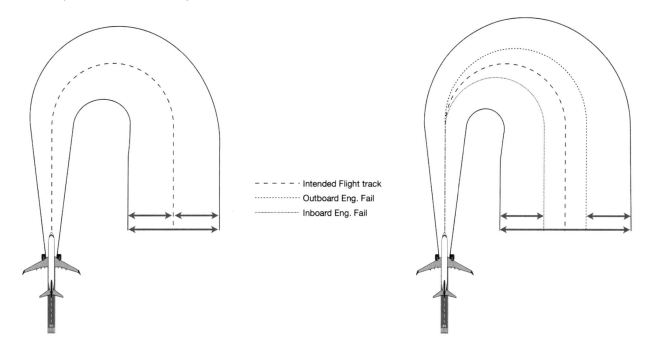

*Figure 232: OAA expansion owing to different radius turn.*

Another problem with the area arises when you specify on the EO-SID that the pilot should start a given turn once reaching a certain altitude. Different takeoff weights will result in varying points at which that altitude is reached. By the way, different weights will also result in very different turn radii. So, my hint is to make the EO-SID have the most precise flight path possible. Lighter aircraft will have to fly that trajectory using small bank angles, and heavier aircraft will have to use steeper bank angles, but at least your area problem will be simpler to address.

### 3.3.4.2 Radius Turn Limited Takeoff Weight

Speaking of turn radius when designing EO-SIDs, that might be one of the issues that will eventually limit your maximum takeoff weight. Let me explain. Say you are departing from Cuzco, Peru. That airport is at a high altitude, with an elevation close to 11,000 feet, and is surrounded by mountains.

When trying to create that EO-SID, you might find that the only option is for the airplane to climb following a path that resembles a figure eight, repeating the pattern until reaching a safe altitude. But even to do that, the mountains are so close to each other that you must keep your turning radius small. The way to achieve this is either with steeper bank angles (which may not be possible because of stall speed) or with smaller weights. There you have it! You will limit your takeoff weight to be able to maintain an acceptable turn radius and avoid crashing into the mountains. This is known as the **Radius Turn Limit Takeoff Weight**.

$$R = \frac{V^2}{g \tan \theta}$$

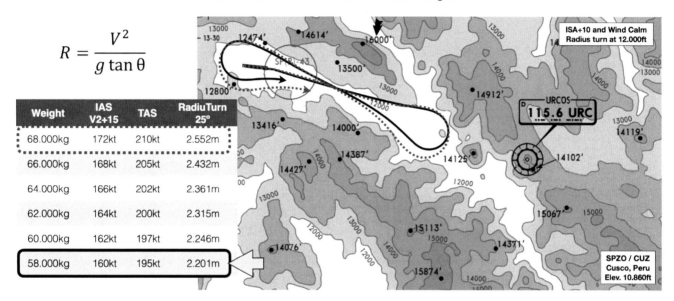

| Weight | IAS V2+15 | TAS | RadiuTurn 25° |
|---|---|---|---|
| 68.000kg | 172kt | 210kt | 2.552m |
| 66.000kg | 168kt | 205kt | 2.432m |
| 64.000kg | 166kt | 202kt | 2.361m |
| 62.000kg | 164kt | 200kt | 2.315m |
| 60.000kg | 162kt | 197kt | 2.246m |
| 58.000kg | 160kt | 195kt | 2.201m |

*Figure 233: Limiting takeoff weight to make radius turn smaller.*

### 3.3.4.3 Announcing Intentions to ATC after an Engine Failure on Takeoff

Many of my students often ask: What about the ATC? Do they know about our EO-SID? Well, no, they do not. Every airline may have a different one, and it is impossible to keep track of them all, especially if they change from time to time. So, it is very important to communicate your intentions clearly! But never forget your priorities: AVIATE, NAVIGATE, and only then, COMMUNICATE.

I have an example of such a situation that I would like to share with you. It happened when a Boeing 747 from British Airways lost its number 3 engine (right inboard) while taking off from Phoenix, USA. The sequence of events is textbook flying and managing! Look for it on YouTube. This video is a MUST-watch.

After becoming airborne, the tower advised the crew of what they saw: "Speedbird 38P heavy, be advised, it looks like your number 3 or 4 engine has sparks coming out of it." To which the pilot replied: "Yes, Speedbird 38P heavy, standby." This means the pilot is now focusing on flying the airplane and dealing with the situation. After a few moments, the pilot came back to ATC and said: "MAYDAY-MAYDAY-MAYDAY, Speedbird 38P, we have an engine shutdown. We are continuing to SPRKY, it will be a right turn direct to Willie, that's IWA, climbing to 6000 feet, and we'll take up the hold at IWA. We will let you know further intentions."

Absolutely brilliant! I have no other words to describe that! The pilot issued the alert (mayday call three times), advised the nature of the problem, and notified their intentions for lateral and vertical navigation! Perfect!

### 3.4.1 Minimum Takeoff Flight Path

Two steps taken. We got off the ground and made sure we did not hit anything. But what if there were no obstacles for takeoff? Would it be possible to depart with a weight that would allow us to get off the ground, but not to go up and force us to fly only by making use of ground-effect, like some seaplanes from the past? No, of course not. Regulations requires minimal airplane climb capability after takeoff, even if there are no obstacles to overcome.

Takeoff was divided into four distinct segments. On each segment, legislators established a minimum amount of excess energy that the airplane must have for a given configuration. This excess of energy is the gradient shown in the comparative table between segments below.

Each segment has its own goal, and the table is showing the way to accomplish that objective. The goal of the first segment is to retract the landing gear. The goal of the second segment is to climb until acceleration altitude. The goal of the third segment is to accelerate the airplane to final takeoff speed, also known as final segment speed. Finally, the goal of the fourth segment is to climb to 1,500ft or reach a safe altitude that clears all relevant obstacles in the area, whichever is higher.

| 1<sup>st</sup> Takeoff Segment | |
| --- | --- |
| Thrust | off Thrust |
| Speed | |
| Climb Grad. | / 0.3% / 0.5% |

| 2<sup>nd</sup> Takeoff Segment | |
| --- | --- |
| Thrust | Takeoff Thrust |
| Speed | V2 |
| Climb Grad. | 2.4% / 2.7% / 3.0% |

| 3<sup>rd</sup> Takeoff Segment | |
| --- | --- |
| Thrust | off Thrust |
| Speed | lerating |
| Climb Grad.* | / 1.5% / 1.7% |

| 4<sup>th</sup> Takeoff Segment | |
| --- | --- |
| Thrust | Max. Continuous Thru |
| Speed | Final Takeoff Speed |
| Climb Grad. | 1.2% / 1.5% / 1.7% |

Several explanations are required on top of this summary table, starting with the fact that for all these minimum gradients, it is assumed that the critical engine has failed at $V_{EF}$. Let me emphasize: the airplane must be able to accomplish all those tasks with one engine inoperative!

1.  In the line referring to Climb Grad, there are always three different values that refer to two-, three- and four-engine aircraft, respectively, always considering their critical engine inoperative since $V_{EF}$.
2.  The acceleration altitude can be any altitude above the minimum value of 400ft above field elevation.
3.  The climb gradient reported in the second segment is not an average value, but a momentary gradient observed at the exact moment that the landing gear has finished being retracted. The airplane will lose thrust as it climbs and this gradient is expected to decrease until reaching acceleration altitude.
4.  The climb gradient reported in the third segment does not seem to make much sense, since starting and ending the segment at the same altitude should represent a 0% gradient. This gradient will be explained in details in a moment.
5.  $V_{FTO}$, Final Takeoff Speed, is a speed at which the airplane will continue to climb after the flap has been retracted. It is also known as Engine Out Takeoff Speed or Final Segment Speed, and must be at least 18% higher than $V_{S1G}$ ($1.18V_{S1G}$) in clean configuration.
6.  The term obstacle free in the fourth segment refers to an altitude at which the aircraft is clear of relevant obstacles, and as mentioned before, this happens once you reach altitudes such as Minimum Vector Altitude (MVA), Minimum Safe Altitude (MSA), or Minimum Enroute Altitude (MEA). The final altitude of the segment will be this one or 1,500ft AFE, whichever is higher.

### 3.4.1.1   *Leveled Flight with 1.2% Climb Gradient! How is that Possible?*

One thing I have not covered yet is how we can measure and calculate such a gradient. Well, since it is a percentage, measuring the gradient is quite simple: it is about how much the airplane can go up or down over a given distance covered. Here is an example:

The plane climbs 60 feet in 500 meters flown forward. The first thing to do is to convert both measurements to the same unit. You can either convert the height to meters or the distance to feet. I chose to convert the height to meters, and to do so, I just multiplied the value by 0.3049. Thus, 60 feet is equal to 18.3 meters. 18.3 divided by 500 is equal to 0.0366, which corresponds to a 3.66% climb gradient. In summary, for every 100 meters traveled forward, the altitude changes by 3.66 meters.

Now that we have established how to measure a climb gradient, can we somehow foresee the gradient that an aircraft could achieve?

Yes! The climb gradient that an aircraft will be able to perform is a reflection of its excess thrust (thrust minus drag) divided by its weight. However, there are two things that an airplane can do when it has excess thrust: either climb or accelerate! Let's take a closer look at this equation: (T-D)/W.

If thrust minus drag results in a positive number, it means the airplane can climb or accelerate. If this number is equal to zero, the airplane can only maintain altitude and speed. Finally, if the result is a negative number, the airplane will either lose speed or altitude! Now, have a look at the following graphic.

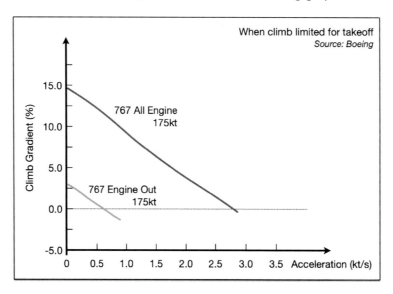

*Figure 234: Acceleration capability versus climb capability.*

This graph shows a Boeing 767 at a given weight, altitude, and speed. At this exact moment, when using all its engines, the airplane is able to achieve almost a 15% climb gradient or accelerate about 2.8 knots per second in level flight. On the other hand, with one engine out, the airplane can only climb at a 2.6% gradient or accelerate 0.6 knots per second. The question is: do you think it is a good idea to try to accomplish both tasks (climb and accelerate) at the same time? The answer is: it depends! It depends on whether we have all engines working or if there is an engine failure.

Considering an all-engine scenario, if we split the excess energy to perform both tasks (50% of that energy to each task), we would still be able to climb at a 7.5% climb gradient and accelerate 1.3 knots per second while climbing. That is what usually happens during everyday takeoffs when the airplane does not lose an engine at V1. However, if the worst happens and we lose one engine during takeoff, the airplane will have so little excess energy that we must do one thing at a time! Upon reaching the acceleration altitude, we must maintain level flight and focus solely on accelerating the aircraft.

Regarding the 1.2% climb gradient on the third segment (for twin engines), pilots often misinterpret this part of the rule. It does not say that the airplane MUST CLIMB with that gradient. It says that the airplane MUST HAVE this excess energy at any point above 400 feet to be ABLE TO ACCELERATE. Legislators could have written it differently, asking for the airplane to have an amount of excess energy equal to being able to accelerate X knots per second. But instead, they ask for excess energy using a unit of climb gradient. The aircraft is not intended to climb during the third segment; it is supposed to use this energy to accelerate.

### 3.4.2   Climb Limited Weight

Finally, the maximum weight in which the airplane is able to accomplish ALL of these four segments is known as **Climb Limited Takeoff Weight**. ANY of the segment's requirements may act as a limiting factor, but the second one is most often responsible for establishing this maximum weight.

The red line in the figure below indicates the area legislators request the manufacturer to demonstrate the airplane has a minimum excess energy that is equivalent to a climb gradient of 1.2, 1.5 or 1.7% depending on the number of engines it has.

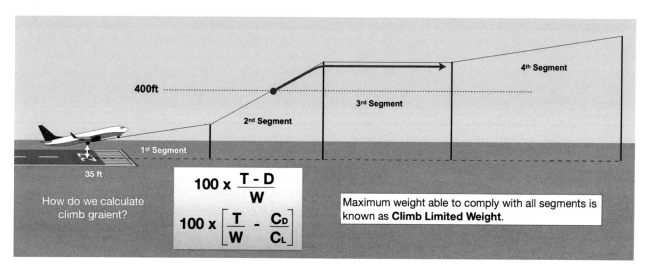

*Figure 235: All four takeoff segments.*

### 3.4.3   Acceleration Altitude and Level Off Limited Takeoff Weight

The acceleration altitude is an interesting point to be studied. It can be any altitude above 400ft, so what makes the operator choose the altitude to be used? Well, several factors must be assessed to answer this question. Let's see some of them.

The presence or absence of obstacles is an aspect that must be taken into account. When there are medium height obstacles relatively close to the runway, it is necessary to choose an acceleration altitude that is higher than these obstacles to avoid heavy weight penalties, or to design complex special procedures (contingency procedures developed by the operator to be performed in case of emergency).

Legislation regarding aircraft engines says that every engine must receive certification for two different aspects:

Maximum takeoff and go around thrust (TOGA): thrust that the engine must be able to maintain for at least 5 minutes without exceeding operational limits.

Maximum continuous thrust (MCT): amount of thrust that the engine must be able to deliver continuously without exceeding operational limits.

Maximum climb and maximum cruise thrust are usually listed in the operations manual, but they are not values that need to be certified by aeronautical authorities, so they are not listed in the AFM (Airplane Flight Manual). The 5-minute limit of TOGA thrust is an issue that must be assessed by the operator, too.

The higher the acceleration altitude is, the longer the aircraft will take to reach the end of the third segment. Remember that the pilot will fly with TOGA until the end of this segment, and only then, thrust will be set to MCT. When the chosen acceleration altitude leaves us at the end of the third segment with exactly 5 minutes elapsed from the start of takeoff run, we say that the takeoff weight was limited because of this choice, that is, **Level Off Limited Takeoff Weight**. It is easier to understand this as a limit if you try to find out what would happen if you chose a higher acceleration altitude. As you would have to climb a bit more, it would take you longer to get there, overshooting the maximum time of 5 minutes. The option would be cutting weight. Then, lighter, you could get to the end of third segment within 5 minutes again.

Now, suppose that at a certain high elevation airport, a high acceleration altitude is chosen – 1,300ft AFE, for example. Since 1,000ft AFE you are already Level Off limited. Repeating: this means that in order to use 1,300ft as acceleration altitude, you were required to reduce the takeoff weight to guarantee the third segment ends within the 5-minute limit of engine thrust. But is there any way to increase the acceleration altitude to 1,300ft while maintaining the same weight that we had with 1,000ft of acceleration altitude and the same takeoff flap?

There is a technique called improved climb, which will be addressed in the next topic, but other than that there are two options that might work. First: it is possible to do an alternate takeoff procedure in which the pilot will use TOGA thrust just until the end of the second segment and then fly the third segment (flap retraction) with MCT. There is no need to purchase any kind of additional certification to do this and only crew training is required to perform this different procedure. The positive side is that you can use all 5 minutes of TOGA that you have available for the sole purpose of climbing (1st and 2nd segments), without having to use this time during acceleration (3rd segment). Such a procedure is known as **Extended Second Segment**.

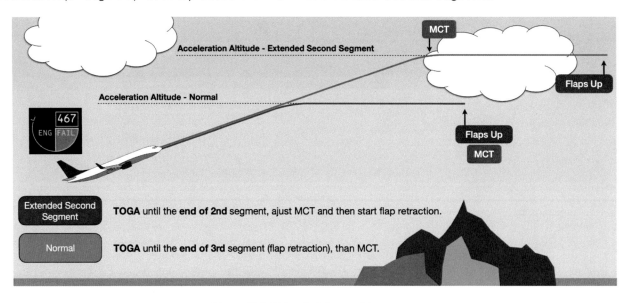

*Figure 236: Extended Second Segment.*

Second: you can search for a different certification (read: more expensive) with the aircraft manufacturer so that you can use TOGA thrust for up to 10 minutes instead of 5. To this end, in addition to paying more money for the aircraft, the airline will have to change some engine maintenance parameters. But aside from paying more and having changes in the maintenance cycles of that aircraft's engine, the plane and the engine are the same as the aircraft with the basic 5-minute TOGA thrust certification.

Of course, when using a 10-minute limit on TOGA thrust you can basically choose whatever acceleration altitude you would like! This certification is often used by airlines operating at very high elevation airports, but we will see more about this in a future chapter.

In addition to the issue of obstacles, the choice of acceleration altitude can have a huge impact on the airline's fuel costs over a year of operation. Let's take as an example a Boeing 737-800 with an average takeoff weight of 65,000kg.

If we consider takeoffs with flaps 5 and departing from sea level, the difference in total fuel consumption for an acceleration altitude of 400ft (the minimum required by law) and 800ft is about 5kg. For a single flight, this is not significant, but suppose a company that operates 1,000 takeoffs per day. In this case, 5,000kg of fuel will be saved every day. Over the course of one year, close to 2,3 million liters of fuel can be saved, considering the average fuel density of 0.8kg/l. Multiply that by the cost of a single liter (let's estimate it at $0.50) and savings can surpass $1,100,000.00.

But if the numbers are so expressive, why don't we always use the lowest acceleration altitude?

There are several reasons for this, ranging from aircraft automation, flight group experience, impossibility due to climb gradients, etc. Regarding the gradient of climb being an impediment, remember that when we studied the limiting obstacles, we saw that the imaginary plane that defined the GFP could not be penetrated in any way. For SIDs, the same happens. Then, consider our aircraft in an All Engine situation to execute an SID with the following climb gradients: 8.5% until 800ft and 4.1% afterwards. See the difference between choosing an acceleration altitude of 400ft and 800ft in the figure below.

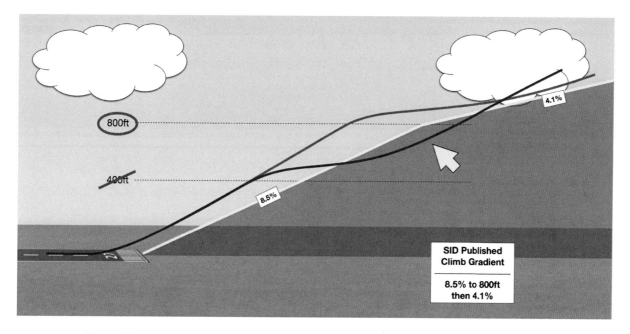

*Figure 237: Unable to choose a low acceleration altitude because of SID climb gradients.*

### 3.4.4    Comparing Climb Excess Energy of Quad- and Twin-Jets

The next graph ends our discussions about Climb Limited Takeoff Weight with some interesting facts. There, we can see a comparison in climb gradients measured at a given moment for two aircraft: a Boeing 767 (2 engines) and a Boeing 747 (4 engines). Note that they both perform almost the same climb gradient with one engine inoperative (only 0.7% difference), but the 767 performs a much higher gradient during takeoff with all engines running. This happens for a very simple reason. All these aircraft are made to be able to take off with one inoperative engine since $V_{EF}$. Then, a Boeing 767 has 100% more thrust than it needs from this point on, while a 747 has 33% of thrust to spare on takeoff with all engines running.

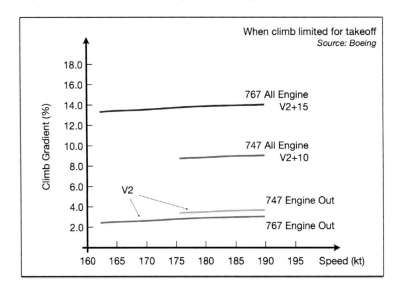

*Figure 238: Climb gradient - twin engine versus four-engine aircrafts.*

That is the reason you will rarely listen to a twin jet asking for a different SID to air traffic control when the clearance given to that airplane includes an SID with a steep minimum gradient of climb. Twin jets are often capable of accomplishing the required gradient. On the other hand, quad-engine airplanes often cannot do the same and ask for a different SID or an alternate procedure, for example, radar vectors.

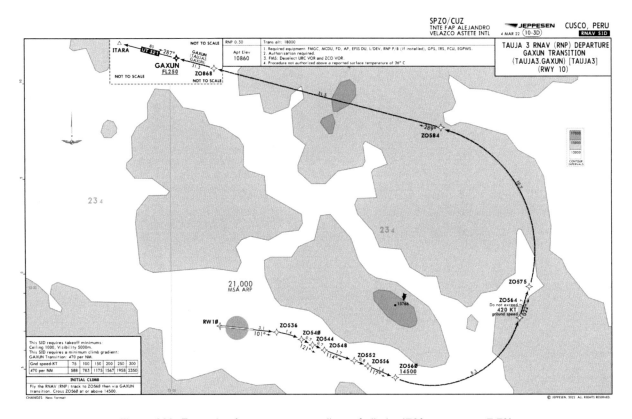

*Figure 239: Example of a very steep gradient of climb. 470ft per nm, or 7.7%.*

The use of the improved climb technique will require higher than normal takeoff speeds (V1, VR and V2). This technique consists in increasing V2 for a better climb gradient (we will see details about this in a moment) and, therefore, V1 and VR will be higher as well. This results in using much more runway than on a "regular" takeoff. That being said, we can deduce that runway length must not be an issue; in other words, our maximum takeoff weight must not be field limited.

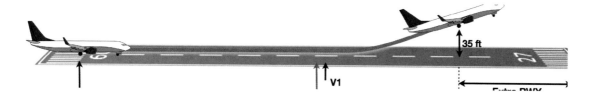

*Figure 240: Condition to use the improved climb technique.*

Before starting any discussion regarding the Improved Climb technique, let's talk briefly about a speed called "best angle of climb" speed. During a flight, pilots might slow down or accelerate the aircraft while maintaining a constant altitude. By doing so, he/she will identify the speed at which less thrust is needed to keep the aircraft stabilized. Lower or higher speeds than this one will require more thrust to maintain steady flight. The reason lies in the balance between two drag curves: induced drag and parasite drag (we saw this in Physics of Flight). By reducing speed, parasitic drag decreases, but induced drag increases, and vice versa. The speed that we need is the one where overall drag has the lowest value, and this speed is going to be the best angle of climb speed.

In the equation that calculates climb gradient, we saw that this gradient is the result of excess thrust (thrust minus drag) divided by the aircraft's weight. Considering thrust and weight as constant values, there will be more excess thrust at the speed at which drag is minimum, that is, we will have the highest climb gradient.

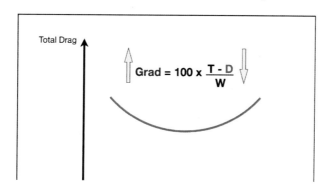

*Figure 241: Minimum drag equals to maximum climb gradient.*

So, let's study a hypothetical situation considering a constant engine thrust during climb and observe what happens to the angle (or gradient) of climb as we change speeds. Basically, the graph for this situation will be a curve mirrored to that of the drag in Figure 241. The closer to a lower drag speed, the higher the climb gradient. This will be our best angle of climb speed.

Imagine a 737-800 taking off from any location. You need to take off weighing 68,000kg, but you are climb limited to 66,000kg. This means that the weight of 66 tons is the highest in which the aircraft will be able to meet the requirements of all four takeoff segments. Although any one of the four segments may be the limiting factor, let's assume that it is the 2.4% gradient imposed by the second segment that has limited our maximum takeoff weight. This is shown in the next figure.

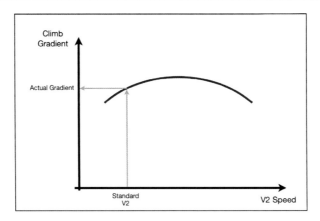

*Figure 242: Standard V2 and climb gradient achieved by it.*

Standard V2 did not allow the aircraft to reach the required gradient at the desired takeoff weight of 68,000kg. However, if we can increase V2, we will gain an extra gradient and will be able to meet the 2.4% rate requested in the second segment.

By how much V2 can be possibly increased is a matter of comparing climb limit and field limit weights. The greater the difference between those two, the further V2 will be increased, and weight gain will also be higher over the climb limited takeoff weight. However, even with the Improved Climb technique, it will never be possible for the new maximum takeoff weight to be equal to the field limited weight. The result will always be something in between the "original" field and climb limits.

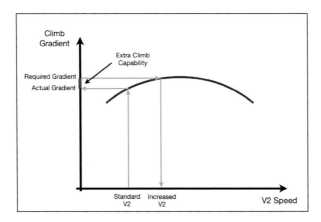

*Figure 243: Increasing V2 and climb gradient.*

When takeoff performance weight is climb limited, we can always execute an Improved Climb and obtain an extra weight. When takeoff is obstacle limited, however, this may or may not be true. We have seen that this technique increases the climb gradient. Well, by increasing the climb gradient, we may assume that the technique can be applied every time performance is obstacle limited. But that is not true. It will be an option to apply improved climb depending on obstacle location, because even if the climb path is steeper, it will commence at a point closer to the end of the runway, i.e., also closer to the obstacle itself. When the obstacle that limits takeoff weight is very close to the runway, the fact that the airplane takes off closer to it means that the aircraft will not be able to overcome this obstacle with the minimum height required by the regulation.

Take a look at the next two figures (244 and 245). They illustrate this explanation clearly. In the first figure, there is a distant obstacle that was not overcome with a normal takeoff, but pilots could perform an Improved Climb technique for that weight and then meet the required gradient and surpass the obstacle with the minimum margin demanded by law.

In the second figure, the obstacle is very close to the runway. When Improved Climb was performed, in this case, the flight path started closer to the obstacle and although the climb gradient was greater than the previous one, the obstacle could not be overcome with the minimum clearance required by regulation.

Figure 244: Improved Climb when obstacle limited by a distant obstacle.

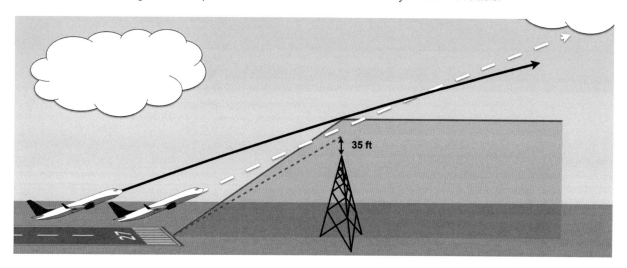

Figure 245: Improved Climb when obstacle limited by a close obstacle.

In short: We can always do Improved Climb when originally Climb limited. We can sometimes perform an IC when the limiting factor is Obstacle. But we definitely can never execute IC when limited by Field, Tire Speed* or Brake Energy*. Performing IC has no influence on Return to Land* limit weight and the weight resulting from the use of the technique is called **Improved Climb Limited Takeoff Weight**. Be patient, will see those three limiting factors marked with an (*) further down below.

Please pay attention to a fact that can sometimes be misleading to pilots. The Improved Climb technique consists of an increase in V2 speed. V1 and VR will also change (they will increase), but it is only a consequence of what had happened to V2. The increase in V1 and VR did not change our climb gradient, V2 did.

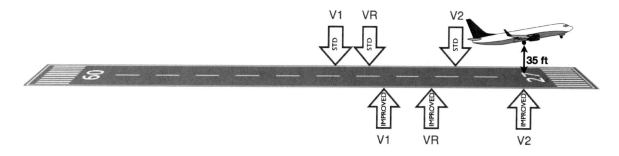

Figure 246: Standard and improved climb VSpeeds.

In addition to increasing the maximum takeoff weight, there are several other advantages in performing an improved climb, and it is highly recommended to do so whenever possible. Here are some of these advantages:

1. It allows a higher assumed temperature.
2. When comparing a takeoff with and without the technique, but with the same takeoff thrust setting, improved climb offers less fuel burn (fuel savings!).
3. The technique offers greater tail clearance, decreasing the chances of tail drag or tail strike.
4. The airplane has more energy, and this allows better controllability in the event of a windshear, for example.

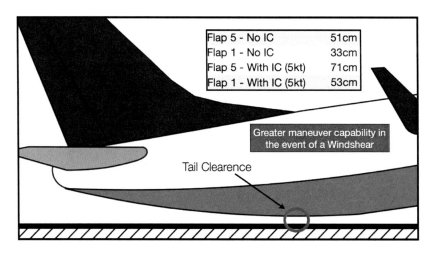

| Flap 5 - No IC | 51cm |
| Flap 1 - No IC | 33cm |
| Flap 5 - With IC (5kt) | 71cm |
| Flap 1 - With IC (5kt) | 53cm |

*Figure 247: Greater tail clearance with smaller flap setting.*

The first item mentioned on the list above was "it allows a higher assumed temperature". We will discuss details on that subject of assumed temperature later, but in short, a higher assumed temperature will result in a smaller amount of thrust being used during takeoff. Let me show you an example of that happening when taking off a Boeing 737-Max8 from Orlando International airport (KMCO).

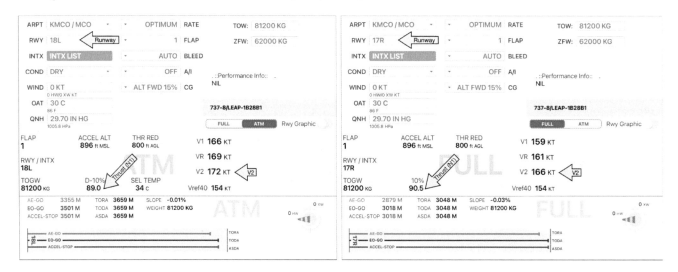

*Figure 248: Performance comparison between Rwy 18L and Rwy 17R at Orlando Intl.*

Runway 17R in Orlando is 10,000ft (3,048m) long, while runway 18L is 12,000ft (3,659m) in length. Importantly, the only difference between both takeoff performance analyses presented above is the runway in use for departure. Weather data and the airplane's weight are the same. This extra 2,000ft of runway allowed the airplane to accelerate a bit more and use a higher V2 (172kt against 166kt). The higher V2 reduced total drag and therefore the airplane was able to reduce takeoff thrust (N1 was reduced from 90.5% to 89.0%), keeping the thrust to drag ratio constant anyway.

As we saw when we discussed takeoff speeds, $V_{LOF}$ can never be higher than tire speed. So, what can happen if the aircraft exceeds $V_{TIRE}$ while still on the ground?

Keeping the plane on the ground at speeds higher than the one suitable for a particular tire poses a serious risk to the aircraft. The most common failure if this occurs is the tire to lose its tread. On aircraft with engines mounted on the tail, it is very likely that this rubber will be ingested by the engine and cause serious damage to it. And this is just one possible problem. Damage to the wing and fuel tank is another example that happened in the Concorde accident. In this tragic event, the tires did not fail because speed was exceeded, but because of FOD (Foreign Object Damage); however, the accident shows the destructive power of a bursting tire.

Aeronautical tires are designed to withstand major deformations at high speeds, but there is a limit. Tires fitted on Boeing 737 and A320 family have a speed limit among 225mph and 235mph depending on the model, BIAS having the lower speed limit and RADIAL, the highest. Specifications require that those tires must be able to withstand the designed speed limit being exceeded **once**.

The greatest chance of a tire failure occurring is during very heavy weight takeoffs, when rotation speed is also very high. When I talk about high speed here, I mean ground speed and not the one shown on the airplane's airspeed indicator. In addition to heavy weight, departing from a high elevation airport on a hot day is another factor that causes an airplane to use high takeoff speeds. Such situations are greatly aggravated in case of tailwind.

When takeoff weight results in a $V_{LOF}$ higher than the Tire Speed, the solution is to restrict VR and, consequently, to restrict $V_{LOF}$. VR restriction will determine your maximum takeoff weight for this scenario and that weight will be called **Tire Speed Limited Takeoff Weight**. You can think of increasing maximum takeoff weight by using a higher takeoff flap setting, but this will certainly decrease climb and obstacle limit weights. Ultimately, one of these two becomes the new limiting factor and MOTW with a larger flap may be lower and, therefore, this is not a solution.

Keep in mind that Tire Speed limit weight is an ALL ENGINE analysis situation. In all takeoff calculations that we have seen so far, we always considered a failure on an aircraft's critical engine at $V_{EF}$. However, when the engine fails, the acceleration rate drops and $V_{LOF}$ will be lower than it would be if all engines were running. As we must always look at the worst scenario in all performance calculations, the worst thing for the tire is lifting from the ground at a higher speed, there is, all engine takeoff.

This is an **ALL ENGINE** situation analysis

re must be able to withstand a **ONE TIME** speed exceedance to a certain value

**Example**

| Max Tire Speed | One Time Exceedance |
|---|---|
| 225mph | 250mph |
| 235mph | 260mph |

**HIGH and HOT**

*Figure 249: Maximum tire speed and tire failure.*

And there is one more thing I need to stress here. When at rotation speed, the pilot is supposed to start rotating the aircraft at a rate between two and three degrees per second. Predicted liftoff speed is based on this action. However, slower rotation rates will significantly affect takeoff distance (which will be much longer) and liftoff speed (which will be much higher).

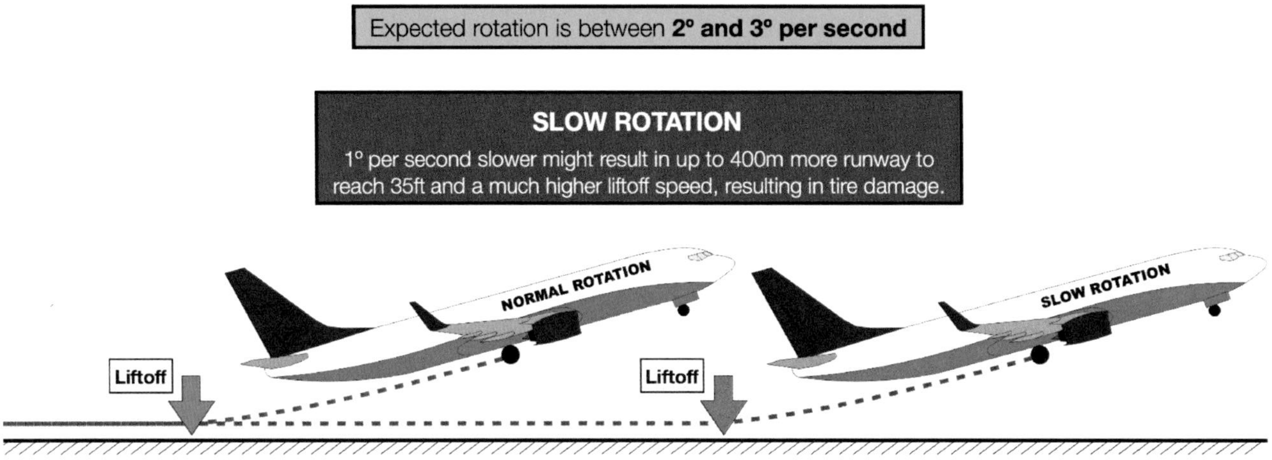

Expected rotation is between **2° and 3° per second**

**SLOW ROTATION**

1° per second slower might result in up to 400m more runway to reach 35ft and a much higher liftoff speed, resulting in tire damage.

NORMAL ROTATION

SLOW ROTATION

Liftoff

Liftoff

*Figure 250: Slow rotation can be very dangerous when you are taking off tire limited.*

As we discussed in the definition of $V_{MBE}$, it is essential that V1 is a feasible takeoff speed, meaning that the pilot can actually interrupt takeoff up to V1. For this to be possible, two factors are required: there must be enough runway ahead to stop, and the brake assembly must be capable of absorbing the RTO (Rejected Takeoff) energy.

A with $V_{TIRE}$, maximum brake energy speed refers to ground speed (GS) and is significantly affected by high elevation airport operations on hot days. These conditions are further aggravated by tailwind and negative runway slope. All these factors, combined with a high takeoff weight, may result in a very low $V_{MBE}$, which in turn means a low V1 and a low maximum takeoff weight.

The operation logic of a wheel brake is quite simple. There is a set of hydraulic pistons that, when activated, move to compress brake pads against a brake disk that spins with the wheel. In the case of a large airplane like the 737-800, each main wheel has five brake disks and ten sets of brake pads (one on each side of each disk). When compressed, the friction between the pads and the disks decelerates the airplane, but also generates a significant amount of heat. And I really mean a lot of heat!

The $V_{MBE}$ test is perhaps the second most expensive test in a certification program. In this test, the aircraft is loaded to the highest takeoff weight that the manufacturer intends to certify. With this weight and a set of 90% worn brakes, it performs a 3-mile taxi with three complete stops until it reaches the runway threshold. With this energy already accumulated in the brakes, the aircraft accelerates on the runway until reaching V1 (equal to $V_{MBE}$ in this test) and then stops. The airplane must demonstrate that it can stop within the previously calculated distance without using any other resource in addition to wheel brakes and speedbrakes. Upon stopping, the overheated brakes cannot compromise the aircraft's safety for the next 5 minutes – this is the estimated time for firefighters to arrive at the scene. Although the test is conducted with 90% worn brakes, the data collected is mathematically extrapolated to represent what would happen with 100% worn brakes. This latter value is used for calculating the aircraft's performance in service.

*Figure 251: Brake system and tire expansion resulting from brake heating.*

The energy of a stop like this is enormous and, as I mentioned, a great deal of it turns into heat in the brake set. This heat is transferred to the gas inside the tire, which expands and greatly increases the tire's internal pressure. To protect the assembly from an ultimate explosion, metal fuse plugs are installed on the wheels. On the 737, there are five plugs on each wheel. One is facing outward, opposite the tire valve, and is an overinflation plug designed to pop once the tire pressure reaches 450 psi (normal tire pressure is 200 psi). The other four are in the inner part of the wheel and are designed to melt at a certain temperature. Both types of plugs have the mission to allow gas to escape from the tire through the hole that is left, preventing an explosion. By the way, the gas inside the tire is not air like in car tires, but nitrogen, an inert gas that does not serve as an oxidizer and does not feed any fire in the brake set.

Having your weight limited by brake energy means that the V1 that determined your weight initially is not allowed because it was above the $V_{MBE}$. V1 was then reduced and weight was adjusted accordingly to accommodate the new V1. When this happens, we call the resulting weight **Brake Energy Limited Takeoff Weight**.

*Figure 252: Fuse pressure plug on the wheel of a Boeing 737.*

*Figure 253: Fuse temperature plug on the wheel of a Boeing 737.*

This takeoff limit applies only to aircraft designed later than 2006, such as Boeing 737MAX, 787, 747-8, Airbus A350, A320Neo, Embraer E2 Series, among others. Aircraft designed previously, regardless of the year of manufacture, are exempt from complying with this limitation.

The line of thought when editing FAR Part 25 and including this new rule was as follows: what if we have to return after takeoff? Although an aircraft emergency was not originally considered, a medical emergency is a possibility.

It was established by FAR 25.1001 that the aircraft must be able to meet the minimum go around gradients established in the regulation that deals with landing performance. There are some criteria:

1. Maximum structural landing weight will not be considered as a limiting factor to return, of course.
2. The aircraft is expected to takeoff, climb to 5,000ft AFE, and then return for landing.
3. Aircraft that do not have a fuel jettison system must consider a fuel burn equivalent to 15 minutes of flight to establish the landing weight that will be used in calculations (ATOW minus 15 min of fuel burn).
4. Aircraft which have a fuel jettison system available must expect 15 minutes of fuel burning and another 15 minutes of fuel dumping to set the landing weight to be used in calculations (ATOW minus 15 min of fuel burn minus 15 min of fuel dump).

After the landing weight has been established, the airplane must be able to meet two requirements known as Landing Climb and Approach Climb minimum gradients. The former considers an all-engine situation and the latter takes into account the critical engine inoperative. The other considerations for each requirement are shown in the figure below. V$_{REF}$ and V$_{REF}$ plus 5kt are the speeds that will be used to check whether or not the aircraft is able to comply with the established gradients. V

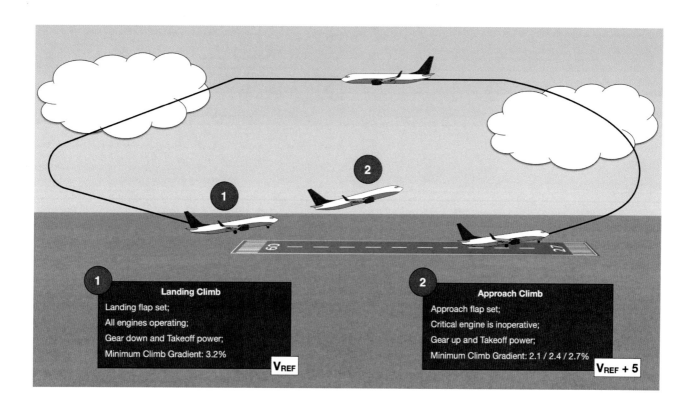

**1** Landing Climb
Landing flap set;
All engines operating;
Gear down and Takeoff power;
Minimum Climb Gradient: 3.2%
V$_{REF}$

**2** Approach Climb
Approach flap set;
Critical engine is inoperative;
Gear up and Takeoff power;
Minimum Climb Gradient: 2.1 / 2.4 / 2.7%
V$_{REF}$ + 5

The objective of this regulation is to ensure that the aircraft can return if necessary, complying with the same go around requirements that must be met by aircraft arriving at their final destination.

The names of those requirements are a bit misleading. The first one, called Landing Climb, refers to landing configuration, i.e., flaps and landing gear extended. There is a single climb gradient of 3.2% to be met by any aircraft because this minimum climb is a requirement that considers all engines operating.

The second requirement, Approach Climb, considers the critical engine as inoperative. With one less engine, an aircraft equipped with 4-engines loses 25% of thrust, while a 3-engine airplane loses 33% and a twin-engine loses 50% of the available thrust. Therefore, it would be unfair to ask everyone to develop the same climb capability in this situation. For this reason, there is a different gradient requirement for each one.

Again, a misleading name. Approach climb requirement refers to a missed approach configuration, that is, missed approach flap setting and landing gear already retracted. In this case, however, critical engine is considered to have failed during a missed approach.

In both cases, performance calculations must be made while considering the actual temperature and the elevation of the runway itself, even if it is reasonable to assume that go around will commence at a slightly higher altitude.

When you are taking off at the maximum weight possible to accomplish the exact minimum climb requirement upon returning to land, either for landing climb or approach climb, after burning the above-mentioned amount of fuel, such takeoff weight is called the **Fuel Jettison Limited Takeoff Weight.**.

That weight is also known as **Return to Land Limited Takeoff Weight**, and it is sometimes used with this name in order not to confuse pilots when this is a limiting factor for takeoff, and the aircraft is not equipped with a fuel jettison system. In the case of the North American manufacturer, Boeing, the name Fuel Jettison is used even for aircraft that do not have the capability of dumping fuel.

*Figure 255: Fuel jettison system in use.*

# 3.9 Reduc

In the event of a small aircraft taking off, such as a Piper Arrow, for example, pilots line up the aircraft with the runway, set engine throttle to maximum thrust, and observe the airplane's acceleration. When reaching a proper speed (VR), they rotate the airplane and take flight. All this without any previous complex calculation that could tell them, more precisely, the speed to be used or the required runway length. They should do all calculations, but they rarely do. Things are often done in this empirical and unscientific way by pilots flying planes of this category.

Aircraft built according to FAR Part 25 rules, however, cannot be operated in the same way. A much more precise method is needed to define whether the aircraft can takeoff at the proposed weight and how takeoff should be performed. In the topics discussed so far, we have seen how to calculate each one of the limiting factors regarding takeoff, but what happens if we are taking off below the maximum allowable takeoff weight? This means that maximum thrust is also not necessary, and we can take off with reduced thrust. However, how much can it be reduced and how does it affect the aircraft? We will see several details about this, starting with the airplane's engine itself.

## 3.9.1 Understanding How a Jet Engine Works

Once again, the Boeing 737NG is used as an example; it is equipped with a CFM56 engine that has several variants. Take the example of the model 7B27B1. The figure below shows several parts highlighted in this engine. Let me walk you through how it works.

The air is sucked into the engine by that first giant blade painted blue. Now it has two paths to follow. Either it goes by the outside of the engine core, or it goes into the core to be compressed and burned when mixed with fuel. In this particular engine model, 5.1 times more air takes the path outside the core than flows into the compressors. We call this the bypass ratio, which is 5.1:1 in this example.

The air that goes into the engine core will start to be compressed by a sequence of moving fans, with each fan having blades closer together then the previous one. However, setting one fan behind the other poses a problem. The second fan in the row will receive air already disturbed by the first. The third will receive even more turbulent air than the previous one, and so on. To solve this problem, between every pair of fans, there are blades that do not rotate around the core; their function is to adjust the airflow to feed the next fan so that the compressor works more efficiently. We call every set of blades that rotate like a fan the "rotary stages" of the compressor. The set of blades that do not move around the core are called the "stationary stages" of the compressor. Stationary blades do not move around the engine core, but they actually move around their own axes, adjusting their angle to the one that best suits their function according to the engine thrust. All stationary stages are colored yellow in Figure 256.

In our example, we have a set of one big fan disk followed by three rotary stages, all painted blue. This blue set is called the low-pressure compressor and is normally referred to as the N1. After that, we have a new set of nine rotary stages and their stationary counterparts. They are painted red and are officially named the high-pressure compressor, but they are often called simply N2.

After being so compressed, the air has increased its temperature and pressure by a significant amount! In fact, by this point, the air is so hot that if you just mix fuel with it, the mixture will burn! So, we now reach the combustion chamber, and the fuel nozzles are right there to spray jet fuel on this hot air. And this burning gas will expand and accelerate a lot! Time to use this energy for some work!

Have you ever had a pinwheel toy? What happens when you blow on it? It spins! Well, there is a lot of gas being blown out of the combustion chamber. Just put a device like a pinwheel at the exit of this chamber and it will spin like crazy! Attach this device via a shaft to the N2, and there you have the power to move all those rotary stages.

The device that works like a pinwheel is called a turbine! If this turbine is used to transfer force and move the high-stage compressor, then it is called the high-pressure turbine, or simply HPT.

A single turbine is used to transfer force and move the N2, but there is too much energy going out of the combustion chamber! Let's put some more turbines in line here and make this new set of four be the workhorse that will move the N1 via a different shaft. A different but concentric shaft, as shown in the figure. What do we call the set of turbines that will be used to drive the low-pressure rotary stages? You guessed it! The low-pressure turbine, or simply LPT.

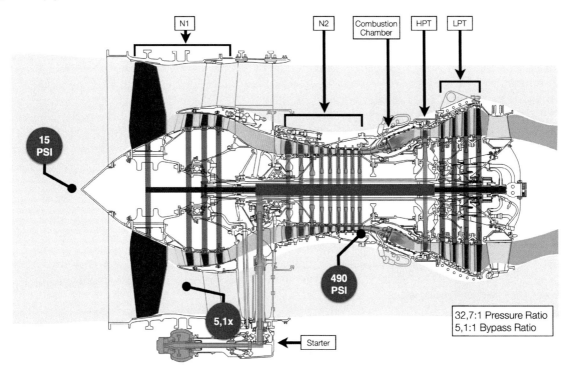

*Figure 256: CFM56-7B27B1.*

I do not know about you, but I have always wondered how to start this engine. After all, for the turbine to be able to move the shaft that drives the N1 or N2, the air must get there first. And the air will only get there after passing through the N1 and N2. So, we have an impasse here! To solve that, something has to help this system transition from being shut down to becoming a self-sustained reaction. This is what a starter does! It is responsible for turning the shaft and allowing air intake to be compressed until it is hot enough to mix with fuel. At a given point, the reaction is able to be sustained without the starter's help, and it is disengaged from the shaft.

We talked about bypass ratio, but there is another property that I believe is important to understand: Pressure Ratio. For example, this engine's pressure ratio is 32.7:1. What does it mean? Well, it means that the air pressure admitted into the engine increases 32.7 times as it passes through three stages of the low compressor and nine stages of the high compressor. At sea level, where atmospheric pressure is just short of 15 psi, we can say that, at maximum thrust, air arrives in the combustion chamber with a pressure of approximately 490 psi.

## 3.9.2   Understanding Engine Parameters

To put in round numbers, let's assume that the maximum rotation speed of N1 is 5,200RPM while that of N2 is 14,500RPM. At this rotation speed, the engine reaches a compression ratio of 32.7:1. Regulations state that the engine must be able to produce the same thrust at any temperature below what will be called the "flat rate temperature" (also known as thrust brake temperature). This temperature has a value referenced to ISA and, in this engine, it is ISA+15. Based on this information, let's see how some engine parameters behave.

At sea level, ISA+15 is equal to 30°C. If we place the engine on a test bench in a controlled environment and provide intake air at this temperature, when we move the thrust levers to TOGA, the engine will develop maximum

RPM, achieve the highest compression rate, and deliver the takeoff thrust that we wanted. However, the combustion chamber cannot receive air at a pressure higher than the value of 490psi that we had calculated. And what happens to the intake air if we cool it down?

Colder air, 10°C, for example, is also denser. If N1 and N2 rotation is maintained, air pressure entering the combustion chamber will be greater than 490psi. To prevent this from happening, the engine N1 and N2 rotation speed is decreased. It does so to ensure the integrity of the engine and not to exceed the maximum internal pressure, but the delivered thrust will be the same, since the pressure difference between the intake and exhaust air will remain the same – we call this pressure difference the EPR (engine pressure ratio), but it is not the same pressure ratio that we discussed previously.

As the air continues to be cooled, the process continues in the same way. The denser the air is, the easier it is to produce the requested thrust, which will be achieved with lower engine RPM in order not to exceed the maximum pressure it can withstand. In this temperature range, below the flat rate temperature (FRT), we say that the engine thrust is limited according to the maximum pressure supported by the combustion chamber, that is, it is a range in which engine thrust is **pressure limited**.

With increasing air pressure as it passes through the compression stages, another physical aspect of air that also changes (increases) is temperature. The air is mixed with fuel and then burned, leaves the combustion chamber, rotates the two turbines (HPT and LPT) and, finally, leaves the engine. The temperature measured at this output point is called EGT (Exhaust Gas Temperature), and a limit is set for it as well.

Still in our example, with an engine on the test bench, at sea level and with controlled temperature, if we consider the air to be very cold at intake, EGT will also be low. As we increase air temperature that is sucked in by the engine fan, EGT also rises and reaches its maximum at the flat rate temperature. It is at this point that it comes closest to its limit and manufacturers purposely leave a margin of some (or many) degrees Celsius between the maximum EGT reached on the test bench and actual design limit. The reason is simple. As the engine ages, it is natural for the measured EGT at a given thrust to be higher and higher approaching the design limit over time. If the two values (EGT at maximum thrust and EGT design limit) had been equal from the start, EGT would likely have exceeded its limit with a very short time of engine usage.

Keeping the safety margin constant as intake air increases temperature is the main goal from this point on. To prevent an increase in EGT with warmer air entering the engine, its compression rate will have to be reduced, and this will be done by decreasing the engine rotation speed. The reduction in compression rate will result in a drastic loss of thrust. This justifies the two names given to this important temperature: "thrust brake temperature", owing to a great decrease in thrust when above that temperature, or "flat rate temperature", because the graph representing engine thrust is nearly a horizontal line (flat) with temperatures below that one. At temperatures above the FRT, as the objective is to maintain the temperature value of the exhaust gases, and we say that engine thrust is **temperature limited**.

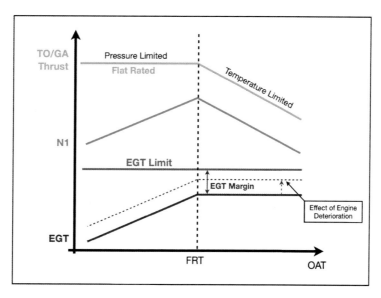

*Figure 257: Engine parameters and flat rate temperature.*

### 3.9.3   Influence of Temperature on Takeoff Performance

Just to round up values, for the time being, let's assume that the FRT of a given engine is ISA and we are at sea level, that is, FRT is equal to 15°C. In this case, as we mentioned before, as the air heats up, its density drops and so does engine thrust.

Now, assuming a given takeoff weight with VSpeeds 140kt, 145kt and 153kt, observe, in Figure 258, the runway length required for the airplane to accelerate, have the critical engine failure at $V_{EF}$, continue, and reach V2. The lower the thrust, the greater the runway length used for EO-GO, that is, the higher the temperature, the greater the runway length that the airplane needs for takeoff.

*Figure 258: Influence of temperature on takeoff distance.*

### 3.9.4   Assumed Temperature Method – ATM

The Assumed Temperature Method (ATM) or, as Airbus calls it, the Flex Temperature method, is a process based on this analysis that we have just made in the previous topic. What would be the threshold temperature for me to takeoff at my current weight? When you answer this question, you find out what the assumed temperature will be for takeoff, but what does "assume a temperature" means?

On most modern airplanes, a computer controls the engine thrust and the RPM required to deliver that thrust. Say it is 15°C outside, but at your current weight you would be able to takeoff at any temperature up to 45°C. When you "talk" to the engine computer you will mention the OAT and the assumed temperature. What the computer will read from that is: "the outside temperature is 15°C in case full thrust is needed, but please, during this particular takeoff, behave as if the OAT were 45°C and deliver the takeoff thrust accordingly".

In other words, assumed temperature means to deceive the engine, telling it that OAT is hotter than it actually is. Thus, it will produce less thrust than maximum. The objective behind such reduction is economic. It is not fuel economy, as some may think. In fact, this process causes the plane to burn a bit more fuel than it does taking off at maximum thrust (more on that when we talk about Thrust Specific Fuel Consumption). Savings are related to engine wear. Engine time on the wing can be more than doubled using the ATM technique on takeoffs and this significantly lowers the costs for aircraft operators.

There is also a second technique that can be used to reduce takeoff thrust, called derate. We will see more about this in a moment, but first let's answer a very common question: is it dangerous to reduce takeoff thrust?

The answer is NO. Quite the opposite. It is absolutely safe and highly recommended to do this whenever possible. The ATM method provides some interesting extra safety margins for our operation. The first margin concerns the engine's thrust. For example, the engine produces a bit more thrust when deceived about outside temperature as being 45°C than when temperature is actually 45°C. The second is related to the "true airspeed effect".

On the next page, you will see an illustration showing the three scenarios that I am going to describe now to explain the effect of TAS on the process. Let's get back to the example of the aircraft that will take off with a given weight and has V1, VR, and V2 equal to 140kt, 145kt and 153kt respectively. Imagine a takeoff in these conditions and with 15°C of air temperature. You could have assumed 45°C for takeoff, but you did not, and took off using maximum thrust. In this case, assuming critical engine has failed at $V_{EF}$, you reach V2 at a point somewhere in the middle of the available runway. To facilitate the analysis, I will now add two pieces of information: the airport is at sea level and the wind is calm. That way, when reaching V2, if I could use a speed trap, like the ones on city roads, I would see that the airplane's ground speed is exactly 153kt, identical to what the pilot sees in the airspeed indicator (IAS equals to GS).

In the second hypothesis, the only thing that changes is the external temperature, which is now 45°C. Once again, takeoff is made at maximum thrust and using the same VSpeeds. If the critical engine fails at $V_{EF}$, the aircraft will reach 35ft exactly at the end of the runway and if the pilot looks at the airspeed indicator, he/she will see 153kt. An external observer looking at the speed registered by the speed trap, however, will see 161kt of ground speed (same as TAS, as the wind is calm). It is a situation in which two factors influenced the result: the engine was producing less thrust owing to lower air density, and the airplane had to accelerate to a higher speed (GS) than in the previous situation, although the indicated airspeed (IAS) was the same.

In the last part of the illustration, the actual temperature is 15°C again, but this time we will use the ATM technique and "lie" to the engine that the temperature is 45°C. Once again, VSpeeds are the same and something interesting happens here. The plane has a critical engine failure at $V_{EF}$, and at 35ft over the runway the pilot will read 153kt on the airspeed indicator. This time, however, which speed would be registered on the speed trap? The same 153kt! Pilots may be able to trick the engine so that it produces less thrust, but there is no way to trick the air around the aircraft. It continues at 15°C and the airplane's ground speed will be unchanged: 153kt (equal to TAS at no wind).

The final result of this simulation is that even if engine thrust at 45°C ATM was equal to that when 45°C was the real temperature – in fact it is slightly higher – the airplane would need to accelerate to a lower speed (153 against 161kt), which is obviously reached sooner. Therefore, it will lift off using a shorter runway length. From this analysis comes the conclusion that ATM is a conservative and safe method of thrust reduction for takeoff.

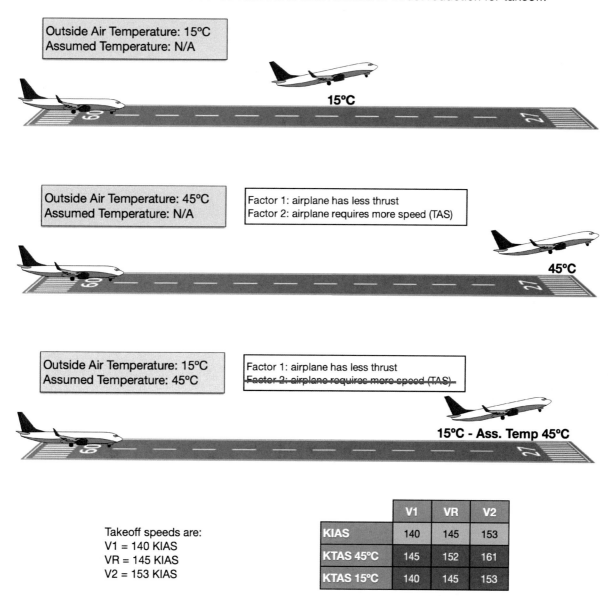

Takeoff speeds are:
V1 = 140 KIAS
VR = 145 KIAS
V2 = 153 KIAS

|  | V1 | VR | V2 |
|---|---|---|---|
| KIAS | 140 | 145 | 153 |
| KTAS 45°C | 145 | 152 | 161 |
| KTAS 15°C | 140 | 145 | 153 |

*Figure 259: Effect of TAS on TOD using ATM.*

By the way, here is a very common question: What to do if and engine fails during takeoff if we are using the assumed temperature method? I will split the question in two parts before answering it.

What **MUST** be done if you lose an engine during takeoff? **NOTHING!** All calculations were made assuming an engine would fail at VEF, therefore, even when using a reduced thrust you will be able to comply with all five take off limitations: field, climb, obstacle, tire speed, and brake energy.

What **CAN** be done if you lose an engine during takeoff? You **MAY** reestablish full takeoff thrust at any time, if you want! However, it is very important to stress that this is optional. You do not need to set full thrust to comply with takeoff limitations (field, climb, obstacle, tire speed, and brake energy).

Back to the advantages of using ATM, according to Rolls Royce, for each degree Celsius used as assumed temperature, EGT can be reduced by something between 3 and 4 degrees. CFM engines have a similar behavior, and this factor is decisive in engine's time on the wing. The less rigorous engine operation is (lower EGT), the lower the maintenance costs and the longer the service life.

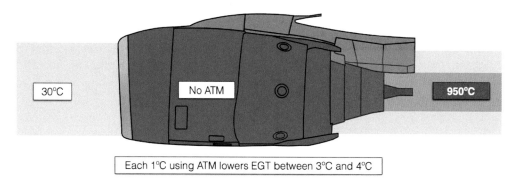

*Figure 260: Influence of ATM on the engine's EGT.*

The idea behind how to perform the assumed temperature can be seen in the following two graphs. The one on the left shows how temperature affects the Climb limited weights and the one on the right shows how it affects Field limited weights. In the case of Climb, there is virtually no variation in the maximum takeoff weight below FRT. This is because this limitation depends exclusively on excess thrust to meet the required gradient. As thrust is nearly constant, maximum climb limit takeoff weight will also be. In case of the Field limited weight, there is some loss of weight when increasing temperature until FRT is reached. After this, such loss becomes much more marked as temperature rises. The reason for that small fall in maximum weight below the FRT is that, even though the engine has relatively constant thrust, the increasingly higher TAS needed for takeoff makes us need more and more runway length. As the runway cannot be stretched, the solution is to reduce weight to get off the ground at a lower speed.

Both graphs show the values of maximum weight and maximum thrust obtained as a function of the actual temperature (orange arrows). We also identified, based on actual takeoff weight (ATOW), the assumed temperature and thrust required for takeoff (purple arrows).

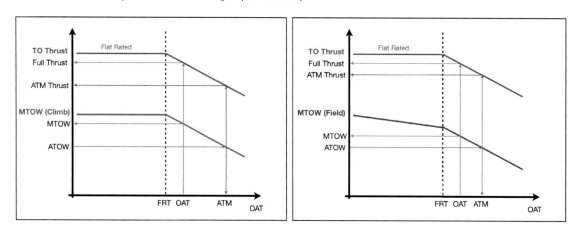

*Figure 261: MTOW for OAT and ATM for ATOW.*

## 3.9.5 Effect of Flat Rate on $V_{1(MCG)}$ and $V_{MCA}$

Now that we know that jet engine thrust does not always drop when temperature increases, can you figure out the true behavior of control speeds such as $V_{1(MCG)}$ and $V_{MCA}$? Well, I maintain what I said: when air density falls, those speeds are reduced, too. But there is something else that I need to say. In the following graph, look at engine thrust as a function of outside air temperature.

CFM 56-7B26 at sea level, static (0kt) and engine bleeds off.

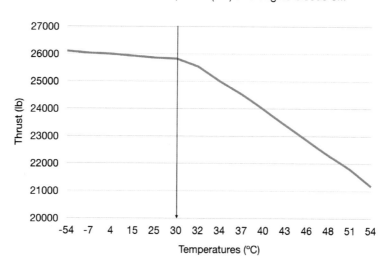

Figure 262: Engine thrust as a function of OAT.

As there is virtually no variation in thrust for temperatures below FRT, it is reasonable to assume that $V_{1(MCG)}$ and $V_{MCA}$ will also remain nearly the same for those temperatures. And this is true. These speeds barely change when they are colder than FRT. And this is due to a specific jet engine behavior imposed by regulations.

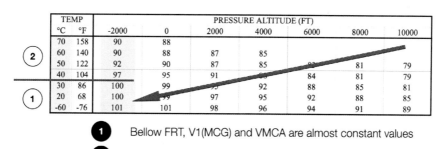

**1** Bellow FRT, V1(MCG) and VMCA are almost constant values

**2** Above FRT, V1(MCG) and VMCA decrease fast

Figure 263: V1(MCG) behavior as a function of FRT.

## 3.9.6 Derated Thrust for Takeoff

Another technique that can also be used to lower engine thrust and reduce engine wear is called Derate. This method consists in adjusting maximum engine thrust to a lower value. To better understand this, let's see in a little more depth how an engine works to deliver the thrust requested by the pilot.

If we open the engine cowl, between pipes, valves and electrical wires passing by, we will find something very similar to a computer CPU tower, the same as the ones we have at home (before they were integrated into the monitor). This unit has different names depending on the engine manufacturer, and I will mention two of them: FADEC, Full Authority Digital Engine Control and EEC, Electronic Engine Control. The latter is a kind of cousin to the former with some fewer functions, but the basic functioning is similar enough to consider them equal in this book.

This computer has a plug with a set of pins attached to it (similar to a computer VGA cable, but round shaped). Depending on the number of pins present in the plug, the computer identifies the maximum thrust the engine must deliver. When the airline buys an aircraft, it usually comes with several engine thrust options. It is like when we buy a car, but unlike this one, the engine is really no different. It is exactly the same engine with a different plug on the computer that electronically tells the engine what maximum thrust it should produce. At any time, the operator can pay an extra and change the airplane's thrust by simply replacing this plug. This maximum thrust is called Engine Rate.

*Figure 264: FADEC on the left and EEC on the right.*

Making a Derate, however, does not mean opening the engine cowl and changing the EEC or FADEC plug. Derate is made from inside the cockpit, from the airplane's flight computer (Flight Management Computer – FMC for Boeing, Flight Management and Guidance System – FMGS for Airbus). With the simple click of a button, you ask the computer to have the engine behave as if it were an engine with a lower thrust plug on it. It is as simple as that. The computer that controls the engine will respond to this request.

One of the main differences (but not the only one) between Derate and the ATM is that in Derate, a new maximum thrust is established, so it is considered as a limiting factor and **MUST NOT** be overcome during takeoff. On the other hand, when using ATM, the smallest thrust is not a limit and, as I said, the pilot is allowed to advance the throttles, recovering maximum thrust at any time during takeoff. The reason for this will be explained shortly.

As can be seen in the following illustration, the maximum Rate for this aircraft is 26,000 pounds of thrust or 26K. When selecting TO-1, the maximum Rate was reduced to 24,000 pounds (24K) and when selecting TO-2 the maximum Rate was reduced to 22,000 pounds. The combination of this technique with ATM is permitted by law, but different manufacturers use different criteria on this subject.

Regulation allows maximum thrust to be reduced up to 25% for takeoff. In Boeing's interpretation, maximum thrust is established by selecting the takeoff Rate and a further 25% reduction can be included in this value using ATM. For example, in the case of FMC in Figure 265, a pilot could, if allowed by the airplane's performance, make a Derate for 22K and assume a temperature that would decrease thrust by another 25%. When doing that, 26,000lb becomes 22,000lb, which will be reduced by 25% through ATM to end up with 16,500lb of thrust (sea level, ISA atmosphere).

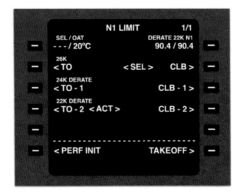

*Figure 265: Engine derate selected on the airplane's computer (FMC).*

According to Airbus, the ATM and the Derate methods cannot be combined. Pilots must choose either Derate or Flex Temperature. That is due to the different thrust lever design by Airbus. I will soon explain that in detail. In any case, a thrust reduction limit of 25% will be established regarding the engine's nominal rate. For an engine with the same thrust as our Boeing example (26,000lb), thrust could be reduced to 19,500lb, either using Derate or Flex Temperature, since we are talking about an engine on an Airbus aircraft.

To find out which assumed temperature generates 25% thrust loss, there is a table on aircraft manuals with this information, but something that we have not mentioned yet is whether or not there is a minimum temperature to assume. Yes, there is! Look at the next illustration and you will see something interesting. Imagine that FRT in this case is 30°C (ISA+15 at sea level). Suppose the OAT is 10°C. Would it be possible to assume 25°C? The answer is no. And the reason is, as often, simple. The objective of using an assumed temperature is to reduce engine thrust. Thrust is only reduced at temperatures above FRT, after all, at any temperature below that, engine thrust is essentially the same. So, why would the computer accept input values lower than 30°C (ISA+15)?

The maximum assumed temperature will be the one which generates a 25% thrust reduction and the minimum assumed temperature is the correspondent FRT for the airport's elevation. But be careful: any assumed temperature must always be higher than the OAT (Outside Air Temperature). There is no way to assume a colder temperature than the real one to try to increase engine thrust. Imagine that the OAT is 33°C within the same scenario. Even if the FRT is 30°C, the lowest temperature we can assume in this case would be 34°C. So, to sum up, minimum assumed temperature is FRT or OAT plus 1°C, whichever is higher.

**Note about ATM:** some airplanes (like B777 and A330) have been granted a special certification that allows thrust reduction up to 40% by using the assumed temperature method, instead of a default 25%.

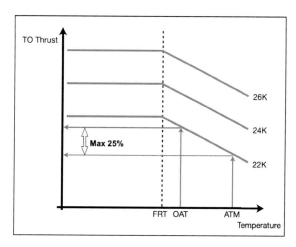

*Figure 266: Maximum thrust reduction.*

## 3.9.7   Limitations regarding the use of ATM and Derate

In addition to the fact that the new thrust is considered as a limit in Derate while in the assumed temperature method it is not, there are other very important differences between the two techniques.

**ATM:** maximum thrust reduction of 25%. Not allowed on sleeper or contaminated runways, or with anti-skid inoperative. $V_{1(MCG)}$ must always be calculated on the basis of the maximum thrust of the selected rate for takeoff.

**Derate:** there are no operational restrictions. It can be used whenever allowed by the airplane's performance. It can, in very specific cases, be used to increase the maximum takeoff weight.

I will get into details and explain how the weakest engine could carry more weight than the strongest one, but first let me explain the operational difference between Boeing and Airbus and why one can combine both methods while the other cannot.

All Boeing airplanes have a freely moving thrust lever. Ranging from idle to full forward (we call it "firewall"), the lever angle is read by a computer and transformed into a thrust setting (N1). Now, let's say our airplane has a couple of engines producing 26,000lb of thrust each, and that thrust is achieved on takeoff when N1 is at 99% with an outside air temperature of 20°C. Now we will analyze three different scenarios.

**ATM, only:** In the first scenario, we used an assumed temperature (ATM) of 45°C and N1 was reduced to 95% during takeoff. What MUST we do if an engine fails on takeoff? NOTHING! But are we allowed to recover full thrust? Yes, we are, and you can push the levers forward to 99% if you like.

**Derate, only:** In the second scenario, we decided to use a derate to 24K, and coincidentally the resulting N1 was the same as before, 95%. What MUST we do if an engine fails on takeoff? NOTHING! But are we allowed to recover full thrust like we did using ATM? NO! Definitely not! This thrust must be considered a new limit during takeoff because control speeds ($V_{MCA}$ and $V_{1(MCG)}$) were calculated based on this new maximum thrust.

**Derate combined with ATM:** In the third scenario, we decided to use a derate to 24K and additionally assume a temperature of 40°C, resulting in an N1 of 89%. What MUST we do if an engine fails on takeoff? NOTHING! But are we allowed to recover full thrust? Yes, but only up to the maximum thrust available for 24K, which is 95% N1! You must be careful not to advance the thrust levers beyond this position during takeoff.

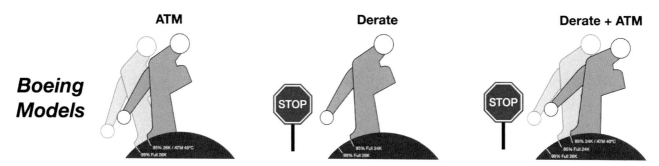

*Figure 267: Why Boeing allows to combine Derate and ATM.*

Now, let's discuss the European counterpart, Airbus. The airplanes designed by Airbus all share a similar thrust lever design (from the A320 onward). That thrust lever is almost redundant. Many pilots flying Airbus often say that a set of push buttons would do the job just as well. Airbus uses a lever mainly because pilots are accustomed to this method for setting thrust. However, by doing so, they introduced a whole new philosophy to the industry and created what they call "thrust detents." These include the idle detent, a very small free range for flying "manually", climb detent (CLB), flex detent (FLEX), and takeoff or go-around detent (TOGA).

When taking off using full takeoff thrust, the TOGA detent should be used. When using a flex temperature, the FLEX detent is the one to select. But what should we do when using derate? Again, the FLEX detent is used! The computer will set the thrust according to the selected parameter, either flex temperature or derate. Now that we know that, let's examine the three scenarios:

**ATM, only:** The pilot will set the thrust lever to FLEX, and the computer will deliver the appropriate N1 and thrust. And what MUST we do if an engine fails on takeoff? NOTHING! But are we allowed to recover full thrust? Yes! You can push the lever forward to the next detent, TOGA.

**Derate, only:** The pilot will set the thrust lever to FLEX, and the computer will deliver the appropriate N1 and thrust. And what MUST we do if an engine fails on takeoff? NOTHING! But are we allowed to recover full thrust as we did using FLEX? No! You MUST leave the thrust lever where it is, at FLEX.

**Derate combined with ATM:** Since there is no detent that allows you to recover the reduced margin from FLEX to the derated thrust, combining both methods is an impossible task.

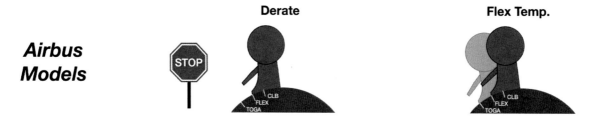

*Figure 268: Why you cannot combine derate and flex thrust on Airbus.*

Is there any exception to the rule of not being able to go full thrust when using derate? Yes, there is one. In the case of terrain or windshear avoidance, all flight crew training manuals always state the same: full throttle! That means TOGA detent for Airbus and Firewall for Boeing! And there is no immediate risk associated with that. Why not? Because there is no asymmetric thrust! Any danger in going full throttle is linked to the loss of directional control, but that risk does not exist if there is no engine failure.

Okay, after that explanation, I am always asked the following question: What if I lose the engine at $V_{EF}$ and encounter windshear just after liftoff? Well, I am awfully sorry to tell you this, but I guess you are the unluckiest pilot in the whole universe, and you must have done something very, very bad to deserve that!

### 3.9.8    $V_{1(MCG)}$ Limited Takeoff Weight

Among the statements made about ATM and Derate, two need to be explained better.

When we talk about $V_{1(MCG)}$ being calculated for the maximum thrust rate, this has everything to do with the fact that thrust can be recovered during takeoff. Remember that $V_{1(MCG)}$ defines the lowest possible V1 and is directly affected by thrust. A high thrust results in a high $V_{1(MCG)}$.

In Figure 269, you can see N1 rotation speed instead of thrust, but you can say that for the same temperature and altitude, N1 is directly proportional to thrust. Therefore, in our example, at a nominal Rate of 26K, the N1 to be used is 99% and $V_{1(MCG)}$ is 106kt.

When we reduce thrust to 24K using derate, $V_{1(MCG)}$ also decreases; however, when we further reduce thrust using the ATM method, $V_{1(MCG)}$ does not change at all. Why? We have the right to advance thrust levers and recover the thrust until the limit of the selected rate. And that is why $V_{1(MCG)}$ must be calculated considering this amount of force! It is done to guarantee lateral control even in a situation in which the pilot chooses to push the throttles forward. Of course, it could go no further than 95% N1 in our example. Remember that thrust derate is considered as a new limit!

|  | N1 | V1(MCG) |
|---|---|---|
| Full Rate 26K | 99% | 106kt |
| Derate 24K | 95% | 99kt |
| 24K ATM 40°C | 89% | 99kt |

*Figure 269: V1(MCG) with derate and ATM methods.*

The second statement that deserves a special explanation is this one: "Derate can, in very specific cases, be used to increase the maximum takeoff weight". It seems an incredible nonsense to say that less thrust will allow greater takeoff weight. In most cases (99.999%) it will be the opposite, with greater thrust offering greater maximum takeoff weight, but as stated, this only occurs in very specific situations.

To understand when and how it occurs, let's first find out how maximum takeoff weight and the takeoff speeds are defined for this weight. Let's consider we are field limited on this takeoff.

The maximum weight is obtained by gathering various pieces of information in a part of the performance manual referred to by Boeing as "Performance Dispatch (PD)", including runway condition (dry or wet), takeoff flap, available runway length, characteristics of the runway (elevation and slope), and weather conditions (temperature and wind).

When we have the information about the maximum takeoff weight in hand, we put these data in another part of the manual called "Performance Inflight (PI)". The weight information is now added, and all other data are repeated: runway condition (dry or wet), takeoff flap, runway characteristics (elevation and slope), and weather conditions (temperature and wind). With all this information, we will obtain our VSpeeds for that takeoff weight.

The software that generates weight and speed values (AFM-DPI, Airplane Flight Manual – Digital Performance Information) follows the same logic of the manual process that I have described. And you always have to validate the results before presenting your "final answer" to the problem. This result validation includes verifying that the calculated V1 is not less than $V_{1(MCG)}$ nor greater than VR or $V_{MBE}$.

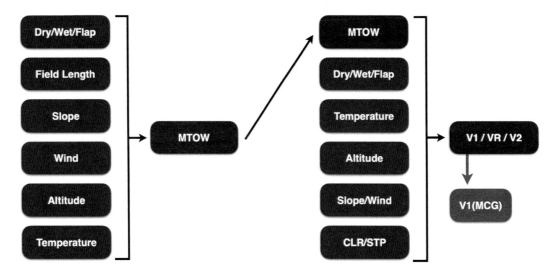

*Figure 270: Workflow to find MTOW and VSpeeds for that weight.*

Now imagine that V1 was below $V_{1(MCG)}$. As this is not allowed, an adjustment would have to be made, i.e., increasing the value of V1 to make it equal to $V_{1(MCG)}$. Assuming that our maximum takeoff weight was field limited and that this limitation was due to the accelerate and stop distance (ASD), the increased V1 creates a serious problem. This new V1 will make it impossible to stop within runway limits and something must be done about it.

Let's put numbers to our example. The values are fictitious and are for exemplification purposes, only.

We have a Boeing 737-300 that will takeoff from an extremely short runway like the one at Santos Dumont airport, in Rio de Janeiro. This runway is only 1,323m long. In the first phase of our evaluation, we determined the weight that we could takeoff from this runway and it was established that, using 22,000lb of thrust, we could depart with 50,000kg and this weight was limited by the ASD.

If the engine had less thrust, say, 20,000lb, the plane could takeoff with 48,000kg and the limitation would be the same. Note that the aircraft with less thrust takes off with less weight. But as we saw before, this is not our final answer. There are still some steps that need to be taken.

In the example of the 22K aircraft, V1 was initially calculated for this weight as 100kt. But when checking $V_{1(MCG)}$, we realize that it is worth 108kt. V1 will have to be increased by 8kt and we will not be able to stop the aircraft if RTO is initiated at 108kt V1. The solution to this problem is to increase the airplane's braking capacity, and this is only possible through one action: reducing the aircraft's weight. A lighter aircraft can accelerate and stop over a shorter distance. In our example, we will say that the weight needs to be reduced by 1,000kg for each knot that V1 is increased by. So, 8kt represents 8,000kg of penalty.

The original field limited weight of 50,000kg has been reduced and it is now worth 42,000kg. As the reduction originated from a penalty due to $V_{1(MCG)}$, we say that this weight is limited by $V_{1(MCG)}$; in other words, this is our **V1(MCG) Limited Takeoff Weight**.

With the 20K engine, initial V1 was also 100kt for the calculated weight of 48,000kg. The validation process identified $V_{1(MCG)}$ as 103kt (as expected, a lower $V_{1(MCG)}$ for 20K then for 22K). Once again, we will be forced to change V1, but now only by 3kt, and this will generate a penalty of 3,000kg.

With the penalty imposed, our new maximum takeoff weight is 45,000kg limited by $V_{1(MCG)}$. The final result of our problem shows that, within this unusual scenario, an airplane using an engine with lower thrust is capable of carrying more weight on takeoff.

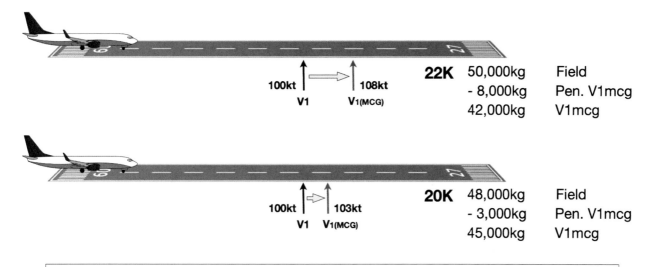

| 22K | 50,000kg | Field |
| | - 8,000kg | Pen. V1mcg |
| | 42,000kg | V1mcg |

| 20K | 48,000kg | Field |
| | - 3,000kg | Pen. V1mcg |
| | 45,000kg | V1mcg |

This new maximum weight resulting from V1 adjustment is called **V1$_{(MCG)}$ Limited Weight.**

*Figure 271: Reducing takeoff thrust can increase takeoff weight.*

To summarize, the situation of increasing maximum weight with reduced thrust (derate) should only occur on very short runways and with some factor that compels the original V1 to be very low, such as a wet, slippery, or contaminated runway. Anyway, whenever the maximum takeoff weight is V1$_{(MCG)}$ limited, it is reasonable to consider a Derate to increase MTOW. It might just work!

In the next figure, you will see a graph that was based on the following premise: airport at sea level, slippery runway (medium to poor braking action - we will see more about that in another topic), and temperature of 28°C. The graphic shows different runway lengths for the presented condition and the maximum takeoff weight that is obtained with three different rates for each available runway length. The rates are 27K, 26K, and 24K for a Boeing 737-800. Note that, on large runways, the aircraft with the highest thrust setting always carries more weight, but on short runways, the scenario changes and there is a drastic drop in the maximum takeoff weight offered by the aircraft with higher thrust (27K). On a 1,825m runway (as the highlight shows), making a Derate to 24K would allow you to take off with almost 10,000kg more, which is equivalent to about 100 passengers and luggage in terms of payload.

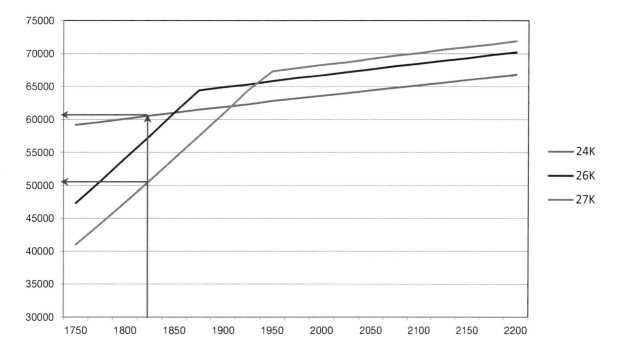

*Figure 272: V1(MCG) limited weight.*

### 3.9.9  Takeoff Bump Thrust

Let's talk about a brief history of the concept of bump using a <u>fictitious story</u>. Some time ago, companies that operated an aircraft like the 737NG on relatively short runways or with very significant obstacles consulted the manufacturer (Boeing) to see if there was any way to increase the available takeoff weight that was limited by the aircraft's performance in these locations. In a study conducted together with CFM, the engine supplier, it was concluded that some extra thrust could be provided by the engine by increasing the RPM and allowing, occasionally, an internal pressure rate higher than the maximum value established initially. The name **Takeoff Pressure Bump** was given to this scenario in which pressure (and thrust) was allowed to be taken a little bit above the value that had been originally defined (the term 'bump' is used here in terms of extrapolation).

I will put fictitious numbers that will better illustrate my explanation. The maximum pressure at combustion chamber intake is 460PSI, and this was achieved with an N1 rotation of 5,000RPM. With pressure bump, the pressure was allowed to reach 490PSI and this resulted in increased available thrust for takeoff. To achieve this new pressure, the engine N1 now spins at 5,200RPM. The problem with this process is that the EGT limit will be reached at a lower temperature than the one used without pressure bump. For example, if FRT is worth ISA+15 in normal engine operation, it drops to ISA with pressure bump (please, that is no rule! That is just one example).

Look at the following illustration. The blue dashed line indicates the new N1 when using pressure bump; the brown line shows the increase in thrust, which was due to an increase in pressure, and the purple dashed line shows the highest EGT. Finally, the black vertical dashed lines indicate where FRT is in normal operation (highest temperature) and with the pressure bump in use (lowest temperature).

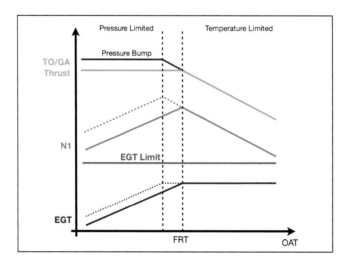

*Figure 273: Engine Takeoff Pressure Bump.*

A little later, airlines operating in places where the temperature often exceeds the FRT asked if there was anything they could do. One more time, the answer was 'yes'! As the operational EGT keeps a certain margin over the actual design limit, engine manufacturers concluded that they could allow a narrower margin in specific situations. By allowing the higher EGT, they could continue increasing the engine's N1 in addition to the original FRT and, thus, maintain constant thrust up to a higher FRT.

Again, let's give some fictitious numbers to solidify the explanation. FRT in a given engine is ISA+15, which is worth 24°C at 3,000ft. However, in a certain location with this elevation, the temperature often exceeds 30°C. In our imaginary engine, when in normal operation, every time air temperature reaches 24°C, the N1 limit of 5,000RPM is also reached and higher OAT values makes RPM (thrust) decrease to keep the EGT constant. The idea that was implemented to meet the request of these airlines is a bump that continues to increase the RPM as air temperature is increased, in order to guarantee that maximum thrust is maintained beyond the normal FRT. The engine's EGT is now much closer to the design limit, and the manufacturer indicates a new temperature at which N1's behavior will reverse.

This last situation I described did not increase engine thrust as it happened in the first; it only enabled maximum thrust to be still available up to a higher temperature value. For this reason, this change to the engine's characteristics is called **Takeoff Temperature Bump**.

Look at the next illustration. The blue dashed line indicates the new N1 when using the temperature bump; the brown line shows that thrust is maintained up to a higher FRT, and the purple dashed line shows the higher EGT. Finally, the black dashed vertical lines indicate where FRT is in normal operation (lowest temperature) and where it is when the temperature bump is being used (highest temperature).

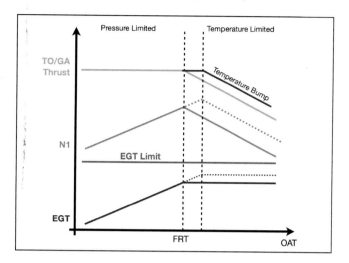

*Figure 274: Engine Takeoff Temperature Bump.*

Finally, there is also the option of combining both factors (temperature bump and pressure bump). In this case, there will be a "constant" thrust until the first FRT (obtained with pressure bump), followed by a slight drop in it between this FRT and the one obtained with temperature bump, and finally followed by a sharp drop in thrust beyond this temperature value. Every engine type or model has its own behavior, which might be a different from this description, but that is the general idea.

The reason for the slight decrease in thrust between the temperatures representing the FRTs of pressure and temperature bump is the engine's RPM limit. Suppose it is 5,200RPM and it was already reached when temperature equaled ISA. This limit can no longer be extrapolated. However, the immediate reversal in the behavior of N1 is not seen in the graph. Between "FRTs", it will remain constant to guarantee maximum pressure up to the highest possible temperature.

Figure 275 shows all of that. The blue dashed line indicates the new N1 when using combined bumps. Note that between the pressure bump and temperature bump FRTs, N1 stabilizes at a single value. The brown line shows the new thrust, and the purple dashed line shows the new higher EGT. Finally, the vertical dashed line to the left indicates what the FRT will be for this combined bump situation. The other two lines of this kind are showing where normal FRT is (center line) and where the temperature bump (rightmost line) was.

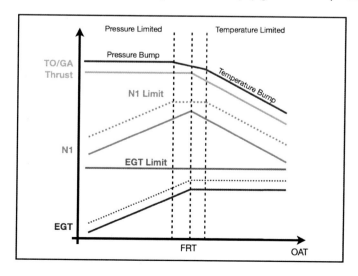

*Figure 275: Engine Takeoff Pressure and Temperature Bump.*

And what would be the difference between the two aircraft represented in the illustration below? One seems to have normal thrust at 27,000lb while the other only has this thrust using the bump. What is going on?

*Figure 276: The customer is always right!*

The biggest difference between these two aircraft is the lease contract of the engine, or putting it more directly, the price the airline pays to lease that engine.

Yes, it may seem weird that I said "lease that engine", but that is correct. Unlike cars, commercial airplanes have separate leasing contracts for the aircraft's cells (airframe) and for the engine. The airline pays a certain amount of money for the airplane and another amount for the engine. In Figure 276, the contract made by the company on the left is certainly more expensive than the one on the right.

Let's start on the right, in which the FMC indicates that normal operation is 26K with the possibility of bumping to 27K. In this case, the use of pressure bump is possible whenever a pilot needs it. However, most likely, the engine's owner monitors this usage. Let's say the contract provides for using pressure bump up to 20 times per month. If used in more situations than these, the operator must pay an additional fee. The extra cost provided for in the contract is all about engine degradation. Excessive use of the bump feature wears out the engine prematurely and therefore contracts become more expensive.

Still on the plane shown on the right, note an interesting detail in the upper left corner of the FMC page. The assumed temperature method cannot be possibly used. Once again, the reason is simple: the airline seeks the manufacturer to ask for more thrust; the manufacturer offers the extra thrust as requested; then, the airline decides to use assumed temperature to reduce thrust. That does not make any sense. Therefore, every time the bump is used, the possibility of using ATM is eliminated.

The plane on the left is a little different. As you may have seen, it does not have the bump function explicitly, but I guarantee that it exists. As I said before, the difference is in the lease contract of the engine. In this airplane, the operator possibly requested the permanent availability of the resource for operating in a very large number of airports that need it. However, it asked the manufacturer to allow the use of ATM for situations that are, let's say, intermediate, meaning that more thrust is needed, but not all the extra thrust that was made available. It is like the operator will so often take off from airports demanding extra thrust and they want this ATM feature to preserve the engine as much as possible.

The owner of this engine knows that this type of use wears out the engine much faster and, therefore, it charges a much higher price. Every airline needs to make a very careful assessment of its actual needs for using takeoff bump; otherwise, paying for this feature when there is no need for it may result in a very large budget deficit.

Here is a final comment about the image of the FMC shown in Figure 276: we can see that there is a selection of climb rate available (shown as <SEL>). The objectives behind Derated Climb will be seen in the Enroute Performance chapter.

# 3.10 Maxim

After going over all the items that can limit the takeoff performance of our airplane, we need to choose the maximum weight that we can use for takeoff. The choice is relatively easy: the smallest among all the evaluated weights. What we have to do is to know the jargon that is used to refer to those weights.

## 3.10.1  Performance Limited Takeoff Weight - PLTOW

First, let's look at the Field, Obstacle, Tire Speed and Brake Energy limits. The smallest among these four is known as **Runway Limited Takeoff Weight**, RLTOW. This will be compared to the only one missing: Climb limit weight. The smaller of the two is known as **Performance Limited Takeoff Weight**, PLTOW.

For aircraft that need to comply with the Return to Land requirement, we must not forget to compare this requirement with the others. Again, the smallest of all will be our Performance Limited Takeoff Weight. Return to Land is not part of the runway limit performance weight (RLTOW); it is a separate item, just like Climb limit weight.

## 3.10.2  Other Takeoff Weight Limits

We are not done yet. We know the weight that our airplane is capable of flying, but we still do not know if it is certified to fly like this with regard to its structural limits. The next assessment should consider Maximum Takeoff Weight (MTOW), Maximum Landing Weight (MLW), Maximum Zero Fuel Weight (MZFW), and the runway's Pavement Classification Rating (PCR – former PCN that is being abandoned in 2024).

PCR is a topic that will be discussed almost at the end of the book, but for now it is enough to know that it is a number that informs pavement strength and, based on that number, we can define the maximum weight for the airplane to run over it without causing damage.

How can MLW and MZFW somehow restrict our takeoff weight? Well, that happens indirectly. MLW defines our maximum landing weight for structural reasons. We are obliged to plan our flight so that, upon arriving at destination, we can land without the need to burn fuel. Therefore, if we add our Trip Fuel to the MLW, we will know the maximum weight that we can use for takeoff to reach the destination at the maximum landing weight. We have to keep in mind that the Maximum Allowable Landing Weight can be lower than the structural MLW, and this is due to landing performance or PCR on the destination's airport runway. However, at this moment, we will consider structural MLW to be the maximum allowed landing weight and after studying the matters relative to landing performance, we will refine this understanding.

MZFW does not limit our takeoff weight, but only the maximum payload. It is considered more as a piece of information than a limit. If you add the takeoff fuel to the MZFW, the result is the takeoff weight that would happen if we were loading the maximum payload. Some do not like to refer to this number as a weight limit because nothing prevents more fuel from being added to the aircraft and increasing takeoff weight. MZFW prevents only additional payload. However, in this book, we will give "weight limit" status to this value.

PCR is just a classification number, not a weight. What we need to do is transform this number into a palpable weight value. We will learn how to do this at the end of the book, but up until then, I will be careful to present PCR as a previously calculated weight. Departing PCR is a value that needs a direct reading, whereas landing PCR will only become a limit at the instant we add Trip Fuel, as we did with MLW.

Among the structural limits that we have seen (MTOW, MLW, MZFW, and PCR), we must choose the lowest value as our weight limit and compare it with the PLTOW that we obtained. The smallest among the smallest will be called Maximum Allowable Takeoff Weight. The following figure shows exactly this flowchart to define the maximum weight allowed for takeoff, but there is an intruder there. Fuel Tankage Limited Weight. We will see more about it in the next topic.

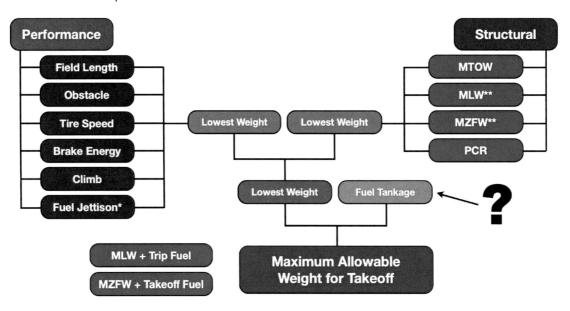

*Figure 277: Flowchart for maximum allowable takeoff weight.*

### 3.10.3 Fuel Tankage Limited Weight

In some cases, the "lowest weight among the lowest weights" needs to be compared with this new value called Fuel Tankage so that, again, the lowest value is defined as our Maximum Allowable Takeoff Weight. I could say that Fuel Tankage plays the role of a new Maximum Zero Fuel Weight. Let's see why this is the case.

To understand what Fuel Tankage means, let's talk about something simpler, like our car. Say you live in Los Angeles, CA and want to spend the weekend in Las Vegas, Nevada. You are alone in the car and without luggage. After driving the 440km connecting these two cities, check your fuel consumption. Let's say you burned 36 liters of gasoline. As you hit the jackpot, let's repeat the same trip on the following weekend, but this time there will be five adults in the car and lots of luggage. Will fuel consumption be the same? Certainly not. On this second trip you spent 40 liters of gasoline.

On an airplane, fuel burn behaves the same way. The heavier it is, the greater the fuel consumption is. So, it is complicated to answer that famous question that many lay people often ask: how far can this plane go? It depends on the weight it takes off with.

Fuel Tankage addresses this relationship between weight and fuel flow. Taking the 737-800 once again as an example: it can carry about 20,600kg of fuel or 26,020 liters, depending on kerosene density. If we need to fly between London and Paris, we will carry less than 5,000kg of fuel and we do not have to worry about Fuel Tankage. But taking off from Montevideo to Panama City is a whole different story. Suppose this flight needs 8 hours and 45 minutes of endurance (including reserves). With the expected payload and on a full tank (20,600kg), all we got is 8 hours of endurance. How can we make this flight feasible if there is no more room for fuel in the tanks?

There is only one answer to this problem. We need to reduce takeoff weight. By decreasing weight, the same amount of fuel now offers greater endurance, and we can possibly get to the required time of 8 hours and 45 minutes.

The chart in the next figure has three distinct threshold moments. For travel distances up to 2,000nm, we are able to carry the maximum payload of the airplane. Between 2,000nm and 2,800nm, payload is no longer limited by MZFW, but it is limited by the MTOW of 79,010kg. In this case, we need trade passengers or cargo for fuel, but the airplane's fuel tank is not full yet.

To fly beyond 2,800nm, the aircraft has topped the fuel tank to its limit. In the example, to carry 145 passengers, the plane will have a weight that limits flight to a distance of 2,950nm – taking off at full tank. If the destination is 3,150nm away from the origin, payload will have to be further reduced, and the flight will take only 110 passengers on this trip. The fuel tank, in this case, did not receive an extra drop of kerosene, as it was already full. The increase in flight range was possible owing to a reduction in takeoff weight, which reduced fuel flow.

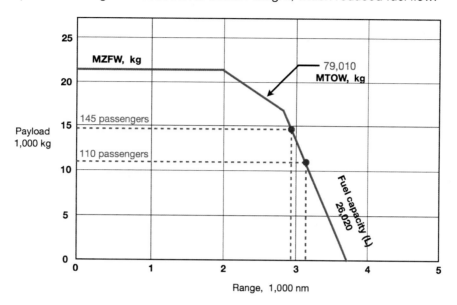

*Figure 278: Range versus Payload.*

This takeoff weight that was established to allow us to have the endurance needed with tanks full of fuel is called **Fuel Tankage Limited Takeoff Weight**. I said that it ends up being a kind of MZFW because, in practice, it establishes a new maximum payload that the flight can carry.

## 3.10.4 *Maximum Certified Takeoff Weight*

Remember when we discussed MTOW and MLW at the beginning of the weight and balance study? We talked about the rate of the descent that the airplane's landing gear must withstand at touchdown, but we also talked about different options for maximum takeoff weight that the operator can acquire when purchasing the aircraft. As an example, I can cite Boeing 737-800 in four different maximum weights: 70,500kg, 72,500kg, 75,000kg and 79,000kg. What is the evaluation made by the operator to make the purchase? Can this value be changed after the acquisition?

There are several reasons for choosing one or the other certification value and it is very important to keep in mind that the only difference between the four "versions" is the written MTOW on the document (AFM) delivered with the airplane. Let me explain that with an analogy. Imagine have you just bought a brand new Toyota Corolla that was on sale! $20,000.00 for the top version! Then, you are ridding it together with your wife and two kids along the road when a police officer makes you pull over just to check on a burned brake light. You handle the officer your documents and suddenly you hear: "sir, I'll have to give you a ticket for being overcrowded! You're only allowed to have two people in this car".

It does not make any sense! There are five seats on the car, only four are occupied and everyone is wearing seatbelts in their seats. "What's going on?" you ask. Then the policeman shows you the car document that says, "2 occupants, maximum". You take the ticket and, feeling furious, you drive back to the store where you bought the car to complain! The salesman explains: "sir, you paid only $20,000.00 for this vehicle. If you wanted to be able to carry 5 occupants you should have paid $27,000.00, but you may go to the cashier and pay the difference if you want. Then we'll update the document".

I know it is a silly story, but that is the way things are in aviation! Not a single bolt or rivet of difference between a 70 and a 79 ton MTOW. Just a different number on piece of paper called the AFM.

An airline must first think of the missions it wants to perform. If the company has a strategy of using aircraft on short haul flights, it can be a big deal to acquire aircraft with a lower certified weight value. See the calculation with rounded numbers for a 737-800 in the next figure. The payload shown in the illustration refers to a flight with 180 passengers and their luggage. Based on the fuel that could be filled with the weight that was still available, an estimation was made of the type of flight that could be made (how far the destination could be).

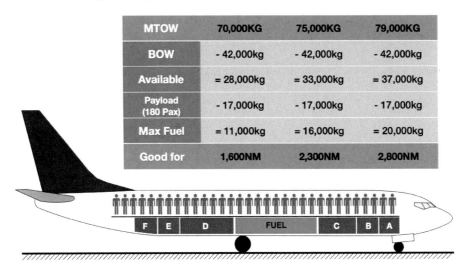

| MTOW | 70,000KG | 75,000KG | 79,000KG |
|---|---|---|---|
| BOW | - 42,000kg | - 42,000kg | - 42,000kg |
| Available | = 28,000kg | = 33,000kg | = 37,000kg |
| Payload (180 Pax) | - 17,000kg | - 17,000kg | - 17,000kg |
| Max Fuel | = 11,000kg | = 16,000kg | = 20,000kg |
| Good for | 1,600NM | 2,300NM | 2,800NM |

*Figure 279: Different maximum certified takeoff weights.*

If the company wants to fly farther, it is imperative to choose the most expensive aircraft with the highest certified takeoff weight, otherwise you will have to fly the routes with very few passengers and a small amount of cargo. It is important to note that the aircraft's operator can change its business model without having to buy another aircraft. As the weight value is a matter of certification, an aircraft with a maximum takeoff weight of 70 tons can be transformed into one of 79,000kg at any time. Of course, the airline will have to pay for the piece of paper that authorizes this change. But as I said, it is just a piece of paper. The rest of the plane remains exactly the same.

Another reason for not buying a more expensive plane if not necessary is the cost that this plane will have in operations. I said that the plane is exactly the same and you must be wondering: how can the cost of operation be higher for an aircraft owing to a simple paper that says it can take off heavier? The difference in operating cost lies in airport fees, radio navigation fees, insurance rates, among others. Landing and parking fees charged by airports, for example, depend on the maximum takeoff weight for which that aircraft is certified. So, even if you always operate at a certain airport with an extremely low weight, the amount of money charged for landing and staying on the tarmac for a couple of hours is higher if your MTOW is higher.

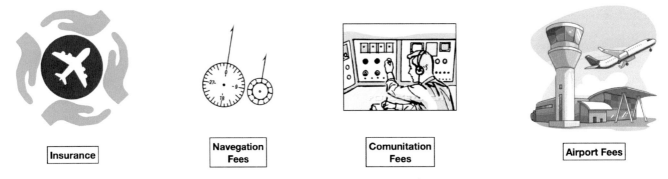

Insurance    Navegation Fees    Comunitation Fees    Airport Fees

*Figure 280: Reasons for carefully choosing your certified MTOW.*

Let's start this discussion by answering a question that you may have asked yourself at some point until now: what is the difference between wet and contaminated runways?

When we say that a runway is contaminated, this contaminant can be loose (also called fluid) or solid. Loose contaminants are: water, slush, snow (wet and dry), or frost. Solid contaminants are ice, wet ice, and compacted snow. Keep in mind that a runway can be covered with more than one type of contaminant at the same time!

*Figure 281: Loose contaminants at the top and solid contaminants at the bottom.*

## 3.11.1 *Effects of Contaminants on Takeoff Performance*

Nowadays all runways are analyzed in three thirds of their length. We will talk about that in more detail when discussing runway condition report (RCR), but for now let's just say that every third of the runway will be reported with a given condition. That condition might be different for every third, for example: wet on the first third, slush on the second third and wet snow on the final third.

Anyway, the third of the runway will be considered contaminated when the contaminant is covering more than 25% of that area. When talking about loose contaminants, their thickness must be greater than or equal to 3mm. And when it comes to water, this is the difference between saying that a runway is simply wet or contaminated with standing water. Manufacturers have the right to determine the depth of the contaminant in which takeoff will be permitted. Both Boeing and Airbus provide charts for contaminant depths between 3 and 13mm and do not recommend taking off with a contaminant thickness greater than this - the original values are in inches, and there are charts for calculation with 1/2in (13mm), 1/4in (6mm), and 1/8in (3mm). Dry snow is an exception! Some manufacturers might consider that it is safe to take off at depths up to 4in (102mm).

In terms of performance, the main difference between a wet and water-contaminated runway is the fact that on a wet runway, the aircraft's acceleration is not compromised, and it is equal to acceleration on a dry runway. Stopping, as we have seen, becomes more difficult owing to the lower friction with the ground. On a water-contaminated runway, however, acceleration is smaller because of the resistance created by the water in front of the tire. When trying to stop, it can be worse or better than on a wet track, depending on the thickness of the water layer on the runway.

Runways covered with solid contaminants (ice, wet ice, and compacted snow) become very slippery. This condition can also occur with a thin layer of water, depending on pavement condition. In both cases, a slippery condition allows close to normal acceleration, but directional control and stopping are extremely compromised. The comparison between them is shown in the next illustration and the same V1 (identified by the yellow arrow) is assumed for all of them.

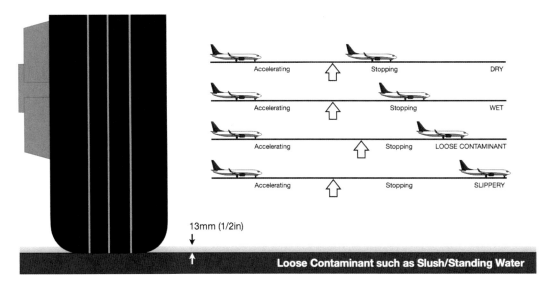

*Figure 282: Differences among dry, wet, or contaminated runways.*

## 3.11.2 Hydroplaning Speed

In addition to the difficulty in accelerating on a runway contaminated with a thick layer of water or slush, we have to consider the real possibility of aquaplaning, either during acceleration, which poses a challenge to the lateral control of the plane, or during deceleration, which also makes stopping difficult. EASA presents an equation to roughly define the speed at which the aircraft is going to aquaplane if the water depth is greater than the groove on the tire rubber, as shown in the figure below.

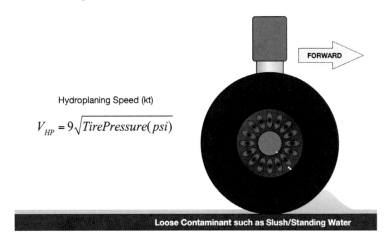

*Figure 283: Hydroplaning speed (in knots) and reasons why acceleration is more difficult.*

## 3.11.3 Aircraft Acceleration

The ability to accelerate an aircraft depends on the excess thrust it has over all factors that are going against this goal: aerodynamic drag, tire friction with the ground, and runway slope. The slope can be either an opposite (uphill) or favorable (downhill) factor to acceleration. Look at the equation in the following illustration.

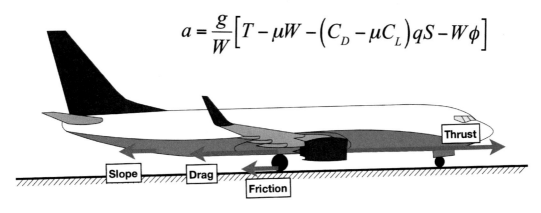

$$a = \frac{g}{W}\left[T - \mu W - \left(C_D - \mu C_L\right)qS - W\phi\right]$$

*Equation 14: Acceleration on the runway.*

On this equation, there are two representations that I have not mentioned yet: the Greek letters "μ" and "φ". The former stands for the friction coefficient between tire and runway pavement, and the latter is the sine of the runway slope. The other elements are already known: a (aircraft acceleration), g (acceleration of gravity), W (weight), T (engine thrust), $C_D$ (drag coefficient), $C_L$ (lift coefficient), S (wing area), and q (air density).

As the plane gains speed, aerodynamic drag increases and thrust decreases; therefore, it is natural that the acceleration rate should also decrease in this period. When one engine fails, available thrust drops dramatically and very suddenly, just when drag increases even more owing to the deflection of control surfaces (rudder).

In a twin-engine aircraft, losing one engine means 50% less thrust, which in addition to increasing drag, makes acceleration drop heavily. In the example below, it dropped from 4kt/s to just over 1kt/s. In some cases, acceleration gets even smaller than that.

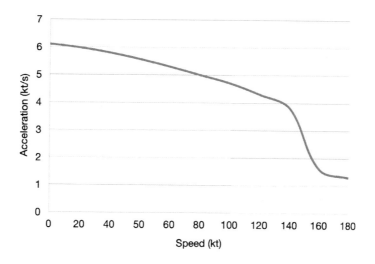

*Figure 284: Example of acceleration before and after engine failure on a twin-engine jet.*

The acceleration rate drops so much that, on a contaminated runway, it can even be negative when one of the engines stops delivering thrust. A study conducted by Boeing considered four different airplane acceleration rates in four different scenarios: dry runway with all engines running (blue), dry runway with one engine inoperative (green), contaminated runway with 6mm slush (yellow) and 13mm slush (red). These last two cases also consider the critical engine inoperative.

Of course, the takeoff weight used in this study would not be allowed for the 737 if the runway were contaminated with 13mm slush. To take this aircraft off the ground in these runway conditions, the weight would have to be drastically reduced, because at this weight used in the study, the aircraft would be actually stopping (negative acceleration), even with the remaining engine at maximum takeoff thrust.

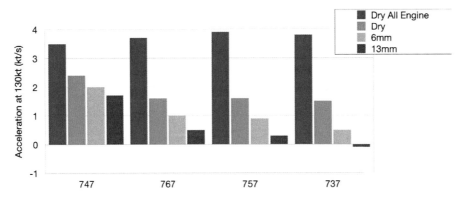

*Figure 285: Acceleration on dry and contaminated runways.*

## 3.11.4 Stopping the Aircraft

Now let's talk about the problem of stopping the aircraft on slippery runways. First, it must be said that a slippery runway can be classified into different levels. Those levels are referenced to braking capacity, or, as used in aviation jargon, braking action. They are named: Good, Good to Medium, Medium, Medium to Poor, and Poor. There are also two other classifications: Dry and Nil; the first one is pretty obvious and the other refers to a runway without any braking capacity at all. It would be like ice skating. We will see more details about this classification in the Landing chapter.

When we were studying weight and balance manifests, the first aircraft we saw in the example was a Piper Seneca. It is a small plane with six seats and a maximum takeoff weight of just 2,150kg. Despite being so small, the manufacturer says that its accelerate and stop distance, considering that the stop is started at a mere 79kt, is almost 1,200m! Why such a light plane uses so much runway to perform this maneuver? Why does a 737 use a lot less, weighing a lot more and using at a much higher speed? The answer is in the next figure: Speedbrakes.

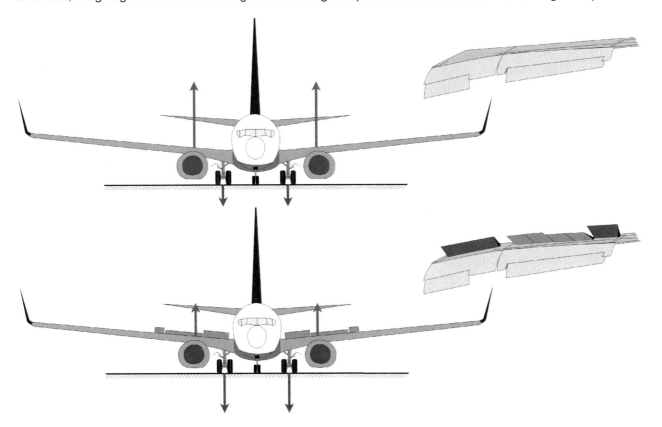

*Figure 286: Brake efficiency largely depends on speedbrakes.*

Regardless of the runway's braking condition, we should keep in mind that the plane stops because of two factors: aerodynamic drag and wheel brakes. The latter will be more efficient depending directly on the weight placed on the wheels to help with friction to the ground. That is why speedbrakes are of vital importance when commanding an aircraft to stop. Although lightweight, Piper Seneca does not have this device, and with 79kt, the wings are producing a lot of lift for this plane. When trying to stop, there is no pressure from the wheels on the ground and there is no efficiency in braking, so Seneca will end up using a lot of runway until it stops.

The following two illustrations provide numbers to illustrate how efficient and important speedbrakes are when it comes to stopping. Numbers refer to a Boeing's study that measured the stopping force produced by a 777 when trying to stop from a speed of 159kt. In the first example, the runway is dry while in the second, it is covered with ice (slippery). See how huge the difference is when using aerodynamic speedbrakes, especially in the slippery condition. Total stopping force with speedbrakes is 63% higher than the force produced without the use of this device on a dry runway. When the runway is slippery, the difference is over 90%. Studies do not consider the use of reverse thrust.

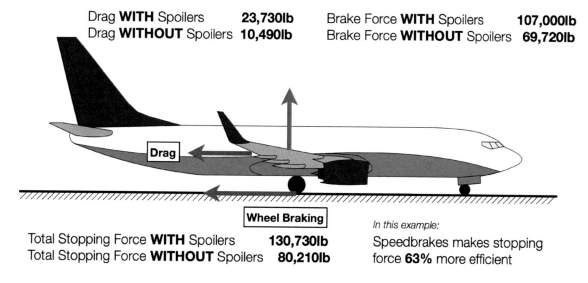

Drag **WITH** Spoilers    **23,730lb**     Brake Force **WITH** Spoilers    **107,000lb**
Drag **WITHOUT** Spoilers   **10,490lb**    Brake Force **WITHOUT** Spoilers   **69,720lb**

Total Stopping Force **WITH** Spoilers    **130,730lb**
Total Stopping Force **WITHOUT** Spoilers    **80,210lb**

*In this example:*
Speedbrakes makes stopping force **63%** more efficient

*Figure 287: Stopping forces measured at a given weight and speed on a DRY RUNWAY.*

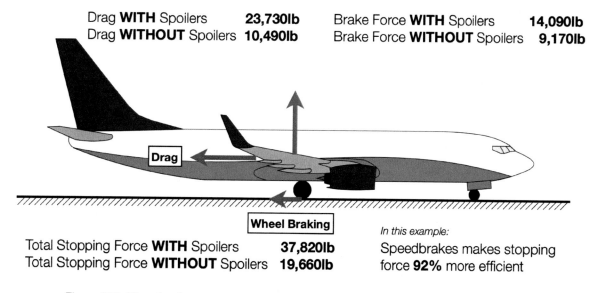

Drag **WITH** Spoilers    **23,730lb**     Brake Force **WITH** Spoilers    **14,090lb**
Drag **WITHOUT** Spoilers   **10,490lb**    Brake Force **WITHOUT** Spoilers   **9,170lb**

Total Stopping Force **WITH** Spoilers    **37,820lb**
Total Stopping Force **WITHOUT** Spoilers    **19,660lb**

*In this example:*
Speedbrakes makes stopping force **92%** more efficient

*Figure 288: Stopping forces measured at a given weight and speed on a SLIPPERY RUNWAY.*

## 3.11.5  Veer Off Risk due to Reverse Thrust

Reverse thrust was not used in the previous example, but of course, it could be used as long as it is available. And this kind of device makes a huge difference in stopping force on a slippery runway, specially at high speed. However, pilots must pay special attention to a small but very real risk involved. Veering off the runway!

Veer off is a technical term used when a runway excursion happens to the side limits of the track. Look at Figure 289. You might think of it as an airplane trying to stop during an RTO or after landing. Anyway, the pilot is using maximum reverse thrust at its and the red arrows indicate the direction of the force being produced by the engine. For some reason, say wind, the airplane deviates to the right of the centerline and the pilot is now trying to get back to it. By applying the left rudder, he/she is able to point the nose to the desired direction – but take another look at the red arrows. They indicate that there is a force against the movement slowing the airplane down, but it also shows that this force produced by the engine's reverse thrust is pulling the airplane off the runway, despite the fact that the airplane's nose is pointing to the center of the runway.

Pilot's Sophie's choice: close thrust reverser to avoid veering off, but risk facing a runway overrun? Or keep reverse thrust to secure complete stop within runway length, but risk veering off the track?

There is no correct answer here. It all depends on how much runway is ahead of the pilot at that very moment. If he/she can guarantee there is enough space left to stop and maybe some space to spare, closing the thrust reverser is the best option. Otherwise, it will be a matter of luck! But being aware of the problem is halfway to make a proper decision!

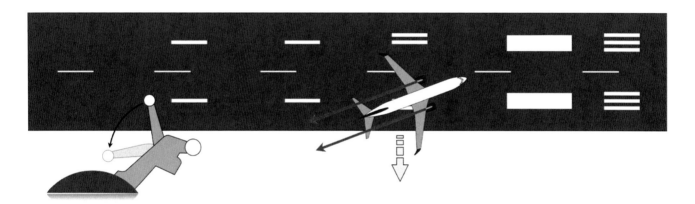

*Figure 289: Veering off because of the thrust reverser on a slippery runway.*

From now on, we will do some exercises using performance manuals to put into practice all the theory relative to takeoff performance that we have seen up to this point. We will look into two types of manuals. The first is called Flight Planning and Performance Manual, FPPM, and it has innumerable performance information, most of which in the form of graphics. The second is called the Flight Crew Operations Manual, FCOM. It basically has the same information as the FPPM, but in a reduced and tabulated form with numbers instead of graphics. For example, on Boeing 737-800 FPPM, you can find graphics for any takeoff flap setting, while in FCOM there are only data for flaps 5 takeoff setting.

As I had mentioned at the beginning of the book, the exercises are no longer within its pages. I will provide them as a PDF file for anyone who requests them. Just send an email to: performance.brenner@gmail.com

The following are just a few topics with explanations of subjects that will arise during the execution of the exercises, such as wind effects, use of anti-ice systems, optimum flap, and definition of VSpeeds.

## 3.12.1  *Wind Effect on Aircraft Performance*

The rule says that we can never give more than 50% credit to headwind, and we are required to consider a least 150% of any tailwind. But be careful. This is already known in tables and graphics, and the results are produced according to this rule. Have you ever noticed that lines representing tailwind always go up in a much steeper way than the headwind lines go down on performance graphics? That is the reason! Therefore, a 10kt headwind will be input as 10kt in the table, and if there is 10kt tailwind, we will do it in the same way. The graphic, table, or software will do the job of considering 50 or 150% for us and the information here is meant to make you aware of it but there is no need to correct the data from the exercises.

It should be noted that this rule applies to all items that will consider wind in performance calculations; however, there are items that completely disregard any wind, such as the calculation of Takeoff Climb Limit Weight or Return to Land Limit Weight. Yes, the wind alters the gradient of the climb, as it changes ground speed, but these two weight limits relate to the excess energy that the airplane must have, without considering proximity to obstacles, for example. Therefore, wind does not matter.

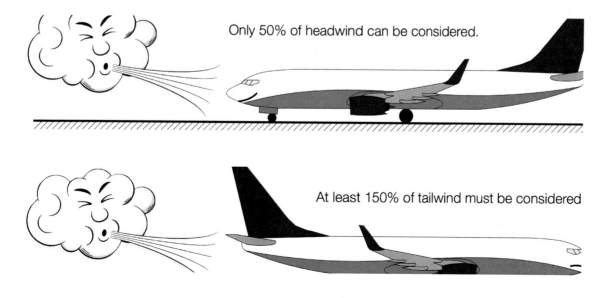

*Figure 290: How wind is used in takeoff performance calculations.*

### 3.12.2 Use of Engine and Wing Anti-Ice on Takeoff

Regarding the use of Engine Anti-Ice and Wing Anti-Ice for takeoff, the first step is to understand when it is necessary. Some aircraft have devices that let pilots know whether it needs to be used or not, but in general, all systems follow the same rule. It is all about combining two factors: temperature and moisture.

The anti-ice system will need to be used during takeoff whenever the outside air temperature is at or below 10°C and there is visible moisture in the form of:

1. Precipitation: rain (RA), drizzle (DZ), snow (SN), or;
2. Water, snow, or slush standing on the apron, taxiway, or runway, or;
3. Mist or fog as long as it is dense enough, so visibility is less than or equal to 1,600m (1sm).

If weather conditions meet these criteria, it will be mandatory to use the anti-ice system for takeoff. Details about cold weather operations will be given in a later chapter. This information is enough at this moment, so you know when to apply weight penalties required by anti-ice operations.

### 3.12.3 Optimum Flap for Takeoff

In performance exercises, a question will be raised about the selection of takeoff flap. You will see that when Field limited, a higher flap setting represents a higher takeoff weight as the airplane uses less runway in this situation. However, when we are Obstacle or Climb limited, the smaller the flap, the greater the takeoff weight. These limits are higher when we have large gradients of climb and we achieve a higher gradient with less drag, that is, less flap. Hence the definition of Optimum Flap (also known as Best Flap): this is the flap that allows you the greatest takeoff weight after analyzing all limitations.

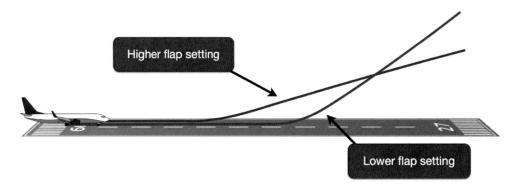

*Figure 291: Influence of takeoff flap.*

Observe the figure below with fictitious numbers for takeoff weights that have been calculated for field, obstacle, and climb limits. For each flap setting, maximum allowed takeoff weight was identified in bold (the smallest of the three limit weights). The flap that allowed the highest takeoff weight is highlighted in red, and this is the Optimum Flap in the example (maximum takeoff weight of 59,400kg). Many pilots think that the best flap will always be either the lowest or the highest setting, but as you can see below, sometimes that optimum flap is somewhere in the middle range of possible flap settings.

| TOW Limit | Flap 1 | Flap 5 | Flap 15 | Flap 25 |
|---|---|---|---|---|
| Field (F) | **55,000kg** | **58,000kg** | 60,500kg | 61,800kg |
| Obstacle (*) | 63,000kg | 61,600kg | **59,400kg** | **57,700kg** |
| Climb (C) | 67,000kg | 65,200kg | 62,000kg | 60,300kg |

*Figure 292: Optimum flap.*

## 3.12.4  Finding V Speeds on FCOM

Finally, at a given point you will be asked to calculate takeoff speeds. To help you solve this exercise, the illustration below shows a kind of flowchart with step-by-step instructions on how to get the result. In these exercises, we will disregard the effect of the clearway and the stopway over V1. That is because, although older FCOM has tables for adjusting V1 for both situations, it does not make any adjustment to the available takeoff weight. This makes the change in V1 pointless. Newer versions of Boeing's aircraft FCOM do not even offer the possibility of performing V1 adjustment.

After the flow chart, there is also a guideline on what to do whenever the VSpeeds validation process goes wrong: $V_{1(MCG)}$ greater than V1 or VR, and V1 greater than VR. I hope it helps solving the exercises.

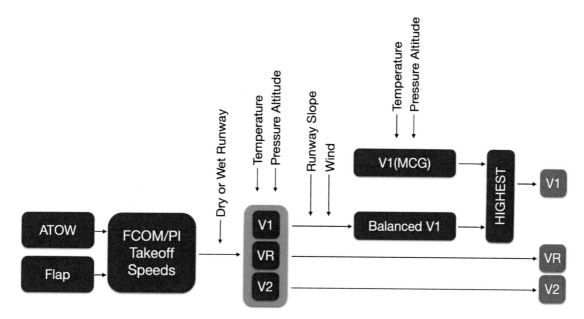

Figure 293: VSpeeds flowchart.

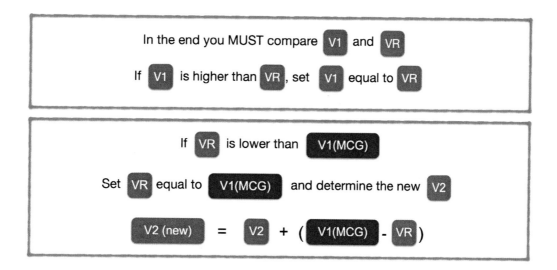

Figure 294: What to do when VSpeed validation goes wrong?

Runway analysis, airport analysis, or takeoff analysis. They are all synonyms that refer to the same thing. Those readers who are willing to do the exercises (just send me an email) will see that it is perfectly possible to manually analyze all takeoff limits using the performance manuals provided by the manufacturer, pick the maximum takeoff weight, and still find the V Speeds of our current weight. Possible, but extremely laborious and a little inaccurate.

Takeoff Analysis is a way to make the whole process simpler. It is a very practical way to establish the maximum takeoff weight, the assumed temperature that we can use with our current takeoff weight, and the VSpeeds (V1, VR, and V2) for this weight.

The analysis does not have a fixed format and can present an enormous amount of information that is arranged in tabulated form. What information will appear in the analysis and in what format it will be displayed is something that must be defined by the operator. In this book, we will look at some possible formats, but not all. As an important note, I would like to point out that a good part of the airlines around the world have already replaced these tabulated analyses with tablets or laptops on board the airplanes with software that is able to make all performance calculations instantly and accurately. This hardware is known as Electronic Flight Bag, EFB.

Figure 295: Examples of EFB Performance software running on iPads.

The illustration below represents a classic format for runway analysis. It has been divided into six parts that will be detailed in sequence. Remember that there may be even more information that I did not mention here, depending on the operator's wishes. All data contained in this table comes from the Airplane Flight Manual (AFM).

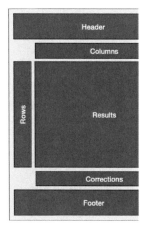

F                                                    runway analysis.

## Header:

- Aircraft type;
- Runway condition;
- Engine bleeds or packs (air conditioning) configuration: although bleeds and packs are not the same thing, performance wise, stating "bleeds off" or "packs off" will end up producing the same result;
- Anti-ice configuration;
- Engine Rate;
- Takeoff flap;
- CG position for performance calculation;
- Type of V1 (maximum, minimum, balanced, optimum, to name a few);
- Runway or intersection;
- Additional information such as airport elevation, magnetic deviation, etc.

## Columns:

- Wind intensity that all results will be based on. Positive values mean headwind and negative numbers refer to tailwind. There might be a separate column for non-runway limited weight, that is, climb or return to land limit.

## Rows:

- Temperatures that all results will be based on;
- N1 value to be used at each temperature.

## Results:

- Maximum takeoff weight for the cross-referenced condition (wind and temperature). The results are normally shown in hundreds of kg or lb (724 meaning 72,400kg);
- A single letter or symbol that represents the limiting factor that resulted in this maximum weight. In Boeing's analysis, those are: Field (F), Climb (C), Obstacle or Level Off (*), Brake Energy (B), Tire Speed (T), Return to Land (J), Improved Climb (**), and $V_{1(MCG)}$ (V);
- V1, VR and V2 for maximum weights at every cross-referenced result from the table. In some cases, these VSpeeds are shown with number 1 suppressed, which means 42 is actually 142kt;
- Might show Climb or Return to Land (the smaller between both) on a separate column, as mentioned.

## Corrections:

- Calculation adjustments that must be applied every time actual QNH is different from the one shown in the results. These tables are often generated with standard QNH (1013hPa), but the operator can choose any value that is more suitable for a given airport.

## Footer:

- Glossary of terms used in these analyses;
- Obstacle information (height, distance, offset) and units for these data;
- TORA, TODA, and ASDA;
- PCR;
- Runway slope (positive is uphill and negative is downhill);
- Line-up distance allowances (if applicable);
- Minimum flap retraction altitude;
- Contingency procedure to follow in case of an engine failure after takeoff.

We will do some exercises using these analyses to see details about the information provided by them.

Heads-up: Do not use these analyses for actual flights. Those are just examples whose data were modified on purpose to represent certain characteristics that are needed in the proposed exercises.

Exercise 1:

Outside Air Temperature: 30°C
Wind: 230° at 10kt
Altimeter Setting: 1023hPa
Maximum Takeoff Weight: **FIND**
Actual Takeoff Weight: 59.500kg
ATM and VSpeeds: **FIND**

```
Elevation: 3497.0 ft              Runway 29R                        SBBR
737-800{W}/CFM56-7B26                              BRASÍLIA, BRASIL

       Derate = Full Rated Thrust          Flaps = Flaps 05
          A/I = Off                           CG = Forward
  Runway Cond = Dry               V1 Policy = Balanced
          A/S = On

*A* indicates OAT outside Environmental Envelope

               Maximum brake release weight - 100 (kg)
    OAT     |                        Wind (kts)
    °C      |    -5.0           0.0            5.0            10.0

    50A     |  570* 30-31-36  579* 31-32-37  582* 32-33-38  585* 32-33-38
    49A     |  574* 30-32-37  583* 32-33-38  586* 32-33-38  589* 33-34-38
    48A     |  578* 31-32-37  588* 32-33-38  591* 33-34-39  594* 33-34-39
    47      |  583* 31-33-38  592* 33-34-39  595* 33-34-39  599* 34-35-40
    46      |  588* 31-33-39  597* 33-34-40  600* 34-35-40  604* 34-35-40
    45      |  593* 32-34-39  602* 34-35-40  605* 34-35-40  609* 35-36-41
    44      |  597* 32-34-40  607* 34-35-41  610* 35-36-41  614* 35-36-41
    43      |  602* 33-35-40  612* 35-36-41  615* 35-36-42  619* 36-37-42
    42      |  607* 33-35-41  617* 35-37-42  620* 36-37-42  623* 36-37-42
    41      |  612* 34-36-41  622* 35-37-42  625* 36-37-43  628* 37-38-43
    40      |  617* 34-36-42  627* 36-38-43  630* 36-38-43  633* 37-38-44
    39      |  622* 35-37-43  632* 36-38-44  635* 37-38-44  638* 38-39-44
    38      |  627* 35-37-43  637* 37-39-44  640* 37-39-44  643* 38-39-45
    37      |  632* 36-38-44  642* 37-39-45  646* 38-40-45  649* 38-40-45
    36      |  637* 36-38-44  648* 38-40-45  651* 38-40-46  655* 39-41-46
    35      |  643* 36-39-45  653* 38-40-46  656* 39-41-46  660* 39-41-47
    34      |  648* 37-39-46  658* 39-41-46  662* 39-41-47  665* 40-42-47
    33      |  652* 37-40-46  663* 39-41-47  667* 40-42-47  670* 40-42-48
    32      |  656* 38-40-46  667* 39-42-47  671* 40-42-48  674* 41-42-48
    31      |  660* 38-41-47  671* 40-42-48  675* 40-42-48  678* 41-43-48
    30      |  664* 38-41-47  675* 40-42-48  679* 41-43-49  682* 41-43-49
    29      |  668* 39-41-48  679* 40-43-49  683* 41-43-49  686* 42-43-49
    28      |  672* 39-42-48  683* 41-43-49  687* 41-43-49  690* 42-44-50
    27      |  675* 39-42-48  686* 41-43-49  690* 42-44-50  694* 42-44-50
    26      |  678* 39-42-49  689* 41-44-50  693* 42-44-50  697* 42-44-50
    25      |  681* 40-43-49  692* 42-44-50  696* 42-44-50  700* 43-45-51
    24      |  684* 40-43-49  695* 42-44-50  699* 42-45-51  703* 43-45-51
    23      |  686* 40-43-50  698* 42-44-51  701* 43-45-51  705* 43-45-51
    22      |  687* 40-43-50  698* 42-44-51  702* 43-45-51  706* 43-45-51
    21      |  687* 40-43-50  698* 42-44-51  702* 43-45-51  706* 43-45-51
    20      |  687* 40-43-50  699* 42-44-51  702* 43-45-51  706* 43-45-51
    19      |  687* 40-43-50  699* 42-45-51  703* 43-45-51  706* 43-45-51
    18      |  688* 40-43-50  699* 42-45-51  703* 43-45-51  707* 43-45-51
    17      |  688* 40-43-50  700* 42-45-51  703* 43-45-51  707* 43-45-51
    16      |  688* 40-43-50  700* 42-45-51  704* 43-45-51  707* 44-45-51
    15      |  689* 41-43-50  700* 42-45-51  704* 43-45-51  708* 44-45-51

QNH Correction (kg/mbar), Ref 1013.0 mbar (based on 1003.0 and 1023.0)
Above Ref      +52              +53            +53            +53
Below Ref      -70              -72            -72            -72

Min Flap Ret Ht    1000 ft

MAX BRAKE RELEASE WEIGHT MUST NOT EXCEED MAX CERT WEIGHT OF    86182 KG
Limit Codes: B=Brake Energy C=Climb F=Field *=Obstacle/Level-off T=Tire
             V=VMCG
TORA is 3200 M, TODA is 3200 M, ASDA is 3200 M
Line-up distances are 0 M for TODA and 0 M for ASDA
Runway slopes are -0.3 % for TODA and -0.3 % for ASDA
                                              OBSTACLES FROM LO-FT/M
Runway    Ht   Dist Offset     Ht   Dist Offset    Ht   Dist Offset
29R      175   2300    0      335   4140    0      344   4860    0
         391   5080    0      482   5355    0      621   5730    0
```

*Figure 297: Runway analysis, Rwy29R SBBR/BSB.*

To solve exercise 1 or any other that requires adjustments to the table because QNH is different from the reference QNH, or because of adjustments imposed by other situations, you do not need to change all result values. There is an easier way.

The following illustration shows that, instead of applying a correction factor to the table (and change a lot of numbers), you can reverse it and apply it to the value that you will seek inside the results chart (making a single calculation). The figure is divided into two parts. There is a green set of blocks that must fit one of the answers (A through E) after all the alternatives have been adjusted by adding one block.

On the left we did as instructed, making adjustments to all five alternatives, just to find out the correct answer is alternative C.

But as I said, you could reverse the procedure and make a single adjustment on the value that is being sought. That way, instead of adding one block to all alternatives, let's remove one block from the green set. We did that on the right and found the same result. Alternative C.

That is what we will do from now on! Always reverse the adjustment factors the make a single step instead of infinite ones!

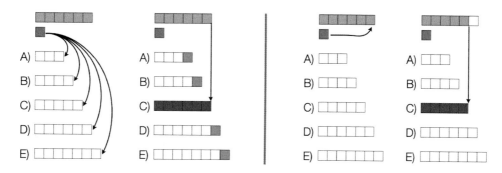

*Figure 298: Reverse adjustment factors to make it MUCH easier!*

As you can see in the example of exercise 1, adding a correction factor of 530kg to all results on the analysis, works the same way as subtracting the same 530kg from the value to be sought on the chart (ATOW).

**Answer to Exercise 1:**

Runway 29R => 290°  
Wind 230° at 10kt  
290° - 230° = 60°  
10kt x cos 60° = Headwind 5kt  
QNH 1023  
1023 - 1013 = 10hPa above Ref  
10 x 53 = 530kg  
MTOW = 67,900kg + 530kg

**MTOW = 68.430kg**  
"Adjusted ATOW"  
59,500kg - 530kg = 58,970kg  
Assumed Temperature is **48°C**  
VSpeeds are:  
**V1 133kt**  
**VR 134kt**  
**V2 139kt**

In Figure 297, in the runway analysis for SBBR Runway 29R, note that after a given temperature (48°C), letter "A" appears next to every temperature value. You must be wondering about the meaning of that letter. The header indicates that temperatures followed by this "A" are those outside the aircraft's environmental envelope. This envelope was addressed in the physics chapter, but I will replicate it next.

The shaded area indicates the temperature and altitude limits for takeoff and landing operations. Temperature values above the indicated one can be used as the assumed temperature, only – hence the reason for using letter "A", Assumed Temperature. Takeoff and landing are prohibited if this is the actual outside air temperature.

The airport of our first exercise is Brasília and, according to the runway analysis, this airport's elevation is 3,497ft. Look at the envelope to find the highest temperature at which takeoff and landing operation is allowed at this airport.

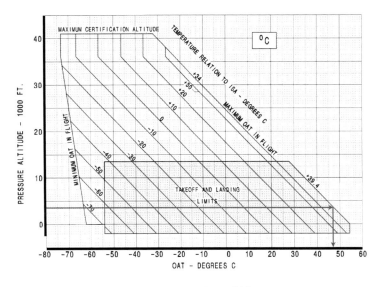

*Figure 299: Finding where the letter "A" starts to appear.*

Answer: 47°C, exactly as pointed out in the runway analysis.

One of the things we saw at the beginning of our study was something called "dry check". To demonstrate the need for this procedure, I will now show you two takeoff analyses for Santos Dumont airport (SBRJ) runway 20L. On the left side, the runway is dry and on the right side, it is wet. The analysis for the wet runway was made without the protection of the Dry Check. See the highlighted result.

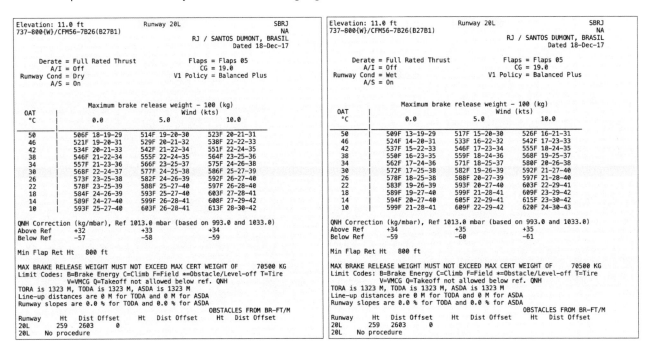

*Figure 300: Runway analysis for dry and wet conditions without dry check.*

Dry check is just the need to compare the result of the wet and the dry runways to confirm that maximum weight found in the dry runway is always greater than or equal to the wet runway analysis, but never less. The software that generates the analysis usually does this check and the values are never higher with the wet runway; however, to demonstrate that it can happen, I made the software ignore this step.

Taking as an example the temperature of 30°C with a headwind of 5kt, we can see in the analysis that the dry runway allows a maximum takeoff weight of 57,700kg, while the wet runway allows takeoff with a maximum weight of 58,200kg. These values are not wrong; on the contrary, they are mathematically correct. But the law prohibits taking off with 58,200kg on a wet runway. I emphasize that the maximum weight on a wet runway cannot exceed the value of the dry runway. Look at the figure below. Now, the wet runway analysis was created with the software's "dry check" protection activated. In this case, with 30°C and 5kt of headwind, the result was 57,700kg limited by field length – the same result obtained with dry runway, as directed by regulations.

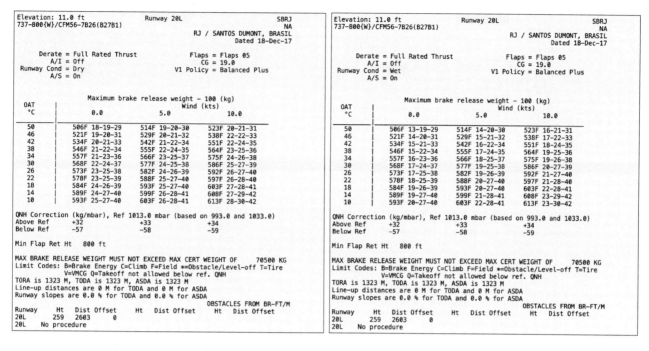

Figure 301: Runway analysis for dry and wet conditions with dry check.

Exercise 2:

Outside Air Temperature: 5°C
Present weather: FOG, visibility 500m
Wind: 110° at 5kt
Altimeter Setting: 1003hPa
Actual takeoff weight: 72,730kg
MTOW, ATM and VSpeeds: **FIND**

Note that, in this exercise, the use of ENG ANTI ICE is required for takeoff, and the analysis was made with anti-ice OFF. This analysis can be used to perform takeoff calculations, as long as you know and apply the correction factor.

| Performance Limited by | Eng or Eng/Wing Anti Ice ON |
|---|---|
| Field (F) | -200kg |
| Climb (C) | -300kg |
| Obstacle (*) | -350kg |

Figure 303: Example of Anti-Ice correction factor.

```
Elevation: 11.0 ft                    Runway 11                        SBPA
737-800{W,SFP}/CFM56-7B27-B1                    PORTO ALEGRE / SALGADO FILHO

        Derate = B27-B1 at 26K Derate          Flaps = Flaps 05
        A/I = Off                              CG = 15.0
  Runway Cond = Dry                            V1 Policy = Optimum
        A/S = On

                Maximum brake release weight - 100 (kg)
                                Wind (kts)
  OAT
  °C        -5.0          0.0          5.0          10.0

   50    645F 35-37-42  666F 39-39-44  673F 40-40-45  680F 41-41-46
   48    654F 36-37-43  675F 39-40-45  682F 40-41-46  689F 41-42-47
   46    662F 37-38-44  684F 40-41-46  691F 41-42-47  698F 42-43-48
   44    671F 38-39-45  693F 41-42-47  700F 42-43-48  707F 43-43-49
   42    680F 38-40-46  702F 41-42-48  709F 42-43-49  717F 43-44-50
   40    689F 39-41-47  711F 42-43-49  718F 43-44-50  726F 44-45-51
   38    698F 40-42-48  720F 43-44-50  728F 44-45-51  735F 45-46-52
   36    706F 40-42-49  729F 43-45-51  737F 44-46-52  745F 45-47-53
   34    714F 41-43-50  738F 44-46-52  746F 45-47-53  754F 46-48-54
   32    722F 41-44-51  748F 44-47-53  756F 45-48-54  764F 46-48-55
   30    730F 42-44-52  756F 45-47-54  764F 46-48-55  773F 47-49-56
   28    733F 42-45-52  758F 45-48-54  767F 46-49-55  776F 47-49-56
   26    735F 42-45-52  761F 45-48-55  769F 46-49-55  778F 48-50-56
   24    737F 42-45-52  763F 46-48-55  772F 47-49-56  781F 48-50-56
   22    740F 43-45-53  766F 46-48-55  774F 47-49-56  783F 48-50-57
   20    742F 43-46-53  768F 46-49-55  777F 47-50-56  786F 48-51-57
   18    744F 43-46-53  770F 46-49-55  779F 48-50-56  788F 49-51-57
   16    747F 43-46-53  773F 47-49-56  782F 48-50-56  791F 49-51-57
   14    749F 44-46-54  776F 47-49-56  784F 48-51-57  793F 49-51-57
   12    752F 44-47-54  778F 47-50-56  787F 48-51-57  796F 49-52-58
   10    754F 44-47-54  781F 48-50-56  790F 49-51-57  798F 50-52-58
    5    760F 45-48-55  787F 48-51-57  796F 49-52-58  805F 50-53-59

QNH Correction (kg/mbar), Ref 1013.0 mbar (based on 1003.0 and 1023.0)
Above Ref       +37          +38          +39          +40
Below Ref       -67          -71          -73          -75

Min Flap Ret Ht   800 ft

MAX BRAKE RELEASE WEIGHT MUST NOT EXCEED MAX CERT WEIGHT OF      86182 KG
Limit Codes: B=Brake Energy C=Climb F=Field *=Obstacle/Level-off T=Tire
             V=VMCG
TORA is 2280 M, TODA is 2280 M, ASDA is 2280 M
Line-up distances are 0 M for TODA and 0 M for ASDA
Runway slopes are 0.0 % for TODA and 0.0 % for ASDA
                                             OBSTACLES FROM LO-FT/M
Runway     Ht   Dist Offset     Ht   Dist Offset    Ht   Dist Offset
11    No obstacles
```

Figure 302: Runway analysis, Rwy11 SBPA/POA.

## Answer to Exercise 2

QNH 1023
1003 - 1013 = 10hPa below Ref
10 x 73 = 730kg
Corrected MTOW
79,600 – 730(hPa) – 200(AI) = **78,670kg**

"Adjusted ATOW"
72,730 + 730 + 200 = 73,660kg
ATM is **36°C**
Takeoff Speeds are
**V1 144kt, VR 146kt and V2 152kt**

## Exercise 3:

Outside Air Temperature: 14°C
Wind: 180° at 10kt
QNH 1013hPa
Actual Takeoff Weight: 61,000kg
MTOW for normal Takeoff: **FIND**
ATM and VSpeeds for normal Takeoff: **FIND**
MTOW for Improved Climb Takeoff: **FIND**
ATM and V Speeds for Improved Climb Takeoff: **FIND**

```
Elevation: 7910.0 ft          Runway 18                          SEQM
737-800{W,SFP}/CFM56-7B27-B1                      QUITO / EQUADOR

      Derate = Full Rated Thrust        Flaps = Flaps 05
         A/I = Off                         CG = 15.0
 Runway Cond = Dry                   V1 Policy = Optimum
         A/S = On

*A* indicates OAT outside Environmental Envelope

OAT  | Climb                            Wind (kts)
°C   | (100 kg)       -5.0            0.0             5.0             10.0

 50A |   551       521*  24-24-28   527*  25-25-28   528*  25-25-28   528*  25-25-28
     |             543** 36-37-40   550** 37-38-41   552** 37-38-41   554** 38-38-41
 46A |   572       541*  26-26-30   547*  27-27-31   549*  27-27-31   549*  27-27-31
     |             564** 38-39-42   570** 39-40-43   573** 40-40-43   575** 40-41-44
 42A |   593       561*  29-29-32   567*  29-29-33   569*  30-30-33   571*  30-30-33
     |             584** 40-42-45   591** 42-43-46   594** 42-43-46   596** 42-43-46
 38  |   614       581*  31-31-35   587*  32-32-35   589*  32-32-36   592*  32-32-36
     |             604** 42-44-47   612** 44-45-48   614** 44-45-48   616** 45-46-49
 34  |   634       599*  33-33-37   605*  33-33-38   608*  34-34-38   610*  34-34-38
     |             623** 44-46-50   630** 46-47-51   633** 46-47-51   635** 47-48-51
 30  |   655       616*  34-34-39   623*  35-35-40   626*  36-36-40   628*  36-36-40
     |             642** 46-48-52   650** 48-49-53   653** 48-49-53   655** 49-50-53
 26  |   666       626*  35-35-40   633*  36-36-41   635*  37-37-41   638*  37-37-41
     |             653** 47-49-53   661** 49-50-54   663** 49-51-54   666** 50-51-55
 22  |   673       632*  36-36-41   640*  37-37-41   642*  37-37-42   644*  38-38-42
     |             660** 48-50-54   668** 50-51-55   671** 50-51-55   673** 50-52-56
 18  |   680       638*  36-37-41   646*  38-38-42   648*  38-38-42   651*  38-38-43
     |             666** 49-51-55   674** 50-52-56   677** 51-52-56   680** 51-52-56
 14  |   687       645*  37-37-42   652*  38-38-43   655*  39-39-43   657*  39-39-43
     |             673** 49-52-56   681** 51-53-57   684** 51-53-57   687** 52-53-57
 10  |   694       652*  38-38-43   659*  39-39-44   662*  39-39-44   664*  40-40-44
     |             681** 50-52-56   689** 52-53-57   691** 52-54-58   694** 53-54-58
  6  |   702       658*  38-39-44   666*  40-40-44   668*  40-40-45   671*  40-40-45
     |             687** 51-53-57   696** 52-54-58   698** 53-54-58   701** 53-55-59

Min Flap Ret Ht   1098 ft

MAX BRAKE RELEASE WEIGHT MUST NOT EXCEED MAX CERT WEIGHT OF      86182 KG
Limit Codes: B=Brake Energy F=Field **=Improved Climb *=Obstacle/Level-off
             T=Tire V=VMCG
TORA is 4098 M, TODA is 4098 M, ASDA is 4098 M
Line-up distances are 0 M for TODA and 0 M for ASDA
Runway slopes are 1.0 % for TODA and 1.0 % for ASDA
                                            OBSTACLES FROM LO-FT/M
Runway    Ht   Dist Offset     Ht   Dist Offset    Ht   Dist Offset
18       650   9100  -624
```

*Figure 304: Runway analysis Rwy36 SEQM/UIO.*

## Answer to Exercise 3

MTOW
No Improved Climb: **65,700 (*)**
With Improved Climb: **68,700 (**)**
ATM No Improved Climb: **34°C**
Takeoff Speeds

**V1 134kt, VR 134kt and V2 138kt**
ATM With Improved Climb: **38°C**
Takeoff Speeds
**V1 145kt, VR 146kt and V2 149kt**

Note that, in exercise 3, there is something that I mentioned when we talked about Improved Climb – a higher assumed temperature. On a "normal" takeoff, the assumed temperature was 34°C. Using Improved Climb technique, assumed temperature was increased to 38°C.

This increase in assumed temperature, you must remember, has some advantages in terms of less engine wear, as it significantly lowers the engine's EGT. This has a direct impact on the airline's cost savings.

In the previous runway analysis, in addition to Improved Climb, as a novelty, note an extra column on the left end of the results field. It has information about the non-runway limit takeoff weight; in other words, Climb. In that example, Climb limit weight was always higher than the Obstacle limit weight shown in the middle of the table. As we must always choose the smaller between the two of them, Obstacle was the limiting factor. But see another example below. This one, from SBSG Rwy12:

```
Elevation: 272.0 ft            Runway 12                         SBSG
737-800{W}/CFM56-7B26                     SÃO GONÇALO DO AMARANTE, BRASIL

          Derate = Full Rated Thrust         Flaps = Flaps 05
             A/I = Off                           CG = Forward
  Runway Cond = Dry                       V1 Policy = Optimum
             A/S = On


 OAT    Climb                              Wind (kts)
 °C     (100 kg)        -5.0              0.0              5.0              10.0

  50      713       723F  46-47-51    745F  46-47-51   753F  47-47-51   760F  47-47-51
                    719** 48-49-53    730** 52-54-57   734** 54-55-59   737** 55-57-60
  45      746       748F  49-50-54    771F  49-50-54   779F  49-50-54   787F  49-50-54
                    747** 49-51-55    759** 53-55-59   763** 55-57-61   767** 56-58-62
  40      778       774F  50-53-57    798F  51-53-57   806F  51-53-57   814F  52-53-57
                                      788** 54-57-61   792** 56-58-62   796** 57-60-64
  35      812       799F  52-55-59    824F  54-56-60   833F  54-56-60   841F  54-56-60
                                      818** 55-58-62   822** 57-60-64   826** 58-61-65
  30      846       818B  52-56-61    848B  56-59-63   857F  56-59-63   862B  56-59-63
                                      847** 56-59-64   851** 58-61-65   856** 59-62-67
  25      851       826B  52-57-62    857F  56-59-64   862B  56-59-64   862B  57-59-64
                                      854** 57-60-65   859** 59-62-66
  20      853       833B  53-57-62    862B  56-59-64   862B  57-59-64   862B  57-59-64
                                      858** 58-61-66
  15      854       840B  54-58-63    862B  57-59-64   862B  57-59-64   862B  57-59-64
  10      856       847B  55-59-64    862B  57-60-64   862B  57-60-64   862B  57-60-64
   5      857       854B  56-59-64    862B  57-60-64   862B  57-60-64   862B  57-60-64

Min Flap Ret Ht    400 ft

MAX BRAKE RELEASE WEIGHT MUST NOT EXCEED MAX CERT WEIGHT OF    86182 KG
Limit Codes: B=Brake Energy F=Field **=Improved Climb *=Obstacle/Level-off
             T=Tire V=VMCG
TORA is 3000 M, TODA is 3000 M, ASDA is 3000 M
Line-up distances are 0 M for TODA and 0 M for ASDA
Runway slopes are -0.09 % for TODA and -0.09 % for ASDA
                                        OBSTACLES FROM LO-FT/M
Runway    Ht  Dist Offset      Ht  Dist Offset      Ht  Dist Offset
12        No obstacles
12        No procedure
```

*Figure 305: Runway analysis, Rwy12 SBSG/NAT.*

Here, there is a bunch of different limiting codes, depending on temperature and wind. Remember to always choose the lowest one, unless you are doing an Improved Climb. Let's see the highlighted example, 30°C.

At 5kt tailwind (-5kt), the indicated weight is 81,800kg. Compared to that of the separate column (Climb – 84,600kg), the lowest value is the Brake Energy limited weight. There is no way to execute and Improved Climb, as this value does not appear on the chart.

On the other hand, wind columns 0kt, +5kt and +10kt all weights are Climb limited, and limit codes vary between Brake Energy and Field. This way, maximum takeoff weight is 84,600kg. Note that even with different weights in these 3 wind columns, VSpeeds are the same. This is because they are referring to the Climb limit weight of 84,600kg.

When executing an Improved Climb analysis, the top line should be disregarded and only the bottom line should be taken into account. Thus, there is no need to perform a weight comparison to select the lowest. The limit weight is really Improved Climb, and VSpeeds are those pointed next to the weight value.

When takeoff analysis is generated, it is essential that some aspects be considered in their worst possible situation. One of the items that assume this characteristic in the analysis is the airplane's center of gravity. Regardless of the actual CG position on takeoff, it is always computed in its most unfavorable position. As you may remember from the CG Considerations section, in the Weight and Balance chapter, the more forward the CG is, the greater the negative lift on the horizontal stabilizer and the greater the lift required to keep the airplane in the air with the same weight.

Let's talk in terms of V2. For example, at a given weight, with CG in the most forward position, I need a given amount of lift that will be produced at a V2 equal to 150kt. If CG were at a more aft position, that would require a little less lift and V2 could be, for example, 148kt. But while this is an interesting and technically correct fact, it is legally prohibited. Maximum takeoff weight and speeds must be calculated using the frontmost CG of the envelope. Unless...

Imagine that over a year or two of operations with this aircraft in your company, you realize that 95% of flights were dispatched with CG at 17% of MAC or aft. When realizing this, the manufacturer offered a purchase option. This option is a certification with a new CG envelope whose forward limit has been changed.

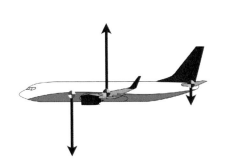

The real CG position for takeoff does not matter for performance computation. Performance is always calculated considering the most unfavorable CG.

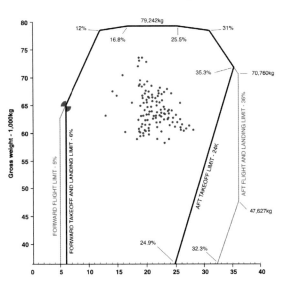

*Figure 306: CG used in takeoff computation (normal envelope).*

Should operators wish to use this new envelope also for landing, they will have to ensure that the CG remains within these new limits at all times between engine start and cutoff. This can affect an aircraft's loading procedure and minimum fuel on board on ferry flights, among other things. For takeoff, however, whenever CG is at or aft that new envelope forward limit, runway analysis can be generated using this new worst possible situation.

We call this new certification **Alternate Forward CG**, which, in my humble opinion, is a little misleading, as it can make some people believe that CG has been moved forward. In fact, the word Forward does not refer to the actual position of the CG, but to the part of the envelope that has been changed. CG envelope has moved its forward limit backwards. So, I would propose a different name with a simple change and would call it Alternate Forward *Limit* CG.

With this change made, there are two ways to analyze the practical result. First, for the same weight, I get lower takeoff speeds and that means that the runway "got bigger". This allows me, for example, to use a higher assumed temperature.

Another possibility, owing to this virtually "longer" runway, is to allow a greater takeoff weight. Note that this is not an absolute truth for every situation. By reducing the takeoff speeds, we "increased" the available runway for takeoff and increased the maximum field limited takeoff weight. But reducing takeoff speeds may not be a good deal when the limiting factor is Climb or Obstacle. In this case, using low speeds may result in weight penalty instead of gain – remember that increasing V2 gets this speed closer to the best angle of climb speed, while reducing it can make you lose some climb capability. That is most likely to be true with alternate forward CG in a very rear position, and for these mid positions often chosen by operators, the reduced drag owing to less required lift will most certainly overcome the problem.

In the next illustration, observe the alternative envelope with modified forward limit. This new limit of 17% will be used for calculating runway analysis – this is just an example as alternate forward CG can be 15, 21, 23% or whichever number the operator is willing to purchase. Note the gain in maximum takeoff weights at Santos Dumont airport: it ranges between 700kg and 800kg, which is equivalent to about 10 passengers by the current standard in Brazil.

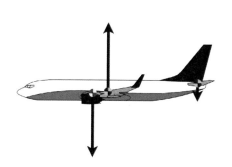

The takeoff CG may move even further aftward without bringing about changes to performance calculation. It was based on the worst scenario for this new envelope.

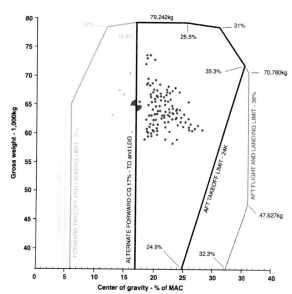

Figure 307: Alternate forward CG envelope.

```
Elevation: 11.0 ft                  Runway 20L                        SBRJ
737-800{W,SFP}/CFM56-7B27-B1                                           NA
                                                    RJ / SANTOS DUMONT, BRASIL
                                                             Dated 27-Jan-19

        Derate = Full Rated Thrust            Flaps = Flaps 15
        A/I = Off                             CG = Forward
Runway Cond = Dry                             V1 Policy = Optimum
        A/S = On

           Maximum brake release weight - 100 (kg)
                              Wind (kts)
OAT
°C        -5.0          0.0           5.0           10.0
  40    533F 14-16-28  560F 18-20-31  568F 20-21-32  577F 21-22-32
  39    537F 15-16-29  563F 19-20-31  572F 20-21-32  581F 21-22-33
  38    540F 15-17-29  566F 19-20-32  575F 20-21-32  584F 21-22-33
  37    543F 15-17-29  569F 19-20-32  578F 20-22-33  588F 22-22-34
  36    546F 15-17-30  573F 19-21-32  582F 21-22-33  591F 22-23-34
  35    549F 15-17-30  576F 19-21-33  585F 21-22-34  594F 22-23-34
  34    551F 16-18-30  578F 20-21-33  588F 21-22-34  597F 22-24-35
  33    554F 16-18-31  581F 20-21-33  590F 21-23-34  600F 23-24-35
  32    557F 16-18-31  584F 20-22-34  593F 21-23-35  603F 23-24-36
  31    559F 16-18-31  587F 20-22-34  596F 22-23-35  605F 23-24-36
  30    561F 16-19-32  589F 20-22-34  599F 22-23-35  608F 23-25-36
  29    563F 16-19-32  591F 20-22-35  600F 22-23-35  610F 23-25-36
  28    564F 16-19-32  592F 21-22-35  601F 22-24-36  611F 23-25-37
  27    565F 17-19-32  593F 21-23-35  603F 22-24-36  612F 23-25-37
  26    567F 17-19-32  595F 21-23-35  604F 22-24-36  614F 24-25-37
  25    568F 17-19-33  596F 21-23-35  606F 22-24-36  615F 24-25-37
  24    569F 17-19-33  597F 21-23-35  607F 23-24-36  617F 24-25-37
  23    570F 17-20-33  599F 21-23-35  608F 23-24-36  618F 24-26-37
  22    572F 17-20-33  600F 21-23-36  610F 23-24-37  619F 24-26-37
  21    573F 17-20-33  601F 22-23-36  611F 23-25-37  621F 24-26-38
  20    574F 18-20-33  603F 22-24-36  612F 23-25-37  622F 24-26-38

QNH Correction (kg/mbar), Ref 1013.0 mbar (based on 1003.0 and 1023.0)

Min Flap Ret Ht   800 ft

MAX BRAKE RELEASE WEIGHT MUST NOT EXCEED MAX CERT WEIGHT OF      86182 KG
Limit Codes: B=Brake Energy C=Climb F=Field *=Obstacle/Level-off T=Tire
             V=VMCG
TORA is 1323 M, TODA is 1323 M, ASDA is 1323 M
Line-up distances are 0 M for TODA and 0 M for ASDA
Runway slopes are 0.0 % for TODA and 0.0 % for ASDA
                                            OBSTACLES FROM LO-FT/M
Runway   Ht   Dist Offset    Ht   Dist Offset    Ht   Dist Offset
20L     259   2877    0
20L   No procedure
```

```
Elevation: 11.0 ft                  Runway 20L                        SBRJ
737-800{W,SFP}/CFM56-7B27-B1                                           NA
                                                    RJ / SANTOS DUMONT, BRASIL
                                                             Dated 27-Jan-19

        Derate = Full Rated Thrust            Flaps = Flaps 15
        A/I = Off                             CG = 17.0
Runway Cond = Dry                             V1 Policy = Optimum
        A/S = On

           Maximum brake release weight - 100 (kg)
                              Wind (kts)
OAT
°C        -5.0          0.0           5.0           10.0
  40    540F 14-16-27  567F 18-19-30  576F 19-20-31  585F 21-21-32
  39    543F 14-16-28  570F 18-19-30  579F 19-21-31  588F 21-22-32
  38    546F 14-16-28  573F 18-20-31  582F 20-21-32  592F 21-22-32
  37    549F 15-16-28  577F 19-20-31  586F 20-21-32  595F 21-22-33
  36    552F 15-17-29  580F 19-20-31  589F 20-21-32  598F 21-23-33
  35    555F 15-17-29  583F 19-20-32  592F 20-22-33  601F 22-23-34
  34    558F 15-17-30  586F 19-21-32  595F 21-22-33  604F 22-23-34
  33    561F 15-17-30  588F 19-21-33  598F 21-22-33  607F 22-23-34
  32    563F 15-18-30  591F 20-21-33  601F 21-22-34  610F 22-24-35
  31    566F 16-18-31  594F 20-21-33  603F 21-23-34  613F 22-24-35
  30    568F 16-18-31  596F 20-22-34  606F 21-23-34  616F 23-24-35
  29    570F 16-18-31  598F 20-22-34  607F 21-23-35  617F 23-24-35
  28    571F 16-18-31  599F 20-22-34  609F 22-23-35  619F 23-24-36
  27    572F 16-18-31  601F 20-22-34  610F 22-23-35  620F 23-24-36
  26    573F 16-19-31  602F 20-22-34  612F 22-23-35  621F 23-25-36
  25    575F 16-19-32  603F 21-22-34  613F 22-24-35  623F 23-25-36
  24    576F 17-19-32  605F 21-22-34  614F 22-24-35  624F 23-25-36
  23    577F 17-19-32  606F 21-23-35  616F 22-24-35  626F 24-25-36
  22    579F 17-19-32  607F 21-23-35  617F 22-24-36  627F 24-25-37
  21    580F 17-19-32  609F 21-23-35  619F 22-24-36  629F 24-25-37
  20    581F 17-19-32  610F 21-23-35  620F 23-24-36  630F 24-25-37

QNH Correction, Ref 1013.0 mbar

Min Flap Ret Ht   800 ft

MAX BRAKE RELEASE WEIGHT MUST NOT EXCEED MAX CERT WEIGHT OF      86182 KG
Limit Codes: B=Brake Energy C=Climb F=Field *=Obstacle/Level-off T=Tire
             V=VMCG
TORA is 1323 M, TODA is 1323 M, ASDA is 1323 M
Line-up distances are 0 M for TODA and 0 M for ASDA
Runway slopes are 0.0 % for TODA and 0.0 % for ASDA
                                            OBSTACLES FROM LO-FT/M
Runway   Ht   Dist Offset    Ht   Dist Offset    Ht   Dist Offset
20L     259   2877    0
20L   No procedure
```

Figure 308: SBRJ takeoff analysis: FWD CG and ALT FWD CG.

When an airplane's takeoff weight is tire speed limited, alternate forward CG can make an even greater difference in MTOW, since you are able to reduce takeoff speeds to keep $V_{LOF}$ within tire limits. Take a look at the next figure. Consider a Boeing 777-300ER departing from runway 34L at Denver, Colorado (USA). The graphic is considering a 5kt tailwind and three different CG envelopes scenarios: FWD, ALT FWD 22%, and ALT FWD 27%. Between the first and the last, the difference in MTOW is close to 9,000kg!

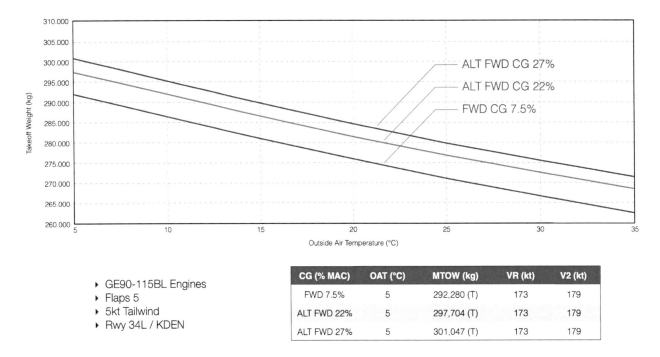

- GE90-115BL Engines
- Flaps 5
- 5kt Tailwind
- Rwy 34L / KDEN

| CG (% MAC) | OAT (°C) | MTOW (kg) | VR (kt) | V2 (kt) |
|---|---|---|---|---|
| FWD 7.5% | 5 | 292,280 (T) | 173 | 179 |
| ALT FWD 22% | 5 | 297,704 (T) | 173 | 179 |
| ALT FWD 27% | 5 | 301,047 (T) | 173 | 179 |

*Figure 309: ALT FWD CG effect on tire speed limit weight.*

# 3.15 Stabili

Light aircraft pilots already know by heart the adjustment of the horizontal stabilizer for takeoff: neutral. At least, this is the case for 95% of smaller planes. Larger aircraft, such as those that we are looking into in this book, have a relatively large CG travel allowance for takeoff and a huge variation in weight and thrust that will be used for takeoff. This requires the horizontal stabilizer adjustment to be studied more carefully and handled more accurately.

What is the purpose of adjusting the stabilizer trim for takeoff?

The rule says that the stabilizer must be trimmed so that three situations can be satisfied:

1.  Provide adequate force in the control column for aircraft rotation.
2.  Aircraft trimmed for V2+Increment on All Engine Takeoff situations.
3.  Aircraft trimmed for V2 on one Engine Inoperative Takeoff situations.

First, let's clarify the expression "V2+Increment". When we assume that the airplane lost thrust on its critical engine in $V_{EF}$, acceleration capability is drastically reduced from this moment on. Either way, it must reach V2 by 35ft above the runway and continue at this speed until the end of the second takeoff segment – assuming a normal rotation rate at VR between 2 and 3°/s. With the same rotation rate during "all engine takeoff", an airplane gets faster between VR and the time it reaches 35ft, exceeding V2 by some knots. How many knots it will exceed V2 is a factor that varies from aircraft to aircraft. While twin-engines can exceed V2 between 15 and 25kt, four-engine aircraft can increase speed between 10 and 20kt. Our model airplane, the Boeing 737-800, usually exceeds V2 by 20kt during a normal all engine takeoff.

Now, it is often not possible to address all three situations with a single adjustment. So, the manufacturer has to compromise and find the best setting to accommodate all three situations. This means that, in some cases, adjustment will not be an accurate trim for both All Engine and One Engine Inoperative takeoffs, but it will be well suited and precise enough for each situation.

The stabilizer trim setting basically depends on 4 factors: takeoff weight (ATOW), CG position, takeoff flap, and engine thrust. For this last item, most aircraft consider the maximum thrust for selected takeoff rate, ignoring the fact that thrust might be lower owing to the assumed temperature method.

In next illustration, we will consider engine thrust as the only force exerted on the airplane and the one that must be counteract by the stabilizer. For this reason, the stabilizer force will be represented as an upward force. In fact, when adding up all forces acting on the aircraft, it should be pointing downward.

You will see the first plane with a 26,000lb engine using full thrust on takeoff. This will produce a pitch up momentum on the airplane, and the horizontal stabilizer will be adjusted to balance this situation.

In the second drawing, engine derate was applied and thrust is 24,000lb now. With less thrust, the pitch up momentum also decreases and, thus, the adjustment of the horizontal stabilizer has to be redefined for takeoff, just as shown.

The third plane in our example will take off with the same 24K derate, but, in addition, pilots used the assumed temperature method to further reduce engine thrust. This decrease caused the nose up momentum also to decrease even further; however, there was no new adjustment in the stabilizer trim for takeoff. The practical result is that the pilots will feel the airplane's nose a bit heavy on takeoff and it will be heavier as assumed temperature is higher and engine thrust is further reduced.

Boeing's recently designed aircraft, such as the 737MAX, 787, and 747-8, started to take into account the reduced thrust resulting from the assumed temperature method, and the stabilizer trim setting on those types of aircraft now accounts for that (actual engine thrust), rather than the maximum thrust of the selected rate.

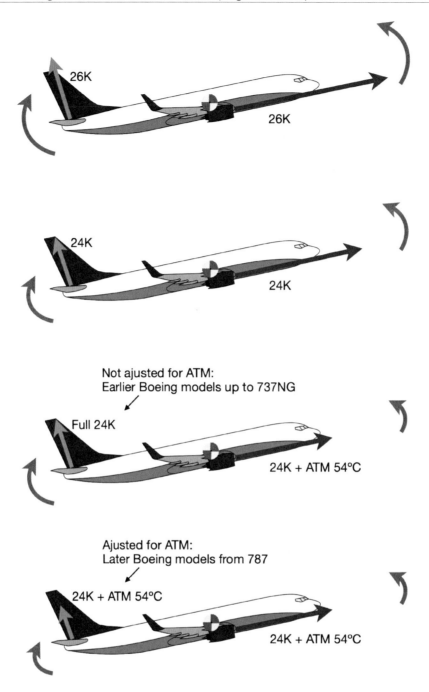

Not ajusted for ATM:
Earlier Boeing models up to 737NG

Full 24K

24K + ATM 54°C

Ajusted for ATM:
Later Boeing models from 787

24K + ATM 54°C

24K + ATM 54°C

*Figure 310: Stabilizer trim setting in older and recent models.*

*Figure 311: Airbus A320 trim setting on the left and Boeing 737NG on the right.*

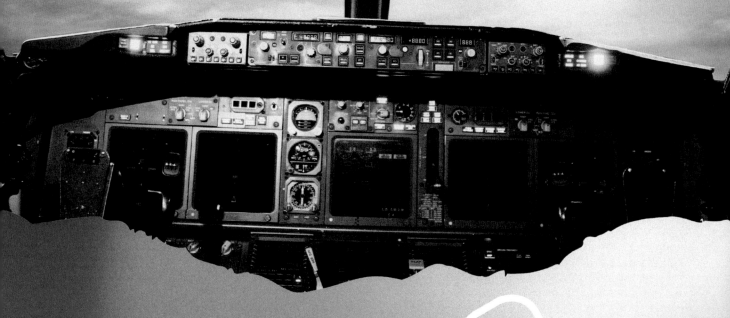

# Enroute Performance

When it comes to climb, we need to know which strategies are available to perform this part of the flight, and which criteria should be adopted for choosing climb speed.

First, let's see when we use $V_X$ (best angle or gradient of climb) and $V_Y$ (best rate of climb) speeds, and how they can be determined.

These two speeds are defined by comparing two different factors. The speed that results in the best angle of climb, $V_X$, is the speed at which the aircraft has the largest amount of excess thrust, which means the greatest value of thrust minus drag. $V_Y$, the best rate of climb, is the speed at which the airplane has the greatest excess of power, meaning the greatest difference between the available power curve and the power required to maintain the flight. Heads-up: even though colloquially, some pilots refer to engine power when they actually mean engine thrust; we need to remember that power and thrust are two absolutely different physical properties. Thrust is a force (Newton is the metric unit) and power is a measure of work in a given time (whose metric unit is the Watt).

Now, although you should know where these speeds come from, we are going to focus on the practical usefulness of information, as promised at the beginning of this book. So, let's see when we use one speed or another.

## 4.1.1 Maximum Angle of Climb Speed

The best angle or the best gradient of climb speed was briefly discussed when we talked about V2. This is the speed that will be used every time you want to reach a given altitude while traveling the shortest possible distance. The best example is when we want to overcome an obstacle, a cloud, or just to be able to comply with an altitude constrain from an SID. Note in the example below that when using any speed other than $V_X$, whether higher or lower, the result will be a shallower angle of climb (indicated by the dashed line).

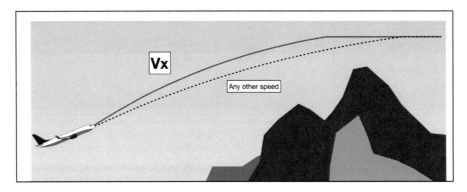

*Figure 312: Best angle of climb speed.*

## 4.1.2 Maximum Rate of Climb Speed

The best rate of climb is the speed that will be used whenever we want to reach a given altitude in the shortest period of time. A typical example of a suitable scenario for using this speed is when an air traffic controller asks us to expedite our climb until crossing or reaching a certain flight level. Another example is when finding turbulence during climb. Sometimes that bumpy ride is only for a few thousand feet and crossing that area vertically as quickly as possible might be a good idea.

$V_Y$ will always be greater than $V_X$, and any speed other than $V_Y$, whether higher or lower, will result in a longer time until the desired altitude is reached.

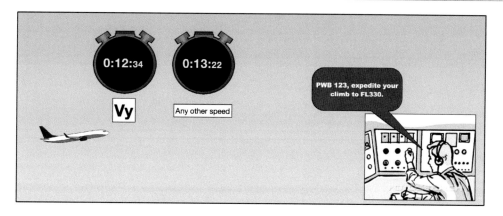

*Figure 313: Best rate of climb speed.*

Bear in mind that these speeds vary with aircraft's weight and altitude. They decrease with a lighter plane and increase with a heavier one. Altitude-wise, it will increase slightly as the airplane gains altitude. During climb, a Boeing 737 can burn more than 2,000kg of fuel and will cross several flight levels. Therefore, it is natural to assume that $V_X$ and $V_Y$ speeds will vary during this phase of flight. This is correct. However, climb speeds calculated by onboard computers of all large commercial aircraft normally select an average speed according to the above-mentioned factors and do not update this value in the short time of a single climb.

To solidify the understanding of the subject, let's analyze both graphs below. They represent a Boeing 757 climbing from sea level up to 30,000ft. The aircraft weighed 100,000kg at the time of takeoff. On the left side you can see the best rate of climb (258kt). Using this speed, time to reach 30,000ft is the shortest. On the right, we can find the best angle of climb speed (220kt), in which the distance covered until reaching 30,000ft was the shortest.

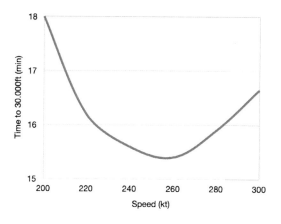
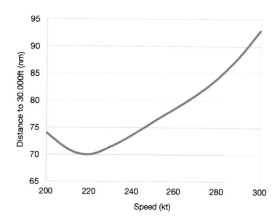

*Figure 314: Example of Vy and Vx for a Boeing 757.*

### 4.1.3 Minimum Fuel Burn Climb Speed

As we are talking about strategies, $V_X$ and $V_Y$ are not the only speeds we have to choose from during climb. We have some other options. One is the speed of lower fuel consumption.

In the example of the previous illustration, the aircraft burns the least amount of fuel to reach FL300 if it maintains 245kt during climb (Figure 315 on the next page), a speed that is less than $V_Y$ (258kt).

However, this is only half the story. At this speed (245kt), the aircraft will burn 1,860kg to reach 30,000ft and is undoubtedly the lowest fuel burn for any speed. However, we can say that this is the **right answer to the wrong question**. The question that should be asked is: which speed generates the lowest fuel burn to get to the destination airport. Let's see what I mean in Figure 316.

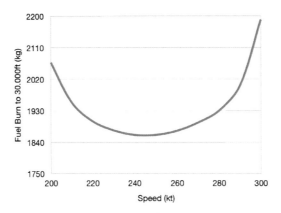

*Figure 315: Speed for minimum fuel burn until reaching 30,000ft.*

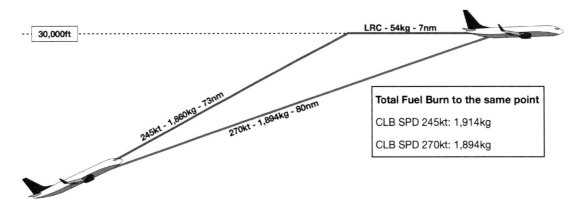

*Figure 316: Minimum fuel burn during climb considering a route from A to B.*

The image above shows that the speed for lowest fuel burn is 270kt and not 245kt. That is because even with a higher fuel burn on the way up, there is a compensation; after all, total fuel burn is lower for the aircraft to be able to achieve a point 80nm downrange (20kg savings).

## 4.1.4   Crossover Altitude - Changing from IAS to Mach

Let's start a discussion about the type of speed that we should use during climb: IAS or MACH? In fact, we use both! When to use one or the other will depend on the altitude we are flying through. So, at which altitude do I stop using IAS and start flying with Mach number?

To answer this question, we will see how these speeds are related. You probably remember the beginning of our studies. In an ISA atmosphere, for a constant indicated airspeed, TAS is greater as altitude increases. In the same scenario, the TAS that represents a given MACH number depends on temperature and, in a standard atmosphere, temperature decreases as we go up, stabilizing in the tropopause. Thus, for the same MACH number, TAS decreases with altitude while below the tropopause and remains constant within this layer of the atmosphere.

Analyzing what I just said, note that when choosing an IAS and a MACH number to climb, these two values will eventually represent the same TAS. It is exactly at this point that we stop flying with one unit and adopt the other, opting for the lowest TAS between both. The altitude at which this occurs is called Change-Over Altitude or Crossover Altitude.

See two examples of this change in speed. Next, we have a graphic where the indicated airspeed is represented by blue lines and the Mach number, by the green lines. On the vertical axis, we have pressure altitude and on the horizontal axis, true airspeed (TAS). So, you can follow a blue line up to any altitude and check which TAS is represented by this IAS by just looking at the horizontal axis of the graphic (in the standard atmosphere). For example, I can see that at 25,000ft, 200kt indicated airspeed is equivalent to 293kt true airspeed (example with red arrows). The same way as the blue line indicates the relationship between IAS, TAS, and Altitude; the thin green line shows the same for Mach/TAS/Altitude. Following the M0.70 line, I can see that 70% of the speed of sound is worth a true airspeed of 412kt at 30,000ft (yellow line).

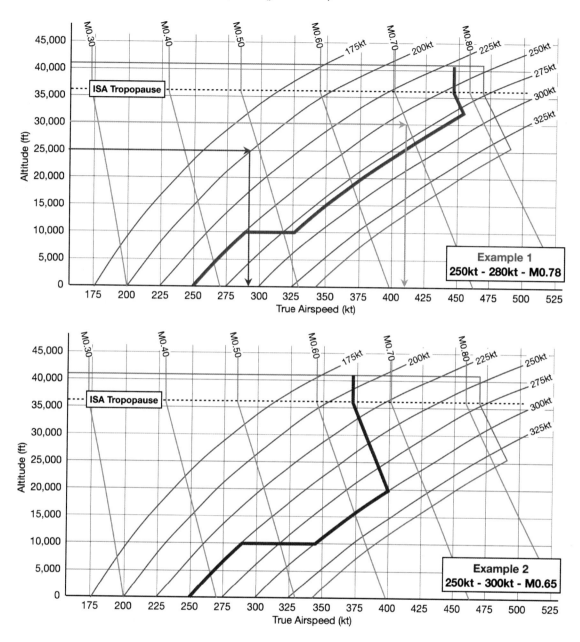

*Figure 317: Change-over altitude examples 1 (32,400ft) and 2 (20,000ft).*

When we talk about indicated airspeed presented in knots, the term KIAS is often used. So, in example 1, shown in Figure 317, we maintained 250KIAS until reaching 10,000ft, accelerated to 280KIAS, and continued climbing with that speed until we found an altitude at which both, 280KIAS and M0.78 (Mach speed we chose to climb), represented the same TAS. This happened at about 32,400ft and the equivalent TAS was 455kt.

In example 2, we kept the same 250KIAS until 10,000ft, accelerated to 300KIAS, and continued climbing at this speed until the Mach number we chose (M0.65) represented the same TAS that we had with 300KIAS. In this case, the altitude at which both were equal was 20,000ft, and TAS was 400kt for both of them.

Maintaining a constant indicated speed until reaching cruise altitude, and disregarding Mach number, will inevitably make us exceed an aircraft operational limit: $M_{MO}$, or Maximum Operational Mach. It happens similarly on a descent path, because if we keep a constant Mach number, the operational speed exceeded will be $V_{MO}$,

Maximum Operational Speed. These speeds ($V_{MO}$ and $M_{MO}$) and the maximum altitude of our model aircraft are represented by the red lines in Figure 317.

Using the equation below, you can determine the altitude at which the transition between Mach and IAS will occur. You must input the chosen Mach number, and the indicated (or calibrated) airspeed that you intend to use (in knots), and the result will be the altitude at which the transition will occur (in feet).

$$h_p = \frac{\left( \left\{ \frac{\left[ 1 + 0.2 \left( \frac{CAS}{661.4786} \right)^2 \right]^{3.5} - 1}{\left( \frac{M^2}{5} + 1 \right)^{3.5} - 1} \right\}^{\frac{1}{5.25588}} \times 288.15 \right) - 288.15}{-0.0019812}$$

*Equation 15: Change-over altitude (in feet).*

A thought that must be running through your head now: "how do I choose the indicated airspeed and Mach numbers to be used during climb?". I am going to explain that.

The indicated airspeed to be used during climb is usually the result of some factors that are entered in the aircraft's flight computer, including weight, expected cruise wind and temperature, and Cost Index (we will see more about Cost Index in an exclusive topic). The Mach number also depends on the same factors, but it is chosen to represent the speed that will be flown during cruise flight, not during climb.

The computer calculates the indicated airspeed you will use when climbing and the Mach number you will use on cruise flight. The result produced by the computer in calculating the cruise Mach number is replicated to be used also during climb. This is done so that there is no need for acceleration or deceleration when leveling the aircraft. Of course, we can edit these speeds and choose others. This is usually done when an air traffic controller makes any speed adjustment request, there is turbulence, or the airplane has a faulty system that restricts its operating speed. But in general, the Mach number used in climb is really the one that will be used during initial cruise flight.

## 4.1.5  Climb Derate

In the images that show the FMC N1 Limit Page of a 737 (when we talk about Derate and assumed temperature), you might have noticed that an adjustment to climb thrust is also available. That is called Climb Derate.

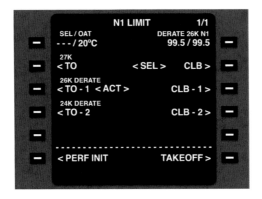

*Figure 318: Climb derate selection.*

In the flight computers of aircraft manufactured by Boeing and Airbus (FMC or FMGS), there is usually the option of two levels of Climb Derate, which are called CLB-1 and CLB-2 on Boeing airplanes. Exemplifying with our model airplane, the 737NG, CLB represents maximum climb thrust, CLB-1 is maximum thrust minus 10% and CLB-2 is maximum thrust minus 20%. But why does climb derate exist?

Originally, the purpose of this feature was to allow aircraft to behave as pilots expected them to. Every pilot, since his/her first flight, takes off with maximum thrust applied and, when reaching acceleration altitude, reduces thrust to a lower level, and this amount of thrust will be used throughout climb path. Remember that takeoff thrust is only available for 5 minutes, as determined by engine certification data.

At some point in time, engines started to become very powerful. Actually, so powerful that pilots did not need to use all available thrust on takeoff. Through the methods we studied, Derate and ATM, engine thrust is reduced to the level that is necessary. In some cases, thrust becomes so low that it is now less than climb thrust. Nonsense happens in these cases. Pilot increase engine thrust instead of reducing it at acceleration altitude.

CLB-1 and CLB-2 were introduced to allow an aircraft's engine to behave as pilots expected and have trained for so long. These extra reductions (10 and 20%) are gradually eliminated during climb, until a certain altitude where the level of thrust being used is already maximum climb thrust again.

| | TOGA | CLB | CLB-1 | CLB-2 |
|---|---|---|---|---|
| **Full Rate 26K** | 98.7% | 95.0% | 92.0% | 89.0% |
| **Derate 24K** | 94.3% | 95.0% | 92.0% | 89.0% |
| **24K ATM 54°C** | 90.3% | 95.0% | 92.0% | 89.0% |

*Figure 319: First reason for climb derate.*

Another question that you may be asking right now is: "does it save fuel"? The answer is no. In fact, total fuel burn increases. But there are other advantages to be considered. Let's talk about them.

Rolls Royce and General Electric, two of the largest jet engine manufacturers in the world (along with Pratt and Whitney), strongly disagree about the advantages of using Climb Derate. GE's vision is very simple: do not use it. For them, it is not worth the extra fuel consumption. RR is a strong advocate for using this resource in all flights, in a very special way, in long-haul flights.

Before proceeding with the explanation why RR defends the use of Climb Derate, look at Figure 320 (left side) to see how it works on a Boeing 777 equipped with these engines. On this aircraft, at 10,000ft or higher, engine thrust is gradually returned to maximum climb regime, reaching this value at 30,000ft. This altitude at which climb thrust returns to maximum is called "Washout Altitude". The British company offers two options of Washout Altitude. In one version, maximum climb thrust is regained at 15,000ft (just as a CFM engine works on a 737NG) while in the other version, a slower thrust recovery occurs, and maximum thrust is available again only at 30,000ft.

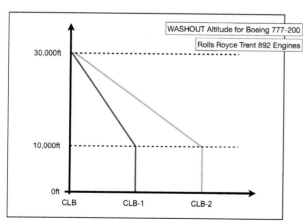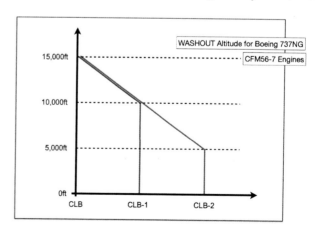

*Figure 320: Engine climb thrust derate washing out (B777-200/RR Trent 892 on the left and B737NG/CFM56 on the right).*

To give more substance to our theoretical study, there is nothing better than a practical example. So, let's make an imaginary flight between two locations 3,000nm apart. We will use a Boeing 777 equipped with RR Trent 892 engines and evaluate some fuel data.

With maximum climb thrust, the airplane climbs faster and reaches cruise altitude sooner. In terms of fuel, climb is much more economical this way, but as we saw earlier in this same chapter, this is only half the story. When using CLB-1 or CLB-2, climb takes longer, and fuel burn is higher, but to be fair, we have to make a comparison of fuel spent to the same point along the route, without evaluating climb path exclusively. This was done and presented in Figure 321. By analyzing the results of this study, we can see that flight time increased by 0.4min when using CLB-1 and by 0.9min when using CLB-2. Fuel burn was 52lb higher using CLB-1 and 144lb higher when CLB-2 was used.

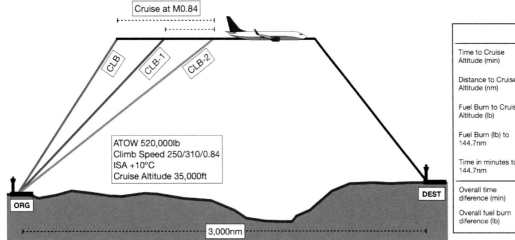

|  | CLB | CLB-1 | CLB-2 |
|---|---|---|---|
| Time to Cruise Altitude (min) | 19.9 | 21.5 | 23.5 |
| Distance to Cruise Altitude (nm) | 123.5 | 132.8 | 144.7 |
| Fuel Burn to Cruise Altitude (lb) | 11312 | 11656 | 12127 |
| Fuel Burn (lb) to 144.7nm | 11983 | 12035 | 12127 |
| Time in minutes to 144.7nm | 22.6 | 23 | 23.5 |
| Overall time difference (min) | Base | +0.4 | +0.9 |
| Overall fuel burn difference (lb) | Base | +52 | +144 |

*Figure 321: Derated climb study.*

Rolls Royce argues that the cost of this extra flight time is negligible and that the cost of the extra fuel, although significant, is outweighed by engine maintenance cost by up to 10 times. According to RR, frequent use of climb derate (CLB-2) in flights significantly reduces turbine gas temperature (TGT or ITT - Internal Turbine Temperature) and, assuming a 777 performing 700 operations per year, this policy would have the effect of increasing up to 3% the time between engine overhauls (more time on the wing). This greater spacing between engine maintenance events will pay off by up to 10 times the cost generated by higher fuel burn.

Indeed, both manufacturers, RR and GE, may be right. It is reasonable to assume that different engines have different consumption and maintenance characteristics, enough to make it more worthwhile for those with GE engines to operate with maximum climb thrust at all times while aircraft equipped with RR engines should preferably be operated using Climb Derate.

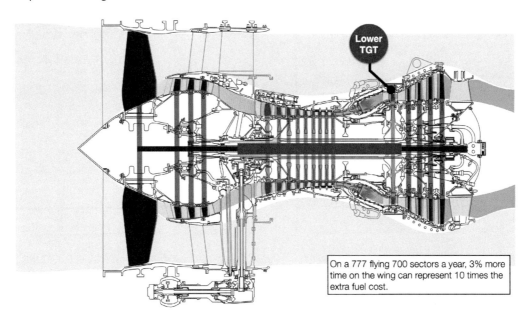

*Figure 322: Lower TGT for longer time on the wing.*

When we think about the time an airplane takes to fly from origin to destination, we have to consider two things: airspeed and altitude. There is a third item to compute, which is the center of gravity, but its influence is indirect, through speed, and we will disregard that. So, I believe that we can divide a possible cruise speed selection into five categories. See the illustration below:

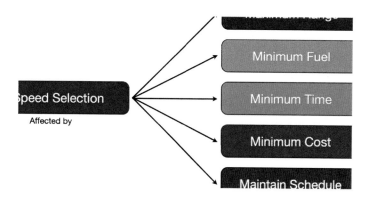

*Figure 323: Possible cruise speeds.*

There is a sixth possibility that was not included in the list, and I will start the discussion showing which one it is and why it was not included. I am talking about the speed that offers the lowest feasible fuel flow and allows for greatest flight endurance.

This speed was not mentioned because we are talking about speeds when navigating from one point to another. I will use a car as an analogy to explain it better. I could say that the speed that offers the longest endurance in my car is 0km/h. That is right. Stopped. With the car parked and the engine running, the fuel flow per hour is very low. Maybe you can leave the car engine running for more than 24 hours before it runs out of gas. Well, just like this car example, the speed that keeps the airplane in the air and offers the greatest endurance is used exactly when you want to keep flying without going anywhere, like when you fly a holding pattern, just waiting for the weather to improve before attempting to land, for example.

## 4.2.1   Fuel Mileage

This is a term that might sound a bit strange for non-English speakers. When we talk about fuel burn to fly from A to B, we are not talking about fuel flow (units of fuel burned per units of time), but fuel mileage! That means how far you can fly with a given amount of fuel burn.

Some may think that the slower we fly, the greater our Fuel Mileage will be. This is not true. Let's go back to the car analogy. Traveling a distance of 200km at 30km/h will result in a hypothetical efficiency of 9km/l. If we increase the speed to 100km/h, this measure jumps to 12km/l. Finally, to further accelerate, say 150km/h, the car's fuel mileage will have a steep drop to 6km/l. An aircraft's behavior is very similar and is based on the drag curve. There is an ideal speed that is neither too slow nor too fast.

Before presenting a graph of an aircraft with fuel mileage as a function of speed, let's go back to those five speed options. Among the five, two represent the same speed. Could you tell which ones?

Maximum Range and Minimum Fuel speed regimes are, in practice, the same thing. After all, to have the greatest range, we need to burn the smallest amount of fuel per mile travelled. About these two, we say that they offer the Optimum Fuel Mileage. We will focus the study of this section on both of them, but first, let's take a quick look at the others.

Minimum Time: to get the shortest flight time, we need to fly at the highest possible speed, which is equivalent to flying at the airplane's $V_{MO}$ or $M_{MO}$.

Minimum Cost: it involves the study of Cost Index, which will be seen in a separate section.

Maintain Schedule: speed based on RTA (Requested Time of Arrival). It occurs when an air traffic controller asks you to pass a certain route fix at a specific time or when the company asks you to adjust the landing time for some special reason.

## 4.2.2 Maximum Range Cruise (MRC) and Long Range Cruise (LRC)

Back to the topic of Maximum Range/Minimum Fuel, the following illustration shows that at the peak of the fuel mileage curve lies its maximum value, allowing us to cover the greatest distance with a specific amount of fuel. This pinnacle value represents our Maximum Range Cruise speed, or simply, MRC. The curve depicted in the illustration pertains to a hypothetical aircraft operating at a designated altitude and weight. It is important to note that altering the weight or altitude will also alter the curve.

A common source of confusion arises, particularly among non-English speakers. Let's delve into the narrative.

During the dawn of commercial aviation's jet era, engine efficiency was notably low, especially at lower altitudes. Aircraft endurance was constrained, making flying in an MRC regime almost imperative to avoid the necessity of making technical landings for refueling.

In the 1970s, the introduction of aircraft equipped with high-bypass turbofan engines (though not as advanced as today's engines) marked a significant improvement in fuel efficiency. Aircraft such as Douglas DC-10, Lockheed L1011 (Tristar), or Boeing 747-200 exemplified this technological advancement. Concurrently, a member of the US Navy (whose name eludes me, regrettably preventing proper credit) undertook a performance analysis of these aircraft to explore the realm of cruise regimes. The study consisted in evaluating if it was worth flying a little bit faster than the MRC to reduce flight time; after all, fuel is the highest, but it is not the only cost of a flight. There were (and still are) other costs related to how long a flight takes from A to B.

The premise adopted by the study was to evaluate what speed gain we have if a penalty of only 1% is applied to the optimum fuel mileage. The result was that, in most cases, there was a gain of between 3 and 5% in cruising speed (on modern jetliners, speed increase is between 2 and 2.5%).

Now, let's consider this perspective together. I will travel 100km that separates any two cities driving at 100km/h in my car. A friend drives the same route in another car at 103km/h. At the end of the trip, it is clear that the faster car arrived first, but time difference was less than 2 minutes. Was it worth the effort?

In another scenario, speeds will also be 100 and 103km/h, but the trip will be longer: 1,000km to go. In this case, the difference between trip times will be 18 minutes, which is a very significant time for flights. Then, the person responsible for the study decided to name this speed regime created from 1% loss over optimum fuel mileage with a name that reflected the kind of flight that it would be best applied to: long-haul flights. He called it Long Range Cruise, LRC.

This term is misleading to many people, who think that it is the speed that can take an airplane to fly the longest distance. This is wrong. LRC takes the airplane up to 99% of the distance it could fly. To travel the longest distance, the speed that must be flown is MRC. Another point that causes confusion is using the Long Range Cruise flight regime in short flights. Some see it as strange, but I assure you that there is nothing wrong. The name suggests the kind of flight in which it is best applied, but it can be used in any flight and there is no such regime called Short or Medium Range Cruise Speed.

When this American fellow did the study, there were still no tools to specify the speed that would show the best relationship between fuel cost and flight time. In modern aircraft, this already exists and is called Cost Index, which will be discussed further on, but for now it is enough to know that when flying is based on typical Cost Index values, the speed that the aircraft develops usually ranges in between MRC and LRC.

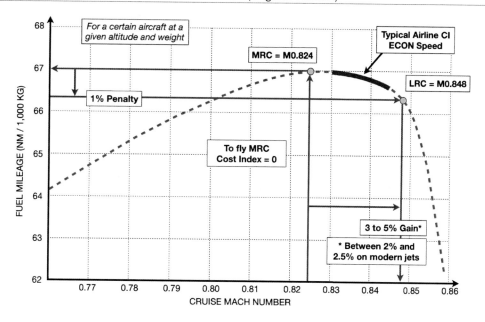

*Figure 324: Difference between LRC and MRC.*

Another relevant piece of information is related to selecting LRC and MRC speeds. The first one is easy. Aircraft flight computers usually have an LRC selection key that just needs to be executed, and that's it: the plane flies at Long Range Cruise speed. For flying at MRC, however, this is not so clear. What should be done is to allow the aircraft to fly on the basis of Cost Index (CI), but set this value to zero. In doing so, the plane will develop Maximum Range Cruise speed.

The reason why CI zero represents MRC speed is simple. For now, let's just say that CI is the ratio between some flight costs and fuel cost, alone. If these flight costs are high and fuel cost is low, the result is a large CI number, and the plane will fly fast prioritizing a short flight time. If flight costs are low and fuel cost is high, we will have a low CI number. Then, the airplane flies at a speed that prioritizes low fuel burn, regardless of the flight time. Then, if I imagine an infinite fuel cost, any number divided by infinite tends to be zero. So, CI zero makes you fly MRC.

Finally, let's see how weight change affects MRC and LRC. Again, simple: the lighter the aircraft, the lower the MRC and LRC speeds. This is because with less weight, the drag curve moves backwards and the speeds have a direct relationship with it. We will see details in a moment, but remember: less weight, less lift, less drag and, of course, less thrust required.

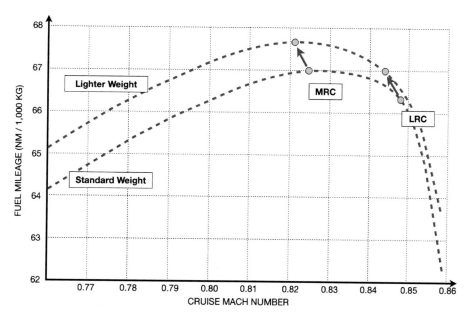

*Figure 325: LRC and MRC as a function of weight.*

### 4.2.3   Wind Effect on MRC, LRC, and ECON Speeds

We talked about how the MRC regime is affected by weight. But how is it affected by wind? For this discussion, let's imagine a glider at some point trying to reach an airport. When we want to fly the longest possible distance, we adjust the best gliding speed, equivalent to the MRC on an airplane in cruise flight. In case of a powered airplane, MRC offers the best distance to be flown in exchange for fuel burned. In the case of gliders, the best gliding speed offers the best distance to be flown in exchange for altitude loss. Let's say the best gliding speed of a given glider is 70kt. With no wind, we can say that any speed different from that (faster or slower) will get us to the ground at a point sooner than flying at the best gliding speed.

Let's disregard the effects of TAS as a function of altitude and pretend that everything happens based on IAS for the purpose of our comparison. With that premise in mind, what would happen if we had a 70kt headwind? Even if maintaining the best gliding speed, our glider would not move at all. We would have to accelerate to actually move forward. It is difficult to imagine how much we should accelerate to have the best gliding speed in this condition, but it is simple to understand that we should fly faster to advance a few meters. For now, this understanding is enough.

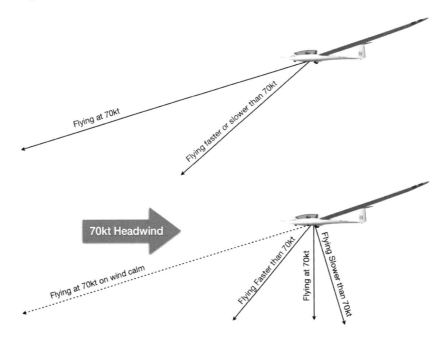

*Figure 326: Best gliding speed for wind clam and headwind.*

The speed that we want to fly on a glider when we are in a thermal is the one that allows us the smallest possible sink rate. In our analogy, it is equivalent to the maximum endurance speed that we use in a holding pattern (maximum time in exchange for fuel on an airplane, and maximum time in exchange for altitude on a glider). Suppose our hypothetical glider has minimum sink speed equal to 60kt. At any speed other than that, it ends up with a higher rate of descent (higher fuel flow for an engine powered aircraft).

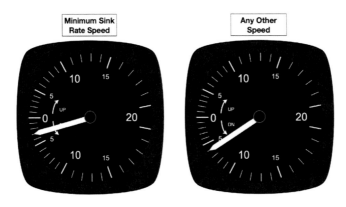

*Figure 327: Minimum sink rate speed.*

Now imagine there is a strong tailwind, instead of a headwind. Since the wind is taking me where I want to go, the most interesting thing would be to take advantage of this situation for as long as possible. Note that I am referring to time, now. In this way, slowing down to our minimum sink speed can take us even further than with maximum gliding speed. This is what we can conclude from these glider-based exercise of imagination: MRC increases with headwind and decreases with tailwind, approaching Maximum Endurance (ME), but never getting below it. Maximum endurance, on the other hand, is not affected by wind.

When analyzing the graph that shows total drag as a function of speed, we can see that it has the shape of a concave curve. Drag starts high, decreases to a certain point, and increases again with speed. This same graph can be used to define the thrust required to maintain level flight, since thrust must be equal to drag in an unaccelerated flight. As thrust is directly proportional to fuel flow, let's look at this chart considering the curve as a representative of these last two factors: fuel flow and required thrust. The lowest point on the curve is the one with the lowest fuel flow and it therefore defines the Maximum Endurance speed. In the same graph, MRC speed is determined when we draw a line that is tangent to the thrust curve and starts from the origin of the system (speed equal to zero). The point where the line touched the graph represents the speed that we are looking for.

To identify how the MRC is affected by the wind, on the same graph we redefine the system's origin based on wind. We move it to the right for headwind and to the left for tailwind. The result confirms what we had imagined would happen.

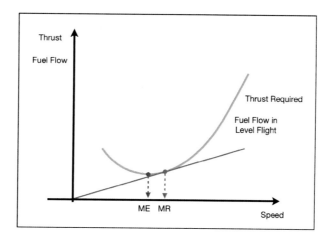

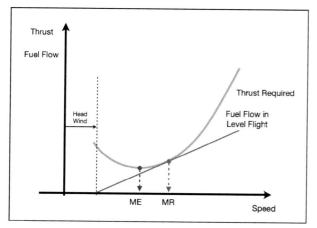
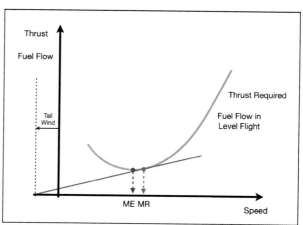

*Figure 328: Wind effect on LRC, MRC, and ECON speeds.*

**Important note:** When we fly based on CI, we say that we are flying with ECON Speed. MRC, ECON, and LRC speeds will all be affected by wind the same way! _HOWEVER_, in practical terms, manufacturers do something different by choice. Boeing's aircraft computers do not correct MRC speeds for tailwinds, just for headwinds (and I believe Airbus and Embraer do the same). ECON speeds for cost index different from zero are corrected for both, headwind and tailwind, but limited to the MRC value for wind calm. Finally, the LRC regime is not corrected for wind at all. It is defined solely based on weight and altitude.

### 4.2.4   Holding Speed and Speed Instability

To explain speed instability, let's revisit the previous graphic. In Figure 329, below, you can see that I have highlighted two speeds, ME and another, much higher one.

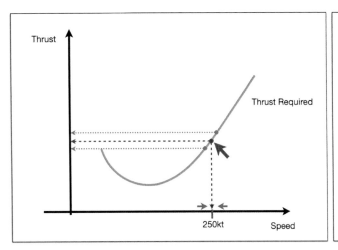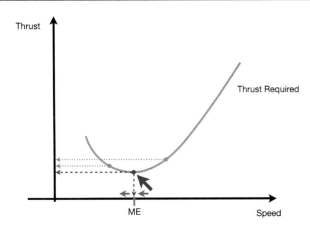

*Figure 329: Stable and unstable speeds.*

Starting with the higher speed on the left graphic (consider it to be 250kt), we can say that it is in a stable region of the graph. To understand that, you need to imagine a small variation in speed, owing to turbulence, for example. Say you lost 3kt flying through bumpy air. You are now flying with 247kt, but you have not changed thrust. As you need less thrust to maintain 247kt, you now have excess thrust, and you will naturally regain speed back to 250kt. If you gain speed instead of losing, say 255kt, you will need more thrust to keep it, but since you did not touch the throttles, speed will soon decrease and set back at the original 250kt. Therefore, it is stable!

Looking at ME on the right graphic now, if you gain some speed for any reason (extrapolated in the figure to show more clearly), as it requires more thrust to maintain and you have not moved the throttles, in a few moments the speed will drop back to original value. However, if you lose a couple of knots, well, you will also need more thrust to keep this lower speed! Remember: you were flying at a speed that required minimum thrust. Flying faster or slower will require more force from the engines. In this situation, speed will drop more and more until a great deal of thrust is applied to regain what was lost. It is a very unstable scenario. For this reason, actual holding speeds are not equal to ME. Yes, I am contradicting myself, but it seemed unnecessary to explain all this before. Now it is time to clarify that. Theoretical ME is not used because it ends up burning more fuel owing to speed instability. So, aircraft usually hold at speeds slightly higher than that, just to do it in a stable region of the graph.

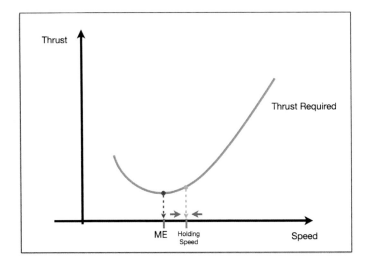

*Figure 330: Actual holding speed is not ME, but a little bit faster.*

It is very important that we take some time to understand how altitude selection affects our flight. We will address two distinct concepts regarding this topic: Optimum Altitude and Maximum Altitude.

## 4.3.1 Optimum Altitude

We had already seen in a previous section that a Fuel Mileage graph is different for each weight and altitude. The following illustration shows these two variations. For a fix weight, note that Fuel Mileage increases as we climb, reaching a maximum at a given flight level, and then it decreases (each blue line represents a different weight). For different weights, the altitude at which the maximum Fuel Mileage occurs also changes. As the airplane gets lighter, the altitude gets higher.

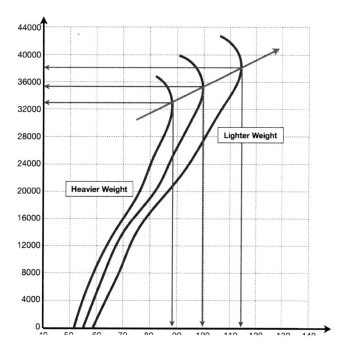

*Figure 331: Fuel mileage as a function of altitude for three different weights.*

Looking at the image above, we find the definition of Optimum Altitude: it is the altitude that offers the highest Fuel Mileage for any given weight. You can see that its variation is linear as the airplane gets lighter. Therefore, we can conclude that the best option for greater fuel savings would be a continuous climb maintaining the aircraft at optimum altitude during the flight. Of course, this solution is utopian and cannot be implemented (there is one exception in commercial aviation history: the Concorde did fly like that). We need to think of a feasible strategy.

Manufacturers have created what they see as the best in-flight fuel economy strategy. In RVSM airspace (Reduced Vertical Separation Minima, in which vertical separation between aircraft is 1,000ft), the recommendation is to make an initial climb to a flight level 1,000ft above the optimum level. This level must be maintained until fuel burn leaves us with an equivalent weight so that current altitude is 1,000ft below the optimum altitude. At this point, we will execute a Step Climb, changing altitude by 2,000ft and putting us back 1,000ft above the optimum level. This process should be repeated as many times as possible, but don't expect too many. For our model aircraft, the Boeing 737NG, this variation of 2,000ft in optimum altitude occurs approximately every 2½ to 3 flight hours, and the average routes flown by this aircraft around the world are shorter than this. In larger aircrafts, making long-haul flights, it is common to make two step climbs during the flight. A third step occurs occasionally.

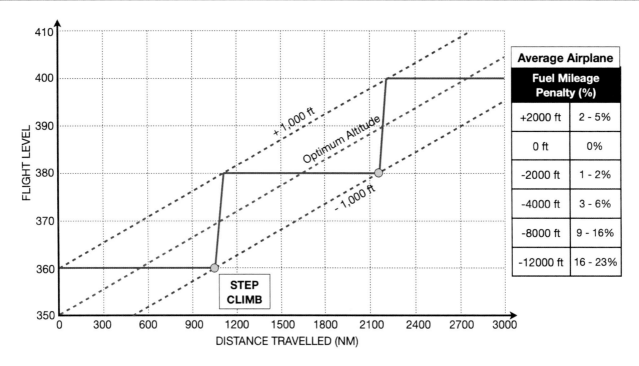

*Figure 332: Step Climb strategy.*

The table on the right side of the illustration above shows how harmful it is to fly away from the optimum altitude. These values may change from plane to plane, and as you see they can increase fuel burn by more than 20% when flying 12,000ft below the optimum level, for example.

An important detail: the optimum flight level may vary depending on the speed selected for cruise flight. If we want to fly between MRC and LRC, for example, Optimum Altitude is about the same for both speed regimes. However, at very high speeds, close to the airplane's $M_{MO}$, this altitude will be significantly lower. For example: a 737-800 weighing 66,700kg has an optimum level of 37,500ft when flying at M0.780. Its optimum flight level drops to 36,500ft when flying at M0.807.

## 4.3.2   Winglets

As we are talking about Fuel Mileage and Optimum Altitude, aircraft with slightly older designs have offered new aerodynamic solutions that directly impact these two topics. On Boeing's side, the 737NG, 757 and 767 line, which originally had no winglets, now does (and aircraft that was purchased without this device can have it installed if desired by the operator). In the case of Airbus, the A319/20/21 line had one type of winglet, but now it has another.

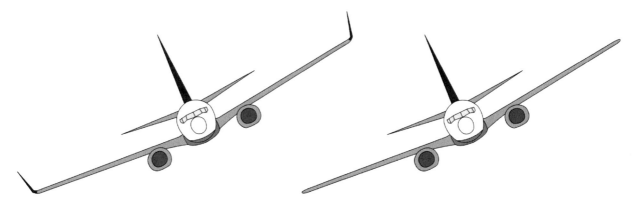

*Figure 333: Boeing 737NG with and without winglets.*

It is important to highlight that the study of aerodynamics is increasingly innovative and what was revolutionary in the past, as a winglet, may not be the best solution for new projects - see Boeing 777, 787 and 747-8 aircraft, for example. However, winglet has been an excellent aerodynamic solution for wings with older design and operators around the world face an interesting dilemma: is it worth paying the cost to install this device?

To help answer this question, you need to know what kind of gains are offered by the winglet. There is an example of gain in increasing fuel mileage of a 737-800, comparing aircraft with and without winglets. The comparison between both of them was made considering the same weight, 75,000kg, and the same cruise flight regime, LRC. The average increase in fuel mileage for this aircraft is over 5.5%. This result is enough to make an evaluation together with two others: the airline must figure how long it intends to use this aircraft in their fleet before passing it on, and how intense their operation is (how many hours per day, on average). With these data, it is simpler to decide whether or not to install these devices on the wings.

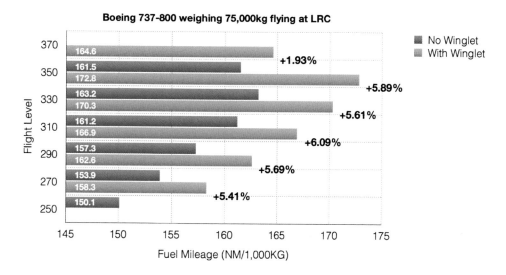

Figure 334: Fuel mileage comparison between 737-800 aircraft with and another without winglets.

### 4.3.3 Flying at Altitudes other than Optimum

Is there any reason why the pilot would choose to fly at an altitude other than the optimum one? Of course, there are always issues related to turbulence or air traffic control, but what about beyond that? Well, there are two basic reasons.

The first is the distance between origin and destination airports. In very short flights, an aircraft's climb and descent paths meet before getting to the optimum altitude. We will be forced to choose between a ballistic flight, or a flight with a lower cruise altitude.

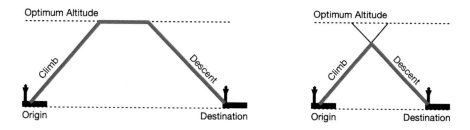

Figure 335: Short flights can make it impossible to reach optimum altitude.

The second case involves some calculations to understand the reason for flying at an altitude other than the optimum one. It is related to different wind layers in the atmosphere. You saw earlier that each aircraft has a different fuel burn penalty, depending on how far away from its optimum altitude it is. Now, imagine that we are at a flight level that penalizes 10% of our fuel mileage, but when comparing to optimum altitude, owing to the more favorable wind at the present flight level, our speed has increased enough to compensate for this penalty, and maybe even more. In this case, the lower altitude is worthwhile. Ways to calculate how much favorable the wind should be at the new altitude will be seen in the last section of this chapter: Practice.

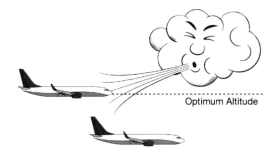

*Figure 336: Flying out of optimum altitude owing to more favorable winds.*

## 4.3.4 Maximum Altitude

We will now begin to discuss Maximum Altitude. Maximum flight altitude is defined on the basis of two distinct parameters: Buffet Margin (or maneuver margin) and Thrust.

### 4.3.4.1 Maximum Altitude – Thrust Limited

Speaking of Thrust, the limit is split in two. The maximum altitude of an airplane can be established by the fact that it has a residual rate of climb of 100ft/min at maximum Cruise Thrust (CRZ), or a residual rate of climb of 300ft/min at Climb Thrust (CLB).

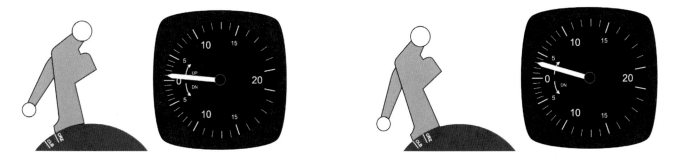

*Figure 337: Maximum altitude - thrust limited.*

### 4.3.4.2 Maximum Altitude – Buffet Limited (Maneuver Margin)

The other aspect that could limit maximum altitude concerns the ability of maneuvering (turning) the aircraft, which we call "maneuver margin". To address this, let's remember what happens to the aircraft as it banks to the side to start a turn in level flight. Well, lift is a force generated perpendicular to the plane of an aircraft's wings; weight is always perpendicular to the ground, no matter what. When wings are leveled, lift and weight are opposite forces, but when the airplane starts to bank, lift starts tilting sideways, too. If it is not increased somehow, the vertical component that is opposite to weight will be smaller and smaller, and the aircraft will lose altitude.

So, we need to find a way of assuring the vertical component of lift to remain equal to weight. The horizontal component of lift is what drives the airplane into the curve, changing its heading. To keep the vertical component equal to weight, total lift needs to be increased. It will be greater and greater as bank is also increased. Then, dividing lift by weight, we can identify the aircraft's "load factor", better known as the G-force.

The greater the G-force, the greater our apparent weight. More weight means we need more lift, and more lift is achieved with more speed. In the following example, we consider an aircraft with a stall speed of 145kt when flying with level wings. See what happens to stall speed (table on the left) and G-force (table on the right) when we bank while maintaining altitude.

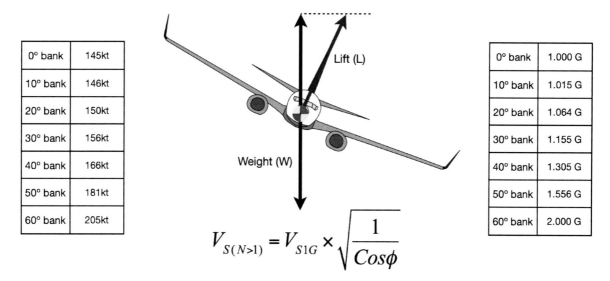

| 0° bank | 145kt |
|---|---|
| 10° bank | 146kt |
| 20° bank | 150kt |
| 30° bank | 156kt |
| 40° bank | 166kt |
| 50° bank | 181kt |
| 60° bank | 205kt |

| 0° bank | 1.000 G |
|---|---|
| 10° bank | 1.015 G |
| 20° bank | 1.064 G |
| 30° bank | 1.155 G |
| 40° bank | 1.305 G |
| 50° bank | 1.556 G |
| 60° bank | 2.000 G |

$$V_{S(N>1)} = V_{S1G} \times \sqrt{\frac{1}{Cos\phi}}$$

*Figure 338: How bank angle relates to stall speed (on the left), and G-force (on the right).*

Regulatory agencies require that maximum flight altitude should have a minimum maneuver margin. For EASA, this value is 1.3G and for FAA, it is 1.2G. Note that these agencies could define minimum margin in terms of bank (EASA 39° and FAA 33°), but it is customary to refer to it according to G-force.

Those who want to receive the proposed exercises (just send me an e-mail to request them) will see that some contain a graph that allows us to calculate this maneuver margin in different situations.

**FAA Minimum Maneuver Margin**

**EASA Minimum Maneuver Margin**

**Long Range Cruise Maximum Operating Altitude**
**Max Cruise Thrust**
**ISA + 10°C and Below**

| WEIGHT (1000 KG) | OPTIMUM ALT (FT) | TAT (°C) | MARGIN TO INITIAL BUFFET 'G' (BANK ANGLE) | | | | |
|---|---|---|---|---|---|---|---|
| | | | 1.20 (33°) | 1.25 (36°) | 1.30 (39°) | 1.40 (44°) | 1.50 (48°) |
| 85 | 32300 | -10 | 34300* | 34300* | 33800 | 32200 | 30800 |
| 80 | 33600 | -13 | 35800* | 35800* | 35100 | 33500 | 32100 |
| 75 | 35000 | -16 | 37100* | 37100* | 36400 | 34900 | 33500 |
| 70 | 36400 | -18 | 38400* | 38400* | 37900 | 36300 | 35000 |
| 65 | 38000 | -18 | 39800* | 39800* | 39400 | 37800 | 36500 |
| 60 | 39600 | -18 | 41000 | 41000 | 41000 | 39500 | 38200 |
| 55 | 41000 | -18 | 41000 | 41000 | 41000 | 41000 | 40000 |
| 50 | 41000 | -18 | 41000 | 41000 | 41000 | 41000 | 41000 |
| 45 | 41000 | -18 | 41000 | 41000 | 41000 | 41000 | 41000 |
| 40 | 41000 | -18 | 41000 | 41000 | 41000 | 41000 | 41000 |

**\*Denotes altitude thrust limited in level flight, 100 fpm residual rate of climb.**

*Figure 339: Example of FAA and EASA minimum maneuver margin on a 737-800W.*

## 4.3.5 Effect of Temperature on Maximum and Optimum Altitude

The previous table (Figure 339) showed the temperature condition "ISA+10 and below". If warmer condition tables were shown, by comparison, you could deduce two things:

First, Optimum Altitude is not affected by temperature. Second, Maximum Altitude is greatly affected by temperature.

And the explanation is simple. With a higher temperature, engine thrust plummets, and when Maximum Altitude is thrust limited, it will also fall fast. Remember that this value is defined as the lowest between thrust limit and buffet limit – or maneuver margin limit, which is the same thing. This fact is so marked that, when temperature is ISA+20, maximum altitude is below the optimum altitude.

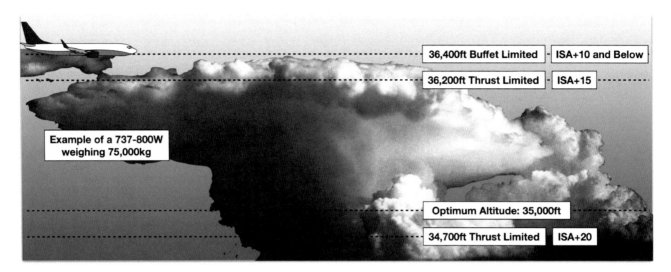

*Figure 340: Effect of temperature on maximum altitude.*

Note regarding how maximum altitude is calculated by Boeing 737's FMC: when we are on the ground, FMC uses temperature information input on PERF INIT (performance initialization) page to indicate maximum altitude. Five thousand feet after takeoff, that information is discarded and actual OAT is used to show maximum altitude. When taking off from hot environments, temperatures are likely to be over ISA+20 even 5,000ft after departure and that will plumb MAX ALT to a much lower level than the one informed on the ground. But don't worry, as the airplane climbs and ISA deviation also falls back to a value closer to the number that had been input on preflight, MAX ALT also starts to climb back to the original number that the FMC showed on ground.

That explanation is likely to be true for other Boeing models, but I cannot say that for sure. Share the information with me if you know!

## 4.3.6    *Maximum Certified Altitude*

What prevents the airplane from going over 41,000ft, as indicated in the Maximum Altitude table? Well, in the case of our model, Boeing 737-800, 41,000ft is its maximum certified altitude. But let's extend the question: why is 41,000ft the maximum certified altitude?

Regulations prohibit the cabin's internal altitude from exceeding 8,000ft. This way, the airframe structure suffers more from differential pressure as an airplane flies higher. If the maximum certified altitude of an aircraft is 43,000ft, this means that it is able, at this altitude, to maintain a differential pressure between the outside and the inside that allows a cabin environment that equates with an altitude of 8,000ft. Boeing 737NG has a maximum differential pressure of 9.1PSI and it was this factor that limited its altitude to 41,000ft.

Another regulation item that can restrict maximum certified altitude of a commercial jetliner is its ability to descend from this maximum altitude to 10,000ft. The law says that this process cannot take more than 10 minutes. If the airplane is unable to descend from the maximum "intended" certified altitude to 10,000ft within the required time interval, its maximum certified altitude will be reduced, so it can comply with this certification item.

An interesting remark: on all Boeing aircraft, the altitude limit is defined according to the maximum differential pressure supported by the fuselage. We will see more about pressurization in a later section.

# 4.4 Coff

## 4.4.1 Low Speed and High Speed Stall

Many authors will argue that a coffin corner is when the airplane is in a situation where low speed stall meets the high speed stall and the pilot runs out of options, having only one possible speed to fly. If speed decreases the airplane stalls. If speed increases the airplane also stalls, they say.

First of all, answer this question: what is the relationship between stall and speed? I will give you a hint: NONE! A wing will stall once the critical angle of attack is reached, regardless of the airplane speed! We have seen this when we discussed maneuvering speed, remember? If not, check topic 1.8.1 in this book. So, if stall has no relation to speed, how can anyone say coffin corner is defined as when low and high speed stall meet each other?

I am sorry, but coffin corner is definitely not that! Stall is the wing reaching its critical angle of attack, period. That can happen at any speed, period. But the idea behind the concept did not come from nowhere. It is likely a misunderstanding associated with one of the symptoms of a wing stalling: buffet!

## 4.4.2 Low Speed and High Speed Buffet

When the airplane is about to stall, that is usually perceived by an airplane vibration that we call buffet. Say we are flying leveled at any given altitude and weight. If we start to reduce speed keeping G-force constant at 1G, buffet will be perceived just before reaching $V_{S1G}$. Let's call this moment the "low speed buffet".

Is there any other reason for an airframe buffet, other than a wing stall? Yes! There is! If the airplane is once again leveled at any given altitude and weight, but this time we start to accelerate keeping G-force constant at 1G, at some point a shockwave will build up on the wing. As speed continues to increase this shockwave will move backwards on the wing and increase its intensity, creating a great deal of disturbance on the airflow and, at some point, airframe buffet will be felt by the pilots. Let's call this buffet the "high speed buffet".

You see, we have one single characteristic that is shared between two different situations. And that, I believe, is the reason behind the confusion of the wrong coffin corner definition I have shown you previously! Coffin corner is in fact a situation when the airplane has no alternative speed to fly, having only one possible speed. Should it lose one knot and the low speed buffet will start. Should it gain one knot and a high speed buffet will hit. Now the difficult question: how can I have a situation where both, low and high speed buffet happen at the same time?

To explain that, I am going to use an example of a fictitious airplane whose stall speed for a given weight is equal to 250kt at clean configuration. Its $V_{MO}$ is 340kt and its $M_{MO}$ is M0.80. On the sequence of graphics in next figure you will see those speeds represented as an orange line (stall), a magenta line ($V_{MO}$), and a green line ($M_{MO}$). The airspeed indicator next to every graphic shows a dashed black and red line representing stall speed at the bottom and $V_{MO}$ or $M_{MO}$ at the top (the smallest between both).

This imaginary airplane will start climbing with 300kt indicated airspeed and at low altitudes you can see on the airspeed indicator that there is a wide range of speed possibilities between minimum (stall) and maximum ($V_{MO}$) speeds – situations 1 and 2. After crossing 24,600ft, $V_{MO}$ is no longer relevant and $M_{MO}$ becomes the new speed limit we must respect. As we keep climbing at 300kt indicated airspeed, the top black and red bar now is the $M_{MO}$ and it represents a smaller IAS every feet we go up, so it starts to get closer and closer to our current speed of 300kt. At 30,600ft the 300kt is equivalent to our airplane's $M_{MO}$ and we can no longer maintain a constant IAS without extrapolating that limit – situations 3 and 4.

Now we need to keep a constant Mach number and that means the IAS will start to decrease. We have no room to accelerate and are getting also closer to stall speed as we climb. At a certain point, more precisely at 38,600ft we have run completely out of options. We cannot decelerate nor accelerate. We are at the coffin corner!

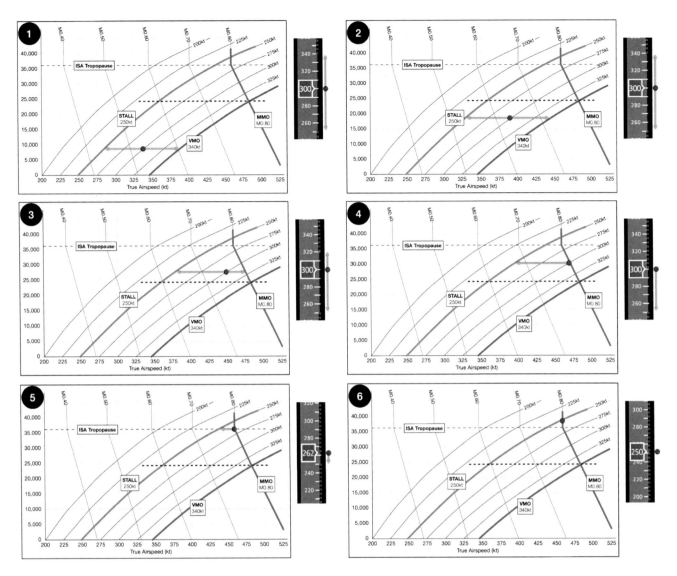

*Figure 341: Climbing to the coffin corner (part 1).*

Alright, I swear I can hear some of you yelling at me right now! I said that coffin corner is a situation where low and high speed buffet meet at the same speed! But what I have shown so far is a situation where low speed buffet meets the maximum operational Mach number. I needed to do that as an introduction to a more complex scenario that I will show you now.

In this new scenario (Figure 342 on the following page), I will show you real data extracted from a Boeing 737-800 weighing 78,000kg. The envelope below shows its stall speed, $V_{MO}$ and $M_{MO}$ using a dashed black and red line. There is a small solid light red line indicating maximum operation altitude of 41,000ft and another red line (a dark one) indicating where high speed buffet happens. The yellow line represents where low speed buffet (stall) and high speed buffet lines would be should the airplane increase its weight by 30%.

Let's start our climb using IAS 300kt and later M0.78. That is indicated by the solid green line. The first situation shows us passing 18,000ft and on our airspeed indicator we can see the airplane's $V_{MO}$ at the top and the yellow band at the bottom (low speed buffet if the aircraft's weight had been increased by 30%).

Different from previous example, this time we made a transition from IAS to MACH at a lower speed than $M_{MO}$. That would leave us a comfortable margin not to exceed this limit in case a sudden wind change increased our speed. From this point onwards we are climbing at a fixed Mach number of M0.78.

Just over 32,000ft something interesting happened! There is a new piece of information showing on the airspeed indicator. There is a yellow band on the top of it, and this yellow line shows where the speed in which high speed buffet will be felt in case our weight is suddenly increased by 30%. And as we keep climbing at M0.78 this line will grow down as the yellow line on the bottom of the airspeed indicator also comes up, closing our operational window more and more, up to a point where both yellow bands, the one from the top and the one from the bottom, meet each other. This IS NOT the coffin corner, despite what many subtitles of Instagram pictures showing an airspeed indicator in a similar situation might say. However, it can become the coffin corner very easily.

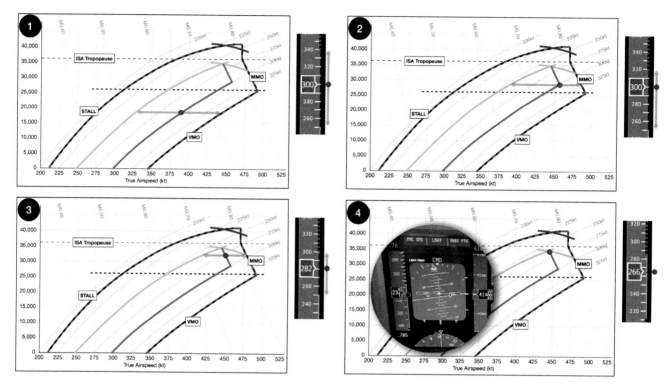

*Figure 342: Climbing to the coffin corner (part 2).*

How can situation 4 of the previous figure turn into a coffin corner, you might wonder. Well, remember what the yellow line represents? It shows where low and high speed buffets will happen should the airplane's weight be increased by 30%. And can you think of any scenarios where this could happen (other than mid-air refueling)? Turns and turbulence! We have just seen that when discussing cruise altitude. A 39° bank leveled turn will increase the airplane's G-load (read: weight) by 30%; in other words, load factor will be 1.3G.

And finally here we are: COFFIN CORNER. High speed buffet if you gain speed (owing to the airflow being disturbed by the shockwave) and low speed buffet if you lose speed (owing to the high angle of attack and stall of the wing). And there is only one way out of this situation: descend to a lower altitude!

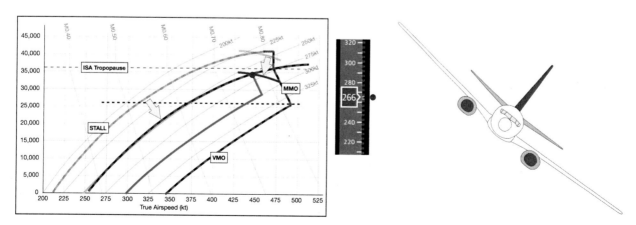

*Figure 343: Finally at the coffin corner.*

Cost Index (CI) is what I consider one of the greatest operational mysteries in aviation. Not because no one knows what it is, as this is relatively simple, but because few, or even no airlines are able to measure their costs with the required precision to use this tool in the most appropriate way.

Do you remember when we talked about LRC in our study of cruise speed? Well, this was the first moment someone decided to question whether it was worth saving fuel by flying MRC or if flying a little bit faster compensated for the extra fuel burn with reduction in other flight costs. There was no calculation of these costs. It was empirical. General feeling was that it was worth it. Technology evolved to a point that it was finally possible to revisit this topic, introducing a new tool called Cost Index. Not that a great deal of technology was required to develop the index, but rather to implement it. After all, cruising speed is now computer controlled.

As always, let's use a practical example to explain this point more clearly. For this purpose, a fictitious company was created, and I lis

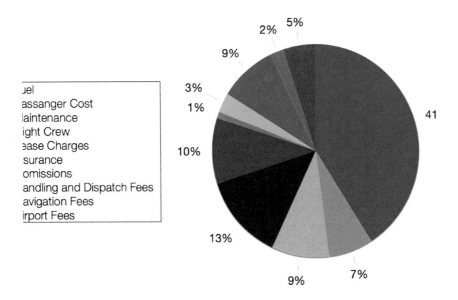

Figure 344: Operating costs of a fictitious airline.

Several items are missing in this list, e.g., ground staff employees, building installations, among others, but the objective is not to be precise (for now); it is just to provide an example to demonstrate how the Cost Index value should be calculated.

Once the "cost pizza chart" has been designed, it is important to rearrange it into three slices only. One will be the fuel slice. Slice number 2 will be the one that includes all fixed operating costs, i.e., those not dependent on flight time. Finally, the third slice will be the sum of all costs that are directly influenced by flight time.

The definition of the first item is the simplest. Determining the other two is more complicated.

As I said before, fixed costs are those that do not vary according to flight time. I can name several here: ground staff salaries, commissions on ticket sales, airport taxes, navigation and radio communication fees, insurance rates, etc. No matter if flight between A and B took one hour or two. These costs will be exactly the same at the end of the month.

Variable costs are the most complex to establish and I will discuss them in a moment. Now, it is important to clarify that I am perfectly aware that none of these pizza slices are exclusively related to variable costs. For maintenance, leasing, crew and other expenses, some costs are fixed while some may depend on flight time.

In this example, we will consider crew, maintenance, leasing, and passenger costs as an exclusive function of flight time (although this is not true, focus is not on accuracy, now) and all other costs as being fixed, except for fuel, of course. The next illustration shows the result of this redistribution.

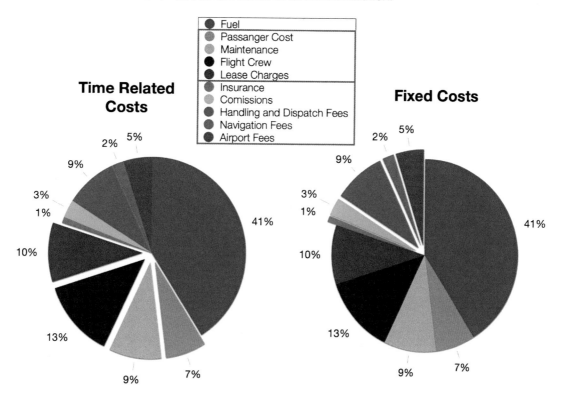

Figure 345: Fixed costs and flight time related costs.

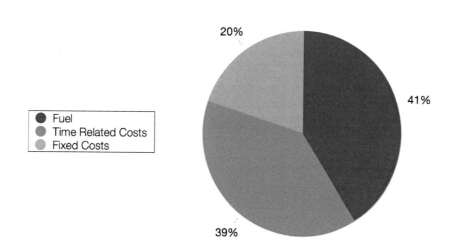

Figure 346: Total cost graph redesigned into three categories.

With our cost graph simplified into just three categories, we came closer to defining the value of Cost Index. For the next step, let's compare Time Related Costs (TRC) and fuel cost. The way this comparison can be made will depend on the manufacturer. Boeing and Airbus work this out in slightly different ways. Boeing divides the cost of an hour of flight per the cost of 100 pounds of fuel to establish the Cost Index. Airbus divides the cost of a single minute of flight per a single kilogram of fuel to find the CI to be applied to its aircraft.

This difference in calculation units will, of course, generate different Cost Index values. Consider, for example, a Time Related Costs value of US$1,350.00 per flight hour and a fuel cost of US$0.54 per pound or US$1.19 per kilogram. When calculating CI, the value entered into a Boeing's flight computer will be 25, while the value to be inserted in Airbus' FMGS will be 19.

$$\text{Cost Index} = \frac{\text{Time Related Costs}}{\text{Fuel Costs}}$$

| Boeing Models | Airbus Models |
|---|---|
| $CI = \dfrac{\text{1 hour TRC}}{\text{100lb of fuel}}$ | $CI = \dfrac{\text{1 minute TRC}}{\text{1kg of fuel}}$ |

Figure 347: Getting to Cost Index value on Airbus and Boeing model aircrafts.

The interpretation of this number is simple. For Boeing, 25 means that 1 hour of Time Related Costs is equivalent to the cost of 2,500lb of fuel. For Airbus, 19 means that 1 minute of TRC equals the cost of 19kg of fuel.

## 4.5.1    Issues Determining Time Related Costs

I might have made it look simple: TRC is divided by fuel cost and that's it! But that is definitely not simple! In fact, it is very, very complex to do this. Determining TRC is one of the most challenging things to do when calculating CI. Allow me to present four problems, some of which are of extreme complexity.

Starting with aircraft leasing. That can be a fixed, variable, or mixed cost depending on the airline's contract with the lessor. Let me explain. Anyone who has rented a car knows that the same vehicle can have two or three different prices at the same rental company. Car "A" can cost the renter US$20.00/day, UsS$40.00/day or US$100.00/day. What is the difference?

When you pay only US$20.00/day, there is no mileage allowance. This means that you will pay the daily rate plus an additional fee for each kilometer you drive. When you are paying US$40.00/day, there is an allowance of 100km per day included, but it will still be necessary to pay an additional fee if this mileage is exceeded. In the last option, US$100.00/day, there is an unlimited mileage allowance. You pay that daily rate and period. No extra penny. The question I would like to ask you is: what is the best contract model? The right answer is: it depends! It depends on the type of use that will be made of the vehicle. The lessee must evaluate, considering the mileage he/she intends to drive, which contract will best suit him/her. An airline works the same way, but just remember that leasing contracts are often separated into engine and airframe (the aircraft itself).

And what is the problem with determining this value within Time Related Costs? The problem is that, frequently, an airline with many airplanes has several different contracts for its fleet, and possibly all three types of leasing are scattered among the company's airplanes. If that is the case, when establishing CI, this will have to be done by aircraft registration number and not by aircraft group.

Leasing

| Aircraft Leasing | Monthly Cost | Allowance | Cost per Extra Hour |
|---|---|---|---|
| Contract 1 | US$ 240,000.00 | 360 h | US$ 850.00 |
| Contract 2 | US$ 280,000.00 | Unlimited | US$ 0.00 |
| Contract 3 | US$ 150,000.00 | 40 h | US$ 2,000.00 |

| Engine Leasing | Monthly Cost | Allowance | Extras |
|---|---|---|---|
| Contract A | US$ 30,000.00 | 240 cicles | US$ 320.00 per cycle |
| Contract B | US$ 20,000.00 | Unlimited | US$ 800.00 per Bump |

Figure 348: Fictitious numbers to exemplify the complexity of leasing contracts.

Another problem that needs to be discussed is maintenance. Aircraft maintenance involves parts that have exchange intervals established in calendar time (1 year, 2 years), parts that must be changed at every few flight cycles (500 cycles, 1,000 cycles – a cycle is a period between engine start and shutdown), or changed at every few flight hours (1,000, 2,000 flight hours). To make things even more complex, most parts have to be changed if any of the three criteria is met, whichever happens first! And what is going to happen first (calendar, flight hours or cycles) will depend on how many flights you fly every day and how long those flights are!

Establishing which part of total maintenance costs is related to flight time and which part refers to fixed costs (flight cycles or calendar time) is a huge challenge for maintenance staff. The problem only grows when the company's fleet involves more than one airplane model. Imagine how complex it is to make this division for each operated model? What ends up happening to many companies is that maintenance departments generate only estimated values to be computed for calculation of CI. Estimates that are often very far from reality.

**Maintenance**

| Aircraft Item | Change every (days) | Change every (hours) | Change every (cycles) |
|---|---|---|---|
| Maintanace Item 1 | 730 | 1,500 | 1,000 |
| Maintanace Item 2 | 365 | 1,000 | 800 |
| Maintanace Item 3 | 180 | 800 | 500 |

*Figure 349: Fictitious numbers to exemplify the complexity of maintenance costs.*

Flight crews are our third problem. They are normally paid per flight hours, but a part of their salary is fixed. Separating one part from the another might be tricky. Beware of the fact that it is important to determine crew wage cost per flight hour, rather than net incomes of the crew members per flight hour – something that is especially different in Brazil. If you consider net incomes per flight hour of R$260.00 for a captain, R$150.00 for a first officer and R$70.00 for a flight attendant, in a crew of six (captain, f/o and four flight attendants), together, they would earn R$690.00 per flight hour, but that is not even close from their actual cost to the airline. Taxes might easily rise this amount by 75%, as show in Figure 350.

One more issue regarding flight crews (in Brazil, at least) is that crew cost varies from one flight to another. A crew member has an hourly cost during daylight flights, another when flying at night and yet another when flights are performed on Sundays and holidays. There may be a single crew on board or, in addition to that, another "deadhead crew" (crew members who are paid, but remain as passengers to take charge of another flight elsewhere).

Let's look at an example: a flight carried out on a Monday morning costs R$1,207.50 per flight hour on "X Airlines". The same flight, carried out on Sunday night and with an entire deadhead crew traveling on board, can multiply the company's cost, adding up to R$7,245.00 per hour.

**Flight Crew**

| | Monday 10 AM | Monday 10 PM | Sunday 10 PM | Sunday 10 PM + 1 DH Crew |
|---|---|---|---|---|
| Captain | R$ 455.00 | R$ 910.00 | R$ 1,365.00 | R$ 2,730.00 |
| First Officer | R$ 262.50 | R$ 525.00 | R$ 787.50 | R$ 1,575.00 |
| Flight Attendant (x4) | R$ 490.00 | R$ 980.00 | R$ 1,470.00 | R$ 2,940.00 |
| Total | R$ 1,207.50 | R$ 2,415.00 | R$ 3,622.50 | R$ 7,245.00 |

*Figure 350: Flight crew cost per flight hour - Brazilian regulation example.*

To conclude the discussion about TRC, we will now talk about the biggest problem of all: measuring what has no tangible value. How much does a flight delay cost? I doubt anyone will answer this question precisely. Delays can create the need to pay for hotel accommodation for passengers who missed a connecting flight; missing passengers will leave empty seats on airplanes, and that is a revenue that is forever lost; as a result of delays, the crew may have to end their workday in an unforeseen location and cancel several flights because of that; this situation may also result in damage to the company's image. The big challenge for airlines is to create their own algorithms that allow them to somehow measure costs of delays and define when and how much it is worth accelerating a flight (burn more fuel) in an attempt to recover from this type of situation.

*Figure 351: Extra costs because of flight delays.*

## 4.5.2   Issues Determining Fuel Costs

You may think that this is not as complex as I made it seem at the beginning of this topic, after all, just take fuel price per liter or gallon at the airport of origin and transform this value into 100lb or 1kg equivalent (depending on whether it is Boeing or Airbus). Well, think about it: how much did the company pay for the fuel in the aircraft's tanks? As I mentioned, some consider the price that is being charged to refuel at the airport of origin, but now I ask you: what about the fuel that was already on board? The one remaining from the previous flight! It has to be taken into account to make the equation and this makes calculation very complex. Imagine the situation shown in the following figure.

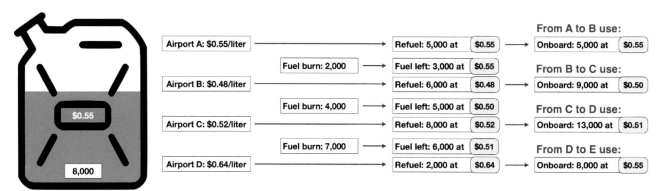

*Figure 352: Fuel price calculation.*

Here, I proposed a sequence of flights between airports A, B, C, D and E. At airport A, the fuel tank was empty and 5,000 liters were filled, costing $0.55 per liter. Starting from this scenario, we will use $0.55 to calculate the CI of the first sector flight, from A to B. Now, observe the next steps of the flight.

A to B: I used 2,000 liters to go from A to B and refueled another 6,000 liters at this location, leaving a total of 9,000 liters on board. Each of the 6,000 liters fueled in B cost $0.48, but as there was 3,000 liters left over from the previous flight, all the 9,000 liters now have an average cost of $0.50, and that is the cost of fuel from B to C.

B to C: I used 4,000 liters to go from B to C and refueled another 8,000 liters at this location, leaving a total of 13,000 liters on board. Each of the 8,000 liters fueled in C cost $0.52, but as there was 5,000 liters left from the previous flight, all the 13,000 liters now have an average cost of $0.51 and that is the cost of fuel from C to D.

C to D: I used 7,000 liters to go from C to D and refueled another 2,000 liters at this location, leaving a total of 8,000 liters on board (represented in the illustration inside the tank). Each of the 2,000 liters fueled in C cost $0.64, but as there was 6,000 liters left from the previous flight, all the 8,000 liters now have an average cost of $0.55.

To fly between airports D and E, the difference between calculating the Cost Index using fuel price at airport D or actual fuel price on the tanks is very significant for the final result. The value to be used in the CI should be $0.55 per liter. Without this progressive control, most airlines worldwide would use fuel price as $0.64 per liter in their calculations. And I will not even dare discussing fuel hedge! This is complex enough already.

## 4.5.3    *Effect of Cost Index on Flight*

Now that we know where the Cost Index comes from, it remains to be seen how it interferes with an airplane's flight. The CI will define the ideal speed for an aircraft to fly. I will give you an example using numbers, but first, let's approach the situation in a more general way.

Basically, the CI will determine the speed to be flown, based on current weight and chosen altitude, using a range of possibilities going from the airplane's MRC (CI=0) to $M_{MO}$ (CI=Max). MRC will vary with weight but $M_{MO}$ will not. Within this range, a scale will be made to identify the correct speed for each selected CI value. This scale is not linear, so smaller CI units have a big impact on speed while the higher CI values do not change it that much.

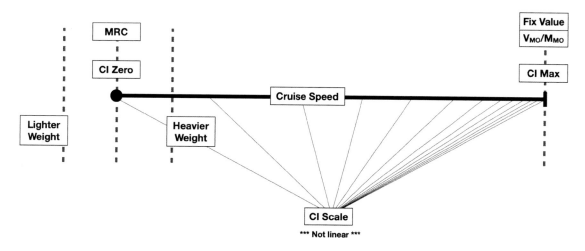

*Figure 353: Speed scale based on cost index.*

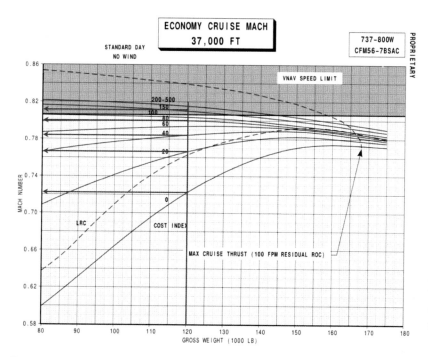

Each aircraft model has its own CI scaling. Among Boeing's aircraft, for example, there are those that range from zero to 200, 500, 999 or even 9,999 units. On the left, I present a real model of this graph extracted from the manuals of our model airplane. For the selected weight (120,000lb), these are the cruising speed variation for CI values: 0, 20, 40, 80 and 160.

Now it is time for our practical example. The respective data are from a Boeing 767. Importantly, they refer to a certain moment of the flight and those values change at all times depending on differences in wind, altitude, weight, etc.

*Figure 354: Example of speed for CI 0, 20, 40, 80 and 160 of Boeing 737-800.*

Consider: Boeing 767-200
Altitude 35,000ft
Weight 310,000lbs

Time related costs: Us$ 1,500.00 / flight hour
Fuel costs: Us$ 0.50 / lbs

$$CI = \frac{1500 / 1}{0.50 \times 100}$$

$$CI = 30$$

To fly 100nm (wind calm), we have the following data:

| Cruise Mach | 0.75 | 0.77 | 0.79 | 0.81 | 0.83 |
|---|---|---|---|---|---|
| Time-hours | 0.231 | 0.225 | 0.220 | 0.214 | 0.209 |
| Fuel-pounds | 2242 | 2230 | 2235 | 2294 | 2451 |
| Segment Cost ($) | | | | | |
| Time related | 347 | 338 | 330 | 321 | 314 |
| Fuel | 1121 | 1115 | 1118 | 1147 | 1226 |
| Total | 1468 | 1453 | 1448 | 1468 | 1540 |

ECON

*Figure 355: Cost index calculation and speed selection example.*

By analyzing the table above, we can see separate lines that identify fuel costs, time related costs, and total costs (sum of the two previous types of cost) to fly for 100nm at 35,000ft in different speed regimes. Flight time and fuel burn (in pounds) are also shown. The obvious thing is time decreasing with faster speeds, but let's analyze the rest of the data.

Observe that the speed at which less fuel is burned to travel 100nm, that is, which offers the best Fuel Mileage, is Mach 0.77. However, this is not the speed that provides the lowest operating cost. To fly the "cheapest flight" after accounting for total costs (fuel and TRC), the speed is Mach 0.79. This Cost Index based speed is known as ECON Speed or economic regime.

Heads-up: the inserted CI value will define ECON Speed. Despite what some may think, ECON does not refer to a speed which intends to save fuel. To save fuel in our example, pilots should fly Mach 0.77. ECON speed is meant to save MONEY! It is the way to make a flight cheaper, even if we have to burn a little more fuel than minimum to achieve this goal. Remember that maximum fuel savings are established by the MRC regime. This, in turn, is obtained by selecting a CI value equal to zero.

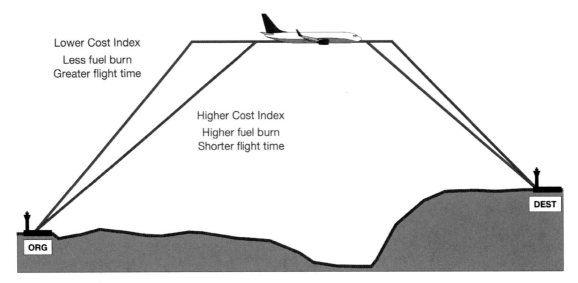

Lower Cost Index
Less fuel burn
Greater flight time

Higher Cost Index
Higher fuel burn
Shorter flight time

DEST

ORG

*Figure 356: CI impact on flight profile.*

To conclude this part of the discussion, look at the next graph, which shows the evolution of costs as a function of speed. The yellow line shows variation in fuel cost, the red one represents TRCs, and the green one is the sum of the previous two. The lowest point on the yellow line identifies the speed which represents the best fuel mileage (save more fuel, CI=0, MRC) and the lowest point on the green line indicates the speed at which the flight would be cheaper to operate.

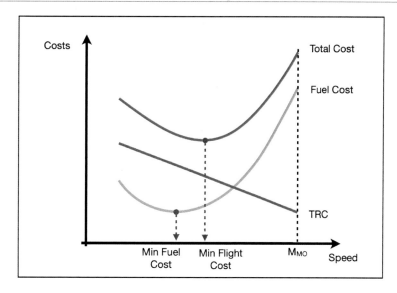

*Figure 357: Fuel costs, TRCs and total cost as a function of speed.*

## 4.5.4    Fuel Tankering

Speaking of fuel costs, just like in gas stations in your city, the price of aviation kerosene is very different from airport to airport. Is it worth refueling more than necessary in one location with cheaper fuel, in order to refuel less or even not refueling at all at the next airport where fuel price is higher? This is a very difficult question to answer, but there is a general rule of thumb that helps.

Remember: more weight equals to more lift required. More lift means more drag, too. More drag requires more thrust. Finally, with higher thrust, fuel burn increases.

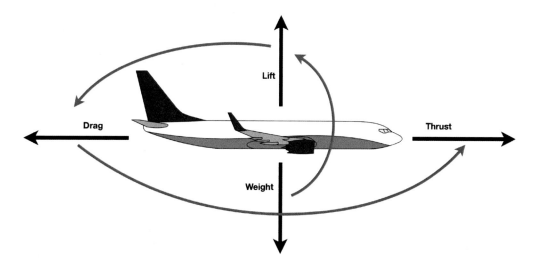

*Figure 358: In the end, weight is directly related to fuel burn.*

In jet aircraft, average excess fuel burn when extra weight (unnecessary fuel) is carried can be predicted as follows: that unnecessary fuel is burned in about 3.5% of its total amount for each flight hour. For example, if we take 2,000kg more kerosene then needed on a 3-hour flight, you are likely to arrive at your destination with an extra 210kg of fuel burn.

Obviously, each plane has its specificities, and this ratio may vary slightly over this reference value of 3.5%. There is a chart in aircraft performance manuals called Brake-Even Price Ratio, which determines what fuel price must be at the destination so that it is worth filling up in excess on departure and still save some money. The table is simple: multiply fuel price at origin by the reported factor (which depends on the air distance between origin and destination) and compare the result with the price of kerosene at destination. If the result is less than the price at destination, putting extra fuel into the tanks will certainly result in financial savings for the company.

In the following illustration, there is a sequence of a seven-sector flight beginning in Porto Alegre (origin) and starting northbound. The first sector is from Porto Alegre to São Paulo and continues in a counterclockwise direction until returning to the same airport. See, for each sector, where it is worth "topping the tank" and where it is not. Most companies call this extra amount of fuel as Fuel Tankering, but there are other names that are also used, such as Policy Fuel, Extra Fuel, Overhead Difference Fuel or some other name.

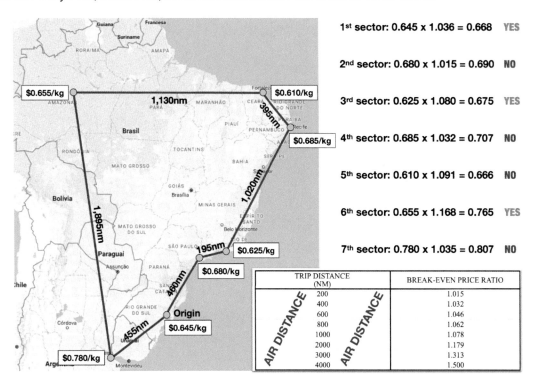

*Figure 359: Example of Tankering Fuel or Overhead Difference Fuel.*

An important factor that is not noted in the table concerns Trip Distance. Although it is not explicit, the distance to be consulted in the table is Air Distance rather than Ground Distance between airports (I made the "air distance" highlight). In the end, it was worth fueling an extra amount on the first, third and sixth sectors of this sequence of seven flights.

Local regulations are yet another factor to be addressed in this discussion! Let me show you an example that also happens in Brazil.

In the early 1990s, in order to improve the country's exports, the Brazilian Government enacted a law dealing with taxes and authorized export products to be exempted from payment of a tax known as ICMS (Tax over Circulation of Goods and Services). Airplanes flying abroad are not exporting fuel, they are not oil supertankers, but according to government, they are contributing positively to the trade balance (not joking). Thus, a plane that takes off from Rio de Janeiro (BRA) to Buenos Aires (ARG) will pay less for fuel than one that takes off from the same place bound for Belo Horizonte (BRA).

The unthinkable happens now! It may be worthwhile to put more fuel than necessary flying both ways on a round trip to Buenos Aires. See the example in the next figure. When departing from Rio, fuel price is $0.625/kg and when comparing with Ezeiza airport ($0.702/kg), we found that it is worth taking extra fuel.

On the return flight, we compare fuel price at Ezeiza ($0.702/kg) with the one at Galeão airport, in Rio. But as the next flight of this aircraft is a domestic flight to Belo Horizonte, the price that we will pay in Rio includes the ICMS and jumps to $0.780/kg. In this case, it is worth fueling some extra, again!

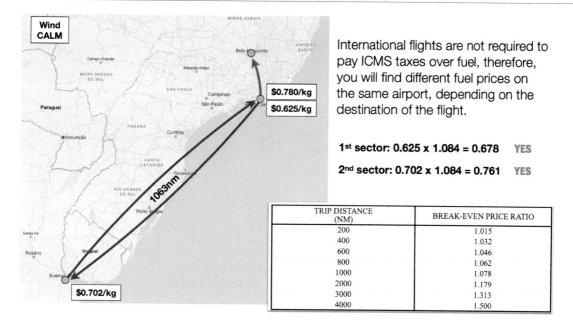

International flights are not required to pay ICMS taxes over fuel, therefore, you will find different fuel prices on the same airport, depending on the destination of the flight.

1st sector: 0.625 x 1.084 = 0.678 **YES**

2nd sector: 0.702 x 1.084 = 0.761 **YES**

| TRIP DISTANCE (NM) | BREAK-EVEN PRICE RATIO |
|---|---|
| 200 | 1.015 |
| 400 | 1.032 |
| 600 | 1.046 |
| 800 | 1.062 |
| 1000 | 1.078 |
| 2000 | 1.179 |
| 3000 | 1.313 |
| 4000 | 1.500 |

*Figure 360: Round trip with tankering fuel in both flights.*

## 4.5.5   Air Distance, Ground Distance, and Great Circle Distance

We have already talked about air miles and ground miles in section 1.3.8. So, the concepts of air distance and ground distance are known by now. Ground distance is the flight distance measured by projecting the flight path on the ground, and air distance is the same, but adjusted for wind effects. Tailwind will make it shorter and headwind will make it longer. But what about this new concept? What is Great Circle Distance?

Great Circle Distance is just a measurement of the distance between origin and destination, considering the shortest distance between these two points. Being on a globe, it is not a straight line, but a curved line, thus the term "great circle" distance. The Flat Earth Society will go crazy with this statement! But this book is not for them, anyway!

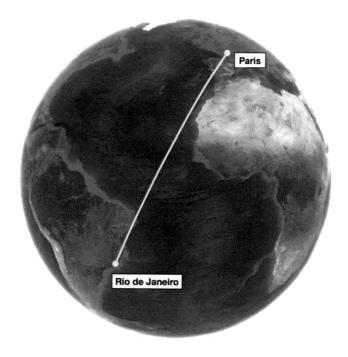

*Figure 361: Great circle distance between Rio de Janeiro and Paris is 4,946nm (Google Earth).*

Specific fuel consumption is a measure that will show us how efficient an airplane's engine is. For jet propulsion engines, we use the term **Thrust Specific Fuel Consumption (TSFC)**. The amount of thrust generated by the engine is an important value to be known, but to establish the efficiency of this engine, what interests the most is to know how much fuel is needed to produce such thrust.

## 4.6.1    The Secret of New Generation Engines

To better understand this point, we are going to compare two different engine generations that equip versions of our model airplane. Pratt & Whitney JT8D-17 was installed in old models, Boeing 737-200, 727-200, among others of this time, and CFM56-7B27B1 was installed in some current models of the Boeing 737-800. The former has maximum takeoff thrust at sea level of 16,000 pounds force (lbf) while the latter reaches 27,100lbf of thrust. The correct term is really "pounds force" and the correct representation is the set of three letters, "lbf". But, so far, we have become used to our purposeful error by calling the thrust only "lb" and the weight only "kg". Let's keep it like that.

When evaluating the fuel flow required by the engine to produce thrust, something is worth of notice: it is almost the same for both engines in our example – 9,854lb/h in the case of the JT8D and 10,325lb/h in the case of the CFM56. The TSFC value is obtained by the ratio of fuel flow to thrust. This means that the lower the value obtained, the more efficient the engine is. In other words, it needs less fuel to produce greater thrust.

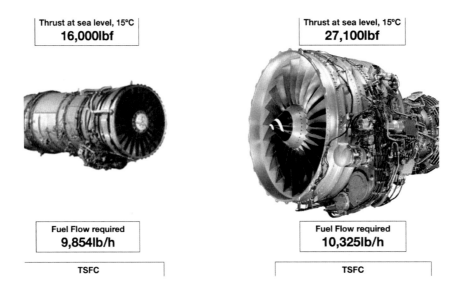

*Figure 362: TSFC - Thrust Specific Fuel Consumption.*

Two common units of measurement for TSFC are: lb/lbf.h, kg/N.h (the order of the denominators can be inverted, lb/h.lbf and kg/h.N). It is not uncommon to see the TSFC being presented with that deliberate error we commented on: lb/lb.h, for example.

Some of you may be wondering where such an increase in efficiency came from. Let's use a little math and physics to answer that. We will need two equations for our discussion: kinetic energy and Newton's Second Law.

Old engines produce thrust taking a small amount of air and throwing it back at a very high speed. Modern engines only give a little speed to a very large amount of air. This is the main secret of success. By using both equations, we will understand the reason.

The example below compares the amount of energy required in both situations to generate the same force. Let's consider that the initial velocity of the air mass is equal to zero and the time between the initial and final velocity is equal to 1 second. This way, we can also consider the acceleration to be equal to the final speed value. After all, it happened in 1 second!

Remember that this is not a physics book. Yes, I know that there should be more variables in the equation – fuel mass, for example – but I will ignore that and go on with the explanation without this level of accuracy, which will not invalidate the idea. In the example on the left, we got 1,000N of force taking a mass of 10kg of air (small) at a speed of 100m/s (large) in 1 second. In the example on the right, we took a mass of 100kg of air (large) at a speed of 10m/s (small) within the same time and obtained the same result (1,000N). But look at the difference in energy spent to produce this force.

$$E_c = \frac{mV^2}{2} \qquad F = ma \qquad a = \frac{V_i - V_o}{t} \qquad \begin{array}{c} V_o = 0m/s \\ t = 1s \end{array} \qquad a = V \qquad F = mV$$

$F_1 = 10kg \times 100m/s$
$F_1 = 1,000N$

$E_1 = \frac{10 \times 100^2}{2}$
$E_1 = 50,000J$

**Same thrust, less energy**
$\longleftarrow \qquad \longrightarrow$

$F_1 = 100kg \times 10m/s$
$F_1 = 1,000N$

$E_1 = \frac{100 \times 10^2}{2}$
$E_1 = 5,000J$

*Figure 363: The secret for modern engine efficiency.*

In the second way, the same force was obtained with the expenditure of one tenth of the energy, compared to the first way. Engineers from the past knew this secret, but there was no technology to develop engines capable of doing that. Technology in design and manufacture of engine blades, fuel injection control, composite materials, electronic controls, etc. – everything helped to make it possible to apply the logic that was already known. See an example of this difference in the figure below. Compare the fan blade of an old engine (left) and that of a modern engine (right).

*Figure 364: Difference in engine blade owing to advances in technology.*

I would like to emphasize that an engine's TSFC varies, depending on speed and altitude. And remember, this number says a lot about the engine, but it does not say much about the airplane. To measure an aircraft's overall efficiency, we have to use another parameter previously studied, which is called "fuel mileage". This will depend on factors other than TSFC, such as aerodynamic efficiency and weight.

To give you a better idea of the evolution of TSFC throughout the last decades, take a look at the following graph. Engine models are disposed in a timeline fashion.

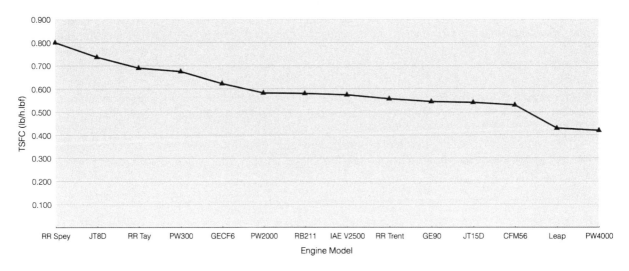

*Figure 365: Evolution of TSFC.*

## 4.6.2 Engine Degradation

Still in the chapter about Takeoff Performance, we talked a lot about some characteristics of the aircraft's engines. Among the issues that we discussed, I mentioned that engine degradation normally occurs. As time goes by, fuel flow and EGT become higher as an engine delivers the same thrust it did when it was new. Some simple techniques can slow down this degradation process.

The first technique is linked to dirt inside the engine. As the engine is used, dust particles accumulate on the compressor's blades. This dirt changes the aerodynamic profile of the blades, affecting the amount of air that is compressed, and this causes the fuel-air mixture to become a little richer than it should be. As a result, TSFC increases.

The following graphic was taken from a Pratt and Whitney's keynote on this subject. According to P&W, over 6,000 cycles, it is common for engines to increase thrust specific fuel consumption by about 4%. Also, according to P&W, washing engine compressors with hot water on a routine basis drastically reduces TSFC, but unfortunately low specific consumption is not maintained for a long time and TSFC tends to quickly increase again and approach the normal degradation that was expected.

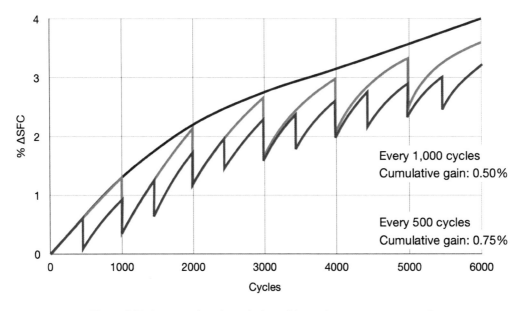

*Figure 366: Less engine degradation with routine compressor wash.*

In the above-mentioned published study, if washing is done every 1,000 cycles, the result at the end of 6,000 cycles is an average gain of 0.5% in TSFC, that is, instead of increasing by 4%, it would increase by 3.5%. If you reduce the wash interval to 500 operating cycles, the gain will be 0.75% in TSFC after 6,000 cycles of engine use.

Wait a second. Could you guess another thing that could improve TSFC by a significant margin? Using assumed temperature during takeoffs! Yes, I said that ATM will increase fuel burn during takeoff instead of saving it, as many pilots think, but the truth is, in the long term, ATM will indeed save fuel! It is estimated that an average 15% thrust reduction on takeoff using ATM could improve TSFC by more than 0.4% over a 1,000-cycle period.

Another simple technique that ensures slower engine degradation is also well within reach of pilots. After a cycle of use (read "after landing"), it is highly recommended that pilots should allow the engine some time to cool before shutting down.

When we do not let the engine cool down, the internal blades end up scraping the fairing that surrounds them owing to different cooling and expansion patterns among materials. This event is not dangerous, but in the long run it ends up creating extra spaces that allow air to pass without being properly compressed. The tips of these blades are also worn, and the entire aerodynamic process is compromised. The result is, once again, loss of engine efficiency and premature increase in TSFC.

Engine efficiency degradation is something expected by manufacturers and operators and it cannot be ignored when planning flights. In this way, a tool called Degradation Factor has been created. This factor is included in performance calculations to define the fuel needed to carry out each flight. The factor can be positive - which means that the aircraft has Fuel Mileage X% worse than the manufacturer's database – or negative, which represents an aircraft with Fuel Mileage X% better than reference data.

There is some confusion about the Degradation Factor. The question is always whether this factor is related to the engine or the airplane. Well, although the engine degradation factor can be evaluated per se, it is much simpler to define it by looking at the system as a whole (airplane plus engine). It does not matter to an operations engineer if a given airplane is burning 2.5% more fuel than the reference amount because the engine is older or the airplane has some extra growth not originally computed (like a Wi-Fi antenna installed on top of the fuselage). What is important is to recognize that this extra consumption exists and needs to be addressed in performance calculations.

Of course, the maintenance engineering department has a different idea about this. They need to know the cause of efficiency loss so that they can figure out whether or not there is any way to mitigate it. Airbus airplanes, for example, are able to input two different degradation factors into the FMGS: the idle factor, related to the engine, and the performance factor, related to the airplane itself. But this is another problem and I do not intend to open discussions in this regard here.

## 4.6.3 Predicting Fuel Flow at Different Weights

When we talked about Tankering Fuel, I mentioned a train of thought using cause and consequence that I would like to repeat here: greater weight creates the need for more lift to maintain the flight. Greater lift implies greater aerodynamic drag. When we have more drag, we will need more thrust, and if thrust is higher, so is fuel flow.

Along the same lines, we can conclude that fuel flow is directly proportional to aircraft weight. So, if we identify that an airplane is burning 2,400kg/h with an actual weight of 70,000kg, we can predict, using a simple rule of three, that fuel flow will be approximately 2,057kg/h when the aircraft weighs 60,000kg. Of course, this calculation is not 100% accurate, as there are other factors involved that are being ignored – CG position, for example. But interestingly, the values we can predict are very similar to those that can be seen in real life.

We have just discussed maximum altitude and optimum altitude. You must remember that maximum altitude is defined by buffet limit or available thrust. Now, imagine a twin-engine aircraft flying close to its maximum altitude when, for some reason, one of its engines stops working. Is it possible to maintain the same altitude?

This section of the Enroute Performance chapter aims to explain what will happen to the aircraft in this situation, what strategies must be planned by engineering and flight dispatch teams and must be carried out be pilots, and how regulations differ for two-, three-, and four-engine airplanes. We will also discuss cabin depressurization and how to handle this emergency from a performance perspective.

## 4.7.1    Driftdown Procedures

Right in the first paragraph of this section, before even asking the question that I now wish to clarify, I gave some tips on the answer. No, we cannot maintain altitude when we lose thrust on one of the engines. After all, we have lost half of the available thrust (in the case of a twin engine) and now thrust minus drag is a negative number! Remember what that means? It means that if we try to maintain altitude, we will lose speed! And if we try to maintain speed, we will lose altitude!

To keep a level flight at constant speed, we need to find a way to regain a little (or a lot of) thrust. The engine needs more air to produce more thrust and we will find that at a lower altitude. Therefore, we will be forced to start a descent; otherwise, the airplane is going to lose speed until it stalls.

*Figure 367: If you try to maintain altitude, you will lose speed, because you have far less thrust then required.*

In the example in the illustration above, we have an aircraft flying at FL330 (33,000ft) with a given weight. To which altitude should we descend? How do we perform such a maneuver? Well, I intend to answer both questions in detail, but I need to lay some groundwork first.

Can you think of a speed to use during descent? Let's suppose you could choose any speed between maximum endurance and $V_{MO}/M_{MO}$. Within this range, the higher the speed you choose, the more thrust will be required to maintain that speed. And where will you find more thrust? At a lower altitude, of course! So, this is the first thing you must keep in mind before making your decision regarding speed. If you choose a higher speed, you will have to level off at a lower altitude.

The second issue is how to perform such a descent, and that might surprise a few, but there is no single answer for that. You could throttle back the remaining engine(s) to idle and descend like that until the new flight level. There is no specific name for this technique; it is basically a normal descent. However, you could execute the maneuver in a different way that involves using thrust on the operating engine(s).

This technique works as follows: set maximum continuous thrust (MCT) on the operating engine(s) and maintain altitude. The airplane will start to lose speed, and when it reaches the speed that you have chosen for descent, let it drift downward slowly, now keeping constant speed. The airplane will descend at a shallower angle as it gets lower and the engine is able to produce a bit more thrust. This will continue for a long time until the airplane reaches an altitude where the required thrust to maintain constant speed at leveled flight is finally available, and it will level off at this point. This slow, thrust-assisted descent is known as <u>DRIFTDOWN</u>. Have a look at the next figure showing this maneuver being performed at different speeds.

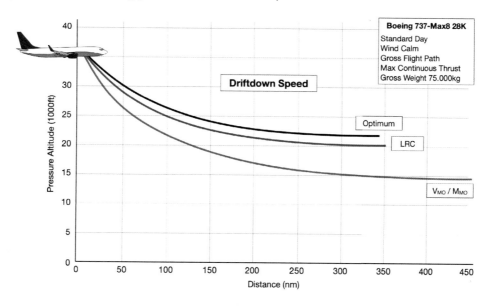

*Figure 368: Driftdown at different speeds.*

You may have noticed that among the three lines presented in Figure 368, there is one called Optimum. That is the Optimum Driftdown Speed, which is basically the best lift-over-drag ratio. This speed will allow you to fly the longest horizontal distance for every foot of altitude lost and will also enable you to maintain the highest altitude with one engine inoperative.

On Airbus and Embraer aircraft, that optimum driftdown speed (maximum L/D) is shown on the airspeed indicator with a green dot, and it is creatively called the Green Dot Speed. On Boeing models, that speed can be found on the flight management computer as shown in the next figure (ENG OUT SPD).

 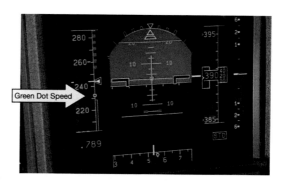

*Figure 369: FMC engine out information and Airbus green dot speed.*

Now, one more question: why would a pilot want or need to execute a driftdown instead of an idle thrust descent after an engine failure? Let's talk about that in a moment, but first, let me show you a driftdown being executed.

Look at the following figure. On it, the airplane shot down the critical engine at FL390, set MCT to the remaining engine (this is a twin-jet), and started drifting down at the best L/D speed (optimum driftdown speed). The blue line shows the airplane's trajectory going beyond the level-off point. In fact, it clearly shows the flight path until the airplane is on an upward path already. This trajectory is called the Gross Driftdown Flightpath, or GDF.

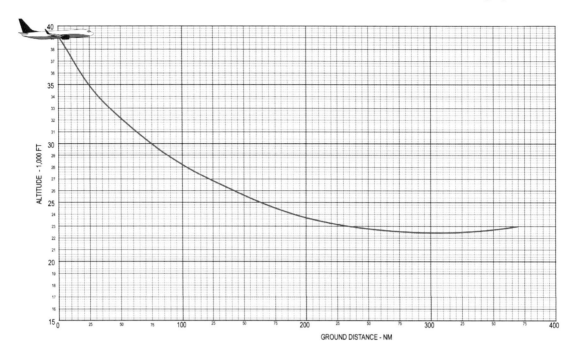

*Figure 370: Flight test driftdown. Actual airplane trajectory shown.*

Now, talking about legislation: I will focus on twin-engine aircraft, and by the end of the discussion, I promise to mention the differences that apply to three- and four-engine airplanes.

Regulations require that any airplane must be able to clear terrain by some margin in the event of an engine failure over obstacles. There you have it! Driftdown is the strategy manufacturers adopt to comply with this terrain clearance requirement. Using the optimum driftdown speed will allow the largest clearance height over any obstacle. But how much terrain clearance is required?

Well, first of all, that minimum clearance is not established over the gross flight path, but rather the NET DRIFTDOWN FLIGHTPATH, or NDF. Let's move back for a moment: what is the NDF?

For twin-engine jets, the NDF is the gross flightpath minus 1.1%. Okay. You probably read that in many books in a different way, stating that the GDF must be 1.1% above the NDF, but it is likely that you had trouble trying to understand that 1.1% margin exactly because, despite the text, it works the other way around. You can only build NDF once you know GDF first. Take the example of Figure 370. Let's analyze that trajectory every 5nm and establish what the gradient performed by the airplane was. Say in the first 5nm the airplane lost 850ft. That means that in this first 5nm the airplane performed a descent path of -2.80%. As the regulation mentions, we must describe a new path called the NDF that is 1.1% below the GDF, so those first 5nm will have a trajectory of -3.9%.

Say that at a given point the airplane lost 500ft over 5nm. That is equivalent to -1.65%, and when drawing the new trajectory we will do so considering a flightpath of -2.75%. An interesting point here: once the airplane has leveled off, the gradient of that 5nm would be 0.0%, but the NDF would still show this airplane descending at negative 1.1%. And if you have wondered why we recorded our flight test until a point where the airplane was already climbing, here is the answer. We have to draw the NDF until the point it shows a 0.0% gradient, and as it is different from the GDF by 1.1%, that implies that when the NDF shows a level flight, the airplane was in fact already climbing at a positive 1.1% gradient. The final result is shown in Figure 371.

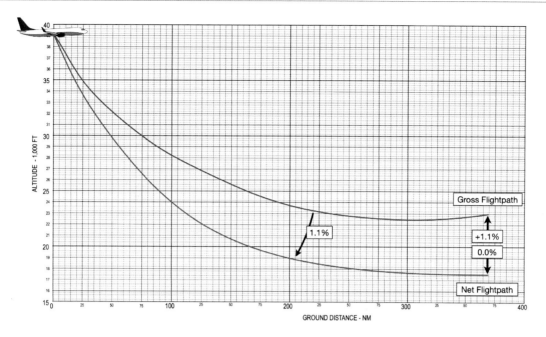

*Figure 371: NDF and GDF show on the same graph.*

Nicely done. One more question answered, time to ask another one! How do we use that NDF?

Should an engine failure happen inflight, during descent to the new flight level we must assure that the airplanes NET driftdown flightpath (the red line) clears any obstacle by 2,000ft. Once the airplane had leveled off, its NDF must clear all obstacles by a 1,000ft margin. The airplane also must be able to keep a holding pattern 1,500ft over the airport where the pilot intends to land. This rule is to ensure the airport chosen to divert is one where the airplane is able to hold altitude and go around if necessary. That means this airport will never be on the airplane's descent phase of the driftdown maneuver.

A common question in my classes: isn't 2,000ft maybe too small a safety margin? Look at the following figure. You will see that because the airplane actually flies on a flightpath 1.1% above the NDF, the real height clearance over obstacles is significantly larger than 2,000ft.

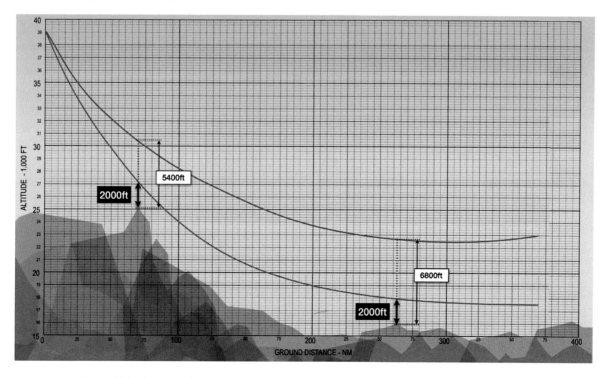

*Figure 372: Actual safety margin is much more than 2,000ft owing to those 1.1% extras.*

I have been talking about twin-engines all the while, but now let me address the differences between this airplane and the others. That difference lies within the gross driftdown flightpath margin. It is 1.1% for twins, but 1.4% for three-engine and 1.6% for four-engine airplanes. On some occasions, the minimum safety gradient for three- and four-engine aircraft will be reduced to 0.3% and 0.5% respectively. This is the case of routes on which we must execute an analysis based on two engines failing instead of just one. We will see that in a moment.

Importantly, at the end of the driftdown procedure, pilots are left with three different alternatives and good judgment will tell which is the best one to be used. Pilots can maintain speed and gradually recover some altitude as the plane becomes lighter (A). Alternatively, they can maintain the altitude and gradually accelerate as weight is reduced (B), or they still have the choice of descending further when clear of obstacles, seeking for a higher speed, for example, Long Range Cruise (C). Everything is summarized in the following figure.

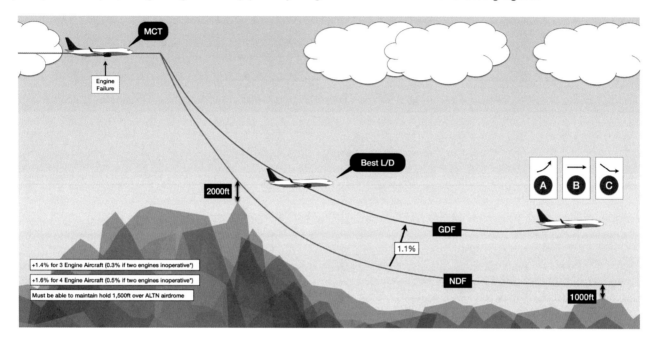

*Figure 373: Engine Failure / Driftdown requirements.*

As you can imagine, all this calculation cannot be made by pilots at the time an engine fails. They should only carry out a plan that has already been developed by flight dispatch personnel. These professionals have a lot of work to do when planning flights like this. That is because calculations do not depend only on the aircraft's weight and initial altitude, but they also heavily rely on weather conditions, especially wind and temperature.

Enroute headwind will make the trajectory much steeper, therefore force the critical decision point to be closer to elevations that we need to overcome, otherwise minimum clearance would be lost. Tailwind allows this critical point to be further away from the elevation we need to surpass (will happen sooner) because the descent trajectory would be shallower. This is represented in the following figure, comparing wind calm (center figure) with the other two situations, all of which are considering engine failure at the same point.

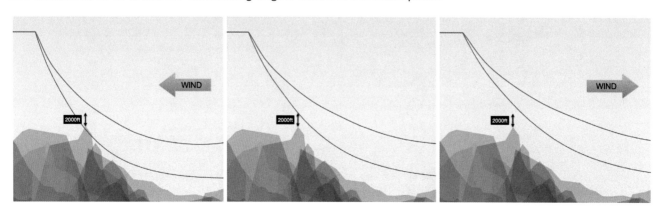

*Figure 374: Wind effect on driftdown flightpath.*

Temperature-wise, a hotter day means a lower altitude capability, because the engine will produce less thrust. This might force the flight dispatcher to greatly decrease the aircraft's weight in some cases (this is called Enroute Climb Limit Weight – we will see details in a moment). Anyway, on flights passing through mountainous regions, pilots must always try their best to follow to the letter all that was computed by the engineering team, fulfilling contingency procedures for engine failures occurring before or after the critical point. Not flying according to what they have planned might put the aircraft and its occupants at risk, drastically reducing terrain separation.

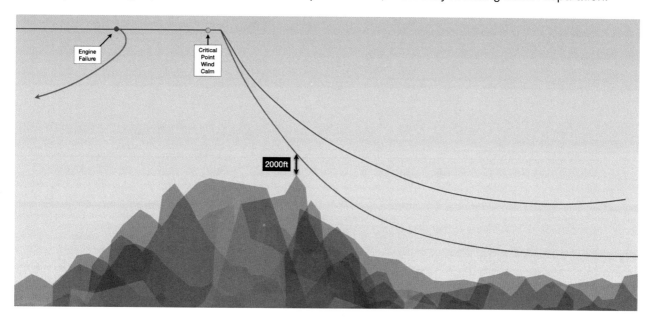

*Figure 375: Pilots must always follow the plan!*

We mentioned that three- and four-engine aircraft, such as MD11, B747 or A380, for example, have to assess the terrain by considering one of its inoperative engines (the critical engine) and execute driftdown with an additional margin of 1.4% or 1.6%. However, in some cases, this assessment needs to consider the failure of two engines on these aircraft, and the extra gradient is decreased.

In order to be sure of whether an evaluation needs to be made in the first or second way, we need to define which alternate airports will be available along the route. These airports have to meet certain criteria and it is not any airport that can be considered. We say that there should be "suitable alternate airports" along the route. The airport must support the aircraft that we are using and have minimum meteorological conditions above those described in FAR 121.197 (these minimums depend on resources available for approach and landing - ILS, VOR, RNAV, etc.).

Once these airports have been determined, the next planning step is to establish an arc around the airport with a radius that represents the distance the airplane is capable of flying in normal cruising condition for 90 minutes with no wind. Suppose a TAS of 450kt: in this case, the arcs will have a radius of 675nm around the airports of choice.

Finally, we draw the desired route. If the route remains within these drawn circle areas at all times, as shown in Figure 376, there is no need to perform a driftdown analysis with two inoperative engines. The analysis is made only with the critical engine inoperative. If the route is at any point outside the "90-minute" arcs, driftdown analysis with two inoperative engines is mandatory.

Our example shows a round-trip flight between two locations using different routes. On the way back, the route passes outside the defined area and the flight dispatcher must make a driftdown analysis with two inoperative engines (Figure 378). This is just an example. We can imagine another situation in which the route would require a driftdown analysis of two inoperative engines. Just think of an alternate airport along the route that has been disqualified as "suitable". This can be due to the weather or another technical factor, such as works on the runway that require that the airport be closed for a given period of time. In any case, Figure 377 shows two airports along the route that were not considered to be suitable that day. This will force pilots to fly beyond the 90min bounded area.

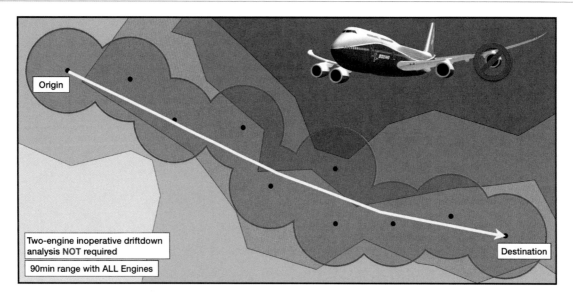

*Figure 376: Dual engine failure analysis is NOT required.*

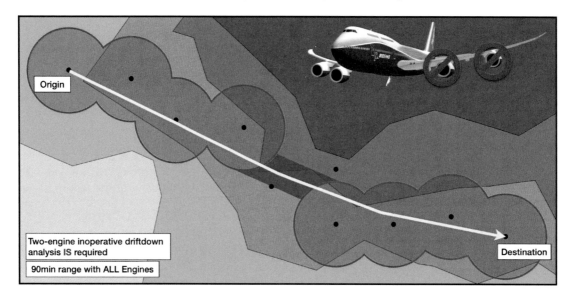

*Figure 377: Dual engine failure analysis IS required (A).*

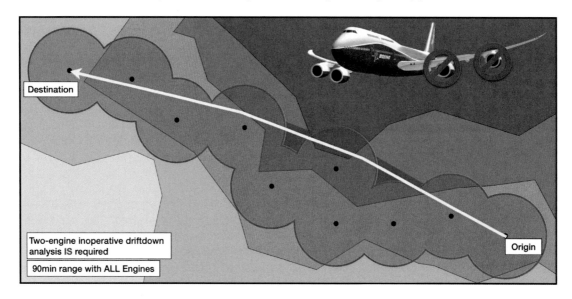

*Figure 378: Dual engine failure analysis IS required (B).*

When performing terrain analysis to define critical points and driftdown strategies, which terrain should be considered? Again, the answer to this question depends on the regulator. The difference is small, but it exists. Take a look at the next illustration.

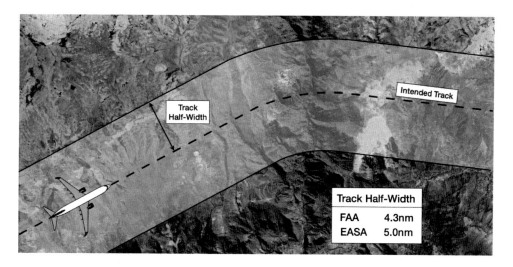

*Figure 379: Track half-width for terrain analysis.*

For EASA, starting from the trajectory planned for the flight, either on the normal or on the contingency routes, it is mandatory to always consider the highest obstacle found in an area that is 5nm on each side of this trajectory. For FAA, the area is slightly smaller: 5sm or 4.3nm for each side of the trajectory's axis.

For even more accurate calculations, we should deal with one more detail regarding the driftdown profile: turning. The path defined for engine failure contingency often involves making a change in direction to be performed after the event. During a turn, in addition to traveling a certain distance that can change the coverage area of terrain analysis, the aircraft has a gradient of descent greater than the one calculated with wings leveled. Boeing offers a performance manual called "Methods to Calculate Turn Performance on Boeing Airplanes", or simply Turn Performance Manual, TPM, which contains data needed to calculate which increase should be expected in the rate of descent during a turn. However, this book will not cover calculations required for this refinement. I just pointed out that the problem exists and has to be addressed by the engineering team during flight planning.

## 4.7.2 Cabin Depressurization and Emergency Descent

We have finished terrain assessments that can affect us on engine failure situations. However, this is not the only emergency that can force the aircraft to descend. Cabin depressurization is another type of emergency that needs to be considered when we talk about terrain clearance. But first things first! Let's begin with oxygen requirements.

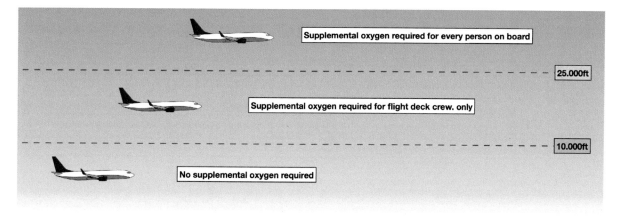

*Figure 380: Supplemental oxygen requirements.*

All commercial aircraft that intend to fly above 10,000ft must have a pressurized cabin. If a particular aircraft is certified for flights over 25,000ft, in addition to cabin pressurization, individual oxygen supply must be available for all occupants in case the cabin loses pressure. Supplemental oxygen must be available for flight deck crew members when they are flying above 10,000ft. The famous oxygen masks shown during flight attendants' safety demonstrations can basically be of two types: a gaseous system, which is very rare (however, this is the standard oxygen supply system for pilots), and the most common system, based on a generator that produces oxygen from a chemical reaction to supply a certain amount of this gas to the passenger for a limited time.

On a curious note: as the air from oxygen masks is mixed with air from the cabin, the pilot will never deploy this system in case of smoke in the cabin! That would only make things worse by forcing passengers to inhale smoke.

Oxygen is produced from a chemical reaction between two elements: sodium chlorate and iron powder. The problem is, when mixing, these substances do not produce only oxygen, but also a lot of heat! It is like burning a candle, and this bottle can easily reach temperatures above 230°C. The result is a weird odor of something burning that can scare some passengers; however, I assure you that it is perfectly normal.

On any row of seats there is often one extra mask. A row with 3 seats, for example, will have 4 masks available. The reason is not associated with a possible mask failure, since all 4 are connected to the same bottle and pulling anyone will pull the trigger that activates the chemical reaction. The reason is simpler. In a row of three, there might by an infant seating on a parent's lap, or a pet (e.g., a small dog) on its owner's lap, or a flight attendant might be on the aisle and he/she will have no time to go to his/her station to get a mask, so they will borrow the closest one available. As some rows have no extra mask, flight attendants must know which rows have it and which ones do not, and never allow the extra person (infant) to be seated there.

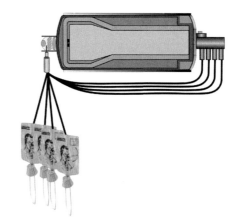

*Figure 381: PSU and oxygen generator bottle.*

The oxygen bottles and masks are installed at points of the aircraft located above passenger's heads. These stations are called Passenger Service Units (PSU). Passengers and flight attendants have the same chemical generator on almost every commercial aircraft and the gaseous system with pure oxygen supply is reserved for the flight deck, only.

| Altitude | TUC (normal ascent) | TUC (rapid decompression) |
|---|---|---|
| 18,000ft | 20 to 30 minutes | 10 to 15 minutes |
| 22,000ft | 10 minutes | 5 minutes |
| 25,000ft | 3 to 5 minutes | 1,5 to 3,5 minutes |
| 28,000ft | 2,5 to 3 minutes | 1,25 to 1,5 minutes |
| 30,000ft | 1 to 2 minutes | 30 to 60 seconds |
| 35,000ft | 30 secs to 1 minute | 15 to 30 seconds |
| 40,000ft | 15 to 20 seconds | 7 to 10 seconds |
| 43,000ft | 9 to 12 seconds | 5 seconds |
| 50,000ft | 9 to 12 seconds | 5 seconds |

*Figure 382: Time of Useful Conscience.*

Supplemental oxygen is required because of human body physiology. We need a given amount of air to breathe, otherwise our body starts to fail. And one of the first functions to fail is our brain's cognitive capacity. The time period between a rapid depressurization and the moment you are no longer capable of responding correctly to basic instructions is called "Time of Useful Conscience", or TUC. This time is shorter and shorter as you climb, ranging between 15 and 20 seconds at 40,000ft.

There are oxygen generators of various capacities, all of which are expressed in time: 12 (minimum), 15, 17, 22 minutes. As mentioned above, oxygen requirements are different for pilots. Oxygen must come from a dedicated cylinder which must be able to supply 100% oxygen through a period of 10min (remember the maximum certified altitude?), considering flow rate used during descent, plus 110min taking into account a normal flow rate at 10,000ft. Of course, this amount of oxygen must be supplied to all occupants on the flight deck. Back to passengers' supply, regardless of the generator capacity available on the airplane, manufacturers always provide an operating envelope for this generator. Let's see an example:

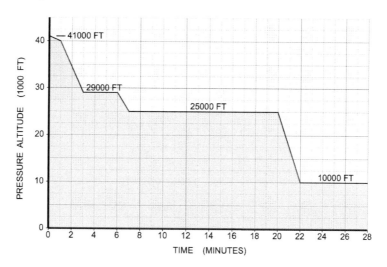

*Figure 383: Operation envelope of a chemical oxygen generator with capacity for 22min.*

Note that this generator with 22-minute capacity does not offer the possibility of flying 22 minutes at any altitude. This is because the higher we fly, the lower the air pressure is and, therefore, a person wearing the mask has a higher demand of oxygen produced by the generator. In this way, the entire operation of the aircraft must be conducted at altitudes within the envelope, which I have highlighted in green.

Also, descending lines of the envelope are very steep and do not necessarily reflect the aircraft's trajectory during descent. This trajectory will vary with airplane's weight. Therefore, it needs to be built backwards, based on the aircraft's descent capability. Next, you can see the most "stretched" operation in the blue line, and a direct descent to 10,000ft in the red one.

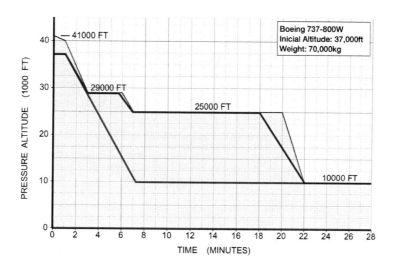

*Figure 384: Maximum and minimum emergency descent flight paths.*

The maximum path (blue line in Figure 384), defined by the aircraft's ability to perform a rapid descent on actual weight, will establish a new maximum envelope for emergency descent that is needed because of depressurization. This model will be used to create our terrain clearance strategy along the route.

An interesting note: next, there is some information about an emergency descent carried out on a flight with no terrain issues. Remember that the regulation requires that the descent should be completed within 10 minutes. As I said, it depends on weight, but it takes between 6 and 7 minutes, on average, for a Boeing 737-800 to descend from 37,000ft to 10,000ft, and the airplane will likely cover between 40nm and 50nm in this process. This descent is carried out at $M_{MO}/V_{MO}$ with speedbrakes deployed. By contrast, a driftdown procedure would take about 1hour and 20min to be performed and would cover about 350nm.

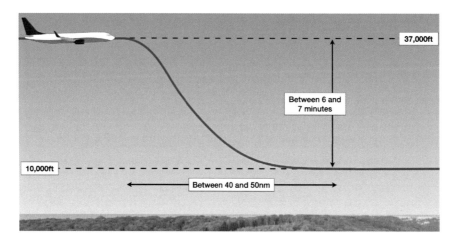

*Figure 385: Example of an average emergency descent.*

## 4.7.3    Sample Flight Planning – Terrain Clearance
### 4.7.3.1    Driftdown Analysis

Our sample flight will be on a Boeing 737-800 flying between Panama City (PTY) and Ezeiza Airport in Buenos Aires (EZE) and is a partial reproduction of a Boeing's keynote on the subject. This route passes over the Andes on two occasions and is a great opportunity to demonstrate the complexity involved in this kind of planning.

Boeing has created a planning suggestion based on a flowchart that I will present at the end of this topic. Initially, I intend to show this subject on a step-by-step approach rather than a flowchart. At each step, I will present the challenges inherent in planning the flight.

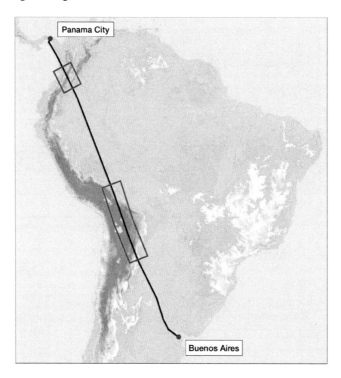

*Figure 386: Terrain clearance analysis on a flight from PTY to EZE.*

## Step 1

The first thing to do is also one of the most challenging: build a terrain profile to be overflown. It is complex because there is a lack of database standardization. There are several ways to build this terrain profile and all of them are correct. The difference lies in the accuracy of each model, which directly impacts our flight, especially when planning for maximum payload and fuel.

Databases that can be used for building this profile include: high and low Jeppesen enroute charts, government land maps, ONC (Operational Navigation Charts), and others. Typically, companies use Jeppesen enroute charts, and the model built is based on the grid MORA (Minimum Off Route Altitude, which guarantees obstacle clearance within the published area by 2,000ft for regions where there are elevations higher than 5,000ft). The problem using this information is that these grids are very large and sometimes, maybe more often than you would like, your flight will be penalized owing to an obstacle that is not part of your route, because it is not within 5nm on each side of your intended trajectory.

The data that I believe to be the most accurate of all come from a project called Shuttle Radar Topography Mission (SRTM). This was a flight made by the Space Shuttle Endeavor in February 2000, when about 80% of the Earth's surface was mapped in detail. The scan took place during 176 orbits, carried out over 11 days, and it collected data in grids of only 30 meters between parallels 60°N and 56°S. The data collected by the mission is available on the following website: https://lta.cr.usgs.gov/SRTM. The problem for operators is to convert the data as is into something that can be used. I do not know of any software for sale on the market that does this job. Boeing, however, has the means to make this conversion and has managed to use this database to make the terrain analysis used in our example. Hint: Google Earth is another nice tool for mapping terrain along a route. But careful, it only maps terrain just below your intended route, not 5nm to each side.

In the following figure, the terrain profile was mapped on the route that will be flown between Panama City and Buenos Aires. The profile traced by SRTM is equivalent to the highest existing terrain considering 5nm on each side of the flight path. The profile drawn in blue represents Jeppesen's published Grid MORA for each quadrant through which the flight will pass. Note that the latter makes the flight much more restrictive and, for this reason, we will consider the SRTM model in the exercise.

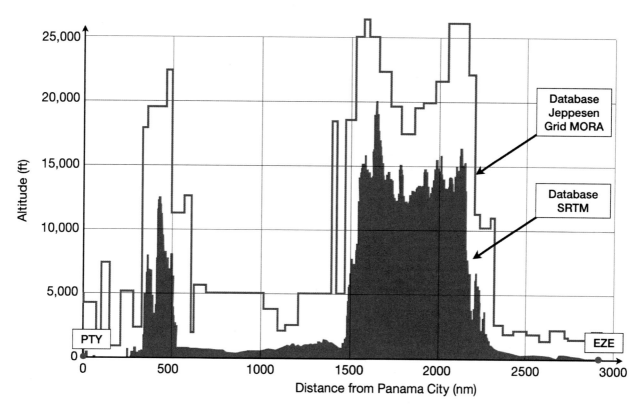

*Figure 387: Terrain analysis from PTY to EZE.*

## Step 2

Now that we know the terrain that we are going to fly over, we need to know how well the airplane can fly these elevations with its critical engine inoperative. To this end, we have a graph from the performance manual that directly informs our Net Level Off Weight. Remember that the airplane will fly higher than that, but it is the NDF that engineers need to worry about, so this graph suits us perfectly. In order to make this calculation, we need two pieces of information: our takeoff weight, which will be 75,000kg, and the weather condition. Suppose that temperature at medium flight levels is predicted at ISA+15°C. If we look at the graph below, using it in reverse, we will see that the aircraft's net altitude capability in this example is 14,400ft in case of a critical engine failure.

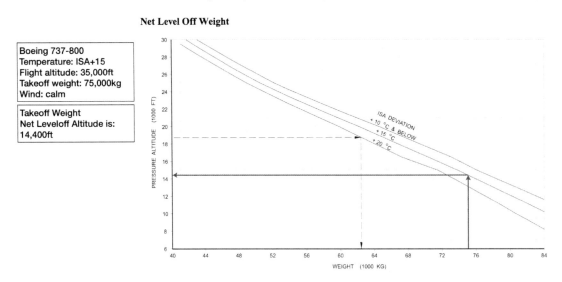

*Figure 388: Net level off altitude for takeoff weight.*

## Step 3

With this valuable information in hand, we now wonder: is there any elevation in our intended route above 15,400ft? Remember that regulations state that our NET trajectory must overcome all obstacles by at least 1,000ft when leveled. So, we can do one of two things: adjust the altitude mentioned in the question to 1,000ft higher or raise all terrain by 1,000ft. For our example, the necessary adjustments will be made to the terrain profile, rising it all by 1,000ft.

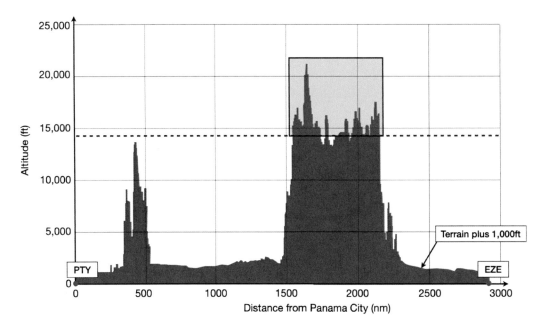

*Figure 389: Terrain on flight path adjusted by an extra 1,000ft.*

## Step 4

If there were no terrain higher than the aircraft's net altitude capability minus 1,000ft, driftdown analysis would be complete; however, as there are obstacles, we will have to refine our calculations. The first analysis was made while considering takeoff weight. But what is my predicted weight when flying over critical terrain?

Consider that the actual weight when flying over the most critical terrain, about 1,600nm after takeoff, is 65,000kg. Again, we need to check the Net Level Off Altitude, but now we will use 65,000kg rather than the takeoff weight. The result is 18,900ft.

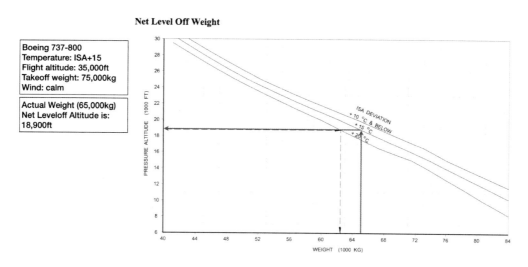

*Figure 390: Net level off altitude for 65,000kg.*

## Step 5

A new terrain assessment must be made to find out if, at this altitude, the airplane is able to clear all obstacles. Remember that our terrain data is increased by 1,000ft.

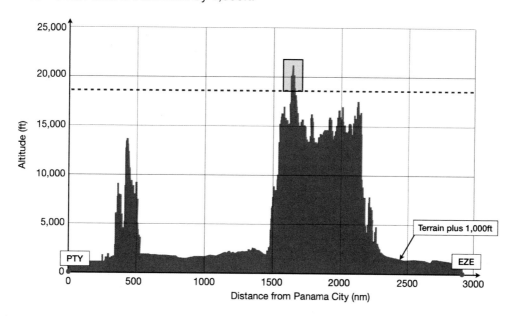

*Figure 391: Terrain analysis number two. Considering actual weight on critical point.*

## Step 6

Again, if there were no terrain higher than net altitude capability minus 1,000ft, driftdown analysis would be completed and we could move on to the oxygen requirements analysis. As there are obstacles indeed, we need to define how the descent path will be like between the proposed cruise level (35,000ft) and 18,900ft, and then check if we can avoid the elevations along this trajectory. For our example, we will consider no wind, but engineers need to think about the forecast wind in those regions as it will significantly change the flight path.

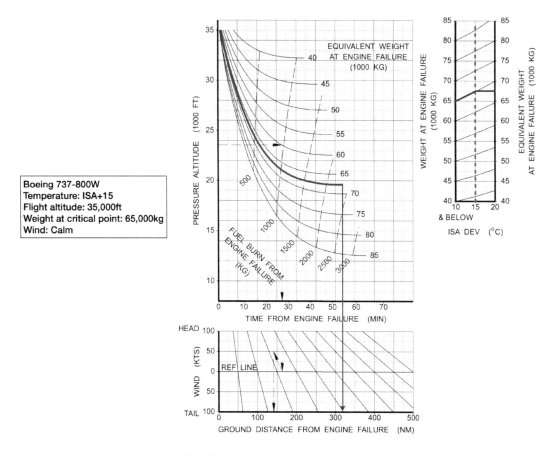

Boeing 737-800W
Temperature: ISA+15
Flight altitude: 35,000ft
Weight at critical point: 65,000kg
Wind: Calm

*Figure 392: Illustration of a net driftdown flight path.*

## Step 7

Based on net driftdown trajectory that we have just created, we will see if we can clear all obstacles below the aircraft during descent when engine failure occurs at the critical point. An important note here: to check if we are free of obstacles during descent, it is mandatory to adjust elevation by 2,000ft as established in the regulation.

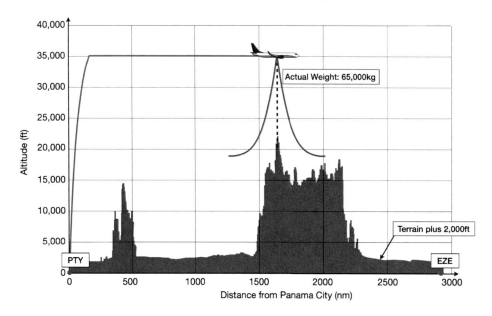

*Figure 393: Analysis of a net driftdown flightpath over terrain.*

**Step 8**

If not all terrain could be cleared after this assessment, the remaining options would be to find another route, reduce takeoff weight to increase Net Level Off Altitude, or create escape routes to the side – not back and forth, as we did. Well, as the obstacles could be overcome, now we need to establish where the critical points are to inform pilots and write contingency procedures that they are supposed to follow.

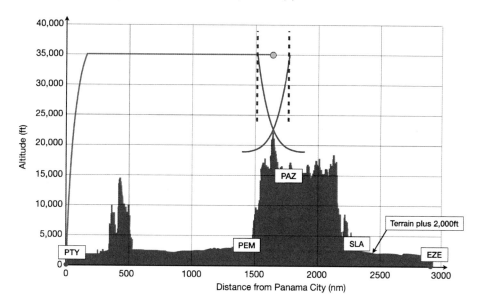

*Figure 394: Margin to establish where the critical point will be.*

Figure 394 shows that the critical point may have a margin to be established, according to the descent profile calculated previously. In our example, it can be as early or as late as identified by the purple dashed lines in the illustration. Between them, you have the option of moving on or returning. Before the first dashed line, you are obliged to return and after the second one you are obliged to proceed. This decision window, even if it exists, must be abandoned in the planning phase and I strongly suggest that the flight dispatcher should always define a clear strategy based on a single point. In our example, VOR PAZ (located in La Paz, Bolivia) is within the area between the purple dashed lines. We will use it as a reference to inform our pilots about our strategy. On this route, there is an airport in Puerto Maldonado (PEM), Peru, just before high elevations begin, and the airport of Salta (SLA), Argentina is located after such elevations. Therefore, the pilots' flight plan could contain the following information in the event an engine fails along this part of the flight:

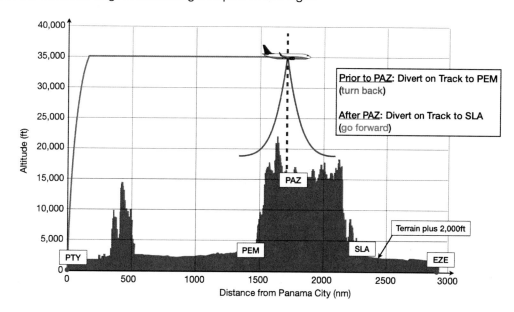

*Figure 395: Strategy that will be presented to pilots.*

Now see the steps described previously as a flow chart to be used in flight planning.

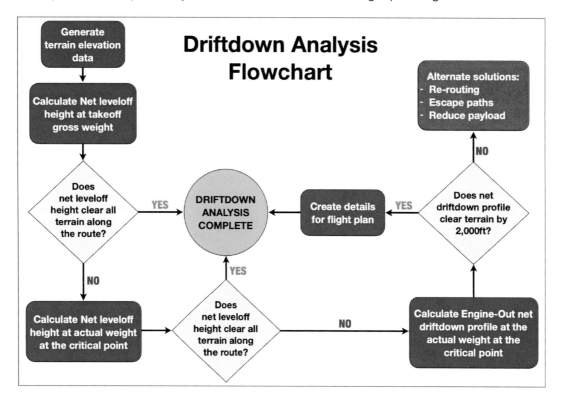

Figure 396: Driftdown analysis flowchart.

### 4.7.3.2 Enroute Climb Limited Takeoff Weight

Before proceeding with oxygen analysis, let me take this opportunity to discuss one extra takeoff weight limitation that is vastly misunderstood. To do that, I will show you three driftdown flight path analyses over the same terrain, but with three different weights (65,000kg, 67,000kg and 69,000kg).

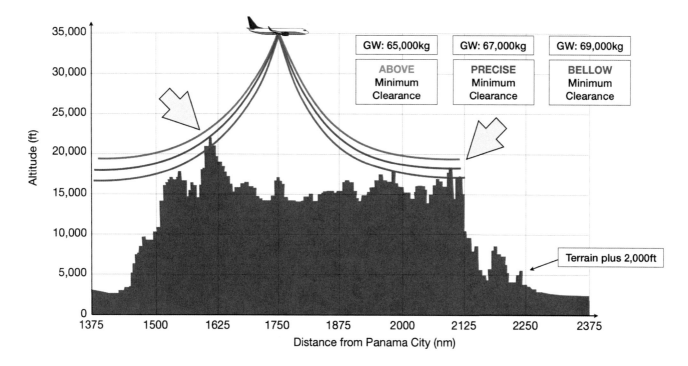

Figure 397: Establishing maximum weight over high terrain.

When we executed the driftdown analysis, I said that one of the solutions, if requirements had not been met initially, would be to reduce weight. In the previous illustration, you can see the reason why. The sequence shows that with a higher weight, the net driftdown flightpath is steeper and steeper. As indicated, when weighing 67,000kg, the aircraft was able to get the exact minimum terrain clearance. When heavier than that, the 2,000ft safety margin was not reached. So, we can conclude that 67,000kg is the maximum weight at which that point of the route should be flown.

This critical point weight limitation is called Enroute Climb Limit Weight. If we add the trip fuel required to get to this point, we now have the **Enroute Climb Limit Takeoff Weight**. Although it is not a takeoff limit, per se, it is a performance limitation that affects maximum allowable takeoff weight, just as maximum landing weight does.

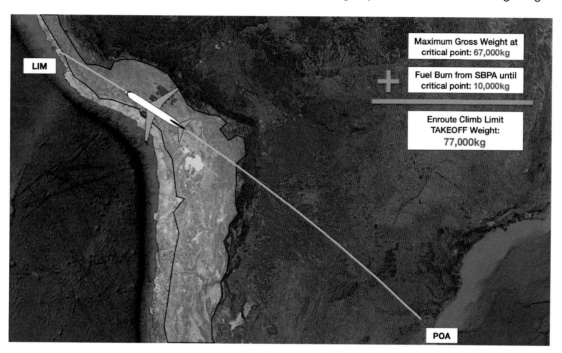

*Figure 398: Example of Enroute Climb Limit Takeoff Weight on a flight from SBPA/POA to SPJC/LIM.*

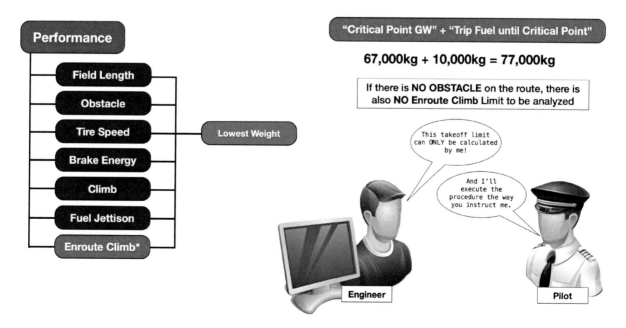

*Figure 399: Quoting Steve Jobs: "There's one more thing" on maximum allowable takeoff weight.*

### 4.7.3.3 Oxygen Requirement Analysis

At this point, we can move on to oxygen requirement analysis. Once again, I will divide our process into steps. Our analysis will be based on the oxygen envelope that we saw earlier, in Figure 384.

### Step 1

When leveled at 10,000ft, we wish to maintain a terrain clearance of 2,000ft while flying to an alternate airport. A simple question: are there any obstacles above 8,000ft on our flight path? The answer is clear in Figure 400.

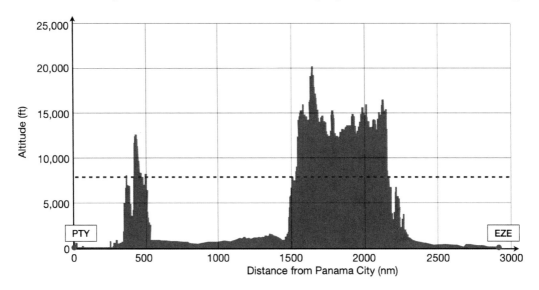

*Figure 400: Obstacles above 8,000ft.*

### Step 2

If there were no obstacles above 8,000ft, our analysis would be complete. As they are, indeed, present, let's use the most stretched emergency descent trajectory, seen in Figure 384, and plot it in our terrain analysis chart, but adding 2,000ft to terrain data (the clearance that we need). Note that two points have been created. One is the latest point that allows us to return to Panama City while the other is the earliest point at which we can continue to Buenos Aires. We need a different contingency plan for everything that exists in between.

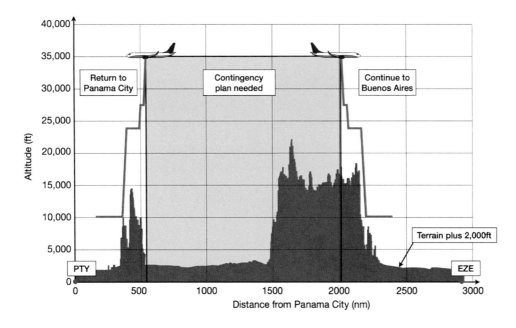

*Figure 401: A contingency plan is required.*

## Step 3

About 900nm after Panama City, there is an airport in a city called Iquitos (IQT), Peru. In the following figure, we determined the latest point along the route at which we are able to divert to Iquitos if cabin pressurization is lost. You will see, however, that there are options regarding the point at which we should start considering diversion to this airport.

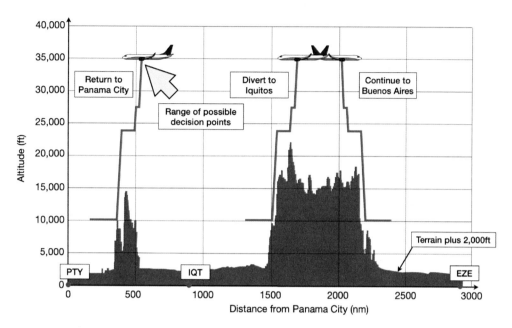

*Figure 402: Where are the earliest and latest points to divert to Iquitos?*

I know we have not yet managed to solve all the problems along the route, but regarding that first mountain to be overflown, we have opportunities for a contingency plan. Figure 403 shows the latest point on the route at which it is possible to return to Panama City, and the earliest point at which it is possible to proceed to Iquitos.

Just as in driftdown analyses, although there is a region where both options are valid, it is crucial that flight dispatchers clearly define a single point along the route for a go/no-go decision. For example, we could use the point where we fly over the top of the hill, about 400nm from Panama City. Before this point, come back to Panama. After this point, proceed to Iquitos!

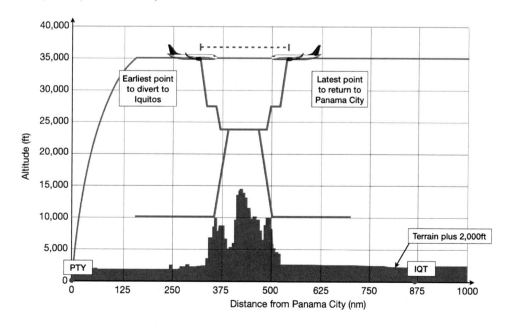

*Figure 403: Establishing a Go/No-go decision point.*

## Step 4

Now, our flight has become quite complicated. We still have to decide what to do in this highlighted region.

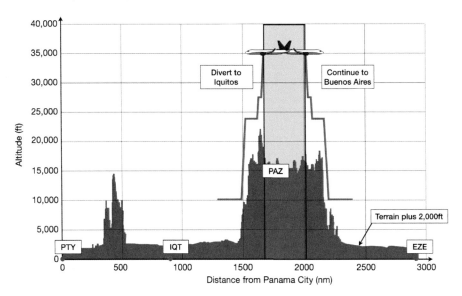

*Figure 404: A contingency plan is still required for the region highlighted (lighter brown area).*

In the red area, which still needs a different strategy to make our flight possible, there is the city of La Paz with an airport situated close to a 13,500ft elevation. Not every airplane or flight crew is certified to operate at that airport, but let's suppose we could land there if we needed to.

In the next figure, you will see that, even though we could operate at this special airport, we still cannot possibly cover the entire route with contingency plans. There is a remaining red area (smaller) that was not covered. We have to look for alternatives using lateral escape routes.

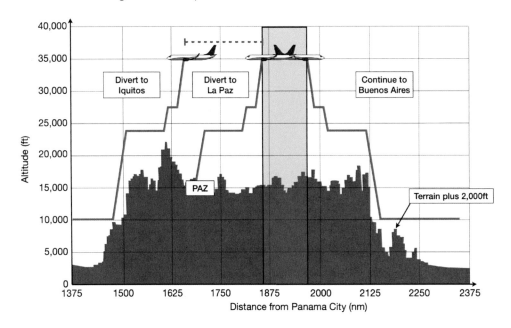

*Figure 405: A contingency plan is still required for the highlighted region (lighter brown area).*

The process of finding lateral escape routes is usually not a first option because it is much more laborious. Some software programs can devise these off-track contingency plans, but often implicating in heavy weight penalties. That is because every software that I know of is only capable of planning for direct alternate routes from any given point along the original flight path. Figure 406 shows what I mean.

Flying shorter distances over the mountains will certainly help! So, one possible strategy is to draw the boundary limits of the high terrain region and ask pilots to fly a heading that can keep them over a dangerous high elevation for a shorter period of time. After surpassing that, the pilots can continue descent to 10,000ft and land safely on an enroute alternate field. Take a look at the analysis below. On the left, there are direct lines from our route to two different alternates, SLVR/VIR (Santa Cruz de La Sierra – Bolivia) and SCDA/IQQ (Iquique – Chile). In the center, high terrain boundaries lines were drawn and flight paths were modified. The third figure in sequence shows the result of the contingency plan that would be handled to the pilots.

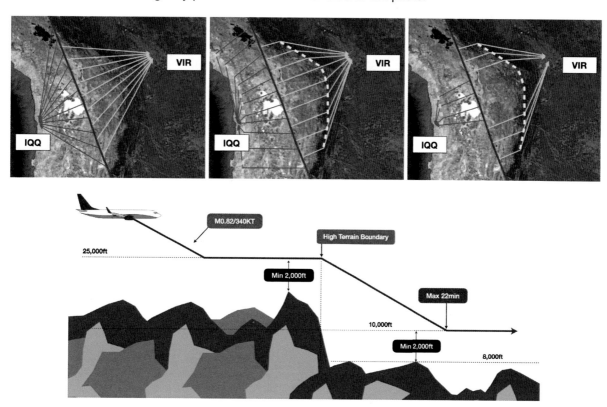

Figure 406: Planning escape routes.

If it is still not possible to meet the requirements for terrain clearance; the only option available to the flight dispatcher is to define a different route (certainly longer and which will require more fuel) in order to make the flight feasible. No flight can be dispatched if ANY requirement is not met. One good example of impractical flights owing to terrain clearance regulations is the Himalayas. There are some flights whose destination is the Tibetan plateau, but they always come from the south (like Delhi, India); there is not a single flight crossing this region into northeastern China, for example, to Beijing.

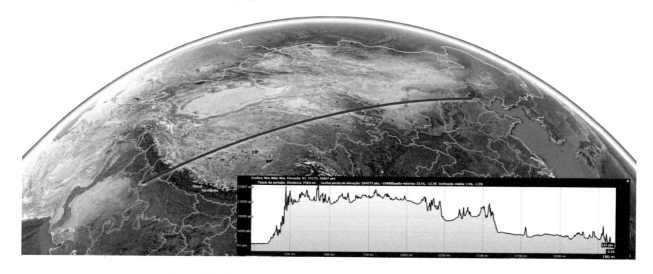

Figure 407: Impossible flight from Delhi to Beijing (Google Earth).

## 4.8.1 Descent Profile

Speed-wise, descent profile is very similar to what we covered during our study about climb. There is an initial phase in which the speed used is Mach, followed by a second phase that is flown using IAS. If IAS is greater than 250kt, when reaching 10,000ft, a speed reduction will need to be computed in most airspaces. Take a look at the example below.

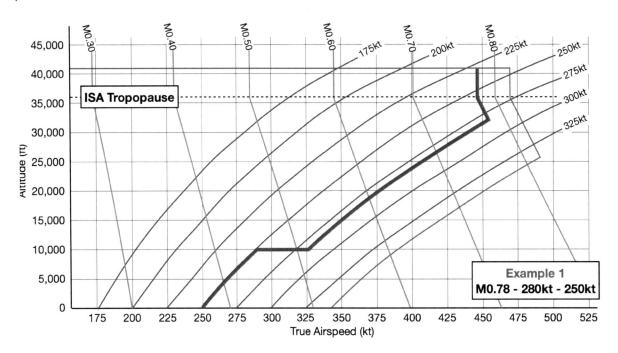

Figure 408: Airspeed during descent.

It is impossible to describe a descent path. There are too many factors varying along a path, for example, speed, attitude, different winds and temperature layers, and so on. Anyway, this book is also intended for use as a study guide, so, let me tell you what regulators want you to believe. They say that the descent profile will look approximately like this: while maintaining Mach, TAS increases and the descent angle tends to increase as well. With constant IAS, TAS decreases, but air density increases lift and slows the rate of descent. In this set, there is a tendency towards nullity and the descent angle remains relatively constant.

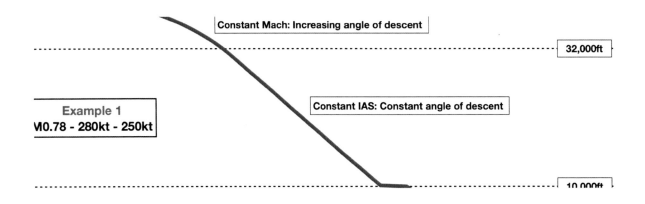

Figure 409: Descent vertical profile. OK for EASA exams, but not real!

## 4.8.2 Descent Speed Strategies

As with cruising speed, there are five possibilities when it comes to defining the speed that will be used in the descent phase. In all of them, the engines are considered to be at idle thrust. Let's go over them:

*Figure 410: Possible speed selection for descent.*

### Maximum Range

It is the speed with the lowest descent angle, which results in the longest possible gliding distance. It is about the same speed as the Optimum Driftdown Speed. Not exactly the same because the latter considers drag of one inoperative engine and the deflection of control surfaces (rudder). This speed increases the descent phase of the flight (using very low fuel flow owing to idle thrust) and reduces the leveled portion of flight (cruise phase), which uses a much higher fuel flow. So, this speed offers the lowest fuel consumption if we consider the overall flight. However, this speed is not recommended for use in a normal flight, as it is usually very low and significantly impacts air traffic control. As previously mentioned, Airbus presents this speed as the Green Dot Speed.

### Maximum Endurance

It is the speed that offers the lowest rate of descent and allows an aircraft to remain in the air for as long as possible, although it does not take it as far as possible. It can be used during a descent towards a fix where some holding is expected, for example. Gliders normally use this speed to gain some altitude when they are inside thermals.

### Minimum Time

It is the speed that results in the shortest possible time to make a descent, that is, it offers the highest possible descent rate. It is used in emergency descents (when cabin pressurization is lost, for example), and it is always the aircraft's $M_{MO}$ or $V_{MO}$ plus drag produced by deployment of the speed brakes.

### Maximum Angle

It is the speed that allows descent at the greatest possible angle. Usually used in landing approaches when the pilot is eventually too high on the intended path and wishes to correct it. But don't push it. Going around to trying again is always an option.

### Company Policy

Descent speed usually based on the Cost Index. It can also be defined in terms of air traffic or any other company policy and will not necessarily coincide with any descent strategy seen before.

## 4.8.3 Top of Descent Calculation – Rule of Thumb

How do we know when we have to start our descent? Most onboard computers on modern aircraft are able to establish the point where descent will begin so that it occurs with engines at idle thrust until final approach has been intercepted for landing. We call this point the Top of Descent (TOD). Calculation to identify how far we will travel during descent will depend on speed, weight, and wind, and it can be done using the airplane's performance charts. However, there is a basic rule that is valid for most jet aircraft and is worth mentioning here. Be advised that on most busy airports around the globe, air traffic control will end up messing up everything that you have planned! They need to guide lots of aircraft in and out of a given airport at the same time, so they will most likely ask a pilot to descend much sooner than he/she had intended. Don't be mad at them. They are just doing their job. But I will tell you how to plan your descent at idle anyway.

If you ever need to calculate how many nautical miles will be required to perform a descent, you can make a simple calculation, and it will give you a good estimate for most airplanes and weights. The rule is as follows:

1. For every 1,000ft that the plane needs to descend, it will fly approximately 3nm.
2. For every 10kt that the plane needs to slow down, it will fly approximately 1nm.

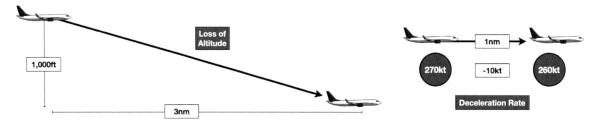

*Figure 411: Descent and deceleration.*

With this rule, let's do a simple mental exercise. We need to go down from 38,000ft to 5,000ft and will intercept final approach at this altitude and with 170kt. Descent will be executed with 280kt until 10,000ft and 250kt below that. At 5,000ft, we will decelerate to 170kt, as requested.

Well, let's solve that: I have to descend 28,000ft (38,000ft minus 10,000ft), and will fly 3nm for every 1,000ft descending (28 x 3 = 84nm). I need to slow down from 280kt to 250kt covering 1nm for every 10kt (3 x 1 = 3nm). Then, I will continue down from 10,000ft to 5,000ft (another 5,000ft of descent) and a further slowdown to 170kt (5 x 3 = 15nm and 8 x 1 = 8nm).

Adding it all up, we have: 84 + 3 + 15 + 8 = 110nm. This means that I need to start descent 110nm before the point at which I want to be at 5,000ft and 170kt. In other words, our TOD is 110nm before that waypoint. Of course this calculation was broken down only for didactic reasons, but this fragmentation is not necessary. We could calculate the entire descent between 38,000ft and 5,000ft (33,000ft is 33 x 3 = 99nm), and then the entire deceleration from 280kt to 170kt (110kt is 11 x 1 = 11nm), and the result would be the same.

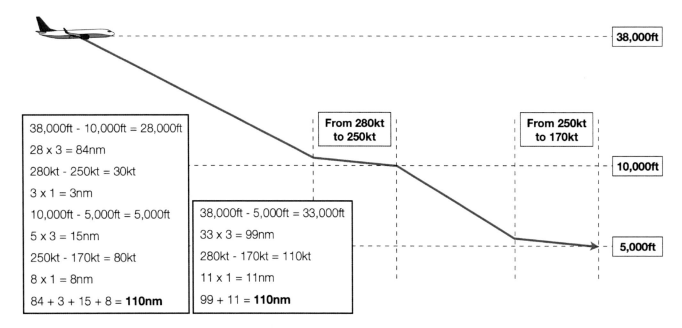

*Figure 412: Example of top of descent calculation using rule of thumb.*

## 4.8.4    Descent Speed Selection effect on Fuel Burn

For commercial airplanes, the descent phase is planned to be always performed on a glided flight, that is, with the engines at idle thrust. As I mentioned, this is not possible at many airports congested with intense air traffic, but for this study, we will consider a descent made just the way it was planned: without using engine thrust beyond idle until stablished at final approach.

For a descent in these conditions, the speed that will offer you the longest gliding distance is the one that provides the best lift over drag ratio (L/D Max). Such speed is usually very low when we are close to our landing weight, maybe less than 230kt. As commercial airplanes end up choosing descent speeds greater than 240kt, we can say that any speed higher than this lower limit (240kt) will result in a steeper descent angle.

We will choose three different speeds to carry out a study about fuel consumption in our airplane model, Boeing 737-800. The speeds are: 240kt, 280kt and 320kt. In this example, the plane weighs 65,000kg and descends from 37,000ft to sea level. During descent, while flying at Mach speed, this will be M0.78. Below 10,000ft, the speed will be 240kt. Now answer: at which speed did we get the lowest fuel burn?

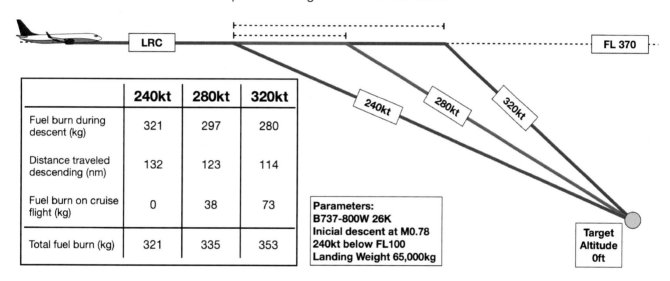

|  | **240kt** | **280kt** | **320kt** |
|---|---|---|---|
| Fuel burn during descent (kg) | 321 | 297 | 280 |
| Distance traveled descending (nm) | 132 | 123 | 114 |
| Fuel burn on cruise flight (kg) | 0 | 38 | 73 |
| Total fuel burn (kg) | 321 | 335 | 353 |

**Parameters:**
**B737-800W 26K**
**Inicial descent at M0.78**
**240kt below FL100**
**Landing Weight 65,000kg**

*Figure 413: Descent speed influence on total fuel burn.*

Again, this study proves that we need to think very carefully about how we can ask the question. Just like what happened when we studied different climb speeds, there may be misinterpretation if we do not pay careful attention to the descent scenario. The faster the descent is executed, the lower the fuel burn will be in this phase of the flight; however, overall consumption increases. This is because a faster descent shortens not only flight time, but also the descent distance to be flown. The result is a slightly longer cruise flight, and we must assess fuel flow at this additional length. With the assessment of total fuel burn in hand, it was found that total fuel consumption was 32kg higher when we made the descent at 320kt compared to the descent executed at 240kt.

This is the reason why the aircraft's flight computer plans increasingly slow descents with low Cost Index values, up to a minimum of 240kt in case of Boeing 737NG. Slower descent speeds, closer to the best L/D, increase flight time, but they also reduce the total amount of fuel burned during this flight.

From now on, we will do some exercises with performance charts to put into practice all theory related to enroute performance that we have seen up to this point. The exercises will use three different manuals: Flight Planning and Performance Manual (FPPM), Flight Crew Operations Manual (FCOM), and Airplane Flight Manual (AFM).

Once again, I would like to point out that the exercises are no longer included in the book. To receive them as a PDF file, just send an email to: performance.brenner@gmail.com.

## 4.9.1    Long Range Cruise Wind-Altitude Trade

There is one single kind of exercise that I would like to show you in detail, here. As I promised, I intend to teach you how to use performance tables to identify whether it is worth changing flight levels from optimum to a lower or higher one owing to more favorable wind conditions. This table is known as "Long Range Cruise Wind-Altitude Trade". Be careful: the name gives you important information that might go unnoticed by some people. The term Long Range Cruise clearly states that this table was designed while considering that the aircraft is flying at this speed regime. If you are flying at a different speed, such as ECON, MRC, or a fixed Mach Number, this table is no longer valid. Either way, onboard computers are able to make this calculation using any speed regime.

The table reproduced in the figure below comes from the FCOM of a Boeing 737-800.

| PRESSURE ALTITUDE (1000 FT) | CRUISE WEIGHT (1000 KG) | | | | | | | | | |
|---|---|---|---|---|---|---|---|---|---|---|
| | 85 | 80 | 75 | 70 | 65 | 60 | 55 | 50 | 45 | 40 |
| 41 | | | | | 30 | 7 | 0 | 4 | 16 | 33 |
| 39 | | | | 22 | 4 | 0 | 4 | 15 | 30 | 45 |
| 37 | | 37 | 14 | 2 | 0 | 5 | 15 | 28 | 43 | 56 |
| 35 | 23 | 7 | 0 | 0 | 6 | 16 | 28 | 41 | 54 | 64 |
| 33 | 2 | 0 | 2 | 8 | 18 | 29 | 41 | 53 | 62 | 68 |
| 31 | 0 | 4 | 11 | 21 | 31 | 42 | 52 | 61 | 67 | 70 |
| 29 | 7 | 15 | 24 | 34 | 43 | 53 | 61 | 67 | 70 | 70 |
| 27 | 19 | 27 | 36 | 45 | 54 | 61 | 66 | 70 | 70 | 68 |
| 25 | 31 | 40 | 48 | 55 | 62 | 67 | 70 | 70 | 69 | 64 |

The above wind factor tables are for calculation of wind required to maintain present range capability at new pressure altitude, i.e., break-even wind.

*Figure 414: LRC Wind-Altitude Trade table.*

Based on this table, we can decide whether or not it is worth flying at a flight level other than optimum, by identifying if more favorable wind speed compensates for a decrease in fuel mileage. It has an explanation on how to use it in the footer. But honestly, I do not like the way the explanation is given, and I created a different approach to the problem. I will share it below with some examples.

My airplane weighs 65,000kg and is flying at FL330 with a 20kt headwind. Is it worth changing to flight level 350, if I know that, at this altitude, there is a 25kt headwind?

In the table, there are several numbers that can be obtained when cross-referencing two pieces of information: weight and altitude. Identify the two numbers that are part of our exercise, that is, the one equivalent to our current flight level and other for the intended flight level.

The trick: "Where do I want to go" MINUS "Where am I" = "Result". In other words, subtract the value found at the current flight level from the value found at the intended flight level.

If "Result" is POSITIVE, the interpretation is as follows: the wind condition **MUST improve AT LEAST** this number of knots to be worth changing altitude. If it improves less, I will stay put in my current FL.

If "Result" is NEGATIVE, the interpretation is as follows: the wind condition **MAY worsen UP TO** this value and it is still worth the change. If it gets even worse, I will stay put in my current FL.

In our example, 6 - 18 = -12. The result, negative 12, should be interpreted as, "even if the wind gets 12kt worse than in the current condition, it is still worth changing the altitude". According to the data presented by the exercise, we had a headwind condition of 20kt and, if we make the switch, the new condition will be 25kt headwind. This is 5kt more unfavorable; however, a worse condition up to 12kt still makes the exchange something positive, so let's go up! We got a credit of 7kt.

Imagine now that the flight takes place at FL370 with a 10kt headwind condition (same weight) and I wonder if it is worth descending to FL330, which has a 15kt tailwind.

In this second example: 18 - 0 = 18. The result, 18 positive, means that the condition MUST improve by at least 18kt for me to consider changing altitude. So, we had 10kt headwind and now we have 15kt tailwind. We can conclude that the situation has improved by 25kt, because not only have I eliminated 10kt against me, but I have also managed to find 15kt helping me. Once again, we have 7kt of credit. Let's go down!

In the third and last example, still with the same weight, say we are flying at FL330 with a 35kt tailwind and we wonder if it is advantageous to climb to FL390 with 15kt tailwind there.

In this case: 4 - 18 = -14. This result, negative 14, means that the wind can worsen up to 14kt and it will still be worth the climb. As there was 35kt of wind in favor and, if climb is carried out, this value will decrease to 15kt, then we will have a real loss of 20kt, compared to a maximum acceptable loss of 14kt. Therefore, it is better to stay put at FL330.

---

### How to use this table

"Intended FL factor" - "Actual FL factor" = "ANSWER"

If "ANSWER" (+), this is the minimum that MUST be improved.

If "ANSWER" (-), this is the maximum that CAN get worse.

---

*Figure 415: Tip on how to use the LRC Wind-Altitude Trade table.*

Intentionally left blank.

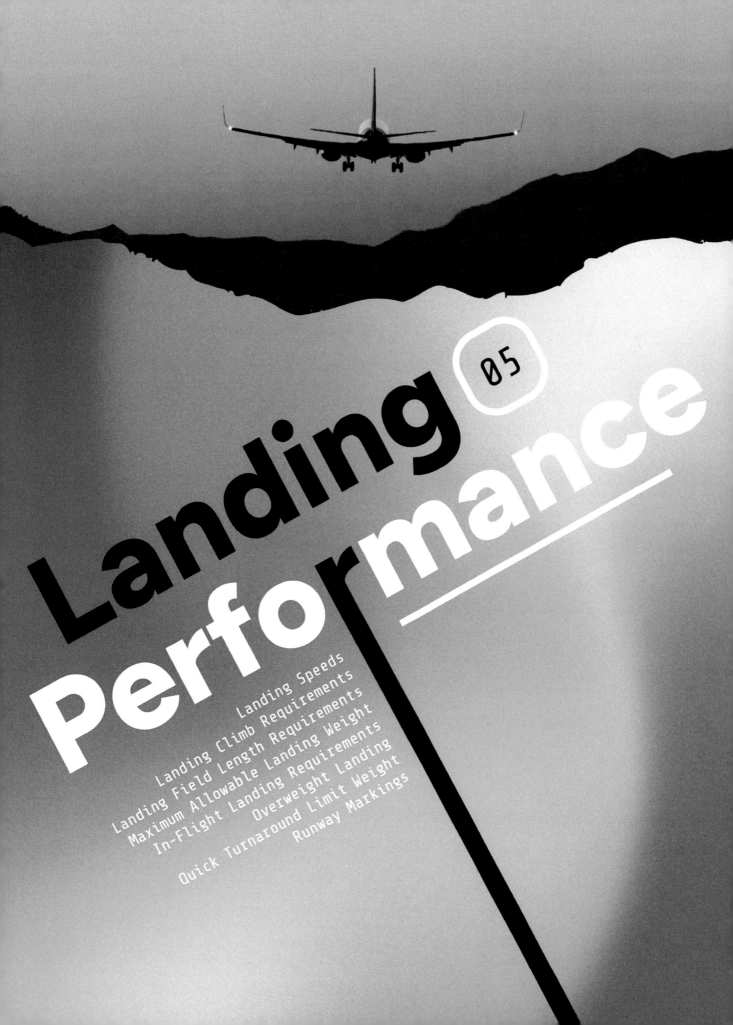

# Landing Performance

05

We will start studying landing performance the same way we did takeoff performance. It is about understanding where the speeds used in calculations and execution of procedures have come from. The first and most "famous" speed is $V_{REF}$.

## 5.1.1 $V_{REF}$ – Reference Landing Speed

This speed is used as a reference for calculation of landing distance and minimum climb gradients. In $V_{REF}$, an airplane must be able to make turns with 40° bank (25° of a normal turn used by commercial jets, plus a 15° protection against an eventual overshoot), considering that it is flying with symmetrical thrust on a descent path 3° downwards.

This speed must never be lower than $V_{MCL}$ (Minimum Control Speed in Landing Configuration), which basically has the same definition criteria as $V_{MCA}$, but in a landing configuration. $V_{REF}$ must always be a speed equal to or greater than $1.23V_{SR}$, that is, 23% higher than the reference stall speed (which is equal to or greater than $V_{S1G}$).

Just remember what I said when we started studying performance: before the existence of $V_{S1G}$, speeds that were related to stall speed had higher parameters. V2 was 1.20VS instead of $1.13V_{S1G}$, $V_{FTO}$ was 1.25VS instead of $1.18V_{S1G}$, and $V_{REF}$ was 1.30VS instead of $1.23V_{S1G}$. So, if you find a contradiction between this book and others on the market, do not be alarmed. I am not wrong in this book, nor the other authors are in theirs. The difference is in the update of materials.

As $V_{REF}$ depends on stall speed, we can conclude that it is directly dependent on aircraft weight. The heavier an airplane, the higher the $V_{REF}$.

## 5.1.2 $V_{APP}$ – Final Approach Speed

Speed used during final approach with landing flap set. It is equivalent to $V_{REF}$ plus a minimum increment. The purpose of this increase in speed is to ensure that neither turbulence, nor anything else that can cause variation in speed, leaves the airplane flying below $V_{REF}$ at any moment during the approach. Most manufacturers recommend a fixed value of 5kt when landing is conducted with a coupled automatic speed control system (such as Autothrottle or Autothrust). If the pilot intends to disengage this system before landing, the following rule must be followed (HWC stands for headwind component):

$$V_{APP} = V_{REF} + increment$$

Increment = 1/2 HWC + Gust

5kt ≤ Increment ≤ 15kt

$V_{APP}$ ≤ Placard Speed - 5kt

*** Maximum increment value was revised from 20kt to 15kt in 2018 ***

*Figure 416: Calculating approach speed.*

To clarify, "Placard Speed" is a name used by Boeing to define all the speeds that are described on placards installed on the aircraft's panel. In this case, it refers to flap maximum operating speed, which is different for each flap setting. The generic term to define this speed is $V_{FO}$ (Flap Operational Speed).

In a previous version of this book, the maximum speed increment was 20kt. In this review, I included the recommendation issued by Boeing in 2018 that decreased the maximum increment from 20kt to 15kt. The reason behind this reduction is the accuracy of current speed measurement systems when compared to those at the time the rule was created, therefore, old models such as the 727 and the 737 Classics (300, 400 and 500 series) should still consider a maximum value of 20kt.

Heads up! The "Gust" described in the rule is not the total value of gust wind, but the difference between the peak intensity and the prevailing wind value. Example: wind blows from 120° at 12kt gusting to 25kt (120/12G25KT) – the "gust" value to be used in calculation is 13kt (25 minus 12). To set this value, you do not need to establish wind components, just calculate the absolute value of the wind.

See some examples to exercise the rule. To solve the examples, consider the landing runway to be 36 (oriented northbound), the aircraft's $V_{REF}$ as 140kt and the Placard Speed of the landing flap to be 163kt.

Examples of reported winds:

360/12          $V_{APP}$: 146kt
12kt headwind. Half the headwind is 6kt. There is no gust. 140 + 6 = 146kt

360/08          $V_{APP}$: 145kt
8kt headwind. Half the headwind is 4kt. There is no gust. 140 + 4 = 144kt. Minimum correction value not reached. Result adjusted to 145kt.

360/06G16          $V_{APP}$: 153kt
6kt headwind. Half the headwind is 3kt. Gust is the difference between the peak and the prevailing wind, regardless of wind direction. 16 - 6 = 10kt of gust. 140 + 3 + 10 = 153kt.

060/08G20          $V_{APP}$: 154kt
Headwind component equals to 8kt x Cos60° = 4kt. Half the headwind is 2kt. Gust is the difference between the peak and the prevailing wind, regardless of wind direction. 20 - 8 = 12kt gust. 140 + 2 + 12 = 154kt.

060/18          $V_{APP}$: 145kt
Headwind component equals to 18kt x Cos60° = 9kt. Half the headwind is 5kt. There is no gust. 140 + 5 = 145kt.

270/14          $V_{APP}$: 145kt
Headwind component equals to 14kt x Cos90° = 0kt. Half the headwind is 0kt. There is no gust. 140 + 0 = 140kt. Minimum correction value not reached. Result adjusted to 145kt.

270/10G22          $V_{APP}$: 152kt
Headwind component equals to 10kt x Cos9° = 0kt. Half the headwind is 0kt. Gust is the difference between the peak and the prevailing wind, regardless of wind direction. 22 - 10 = 12kt gust. 140 + 0 + 12 = 152kt.

360/16G30          $V_{APP}$: 155kt
Headwind of 16kt. Half the headwind is 8kt. Gust is the difference between the peak and the prevailing wind, regardless of wind direction. 30 - 16 = 14kt gust. 140 + 8 + 14 = 162kt . Maximum correction value of 15kt exceeded. Corrected result to 155kt.

180/08          $V_{APP}$: 145kt
Headwind component equal to 8kt x Cos180° = -8kt (tailwind). Half the headwind is 0kt. There is no gust. 140 + 0 = 140kt. Minimum correction value not reached. Result adjusted to 145kt.

## 5.2.1 Approach Climb and Landing Climb Limited Weight

You might as well remember the "Return to Land Requirements" that we studied in takeoff performance chapter. That limitation was specific to new design aircraft, but it originated in an older rule. Landing Climb and Approach Climb requirements apply to any aircraft upon landing. What FAR 25.1001 did was to enforce that this existing rule be applied to aircraft taking off that would, for some reason, wish to return to land at the same airport shortly after departure

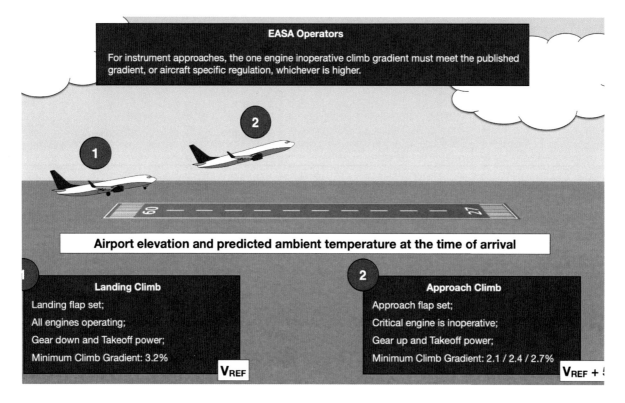

The description of the two requirements repeats what was said about Return to Land. Landing Climb refers to climb capability in landing configuration, that is, flaps and landing gear down. There is a single gradient of 3.2% to be met by any aircraft because this minimum climb requirement considers that all engines are running.

The second requirement, Approach Climb, considers the critical engine inoperative. With one less engine, a four-engine aircraft will lose 25% of thrust, a three-engine airplane will lose 33%, and the twin-engine will lose 50% of the available thrust. For this reason, there is a different gradient requirement for each of them.

The speed for measuring climb capability in each requirement is $V_{REF}$ and $V_{REF}+5kt$, respectively.

If you looked at the table of contents and came straight to this point of the book you probably missed my explanation about the (misleading) name of this requirement. How can I make an approach or land when still climbing? I am not sure if that is easy for native speakers to understand, but for non-English speakers that is confusing, for sure. Let me explain that again.

Landing climb should be renamed as "landing configuration climb capability", and approach climb should also be rebranded as "missed approach configuration climb capability". Those names would give a much clearer idea of what the requirements represent. Both are just ensuring a minimum excess energy to guarantee that the airplane will be able to climb if you need to give up the approach. The first scenario is thinking about the start of a missed approach in landing configuration (landing flaps and gear down), and the second scenario is considering that, as soon as the airplane is in a missed approach configuration (missed approach flaps and gear up), a sudden failure on the critical engine happened and the airplane is still able to continue climbing.

Although it is reasonable to assume that most missed approaches will commence at a higher altitude than airport elevation, both requirements are measured considering that a missed approach initiates at airport elevation and must use the OAT predicted for time of arrival to determine climb capability.

As in our study about takeoff performance, the same thing happens to landing. Climb gradients specified on the four takeoff segments, and obstacle requirements are unrelated to those published on SID charts. Similarly, landing Climb and Approach Climb minimum gradients have nothing to do with the go around gradient published on approach charts.

According to ICAO DOC 8168, the entire go around procedure of an instrument approach is built while considering a minimum climb gradient of 2.5%. If any landing procedure requires a higher gradient, this gradient must be informed on the approach chart (IAC – Instrument Approach Chart).

Note that go around values are higher than the Approach Climb Gradient for two- and three-engine aircraft. I wish to make it clear that these are rules with different intentions and that they do not "talk to each other". On the one hand, IAC's go around procedure is intended to ensure that no aircraft dangerously approaches any obstacle. On the other hand, the legislator only wanted to guarantee a minimum climb capability for airplanes in the event of a critical engine failure at the time of a missed approach. However, only some regulatory agencies – as far as I know – have regulated on this discrepancy; for example, the European regulatory agency has.

For EASA (European Union Aviation Safety Agency), every time the airplane is performing an instrument approach procedure, the Approach Climb Limit Weight must be calculated according to the published gradient or the airplane's specific criteria, whichever is higher. For example, a regular IAC has a minimum missed approach climb gradient of 2.5%. A twin-engine airplane would have to comply with that gradient, but a four-engine aircraft would have to be able to comply with its own requirement, which is a bit higher: 2.7%.

If the airplane is unable to comply with IAC's missed approach climb gradient, an alternate go around procedure can be used in case there is an engine failure, but it is the operator's responsibility to design such procedure, just as it is with Engine Out SIDs.

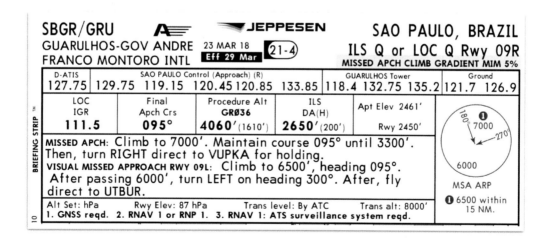

*Figure 418: A missed approach climb gradient higher than normal is explicitly informed on the IAC.*

That maximum weight at which the aircraft can meet the gradient of climb in landing configuration will be called **Landing Climb Limited Weight**. Maximum weight at which the aircraft can meet the gradient of climb in missed approach configuration with its critical engine inoperative will be called **Approach Climb Limited Weight**.

It is very common for the two of them to be combined and the lowest value between them to be simply called **Approach/Landing Climb Limited Weight**.

## 5.2.2   Critical OAT

A higher temperature decreases air density. The lower air density decreases the engine's ability to produce thrust. This train of thought is not new. We know that this kind of low density/low thrust situation will happen at high elevation airports on hot days. So, in most cases, neither landing climb nor approach climb limit weights will restrict an airplane's maximum landing weight.

Imagine a flight dispatcher who needs to perform calculations for 7 or 8 flights every hour. It is a lot of work to be done in a very short time. In order to find out  the maximum landing weight for an aircraft to be allowed to land at destination, he/she needs to check the predicted temperature at ETA (estimated time of arrival) and analyze landing and approach climb limits. To slightly reduce workload, the term Critical OAT has been coined.

The maximum weight allowed to land at a given airport will be the lowest of all weights that will be analyzed. So far, we know of three scenarios that need to be addressed for this definition: maximum certified landing weight (MLW), Approach Climb, and Landing Climb Limited Weight. There are two more factors that are runway length and PCR, but we will focus on the first three.

If you look at the generic table in Figure 419, you will see that both climb limits (landing and approach) are falling as temperature rises. The value for the certified MLW, however, remains constant. At a given temperature, one of the performance limitations (either Landing Climb or Approach Climb) equals the certified MLW. The temperature at which one of those limits (either one) is equal to the aircraft's certified MLW is our Critical OAT. Based on this temperature, a flight dispatcher will be able to tell if the maximum landing weight is certainly no longer the certified MLW, but a lower value than that.

By tabulating critical temperature values for all airports, the dispatcher reduces his/her workload. He/she only needs to find out the predicted temperature for time of arrival at the destination airport. If it is less than or equal to Critical OAT, they do not even need to calculate Approach/Landing Climb Limited Weight values, as they are absolutely sure that the Certified MLW is a smaller value and will limit landing weight anyway. If the predicted OAT is higher, then the flight dispatcher will calculate both performance limitations.

In our example, Critical OAT is 40°C.

|  | 25°C | 30°C | 35°C | 40°C | 45°C |
|---|---|---|---|---|---|
| **Approach Climb** | 78.2 | 75.1 | 70.2 | 65.3 | 60.4 |
| **Landing Climb** | 80.4 | 78.0 | 74.3 | 69.9 | 66.7 |
| **MLW Structural** | 65.3 | 65.3 | 65.3 | 65.3 | 65.3 |

*Figure 419: Critical OAT is 40°C in this example (weights in 1,000kg).*

Of course, this tabulation of critical OAT does not make sense for flight dispatchers using any performance software nowadays. That strategy is meant to be used for those who are still using performance charts to manually establish maximum takeoff and landing weights. Personal opinion: I strongly suggest that every flight dispatcher manually dispatch a flight every once in a while to keep their abilities sharp for any event when this might be required.

The last issue that defines landing performance for dispatching an aircraft is the runway length available to execute this landing. In the same way as we did when studying takeoff performance, we can look at this part of the content in two different ways. We can take a certain weight and find out the minimum runway length needed to land with that weight, or we can take a given runway and find out the maximum weight to land on it. In the latter case, this weight is called **Landing Field Limited Weight**.

Although it is more practical to define a certain weight according to the available runway we have (after all, the runway cannot be changed but our weight can), we will start by doing the opposite to understand how minimum landing distance is established. Pay attention to the rules that have recently changed; I will address the old and the new ones here. The new rule applies to aircraft with a recent design such as 737MAX, 787, 747-8, A350 and Embraer's E2 family.

The landing distance starts to be computed from the point at which the aircraft is 50ft above the runway. The speed at this point, for calculation and certification purposes, is $V_{REF}$.

According to the old regulation, landing flare was minimal, and the aircraft's main gear would touch the runway 1,000ft (305m) after the point where it reached the height of 50ft. Touchdown should happen in a speed between $V_{REF}$ and $V_{REF}$-5kt.

According to new legislation, landing flare has no specific length value, but it lasts between 4.2 and 4.6 seconds. The speed at the moment of touchdown is $V_{REF}$ minus a speed bleed off between 1 and 2%. With the new rule, air distance (length of runway between 50ft height and touchdown) depends on $V_{REF}$, and is no longer a fixed value of 1,000ft. The items I mentioned in this paragraph are highlighted in Figure 420 and are the only differences between old and new regulations. Everything else remains the same.

Landing touchdown is performed aggressively, avoiding a landing flare that would extend landing distance unnecessarily, and occurs at a rate of descent between 4 and 6ft/s. After touching down, rules for defining the ground roll portion of the landing distance requires the test pilot to use maximum manual wheel braking and aerodynamic brakes until the aircraft has come to a complete stop.

For stopping distance calculations, the transition period between touchdown and the moment when maximum braking capacity is available must be the highest value between one second and the period observed in flight tests. This landing must be demonstrated on a dry, paved, and level runway, in ISA condition and with no wind. The use of other features that assist in stopping, such as engine thrust reversers, are prohibited. Of course, this does not mean that the pilot will not use it for normal airplane operation.

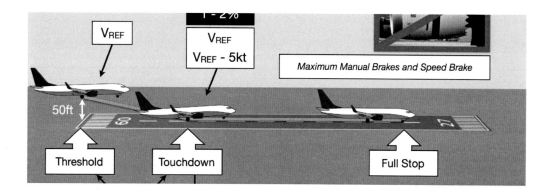

*Figure 420: Flight test landing field length.*

## 5.3.1   *Certified Landing Distance for Dry and Wet Runways*

Obviously, Figure 420 is an extreme condition to define the minimum runway length required to land an aircraft, and there are a lot of factors that on regular day operations can make the actual landing distance to be much, much longer. Let's analyze some of these factors:

1. The runway was considered to be leveled. But what if it is downhill? That would increase the landing distance by some meters.
2. The temperature was considered to be ISA. But what if it is warmer? That would increase ground speed and make landing distance increase by some meters.
3. The pressure was considered to be ISA. But what if it is lower? That would increase ground speed and make landing distance increase by some meters
4. The wind was considered to be calm. But what if we find an unexpected tailwind? That would increase ground speed and make landing distance increase by some meters.
5. The touchdown was considered to be 305m after the threshold. But what if landing flare is a little longer than that? It would increase our total landing distance in some meters.
6. The approach speed was considered to be $V_{REF}$. But we do our approach using $V_{APP}$, or maybe, unintentionally, some knots more. What would happen to our landing distance? That would increase it by some meters.
7. The pilot used maximum manual braking effort. What if we use less than that? That would increase it by some meters.

You see, there are a lot of "some meters" to increase in our landing distance and of course no regulator in the world would allow normal operations to be carried out on runways with LDA equal to what was demonstrated in flight tests. There has to be an extra safety margin!

Then, it was agreed that an extra two thirds over the flight test landing distance should account for all those extra "some meters" that we have discussed. So, multiply the flight test landing distance by a factor of 1.67 (it should be 1.666666…, but let's round the number to 1.67) and you will find the **Certified Landing Distance**, CLD-DRY. That is the minimum required LDA to land an airplane with the calculated weight. But did you notice I wrote the word DRY next to CLD?

One of the many assumptions made during flight tests was that the runway was dry! And we all know that friction between pavement and landing gear is reduced when the runway is wet. So, I ask you: by how much is the landing distance increased when the runway is wet? I know the answer many pilots will give, which is 15%! Sadly, this answer is wrong, however! There is no way of knowing for sure how much that distance will increase. Not all pavements are equal, therefore, not all of them have the same friction. Some runways could accumulate more water than others. So how could you say it is 15%?

Well, the thing is, despite the interpretation of some people when reading the FAR, no one really said that; 15% is not the amount of runway used by the airplane that is going to be increased! 15% is the amount of extra runway that was arbitrarily added by law to CLD-DRY to operate under wet or slippery conditions! As simple as that! And this extra length will hopefully be enough to account for the extra stopping distance the airplane will demand. By the way, I emphasize that 15% must be added over the CLD-DRY and that brings us to a new discussion: math!

A question that is frequently asked: how much longer is the Certified Landing Distance for WET runways when compared to the flight test landing distance? Let's do the math to find out: flight test landing distance plus 67% plus 15% equals to 82%, right? No, definitely not. When adding percentages, the sum is not that simple. Let me show you 10 plus 10 not being equal to 20. Say you put $100 in an investment with 10% interest over a given time. After that time, you have $110. Say you leave the money there and wait more time for another 10%. How much do you have now? $121! You gained 10% over the new amount of $110, which is $11. So, 10% plus 10% equals 21%. The same applies for CLD-WET. 15% is added over the CLD-DRY which already was 67% longer than flight test landing distance. Conclusion: CLD-WET is 92% greater than the original distance measured in flight tests.

The other point I need to clarify is about that value of 67%. That is written nowhere in the regulation. So where did it come from? In fact, it is written in a different way on the FAR. There it reads that flight test landing distance must not be greater than 60% of the landing distance available for landing on a dry runway condition. It is basically the same thing but with a different perspective. Remember when I told you that we could use the airplane or the runway as a reference? So, saying LDA must be at least 67% longer than flight test landing distance or saying that flight test landing distance must not be greater than 60% of the LDA is exactly the same thing.

To end this initial discussion about landing distance, I bet most of the readers have never heard of certified landing distance, but rather heard a different name pilots often use to refer to CLD. To get from flight test landing distance to CLD, we added a safety margin. Engineers refer to that as a safety "factor". So, the flight test landing distance is the **UNFACTORED** landing distance and the CLD is the **FACTORED** landing distance.

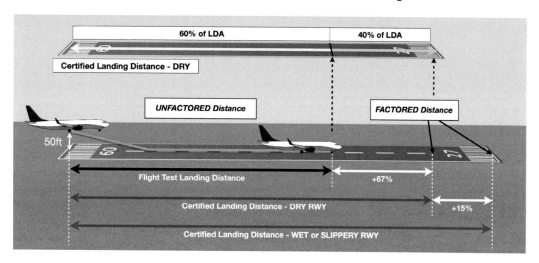

*Figure 421: Factored and unfactored landing distance.*

## 5.3.2  *Alternative Method for Establishing Certified Landing Distance on Wet Runways*

There is another method for establishing Certified Landing Distance for Wet Runways. Heads up: this method is only valid for wet runways (braking action Good) and cannot be used for slippery runways. In this method, instead of taking a dry runway CLD and adding 15% to that distance, you can perform an alternative calculation, provided that the manufacturer has published specific wet runway landing performance data.

In the alternative method, the runway is considered to be wet and, in possession of the data provided by the manufacturer, we measure the stopping distance using the intended landing weight. The approach speed used in this methodology is $1.33V_{SR}$, instead of normal $V_{REF}$ ($1.23V_{SR}$). To the resulting distance, we will add a safety margin of 15%. If this runway length is less than the runway length calculated when adding 15% to the dry runway CLD, the shorter distance can be used as the wet runway CLD. This usually occurs on tracks with a grooved surface and with SKR (Skid Resistant Runway) certification. In Brazil, there are two airports with this certification so far: Santos Dumont airport, in Rio de Janeiro, and Congonhas Airport, in São Paulo.

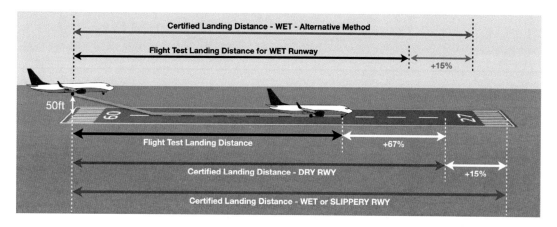

*Figure 422: Alternative method for Wet Runway CLD.*

Once again, Dry Check is a relevant issue. This alternative calculation method may eventually result in a smaller Wet CLD than the usual method for calculation of Wet CLD, but we can never use a result that is less than Dry Runway CLD. See the illustration below. When this occurs, Wet CLD becomes the same as Dry CLD.

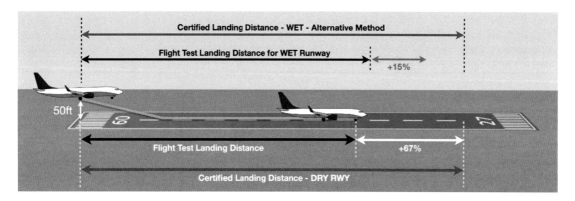

*Figure 423: When Dry Runway CLD becomes Wet Runway CLD.*

To establish the maximum allowable landing weight when dispatching an aircraft, there is a flowchart that goes through all the requirements that we have seen so far. This flowchart follows the same format as the one we saw earlier when looking into maximum allowable takeoff weight.

Again, the maximum weight allowed for landing will be the lowest of all values found. Of course, this is only for dispatching the aircraft. In emergency conditions, this rule no longer applies. The result found in this flowchart is to be used by flight dispatchers for fuel and maximum payload calculations. A flight dispatcher cannot plan a flight that allows the airplane to reach its destination above the maximum weight found here.

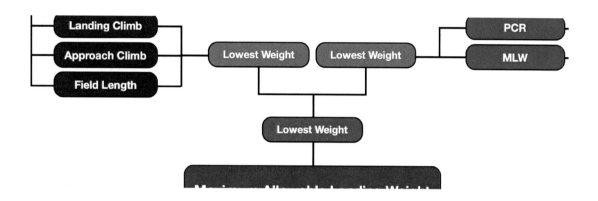

*Figure 424: Flowchart for maximum allowable landing weight.*

## 5.4.1   *Alternate Forward CG on Landing*

Alternate Forward CG can be used for increasing maximum landing weight, but under certain conditions. Just as V2 on takeoff, the reference speed, $V_{REF}$, is calculated while considering CG in the worst possible position, that is, the frontmost CG of the envelope. We can think of it like this: to keep the airplane in the air, a certain amount of lift needs to be produced. You need more lift when you have a forward CG and you get more lift with more airspeed, so $V_{REF}$ will be calculated for this scenario. The actual CG position, as in takeoff performance, does not matter.

However, if we use an envelope with Alternate Forward CG on the load sheet, we already guarantee that CG will stay within these new limits throughout all flight (from takeoff weight until zero fuel weight). We could, then, consider the new forward limit and recalculate $V_{REF}$ with this more aft position. The premise is true, but to use credit provided by Alternate Forward CG, pilots must have a way to calculate the new lower $V_{REF}$, since on-board computers (FMC or FMGS) are not able to do that. They always provide $V_{REF}$ based on normal CG envelope.

Let's exemplify with some numbers extracted from our model aircraft. Consider a very short runway operated by a Boeing 737-800, such as that of Santos Dumont airport (SBRJ), with only 1,323m (4,340ft) of landing distance available.

Maximum landing weight is field limited at this airport. It is worth 57,319kg for a dry runway. This value was based on the fact that approach would be flown with $V_{REF}$ of 127kt and that the plane would use 793.8m to come to a complete stop on the runway. This value is equivalent to 60% of the landing distance available, exactly as required by law. With 17% Alternate Forward CG (meaning the new forward limit of the envelope is now 17% MAC and not 6%), I could land at this same airport weighing 58,348kg. How?

When checking the airplane's FMC, the pilot would observe that $V_{REF}$ for 58,348kg is 128kt. A heavier and faster plane is bound to use more runway to stop. There is no magic that can be done if these factors do not change. What needs to be done is to consult a source that is able to calculate the new $V_{REF}$ for the alternate forward CG (AFM-DPI, OPT, PET, or any other approved software). With the aft CG, less lift is required and if we need less lift, we need less speed. New $V_{REF}$ obtained through one of these software programs will be 126kt. With this speed, even if the plane weighs 58,348kg, it will be able to stop using 793.8m of runway and comply with the law.

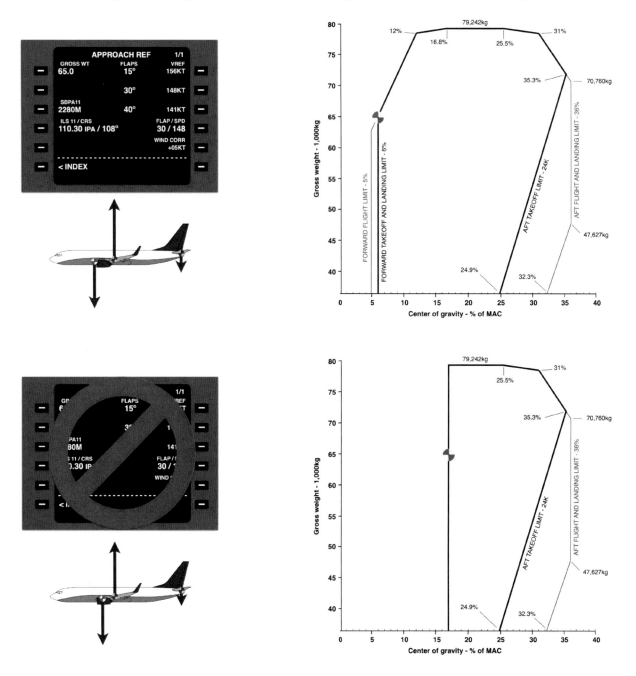

*Figure 425: Using Alternate Forward CG for landing. VREF from FMC is no longer valid.*

## 5.4.2   Influence of Different Brakes and Tires on Landing Weight

Aircraft such as the Boeing 737NG offer two different models of brakes and tires to operators. Brakes can be made of steel or carbon. Tires can be Radial or BIAS. Using carbon brakes and radial tires allows maximum landing weight to be greatly increased when it is field limited, but I believe that an assessment should always be made by the company's flight safety department before implementing these higher weight values. The reason lies in the difference between the calculation made by engineers and the way pilots actually fly the airplane. As we have seen before, when these two things are not the same, it can be dangerous.

Carbon brakes, for example, can increase the airplane's maximum landing weight between 700kg and 1,000kg. But how does it happen? Let's imagine two Boeing 737-800 on approach to land at SBRJ, each at its maximum landing weight (58,348kg and 59,182kg, for Runway 20L). The only difference between them (in addition to weight) is that the heavier aircraft is equipped with carbon brakes while the lighter, with steel brakes. On this landing, the pilots will use Autobrake at maximum level. Will they stop at the same distance?

The answer is "no". The heavier aircraft approaches at a higher speed and as the Autobrake system is designed to provide a fixed deceleration rate (we will see further details in a moment), the faster one will need more runway length to stop. Anyway, it is legally allowed to land with more weight using credit for different brakes and tires. This is because landing calculation is not made using automatic brake systems, but maximum manual braking. In this case, the carbon brake is actually more efficient and both aircraft would stop at the same distance, despite the difference in weight.

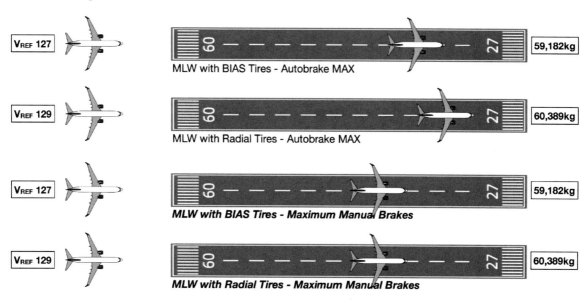

Figure 426: Difference among tires in terms of stopping distance: BIAS vs radial.

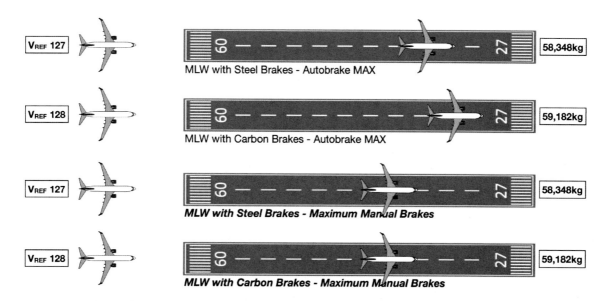

Figure 427: Difference among brakes in terms of stopping distance: steel vs carbon.

The extra weight was possible precisely because manual breaking was taken into account; however, as pilots do not operate this way, one needs to make a safety assessment before adopting these policies and try to check if the 40% safety margin is not being excessively compromised when these legal "amendments" are used to increase maximum allowed landing weight. A program named TALPA will do just that, and we will talk more about this program in a moment.

So, how can radial tires be more efficient than BIAS? Well, tires of this type have a "less rounded shape" on the edges and are flatter than the others (Figure 428). This is possible due to the different structure of the tire, where the sides are not linked to the tread in the same way as in BIAS. As it happens, when the airplane is trying to stop, either after landing or after an RTO, tires withstand a huge stress and their shape is deformed. To make it simpler, think of a piece of rubber being twisted by you. When you release the rubber, it comes back to its original format. This behavior also happens on a tire. It is trying to resume its original shape and by doing so, it acts like a spring. For that reason, not all weight is transferred to the ground and the braking is less efficient.

Well, that being said, owing to the different structure previously mentioned, radial tires are subject to much less deformation then BIAS ones, that is, they are able to transfer more weight to the ground and brake more efficiently.

So, once again, the problem is the difference between operation and engineering calculation. Since the automatic braking system is set to provide the airplane with a specific deceleration rate, a heavier plane will approach faster and will stop further away after landing. Again, the extra weight was established on the basis of maximum manual braking.

*Figure 428: Different tire models.*

I would like to emphasize that I am not personally against using these resources to increase an aircraft's maximum landing weight. Actually, I am all for it! But having said that, I think those special operations must be treated as such also by pilots. For this reason, it is essential that they be aware of the premises established when calculating maximum landing weight.

A few years ago, a wave of concern began with increasing events involving runway excursion on landing. The singular event that sparked these discussions was an accident at Midway Airport, in Chicago, USA, in which an aircraft overshot the end of the runway after landing, broke a wall and stopped by a highway next to the airport. There were no casualties on the aircraft, but tragically, a child was killed when the aircraft hit the car she was in.

*Figure 429: Chicago Midway runway excursion, December 2005.*

## 5.5.1  Takeoff and Landing Performance Assessment – TALPA

I do not intend to address all details of discussions that followed the accident. I aim at the final result. The Federal Aviation Administration (FAA) has implemented a program called TALPA-ARC (Takeoff and Landing Performance Assessment - Aviation Rulemaking Committee) that was especially concerned with "time of arrival performance assessments" for landing calculations. This regulatory committee intended to establish parameters that were more accurate with respect to the actual stopping distance on landing. As we have seen before, when calculating the runway length required for landing, a flight dispatcher makes several assumptions that cannot be implemented in many cases. Do you remember our briefing, when we emphasized the importance of pilots flying according to plan to ensure safety in operations? In many landing situations, however, pilots do not fly according to plan, and that is due to impossibility rather than negligence.

There is nothing better than an example to explain the result of this debate. Consider that our model aircraft is about to land on runway 02R, at Santos Dumont airport, in Rio de Janeiro, Brazil. Remember that, when calculating maximum landing weight, the flight dispatcher makes several assumptions, for example: $V_{REF}$ without additions, wind calm, leveled runway, ISA condition, maximum manual braking and a touchdown that occurs exactly at 305m (1,000ft) after crossing the runway threshold.

Based on these premises, it could be established that an airplane weighing 58,400kg will use 794m to stop, that is, 60% of the available runway. So, this is our maximum allowable landing weight.

In addition to this data, let's consider the following conditions: landing distance available on runway 02R is 1,323m; wind blows from 020° at 8kt gusting to 19kt; pilots will use the autobrake system set to maximum; outside air temperature is 35°C; landing will be performed using flaps 40 and both reverse thrusts are operating normally.

Bearing in mind that pilots do not necessarily fly according to what had been calculated as a matter of impossibility, let's see what the actual stopping distance would be for the conditions that we mentioned, including the correction in our approach speed and the braking capacity of the automatic brake system and all environmental factors that we also mentioned before.

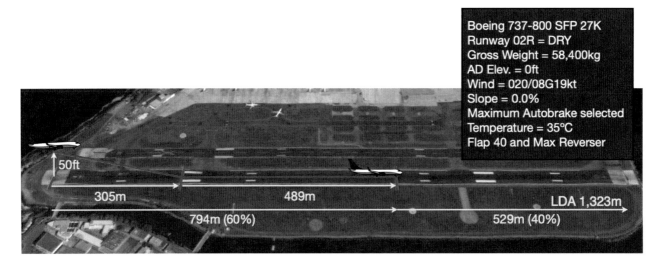

*Figure 430: Landing distance as imagined by the flight dispatcher's calculations.*

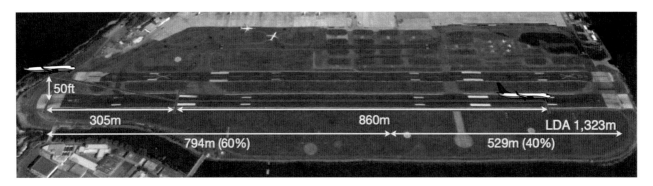

*Figure 431: Actual landing distance if touchdown occurs at 305m.*

Figure 431 shows that the airplane used more runway to stop than originally planned (1,165m actually used).

Quick review: why is there an extra runway margin imposed by legislation? Because weather condition is not always ISA (35°C is ISA+20), the wind is not always calm (good news, 8kt headwind), approach speed is not always $V_{REF}$ ($V_{REF}$+15kt due to gusty winds), runway slope is not always zero (in this example it is 0%), and the pilot does not always use maximum manual brake on landing (autobrake set to MAX). All these factors contribute to the aircraft using more runway to stop after landing. So, 67% safety factor is not there for nothing. It will be used whenever any condition is different from what had been planned.

However, the committee started to worry about other aspects and the first to be noticed was the 305m between the 50ft point above the runway and touchdown. This considers an aggressive touchdown technique and ignores a number of factors that may be present causing the airplane to float a little, using a longer runway length to touchdown. Regulator's studies shows that an extra 500ft credit should be given to air distance (from 305m to 457m), and that would be something much more realistic and likely to be performed.

Figure 432 shows that actual landing distance (1,317m) is now virtually the exact length we have available to land (1,323m). The committee understood that there may still be factors other than those mentioned that will impact the actual stopping distance after landing, but they cannot be predicted in calculations, e.g., the pilot's own imprecision, low level turbulence, wind shifts, or any other aspect. All these items increase the landing distance even more. And by a significant amount.

For this reason, TALPA-ARC established that every pilot should calculate their required landing runway length based on actual runway and airplane conditions (slope, wind, temperature, autobrakes, etc.) before starting the approach, and over this value, they should add a safety margin of 15% for unforeseen events. In our example, "factored actual landing distance" would be 1,515m. The committee strongly recommends against any landing attempt when "factored actual landing distance" is greater than LDA (Landing Distance Available), and this is exactly what happened in our example.

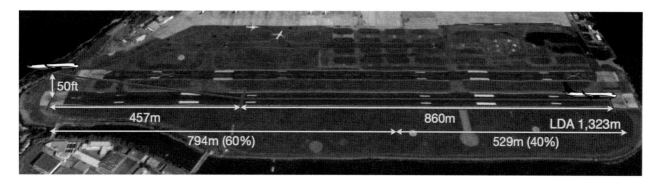

*Figure 432: Actual landing distance with adjusted air distance.*

Please note that the TALPA rule came as a safety recommendation for operators and the published document (SAFO – Safety Alert for Operations number 06012, August 2006) establishes that it is highly recommended that you do not attempt to land on any runway when this runway is not at least 15% longer than necessary to stop the aircraft, considering the actual conditions at time of arrival. This means that, in our example, pilots would be legally right if they decided to land. TALPA is just a warning at this point, as the documents published by the regulatory committee are not legally binding. In addition to SAFO, there are two advisory circulars dealing with the subject. AC number 25-32 and 91-79 A, in case you want to read them.

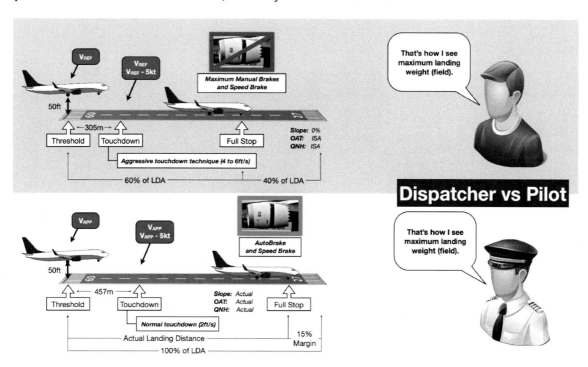

*Figure 433: Different views for establishing maximum landing weight.*

As we have seen, these ACs have also changed the way landing distances are measured. The main difference is in Landing Flare, which is the air distance on landing (between 50ft and touchdown). When calculating the actual stopping distance, old models that decided to adopt TALPA recommendations changed air distance from 305m to 457m. New models have to compute landing flare as a function of time and speed. TALPA recommends air distance of 7 seconds with 4% speed bleed off during flare – a little bit different from the dispatch rule that calculates 4.6 seconds flare with 2% speed bleed off. The additional 15% margin is an item that old and new aircraft must observe. I emphasize that we are talking about the actual stopping distance; therefore, engine reverse thrust can be used in the calculations.

It is obvious, but it is worth mentioning anyway. These margins are recommendations valid for NORMAL OPERATIONS, only. In an emergency situation, the rule described above is no longer valid. In this case, the airport runway is already considered as adequate whenever it is possible to land and stop within its LDA, and there is no need to add any extra margin or to calculate the landing with extended landing flare (7s or 457m).

## 5.5.2 Flat Approach and Steep Approach

Some pilots instinctively fly shallower approach paths when landing on short runways. This flat approach is definitely not a good idea! First because you can undershoot your target and "land" before the runway, and second because, in most cases, it will actually increase landing distance instead of making it shorter. The reason is simple. Regardless of flying a flat, normal, or steep approach path, your approach speed will be the same. As a result, engine thrust setting on approach will be different. Airplane flight characteristics (landing flare included) designed by engineers and tested by pilots are based on certain parameters. The ground effect that is predicted to occur during landing flare assumes a given amount of engine thrust, but this effect can be significantly higher if engine thrust is excessive. Take a look at next couple of figures and see the difference in thrust setting between a normal approach (Figure 434 on the left) and a flat (Figure 434 on the right) or steep approach (Figure 435).

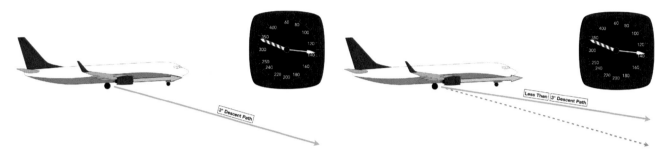

*Figure 434: To perform a flat approach, the pilot will use more engine thrust.*

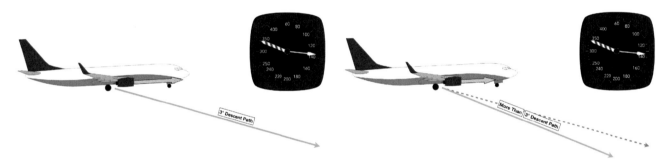

*Figure 435: To perform a steep approach, the pilot will use less engine thrust.*

As you will use more thrust on a flat approach, the most likely result is an unwanted long flare, and of course, a longer total landing distance! But that does not mean that a steep approach is a better solution! It is not! Steeper approaches are responsible for most of the hard landing events unrelated to weather conditions. When performing a steeper approach, pilots use far less thrust than normal. The ground effect is also less intense and flare maneuver will sometimes make things even worse! Let me explain that in more detail.

Control column inputs back and forth change elevator position. Pulling the yoke will deflect the elevator upward and produce a downward force on the tail. This force rotates the aircraft on its lateral axis, projecting the main gear down! It also briefly increases "airplane weight" (not weight itself, but the sum of forces pointing down). When both factors are combined, sometimes (and more often than you think) the airplane hits the ground with stronger intensity than expected! Pilots yelling bad words after touchdown is not uncommon!

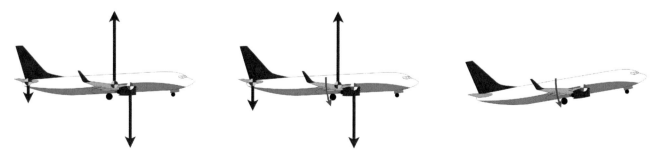

*Figure 436: Making a hard landing even harder.*

### 5.5.3 Autobrake System and Reverse Thrust Effectiveness

As we are addressing the subject of landing, let's talk about the efficiency of thrust reversers in stopping the aircraft. This is an interesting subject and one that often raises a great deal of doubt. To begin the explanation, you need to understand how an aircraft's automatic brake system works. I had already mentioned it, but now we are going discuss it in more detail.

First, a note: the pilot, using maximum manual braking, is always able to brake more effectively than the automatic brake can when the runway is dry. This is because the automatic brake system is not designed to exert any given amount of pressure on the brakes; it works with a deceleration target, that is, it applies the necessary force on the brakes to achieve the desired deceleration. If a parachute were deployed after landing, deceleration would be way above target and brake pressure would drop to zero, as wheel brakes are unnecessary to reach the desired deceleration rate.

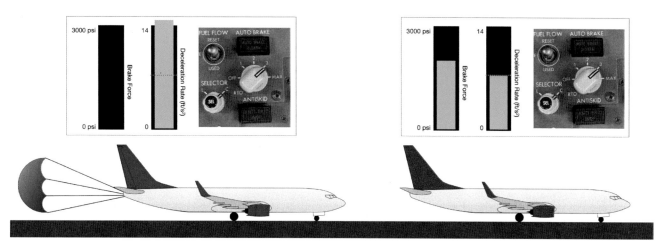

*Figure 437: Wheel brake force with and without a parachute to slow down the airplane.*

On a leveled runway, deceleration will happen because of aerodynamic drag ("DG" in the figure), braking force (red bar for autobrake and green bar for manual braking in the figure) and thrust reverser ("RE" in the figure). The autobrake system of our model aircraft, the Boeing 737NG, has a deceleration target of 8.3kt/s (14ft/s$^2$) on its maximum setting and 4.3kt/s (7.2ft/s$^2$) with level 3 setting. On a dry runway, brakes alone are capable of reaching this parameter, so, when we use engine reverse thrust, brake pressure is reduced in the set of discs and pads to maintain the same deceleration rate. In this case, it is clear that reverse thrust does not change stopping distance at all; it only reduces brake wear. When pilots use manual brakes, however, they are not aiming for a deceleration target; they are simply braking. In this case, wheel braking and thrust reverser are added and stopping distance also changes, as shown below.

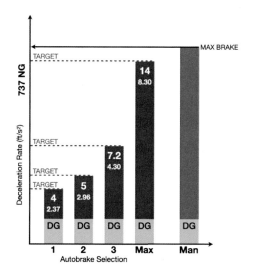 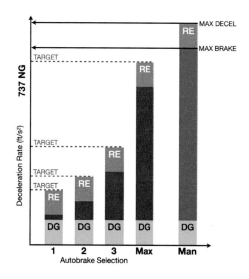

*Figure 438: Dry runway without thrust reverser on the left and with thrust reverser on the right.*

On the other hand, when the runway is wet, friction between the airplane's wheels and the ground surface decreases and a problem begins to occur. As much as I try to brake manually, the airplane's anti-skid system (equivalent to ABS in cars) does not allow the wheels to lock and relieves pressure on the brake automatically. We say that the ability to slow down is limited by the anti-skid system. In some cases, this capacity is below maximum autobrake deceleration target.

When this happens, the thrust reverser changes stopping distance even when automatic brakes are used. But we continue to depend on how much our braking capacity has been affected.

In Figure 439 (right), the reverser increased deceleration and changed the aircraft's stopping distance when the pilot is using maximum manual or maximum automatic brakes. When autobrake was set to 2 or 1, deceleration target was reached even on wet pavement, and the thrust reverser did not change the deceleration rate nor the landing distance; it only reduced brake wear. For autobrake 3, thrust reverser helped to reach the desired deceleration rate, but it was not as effective as for autobrake maximum. Remember that this is just an example. It will all depend on how much friction the runway has when wet.

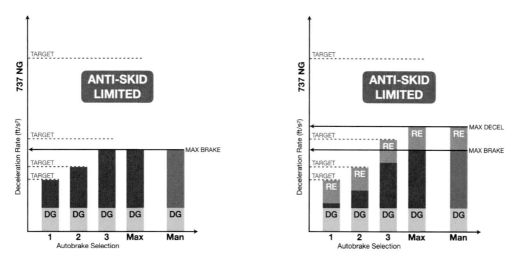

*Figure 439: Thrust reverser effectiveness when the runway is wet.*

## 5.5.4    Carbon Brakes and Low Level Autobrake Settings

As you can see in the illustration that dealt with Autobrake usage (Figures 438 and 439), if we use the thrust reverser with lower autobrake settings, the work done by wheel brakes ends up being very light. So light, in fact, that the sensor that records an aircraft's deceleration sends many signals, both to increase and reduce brake pressure. This instability, which is due to inaccurate measurement, generates many cycles of application on the brakes during deceleration after landing. According to Boeing, carbon brakes have a more pronounced wear depending on the number of times the brakes are applied than by the pressure exerted on them. Therefore, the use of the automatic brake at a low level (example: level 1 or 2 for 737NG) is only recommended if no reversers are used! In this way, pressure applied to the brake is steadier and brake wear is reduced.

## 5.5.5    Braking Action Report and Runway Condition Code (RCC)

The biggest problem with respect to calculating the actual stopping distance is how to determine runway braking action. For a long time, this report was extremely subjective, and relied on pilots' reports, which had no standardization whatsoever. Two pilots landing under the same conditions could make very different braking action reports. However, TALPA-ARC decided to create a table with codes to help make this assessment a little more objective. Now pilots have a guideline to follow before reporting runway braking action. There are 5 braking action levels, in addition to dry runway. The table below (Figure 440) includes a seventh option that was called "nil", which would be equivalent to no braking action at all! Needless to say, it is not a good idea trying to land in these conditions.

The table known as Runway Condition Code (RCC) describes braking action characteristics, which are named as follows: Dry, Good, Good to Medium, Medium, Medium to Poor, Poor, and Nil. Each one presented in the table below has an expected braking coefficient, directional control, and braking characteristics that can be anticipated by the pilots, and there are examples of weather conditions and contaminants that normally represent such braking action conditions.

| Braking Coefficient | Description and Examples | Braking Action | Rwy Cond Code |
|---|---|---|---|
| ... | ...<br>Runway is Dry | DRY | 6 |
| ≥ 0.40 | Braking deceleration is normal for the wheel braking effort applied. Directional control is normal.<br>Damp / Frost / Wet (3mm or less of water) / Slush, Dry Snow and Wet Snow (depth of 3mm or less) | GOOD | 5 |
| 0.36 - 0.39 | Brake deceleration and controllability is between Good and Medium<br>Compacted Snow with OAT colder than -15°C | GOOD TO MEDIUM | 4 |
| 0.30 - 0.35 | Braking deceleration is noticeably reduced for the wheel braking effort applied. Directional control may be reduced.<br>Slippery when Wet / Dry or Wet Snow over Compacted Snow / Dry or Wet Snow more than 3mm / Compacted Snow with OAT warmer than -15°C | MEDIUM | 3 |
| 0.26 - 0.29 | Brake deceleration and controllability is between Medium and Poor. Potential for hydroplaning exists.<br>Slush or Water in greater depth than 3mm | MEDIUM TO POOR | 2 |
| 0.21 - 0.25 | Braking deceleration is significantly reduced for the wheel braking effort applied. Potential for hydroplaning exists. Directional control may be significantly reduced.<br>Ice | POOR | 1 |
| ≤ 0.20 | Braking deceleration minimal to non-existent for the wheel braking effort applied or directional control is uncertain.<br>Wet Ice / Slush over Ice / Water over Compacted Snow / Dry Snow over Ice | NIL | 0 |

*Figure 440: Runway Condition Assessment Matrix - RCAM.*

In United States, FAA informs runway conditions using a standard message known as FICON (Field Condition Reporting). FICON is used to report conditions of tarmac, taxiways, and runways. The coding in Figure 440, however, is intended only for runways, not tarmac or taxiways. Runway condition reports are published by dividing the runway into three equal parts, for example, FICON RWY 09 3/3/5. This means that runway 09 has MEDIUM braking action in the first and second third, and GOOD braking action in the last third. The type of deposit that causes the reported braking action can be informed separately. For example: DRY SN 75PC, which means dry snow in 75% of the section.

Runway Condition Reports (RCR) are becoming more common all around the world as time goes by. Different countries might name their report differently, that is, not necessarily FICON, but they all follow the same report structure (thanks to Global Reporting Format – GRF), splitting the runway into three equal parts and using the same braking action codes. We will see some other details in the last chapter, in a section named Cold Weather Operations.

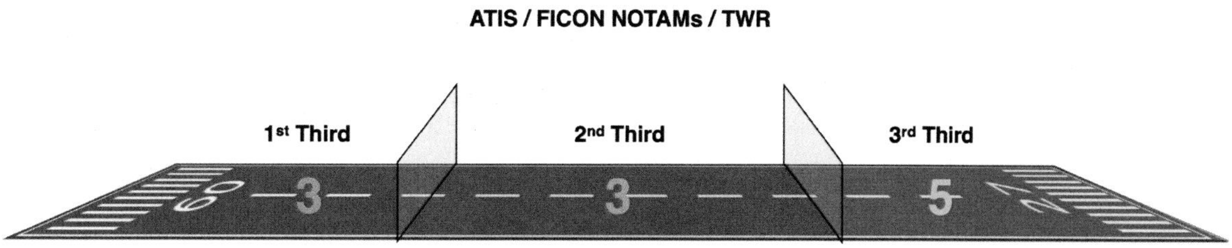

**ATIS / FICON NOTAMs / TWR**

*Figure 441: FICON example.*

As you might remember from the Weight and Balance chapter, every airplane is certified with a maximum takeoff and a maximum landing weight, and they are often different from each other by a large amount! Let's revisit the topic briefly.

The landing gear of the airplane is designed to withstand tremendous loads. At maximum structural takeoff weight the landing gear must be able to resist a landing at 6ft/s at the moment of touchdown. At maximum structural landing weight the landing gear must withstand a landing with vertical speed of 10ft/s on touchdown.

As you can see, maximum structural takeoff weight is set with a landing situation in mind! However, why is maximum takeoff weight greater than maximum landing weight anyway? The answer is quite simple. The airplane will get lighter during the flight as it burns fuel! So it is reasonable to think of a lighter weight to comply with the aggressive 10ft/s descent rate required by the regulations.

Sometimes, when the difference between MOTW and MLW is too big, the manufacturers choose to build a fuel jettison system to that airplane. But mid-size jets such as the Boeing 737 and Airbus A320 has no such device. So, now let's think of a situation where the airplane has just taken off, well above maximum landing weight, and for whatever reason needs to return to the departure airport. What should the pilot do? Burn fuel to get under maximum landing weight? Or land overweighted?

Well, first things first. The airplane is definitely able to land with overweight. As we have seen, it is designed to do so. The A320 overweight landing checklist even reminds the pilots not to exceed 360ft/min (same as 6ft/s) on touch down. However, landing overweight has two issues that we need to talk about. And what I am about to say here is what happens in most of the jet airliners, but not necessarily all of them. So, always use the airplane manual as the authoritative source of information.

When attempting to land at weights close to maximum takeoff weight, it is very likely that you will not be able to land using full flaps. Every flap setting has its own maximum operational speed, and at MTOW the speed required to fly with full flaps is often above (or very close to) the maximum allowable speed for that flap. So, the checklist will instruct the pilots to use a lower flap setting. For example, to use flaps 30 instead of flaps 40 on the Boeing 737, or flaps 3 instead of flaps full on an Airbus A320. The second issue is related to brakes! After landing the brakes can become extremely hot, potentially causing the tire to deflate. That being said, it is basically a normal landing.

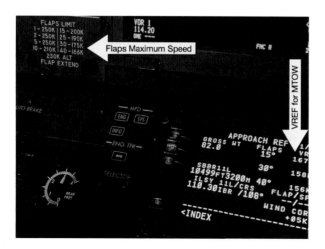

*Figure 442: On the Bc*            *an VREF for the same flap at MTOW.*

After reading all of that, one might think I am saying that it is okay to land overweight in any situation. Definitely not. But, when is it recommended to execute one and when not to land overweighted? Well, I will give you some tips, however I would like to make it clear that what I am about to say is just my personal opinion! Feel free to do anything different and even share your thoughts on this subject with me via e-mail.

I believe that once you are faced with a situation when returning to the departure airport is necessary, that are three possible scenarios. First: after assessing the reason that made you decide to come back you realized that flying is not a threat, but the landing itself is. For example: you have an unsafe landing gear situation, or your flaps are jammed at a very low setting. In those cases, I would recommend any pilot to burn off fuel and land at the lowest possible weight.

Second: keeping the airplane in the air is now a threat, either to the airplane or the people onboard. For example: you have had an engine failure, or a cargo fire indication, or a passenger needs immediate medical assistance. I would recommend any pilot to execute an overweight landing on those cases. Exception made to the situation where the aircraft that had the engine failure has a fuel jettison system.

Finally, if the situation presented is not a threat for landing, nor to keep the airplane flying. For example, the airplane failed to pressurize after takeoff for whatever reason. Well, in that case we have what I believe is a judgement call from the airline manager. Contact flight operations center and see what they have to say. They may find useful to ask you to land overweighted, or they may ask you to burn off the fuel until you are under maximum landing weight. But the important thing is, in this kind of situation I would share the decision making process with people that has more information than I do (such as information about passenger connecting flights, maintenance personnel and tools, among others).

Every time we use aircraft brakes, whether during landing, taxiing, or a rejected takeoff, they accumulate energy in the form of heat. There is a limit to how much energy brakes are able to absorb and how fast they are able to dissipate that energy to the environment. Some airplanes have brake fans systems that help with such energy dissipation; the Airbus A320 family, for example.

The energy absorbed by the braking system is cumulative with each brake application, and the Maximum Brake Energy test shows what happens when we get close to the energy limit that brakes are able to sustain. A specially designed fuse plug is installed on every wheel to protect the tire against an explosion. It melts at a given temperature and allows the nitrogen inside the tire to escape without blowing it.

Quick Turnaround Limit Weight (QTLW) makes the pilot aware of the maximum weight with which he/she can land the airplane (using maximum manual brake, on a dry runway and without using thrust reversers) and perform a new immediate takeoff without having a minimum cooling time of the brakes, assuring that, during this process, the protective fuse will not reach the temperature at which it melts.

Pay close attention to the fact that QTLW does **NOT** guarantee that brakes are capable of withstanding an RTO during a new takeoff. This limit weight only guarantees that, during takeoff, fuse plugs will not melt and leave the airplane with a deflated tire.

There are tables and graphs that show pilots the minimum time to wait for brakes to cool down after using them, either after landing or RTO event. But on Boeing airplanes, even these tables, called Brake Cooling Schedule, do **NOT** guarantee that after the cooling period, brakes are able to absorb the heat generated by a high energy RTO, close to Brake Energy limit weights (typically above 120kt).

Old model aircraft, like McDonnel Douglas MD-11, used to have some complicated, but very useful charts to determine cooling time that would indeed guarantee a new RTO. These charts accepted data inputs of intended takeoff weight and V1 to establish minimum cooling time. I honestly wonder why Boeing does not use this kind of chart (with a software interface) in recent models.

Note 1: Boeing uses the speed of 80kt as a divider of what it considers high and low energy to be. Airbus makes the same division at 100kt, but the plane's brakes rarely fail to stop the aircraft when RTO is commanded below 120kt. In most runway excursion events that occurred after RTO maneuvers, the speed was higher than that.

Note 2: Taxiing adds a lot of heat to brake assembly! **Do not attempt to taxi in order to cool down the brakes**, as it will only make them hotter! On October 1st, 2018, a Boeing 767 tried to do just that after an RTO at JFK airport, and after taxiing for about 10min and almost 6 miles, the brakes caught fire and badly damaged the airplane.

*Figure 443: All fuse plugs were melted after this VMBE test, and all tires were deflated because of that. Very successful test.*

Runway markings (painting or lights) can provide a lot of information to the pilot, especially when landing. It is very important to know how to read this information, and quite nice to know the premises in which it was developed. In this section, we will talk about the paintings and lights that are present on the runway.

Let's begin with Displaced Threshold markings. In Brazil, there are some unusual situations regarding this matter. I will talk about them later.

## 5.8.1   Displaced Threshold

Just as there is an area defining which obstacles may be critical on takeoff, there is also an area that must be observed in relation to an aircraft's approach path. It has a similar shape as the Obstacle Accountability Area, OAA, starting 60m beyond the runway threshold with a half-width of 150m and widening at a 15% ratio to each side for as long as 15km. Once again, I am showing the most comprehensive area of all. Depending on the airport's intended type of operation or runway classification, this cone may be much narrower and less restrictive. Check ICAO Annex 14 for details.

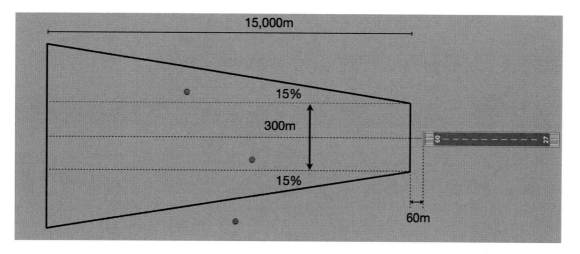

*Figure 444: Approach cone (not to scale).*

All obstacles found within this area must undergo the following assessment: from the top of the obstacle, a 2% gradient path towards the ground must be projected. This gradient is for IFR (Instrument Flight Rules) operations. If the airport intends to operate only VFR (Visual Flight Rules), the gradient changes to 2.5%. The point at which this projection meets the runway level must be 60m before the runway threshold. If this projection touches a point within that 60m limit or even inside the runway, the threshold must be displaced for landing, starting 60m ahead of the place where the obstacle projection met the level of the runway.

During a normal approach, the airplane descends on a 3° slope that is equivalent to 5.2% downward gradient. This trajectory is not aiming exactly at the beginning of the runway, but at an advanced point between 300 and 450m after the start of the Landing Distance Available.

Based on this information, we can measure how high an obstacle that was responsible for threshold displacement will be overflown. For example: consider that the aircraft is projecting its downward path to touchdown the runway 300m beyond the beginning of the LDA. There is a 60m height obstacle that displaced the runway threshold by some amount. On a 5.2% normal slope, how high are we going to fly over this obstacle? The solution to the problem is in the following illustration.

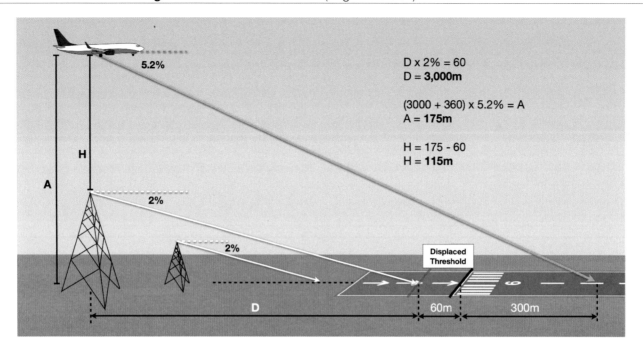

*Figure 445: Flying over obstacles on the approach path.*

The way threshold displacement is informed to pilots sometimes can cause a bit of confusion. Dangerous confusion. Below, I show three markings that can appear at the beginning of the runway and have completely different meanings. All landing distances begin at the same point, in the upper third of the illustration. Takeoff, however, is allowed to start at different points, as indicated.

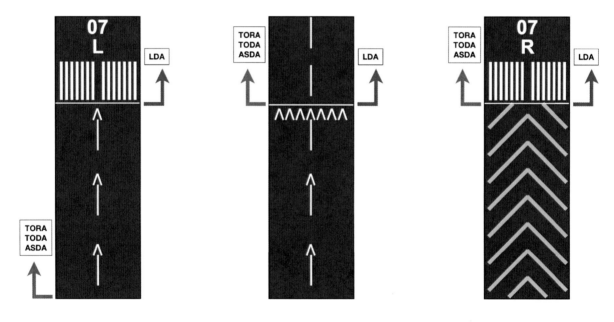

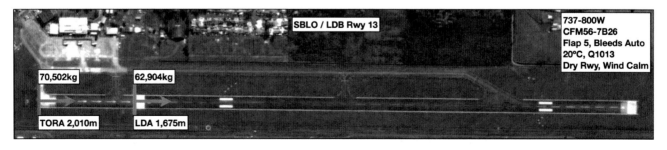

*Figure 446: Where to start takeoff run?*

In the previous figure, the left runway represents a classic displaced threshold, motivated by obstacles on final approach, just as we have studied so far. That mark **ONLY** displaced the beginning of the landing distance available! If a takeoff analysis was made for the full length, the pilot **MUST** initiate takeoff roll from the point indicated in red. To show you how dangerous a misinterpretation is, there is an example from runway 13 in Londrina (SBLO/LDB). In that scenario, described in Figure 446, a Boeing 737-800 is able to takeoff from this runway with a weight of 70,502kg. Now, suppose you are about to takeoff weighing just that and, for some reason, you decide to taxi until the end of that displacement mark before setting takeoff thrust. Taking off from this point, your performance is significantly reduced. You could only takeoff from this point with 62,904kg. There is roughly a 7,600kg penalty, here! You will have a big surprise at the end of the runway. On all engine takeoff, with some luck, you will be airborne. If an engine fails just after V1, you will certainly overrun that runway before liftoff!

The runway in the middle of Figure 446 has a similar marking. The difference is that, in this case, runway displacement possibly happened because works were being executed at an earlier point of the runway. This marking shifts the beginning of the runway for both operations, takeoff and landing, therefore changing TORA, TODA, ASDA, and LDA. This marking is something temporary, not permanent, and it is there to prevent jet blast from endangering workers' safety. Sometimes, pilots are allowed to taxi over this part of the pavement, but they should be aware to only set takeoff thrust at the appropriate point. The rightmost runway of the figure is not a runway threshold displacement, but a stopway (the area is also called "blast pad"). In this part of the runway, any aircraft movement is prohibited, either for taxiing or takeoff. It is there to be used in case of an RTO (Reject Takeoff) for an aircraft taking off in the opposite direction, only.

## 5.8.2   Touchdown Zone
### 5.8.2.1   Touchdown Zone Markings

Except for runway numbers, responsible for identification, all other markings are intended to guide the pilot on landing. There is no mark with a specific purpose during takeoff.

The first thing that is very important to note is that the ICAO (International Civil Aviation Organization) sets a standard that may or may not be followed by signatory countries. All airport recommendations, including runway horizontal painting, are in ICAO's Annex 14. Any country might decide to do something different from what is written there, but they must publish these differences so that a foreign pilot would know what to expect when flying there. I will show you some differences between ICAO standard and FAA standard.

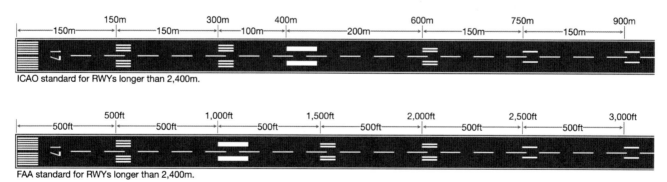

*Figure 447: Touchdown zone marks. Differences between FAA and ICAO standards.*

In Figure 447, what you see are touchdown zone runway markings (TDZ). In this figure it is assumed that the runway landing distance available is 2,400m or longer and in this case, TDZ will be 900m (3,000ft) long, starting at the beginning of the LDA. Among those bands painted on each side of the center line, a mark stands out for being wider and longer than the others. Technically named the "aiming point", it is also known as the "one thousand feet mark", but this name does not reveal its true location. At least, not always. This name is due to the fact that, according to FAA standards, this strip is always located 1,000ft away from the threshold. However, according to ICAO standards, when a runway is 2,400m or longer, the "one thousand feet mark" is, in fact, 400m or 1,312ft away from the threshold.

According to ICAO's recommendation, the aiming point will only be positioned at 1,000ft when the runway landing distance available is longer than 1,200m and up to, but not including, 2,400m. And that is not the only difference when a runway is shorter. In these cases, TDZ also changes, and there is a smaller number of markings identifying this area. Observe some examples in the next figure.

6 markings for RWY longer than 2,400m. Aiming point at 400m.

4 markings for RWY longer than 1,500m up to, but not including 2,400m. Aiming point at 300m.

3 markings for RWY longer than 1,200m up to, but not including 1,500m. Aiming point at 300m.

*Figure 448: Different touchdown zone markings for different runway lengths according to ICAO standards.*

### 5.8.2.2 Touchdown Zone Lights - TDZL

Next, you will see what is known as the touchdown zone lights (TDZL). They are a set of three white lights on each side of the runway centerline (it can be a set of four lights on each side if the runway is 60m wide) that serve to identify touchdown zone on night landings as well as in low visibility. That being said, everything leads us to believe TDZL extend from the runway threshold to the base of the last painted strip that identifies the end of touchdown zone. But that is not exactly what happens.

Annex 14 shows something somewhat surprising regarding TDZL. Touchdown zone lights must be placed from the beginning of the LDA up to 900m away from this point. There is no extra observation dealing with runway length, except for one small detail: on runways less than 1,800m long, lights will be placed only until half this length.

Please note that regardless of the actual size of the touchdown zone, touchdown zone lights will always be installed up to 900m, just as it happens with TDZ when the runway LDA is 2,400m or longer (with the exception I mentioned of runways shorter than 1,800m).

For example, consider a runway whose LDA is equal to 2,100m. TDZ markings on this runway will be 600m long, but at night and specially with low visibility, pilots will easily be cheated to believe the touchdown zone is 300m longer, that is, ending where indicated by the lights (as shown in the next figure).

Should TDZL be installed on a runway with LDA of 1,500m, those lights would extend to 750m down the runway, the exact half of its length.

Example of TDZL on a runway with LDA of 2,400m.

Example of TDZL on a runway with LDA of 2,100m.

Example of TDZL on a runway with LDA of 1,500m.

*Figure 449: Touchdown zone LIGHTS going 300m beyond the actual touchdown zone.*

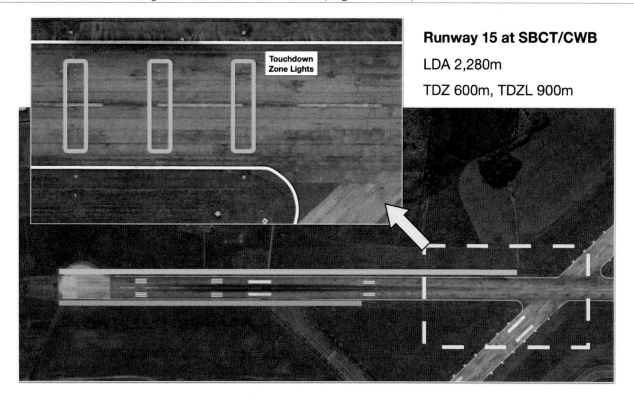

**Runway 15 at SBCT/CWB**

LDA 2,280m

TDZ 600m, TDZL 900m

*Figure 450: Runway touchdown zone lights going 300m beyond the touchdown zone (Google Earth).*

Ignoring the fact that the touchdown zone is painted in a non-existing pattern, at least it has the correct length, which is 600m. And as you can see in the highlighted area, TDZL goes until 900m down the runway.

### 5.8.3   Runway Edge and Center Lights

The last set of lights that needs to be identified in our study is Runway Center Lights (RCL) and Runway Lights (RL), with the latter being located on the edge of the runway. Runway lights are white and can be between 30 and 60 meters apart, and they are a good indicator to estimate visibility when there is fog.

These lights can warn pilots when there is only 600m of runway left ahead of them, turning all amber instead of white. Runway center lights are all white until getting to the last 900m of the runway. At this point, they start alternating red and white lights for the next 600m. With 300m left to the end of the runway, they turn all red. All these settings are show in Figure 451 below.

## ICAO Standard

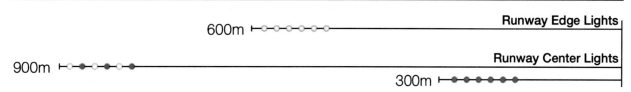

*Figure 451: Runway lights and center lights close to the end of the runway.*

## 5.8.4 Fun Facts regarding Runway Markings

As I had promised, let me tell you some fun facts that happens only in Brazil (as far as I know, at least). I have seen the first one in three different places: Goiânia, Manaus, and Foz do Iguaçu airports (ICAO code SBGO, SBEG and SBFI). For reasons I am not entirely sure, there was a NOTAM (NOtice To Air Men) at those airports stating that takeoff could only be started a few meters beyond the threshold. It is an interesting challenge for an airport authority to make a runway marking that indicates this position, as there is no provision in Annex 14 for a marking displacing the threshold only for takeoff and continuing to allow landing.

The solution found was a simple dashed or continuous white line from side to side indicating the exact point where takeoff could be initiated. In the next figure you can see what I mean. The blue arrow shows where LDA begins, and although very weirdly, the yellow one indicates where TORA, TODA, and ASDA begin. By the way, this condition is no longer present in any of the mentioned airports nowadays.

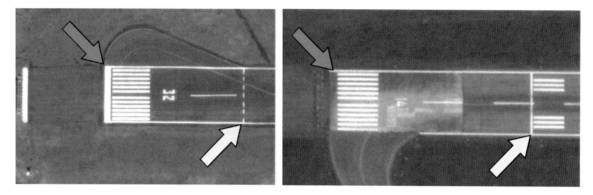

*Figure 452: Google Earth image. Foz do Iguaçu on the left and Goiânia on the right.*

Another Brazilian fun fact (this one still present): airport authorities are often confused about which TDZ standard they should follow: ICAO or FAA. Although there is no published document indicating differences with regard to those markings in Brazil, there is an expressive number of airports around the country painted according to FAA standards. Even some airports which are following ICAO's standard have the aiming point painted in the wrong place. As an example, I can cite two of the major airports in the country: Guarulhos (SBGR/GRU) and Galeão (SBGL/GIG).

Over the past few years, some runways have been repainted to adhere to correct standard, but Confins (SBCF) deserves a picture, because no one would simply believe if I told them and did not show any evidence. At this airport, opposite ends of the same runway (16/34) follow different standards.

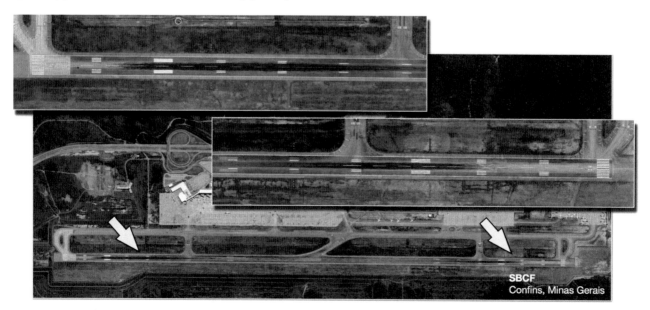

*Figure 453: Google Earth image from Confins airport, runways 16 and 34 with different standards (SBCF/CNF).*

I wish I could tell you that was the only airport you could encounter this kind of situation, but it is not. Another example is the airport of São Luis, state capital of Maranhão, Brazil. Runway 06 and 24 are different from each other just as it happened in Confins. Be aware that I am not saying that different markings on opposite runways cannot exist in a correct way! That may happen if LDA is different owing to some displaced threshold: 2,500m on one side and 2,300m on the other, for example. But that is not the case in these two airports that I mentioned.

## 5.8.5    PAPI, GS, TCH, and MEHT

First of all, let me introduce you to these acronyms, and then I will discuss them.

PAPI: Precision Approach Path Indicator. This is a set of four lights located on the side of the runway. Those lights may be shown as red or white to the pilot. Four red lights mean that you are too low compared to a normal approach path. Three red lights and one white mean you are slightly low. Two and two mean you are just fine. Three white lights together with one red means you are slightly high and finally, four white lights mean you are too high! The approach corridor shown by each of those combinations might be calibrated to 20', 25' or even 30' wide. The example in Figure 454 below shows a 20' corridor.

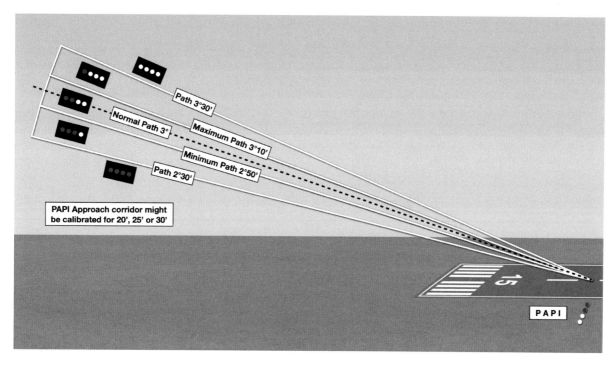

*Figure 454: PAPI calibration.*

GS: Glide Slope. This is an antenna located in a similar point as PAPI and that electronically guides the pilot on an ideal approach path until touchdown.

TCH and MEHT: Threshold Crossing Height and Minimum Eye Height over Threshold. I will explain those terms during our debate over the subject in the next paragraphs.

So, let's begin with PAPI calibration. As mentioned, each corridor (on path, slightly below, and slightly above) can be 20', 25' or 30' wide. The authority will take the lowest angle of the corridor indicating "on path" (known as minimum path) and subtract 2 minutes from this angle (as shown in Figure 455). In our example, 2°50' minus 2' equals 2°48'. This minimum path minus 2' will be the path used to determine what the MEHT (Minimum Eye Height over Threshold) is. That is where the pilot just starts to see three red lights.

Figure 456 shows that every pilot that just started to see the three red lights and the white one, will be seating at the same height, regardless of the size of the airplane, but that does not mean that every airplane will be at the same height from touching the ground.

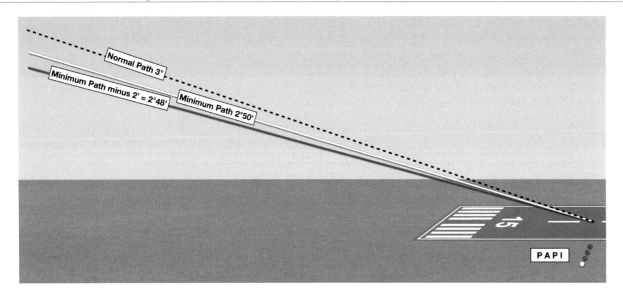

*Figure 455: Minimum path minus 2'.*

The airport authority must always think about another important measure: Minimum Wheel Clearance (MWC)! If you take a Boeing 737-800 and compare it to a Boeing 747-8, you will see that both pilots can see the same, but their airplanes are in a very different situation! So, the main concern of authorities when calibrating PAPI should always be the most limiting aircraft operating on that particular runway.

Keep in mind that considering a normal approach flight path of 3° (at the center of the corridor), the only way of changing MWC is shifting the location of PAPI. Move it further down the runway to increase MWC. As an example, should a 3° angle PAPI be installed at 1,000ft from the threshold, a Boeing 747-8 will have a minimum wheel clearance of only 12ft. If the same PAPI is positioned 1,500ft from the runway threshold, the Jumbo's main landing gear will clear the runway by 36ft when crossing it.

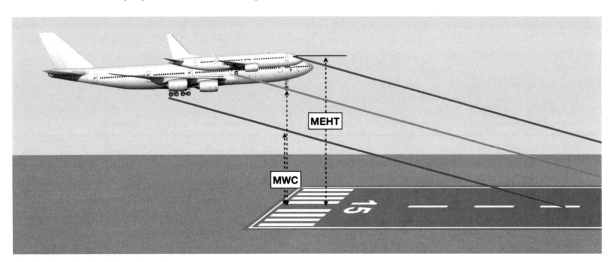

| Height based on 3° Glideslope | Pilot Eye Height (feet) | Main Gear Height (feet) |
|---|---|---|
| B737NG | 49 | 34 |
| B747-400 | 47 | 12 |
| B777 | 48 | 19 |

Visual aid runway intersection distance from the threshold 1,000ft

| Height based on 3° Glideslope | Pilot Eye Height (feet) | Main Gear Height (feet) |
|---|---|---|
| B737NG | 75 | 60 |
| B747-400 | 73 | 36 |
| B777 | 74 | 35 |

Visual aid runway intersection distance from the threshold 1,500ft

*Figure 456: MEHT must guarantee a safe minimum wheel clearance.*

I told you that Glide Slope is an antenna that electronically guides the pilot to touchdown, but now we need to know the location of the receiving antenna on the airplane. And you might wonder why that is important. Well,

Threshold Crossing Height (TCH) published on approach charts is a piece of information based on what height the receiving antenna is crossing the runway threshold when following the GS signal. Smaller aircraft normally have this GS receiving antenna on their nose cone, while bigger airplanes have it just in front of the nose gear, as shown in Figure 457 below. The 747 has actually two GS antennas but the one in front of its nose gear is the one being used on this stage of flight.

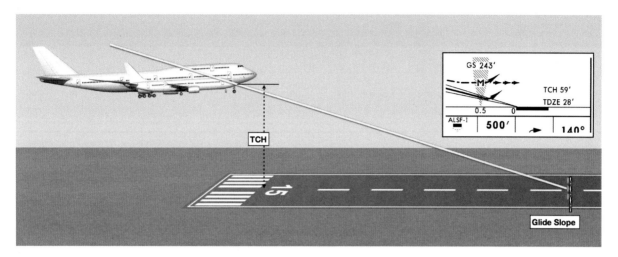

*Figure 457: Glide slope signal and TCH.*

So, let's analyze what we have seen so far. Figure 456 shows both airplanes at the same eye height following the PAPI indication. Figure 457 shows both pilots at different eye heights following the glide slope signal. Which one is correct?

Both of them! Pilots must understand that all this information, visual and electronic, is coincident when they are far from the runway, but as they get closer, especially when crossing the runway threshold, it is perfectly normal that they start mismatching each other. So, do not worry about that. If you are flying manually, when about to fly over the threshold, sight the aiming point and follow flight crew training manual techniques on flare, regardless of glide slope or PAPI indications from this moment on.

Intentionally left blank.

# Miscellaneous

06

ACR / PCR
Reclearance In Flight
ETOPS
Minimum Equipment List
Cold Weather Operations
Narrow Runway Operations
High-Altitude Airports

## 6.1.1   PCR – Pavement Classification Rating

Time to move on! As of November 2024, the old PCN (Pavement Classification Number) will give way to the new Pavement Classification Rating (PCR). PCR is a number that expresses the load-carrying capacity of a pavement for unrestricted operations, and as it was for PCN, this classification method only applies to aircraft with maximum gross weight greater than 5,700kg. If you would like to go deeper into this subject, I suggest you read the following document: AC 150/5335-5D.

Important notice: there is no mathematical correlation between the previous ICAO pavement strength reporting ACN-PCN and the new ICAO ACR-PCR system. PCR and ACR are now larger numbers (often three digits compared to the two-digit PCN and ACN), but it is not a simple factor of 10 as a few articles about the topic have suggested (yes, some ACR will be 10 times ACN, but that is no rule). Look at the following example comparing old PC

Florianópolis, Brazil (SBFL / FLN)

Former PCN Rwy 14/32: 78 F / A / X T

Current PCR Rwy 14/32: 550 F / A / X T

*Figure 458: No mathematical correlation between PCN and PCR.*

The strength of a pavement is reported in terms of the load rating of the aircraft which the pavement can accept on an unrestricted basis. The term unrestricted operations in the definition of PCR does not mean unlimited operations. Unrestricted refers to the relationship of PCR to the aircraft's ACR (Aircraft Classification Rating, which we will discuss in a moment), and that it is permissible for an aircraft to operate without weight restriction when the PCR is greater than or equal to the ACR.

Just as it happened to PCN, PCR is not only a number, but a number followed by 4 letters. Before going into details about the number, let's check out the meaning for those four letters using an example: **PCR 440/F/B/X/T**.

Determination of the numerical PCR value for a particular pavement can be based upon one of two procedures: the "Using aircraft method" or the "Technical evaluation method". Whichever methodology was used must be reported as part of the posted rating. The information will be shown on the last of the four letters, using "T" or "U" (Technical evaluation method or Using aircraft method).

Honestly, that is just saying how the airport authority came up with the final result, but that information is completely useless for operations. Nobody on the airplane cares how or who came up with the PCR.

The second to last letter refers to maximum tire pressure. The option is any of the last four letters of the alphabet: "W", "X", "Y" or "Z". Each letter represents a maximum tire pressure allowed on the main gear of the airplane to operate over that pavement. Check the numbers in Figure 459.

I normally say that this tire pressure letter is a GO, NO GO piece of information. That is because the information will basically tell us whether we can or cannot operate over that pavement, but without telling us with how much weight. Should the airplane's tire pressure be over the limit, it will not be allowed to go over that pavement, regardless of the airplanes weight. On the other hand, if tire pressure is under the limit, you can go over there, but we need more information to determine the maximum weight.

The first letter could be either "F" or "R", and it indicates the kind of top layer of that pavement: flexible or rigid. Let's talk straight here: it actually means asphalt (flexible) or concrete (rigid).

The letter that follows can be any of the first four letters of the alphabet: "A", "B", "C", or "D". Each letter represents the strength of the subgrade, which is basically what is beneath the asphalt or concrete. I mean, it will state the density of the raw ground under the layers that were actually built. Typically, engineers will construct runways with the following layers from top to bottom: surface course, binder course, base, subbase and then the subgrade (there might be additional layers in the mix, but this is the general idea).

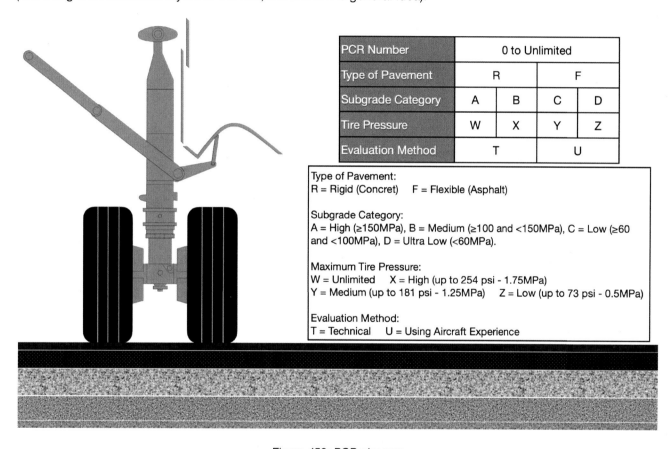

| PCR Number | 0 to Unlimited | | | |
|---|---|---|---|---|
| Type of Pavement | R | | F | |
| Subgrade Category | A | B | C | D |
| Tire Pressure | W | X | Y | Z |
| Evaluation Method | T | | U | |

Type of Pavement:
R = Rigid (Concret)    F = Flexible (Asphalt)

Subgrade Category:
A = High (≥150MPa), B = Medium (≥100 and <150MPa), C = Low (≥60 and <100MPa), D = Ultra Low (<60MPa).

Maximum Tire Pressure:
W = Unlimited    X = High (up to 254 psi - 1.75MPa)
Y = Medium (up to 181 psi - 1.25MPa)    Z = Low (up to 73 psi - 0.5MPa)

Evaluation Method:
T = Technical    U = Using Aircraft Experience

*Figure 459: PCR glossary.*

Finally, the number itself! It will be determined based on the most limiting aircraft which operates over that pavement. It will take into account the cumulative damage factor (CDF) which intends to maximize opportunities while actually predicting the traffic that will operate over that particular pavement along a specific amount of time. Interesting note: as the PCR analysis is tailor made to every airport condition, two runways that had equal PCNs may now have different PCRs.

Heads up for the fact that I never said PCR is a number that guarantees unlimited operations. I only said unrestricted. The term 'unlimited operations' does not take into account pavement life. The PCR to be reported is such that the pavement strength is sufficient for the current and future traffic being analyzed, and it should be re-evaluated if traffic changes significantly. A significant change in traffic would be indicated by the introduction of a new aircraft type or an increase in current aircraft traffic levels not accounted for in the original PCR analysis.

## 6.1.2   ACR – Aircraft Classification Rating

ACR is the aircraft's classification rating, which must be compared to PCR to determine whether or not the aircraft can be operated with a specific weight, on that runway, taxiway, or tarmac. There is an equation for establishing an aircraft's current ACR, based on maximum gross weight and basic empty weight ACR as provided by the manufacturer.

Well, now I ask you: where does ACR comes from?

ACR is defined by using a method called Derived Single Wheel Load (DSWL). Approximately 95% of the aircraft's total weight, when CG is as far back as possible, ends up being supported by the main landing gear while the remaining 5%, by the nose landing gear. Assuming that this is true for our model aircraft, 95% of its maximum takeoff weight (79,000kg), is equal to 75,050kg, and this weight is over its 4 wheels on the two legs of the main landing gear. This means that the load on each wheel is about 18,800kg.

ACR of a given weight will be equivalent to two times the DWSL, establishing the landing gear and pavement interaction, using a standard tire pressure of 1.50MPa (218psi), computed for 36,500 passes over that pavement.

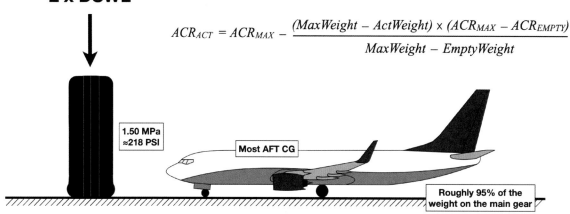

$$ACR_{ACT} = ACR_{MAX} - \frac{(MaxWeight - ActWeight) \times (ACR_{MAX} - ACR_{EMPTY})}{MaxWeight - EmptyWeight}$$

*Equation 16: Actual ACR.*

Once again, taking our model airplane as an example and using the ACR reference table in Figure 460 (provided by the manufacturer), we will use the equation above to find what the current ACR is so that we can figure out whether or not we can operate on a runway with PCR 440/F/B/X/T and actual gross weight of 62,000kg. In the ACR table, the first row represents maximum weight and ACR MAX values, while the second row has the empty weight and ACR EMPTY values. For an ACR/ACN comparison, the former ACN table is also shown.

$$ACR_{ACT} = 410 - \frac{(79,242 - 62,000) \times (410 - 198)}{79,242 - 41,413}$$

$$ACR_{ACT} = 313$$

$$ACR_{ACT} = ACR_{MAX} - \frac{(MaxWeight - ActWeight) \times (ACR_{MAX} - ACR_{EMPTY})}{MaxWeight - EmptyWeight}$$

### 440 F / B / X / T

| Boeing 737-800 current ACR table | | | | | | | | |
|---|---|---|---|---|---|---|---|---|
| Weight | Flexible | | | | Rigid | | | |
| | A | B | C | D | A | B | C | D |
| 79242 | 377 | 410 | 448 | 507 | 502 | 524 | 539 | 556 |
| 41413 | 191 | 198 | 206 | 224 | 231 | 243 | 252 | 262 |

| Boeing 737-800 former ACN table | | | | | | | | |
|---|---|---|---|---|---|---|---|---|
| Weight | Flexible | | | | Rigid | | | |
| | A | B | C | D | A | B | C | D |
| 79242 | 43 | 45 | 50 | 55 | 49 | 52 | 54 | 56 |
| 41413 | 20 | 21 | 22 | 26 | 23 | 24 | 25 | 27 |

*Figure 460: Current ACR based on PCR and actual gross weight.*

ACR (313) was lower than PCR (440), and this tells us that our operation is allowed in this location, as long as tire pressure is less than 254psi (category X). Another way to face the problem is to look for the maximum gross weight to enable operation with that PCR and compare the result to our current gross weight. So, we have two possible approaches:

1. Determine ACR based on current gross weight and check if we are allowed to operate at that pavement by comparing it with the published PCR (as we just did), or
2. Using the runway's PCR, find the maximum gross weight for operation.

When we isolate the Actual Weight variable in the equation and match $ACR_{ACT}$ to the published PCR, when we find the Actual Weight value, the result will actually be the aircraft's maximum operating weight on that pavement (Limit Weight variable on the equation below). Check the example for PCR 490 R/C/X/T.

$$LimitWeight = MaxWeight - \frac{(ACR_{MAX} - PCR) \times (MaxWeight - EmptyWeight)}{ACR_{MAX} - ACR_{EMPTY}}$$

$$LimitWeight = 79,242 - \frac{(539 - 490) \times (79,242 - 41,413)}{539 - 252}$$

$$LimitWeight = 72,783kg$$

## 490 R / C / X / T

| Weight | Flexible | | | | Rigid | | | |
|---|---|---|---|---|---|---|---|---|
| | A | B | C | D | A | B | C | D |
| 79242 | 377 | 410 | 448 | 507 | 502 | 524 | 539 | 556 |
| 41413 | 191 | 198 | 206 | 224 | 231 | 243 | 252 | 262 |

Boeing 737-800 current ACR table

*Equation 17: Finding maximum weight to operate on a given PCR.*

In many countries, operations are occasionally allowed when ACR is greater than PCR, as long as ACR stays within 105% of PCR on rigid pavements and within 110% on flexible ones. This overload is limited to 5% of the airport's annual operations (last 12 months) and overweight operations must be scattered along that period. Check another example in Figure 461 below.

| Flexible Pavement | Rigid Pavement |
|---|---|
| ACR 10% greater than PCR is allowed | ACR 5% greater than PCR is allowed |

Example: **350/F/B/X/U**

350 + 10% = **385**

Maximum Weight for PCR 350: **68,536kg**

Maximum Weight for PCR 385: **74,781kg**

*Figure 461: When ACR is higher than PCR.*

There are two interesting facts regarding this subject now. First: can the wheel load be higher on smaller airplanes? Well, yes it can! And I will give you an example. Let's compare the ACN of two different aircraft models: Boeing 787-9 and Airbus A380. Keep in mind that those airplanes have very different landing gear structures. The Boeing model has a set of two legs on the main gear, each with four wheels, that is, eight wheels overall (disregarding the nose gear). A380, however, has four legs on its main gear. Outboard legs are fitted with four wheels each and inboard legs have six wheels each, in a total of 20 wheels on the main gear!

Now, when you get 95% of the maximum takeoff weights of both aircraft and divide it by the number of wheels on the main gear, you will see that the load in each of B787-9's wheels is about 30,110kg, while on A380, each wheel has to withstand about 26,695kg.

That being said, the load distribution will generate bigger ACR for the 787 than for the A380 on almost every pavement, except for R/C and R/D, as shown in Figure 462. I am not sure of the reason, but that is interesting.

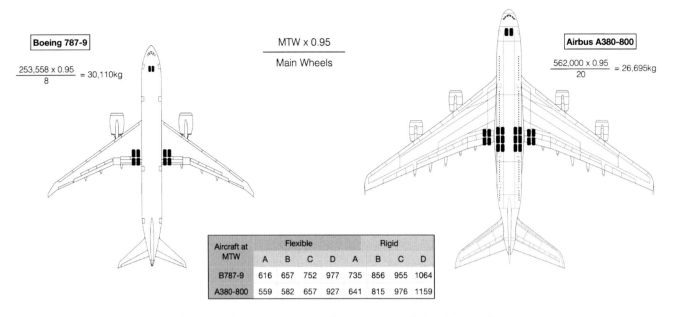

*Figure 462: ACR comparison between a B787-9 and an A380.*

The second interesting thing: in what moment does the greatest pressure on pavement occur? Unlike what many people may think, the greatest pressure exerted on pavement happens during taxi to the runway and initial takeoff roll, when the airplane is heavier. Upon landing (on touchdown), this pressure is about 38% of the maximum pressure exerted on takeoff and gradually increases during deceleration up to a maximum pressure of around 83% of the highest pressure on takeoff.

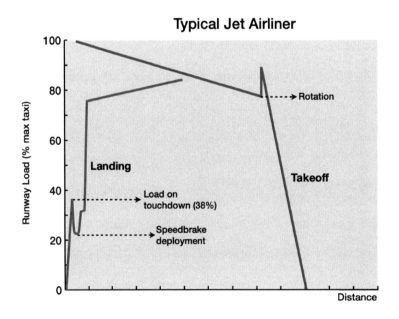

*Figure 463: Typical jet airliner pressure over pavement during takeoff and landing.*

If you are interested in learning more about the ACR of several airplane models, you can access FAA's website and download the FAARFIELD 2.1.1 (current version as I am writing this book).

## 6.2.1   Reducing Fuel Quantity on Board

The first step before talking about Reclearance In Flight (RIF) is to review what regulations say about minimum fuel requirements. I decided to use the basic FAA rule for international flights in our example (reserve fuel equal to 10% of the flight time). However, the premise I will present to you applies to all other regulations. Look at the diagram below.

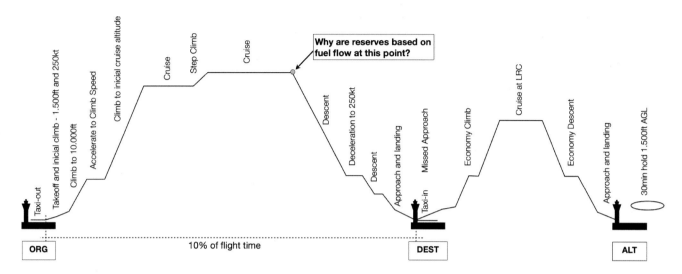

Figure 464: Minimum fuel required on takeoff.

First, can you think of any particular reason for computing reserve fuel (10% of the flight time between A and B) using fuel flow calculated just before top of descent? Well, as we saw before, the airplane's thrust is directly proportional to its weight, that is, a heavier plane needs to produce more thrust to keep a particular flight level at a given speed. At this point of flight, the airplane's weight is considerably lighter than at takeoff, and this makes a huge difference in engine fuel flow. Here is an example of a Boeing 777 flying LRC regime:

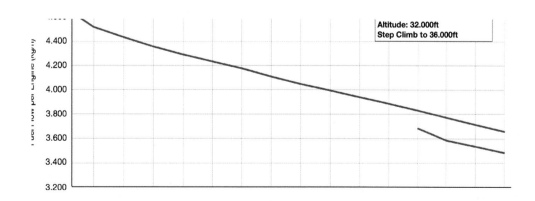

Figure 465: Fuel flow variation along the route.

In this graph, at about 500nm travelled, the airplane had a fuel flow per engine of just over 4,500kg/h. Six thousand miles later (6,500nm from the origin) and after a Step Climb to 36,000ft, fuel flow plummeted to less than 3,600kg/h/eng – a difference of 1,800kg/h in total fuel flow. Calculating reserves with this lower fuel flow is very important to the financial health of any airline, as it reflects the need to put a much smaller amount of fuel inside an aircraft's tanks.

Even though this is an "advantage" allowed by regulations (reserve fuel based on the last cruise fuel flow), a good opportunity was found for greater fuel savings. When flying long-haul flights, compliance with regulatory fuel requirement often results in a large amount of fuel reserves, after all, 10% of a large number is also a large number. That extra fuel sometimes limits the total payload that the flight could carry. So, what we know as Reclearance In Flight, or RIF, was implemented.

Understanding RIF requires a bit of imagination, and sometimes that can be a difficult thing to do, but I will do my best to shed some light over this topic using an example of a fictitious flight between Los Angeles Intl. (LAX) and Guarulhos Intl. (GRU). That flight will have Galeão Intl. (GIG) as its alternate airport. The flight will be performed by a Boeing 777 departing from LAX weighing 291,600kg (payload of 38,551kg – 215 passengers and cargo).

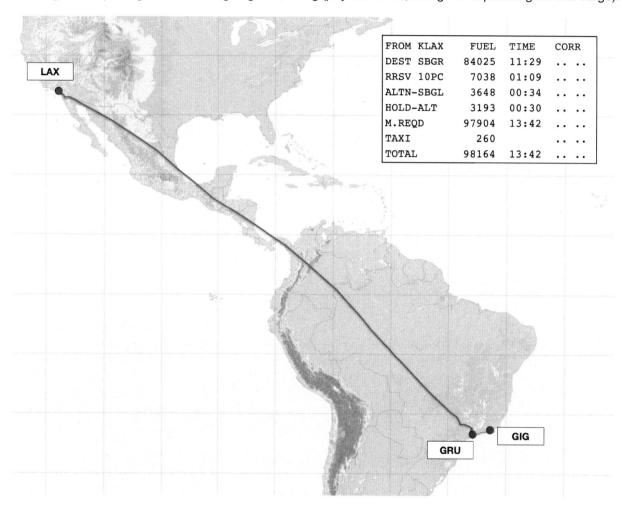

| FROM KLAX | FUEL | TIME | CORR | |
|-----------|------|------|------|------|
| DEST SBGR | 84025 | 11:29 | .. | .. |
| RRSV 10PC | 7038 | 01:09 | .. | .. |
| ALTN-SBGL | 3648 | 00:34 | .. | .. |
| HOLD-ALT | 3193 | 00:30 | .. | .. |
| M.REQD | 97904 | 13:42 | .. | .. |
| TAXI | 260 | | .. | .. |
| TOTAL | 98164 | 13:42 | .. | .. |

*Figure 466: Flight release without RIF from LAX to GRU.*

As you can see on the flight release shown above, the flight will require a trip fuel of 84,025kg. And here is a clear example of the difference between 10% of the fuel amount (Brazilian rule) and 10% of the flight time between origin and destination (FAA). Contingency fuel is set to be 7,038kg, way less than 10% of 84,025. However, that is equivalent to an endurance of 1 hour and 9 minutes, exactly 10% of the trip time of 11 hours and 29 minutes. Takeoff fuel was stablished at 97,904kg, which represents an endurance of 13:42.

Now let's use the same route we used to fly from LAX to GRU, but we will land at an intermediate airport, Manaus (MAO). Note in the following figure that we just deviated to land in MAO when passing abeam this airport, at a fix that for now we will just call RF. On that flight, our alternate airport is Boa Vista (BVB).

Here, things start to get weird. After creating that route from LAX to MAO, we now have to create another flight that departs from cruise flight already! It is like the departure airport is at flight level 370, and this departure point is not an airport but a fix, it is the RF we have mentioned before. From RF we will fly to GRU and the alternate airport is, once again, Galeão Intl. (GIG).

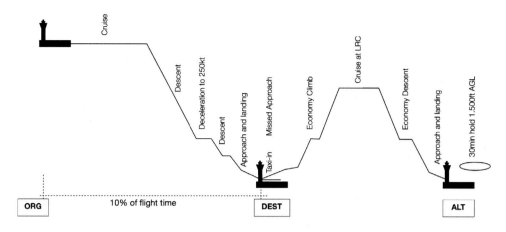

*Figure 467: Use your imagination to create a flight that has departed already from cruise flight.*

In the next figure, those two routes were drawn and calculated. For the first one between LAX and MAO, minimum fuel required was 81,208kg. For the second one between RF and GRU, minimum fuel required was 28,183kg. Both calculations are following the fueling rule exactly is we know so far: enough fuel to go from A to B, plus 10% of the time used from A to B based on the last cruise fuel flow, plus fuel to go around at B and divert to C, plus 30min of fuel endurance based on holding fuel flow 1,500ft over C.

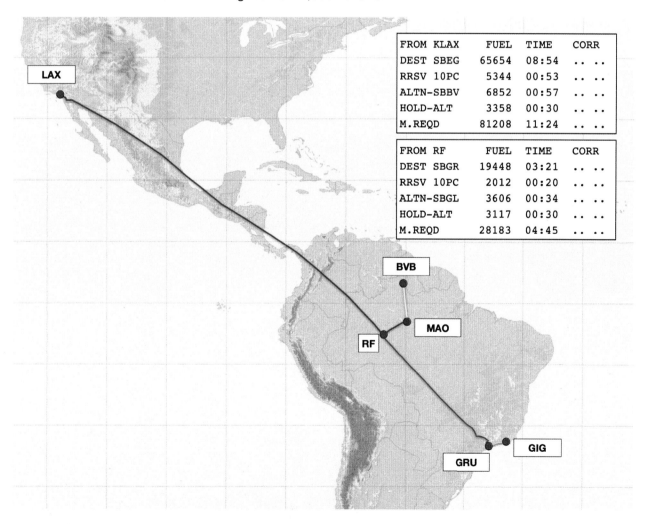

| FROM KLAX | FUEL | TIME | CORR |
|---|---|---|---|
| DEST SBEG | 65654 | 08:54 | .. .. |
| RRSV 10PC | 5344 | 00:53 | .. .. |
| ALTN-SBBV | 6852 | 00:57 | .. .. |
| HOLD-ALT | 3358 | 00:30 | .. .. |
| M.REQD | 81208 | 11:24 | .. .. |

| FROM RF | FUEL | TIME | CORR |
|---|---|---|---|
| DEST SBGR | 19448 | 03:21 | .. .. |
| RRSV 10PC | 2012 | 00:20 | .. .. |
| ALTN-SBGL | 3606 | 00:34 | .. .. |
| HOLD-ALT | 3117 | 00:30 | .. .. |
| M.REQD | 28183 | 04:45 | .. .. |

*Figure 468: Splitting previous route into two parts.*

In the following figure, I have summarized all three scenarios, and from there I will pick up the highlighted values to create a new total amount. I will ignore the 10% of the sector between LAX and GRU and substitute that amount per the 10% calculated on the sector between RF and GRU.

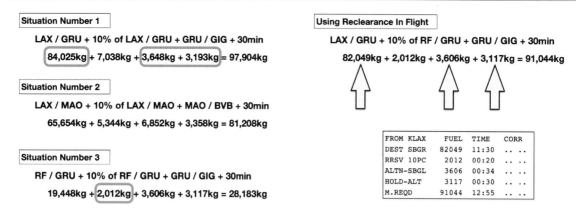

| Situation Number 1 |
| --- |

LAX / GRU + 10% of LAX / GRU + GRU / GIG + 30min

84,025kg + 7,038kg + 3,648kg + 3,193kg = 97,904kg

| Situation Number 2 |
| --- |

LAX / MAO + 10% of LAX / MAO + MAO / BVB + 30min

65,654kg + 5,344kg + 6,852kg + 3,358kg = 81,208kg

| Situation Number 3 |
| --- |

RF / GRU + 10% of RF / GRU + GRU / GIG + 30min

19,448kg + 2,012kg + 3,606kg + 3,117kg = 28,183kg

| Using Reclearance In Flight |
| --- |

LAX / GRU + 10% of RF / GRU + GRU / GIG + 30min

82,049kg + 2,012kg + 3,606kg + 3,117kg = 91,044kg

| FROM KLAX | FUEL | TIME | CORR |
| --- | --- | --- | --- |
| DEST SBGR | 82049 | 11:30 | .. .. |
| RRSV 10PC | 2012 | 00:20 | .. .. |
| ALTN-SBGL | 3606 | 00:34 | .. .. |
| HOLD-ALT | 3117 | 00:30 | .. .. |
| M.REQD | 91044 | 12:55 | .. .. |

*Figure 469: The recipe for fueling the airplane using RIF.*

Check the values pointed by the yellow arrows above. I just said that all I would do is substitute the 10% of situation 1 (7,038kg) for the 10% in situation 3 (2,012kg), so, why did the other values also change? Again, the answer lies in weight and fuel flow. As we are now five thousand kilograms lighter, the airplane will burn less fuel during the flight, and that is a kind of good vicious circle because trip fuel will be smaller, as well as alternate fuel and final reserve fuel.

Anyway, we put 91,044kg of fuel into the airplane's tanks. I believe you understood that, but you are probably thinking: how is that legal?

When you request our ATC clearance in LAX, the controller will grant you clearance to fly to GRU as filed on your flight plan. However, pilots must understand that they are committed to a different destination upon airborne, and that is Manaus (MAO).

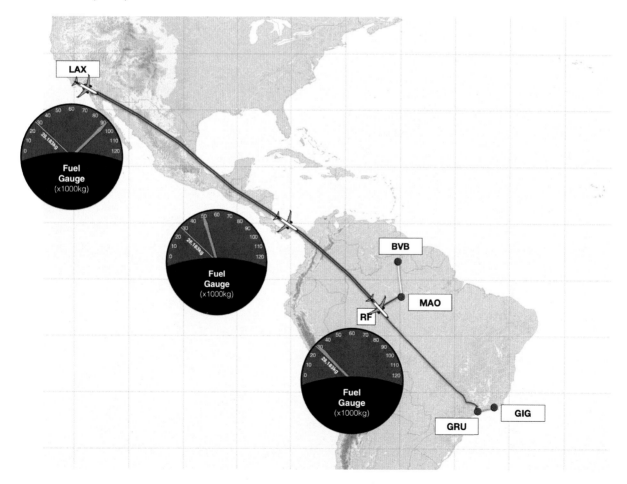

*Figure 470: Biting your nails until crossing the line!*

When we took off from LAX our fuel onboard was 91,044kg, and to go to MAO, the minimum fuel required, including contingency fuel, alternate fuel, and final reserve fuel, was 81,208kg. You see, we actually departed with 9,836kg of extra fuel to make this flight! But why are we committed to MAO instead of GRU? Our ATC clearance was for GRU and all passengers purchased their tickets to fly to GRU.

As it happens, ATC clearance is one thing, and being dispatched by the flight dispatcher is another. Despite the ATC, the airline flight dispatcher has dispatched you to fly to MAO, but that guy is a nice guy. And he/she gave you another dispatch clearance together with the one to MAO. They said that, if you have 28,183kg or more of fuel onboard the moment you cross RF you will be <u>redispatched</u> to fly "a new sector" from RF to GRU. After all, if you look at situation 3 in Figure 469, that is the minimum fuel required to fly from RF to GRU, including contingency fuel, alternate fuel, and final reserve fuel.

And I always get the following question from my students: what if we cross RF with less than 28,183kg? Say 27,500kg. What should be done?

I am sorry to tell you that, but you will have to continue to MAO, the airport you were committed to go since the beginning. GRU was always an IF! You would only go to GRU if you managed to cross RF with 29,183kg of fuel or more. There is an option of trying to contact your company dispatch center and ask for an update on those numbers, and maybe, just maybe, rerunning the operational flight plan on the computer the flight dispatcher will have a new minimum fuel for you that is smaller than the previous one. That can happen if actual winds are more favorable than predicted hours ago, or if you chose a closer alternate, but if the dispatcher is unable to change the minimum fuel to a smaller value than the amount you have in fuel tanks, you must land on the intermediate airport.

So, great deal to use redispatch! Without that your minimum fuel required was 98,164kg (Figure 466). By using redispatch, we were able to reduce the minimum fuel required to 91,044kg, a difference of 7,120kg of fuel!

There is more thing to mention. The pilot will always receive the flight plan with three different pieces of flight release information. The first is the flight from origin (LAX) to intended destination (GRU), but using that small amount of contingency fuel. The second is from origin (LAX) to intermediate airport (MAO), and the third is from RF to intended destination (GRU). The first and second flight releases must result in the same amount of fuel. And of course that is very unlikely! So, after both calculations are complete, we just add to the smallest value a given amount to make that total equal to the highest value. This additional fuel on your flight release is called "reclearance fuel". Heads up to the fact that the highest value may be any of the first two. In my example it was the first, but it can just as easy be the second. Anyway, they must be equalized by adding this extra line: RCR FUEL.

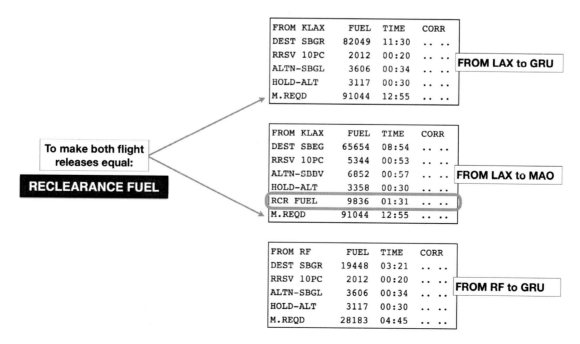

*Figure 471: Making flight release 1 equal to flight release 2 with reclearance fuel (RCR FUEL).*

## 6.2.2 Optimum Redispatch Point

Next, I will explain what an Optimum Redispatch Point means. The first thing you can see in Figure 472 is that RF can be anywhere between the origin and the intended final destination. The flight dispatcher's objective, however, is to establish an RF such that, when crossing over this point, the amount of fuel necessary to proceed to the intermediate airport and to destination is the same. When this happens, another interesting thing happens as well: the minimum fuel required in situation 2 is equal to the minimum fuel required for the mission itself. As a result, there will be no Reclearance Fuel added to this flight plan.

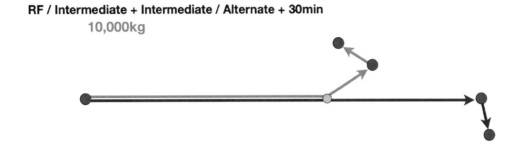

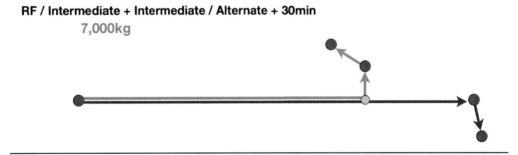

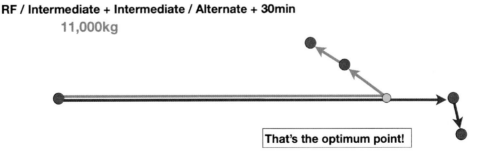

*Figure 472: Finding Optimum Redispatch Point.*

## 6.2.3 Improving Payload Capacity

I said that by using redispatch, we could reduce fuel on board or increase the aircraft's payload capacity. Now, we will use another example to show how payload can be increased; this time, on a Boeing 737-800 flying from PUJ (Punta Cana, Dominican Republic), to GRU (São Paulo, Brazil).

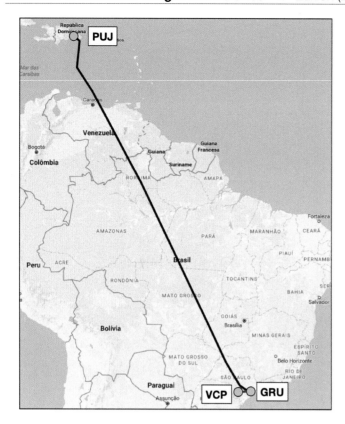

**WITHOUT RIF**

```
FLT NUMBER  GLO 1111 MDPC/PUJ TO SBGR/GRU     VM   CRZ
                  ELEV 47   FT       2461 FT      AVG W/C H3   ISA DEV P05

COMP2057Z FOR ETD0040Z/07JUN17  REGN PR-GTA    B737-800SF ECO/C.I. 012
                                DEG  6.0 PC    CFM56-7B27B1            KGS

             FUEL TIME  CORR      BRWT    LDGWT     ZFWT     BOW     PLD
DEST SBGR   16950 0647  .. ..     73300   56350    52850    41720   11130
RRSV 10PC    1440 0041  .. ..             LDGWT INCLUDES RESERVE FUEL
DEST-MNVR       0 0000  .. ..
ALTN-SBKP     990 0022  .. ..
HOLD-ALT     1070 0030  .. ..
M.REQD      20450 0820  .. ..
TAXI          150       .. ..     FLIGHT TIMES ETD 0040 ATD ....
TOTAL       20600 0820            ETA 0727 ATA ....

ALT-1 SBKP FL 160 DIST  89NM TIME 00.22  WC H14  FUEL  990 MFOD 2060
SBGR CG01A SCB DCT CPN DCT SBKP
```

Minimum Fuel Required: **20,450kg (8:20)**
Brake Release Weight: **73,300kg**
Payload: **11,130kg**
Reserve: **1,440kg (0:41)**

*Figure 473: Flight plan without RIF.*

Above, there is a flight release, with fueling details of our proposed flight. In this document, we can see two interesting pieces of information that are highlighted: Minimum fuel required for takeoff is 20,450kg (which represents 8 hours and 20 minutes of endurance) and available payload is 11,130kg.

Note: the maximum fuel capacity of this aircraft's tanks is exactly 20,600kg and includes taxi fuel.

If there is a need to take more cargo or passengers, that means a heavier takeoff. Taking off at higher weights means burning more fuel, as well. The problem is, there is no room for extra fuel; after all, we have already topped the tank. Question: how can I carry more payload?

In a second Flight Release, shown in Figure 474, total fuel onboard for takeoff is also 20,450kg, but there is something strange going on. Maximum payload now is 14,780kg. As predicted, fuel endurance has been reduced to 7 hours and 55 minutes. But how is that still legal?

The answer lies in redispatching, again! Reclearance in flight made it possible to reduce the amount of reserve fuel from 41 minutes (1,440kg) to just 15 minutes (550kg). As minimum fuel endurance is lower, we are able to increase payload despite the increase in fuel flow generated by the extra weight. Note that, in the first part of the assessment, trip fuel between Punta Cana and Guarulhos was 16,950kg and it has now increased to 17,720kg, but flight time is still the same.

The final result is that we have a flight that needs less endurance, but requires the same amount of fuel as it took a larger payload. Figure 474 shows the route and all three flight plans.

In this example, the reclearance fix, RF, is a waypoint along the airway called TAROP. Minimum fuel required over TAROP to proceed to Guarulhos is 7,850kg. This RF is not the Optimum Redispatch Point and we can see that we have 1,600kg of Reclearance Fuel (RCR FUEL) onboard.

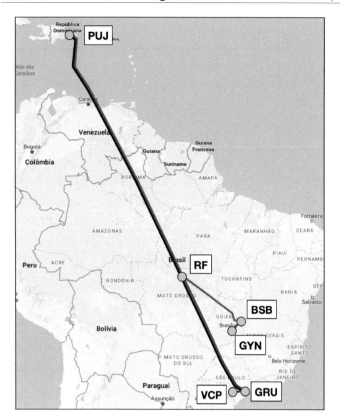

**WITH RIF**

```
FLT NUMBER  GLO 1111 MDPC/PUJ TO SBGR/GRU    VM  CRZ
                     ELEV 47   FT      2461 FT      AVG W/C H4    ISA DEV P07

COMP2047Z FOR ETD0040Z/07JUN17   REGN PR-GTA    B737-800SF ECO/C.I. 012
                                 DEG  6.0 PC   CFM56-7B27B1           KGS

MDPC/SBGR      FUEL TIME  CORR      BRWT     LDGWT      ZFWT    BOW    PLD
DEST SBGR     17720 0647  .. ..    76950     59230     56500  41720  14780
RRSV 10PC       550 0015  .. ..              LDGWT INCLUDES RESERVE FUEL
DEST-MNVR         0 0000  .. ..
ALTN-SBKP      1050 0023  .. ..
HOLD-ALT       1130 0030  .. ..
M.REQD        20450 0755  .. ..
TAXI            150        .. ..   FLIGHT TIMES ETD 0040 ATD ....
TOTAL         20600 0755  .. ..                 ETA 0727 ATA ....

ALT-1 SBKP FL 140 DIST  89NM TIME 00.23  WC H15  FUEL 1030 MFOD 2160
SBGR CGO1A SCB DCT CPN DCT SBKP
```

Minimum Fuel Required: **20,450kg (7:55)**
Brake Release Weight: **76,950kg**
Payload: **14,780kg**
Reserve: **550kg (0:15)**

Minimum Fuel Required: **20,450kg (8:20)**
Brake Release Weight: **73,300kg**
Payload: **11,130kg**
Reserve: **1,440kg (0:41)**

```
MDPC/SBGR    FUEL TIME  CORR      BRWT     LDGWT      ZFWT    BOW    PLD
DEST SBGR   17720 0647  .. ..    76950     59230     56500  41720  14780
RRSV 10PC     550 0015  .. ..              LDGWT INCLUDES RESERVE FUEL
DEST-MNVR       0 0000  .. ..
ALTN-SBKP    1050 0023  .. ..
HOLD-ALT     1130 0030  .. ..
M.REQD      20450 0755  .. ..
TAXI          150        .. ..   FLIGHT TIMES ETD 0040 ATD ....
TOTAL       20600 0755  .. ..                 ETA 0727 ATA ....

ALT-1 SBKP FL 140 DIST  89NM TIME 00.23  WC H15  FUEL 1050 MFOD 2180
SBGR CGO1A SCB DCT CPN DCT SBKP


MDPC/SBBR    FUEL TIME  CORR      BRWT     LDGWT      ZFWT    BOW    PLD
DEST SBBR   15340 0544  .. ..    76950     61610     56500  41720  14780
RRSV 10PC    1330 0034  .. ..              LDGWT INCLUDES RESERVE FUEL
DEST-MNVR       0 0000  .. ..
ALTN-SBGO    1050 0025  .. ..
HOLD-ALT     1130 0030  .. ..
RCR FUEL     1600 0034
M.REQD      20450        .. ..
TAXI          150        .. ..
TOTAL       20600 0747  .. ..


ALT-1 SBGO FL 180 DIST 113NM TIME 00.25  WC T10  FUEL 1050 MFOD  2180


RECLEAR FIX TAROP    TO SBGR
            FUEL TIME  CORR          LDGWT
DEST SBGR    5140 0228  .. ..         59230
RRSV 10PC     550 0015  .. ..        LDGWT INCLUDES RESERVE FUEL
ALTERNATE    1050 0023  .. ..
HOLD-ALT     1130 0030  .. ..
M.REQD       7850 0335  .. ..
```

*Figure 474: Detailed flight release from PUJ to GRU using Reclearance In Flight.*

### 6.3.1   Historical Aspects of the Regulation

Modern turbofan engines and airplane systems have achieved high levels of reliability in aviation history, but it took many years for the aviation industry to learn how to develop such reliability. At early stages of commercial aviation, in the 1920s, airplanes were usually equipped with several engines. But as it happens, the number of engines does not measure an airplane's reliability. More engines could not overcome the several deficiencies in the systems of these early aircraft.

Advances in powerplant and systems technology greatly improved in the 1940s, and air transport airplanes started to grow in size and weight to carry more and more passengers. However, a larger airplane requires a more powerful engine and, by the 1950s, piston engines had reached their limits. Statistics clearly showed that the more horsepower a piston engine was required to produce, the greater the risk of failure. This risk prompted a new regulation in 1953, requiring commercial twin-engine and three-engine airliners to be within 60-minute flying time of a suitable airport at all times. This 60-minute rule of the piston engine era is still in effect today, although in 1964 three-engine airplanes were released from that requirement.

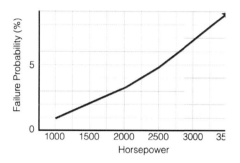

Figure 475: Piston engine failure probability.

Engine failure probability was so high at that time (compared to modern engines) that one of the most iconic airliners of all times, the four-engine airplane Lockheed Super Constellation, was known as the best three-engine airplane ever. This can give you a perspective of how often one of its engines was seen with propellers feathered.

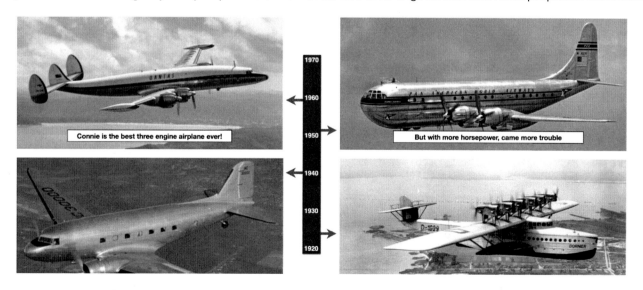

Figure 476: Evolution of piston engines and aircraft systems.

In the mid-1980s, with the introduction of a new long-range twin-engine aircraft on the market, the Boeing 767, and in recognition of the increasing reliability of modern turbofan engines and aircraft systems, international regulatory agencies began to make exceptions, that is, pilots started to fly twin-engine aircraft farther than 60 minutes from a suitable airport.

Known as ETOPS (Extended Twin OPerationS), these exceptions allowed qualified operators to fly first up to 90 minutes, and then 120 minutes away from a suitable airport. As airline experience and airplane reliability continued to increase, approvals were granted to ETOPS flights up to 180 and even 330 minutes from a suitable airport. By the mid-1990s, ETOPS had already proven to be a routine, safe, and highly successful way to conduct flight operations.

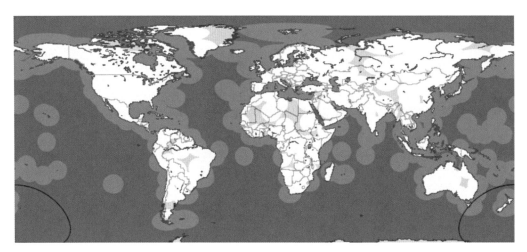

*Figure 477: ETOPS 60 according to Great Circle Mapper.*

The illustration above shows something that may seem strange. Many consider ETOPS to be like a restriction on flights over water, but that is not what the rule says. Regulations make it clear that the restriction is about not allowing a twin-engine airplane to be more than 60 minutes away from a suitable airport. This ultimately makes it impossible to fly long distances in direct routes over continental areas as well. Check the dark shaded areas over South America, Africa, Asia, and Australia (this illustration is old, and this is not necessarily true nowadays).

## 6.3.2   ETOPS Strategy

Let's resolve the first issue imposed by the rule. It mentions a maximum time away, but it does not impose any specific distance from the airport. At which speed should we calculate this distance? It must be calculated based on speed and altitude compatible to flying with one inoperative engine, ISA conditions, and wind calm. With this information in hand, the operator must define its "ETOPS strategy", that is, at which speed the pilot should fly after a potential engine failure. If you choose a low speed, 60-minute circles around those suitable airports will be small. At a higher speed, circles will be larger. We are going to propose a sample strategy for an aircraft with a certain weight flying with Mach 0.79 and 310kt.

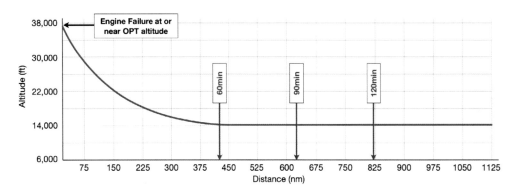

*Figure 478: Maximum distance from a suitable airport with a M0.79/310kt strategy.*

The previous figure shows how large the circle radius is, depending on ETOPS time. ETOPS 60 (this term does not really exist, but I am using it to show the standard rule for every twin-engine) allows us to be away up to 425nm from a suitable airport. As you can see on the first map (Figure 479), this is not enough, for example, to allow some oceans to be crossed by twin-engine aircraft. In fact, the Atlantic and Pacific Oceans could only be crossed through a far north route, making many routes economically unfeasible.

The Boeing 767 was the first to receive the new ETOPS 120 certification. This meant that it was cleared to fly routes that had a suitable airport for landing within a radius of up to 120 minutes of flight, which, as you can see in the previous graph, expands the area of operation from 425 to 825nm radius.

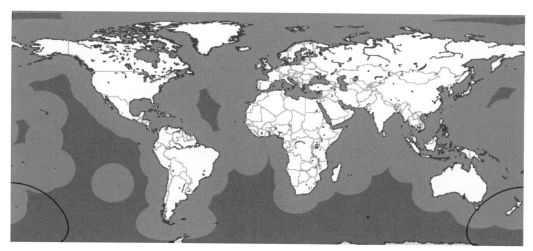

*Figure 479: ETOPS 120 according to Great Circle Mapper.*

Some impossible flights were made possible and many others were to come with larger ETOPS certifications granted to new aircraft and airlines as reliability increased. In fact, by 1995, there had been more than 600,000 ETOPS flights from Boeing 767 alone! From this total, 99.8% reached their final destination without any issues. The few flights that needed to divert had, in most cases, problems with systems, not engines. And these systems are also installed in three- and four-engine airplanes.

When the Boeing 777 received ETOPS 180 certification, a new world opened up for airlines. An aircraft with only two engines (low fuel burn) carrying almost the same number of passengers as another with four engines (high fuel burn) was able to virtually fly the same routes, maybe even increasing flight frequency. This way, a flight that used to be operated three times a week, became a daily one.

ETOPS certification might seem a bit expensive for airlines to obtain at a first glance, but the resulting flexibility, in addition to much lower costs with twins than with three- and four-engine airplanes, hugely pays off! In fact, just before COVID-19 pandemic hit aviation, twins making ETOPS flights already accounted for more than 70% of long-range flights.

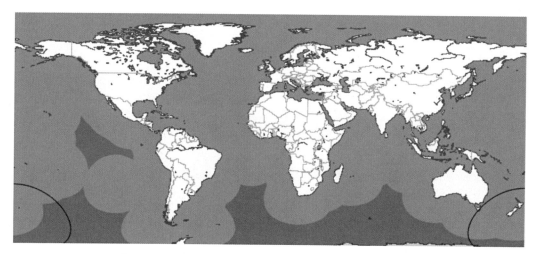

*Figure 480: ETOPS 180 according to Great Circle Mapper.*

## 6.3.3 Flying ETOPS

It is not a simple task getting an ETOPS certification. It is necessary to address a great deal of maintenance, flight planning, and operation requirements to carry out this type of operation. Let's discuss some operating issues, starting with selection of ETOPS alternate airports. These are airports that will be used to draw those large circles, and the aircraft is not supposed to fly outside the area established by them.

Let's plan a hypothetical flight to see how flight planning is handled.

First, you need to understand what kind of flight needs this detailed ETOPS planning. Remember that any twin-engine aircraft without special certification is treated as "ETOPS 60", that is, it can fly up to 60 minutes away from a suitable airport. We only refer to a flight as an ETOPS flight if the aircraft intends to fly beyond those standard 60 minutes. Brazilian aviators, heads up to the fact that in Brazil this default value is 75min instead of 60min. So, following Brazilian rules you will only need ETOPS certification to fly farther than 75min from a suitable airport. There may be other places in the world with a similar difference, but I am not totally sure of anyone to mention here.

In our example, the aircraft is certified as ETOPS 120, and between origin and destination, we selected four alternate airports that are suitable for our aircraft. We should stress the word "suitable". It will make a great deal of difference in flight planning, depending on the aircraft that is going to be used to accomplish that mission. An airport can be suitable for a Boeing 737, but not suitable for a Boeing 777. So, the flight dispatcher must first select airports with characteristics that match the specifications of the airplane (runway length, slope, width, elevation, PCR, etc.). In the next figure, the inner circles represent the area that would be 60min away from the airport and the outer circles are the operating limit of 120min. To fly this mission, we must remain within the area bounded by the outer circle at all times.

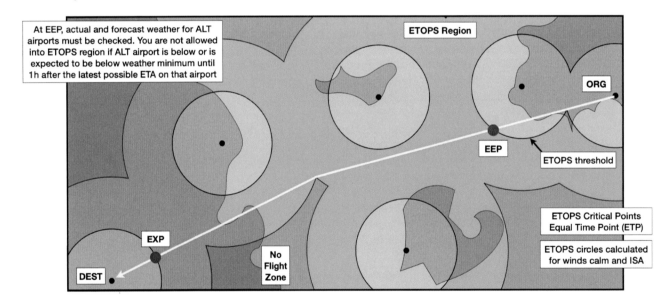

*Figure 481: ETOPS flight example. ETOPS entry and exit points.*

Every time we leave the inner circle (60min), we say that we are entering an ETOPS region of the flight. This point is called ETOPS Entry Point (EEP). Every time we approach a suitable airport again, if we stay less than 60 minutes away from it, we stop being in an ETOPS region; therefore, we call this point ETOPS Exit Point (EXP).

Always before entering an ETOPS region (before EEP), regulations oblige pilots to check for current and forecast weather conditions at the ETOPS Alternate Airport. It must be satisfactory from the moment you cross ETOPS threshold until one hour after the latest possible estimated time of arrival (ETA) on that airport, should you use it as an alternate. If the conditions are not satisfactory, you cannot enter the ETOPS region.

Of course, it is a natural thing to change alternate airports from time to time along the route. We normally change from one to another at every ETOPS Critical Point. These are the points along the route that will leave us at the same flight time between two possible alternates. Because of this characteristic, we call these points Equal Time

Points (ETP). Unlike ETOPS circles, which are drawn considering wind calm, ETPs take into account enroute weather forecast. In our example, we considered no wind, so ETPs are equidistant from ETOPS Alternate Airports.

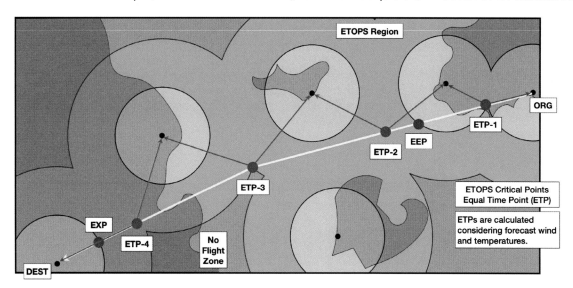

*Figure 482: ETOPS flight example. ETOPS critical points - equal time points.*

An interesting thing about the selection of an ETOPS alternate: the weather! Let's say we have a Boeing 777-300 and an Embraer E2 190 flying along the same route. They are both certified ETOPS 90 (yes, I know it is too little, but it is just an example), and when checking for suitable airports along the route, the Embraer was able to find two additional airports that were not considered suitable for the bigger Boeing twin owing to runway characteristics at those airports. For this reason, a direct route from origin to destination will be an ETOPS flight to the 777 and will not be an ETOPS flight to the E2.

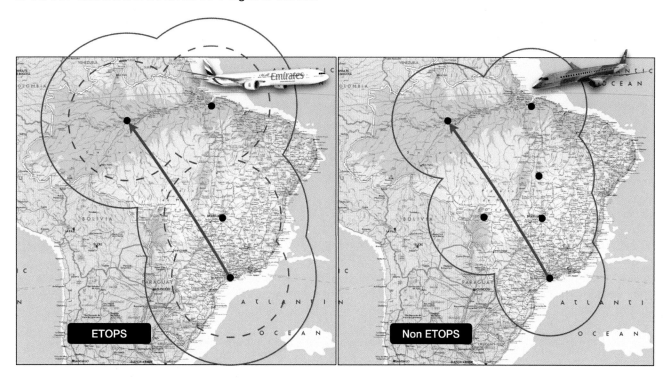

*Figure 483: The same route might be an ETOPS flight for one, but not for another airplane type.*

Now, suppose a big area of dense fog is all over that gigantic region – please, I know it is not realistic, I am just trying to make a point here. Except for origin and destination airports, all alternate airports shown in the figure are below weather minima, with visibility of only 100m. That would put us in a very strange situation. Those airports are no longer suitable to be used as alternates for an aircraft flying ETOPS (the Boeing 777), but for non-ETOPS flights that is not an issue! Selecting suitable airports just to stablish the 60min arc does not require a weather analysis, and only infrastructure is evaluated. So, as crazy as it may seem, the E2 would still be allowed to make that flight while the 777 would have to look for a different alternate airport along the route with good weather to be able to accomplish the proposed flight.

For that reason, a different term was coined. There is the SUITABLE airport: when we look for an airport with infrastructure suitable to the needs of our airplanes. And there is the ADEQUATE airport: when we evaluate if a suitable airport can be used as an ETOPS alternate, checking for weather forecast. Note that any airport to be used as an ETOPS alternate must be listed on the airline's "ops specs" document.

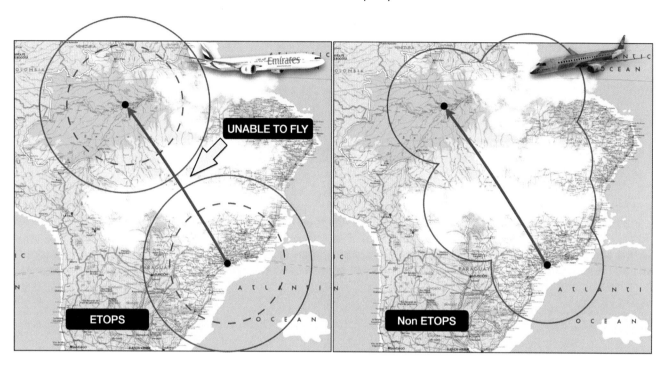

*Figure 484: Weather is not a concern for non-ETOPS flights.*

## 6.3.4  ETOPS Critical Fuel

For each ETP along an ETOPS flight route, three different situations must be addressed: engine failure, cabin depressurization, and engine failure with cabin depressurization at the same time. At every ETP, the airplane must have sufficient fuel onboard to fly according to the parameters described in the next paragraph and on the worst condition out of the three situations that I have just presented.

The aircraft must have enough fuel to divert to a suitable alternate airport, hold for 15 minutes, execute one IFR (instrument) approach, perform a go around, and execute a new VFR (visual) approach. Moreover, 5% extra fuel should be added to account for weather different than planned and another 5% for eventual performance penalties also unaccounted for. If there is ice forecast, once more, an additional amount of fuel must be added to account for that.

Now, you are probably thinking: but what does this have to do with minimum dispatch fuel? I will show you.

In Figure 485 on the next page, the solid blue line shows the amount of fuel on board during the flight according to the initial flight plan. As we progress, we have less and less fuel in the tanks; after all, it is being burned. The red lines represent the amount of fuel required to deal with the worst of the three scenarios and divert to the alternate airport.

When passing ETP1, if the worst emergency happens, we need less fuel to divert than the amount we have on board, so there is no problem. The same is true for all other ETPs except ETP4. When we fly over this point, we get enough fuel to go on in a normal situation. However, if we face the worst of the three emergencies, we will need more fuel to divert (and the extras mentioned above) than we have onboard. For this reason, we have to make an adjustment, adding fuel on takeoff so there is enough fuel on ETP4 to comply with regulatory requirements. This additional fuel is called ETOPS Critical Fuel. New minimum takeoff fuel and adjusted fuel at every checkpoint are both represented by the dashed blue line.

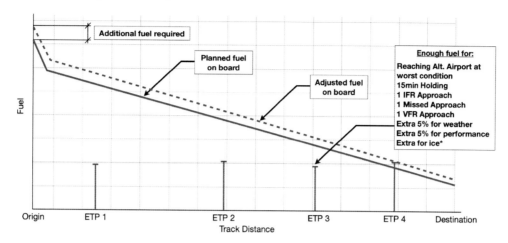

*Figure 485: ETOPS critical fuel.*

Below is an example for a Boeing 787-8 aircraft, showing all three scenarios and pointing the amount of fuel needed in each one to fly 1,000nm weighing 200,000kg at the moment of the emergency. Note that, depending on speed strategy, one or another event can be the most restrictive.

| | All Engine Decompression Fuel (LRC) | Engine Inoperative Speed | Engine Inoperative Driftdown Fuel | Engine Inoperative Decompression Fuel |
|---|---|---|---|---|
| **Engine Failure** — Flying at planned speed on still air | 16,571kg | 290kt => | 13,146kg | 16,240kg |
| | 16,571kg | 300kt => | 13,507kg | 16,225kg |
| **Cabin Decompression** — Flying at 10,000ft and LRC on still air | 16,571kg | 310kt => | 13,812kg | 16,522kg |
| | 16,571kg | 320kt => | 14,242kg | 16,702kg |
| **Engine Failure and Cabin Decompression** — Flying at FL100 and planned speed on still air | 16,571kg | 330kt => | 14,701kg | 16,956kg |
| | 16,571kg | 340kt => | 15,111kg | 17,478kg |

*Source: Boeing*

*Figure 486: ETOPS fuel sample. Boeing 787-8 weighing 200,000kg and diverting to an airport 1,000nm distant.*

## 6.3.5 Extended Diversion Time Operations - EDTO

In 2003, there was a change in ETOPS regulation. It ceased to be an exclusive certification for twin-engine aircraft and became a certification requested for any passenger transport aircraft. The acronym became "Extended Range Operations", and some started calling it EROPS. ICAO, however, abandoned the term and now refers to this type of certification as EDTO, or Extended Diversion Time Operations. The basic difference in the rule between two-engine aircraft and those with more than two, refers to the "standard certification". As mentioned previously, it is 60min for twin-engines, and it was set at 180min for aircraft with more than two engines.

The concern of legislators no longer lies exclusively in a potential engine failure, but any emergency situation that compromises systems that cannot support a great deal of time in flight. The classic example that restricts ETOPS certification is an aircraft's ability to suppress a fire situation on cargo holds. In that case, ETOPS certification is limited to maximum suppression time minus 15min, considering actual weather forecast. And yes, despite the new name given by ICAO (EDTO), many documents and even airlines around the globe still refer to this certification as ETOPS, and so do I. No problem with that. Everybody will understand. Once a name has stuck, and it has been around for more than 60 years, it is very hard to change it!

> **Cargo fire suppression time minus 15min, flying at all engines speed and on forecast winds and temperatures.**

*Figure 487: EDTO regulation deals with the most limiting system, and for most airliners that is the fire suppression system.*

As I mentioned at the beginning, ETOPS 330 is the ETOPS certification that currently allows aircraft to fly the farthest distance from a suitable airport. Incidentally, this is actually the certification received by the 747-8, 787, and 777 (which flew for six hours and 29 minutes with a single engine running on a test flight to earn this certification). This virtually allows a straight line between origin and destination on almost the entire planet.

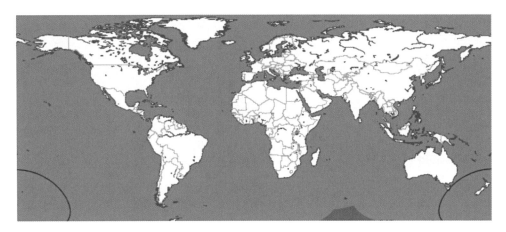

*Figure 488: ETOPS 330 according to the Great Circle Mapper.*

## 6.3.6 Notes regarding ETOPS

A historical note: the longest single-engine flight, owing to a real failure in the other engine, was flown by a United Airlines Boeing 777 on March 17th, 2003. The aircraft flew over the southern Pacific Ocean and was carrying 255 passengers. It flew for 192 minutes relying on a single engine running until it landed.

A 2003 statistical note pointed out that engine failure rate on airplanes flying ETOPS was less than 1 for every 100,000 flights, and it has improved ever since.

## 6.3.7 Sample for a Real ETOPS Flight

Finally, let's make a real ETOPS flight between Los Angeles (USA) and Sidney (Australia). There is a map of this flight on the next page. There you will be able to identify every aspect of an ETOPS flight that we have just studied.

Check the ETOPS Entry and Exit points, inner circles showing ETOPS thresholds and outer circles showing the limit of ETOPS region, and four different ETPs along the route.

You can see on flight release that this flight is using redispatch and additional ETOPS fuel was required. That 1,413kg extra fuel is there to make sure that on ETP4 the airplane will have the minimum fuel of 19,653kg to deal with the worst possible emergency. In this case, it was an engine failure followed by cabin decompression. The airline ETOPS strategy for that emergency is to fly at Mach 0.84 and 320KIAS during descent until reaching 10,000ft, and then flying at 250KIAS at that altitude.

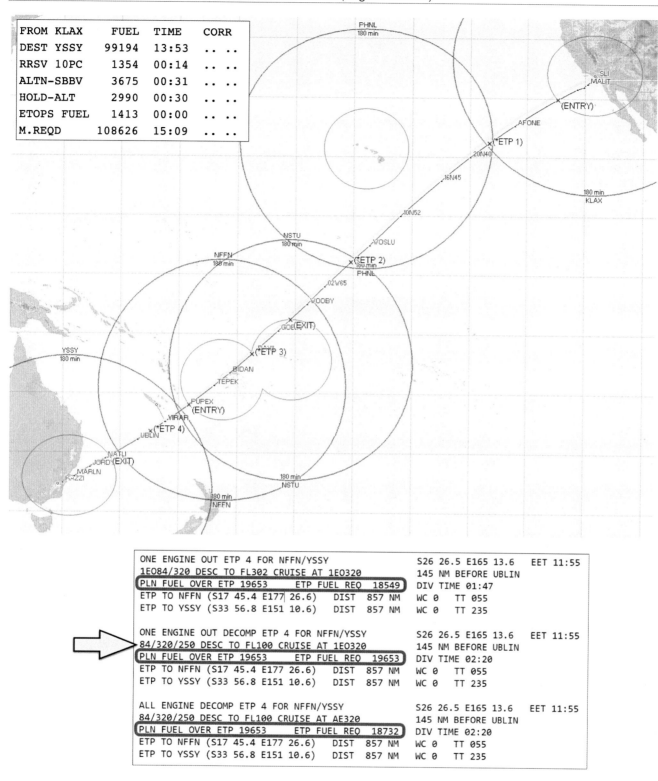

| FROM KLAX | FUEL | TIME | CORR |
|---|---|---|---|
| DEST YSSY | 99194 | 13:53 | .. .. |
| RRSV 10PC | 1354 | 00:14 | .. .. |
| ALTN-SBBV | 3675 | 00:31 | .. .. |
| HOLD-ALT | 2990 | 00:30 | .. .. |
| ETOPS FUEL | 1413 | 00:00 | .. .. |
| M.REQD | 108626 | 15:09 | .. .. |

```
ONE ENGINE OUT ETP 4 FOR NFFN/YSSY              S26 26.5 E165 13.6   EET 11:55
1EO84/320 DESC TO FL302 CRUISE AT 1EO320        145 NM BEFORE UBLIN
PLN FUEL OVER ETP 19653      ETP FUEL REQ  18549   DIV TIME 01:47
ETP TO NFFN (S17 45.4 E177 26.6)    DIST  857 NM  WC 0   TT 055
ETP TO YSSY (S33 56.8 E151 10.6)    DIST  857 NM  WC 0   TT 235

ONE ENGINE OUT DECOMP ETP 4 FOR NFFN/YSSY       S26 26.5 E165 13.6   EET 11:55
84/320/250 DESC TO FL100 CRUISE AT 1EO320       145 NM BEFORE UBLIN
PLN FUEL OVER ETP 19653      ETP FUEL REQ  19653   DIV TIME 02:20
ETP TO NFFN (S17 45.4 E177 26.6)    DIST  857 NM  WC 0   TT 055
ETP TO YSSY (S33 56.8 E151 10.6)    DIST  857 NM  WC 0   TT 235

ALL ENGINE DECOMP ETP 4 FOR NFFN/YSSY           S26 26.5 E165 13.6   EET 11:55
84/320/250 DESC TO FL100 CRUISE AT AE320        145 NM BEFORE UBLIN
PLN FUEL OVER ETP 19653      ETP FUEL REQ  18732   DIV TIME 02:20
ETP TO NFFN (S17 45.4 E177 26.6)    DIST  857 NM  WC 0   TT 055
ETP TO YSSY (S33 56.8 E151 10.6)    DIST  857 NM  WC 0   TT 235
```

*Figure 489: A real ETOPS flight plan between LAX and Sidney.*

To talk about the Minimum Equipment List (MEL), first, we need to understand what this document is not about. The MEL is not a list of minimum equipment that must be installed on the aircraft to perform a flight. This concept, often heard in aviation chats, is completely wrong. The Minimum Equipment List (MEL) is the authorizing document that legally allows dispatch in a non-standard configuration for a temporary period of time.

"If any equipment is not listed in the MEL, then dispatching the aircraft is prohibited until this item is repaired". This statement is only partially true; after all, the MEL does not include items that are not related to airworthiness, such as non-essential equipment and furnishings (known as NEF items). When a system is not working properly and is not listed in the MEL, then we say that this is a "no go" and the aircraft is grounded, or its status is AOG, which stands for Aircraft On Ground.

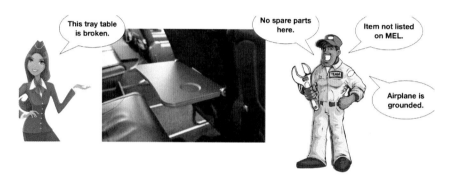

*Figure 490: By the way, that is a joke! Tray table is a furnishing equipment, not listed in MEL but a proper list named NEF.*

The MEL can authorize an airplane to be legally dispatched, but it can never jeopardize its safety. Therefore, it ensures safety by applying some particular practices, namely:

1. Operational limitations or restrictions. For example: an aircraft cannot be operated in icing conditions.
2. Transferring functions from an inoperative device to another that is operating normally. For example: an audio panel is not working and its function will be taken over by two others that are working normally.
3. Performance penalties. For example: maximum performance takeoff weight is reduced by 2,000kg.
4. And there is always a limit repair interval. For example: repair must be performed within 2 calendar days.

**More restrictive operational limitations**

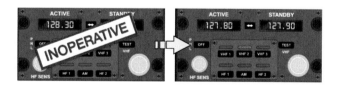

**Transfer of function to another operating component or instrument**

**Performance adjustments**

**\*\*\* All items have limited repair interval \*\*\***

The repair interval is divided into four categories, named as A, B, C, or D. Category A is a non-standard period and is always specified in the "remarks" field in the MEL. It can be something like "repair must be made within three flight days". A flight day is a 24-hour period (from midnight to midnight), either UTC or local time, as established by the aircraft's operator, during which at least one flight is initiated for the affected aircraft.

Categories B, C, and D are standard periods, those being 3, 10, and 120 consecutive calendar days, respectively, but always excluding the day when the malfunction was recorded in the aircraft's maintenance logbook. Categories B and C are eligible to be granted with a one-time extension period; however, the operator must notify the regulatory agency of the reason for the extension.

| Category | Time Interval |
|---|---|
| A | As specified on "Remarks" |
| B | Repair within 3 consecutive calendar-days (72h) |
| C | Repair within 10 consecutive calendar-days (240h) |
| D | Repair within 120 consecutive calendar-days (2880h) |

One-time extension period may be granted

Excluding the day when the malfunction was recorded in the aircraft's maintenance logbook

*Figure 492: Repair interval category.*

When manufacturers design their airplanes, one of the topics they should carefully address is how to enable such aircraft to be dispatchable in as many situations as possible, avoiding an AOG status. When allowed to postpone the repair of particular items, airlines can maintain a continuous flow of operations, which has a great economic impact for them. Other benefits include the possibility of stocking a smaller number of spare parts and concentrating this stock in some specific bases; a decrease in delays and flight cancellations, and increased customer satisfaction.

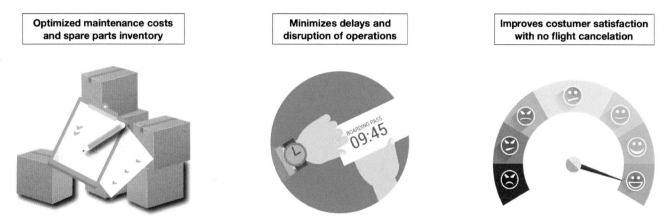

**Optimized maintenance costs and spare parts inventory**

**Minimizes delays and disruption of operations**

**Improves costumer satisfaction with no flight cancelation**

*Figure 493: Some dispatchability advantages.*

To clearly understand how crucial it is for operators to ensure an aircraft's dispatch in non-standard conditions, watch out for the number of flights dispatched with some MEL item at any given moment. In low season, it is estimated that about 20% of flights around the globe are being carried out thanks to the dispatchability offered by this manual. In the high season, this number easily exceeds 50%.

Regardless of the manufacturer, document layout is approximately the same. In fact, FAA Master MEL has one layout while EASA has another. I will show you both of them.

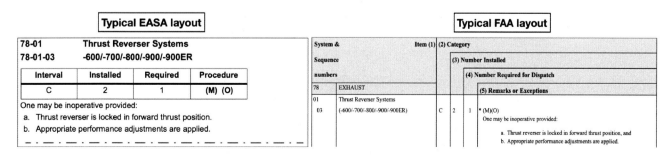

**Typical EASA layout**

| 78-01 | **Thrust Reverser Systems** | | |
| 78-01-03 | **-600/-700/-800/-900/-900ER** | | |

| Interval | Installed | Required | Procedure |
|---|---|---|---|
| C | 2 | 1 | **(M) (O)** |

One may be inoperative provided:
a. Thrust reverser is locked in forward thrust position.
b. Appropriate performance adjustments are applied.

**Typical FAA layout**

System & Sequence numbers | Item (1) | (2) Category
(3) Number Installed
(4) Number Required for Dispatch
(5) Remarks or Exceptions

| 78 | EXHAUST | | | | |
| 01 | Thrust Reverser Systems | | | | |
| 03 | (-600/-700/-800/-900/-900ER) | C | 2 | 1 | * (M)(O) |

One may be inoperative provided:
a. Thrust reverser is locked in forward thrust position, and
b. Appropriate performance adjustments are applied.

*Figure 494: Different MEL layouts.*

In the example, you can see that our model aircraft has two thrust reverser systems (one for each engine) and that flight is dispatchable with one of them inoperative, as long as the system is locked in forward position and appropriate performance adjustments are applied. The symbols (M) and (O) indicate that there are Maintenance procedures (maintenance personnel) and Operational procedures (flight crew) to be taken. Those procedures are described just below this header, and can be straight forward or even refer to another manual, such as in our example.

**MAINTENANCE (M)**
1. Deactivate and secure the associated thrust reverser (AMM 78-00-00/901).
   NOTE: With the thrust reverser secured closed, one or both sync locks may be inoperative provided the sync lock is verified to be in the locked position.
2. Prevent movement of the reverse thrust handle by any appropriate means (e.g. lockwire the thrust reverser handle to the appropriate forward thrust lever).

**OPERATIONS (O)**
NOTE: Thrust reverser deactivation per AMM can result in the illumination of the MASTER CAUTION and ENG annunciation when performing a Master Caution recall.
1. Use of reverse thrust is left to the discretion of each carrier. Techniques for controlling the aircraft with unsymmetrical reverse thrust should be developed and used in training.
2. The wet runway/obstacle limited weight and associated V1 must be reduced to account for the inoperative thrust reverser. Refer to the Takeoff and Landing Section of the Flight Planning and Performance Manual for the appropriate penalties.

**Thrust Reverser Inoperative**

When dispatching on a wet runway with both thrust reversers operative, an operative anti-skid system, and all brakes operating, regulations allow deceleration credit for one thrust reverser in the engine failure case and two thrust reversers in the all engine stop case.

When dispatching on a wet runway with one thrust reverser inoperative, the runway/obstacle limited weight and V1 must be reduced to account for the effect on accelerate-stop performance. A simplified method, which conservatively accounts for this, is to reduce the normal wet runway/obstacle limited weight by 850 kg and the V1 associated with the reduced weight by 2 knots.

If the resulting V1 is less than minimum V1, takeoff is permitted with V1 set equal to V1(MCG) provided the accelerate-stop distance available corrected for wind and slope exceeds approximately 1200 m.

Detailed analysis for the specific case from the Airplane Flight Manual may yield a less restrictive penalty.

*Figure 495: Information from MEL on the left and FPPM on the right.*

Attention: the MEL document is used for dispatching aircraft in a non-standard situation; therefore, the information contained in this document is only relevant for a flight that has not yet taken off. For this reason, it is very important to establish what we consider a Point of Dispatch to be. If, at any time before this point, the crew members perceive a failure in any system, they need to be able to solve the problem or check the MEL before starting takeoff (if applicable, after all the inoperative item can be "no go"). After the point of dispatch, any abnormality should be referred only to the appropriate checklist (QRH – Quick Reference Handbook).

The point of dispatch is a different point depending on the operator's choice. It can be the moment that doors have been closed and the airplane is ready to start the engines; it can be when engines are already up and running, or when thrust is applied with the intention of commencing takeoff roll. Let's consider this last example as our point of dispatch in this book, just before takeoff.

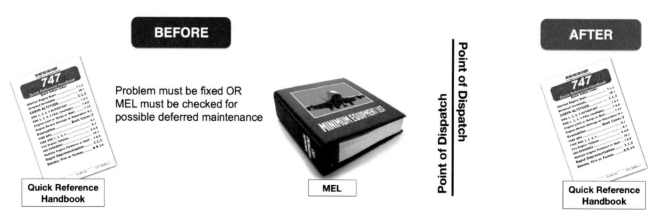

*Figure 496: Procedures before and after the point of dispatch.*

However, even in flight, it is usually a good idea to check the MEL when identifying an abnormal situation. This will allow the flight crew to anticipate any kind of problem with flight dispatch in the next flight. For example: you took off from Brasília to Belém with a stop in Marabá (they are all Brazilian cities). You are "tankering" fuel in Brasília because there is a NOTAM advising there will be no fuel available in Marabá for the next 10 days. When cruising between these two cities, a master caution is activated. You have an aft "fuel pump low pressure". After reading the checklist, you realize it is no big deal. Just set the fuel pump switch to OFF and continue normal operation. Well, if you do only that and land in Marabá, you will not have done anything wrong, but you definitely put yourself in trouble. Marabá is a small town that your airline flies only once a day. There might be some spare parts there, like a tire to be changed once in a while, but there is no fuel pump for sure! Well, the aircraft must now be dispatched using the MEL, and that is perfectly ok. However, when consulting this document, you see that a great amount of ballast fuel will be required. Huge problem! There's no fuel in Marabá! Remember the NOTAM?

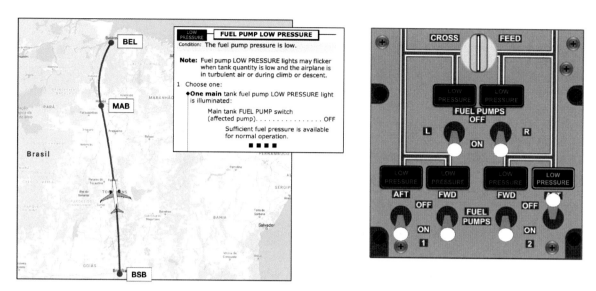

*Figure 497: Fuel pump failure in flight is no big deal.*

In this scenario, the aircraft would be grounded in Marabá until fuel is available again, or until proper maintenance has been performed. However, if the MEL had been checked during the flight (even though that was not a mandatory procedure), you would have been able to contact the company's flight operations center with valuable information, and possibly deal with the problem in a different way, maybe not landing in Marabá and diverting directly to Belém.

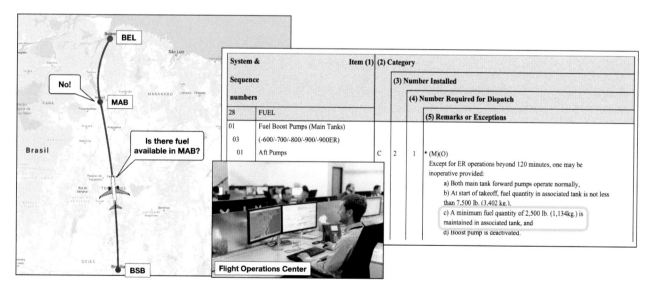

*Figure 498: It is always a good idea to check the MEL and be prepared to deal with problems that may appear.*

As this is a book about aircraft performance, let me show you examples of some systems that, when inoperative, can cause performance penalties on a Boeing 737NG:

1. Engine Thrust Reverser inoperative: weight penalties when taking off on wet runways and Field or Obstacle limited. V1 will have to be reduced in these cases.
2. Anti-Skid inoperative: takeoff is allowed only on dry runways. Weight penalty for takeoff and landing. Great reduction in V1 for takeoff. The use of the assumed temperature method is prohibited, but derate is allowed.

3. Engine Bleed or Air Conditioning Pack inoperative, or any condition that requires flying with this system off: maximum flight altitude is limited to a lower level and fuel burn is increased.

4. Auto Speed Brake inoperative: maximum field limited landing weight penalty owing to increased stopping distance.

5. Leading Edge Flap Transit Indicator inoperative: maximum cruise speed limitation is imposed, possibly causing limitation to maximum altitude as well.

6. Anti-ice valve inoperative in open position: takeoff performance weight penalty; altitude capability is also reduced in case of engine failure. There will be an increase in fuel burn, too.

7. APU (Auxiliary Power Unit) inoperative: ETOPS flights are prohibited.

8. EEC Normal Mode inoperative: flight must be conducted with this device in alternate mode. Depending on engine rate, takeoff performance adjustments might apply. The use of assumed temperature is prohibited.

9. Tail Skid Extended: VR speed will increase and weight penalty to performance takeoff weight must be applied.

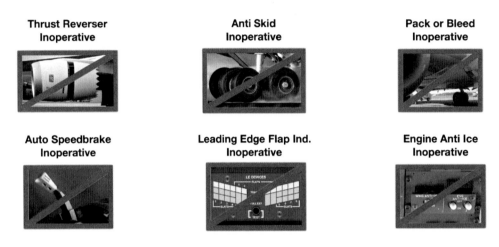

*Figure 499: Examples of inoperative items that will affect performance on a Boeing 737NG.*

Those are just a few examples and the values of each penalty should be checked directly on the aircraft's MEL. This document, by the way, must always be available to pilots, so there must be an updated copy on the flight deck.

An airline's MEL is, in fact, a sum of two documents: Master MEL and CDL (Configuration Deviation List). Both documents are written by the manufacturer and approved by the local regulatory agency. The MEL is based on FAR parts 25 and 121 (design and operating regulations), while the CDL is only based on part 25, so it is included as an Appendix of the AFM. That is because the CDL is not a manual focused on systems, but rather on secondary airplane exterior parts that may affect an airplane's total drag or stall speeds. As the airplane's AFM is certified to allow the airplane to fly in these conditions, CDL items often are not limited by any repair interval.

*Figure 500: The CDL is focused on secondary external parts.*

When the Master MEL (MMEL) is merged with the CDL, the resulting new manual is called Dispatch Deviation Guide, or DDG. This document is handled to the operator and every operator MUST propose and make changes to it. The changes are related to company policies, operation standards, and procedures, and they are executed in coordination with the local regulatory agency. After changes, DDG is finally turned into the Airline's Minimum Equipment List.

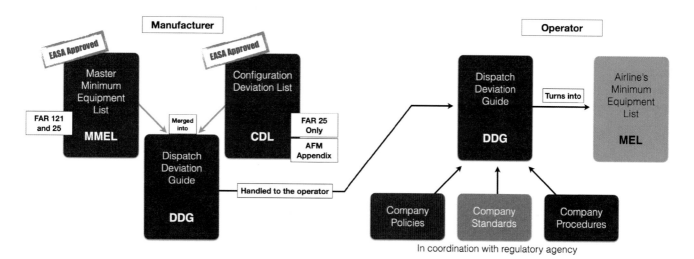

*Figure 501: Process for transition from MMEL to Airline MEL.*

On January 13th, 1982, a Boeing 737-200 operated by Air Florida was preparing for takeoff from Washington to Fort Lauderdale, with a stopover in Tampa, on a domestic flight in the USA. However, shortly after takeoff, the aircraft quickly lost altitude, hit a bridge, and crashed into the Potomac River about three kilometers from the White House. Only five of the 74 people on board survived, and in addition to those who perished on the airplane, there were four other fatal victims on the ground – all of them were occupants of vehicles traveling on the bridge hit by the airplane. The day was cold, -4°C, and it was snowing at the time of takeoff.

The reason for this tragedy was ice! No accident has a single cause, and this is no exception. The pilots' actions also contributed to the accident, but we will focus on ice to develop this discussion. So, before we continue the study of cold weather operations, let's talk a little bit about how ice can affect our flight.

You must remember from the beginning of this book that an airplane is capable of flying owing to deformations that the air flow undergoes when passing by the airplane's wings. These wings are meticulously designed, so these deviations in aerodynamic flow occur as intended. If we put ice on the wings, the airfoil shape is drastically changed, and the result can be catastrophic. A wing that is supposed to produce lift now produces only an aerodynamic mess that is not able to keep an airplane flying. In addition, the extra weight that the airplane carries with the ice accumulated on it makes that the perfect recipe for a disaster (drag is estimated to increase by more than 40% and lift is reduced by up to 30%, severely increasing stall speed).

**Attention!** Stall warnings are calibrated as a function of the angle of attack on the airplanes. When ice is detected, the **stall warning is reset to a lower angle of attack**. However, this new value is an **ESTIMATE** based on flight testing, and depending on the ice accumulation on the wing, the airplane can stall before any warning is given to the pilots! The ice will accumulate on the leading edge of the wings and can assume many different forms, causing different disturbances to the air flow. One kind of shape that the ice can build up is known as "horn shaped ice", owing to the oddly format resembling a pair of bull horns.

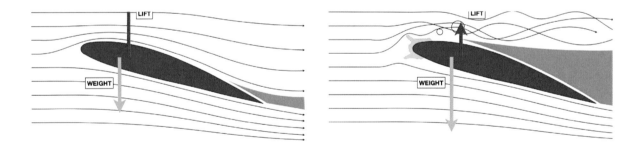

There are several types of ice accumulation that might happen on an aircraft's surface. For example, overnight frost, clear ice (hard to detect because it is transparent and usually results from frozen water patches or snow that melts and then freezes up again), rime ice (mostly experienced during climb and approach phases), mixed ice (generally built up on airplanes that are parked for a long time, when other types of ice happen, slightly melt and freeze again, over and over).

*Figure 503: Examples of ice accumulation.*

There is no device on airplanes that can remove ice on the ground. Anti-icing systems are designed to prevent formation of ice at very specific points, such as probes used in measurement of speed and temperature, flight deck windows, engine cowl and leading edge of the wings. In other words, these systems are very useful during a flight, when speed prevents ice accumulation on the wings and fuselage.

But what can we do when ice is all over the airplane before takeoff? In this situation, there is an aircraft de-icing service which is offered (and charged) by some airports to operators so that they can deal with extreme weather situations. It is an expensive process for airlines, but it is absolutely necessary.

*Figure 504: Anti-ice and de-ice airplane systems (in red) are design to protect aircraft parts during the flight.*

In situations such as the one shown above, after passengers are boarded and cargo is loaded, the plane proceeds, towed or under its own power, to a designated area of the airport called the "deicing pad", normally close to the runway in use. In this place, the aircraft will be sprayed with a liquid substance that will remove ice and, depending on the type, still prevent the formation of a new layer of ice for a given amount of time. The time period that shows how long new ice accumulation can be delayed is known as "Holdover Time" (HOT). Deicing services can be executed on the gate as well, but in this case, things can get a bit complicated, because the pilot will still have to taxi all the way to the runway, and ice may build up on the airplane again in the meantime.

There are four types of fluids that can be used to deice an aircraft. They are identified simply by the title Type I, Type II, Type III, and Type IV. Those are propylene glycol-based fluids (which are toxic, so, do not allow them into the air conditioning system) and act as freezing point depressors. Each has a different color, namely orange, white, yellow, and green, respectively. Next, we will see some small details about each of the four types and then we will briefly discuss how to use the holdover time table.

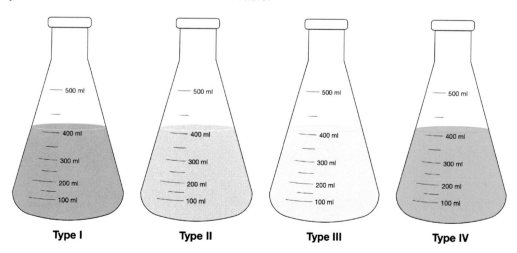

*Figure 505: Types of deicing fluids.*

## 6.5.1   Type I Fluid

This type of fluid is applied hot and under high pressure on the aircraft. It is used to remove ice only, having no anti-ice properties, and it is the most common fluid found in airports that offer deicing services. To have no anti-ice quality means it cannot prevent new ice accumulation over a long period of time after application. For that reason, it is used when there is no precipitation or in combination with another type of fluid (Type II or IV).

*Figure 506: Type I orange deicing fluid.*

## 6.5.2   Type II Fluid

This type may be applied in a single process just to remove ice that is already on the airplane. This happens when there is no precipitation that may build up a new layer of ice on the aircraft. It can also be applied in a two-step process. There are two options now. We can use Type II in both steps, being heated at first (to clean the airplane), but not heated in the second step. Alternatively, we can remove ice by using Type I first and then we apply Type II only in the second step of the deicing service, preventing new ice build-up for a given amount of time.

## 6.5.3   Type III Fluid

This type of fluid has similar properties to those of fluids I and II, that is, it is used for deicing and anti-icing, but it is applied in a single process and is intended to be used by turboprop aircraft, for example, ATR-72 or Dash-8. Pilots flying this type of aircraft have to be very attentive to ice that may settle on the propellers, since ice accumulated there, if any, is very likely to be thrown against the aircraft's fuselage when the engine is rotating at a high speed, as in takeoff, for example. In fact, that is the reason why this kind on aircraft has a reinforced structure on the fuselage, just next to the propeller. It is intended to protect the fuselage against the impact of ice that may be ultimately thrown by the rotating blades.

*Figure 507: Type III yellow deicing fluid for turbo props.*

Figure 508: Reinforced structure on the fuselage.

## 6.5.4   Type IV Fluid

This type of fluid is denser than the others and should be used as an anti-ice product, only. So, it is applied in a two-step process, together with either type I or II. Of course, the deicer is applied first and Type IV, afterwards. Types II, III and IV are fluids that can be applied mixed with hot water in different concentrations depending on the temperature: 100% (no water, just deicer), 75/25, or 50/50. The concentration being applied on the aircraft will always be informed by the fellow that is doing the job (sometimes nicknamed "iceman").

Figure 509: Type IV green anti-ice fluid.

## 6.5.5   Holdover Time Tables (HOT)

These tables indicate how long the aircraft surface is expected to resist new ice buildup. It works as follows: an "iceman" informs the pilot about the exact moment when fluid application has started and what type of fluid is being used (and concentration, too). The pilot checks the appropriate table and identifies the holdover time. This time period is valid from the beginning of the application, not from the end, but in a two-step application, time is running after the anti-ice fluid application starts. Let's look at some examples on how to use this table.

To use it, pilots will need the following information: air temperature, type of precipitation, visibility, type and concentration of the fluid. If you look at a Type I HOT table, you will see that there is no need to enter fluid concentration. That is because, as I said before, Type I is a deicer, only, so it is always 100% and information on concentration is only required when using types II, III, or IV.

Another thing that I mentioned but does not appear in the table shown in Figure 510 is visibility. This is because it is not in this table that we use visibility, but in another one. Don't worry, I will explain that. It turns out that intensity of snowfall or water precipitation (rain) has a lot to do with visibility and temperature. The same level of precipitation can offer very different levels of visibility during daylight if compared to nighttime, and visibility at night is much greater. So, we have a second table (shown in Figure 511) that must be assessed only at night and if there is precipitation.

Consider the following weather data: light snow precipitation, visibility of 1,600m, and temperature at -5°C (METAR 04010G20KT 1600 –SN OVC003 M05/M06 Q1013). If this flight is happening at night, we should use the table in Figure 511. Look at the third row (Night - Colder / Equal -1°C) and at the sixth visibility column (1,600m). As highlighted, what is considered light precipitation during daylight should be considered moderate at night!

Back in Figure 510, we will find HOT information. If we were using Type IV at a 75/25 concentration level, cross-referencing temperature and precipitation data, we would get between 1 hour and 1 hour 50 minutes of holdover time since application started. That is for a daylight takeoff. This time would decrease to something between 30 minutes and one hour at nighttime.

Although not shown in the figure, if we used type I fluid, the result would be between 5 and 8 minutes during daylight. This is almost nothing, considering that this is about the time it takes to deice the airplane. As I said, Type I fluid does not offer almost any anti-ice capability and, in our example, takeoff would have to be performed immediately after application.

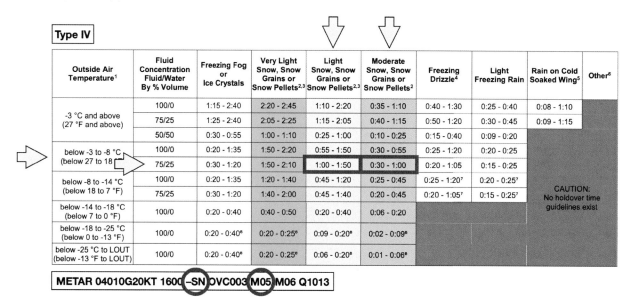

Figure 510: Holdover time table for Type IV fluid.

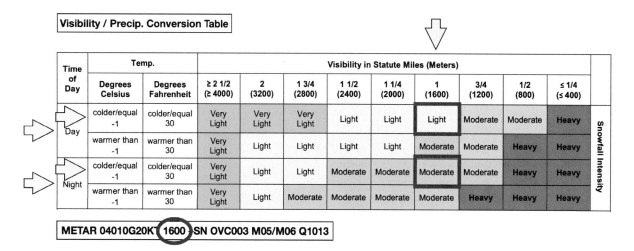

Figure 511: Conversion table for Visibility / Precipitation intensity.

### 6.5.5.1 Considerations about HOT Tables

As you can see, there can be very large "windows" between the minimum and maximum times shown in these tables. Most airlines advise their pilots to play safe and always use the minimum value as a reference. Even so, be aware that this information should be used more as guidelines than as effective data. Anytime a pilot suspects that ice has already built up on the aircraft's wings or stabilizer, a new deicing procedure must be performed. And there are many factors that might shorten this time presented in HOT tables. Let's see some of them below:

1. Jet blast from another aircraft taxiing in front of your airplane might expedite the removal of the fluid protective layer from your wings, just as high wind velocity will do.
2. After extending flaps for departure, you will expose an unprotected part of the wing to precipitation; this way, many airplane manuals tell pilots to do that only when they are about to join the runway for takeoff (when operating in this kind of weather).
3. Airport facility trucks deicing the runway may be a problem, too. This product can be poured by the wind over the airplane waiting for departure at the runway holding point. That significantly decreases the deicing effect of the fluid.
4. Even different types of aircraft materials can produce very different holdover times. For example, previous studies have shown that HOT for composite materials are 30% shorter when using type I fluid, in comparison to airplanes made from aluminum.

Note: because of this difference, we now have two different kinds of holdover time tables. One for aluminum and another for composite materials.

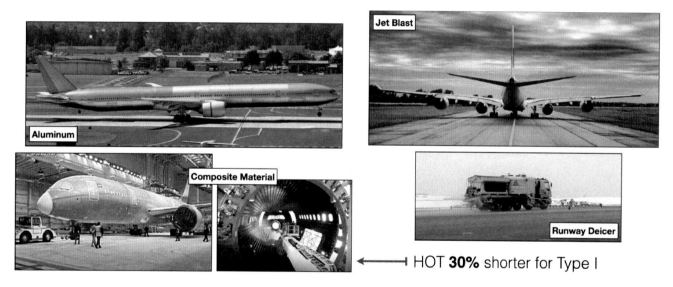

*Figure 512: Factors that can affect HOT.*

## 6.5.6 Issues about Deicing Fluids

Ice can be very dangerous and must be fairly addressed in cold weather operations. Pilot must never take off if they are unsure about ice formation over the aircraft, especially on wings, flight controls and stabilizers. However, even though deicing fluids are a good way to remove and/or prevent ice, there is a collateral effect.

When thickened airplane deicing/anti-icing fluids dry, they may leave a very fine, powdery residue on the above-mentioned critical areas. This residue can rehydrate and expand into gel-like materials that may freeze during the flight and impair the operation of flight control systems. A two-step deicing/anti-icing process helps to reduce the amount of fluid residue on the wings and stabilizers.

Deicing trucks are also a very important resource. Without them, runways can become very contaminated and very slippery, very fast! But, once again, there is a kind of backfire in this process. Carbon brakes can have a very short service life owing to catalytic oxidation caused by the product used as a runway deicer (salt).

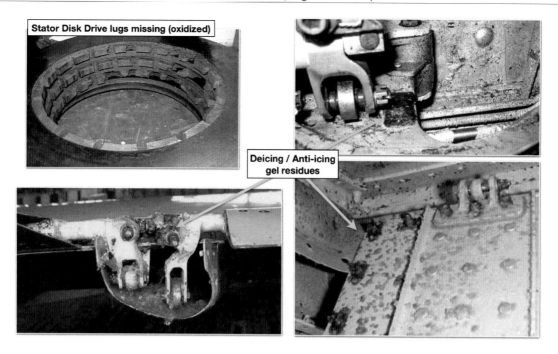

*Figure 513: Maintenance issues involving deicing fluids.*

## 6.5.7  Deicing Fan Blades

When doing a walk around as part of preflight procedures, pilots should carefully check the fan blades of the jet engine, front and back! If there is ice on it, as shown on the left image of the next figure, it must be removed before engine start. However, it must be done with hot air, not deicing fluid!

Fan blades might have ice on the leading edge of each blade, as shown in Figure 514 (right side). That is acceptable, as long as the fan disk is free to rotate and the snow or ice is removed using the ice shedding procedure during taxi-out and before setting takeoff thrust. This procedure is commonly known as "Fan Ice Removal".

*Figure 514: Ice accumulation on engine fan blades.*

## 6.5.8  Cold Soaked Fuel Frost (CSFF)

I mentioned frost as one kind of ice that should be removed from airplane wings before takeoff. And I stand by what I said. However, there is one exception.

If you ever poured alcohol in your hands (and I bet you did it a lot in 2020), you probably had a refreshing feeling. Well, that is because alcohol turns into vapor very quickly, and this vapor takes away some body heat with it, momentarily cooling the surface. Now, imagine a tank full of fuel. This fuel tends to take heat away from the surface as well as the alcohol did to you. So, the fuel tank surface is naturally colder than the rest of the airplane.

Aware of that, manufacturers allow some frost buildup on the wings, over or under them, as long as it is limited to a predetermined area. Figure 515 shows this area highlighted in red, but it is actually painted black on the airplane.

There are other conditions to allow takeoff with frost in that area: there must be no precipitation, air temperature must be at or above 4°C, and fuel tank temperature must be at or above -16°C.

*Figure 515: Cold soaked fuel frost (CSFF).*

## 6.5.9 Using Aircraft Anti-Ice Systems
### 6.5.9.1 How and when ice will buildup on an airplane

Have you ever wondered how ice can build up on an airplane? While in flight, ice present in the atmosphere is not typically a direct threat to the aircraft. Let me clarify: no one would fly into a cumulonimbus cloud with baseball-sized hailstones and expect to emerge unscathed. That's a serious hazard, but it is usually avoidable with weather radar.

What I mean is that ice particles in the air generally do not stick to the airplane; they bounce off and disperse. The real threat is water in a liquid state at temperatures below 0°C. Yes, that can happen! Have you ever left a bottle of beer in the freezer too long? When you finally retrieve it, you might initially be relieved it has not frozen, but a slight shake suddenly turns it solid. Water requires low temperature, a condensation nucleus, and sometimes a "little push" to transition from liquid to solid.

So, when an airplane flies through a cloud full of supercooled liquid droplets, that is where the real trouble lies. The airplane acts as the condensation nucleus and the disturbance needed to turn that liquid water into ice. This is especially true when flying in regions with supercooled large droplets, known as SLD. A typical cloud droplet is around 10 microns in diameter, but SLDs are larger than 50 microns and can reach up to 1,000 microns. These SLDs quickly turn to ice upon contact with the airplane, building up on pitot tubes (remember the Air France 447 accident – Airbus A330), windshields, propellers, engine cowls, and the leading edges of wings and stabilizers.

The region of the atmosphere where SLD is most likely found is between the altitudes with temperatures of 0°C and -15°C. To prevent ice buildup, anti-ice systems should be used whenever both temperature and moisture conditions are met. I will outline these conditions for each phase of flight, starting with takeoff.

### 6.5.9.2 Takeoff and Ground Operations

Anti-ice systems must be used during ground operations (taxiing) and when taking off whenever air temperature is at or below 10°C and there is visible moisture present in one of the following ways: precipitation of any kind (rain, drizzle, or snow); standing water, snow or slush on the runway, taxiways or tarmac; and mist or fog, as long as it is dense enough to restrict visibility to 1,600m (1 statue mile) or less.

### 6.5.9.3 Climb and Cruise

Engine anti-ice systems must be used during climb and cruise flight whenever TAT is at or below 10°C and SAT is at or above -40°C, and there is visible moisture present in the form of cloud or precipitation. Pay attention to the existing temperature window. When air is cooler than -40°C, the system does not need to be used, since at these temperatures, it is assumed that there is no water in liquid state on the atmosphere, and as I said earlier, any ice in the atmosphere does not adhere to the aircraft's surface.

Wing anti-ice systems do not follow such a clear rule. Manufacturers say this system should be used only in situations of stronger ice formation. Some airplanes, e.g., those from Airbus, have a small metal stick right in front of the pilots' window that indicates the need to use wing anti-icing when this stick is covered by ice. Boeing 737 operators are instructed to look at the windshield wiper holder. If there is ice accumulated either there or on the window, the system must be turned on.

### 6.5.9.4 Descend

Disregard SAT. During the descent phase temperature will increase rapidly, so, it doesn't really matter if it is below -40°C, SAT will soon be above that value. Then, whenever TAT is at or below 10°C and there is visible moisture, turn on the engine anti-ice system. Wing anti-icing follows the same rule as in climb or cruise. Look for these cues on the window before turning it on.

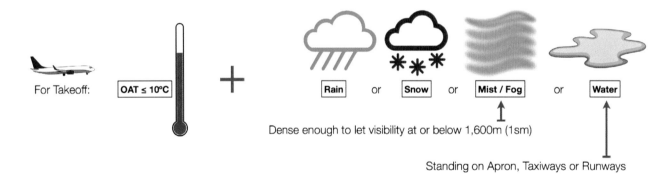

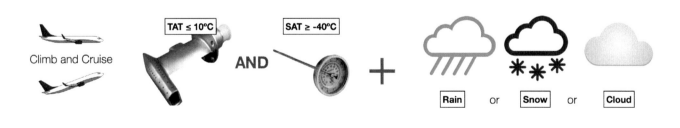

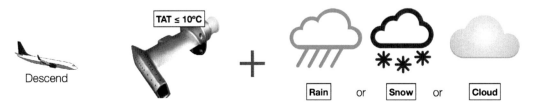

*Figure 516: When to use engine anti-ice systems.*

## 6.5.10  Difference between Deicing and Anti-Ice System

Lighter aircraft, such as turboprop ATR 72, has no wing anti-ice system. What they have is a deicing system. You might wonder: what is the difference? Well, let's take a closer look at a traditional jet engine anti-icing system.

Most jet airliners bleed air from their engines and direct this heated air to the engine cowl or the leading edge of the wing. The air then escapes through small holes to relieve pressure from the system. This way, the surface stays warm and prevents any ice accumulation.

*Figure 517: The wing anti-ice system of most jetliners work like this.*

Most anti-ice systems of jetliners work like this, but that of Boeing 787 is an exception. This airplane's system works by electrically heating the leading edges, which is a much more fuel-efficient solution, because you do not need to bleed air from the engine, as it will take some thrust away with it.

Engine anti-ice systems should always be used just as this: an ANTI-ice device, or something to prevent ice from building up at any time. Allowing ice to buildup on the engine cowl and just then switching on the anti-ice system might release large chunks of ice into the engine and severely damage it. Wing anti-icing, however, can be used in two different ways: for pre-heating the surface and preventing ice buildup, or as a deicing system, letting some ice accumulation occur and just then, turning it on to remove it.

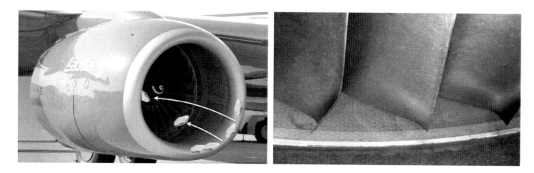

*Figure 518: Allowing ice first to build up and only then turning on the anti-ice may release ice chunks into the engine and badly damage it.*

The wings of some lighter jets and of almost every turboprop have a deicing system only. It cannot, under any circumstances, be used as anti-ice protection. Those aircraft have rubber bags on the leading edge of the wings, called rubber boots (maybe because they are intended to "kick" the ice off the wing), which will inflate with air and expel the ice that has already been formed there. Therefore, we need to wait for ice to accumulate and then remove it from the wing. If those "boots" are already inflated by the time ice has built up, they will have no effect after that, deflating and inflating again without being able to break the ice that is now beyond their reach.

*Figure 519: Rubber boots must be used as deicers only.*

Again, most jetliners have no anti-icing or deicing system on their tail (horizontal and vertical stabilizer). In fact, most of them do not even have this system on the whole wing, but only in part of it. Don't worry. Every single aircraft must demonstrate that it is able to maintain its flying characteristics with up to 3in of ice accumulated on any unprotected surface. You can see that most turboprops, in comparison, have the same wing rubber boots installed on the vertical and the horizontal stabilizers.

*Figure 520: Deicing rubber boots installed on vertical and horizontal stabilizer.*

## 6.5.11 Ice Crystal Icing

Is there any ice that is hazardous at temperatures below -40°C? Not usually. But in the past few years, a phenomenon called Ice Crystal Icing has been the object of a great deal of research in the aviation industry. It can happen in various temperature ranges, including below -40°C, even though it is more common in warmer air.

Cumulus Nimbus (CB) clouds are stormy clouds with great vertical development and a low altitude base, and whose top reaches altitudes well beyond 40,000ft in tropical latitudes. This classic format of storm is easily identified on weather radars and can be avoided by simply turning around (sometimes it is not that simple to find a way around it, but that is another story).

Occasionally, a pilot is caught flying near a "non-classic" system. There are CBs all around, but none with great vertical development. Looking on the weather radar screen, there is nothing to worry about – just a scattered green area ahead. By the way, precipitation and turbulence intensity on radar varies from none (black) to light (green), moderate (yellow), heavy (red), and extreme (magenta).

Flying on green in these situations might be a trap. The storm is not strong enough to develop vertically, but very tiny icy particles are easily lifted by upstream to altitudes far beyond the top of the cloud. These particles are too small and the air is too cold for them to adhere to the airplane. However, as they get ingested by the engine, a sequence of events starts to make things more interesting.

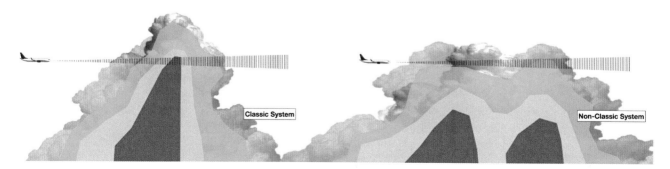

*Figure 521: Classic and non-classic system of CBs.*

The air taken in by the engine passes through several compressor stages and its temperature increases at each stage. As temperature rises, it gets warm enough for those ice particles to stick to a metal structure, like a stator vane between compressor stages. Ice starts building up at this point until airflow gets disturbed enough to make the engine lose thrust. The situation can progress to a point at which a block of ice has already formed inside the engine and, if it is suddenly released, it can violently hit a rotor blade, causing a great deal of damage to the engine and significant thrust deterioration or even a flame out.

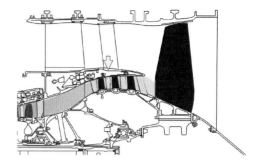

Figure 522: Engine internal ice buildup.

However, that is not the only situation in which this problem can occur. In fact, as I had mentioned, it can happen much more frequently in warmer air, with a greater presence of water particles in very small size. When Ice Crystal Icing (ICI) is present, pilots often perceive one or more of the following: rain on the windshield, small collection of ice on the wiper post, a "shhh" sound, TAT near zero, humid cockpit, ozone smell, St. Elmo's fire (static discharge that looks like lighting happening right on the windshield), and increasing engine vibration.

Figure 523: St Elmo's fire.

### 6.5.12  Fuel Freezing Point

On January 17th, 2008, a British Airways Boeing 777 coming from Beijing to London crashed when it touched the ground a few hundred meters before runway 27L, at Heathrow airport. The crew was surprised with a dual engine loss of thrust on short final and did a tremendous job getting the airplane down and everybody out of it. There were no casualties in that accident.

Investigation pointed to a design flaw on the fuel heater exchange as the main reason for the accident, but low fuel temperature was also a contributing factor. And let's talk about that!

There are three types of jet fuel that are used in commercial aviation. JET A, JET A-1, and JET B. The latter is used only in remote areas of Canada and Russia, so let's focus on the other two. JET A-1 is the fuel type most used around the world. In fact, it is used everywhere but in USA, Brazil, and those remote parts using JET B. JET A-1 has a freezing point of -47°C and JET A, used in USA and Brazil, has a fuel freezing point of -40°C.

Figure 524: Fuel freezing point of jet engine fuel.

There are two issues that we are going to discuss. First, how low can fuel temperature get during a flight and how can I increase its temperature if needed? Second, travelling to and from USA, which fuel freezing point should I stick to: -40°C or -47°C?

When flying at a high altitude, air temperature can get extremely low. At 38,000ft, close to tropical latitudes, it is normally around -56°C, but in the case of the above-mentioned event, that aircraft was flying close to the North Pole, where the air was at -74°C! So, it is only natural that the aircraft's "skin" gets colder and the fuel temperature starts to drop as well. Now, if outside air temperature is -74°C, that means fuel temperature will eventually fall to the same value, right? No, not quite. I will tell you why, but let me talk about fuel temperature probe first.

Fuel temperature drops because fuel is exposed to very cold air. Fuel on the wings is much more exposed to such cold than fuel in the center tank, where it is "protected" by the passenger cabin in the upper part. Some aircrafts have fuel temperature probes in every single fuel tank, however, when an aircraft is designed with a single temperature probe, it is placed on the wing to measure the worst-case scenario. On the Boeing 737, for example, the fuel temperature probe is located on the left-wing fuel tank.

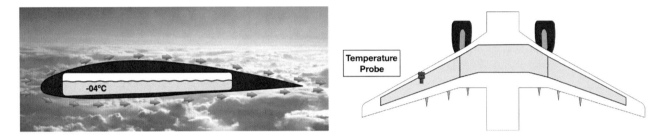

Figure 525: Fuel inside wing tanks will lose heat faster than in center tanks.

Let's get back to how low fuel temperature can get. Temperature needs equilibrium. If you put ice in your soda, it gets colder while ice melts, until a point where both the ice and the soda are at the same temperature. Well, air friction has increased the temperature of the wing skin to some extent, so it is not as low as the outside air temperature (OAT). The skin temperature is fairly the same as that of the total air temperature (TAT), so it is reasonable to deduce that equilibrium will be achieved in this value, and fuel temperature is not going to be lower than TAT.

Engine manufacturers will determine which the lowest allowable fuel temperature is. Most of them say that fuel temperature should never be colder than 3°C above its freezing point, or else there should be a specific limit value, whichever is warmer. Take the 737 as an example: minimum fuel temperature is 3°C above fuel freezing point or -43°C, whichever is higher. If using JET A, that limit would be -37°C, but if using JET A-1, the minimum temperature would be -43°C. As an American company, Boeing set the alarm to trigger on their airplanes at minus 37°C (3°C above the freezing point of JET A fuel).

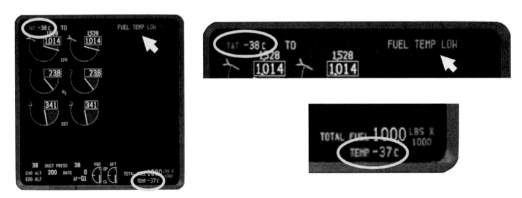

Figure 526: EICAS message of 'Fuel Temperature Low', on a B777.

When that happens, pilots must find a way to increase fuel temperature, and the only way to do that is by increasing TAT. But how? Well, there are two clear options: increase airspeed or descend to a lower altitude. Increasing airspeed will increase air friction and TAT will rise. It is expected to increase between 0.5 and 0.7°C for every 0.01 Mach number that an aircraft accelerates. If the pilots choose to descend, TAT should increase by about 8°C for every 4,000ft the airplane descends while keeping a constant Mach number. No option is a perfect option, and that is because both of them will result in higher fuel burn. For this reason, there is no correct answer to that. You will have to address the best course of action in a case-by-case analysis.

And to answer the final question about fuel freezing point, Boeing recommends that you stick to the highest value (-40°C of JET A) until the third consecutive refueling process with JET A-1. Only then you can consider -47°C as your new fuel freezing point. In the example in Figure 527, for taking off from Lisbon (LIS) to Miami (MIA) you fueled the airplane with JET A-1 and will use -47°C as fuel freezing point. After departing from Miami, you will use -40°C as a reference. No big deal up to this point. However, even if you refuel JET A-1 in London (LHR) to go to Delhi (DEL), and use the same fuel again to go from there to Singapore (SIN), you will have to consider the fuel freezing point to be at -40°C on both flights. Only then, on a third consecutive flight with JET A-1 (bound for Beijing, PEK), should you change this value back to -47°C.

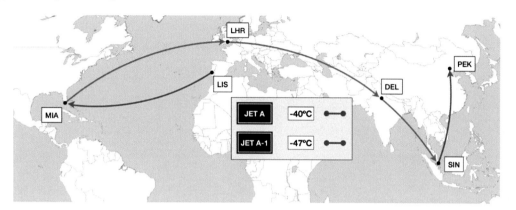

*Figure 527: Fuel freezing point when mixing fuel types.*

## 6.5.13  Snowtam

NOTAM is a coded message issued to warn pilots about most diverse subjects. For example, a runway that will be closed for a certain period, an airspace that will be closed owing to military exercise, a radio aid that is out of service, among other possible messages. The name is an acronym for the expression NOtice To AirMen.

For cold weather operations, a similar type of coded message was created and nicknamed SNOWTAM, as a pun with the word SNOW mixed with NOTAM. This is a special series NOTAM given in a standard format providing a surface condition report notifying the presence or cessation of hazardous conditions due to snow, ice, slush, frost, standing water, or water associated with any of the previous conditions on the movement area.

This message contains up to seventeen different fields of information and nobody expects pilots to known them by heart. For this reason, I present a summary that you can consult at any time, but be aware that not all 17 fields need to be included in a SNOWTAM. Those without relevant information will not appear. This message is valid for 8 hours and has also been through some changes when standardized GRF (Global Reporting Format) was implemented.

Now, SNOWTAM has two different sections, namely the "airplane performance section" and the "situational awareness section".

The Runway Condition Code (RCC on item D) is available to you on this book in Figure 440 (section In-Flight Landing Requirements). As I told you there, the code varies from 6 to 0, and the lower the number, the lower the braking action. To determine the runway braking action, the airport authority will assess the contaminant present on each third of the runway. Every type of contaminant is expected to affect aircraft performance in a given way, and in the same figure you will find this correlation, showing what kind of braking and lateral controllability issues are anticipated for several contaminants.

Pilot reports (PIREPS) are still very important. Depending on those reports, the airport authority may elect to degrade braking action report even further. And now one question arises about the braking action report. If I find more than one braking action report on the runway, which should I use to calculate my aircraft's performance, as performance software only accepts one input value?

| | SITUATIONAL AWARENESS SECTION | |
|---|---|---|
| I | **REDUCED RUNWAY LENGTH**<br>Example: "RWY 16R REDUCED TO 2000" | |
| J | **DRIFTING SNOW ON THE RUNWAY**<br>Example: "DRIFTING SNOW" | |
| K | **LOOSE SAND ON THE RUNWAY**<br>Example: "RWY 09 LOOSE SAND" | |
| L | **CHEMICAL TREATMENT ON THE RUNWAY**<br>Example: "RWY 15L CHEMICALLY TREATED" | |
| M | **SNOW BANKS ON THE RUNWAY**<br>Example: "RWY 27 SNOW BANK L20 FM CL" (snow bank 20 metres to the left of the centreline of runway 27); if the banks are on both sides, LR is used. | |
| N | **SNOW BANKS ON THE TAXIWAY**<br>Example: "TWY A SNOW BANK" | |
| O | **SNOW BANKS ADJACENT TO THE RUNWAY**<br>Example: "RWY 12L ADJ SNOW BANKS" | |
| P | **TAXIWAY CONDITIONS**<br>Reporte only when conditions are poor. Example: "TWY B POOR" or "ALL TWYS POOR" | |
| R | **APRON CONDITIONS**<br>Reporte only when conditions are poor. Example: "APRON POOR" or "APRON EAST POOR" or "ALL APRONS POOR" | |
| S | **MEASURED FRICTION COEFFICIENT**<br>Includes the measured friction coefficient and measuring device. This is only used if the State has an established programme of runway friction measurement using a State-approved measuring device. | |
| T | **PLAIN LANGUAGE**<br>Plain language remarks. | |

| | AIRPLANE PERFORMANCE SECTION | |
|---|---|---|
| A | **AIRDROME**<br>Aerodrome location indicator (the four-letter location indicator according to ICAO Doc 7910). This item is mandatory. | |
| B | **DATE AND TIME**<br>Date (mmdd) and Time (hhmm) of completion of measurement in GMT. This item is mandatory. | |
| C | **RUNWAY DESIGNATORS**<br>Lower runway designator number (e.g. 09, 04L, etc.). Only one runway designator is inserted for each runway and always the lower number. This item is mandatory. | |
| D | **RUNWAY CONDITION CODE**<br>Runway condition code for each runway third. Only one digit (0-6) is used for each runway third (e.g. 6/4/5). The runway condition code depends on the type and depth of the contaminant and the outside air temperature. Higher numbers indicate better braking action. This item is mandatory. | |
| E | **PER CENT COVERAGE FOR EACH RUNWAY THIRD**<br>This information is provided only when the runway condition for each runway third (Item D) has been reported as other than 6 and there is a condition description for each runway third (Item G) that has been reported other than DRY. In this case, values 25, 50, 75 or 100 for each runway third are given (e.g. 75/100/50). When the conditions are not reported, "NR" is used instead of numbers. | |
| F | **DEPTH OF CONTAMINANT**<br>Depth of loose contaminant for each runway third in millimetres (e.g. 10/12/10). When the conditions are not reported, "NR" is used. This information is only provided for:<br><br>STANDING WATER      WET SNOW<br>SLUSH      DRY SNOW | |
| G | **CONDITION DESCRIPTION FOR EACH RUNWAY THRID**<br>This item is mandatory. When the conditions are not reported, "NR" is used. The following words and phrases are used:<br><br>COMPACTED SNOW      WATER ON TOP OF COMPACTED SNOW<br>DRY SNOW      WET<br>DRY SNOW ON TOP OF COMPACTED SNOW      WET ICE<br>DRY SNOW ON TOP OF ICE      WET SNOW<br>FROST      WET SNOW ON TOP OF COMPACTED SNOW<br>ICE      WET SNOW ON TOP OF ICE<br>SLUSH      DRY (only reported when there is no contaminant)<br>STANDING WATER | |
| H | **WIDTH OF THE RUNWAY TO WHICH RCC APPLY**<br>Width of runway to which the runway condition codes apply. This item is included if the value in metres is less than the published runway width. | |

*Figure 528: SNOWTAM summary – Airplane performance and situational awareness sections.*

Well, first of all, follow your airline policy! I cannot know what kind of recommendation they have for you, but I will present some options here.

Of course, you can always "play safe" and use the worst condition reported. Let's use one example. Say a given runway braking action is reported as 4/4/3. For takeoff, I would definitely recommend that you should use braking action 3. That is because the last third of the runway is the part of it where you will be braking in the event of a rejected takeoff. However, on a landing assessment, I could use braking action 4 (good to medium) if I could guarantee that I would only use the first two thirds of the runway for landing.

Anyway, here are just my thoughts on the subject, but please, I reaffirm the importance of following your company's policy over this matter.

Before we start a discussion about operations on narrow runways, we have to define what can be considered as a narrow runway. There is no requirement in any regulation to establish a minimum runway width for aircraft operations. In any case, we can assume that the aircraft must at least fit the runway on which it is going to takeoff or land. However, this is only common sense, not law.

One item that is definitely relevant to this topic is the definition of $V_{1(MCG)}$. It says that the aircraft control must be re-established by deviating no more than 30ft (9.14m) from the runway centerline. If we add this rule to the "common sense" that we just talked about (not letting any wheels off the runway), we will find a method of at least recommending a minimum runway width for operation. Please note that minimum width is a recommendation, only, and let's take our model airplane as an example.

Boeing 737NG is approximately 7m wide between the external faces of the outboard wheels of the main gear, that is, 3.50m for each side of its longitudinal axis. By adding maximum centerline deviation allowance (9.14m) to that, we now got 12.64m. Boeing and Airbus voluntarily provide 2m of initial offset to establish any recommendation (other aircraft manufacturers might do that, too), so let's add 2m to our findings, and now we have 14.64m of minimum runway halfwidth. Rounding up these numbers, minimum runway width would be 30m.

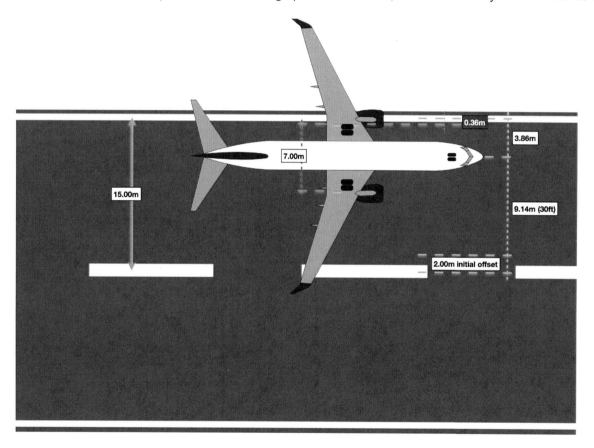

*Figure 529: Minimum runway width recommendation.*

After looking at this figure, some might say that operating on runways narrower than 30m can be dangerous. Well, let's dig a little dipper and look at some statistics before coming to any conclusions.

According to Boeing, between 1995 and 2002, there were 117 incidents of "sideway" runway excursion (known as "veer-off"). Of these, 15 occurred while taxiing, 87 occurred during landing and only 15 occurred during takeoff. In addition, 115 of the 117 events took place on 45m wide runways or even wider ones (60m). One veer-off happened on a 42m wide runway and only one single event happened on a 30m wide track.

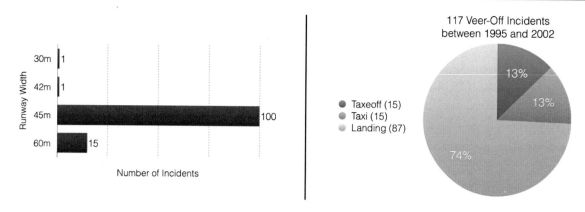

Figure 530: Runway veer-off events between 1995 and 2002.

Reasons for veering off were as varied as possible, including rain, wind, system failures, engines, deviations of instrument landing system locator signal and even intentional events. However, we can see that runway width had very little influence on the occurrences, and despite the fact that our first approach to the problem was a concern with the takeoff phase, only 13% of the events happened at such moment. Also, when I first read this study, the main reason for veer-off on takeoff caught my attention: asymmetric spin-up. Let's see what that means.

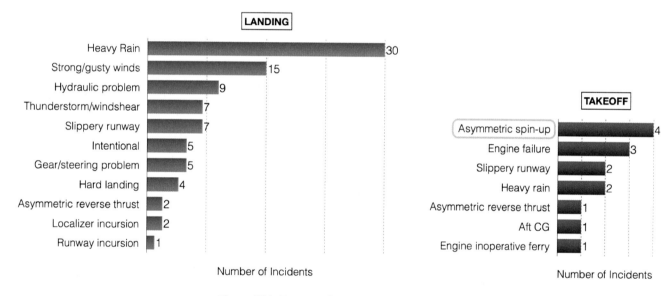

Figure 531: Reasons for veering off the runway.

## 6.6.1   Engine Spool Up

A standard procedure when setting takeoff thrust is as follows: advance thrust levers a bit and wait until %N1 (engine first stage rotation) has stabilized at about 40%. As soon as all engines have achieved these level, push TOGA (Takeoff/Go Around) in case of Boeing airplanes, or advance levers to Flex position in case of Airbus models. But why should pilots make this brief and, very important, "stop" at about 40% N1?

A piston engine is quite different from a turbo fan jet engine in many aspects, including response time. When pilots set throttles from idle to full forward on a piston engine aircraft, this engine responds almost immediately to that command. On a jet engine, however, acceleration time from idle to full thrust is not linear. It starts gaining rotation speed very slowly, and then it suddenly reacts fast!

On a multiengine aircraft, if a pilot advanced throttles rapidly and in a continuous move, and if one engine got to that "changing point" in behavior before the other, it would go to full thrust while the other would stay behind.

That big asymmetry at hardly no speed has no way of being counteracted, as the rudder is not producing any aerodynamic force yet.

The next figure shows the rotation speed of a jet engine (%N1) versus the time it takes to reach this rotation once thrust levers are moved forward. You can see that there is an idling band, a slow and a fast acceleration band. This drawing shows two engines accelerating on the same aircraft, but one of them reached the changing point (slow to fast acceleration) one second earlier. This means that, two seconds later, one engine would be at 92%N1 while the other, still at 52%N1. That is too much difference to be handled by the pilot. Most likely, this aircraft would veer off the runway at the very beginning of takeoff roll.

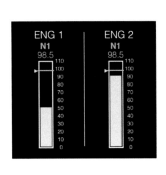  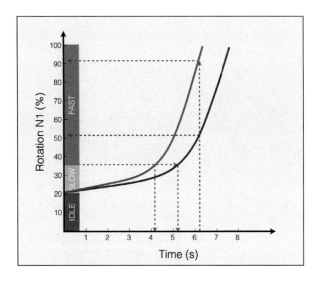

*Figure 532: Why stop and wait at 40%?*

We call this delay in acceleration the "engine spool up", and its delay in deceleration is the "engine spool down". Although asymmetric spin-up was responsible for only 4 veer-off events in the above mentioned 7-year period, it is responsible for a lot of scary moments every single year! Luckily, most pilots are able to react fast by retarding throttles back to idle and regaining control using nose wheel steering before exiting the runway. But, yeah, I could not state that this is a rare type of event.

### 6.6.2 Changing $V_{1(MCG)}$ Method

Anyway, if the operator wants to takeoff on runways narrower than 30m (for our example), safety margins can be increased in regard to $V_{1(MCG)}$ criteria, and there are two possibilities to consider.

The first is linked to 30ft maximum deviation from the centerline. It can be reduced to 20ft and $V_{1(MCG)}$ can be reestablished on the basis of this new parameter. Obviously, this will make $V_{1(MCG)}$ considerably higher and a new problem arises: the runway may be narrow, but at least it will have to be long. For a 737-700, changing $V_{1(MCG)}$ criteria from 30ft to 20ft, generally increases this speed between 4 and 6kt, depending on the airport's altitude and temperature.

Here is an interesting thing about Boeing aircraft with respect to $V_{1(MCG)}$: this speed definition does not imply taking into account any crosswind. However, when operating on a 45m wide runway, Boeing guarantees that maximum crosswind conditions demonstrated on test flights and published in FCOM are adequate in the event of an engine failure at $V_{1(MCG)}$.

As a second option, the operator could set CG as forward as possible when executing weight and balance. There are no allowances for an aft curtailment as in ALT FWD CG, so the calculated $V_{1(MCG)}$ will stay the same, but the actual speed will be significantly lower, and that can provide extra comfort and make airplane controllability easier for the pilot in the event of a real engine failure.

To end the discussion about this subject, the next figure summarizes all main issues that operators should address when taking off, landing or simply taxiing on narrow runways. One of these topics is about the possibility of foreign object damage caused to wing-mounted engines. The last image clearly shows why this should be a concern! All 4 engines of this Boeing 747 are out of the paved area and over grass and gravel. Of course, this is not a regular operation. It was a one-time thing when this Boeing 747SP from South African Airways was being retired and delivered to a museum. This was the museum's runway, not intended for this kind of aircraft!

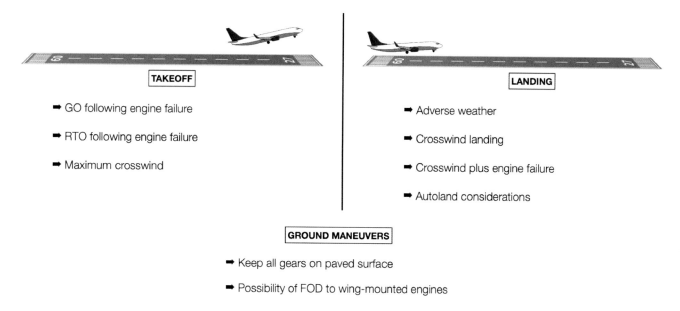

**TAKEOFF**

➡ GO following engine failure

➡ RTO following engine failure

➡ Maximum crosswind

**LANDING**

➡ Adverse weather

➡ Crosswind landing

➡ Crosswind plus engine failure

➡ Autoland considerations

**GROUND MANEUVERS**

➡ Keep all gears on paved surface

➡ Possibility of FOD to wing-mounted engines

*Figure 533: Issues to be addressed when operating on narrow runways.*

*Figure 534: Boeing 747SP landing on a VERY narrow runway.*

Operation at high elevation airports is not much different from that of airports closer to sea level, except for higher true airspeeds and less available engine thrust. Well, to be fair, these two factors will make this kind of operation a special one, indeed. And pilots must be very aware of this. Speed-wise, we need to remember that indicated airspeed might be the same as at a low altitude airport; however, there is a huge difference between an aircraft's IAS and its TAS or GS. Let's think about some scenarios to learn about the effects of altitude.

However, let me make one thing clear, first. There is no such a definition of what a high-altitude airport would be. Boeing classifies an airport as of high altitude every time its elevation exceeds their aircraft's standard certification envelope for takeoff and landing. By the way, this number is 8,400ft. Off-topic: Boeing conducts most of its takeoff and landing test flights at Edwards Air Force Base (USA). Runway elevation is just short of 2,400ft and regulation says that numbers obtained in those tests can be extrapolated up to 6,000ft to predict airplane behavior in other airport elevations. That is why their standard is 8,400ft. However, as far as I know, Airbus conducts most of their tests in Toulouse (FRA), which is only 500ft high and, despite that fact, their standard certification for takeoff and landing is 9,200ft. I am curious to find out where else they do their tests! Let me know if you have the answer.

Back to the subject, I will split it into two parts: "takeoff and initial climb" and "approach and landing". But that does not mean that what I say in the first part is not valid for the second. Thrust is low and speed is high whether you ar

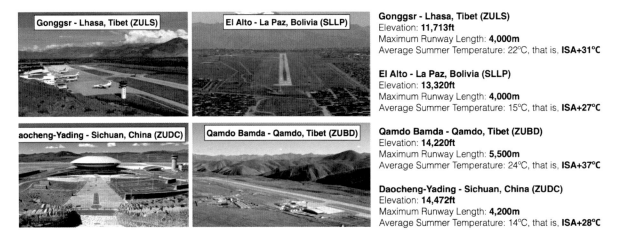

**Gonggsr - Lhasa, Tibet (ZULS)**
Elevation: **11,713ft**
Maximum Runway Length: **4,000m**
Average Summer Temperature: 22°C, that is, **ISA+31°C**

**El Alto - La Paz, Bolivia (SLLP)**
Elevation: **13,320ft**
Maximum Runway Length: **4,000m**
Average Summer Temperature: 15°C, that is, **ISA+27°C**

**Qamdo Bamda - Qamdo, Tibet (ZUBD)**
Elevation: **14,220ft**
Maximum Runway Length: **5,500m**
Average Summer Temperature: 24°C, that is, **ISA+37°C**

**Daocheng-Yading - Sichuan, China (ZUDC)**
Elevation: **14,472ft**
Maximum Runway Length: **4,200m**
Average Summer Temperature: 14°C, that is, **ISA+28°C**

*Figure 535: Some of the highest elevated airports in the world.*

## 6.7.1   Takeoff and Initial Climb Considerations
### Acceleration

We already know that engine thrust goes down as we increase altitude. A higher altitude means less air, and if an engine has less amount of air to accelerate when throwing backwards, it will produce less thrust.

*Figure 536: Less air to throw back equals less thrust to push forward.*

Operating at a higher airport means having far less thrust available for takeoff. A pilot who is used to operating at sea level may even be startled by the difference in the airplane's acceleration when taking off from a higher airport for the first time. Let's exemplify: time to go from standing still to rotation speed at a given airplane and takeoff weight at sea level is about 30 seconds. However, when taking off from an airport at 8,000ft, this time can easily reach 50 seconds for that same airplane and weight. It is quite distressing to look at the airspeed indicator and not to see those numbers increase at the rate you are used to. And this thrust situation can get even worse at high temperature! Look at the next figure.

| CFM56 -7B26 | 0ft | 2,000ft | 4,000ft | 8,000ft |
|---|---|---|---|---|
| ISA | 25,928 LB | 24,616 LB | 23,095 LB | 19,259 LB |
| ISA+15 | 25,827 LB | 24,548 LB | 23,046 LB | 19,184 LB |
| ISA+31 | 22,856 LB | 22,163 LB | 21,364 LB | 16,977 LB |

Thrust (LB) at 0kt and given Altitude and Temperature

*Figure 537: From 0ft and ISA to 8,000ft and ISA+31, engine thrust decreased by almost 31%.*

### 6.7.1.2 Takeoff Distances

As acceleration is much lower, takeoff distances are expected to increase considerably. That is exactly what happens. Pilots need to keep in mind that both Accelerate STOP and Accelerate GO distances will be much greater than the ones closer to sea level.

### 6.7.1.3 Tire Speed and Brake Energy

If you remember our discussions about tire speed and brake energy in the chapter about takeoff performance, you will also remember that I said that those requirements often limit takeoff weight when departing from high and hot airports. Well, we are talking about the higher airports now, so it is natural to find brake energy and tire speed as our performance limits here. The reason behind that? Very high speeds!

Although indicated speed is not significantly different for a given weight, ground speed will be very different! Specially if departing in tailwind conditions and on a hot day. That can make the initial calculated $V_{LOF}$ higher than $V_{TIRE}$ or V1 higher than $V_{MBE}$. Of course, that is not allowed and a weight penalty applies to make speeds feasible again. Final result: performance weight is tire speed limited or brake energy limited.

| | 0ft ISA+20 | 5,000ft ISA+20 | 14,000ft ISA+30 |
|---|---|---|---|
| 150 kt | 155kt | 167kt | 196kt |

TAS for a given CAS, FL and ISA deviation

*Figure 538: TAS increases with higher altitudes and temperatures.*

### 6.7.1.4 Climb Gradient

Perhaps the biggest problem is the lack of climb capability after liftoff. Operating at high elevation airports is usually linked to operating in regions surrounded by mountains and obstacles. As engine thrust is considerably lower, the aircraft's available climb gradient will also be very small – precisely in a region where we wish it were high. This implies a lot of work for an airline's operations engineering team. They must develop contingency procedures to allow taking off or landing in those places even with very little climb capability. They need to establish flight paths that do not conflict with obstacles and that will be followed in the event of an engine failure. Believe me, this can be very complex. An example is Paro Airport, in Bhutan. It is located on a small plateau 7,300ft above sea level and is surrounded by mountains with peaks that reach 18,000ft. The airport receives scheduled commercial flights operated by Airbus A319. Contingency procedures here are extremely complex and detailed.

1,500ft                    14,000ft

*Figure 539: Climb capability is very different when comparing situations at 1,500ft and 14,000ft.*

*Figure 540: Paro Airport, Bhutan.*

## 6.7.2   Approach and Landing Considerations
### 6.7.2.1   Radius Turn

When making curves to intercept, for example, the final approach course, we need to keep in mind that a higher speed (TAS) will make the turn radius much larger than you might be used to. We may have to anticipate some configuration changes (flaps) in order not to overshoot lateral limits in a landing procedure.

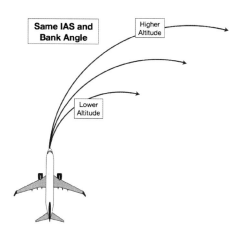

| Bank 25° | 0ft ISA+20 | 5,000ft ISA+20 | 14,000ft ISA+20 | 20,000ft ISA+20 |
|---|---|---|---|---|
| **140 kt** | 1,217m | 1,408m | 1,875m | 2,269m |
| **180 kt** | 2,002m | 2,315m | 3,062m | 3,734m |
| **210 kt** | 2,715m | 3,169m | 4,157m | 5,036m |

Radius turn for a given CAS, FL and ISA deviation

Radius trun is roughly **60%** greater at FL200 compared to FL50

*Figure 541: Radius turn with higher TAS.*

### 6.7.2.2 Deceleration

When we are flying at a high altitude, TAS is much higher than when we are near sea level. This means that the pilot will need to manage his/her airplane's energy more carefully. That rule of thumb that says you can decelerate 10kt when flying 1nm forward might well exceed this 1nm. So, always plan an extra distance to decelerate.

### 6.7.2.3 Rate of Descend on Final Approach

International agencies dealing with flight safety have established some operating windows with parameters that must be followed to avoid serious occurrences, such as a runway excursion after landing. One of the premises is the fact that final approach to land is carried out in a stabilized manner below a certain altitude.

Many criteria are used to define whether an approach is stabilized or not. One of them establishes that rate of descend should not be higher than 1,000ft/min. However, "if an approach requires a sink rate greater than 1,000 feet per minute (due to steep descent paths or higher approach speeds), a special briefing should be conducted highlighting this fact".

Now, imagine a final approach being flown at 150kt (IAS) to land at an airport situated 8,000ft above sea level. When passing 1,000ft AFE (Above Field Elevation), considering ISA+5°C, the aircraft's TAS will be 173kt. Consider a 10kt tailwind and we get a ground speed of 183kt. At this speed, to maintain a normal flight path angle of 3°, the rate of descend must be 952ft/min. Any slight variation will cause the airplane to exceed the 1,000ft/min value that had been set as our limit. So, approaches in "High and Hot" locations are excellent examples of where these special briefings need to be executed.

| Descent Path 3° | Rwy at 0ft | Rwy at 5,000ft | Rwy at 10,000ft | Rwy at 14,000ft |
|---|---|---|---|---|
| **130kt** | 724 ft/min | 781 ft/min | 844 ft/min | 914 ft/min |
| **140kt** | 780 ft/min | 840 ft/min | 908 ft/min | 984 ft/min |
| **150kt** | 835 ft/min | 900 ft/min | 973 ft/min | 1,054 ft/min |

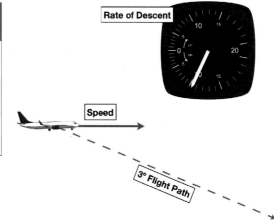

Descent rate for a given CAS from 2,000ft AFE to ground (wind calm, ISA+20).

**Special briefing required!**
Likely to exceed **1,000ft/min** on final approach

*Figure 542: Rate of descend expected on final approach.*

### 6.7.2.4 Missed Approach Climb Gradient

High altitude airports are typical locations where Landing Climb and Approach Climb requirements are the most restrictive performance requirements for landing. Special attention must be given to the fact that these limits do not guarantee any kind of terrain separation; they only assure minimum climb capability. Therefore, it is highly recommended that airlines should develop special procedures to fly the aircraft free of obstacles in the event of an engine failure.

One possibility to increase maximum landing weight when it is limited by Approach or Landing Climb in these situations is to reduce the landing flap. In case of Boeing 737NG, the most restricted option is landing with flap 40 and going around with flap 15. Flaps 30 is a better option, no doubt. Another possibility is landing with flaps 15 and going around with flaps 1 or even landing with flap 30 and going around with flap 5 (option available for 737MAX).

Anyway, high altitude airport operations require more planning and attention, but they are perfectly safe if these precautions are taken by operations engineering team and pilots. Another good tip about operating in these locations is to schedule them to be carried out in the coldest hours of the day, trying to mitigate loss of thrust in some way.

# Epilogue

I was a student pilot having my final flight lessons, about to get my commercial pilot's license. I was flying a Piper Arrow from Porto Alegre (SBPA/POA) to Curitiba (SBBI/BFH) with a touch and go in Florianópolis (SBFL/FLN). There were only two people on board: me and my flight instructor. Upon landing in Curitiba, we shut down the engine at the general aviation apron and stepped out of the airplane to stretch our legs, refuel (to a full tank), and grab a bite to eat. Our next sector was a nonstop flight back to Porto Alegre, a journey that would last about 2 hours and 30 minutes.

My instructor met two friends in Curitiba who were trying to get back to Porto Alegre. They were also pilots, and we invited them to join us on our flight back. Now, imagine the situation: four men, two heavy pieces of luggage, on an aircraft topped with enough fuel for seven and a half hours of flying. We were obviously very overweight! But that's not all. We were departing from a runway that is uphill and situated at 3,000 feet elevation. Was there any chance of that going right? Of course not.

The problem was, no one actually thought about the performance issue. We simply boarded the airplane, performed the engine check and warmup, lined up from an intersection (just to make things even worse), and started rolling. I was about 10 knots shy of the rotation speed, and the runway was about to end. I had no other option but to rotate and pray! The stall warning started to buzz the moment I pulled the yoke. As the airplane lifted off, I immediately retracted the landing gear, but it didn't help much. I was still unable to gain altitude or speed. Then, things finally started to turn around! At the end of the runway, there is a valley, and the terrain is significantly lower than where the runway is situated. I had no doubt in my mind about what to do: descend! Going down and letting gravity help me gain some badly needed speed.

That was the first — and hopefully last — downward takeoff I ever made. It was a decisive moment in my professional life. I promised I would never put myself in that kind of situation again, a situation where a complete lack of knowledge almost killed me.

There's a saying that when we are young, we have a lot of luck. As we grow older, we gradually run out of it, and we compensate with wisdom. So, run and gather all the knowledge you can before your luck completely vanishes.

From that day on, I started to study airplane performance. I would never allow myself to fly an airplane without knowing in advance what to expect from it: takeoff distance, rate of climb, service ceiling, everything. Many years later, I became a college professor with a mission to pass all the knowledge I have accumulated to my students.

I did my best to go one step further with this book, sharing everything I know about this subject with my readers. I hope you have enjoyed reading it as much as I enjoyed the challenge of writing it. And what a challenge it was! Writing in a foreign language and trying to maintain a conversational, storytelling style was no easy task. I aimed to create something different. There are many books about aircraft performance, but they often follow the same structure, presenting the subject as a set of regulations. This has its advantages, no doubt, as it allows for quick searches on any given topic to find the list of requirements. However, those books share a common flaw: they do not explain the subject.

That was my main goal — to make the reader feel as if they are in a classroom, listening to me explain and asking questions (rhetorical, of course) about this fascinating, and yet challenging theme: Aircraft Performance Weight and Balance!

# References

## Books

BLAKE, Walt. **Jet Transport Performance Methods**. Seattle, USA, 2009.

AIRBUS, Flight Operations Team. **Getting to Grips with Aircraft Performance**. Toulouse, France, 2002.

HURT, Hugh H. **Aerodynamics for Naval Aviators**. Renton, USA: Aviation Supplies and Academics, 1992.

HULSHOF, Maurits. **Performance Reference Handbook: Boeing 737. FAA edition**. Netherlands, 2010.

WARD, Donald T., STRGANAC, Thomas W. **Introduction to Flight Teste Engineering – 2nd Edition**. Kendall Hunt Publishing Company, EUA, 2001.

ANDERSON, John D. **Introduction to Flight – 7th Edition**. Washington, USA. 2012

OXFORD AVIATION ACADEMY. **Flight Performance and Planning – Mass & Balance and Performance**. Singapore, 2014.

EASA. **ATPL Mass and Balance - Version 2.6**. Slate Ed. Limited, Gloucester, UK, 2015.

EASA. **ATPL Aeroplane Performance - Version 2.3**. Slate Ed. Limited, Gloucester, UK, 2012.

US Department of Transportation, FAA. **Aircraft Weight and Balance Handbook**. Washington, 2007.


## Airplane Manuals

BOEING. **Boeing 737NG: Flight Crew Training Manual**. Seattle. Boeing Commercial Airplane Group, 2018.

BOEING. **Boeing 737NG: Flight Crew Operations Manual**. Seattle. Boeing Commercial Airplane Group, 2018.

BOEING. **Boeing 737NG: Flight Planning and Performance Manual**. Seattle. Boeing Commercial Airplane Group, 2018.

BOEING. **Boeing 737NG: Airplane Flight Manual**. Seattle. Boeing Commercial Airplane Group, 2018.

BOEING. **Boeing 737NG: Minimum Equipment List**. Seattle. Boeing Commercial Airplane Group, 2018.

BOEING. **Boeing 737NG: Weight and Balance Manual**. Seattle. Boeing Commercial Airplane Group, 2018.

BOEING. **Methods and Data to Calculate Turn Performance of Boeing Airplanes**. Seattle. Boeing Commercial Airplane Group, 2011.

AIRBUS. **Airbus 318/319/320/321 Flight Crew Operating Manual**. Blagnac Cedex. Airbus Training and Flight Operations Support and Services, 2003.

AIRBUS. **Airbus 330 Performance Training Manual**. Blagnac Cedex. Airbus Training and Flight Operations Support and Services, 2010.

AIRBUS. **Airbus 318/319/320/321 Performance Training Manual**. Blagnac Cedex. Airbus Training and Flight Operations Support and Services, 2005.

RYANAIR. **Winter Operations Guide**. 2019

## Magazines

BOEING. **Aero Magazine**. Seattle, USA. Boeing Commercial Airplane Group, editions 18 to 56.

AIRBUS. **Safety First Magazine**. Blagnac, France. Airbus S.A.S., editions 1 to 29.

Personal note: those magazines are top quality in articles related to aviation performance. It is impossible to cite every single article that I read to build this material, and despite mentioning some individually, I need to point that all writers on these two magazines have contributed to build my knowledge. Thank you all!


## Aviation Articles

MACKINNON, Robert. **Rejected Takeoff Studies**. Aero Magazine N°11. Seattle. Boeing Commercial Airplane Group. 2000.

EKSTRAND, Chester. **New ETOPS Regulations**. Aero Magazine N°22 Qtr 02. Boeing Commercial Airplane Group, 2003.

ODA, H. Et Tal. **Safe Winter Operations.** Aero Magazine Qtr 04. Seattle. Boeing Commercial Airplane Group, 2010.

ROHNER, Allen. **737-700 Technical Demonstration Flight in Bhutan**. Aero Magazine N°23 Qtr 03. Boeing Commercial Airplane Group, 2003.

ROBERSON, Bill. **Fuel Conservation Strategies**. Aero Magazine Qtr 02. Boeing Commercial Airplane Group, 2007.

WAKEFIELD, Ingrid. **Exceeding Tire Speed Rating During Takeoff**. Aero Magazine Qtr 02. Boeing Commercial Airplane Group, 2009.

COLLELA, Rick. **Overweight Landings**. Aero Magazine Qtr 03. Boeing Commercial Airplane Group, 2007.

COOK, A. Et. Tal. **Dynamic Cost Indexing**. 6th Eurocontrol Innovative Research Workshops & Exhibition, 4-6 December 2007.

MACKNESS, Bob. **Managing Uneven Brake Temperatures**. Aero Magazine. Boeing Commercial Airplane Group.

KOTKER, David. **New Deicing Anti-Icing Fluids**. Aero Magazine. Boeing Commercial Airplane Group.

Unkonwn. **Erroneous Takeoff Speeds**. Aero Magazine. Boeing Commercial Airplane Group.

JAMES, W., O'DELL, P. **Derated Climb Performance in Large Civil Aircraft**. Rolls Royce, Article 6. 2005.

DONALDSON, Et Tal. **Economic Impact of Derated Climb on Large Commercial Engines**. General Electric, Article 8. 2007.

STOPKOTTE, Jack. **Reduced Thrust for Increase Benefits – Parts 1 and 2**. Boeing Performance and Flight Operations Engineering Conference. Seattle. 2003.

MIHALCHIK, Andy. **Reduced Thrust Takeoff**. Boeing Performance and Flight Operations Engineering Conference. Seattle. 2010.

TING, Dennis. **Takeoff Performance Optimization**. Boeing Performance and Flight Operations Engineering Conference. Seattle. 2010.

DAVIS, Catherine. **Driftdown and Oxygen Procedures over High Terrain Requirements and Analysis Methods**. 2003.

BROWN, Scott. **Improved Climb Benefits, Method and other Considerations**. Boeing Performance and Flight Operations Engineering Conference. Seattle. 2007.

BOONE, Pat. **Fly the Dog**. August, 2013.

Unknown. **The Effect of High Altitude and Center of Gravity on The Handling Characteristics of Swept-wing Commercial Airplanes**. The Boeing Company. 1998.

FAA. **Holdover Time Guidelines**. August, 2018.

DANEY, Jean. **Runway Excursions at Takeoff**. Safety First Magazine #02. Airbus S.A.S., September 2005.

BONNET, Catherine. **Incorrect Pitch Trim Setting at Takeoff**. Safety First Magazine #09. Airbus S.A.S., February 2010.

KORNSTAEDT, L., LIGNEE, R. **Operational Landing Distances - A new standard for in-flight landing distance assessment**. Safety First Magazine #10. Airbus S.A.S., August 2010.

WILLIAMS, Alum. **Flight Crews and De-Icing Personnel – Working together in temporary team work for safe skies**. Safety First Magazine #16. Airbus S.A.S., July 2013.

URDIROZ, Albert. **Low Speed Rejected Take-off upon Engine Failure**. Safety First Magazine #16. Airbus S.A.S., July 2013.

BONNET, C., BARRIOLA, X. **Understanding Weight and Balance**. Safety First Magazine #19. Airbus S.A.S., January 2015.

DUMOLLARD, Yannick. **A Recall of the Correct use of MEL**. Safety First Magazine #25. Airbus S.A.S., January 2018.

HIRTZ, N., BOUSQUET, X., LESCEU, X., KAHLOUL, S., GUPTA, S. **Engine Thrust Management - Thrust Setting at Takeoff**. Safety First Magazine #27. Airbus S.A.S., January 2019.

ATR Costumer Service. **Cold Weather Operations – Be Prepared for Icing**. March 2011.

## *Legislation*

ICAO. **Procedures for Air Navigation Services – Flight Operations (PANS-OPS) Doc 8168**.

ICAO. **Annex 6 – Operation of Aircraft**.

ICAO. **Annex 14 – Aerodrome**.

BRAZIL. **RBAC 25 - Requisitos de Aeronavegabilidade: categoria transporte**.

BRAZIL. **RBAC 121 - Requisitos Operacionais: Operações Domésticas, de Bandeira e Suplementares**.

BRAZIL. **RBAC 91 - Regras Gerais de Operação para Aeronaves Civis**.

BRAZIL. **Instrução Suplementar 153.103-001** - Orientações para aplicação do método ACN/PCN.

USA. **Federal Aviation Regulation, Code of Federal Regulations Part 25**.

USA. **Safety Alert for Flight Operations 06012**. Time of Arrival Landing Performance Assessment.

USA. **Advisory Circular 25-32**. Landing Performance Data on TALPA.

USA. **Advisory Circular 91-79A**. Mitigating the Risks of a Runway Overrun Upon Landing.

USA. **Advisory Circular 120-91**. Airport Obstacle Analysis.

USA. **Advisory Circular 150/5335-5D**. Standardized Method of Reporting Airport Pavement Strength - PCR

UE. **EASA CS-25** Large Aeroplanes.


## *Main Websites*

https://www.ecfr.gov/current/title-14/chapter-I

https://www.faa.gov/regulations_policies/advisory_circulars/

https://www.anac.gov.br/assuntos/legislacao/legislacao-1/rbha-e-rbac/rbac

https://www.easa.europa.eu/en/regulations

https://regulatorylibrary.caa.co.uk/


## *Accidents / Incidents Related to Performance*

Below, there's a short list of aeronautical accidents and incidents related to Aircraft Performance Weight and Balance content presented in this book. There are records of hundreds of these kind of events and I chose only 10 to illustrate. I hope to instigate your curiosity and make you look for them on the internet and see what happened on each one of them. You will be surprised.

**FineAir 101**, Douglas DC-8, Miami, USA, 7 August 1997.

**Air Florida 90**, Boeing 737-200, Washington, USA, 13 January 1982.

**US Airways 1702**, Airbus 320, Philadelphia, USA, 13 March 2014.

**Thompson Airways 2453**, Boeing 737-800, Malta, Spain, 28 September 2017.

**El Al 27**, Boeing 787-9, Tel Aviv, Israel, 29 March 2018.

**Qantas 87**, Airbus A330-300, Sydney, Australia, 6 March 2009.

**Arik 6656**, Boeing 737-700, Southend, England, 21 November 2010.

**Titan 16V**, Boeing 737-300, Edinburgh, Scotland, 19 November 2013.

**EasyJet 186**, Airbus A319, Belfast Northern Ireland, 25 June, 2015.

**Virgin Australia 127**, Boeing 737-800, Christchurch, New Zealand, 15 July 2015.